COGNITION

The text of this book is composed in Adobe Minion
with the display set in Adobe Myriad.
Composition by University Graphics, Inc.
Manufacturing by Courier, Westford.
Book design by Jack Meserole.
Cover illustration: James Crable. "2nd Avenue, New
York, New York," 1989. Photocollage. Courtesy
J. J. Brookings Gallery, San Francisco.
Cover design by Paul Moran.

Library of Congress Cataloging-in-Publication Data

Reisberg, Daniel.
    Cognition / Daniel Reisberg.
        p.   cm.
    Includes bibliographical references and index.
    ISBN 0-393-96925-8
    1 Cognitive psychology.   I. Title.
BF201.R45   1996
    153—dc20   95-47058
ISBN 0-393-96925-8
W. W. Norton & Company, Inc., 500 Fifth Avenue, New York, N.Y. 10110
    http://web.wwnorton.com
W. W. Norton & Company, Ltd., 10 Coptic Street, London WC1A 1PU
1 2 3 4 5 6 7 8 9 0

DANIEL REISBERG

Reed College

COGNITION
Exploring the Science of the Mind

W · W · Norton & Company

New York · London

For Mim and Leo

Contents

Preface

I was a college sophomore when I took my first course in cognitive psychology, and I've been excited about this field ever since. Why? First, cognitive psychologists are asking terrific questions. Some of the questions concern broad issues that have intrigued humanity for thousands of years. Why do we think the things we think? Why do we believe the things we believe? What are the limits of human ability? How can we make ourselves better, as individuals, and as a species?

Sometimes, though, the questions are of a more immediate, personal, concern: How can I help myself to remember more of the material that I'm studying in school? Is there some better way to solve the problems I encounter? Why is it that my roommate can study with the radio on, but I can't?

And sometimes the questions have important consequences for our social institutions: If an eyewitness reports what he saw at a crime, should we trust him? If a newspaper raises questions about a candidate's integrity, how will the voters react?

Of course, we want more than interesting questions: We would like some *answers* as well, and this is the second reason I find cognitive psychology so exciting: In the last half century, the field has made extraordinary progress on many fronts, providing us, now, with a rich understanding of the nature of memory, the processes of thought, and the content of knowledge. There are, to be sure, many things still to be discovered—that's part of the fun. Even so, we already have something to say about all of the questions just posed, and many more as well. We can speak to the specific questions and to the general, to the theoretical issues and to the practical. Our research has provided data of interest to scholars engaged in a range of intellectual pursuits; we have uncovered principles useful for improving the educational process; and we have made discoveries of considerable importance for the courts. What I've learned, as a cognitive psychologist, has changed how I think about my own memory; it's changed how I make decisions; it's changed how I draw conclusions when I'm thinking about events in my life.

On top of all this, I'm excited about the intellectual connections that cognitive psychology makes possible. In the modern academic world, intellectual disciplines are becoming more and more sophisticated, with their own methods, and their own conceptual framework. As a consequence, these disciplines often become isolated from each other, regularly working on closely related problems without even realizing it. In contrast, cognitive psychology has, in the last decades, actively sought out contact with neighboring disciplines, and so, in this book, we will touch on topics in philosophy, economics, biology, linguistics, politics, computer science, and medicine. These connections bring obvious benefits, since insights and information can be traded back and forth between the domains. In addition, these connections highlight the *importance* of the material we will be examining, and provide a strong signal that we are working on a project of considerable power and scope.

I have tried, in this text, to convey all this excitement. I've done my best to put in view the questions being asked within my field, the substantial answers we can provide for these questions and, finally, some indications of how cognitive psychology is (and has to be) interwoven with several other intellectual endeavors.

I have also had other goals in writing this text. In my own teaching, I work hard at maintaining a balance among several different elements—the nuts and bolts of how our science proceeds; the data provided by the science; the practical implications of our findings; and the theoretical framework that holds all of these pieces together. I've tried to find the same balance in this text. In particular, I've tried to make certain that the presentation of our science—the procedures we use, the exact nature of our data, and so on—is fully integrated with a presentation of the ideas and theories that derive from cognitive psychology research. These ideas provide the narrative that binds the pieces of the science together, and, indeed, it is these ideas that make the research interesting; it is these ideas that drive our endeavor forward. Therefore, I have tried, within each chapter, and from one chapter to the next, to convey how the various peices fit together into a coherent package. In short, I have tired to emphasize what the results *mean*, and what the science is telling us.

I have also aimed at a text that is broad in its coverage and up-to-date in its presentation. Our field changes quickly, and students are entitled to a text that stays close to the current state of the art. Moreover, our theories are often rich and subtle in their treatment of a topic, and students deserve a text that conveys this sophistication. I've therefore tried, overall, to write a book that is deep enough, serious enough, but also *clear enough* so that by the book's close, students will have a full, rich, and contemporary understanding of cognition.

Perhaps most important, I have tried to write this book with language that is compatible with all these goals. To help students see how the pieces of our field fit together, the prose needs to emphasize the flow of ideas in research. To help students grasp the technical material, the prose needs to be approachable, but, to provide real understanding of these issues, the prose needs to be precise. I hope my writing style will achieve these aims, but you, the reader, will need to be the judge of this.

Indeed, in general, others will have to decide whether I've accomplished what I set out to. In fact, I look forward to hearing from my readers—both the students I'm hoping to reach, and the colleagues I'm hoping to serve. I would be happy to hear, from both constituencies, what I have done well in the book, and what I could have done better; what I've covered (but should have omitted) and what I've left out. It is unlikely that I'll be able to respond to every comment, but I do welcome the comments, either via regular mail (through W.W. Norton) or via the internet (cogtext@reed.edu).

The book's fourteen chapters are designed to cover the major topics within cognitive psychology. Chapter 1 provides the conceptual and historical background for the subsequent chapters. In addition, this chapter seeks to convey the extraordinary scope of this field, and thus why research on cognition is so important. This chapter also highlights the relationship between theory and evidence in this domain, and discusses the logic on which the field of cognitive psychology is built.

Chapters 2 and 3 then turn to the broad problem of how we gain information from the world around us. Chapter 2 examines the topic of pattern recognition; Chapter 3 discusses what it means to "pay attention," with the first half of the chapter concerned with "selective attention," in which one seeks to focus on a target while ignoring distractors, and the second half of the chapter concerned with "divided attention," in which one seeks to focus on more than one target, or more than one task, at the same time. In these chapters, I try to make it clear that seemingly simple processes often turn out to be far more complicated than one might suppose. These chapters also introduce the idea of "cognitive short cuts" as an essential element of our intellectual functioning, and how these "short cuts" are guided by (and sometimes misled by) our prior knowledge. Also crucial here is a discussion of how this knowledge is used, and this allows me to introduce the concepts of network processing and distributed knowledge. These chapters also emphasize a theme that runs throughout the book, namely, the diverse research strategies and the diverse forms of evidence available to cognitive psychologists. Thus, for example, these chapters include discussion of neuropsychology and data from brain-imaging studies.

Chapters 4, 5, and 6 discuss the topic of *memory*, starting with a discussion of how information is "entered" into long-term storage, but then turning to the complex interdependency between how information is first learned and then how that same information is subsequently retrieved. In short, a recurrent theme in this section is that learning that is effective for one sort of task, one sort of use, may be quite *in*effective for other uses. This theme is examined in several contexts, and leads to a discussion of current research on "memory without awareness." These chapters also offer a broad assessment of human memory: How accurate are our memories? How complete? How long-lasting? These issues are pursued both with regard to theoretical treatments of memory, and also the practical consequences of memory research, including the application of this research to the assessment, in the courtroom, of eyewitness testimony.

The book's early chapters emphasize the fact that we are, in many ways, guided in our thinking and experiences by the broad pattern of things we already know. This invites the questions posed by Chapter 7, 8, 9, and 10: What is knowledge? How is it represented in the mind? Chapter 7 examines the idea that knowledge can be represented via a complex network, and includes a discussion of associative networks in general, and connectionist modeling in particular. Chapter 8 turns to the question of how "concepts," the building blocks of our knowledge, are represented in the mind. Chapters 9 and 10 focus on two special types of knowledge: In Chapter 9, I examine our knowledge about language, with discussion both of "linguistic competence" and "linguistic performance." Chapter 10 considers "visual knowledge," and examines what is known about mental imagery.

The next three chapters are concerned with the topic of *thinking.* Chapter 11 examines how each of us draws conclusions from evidence—including cases in which we are trying to be careful and deliberate in our judgments, and also cases of informal judgments, of the sort we often make in our everyday lives. Chapter 12 turns to the question of how we reason from our beliefs—how we check on whether our beliefs are correct, and how we draw conclusions, based on things we already believe. Both of these chapters examine the strategies that guide our thinking, and also some of the ways that these strategies can, on occasion, lead to *error.* The chapters then turn to the pragmatic issue of how these errors can be diminished, through education. Chapter 12 also discusses how we make decisions and choices, with a special focus, first on "economic" theories of decision making, and then, second, on some of the seeming "irrationality" in human decision making. Finally, Chapter 13 considers how we solve problems. The first section of the chapter discusses problem-solving strategies of a general sort, useful for all problems; the chapter then turns to more specialized strategies, and with this, the topic of "expertise." The chapter concludes with a discussion of the role of creativity and insight, within problem solving.

The last chapter in the book does double-service. First, this chapter pulls together many of the strands of contemporary research relevant to the topic of *consciousness*—what consciousness is, and what consciousness is for. In addition, most students will reach this chapter at the end of a full semester's work, a point at which students are well-served by a review of the topics already covered, and also a point at which students are often ill-served by the introduction of much new material. Therefore, this chapter draws most of its themes and evidence from previous chapters, and in that fashion serves as a review for many points that appear earlier in the book. By the same token, Chapter 14 highlights the fact that we are using these materials to approach some of the greatest questions ever asked about the mind, and, in that way, this chapter should help to convey some of the power of the material we have been discussing throughout the book.

Finally, let me turn to the happiest of chores—thanking all of those who have contributed to this book. I've had the benefit of help from many sources. Two colleagues, Bob Crowder (Yale University) and Bob Logie (University of Aberdeen), read through the entire text, and I am deeply grateful for their comments, their insights, and their corrections. In addition, a number of colleagues helped me with specific chapters, and the book is much improved for their efforts. Therefore, let me offer sincere thanks to Paul Rozin (University of Pennsylvania) (Chapters 1 and 2), Mike McCloskey (Johns Hopkins University) (Chapters 2, 3, and 4), Hal Pashler (University of California–San Diego) (Chapters 3 and 4), Henry Gleitman (University of Pennsylvania) (Chapters 4, 5, 6, and 14), Peter Graf (University of British Columbia) (Chapter 5), Frank Keil (Cornell University) (Chapters 7, 8, and 10), Enriqueta Canseco-Gonzalez (Reed College) (Chapter 9), Lila Gleitman (University of Pennsylvania) (Chapter 9), and Steve Pinker (MIT) (Chapter 9). Finally, I received a range of useful suggestions from three colleagues who read the almost-finished volume, and so thanks also go to Rich Carlson (Pennsylvania State University), John Henderson, (Michigan State University), and Jim Hoffman (University of Delaware).

In addition, I owe a more global debt to several other individuals. Many of the chapters here build on chapters I'd written for a text I co-authored with Barry Schwartz, and I'd like to express my thanks to Barry—for his comments on those chapters in the earlier book, and for the psychology he has taught me over the last two decades. I'm also boundlessly grateful for the manner in which Jacob and Solomon have—with grown-up grace—accepted their father's absences (sometimes physical, sometimes mental) as he worked on these pages; they've made this book possible, and they make my days worthwhile. Finally, there's one individual who's done "all of the above"—commented on chapters; tolerated my absences; taught me endlessly, over the years, about psychology, and teaching, and publishing; and, above all, who's filled my life with treasure. For all of that, thanks to Friderike Heuer. In the broadest sense, none of this would be possible without her.

Reed College was generous in its support of this book, and I'm also delighted to thank all at the MRC's Applied Psychology Unit, in Cambridge. My months there were productive, and stimulating, and great fun.

Daniel Reisberg
Portland, Oregon

COGNITION

1

The Science of the Mind

This is a book about intellectual functioning. It will take us several pages to spell out just what this means, but some of the questions to be asked are obvious from the start:

There you are, studying for next Wednesday's examination but, for some reason, the material just won't "stick" in your memory. You find yourself wishing, therefore, for a better strategy to use in studying and memorizing. What would that strategy be? Is it possible to have a "better memory"?

While you're studying, your friend is moving around in the room, and you find this terribly distracting. Why can't you just "shut out" your friend's motion? Why don't you have better control over your attention and your ability to concentrate?

An attorney is interviewing a witness to a crime and is amazed by how little the witness remembers. An individual is working with a therapist, trying to reconstruct an event that took place years earlier. The individual is frustrated, though, by how much of the event has been forgotten. You've been introduced to a woman at a party, but, minutes later, you realize (to your embarrassment) that you have forgotten her name. Why do we forget? What sorts of things are we likely to forget, and what sorts of things are we likely to remember?

You pick up the morning newspaper, and you're astonished to read the President's views on some key issue. Why didn't the President draw the same conclusions from the facts that you did? Indeed, how, in general, do people go about drawing conclusions from evidence? If people make errors in drawing conclusions, what causes these errors?

Your newspaper also reports the results of a recent opinion survey, and you are horrified to learn how many people have decided to vote for Candidate X. How do people make these decisions? For that matter, how do people decide what college to attend, or which car to buy, or even what to have for dinner? What forces drive our decisions?

Cognitive psychologists know an enormous amount about all these topics and, before we are through, we will have considered evidence pertinent to each of the scenarios just mentioned. In addition, note that, in the cases just described, things aren't going as you might have wished: You fail to remember; you are unable to ignore a distraction; the voters make a choice you don't like. But what about the other side of things? What about the great intellectual feats that humans produce—great deductions, or extraordinary feats of memory, or incredibly creative solutions to problems? Before we are done, we will also have a lot to say about how these are possible, and thus how it is that we accomplish the great things we do.

The Psychology of the Ordinary

It has been said that poetry serves "to make the mysterious familiar and the familiar mysterious." We might debate this claim about poetry, but it is, in any case, a claim surely true of psychology. In this book, we will discover that many phenomena which appear complex at first inspection, are actually rather simple, when examined closely. This will be true, for example, when we consider how people make judgments about facts they have observed, or evidence they have encountered. As we will see, a few unsophisticated strategies lie at the heart of an extraordinary range of judgments; if we understand these strategies, we understand a great deal. Likewise, our ability to solve problems often seems subtle and mysterious; here, too, we will discover that much of the work is done by means of a few simple strategies. In that sense, then, we will make the mysterious seem familiar.

We will discover also that apparently simple achievements are, in fact, remarkably complicated. You look at this page, read the words, and know what they mean. You choose to stop reading, and pay attention instead to some sound that is reaching your ears. Or perhaps you choose instead to think about how you spent last weekend, and you spend a minute remembering. These seem like ordinary accomplishments. You take no pride in reading—all college students can read. Likewise, it's usually no trick to pay attention to this or that; you have been able to control your attention, with only occasional lapses, ever since you were a child. Similarly, the remembering is immediate, effortless; there's no indication of any complexities here.

When closely examined, though, these accomplishments are complex, and amazingly so. We will spend most of Chapter 2 describing the processes needed to recognize the words on a page; in Chapter 9, we'll examine the further steps required when you put these words together into meaningful sentences. In Chapter 3, we'll see that the simple act of "paying attention" involves a mechanism with many parts; attending is possible, therefore, only when all of these "components" are working properly together. In these ways, then, we will discover that our ordinary achievements are less straightforward than one might guess. The familiar, in other words, is remarkably mysterious.

The Complexity of Cognition: An Example

As one way of conveying these points, consider this little story (adopted from Charniak, 1972) : "Betsy wanted to bring Jacob a present. She shook her piggy bank. It made no sound. She went to look for her mother."

No one has any trouble understanding this four-sentence tale, but you should reflect for a moment on what makes this possible. The story is comprehensible, indeed, is *coherent*, only because you provide some important bits of background. For example, in order to understand this story, you need to know these facts:

1. The things one gives as presents are often things bought for the occasion, rather than things already owned. Otherwise, why did Betsy go to her piggy bank at all? (Surely you did not think she intended to give the piggy bank as the present, or its contents!)
2. Money is kept in piggy banks. One often does not keep track of how much money is in the bank, and one cannot simply look into a piggy bank to learn its contents. Without these facts, how could we explain why Betsy *shook* the bank?
3. Piggy banks are made out of hard material. It's usually coins, not bills, that are kept in piggy banks. Coins make noise when they contact hard material. Otherwise, why would it be informative that the bank made no sound?
4. Children, not adults, are the ones who keep piggy banks, and children tend not to have credit cards. Otherwise, Betsy could compensate for her lack of cash by pulling an American Express card out of her wallet. If you didn't know this, then you wouldn't understand why she went to see her mother!

This list of relevant facts could easily be expanded, but by now the point is clear: The story makes sense only because of the knowledge you bring to it. Without this knowledge, you would be unable to see why the second sentence of the story is a logical sequel to the first, why the third sentence conveys any information at all.

This story, therefore, starts to reveal some of the complexities involved in our moment-by-moment intellectual commerce with the world. Anyone, even a child, could understand this brief story. Nonetheless, in order to understand it, you must engage in some (usually unnoticed) activity—dredging information out of your memory, integrating that information with the sentences you are reading, making some inferences, and so on.

Moreover, let's emphasize that these background facts, needed to understand this story, are supplied *by you*. Therefore, these facts must be drawn from your storehouse of remembered information—that is, from your memory. And, of course, the knowledge at issue here is knowledge of a common-sense sort—e.g., the fact that coins are kept in children's piggy banks, or the fact that metallic objects make a noise when they bump into other hard objects. Surely, you know a vast number of these low-level facts: You know that ceilings are above floors, not below them; you know that it's generally cold in the winter; you know that one usually invites friends to birthday parties, not enemies or total strangers; you know that 2 + 2 = 4, that red is a color, that there's no royal family in the U.S., and on and on and on.

These commonsense facts are referred to as **generic knowledge**—knowledge about how things work in general. Also in memory is a wide range of **episodic knowledge**—knowledge about specific episodes within your life. You remember how you spent last summer, what you had for breakfast this morning, and a huge number of other episodes as well. It seems, then, that there is actually an enormous quantity of information in your memory: generic knowledge, episodic knowledge, and (as we'll see) more. This vastness of knowledge is impressive, but it also creates a problem: With all this information stored in memory, how do you manage to find just the information you need? Moreover, how do you manage to find the information rapidly— so rapidly, in fact, that you don't even realize you've just pulled information out of memory? (In the Betsy and Jacob story, for example, you probably didn't notice your "contribution" until we pointed it out.)

Many people speak of memory as though it were a "library," or "filing system," not so different in its functioning from an actual library or filing system. As we'll see in later chapters, these comparisons are somewhat misleading, but let's pursue them for a moment. Who serves the role of librarian, or file clerk? When you need some information from memory, you're usually not aware of searching for it; instead, the sought-after information simply "pops" into mind for you. Therefore, it would seem, it is not the conscious self doing the memory search. As Flanagan (1991, p. 176) puts it, then,

> "perhaps this is evidence for a secretarial homunculus [literally: "little man"], a sort of mental office manager, who races around performing the boring matches and searches and only passes on information to me when I, as the executive director of the operation, really need it. But if there really is such an office manager in my mind, he or she or it is really quite a bit smarter than I am, and possesses skills that I certainly don't have. It is inconceivable to me that I could figure out a filing and retrieval system, as well as perform the filing and retrieval, for the 100 trillion bits of information which, according to some estimates, are encoded in my brain."

Once again, therefore, there is a puzzle to be figured out. The comprehension of even a simple story requires the integration of that story with prior knowledge. This in turn requires that the knowledge be drawn from memory and, in fact, be drawn rapidly enough so that the process doesn't derail the comprehension of the story itself. But, given how much is in memory, how much there is to be searched through, this knowledge retrieval is far from trivial. What is the filing system? Who runs it? Is the retrieval reliable—does it always succeed, or does it occasionally fail to locate the sought-after information? These are questions we must answer if we're to understand even the simplest bit of our intellectual functioning, such as the comprehension of a simple child's story.

The Scope of Cognitive Psychology

The processes we've mentioned so far—remembering, comprehending text, making judgments about evidence, solving problems—all fall squarely within the realm of cognitive psychology. In its modern form, cognitive psychology is an enterprise only three or four decades old. Classic, pioneering research was done in the 1950s (e.g., Broadbent, 1958; Bruner, Goodnow & Austin, 1956; Miller, 1956); the first modern textbook was published only in 1967 (Neisser, 1967). In these early works, cognitive psychology was often understood as the scientific study of *knowledge*. How is knowledge acquired? How is knowledge retained, so that it's available when needed? How is knowledge used, as a basis for action, or as a basis for generating further knowledge? This first of these questions (how is knowledge acquired?) leads us to be interested in the processes of perception, and how perceived objects are categorized and understood. The second question (how is knowledge retained?) leads to the study of memory—both the formation of memories, and then the subsequent retrieval of information from memory. The third question (how is knowledge used?) invites the study of decision-making, judgment, and inference.

These topics continue to define the broad outlines of cognitive psychology, and thus the selection of topics covered in this book: Chapters 2 and 3 will be largely concerned with our acquisition of new information from the world, obviously an important source of our knowledge. Chapters 4, 5, and 6 will then examine the nature of memory—how memories are created, how memories are retrieved when needed. Chapters 7 and 8 will seek to characterize our knowledge itself: How is the knowledge recorded within our minds, within our memories? Chapter 9 will examine a special type of knowledge—our knowledge about language. Chapter 10 then focuses on visual knowledge and visual imagery, and we'll consider the contrast between these and knowledge that's more verbal in character. The remainder of the book will then be concerned with how our knowledge gets used: In Chapter 11, we will consider how we make judgments or draw conclusions about things we have experienced. In Chapter 12, we will ask what we *do* with our knowledge, once we've got it. What implications do we consider? How do we then make decisions, based on our knowledge, and based on our perceptions of our various options? Then, once we have made a decision and chosen a goal, how do we select a path toward that goal? This will be our focus in Chapter 13. Finally, in Chapter 14, we will gather together some strands that will have run throughout the book, considering in particular just how much of our thought is *unconscious*. In the process, we will consider what consciousness *is for*.

The Wide Implications of Cognition Research

This catalogue of topics should convey the considerable breadth of cognitive psychology. Perhaps a better way to convey this breadth, though, is to look "within" these topics, examining what each includes. Consider, for example, the study of memory: When we study memory, what are we studying? Or, to turn this around, what tasks rely on memory? When you are taking an exam, you obviously rely on memory—memory for what you have learned during the term. Likewise, you rely on memory when you are at the supermarket and are trying to remember the cheesecake recipe, so you can buy the ingredients. You rely on memory when you are reminiscing about childhood. But what else draws on memory?

The "Betsy and Jacob" story, earlier in the chapter, should have made clear that we also rely on our memories to supplement materials we read, tales we hear, scenes we examine. Without this use of memory, anyone *telling* the Betsy and Jacob story would need to spell out all the connections, and all the assumptions. That is, the story would have to include all the background facts that we earlier enumerated, background facts that, with memory, are supplied by you. In this case, the story would have to be fifty times longer than it currently is, and the telling of it fifty times slower. The same would be true for every story we hear, every conversation we participate in. In short, without memory, conversation and reading would be impossibly slow. Memory is crucial for each of these activities. Likewise, without memory, you wouldn't be able to *retain* anything you've learned—and so, no memory, no learning; no memory, no ability to benefit in any way from experience.

Here is a different sort of example: In Chapter 5, we will consider various cases of clinical **amnesia**—cases in which someone, because of brain damage, has lost the ability to remember certain materials. These cases are fascinating at many levels, including the fact that they give us key insights into what memory is for: Without memory, what is disrupted?

One well-studied amnesic patient was a gentleman identified as H.M. We'll have much more to say about H.M. in Chapter 5, but let us here make a few observations: H.M.'s memory loss was the unanticipated byproduct of brain surgery (surgery intended to control his epilepsy). The memory loss is quite profound: H.M. remembers well events prior to the surgery, but seems unable to recall any event that has occurred subsequent to the surgery. This has, of course, had massive consequences for his life, and some of the consequences are perhaps surprising. For example, H.M. had an uncle of whom he was very fond, and H.M. often asks about his uncle: How is he? What's he doing these days? Unfortunately, the uncle died sometime after H.M.'s surgery. H.M. can (and does) learn of this fact, but he cannot remember it. As a result, each time H.M. hears about his uncle's death, he is hearing the news "for the first time,"—with all the shock, all the grief. Because of his amnesia, he soon forgets that he has heard this terrible news, and so has no opportunity to "live with" the news, to adjust to it. Hence, his grief cannot subside. Without memory, H.M. cannot come to terms with his uncle's death.

A different glimpse of memory function comes from H.M.'s poignant comments about his state and about "who he is." Each of us has a conception of who we are, of what sort of person we are. That conception is supported by numerous memories: We know whether we're deserving of praise for our good deeds or blame for our transgressions, because we remember our good deeds and our transgressions. We know whether we've kept our promises, or achieved our goals, because, again, we have the relevant memories. None of this is true for amnesics, and H.M. sometimes comments on the fact that, in important ways, he doesn't know who he is. He doesn't know if he should be proud of his accomplishments or ashamed of his crimes; he doesn't know if he's been clever or stupid, honorable or dishonest, industrious or lazy. In a sense, then, it would seem that, without a memory, there is no self. (For broader discussion, see Hilts, 1995.)

What, then, is the scope of cognitive psychology? As we mentioned earlier, this field is sometimes defined as the scientific study of the acquisition, retention, and use of knowledge. This makes it sound like the field is concerned with purely intellectual matters; it makes it sound like the field has a fairly narrow scope. We have just considered some examples, though, that show the opposite to be true: Our self-concept, it seems, depends on our knowledge (and, in particular, on our episodic knowledge). Our emotional adjustments to the world, as we have seen, rely on our memories. Or, to take much more ordinary cases, our ability to understand a story we've read, or a conversation, or, presumably, *any* of our experiences, depends on our supplementing that experience with some knowledge.

In short, cognitive psychology, and a reliance on our knowledge, on our ability to learn, to remember, and to make judgments, is relevant to virtually every waking moment of our lives. Activities that don't, on the surface, appear "intellectual" would nonetheless collapse without the support of our cognitive functioning. This is true whether we're considering our actions, our social lives, our emotions, or almost any other domain. This is the scope of cognitive psychology and, in a real sense, is the scope of this book.

A Brief History

We have already mentioned that cognitive psychology is a relatively young endeavor—about 35 years old, making it one of psychology's youngest branches. Despite this youth, cognitive psychology has had an enormous impact on the field—so much so that many speak of the "cognitive revolution" within psychology. This (alleged) revolution, taking place across the late 1950s and 1960s, represented a striking change in the style of research and theorizing employed by psychologists. The new styles were intended initially for studying problems we have already met: problems of learning, memory, and so on. But these new styles were soon "exported" to other domains, and have provided important insights into these domains. In important ways, then, the Cognitive Revolution has changed the intellectual map of our field.

The Years of Introspection

To understand all of this, we need some historical context. In the late nineteenth century, scholars—notably Wilhelm Wundt (1832–1920) and his student, Edward Bradford Titchener (1867–1927)—launched the new enterprise of research psychology, defining their field for the first time as an endeavor separate from philosophy or from biology and physiology.

In these years, psychologists were largely concerned with the study of conscious mental events—our feelings, our thoughts, our perceptions, our recollections. Moreover, there was just one way, they argued, to study these events: Let's start by noting that there is no way for you to experience my thoughts, or I yours. The only person who can experience or observe your thoughts is *you*. Thus, the only way to study thoughts is for each of us to **introspect**, or "look within," to observe and record the content of our own mental lives, and the sequence of our own experiences.

If psychology is to study thoughts, recollections, and sensations, therefore, introspection must be our method. Wundt and Titchener insisted, though, that the introspection cannot be casual. Instead, introspectors had to be meticulously trained—they were given a vocabulary, to describe what they observed; they were trained to be as careful and as complete as possible; and above all, they were trained simply to report on their experiences, with a minimum of interpretation.

Psychologists quickly became disenchanted with this style of research, and it is not hard to see why. As one concern, debate soon emerged about unconscious thought. If such thought existed, then introspection was necessarily inadequate, since introspection, by its nature, is the study of conscious thought and so only works for conscious experiences! In fact, present-day scholars are convinced that unconscious thought plays a large part in our mental lives. For example, what is your phone number? Now, how did you find this out? One might expect that you used some system or strategy for "looking up" this information in your memory and then bringing this information into awareness. Indeed, we'll see in later chapters that a complex series of steps is required even for this simple bit of remembering. None of these events, however, is part of your conscious experience. Instead, the telephone number simply "comes to you," without any effort, without any noticeable steps or strategies on your part. If we relied on introspection as our means of studying mental events, then we would have no way of examining these processes.

As a different concern, it seems clear that science needs some way of testing its assertions, of confirming or disconfirming its claims. Hand in hand with this, science needs some way of resolving disagreements: If you claim that there are ten planets in our solar system, and I insist that there are nine, we need some way of determining who is right. Otherwise, we have no way of locating the fact of the matter, and so our "science" will become a matter of opinion, not fact.

With introspection, though, this "testability" of claims is often unattainable. Let's imagine that you insist that your headaches are worse than mine. How could we ever test your claim? It might be true that you describe your headaches in extreme terms—you talk about your "unbelievable, agonizing, excruciating" headaches. But that might simply mean that you are inclined toward extravagant descriptions—it might reflect your verbal style, not your headaches. Similarly, it might be true that you need bed-rest whenever one of your headaches strikes. Does that mean your headaches are truly intolerable? It might mean instead that you are self-indulgent and rest even in the face of mild pain. Perhaps our headaches are identical, but I'm stoic about mine, while you're not.

In fact, there's only one way to test your claim about your headaches: We'd need some way of comparing your headaches to mine. That would require that we somehow "place" the headaches side-by-side so that we can compare them. Then we could separate the facts from the reporter and get some objective assessment of the headaches. But there is obviously no way to do this, leaving us with no way to determine if your reports of your headaches are exaggerated or not, distorted or accurate.

For purposes of science, this is just not good enough. For science, we need objective observations, observations that we can count on. We need observations that aren't dependent on a particular point of view, or a particular descriptive style. It is not enough to consider "the world as one person sees it." Instead, we want to consider the world as it objectively is. In scientific discourse, we usually achieve this objectivity by making sure all the facts are out in plain view, so that you can inspect my evidence, and I yours. In that way, we can be certain that neither of us is distorting, or misreporting, or exaggerating, the facts. And that is precisely what we cannot do with introspection.

The Years of Behaviorism

The concerns just raised led many psychologists, particularly those in the United States, to abandon introspection as a research method. One could not do science, they argued, with introspective data. Instead, psychology needed *objective* data. That means we must focus on data that are out in the open, for all to observe.

An organism's behaviors fall into this category: You can watch my actions, and so can anyone else who is appropriately positioned. Therefore, data concerned with behavior will be objective data, and so are grist for the scientific mill. Likewise, stimuli in the world are in this same "objective" category: These are measurable, recordable, physical events. Moreover, you can arrange to record the stimuli I experience today and also the behaviors I produce. The same is true for stimuli and behaviors tomorrow and the day after. This will allow you to record how the pattern of stimuli and behaviors changes with the passage of time and with the accumulation of experience. Thus, my *learning history* can also be objectively recorded and scientifically studied.

Of course, my beliefs, my wishes, my goals, and my expectations are all things that cannot be directly observed and cannot be objectively recorded. Thus we need to rule out any discussion of these **mentalistic** notions. These can be studied only via introspection (or so the argument goes), and introspection, we have suggested, is worthless as a scientific tool. Hence, a scientific psychology needs to avoid these "invisible" internal processes or events.

It was this perspective that led researchers to the **behaviorist** movement, a movement that dominated psychology in America for roughly the first half of the twentieth century. This movement produced some notable gains— broad principles concerned with how our behavior changes in response to different configurations of stimuli (including stimuli we often call "rewards" and "punishments"). These principles apply in a wide range of settings, to a wide range of behaviors and, as it turns out, to a wide range of organisms. Many of these principles remain in place within contemporary psychology, and provide the base for an impressive theoretical enterprise, as well as a range of practical applications. (For a description of these principles, see Schwartz & Robbins, 1995.)

However, by the late 1950s, psychologists were convinced that a great deal of our behavior could not be explained in this way. The problem in a nutshell

reaction = understanding of stimulus + response

is this: When you respond to some stimulus in the world, your reaction is usually guided by your understanding of the stimulus, and not by the stimulus itself. Therefore, if we try to predict your behavior by focusing on the stimulus *per se*, by focusing on the objective situation, then we will regularly make the wrong predictions. In the same way, your choice of a response is generally guided by what the response means—that is, by how you understand the response, and by how you believe others will understand the response. Once again, therefore, if we want to predict your behavior, we need to consider more than the objectively defined response; we also need to consider your *understanding* of the response.

These broad claims spell trouble for the behaviorists' program. The behaviorists, in striving for objectivity, sought to exclude such invisible entities as "beliefs" or "understanding" (not to mention plans, strategies, preferences, perceptions, and the like). Yet, it seems, we need these mentalistic notions if we're to achieve the prediction and scientific understanding of human actions. Thus we *can't* study these mentalistic notions within the behaviorists' perspective, but we *must* study these notions if we're going to understand behavior.

The evidence for these assertions is threaded throughout the chapters of this book. Over and over, we will find it necessary to mention subjects' perceptions and strategies and understanding, as we strive to explain *why* (and *how*) subjects perform various tasks and accomplish various goals. Indeed, we've already seen an example of this pattern: Imagine that we present the "Betsy and Jacob" story to subjects and then ask them various questions about the story: Why did Betsy shake her piggy bank? Why did she go to look for her mother? Subjects' responses will surely reflect their understanding of the story, which in turn depends on far more than the physical stimulus—i.e., the 29 syllables of the story itself. If we wanted to predict subjects' responses, therefore, we would need to refer to the story but also to the subjects' knowledge, and their understanding of, and contribution to, this stimulus.

Here's a different example, that makes the same general point: There you sit in the dining hall. A friend produces this physical stimulus: "Pass the salt, please." You immediately produce a bit of salt-passing behavior. So far, all is fine from the behaviorists' perspective: There was a physical stimulus and an easily-defined response. But notice that things would have run off in the same way if your friend had offered a different stimulus. "Could I have the salt?" would have done the trick. Ditto for "Salt, please!" or "Mmm, this sure needs salt!" If your friend is both loquacious and obnoxious, the utterance might have been, "Excuse me, but after briefly contemplating the gustatory qualities of these comestibles, I have discerned that their sensory qualities would be improved by the addition of a number of sodium and chloride ions, delivered in roughly equal proportions and in crystalline form; could you aid me in this endeavor?" You might giggle (or snarl) at your friend, but you would still pass the salt.

Now let's work on the "science of salt-passing behavior." When is this behavior produced? Since we've just observed that the behavior is evoked by all of these stimuli, we would surely want to ask: What do these stimuli have in common? The answer, quite simply, is that they have very little in common at the level of observable, objective data. After all, the actual sounds being produced are rather different in "Pass the salt" and "Could I have the salt?" Indeed, many *similar* sounds would lead to rather different effects. Imagine that your friend said, "Salt the pass." Or perhaps your friend said, "She has only a small part in the play. All she gets to say is, 'Pass the salt, please.' " In these cases, you wouldn't pass the salt. Hence physically dissimilar stimuli do the trick; physically similar ones don't.

Of course these stimuli do have something in common with each other: They all mean the same thing. These utterances may have different physical forms and different *literal* meanings, but in our culture they're all understood as ways of requesting salt. In order to produce a "science of salt-passing" or, more modestly, to predict your behavior in this situation, we need to consider what these stimuli mean to you. This seems an extraordinarily simple point, but it is a point, echoed over and over by countless other examples, that indicates the impossibility of a complete behaviorist psychology.[1]

The Roots of the Cognitive Revolution

We seem to be nearing an impasse: If we wish to explain or predict behavior, we need to make reference to the mental world—the world of perceptions, understandings, and intentions. We could study this mental world via introspection, but we've argued that introspective data are (at best) problematic. The world of the objective seems (for our purposes) inadequate, and the world of the subjective seems unstudy-able.

The solution to this impasse is actually one suggested many years ago, perhaps most clearly by the philosopher Immanuel Kant (1724–1804). It is his method that, in many ways, led to the principal research strategy of cognitive psychology. To use Kant's transcendental method, one begins with the observable facts. For Kant, these included the fact that humans can and do reason about spatial and temporal relations, and also the fact that we can and

---

[1] We should mention, as a fast side-comment, that the behaviorists themselves quickly realized this point. Hence modern behaviorism has abandoned the radical rejection of mental terms, and, indeed, it's hard to draw a line between modern behaviorism and a field often called "animal cognition," a field that often employs mentalistic language! The behaviorism being criticized here is a historically defined behaviorism, and it's this perspective that, in large measure, gave birth to modern Cognitive Psychology.

do reason about cause and effect. Kant's research strategy was then to work backwards from these observations. Given these "effects," what can we figure out about the "causes"? What must the mental world be like in order to make these observations possible? In essence, Kant asked, "How could the observed state of affairs have come about?" (See Flanagan, 1991, for further discussion of this method.)

This method is sometimes called "inference to best explanation," since what one seeks is the best possible explanation of all the available facts. As it turns out, this method is crucial for a great deal of modern science. Physicists, for example, do not observe electrons directly. They instead infer electron activity from the "tracks" electrons leave in orbitals, and by momentary fluctuations in magnetic fields, and so on. From these *effects* of electrons, physicists figure out what the *causes* must be like, and in this fashion they infer the properties of the electron (or any other particle). Thus physicists, too, are using Kant's research strategy, and "doing science on the invisible." In this way, they are making important discoveries about particles that no one has ever seen, reaching firm conclusions about events they have never observed. Kant's method is a powerful one and, in using it, cognitive psychologists are in good company.

The Computer as Metaphor

In Kant's method, one starts with observed data and seeks to reconstruct the unseen processes that led to these data. But where does one begin? What sort of mechanisms might one propose for our ability to remember, or our ability to solve problems? Should we seek to explain the data in terms of magnetic fields, or biochemistry, or divine intervention? If we seek the "best explanation" for the observed data, then in what terms should that explanation be cast?

In the 1950s, a new approach to psychological explanation became available, and turned out to be immensely fruitful. This new approach was suggested by the rapid developments in electronic information processing, including developments in computer technology. It quickly became clear that computers were capable of immensely efficient information storage and retrieval ("memory"), as well as performance that seemed to involve decision-making and problem-solving. Psychologists therefore began to explore the possibility that the human mind employed processes and procedures similar to those used in computers, and so psychological data were soon being explained in terms of "buffers" and "gates" and "central processors," all terms borrowed from computer technology. (See, for example, Broadbent, 1958; Miller, Galanter & Pribram, 1960.)

The computer metaphor provided a new language for describing psychological processes, explaining psychological data. Given a particular performance, say, on a memory task, one could hypothesize a series of **information processing** events that made the performance possible. As we will see, hypotheses framed in these terms led psychologists to predict a host of new observations, and thus both organized the available information and led to many new discoveries.

In essence, then, the computer metaphor allowed us to run the Kantian logic: Given a set of data, one could propose a particular sequence of information-processing events, as the hypothesized source of those data. One could then ask whether some other, perhaps simpler, information-processing sequence could also explain the data, or whether some other sequence could explain both these data and some other findings. (Recall that we're seeking the *best* explanation.) More important, one could then *test* these proposed sequences: If such-and-such mechanism lies behind these data, then things should work somewhat differently in this circumstance, or that one. (We'll offer an example of how this works in just a few pages.)

In these ways, the influence of the computer metaphor led to a blossoming of psychological research in the 1960s and 1970s, and this provided a major impetus for the development of modern cognitive psychology. It is worth noting that the use of this metaphor does not commit us to claiming that "the mind is just like a computer," or "the mind is nothing more than a complex computer." These claims may or may not turn out to be true; for now, these claims remain highly controversial. (See, for example, Charniak & McDermott, 1987; Churchland, 1988; Dreyfus, 1979; Haugeland, 1981, 1986; Pylyshyn, 1984; Winston, 1984.) For now, it is sufficient to argue that the mind is *enough* like a computer that we can profitably explain much about the mind by using the language of computer processing. Likewise, the mind seems to be enough like a computer so that the use of such language leads to the discovery of new facts about intellectual performance.

Multiple Levels of Description

We should be clear, though, about just what is meant by the language of computer processing. There is, in fact, considerable flexibility here: Consider, for example, a computer designed to play the game of chess; how should we understand this computer's functioning? The answer to this depends on our *purposes* and on just what it is we are seeking to understand. Imagine, for example, that the computer is broken. No matter what you do, it produces no response. No matter what program you try to run, the result is the same—still no response. In this case, you might investigate the machine's hardware: Is it properly connected? Is it receiving electricity?

Imagine, as a different case, that the computer functions reasonably well, most of the time. Every so often, however, it produces a sequence of bizarre moves, each of which simply undoes the move before. (The Queen moves one space left, then one space right, then one space left, then right again.) In this case, you might suspect that the problem lies in the computer's program or software. If the computer is doing *other* tasks perfectly well, you'll probably reason that the problem doesn't lie in the wiring or in some defective component. Instead, somewhere within the chess-playing program, someone has given the computer the wrong instruction. Hence, to fix the "bug," you would probably call a programmer, not an electrician.

Imagine, as yet another case, that you're playing *against* this computer in a chess tournament. For this purpose, you will probably care about the strategies and goals contained within the computer's program. What gambits is the machine likely to try? What traps will it detect, and what traps will it fall into? You probably won't care about the hardware—your response to a "pawn gambit" will be the same whether the computer is built out of silicon chips or out of relays. You also might not care exactly how the computer was programmed. You won't care, for example, what language the computer's instructions are written in. If there are bugs in the program, you want to know about them, but perhaps no bugs have been detected. You won't care how the computer's strategies are labeled, or in which "memory registers" the strategies are listed. This information isn't useful to you in deciding what moves you should make, and what strategies you should try.

Each of these levels of description—at the level of hardware, at the level of the program, or at the level of goals and strategies—is legitimate and often useful. Which level of description you use will depend on your situation. Thus, the "language of computer processing" is, in an important way, opportunistic: You use the language appropriate to your goals.

The same is true within cognitive psychology. In many cases, our understanding of mental function depends on close consideration of neurological or physiological mechanisms. In these cases, we will need to consider the "hardware" of the mind—i.e., the brain. In other cases, we will find it useful to offer a more abstract level of analysis—making reference to beliefs and assumptions and strategies, terms familiar to us all. In still other cases, we will use an intermediate level of analysis to explain the data in terms of "memory buffers" and "response selectors" and the like.

Our choice among these levels of description will be governed, throughout, by the same Kantian logic. For each phenomenon, we will begin with the observable facts, and ask what unseen mechanism makes these facts possible. When an explanation in terms of "hardware" seems the best account of the facts, that is the idiom we will use. When an explanation in terms of beliefs or strategies seems more economical, more straightforward, then we will shift to that level. In each case, though, we will then seek to test our account by asking what new predictions we can derive from it. In this sense, our enterprise is based on inference, but our inferences must themselves be testable.

Research in Cognitive Psychology—An Example

Our discussion of research in cognitive psychology has so far been rather abstract, and so it may help at this point to provide a concrete example. We will return to this example in Chapter 4, and there put it into a richer theoretical context. For now, though, our focus is on the method, rather than the theory itself.

As we turn to method, though, let us emphasize that what characterizes cognitive research is not a particular group of experimental procedures or a particular laboratory paradigm. Instead, the research is characterized largely by the logic of the methods used and, to a smaller extent, by the types of data that are typically collected. With that proviso in place, let us turn to the example.

Working Memory: Some Initial Observations

Many of the sentences in this book—including the present one, which consists of nineteen words—are rather long. In many of these sentences, words that must be understood together (such as "sentences . . . are . . . long") are widely separated (note the 12 words interposed between "sentences" and "are"). Yet you have no trouble understanding these sentences.

This simple observation implies a form of memory in use as you read a sentence: You must somehow remember the early words in the sentence as you forge ahead in your reading. Then, once you have read enough, you can integrate what you have decoded so far. In this section's very first sentence, you needed to remember the first seven words ("Many of the sentences in this book"), while you read the interposed phrase ("including . . . nineteen words"). Then you had to bring those first seven words back into play, to integrate them with the sentence's end ("are rather long").

Psychologists have proposed that the memory relevant to this task is *qualitatively* different from the memory used for storing, say, your recollection of last summer, or for storing your "mental encyclopedia," in which you store your generic knowledge. These latter examples are drawn from *long-term storage*, a vast repository holding all your knowledge in "dormant" form. In contrast, our example of sentence-reading relies on *short-term storage*, or in the terms we'll use, it relies on *working memory*. Working memory is relatively small in size, but holds information in an easily accessible form. Working memory, in effect, keeps information "at your fingertips," so that it is instantly available when you need it. Thus, having decoded the first part of a sentence, you store its semantic content in working memory, so that it is ready at hand a moment later, when you are all set to integrate this content with the sentence's end.

We'll have much more to say about long-term memory and working-memory in Chapter 4. There we'll consider evidence for the claim that these memories are, in fact, qualitatively different from each other; we'll also provide a more refined view of how these memories interact. For now, though, let's consider just a few facts—some basic observations about working-memory's size and its function.

First, working memory's capacity is sometimes measured via a span test. In this test, you read a subject a list of, say, four items, perhaps four letters ("A D G W"). The subject has to report these back, immediately, in sequence. If the subject succeeds, we try it again with five letters ("Q D W U F"). If the subject can repeat these back correctly, we try six letters, and so on, until we find a list that the subject can not report back accurately. Generally, subjects start making errors with sequences of 7 or 8 letters. Subjects' **letter span**, therefore, is about 7 or 8.

Interestingly enough, when subjects do make errors, their errors are often systematic. Often subjects will inadvertently substitute one letter for another with a similar sound. For example, having heard "S" they'll report back "F," or having heard "V" they'll report back "B." The problem is not in hearing the letters in the first place: We get similar sound-alike confusions if the letters are presented *visually*. Thus, having seen "F" subjects are likely to report back "S." They are not likely, in this situation, to report back the similar-*looking* "E."

Working Memory: A Proposal

Alan Baddeley and Graham Hitch proposed a model to explain the facts we've just described, and a variety of other data as well. Their model starts by stipulating that working memory is not a single entity. Instead, working memory has several separate parts, and so they prefer to speak of a **working-memory system**. At the heart of the system is the **central executive**. This is the part that runs the show and that does the real work.

The executive often calls on a number of **slave systems**. These "slaves" are not very sophisticated—they are useful for mere storage of information and not much more. If any work needs to be done on the information—

interpretation or analysis—the slave can't do it; the executive is needed. Nonetheless, these slave systems are highly useful: Information that will soon be needed, but isn't needed right now, can be sent off to the slaves for temporary storage. Therefore, the executive isn't burdened by the mere storage of this information, and is freed up to do other tasks.

In effect, the slave systems serve the same function as a piece of scratch-paper on your desk. When you're going to need some bit of information soon, you write it down on the scratch-paper. Of course, the scratch-paper has no mind of its own, and so it can't do anything with the "stored" information; all it does is hold on to the information. But that's helpful enough: With the information stored in this manner, you can cease thinking about it, and so are free to think about something else instead. That is the gain. Then, once you are ready for the stored information, you glance at your notes, and there the information is.

One of working memory's most important slaves is the **articulatory rehearsal loop**. This slave is used for storing verbal materials, or nonverbal materials that can be "translated" into some verbal code. To use this slave, the central executive launches the activity of *pronouncing* the to-be-remembered items. The pronunciation isn't out loud; instead, you "talk to yourself"—you go through the motions of speaking but without making a sound. This is referred to as **subvocalization**. Even though it is silent, subvocalization does cause a record of this "speech" to be loaded into a sort of echo box, a passive repository that is part of the mental apparatus normally used for hearing. You can think of the "inner voice" loading a record into the "inner ear." More technically, subvocalization creates a record in a **phonological buffer**. Once in that buffer, however, the record begins to fade away. At this point, the executive must intercede: The executive "reads" the contents of the buffer, and launches another cycle. (See Figure 1.1.)

Note, then, that this loop—from executive to subvocalization to buffer, and then back to executive—places only an intermittent demand on the executive, that is, for the launching of each cycle. Once launched, though, the inner voice can run pretty much on its own, thanks to the fact that speech is enormously well-practiced and thus largely automatic. Likewise, the phonological buffer is a passive storage device—information simply arrives there, and starts to decay, with no action needed. Therefore, for most of the duration of the rehearsal cycle, the executive is free to work on other matters, which is the advantage of using this loop.

Evidence for the Working-Memory System

This proposal neatly handles the observations we've already offered, and leads to many new predictions. For example, notice that the rehearsal loop employs

Figure 1.1

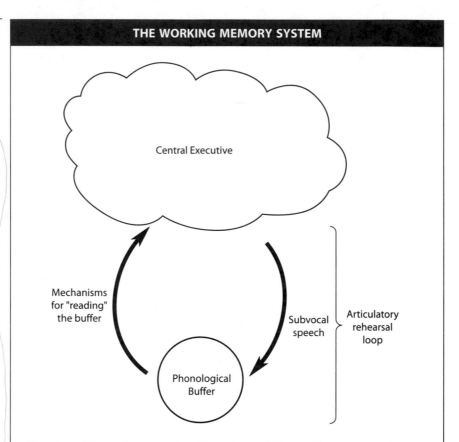

The following handwritten notes appear in the left margin:

Item
↓
subvocalize item
↓
rehearse subvocalization
(∴ loading buffer)
↓
buffer begins to decay
↓
executive reads buffer
before it decays
↓
executive pronounces
item
↓
Next item

THE WORKING MEMORY SYSTEM

Central Executive

Mechanisms
for "reading"
the buffer

Subvocal
speech

Articulatory
rehearsal
loop

Phonological
Buffer

The Central Executive controls all functions within working memory, but the executive is supported by a number of slave systems. One slave system, the articulatory rehearsal loop, involves two components—subvocal speech (the "inner voice") and a phonological buffer (the "inner ear"). Items are rehearsed by using subvocalization to "load" the buffer. While this is going on, the executive is free to work on other matters. However, the executive is needed to "read" the contents of the buffer before they decay; the executive can then pronounce the items again, launching another cycle through the loop.

some of the mechanisms of hearing: The "inner ear" is literally part of the auditory system. Consequently, letters that sound alike, when heard, also sound alike in the inner ear. It is no wonder, then, that "sound alike" errors crop up in working memory—these errors are the result of using the loop.

Against this backdrop, imagine that we ask subjects to take our span task while simultaneously saying "tah-tah-tah" over and over, out loud. This **concurrent articulation task** obviously requires the mechanisms for speech production. Therefore, these mechanisms are not available for other use, including subvocalization. (See Figure 1.2.) One can't subvocalize one sequence while overtly vocalizing something else.

According to the model, how will this matter? First, note that our initial span test measures the *combined capacities* of the central executive and the loop. That is, when subjects take a span test, they store some of the to-be-

Figure 1.2

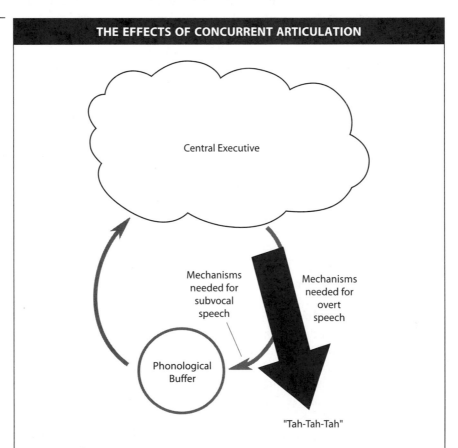

THE EFFECTS OF CONCURRENT ARTICULATION

Central Executive

Mechanisms needed for subvocal speech

Mechanisms needed for overt speech

Phonological Buffer

"Tah-Tah-Tah"

The mechanisms needed for subvocal speech (the "inner voice") overlap heavily with those needed for actual, overt speech. Therefore, if these mechanisms are in use for actual speech, they are not available for subvocal rehearsal. Hence, many experiments block rehearsal by requiring subjects to say "tah-tah-tah" out loud.

remembered items in the loop, and other items via the central executive. (This is an extravagant use of the central executive, which is capable of vastly more than mere storage. It's akin to using a super-computer to record your shopping list. But mere storage is all that the span task requires.) With concurrent articulation, though, the loop isn't available for use, and so we are now measuring the capacity of working memory *without* the rehearsal loop. We should predict, therefore, that concurrent articulation, as easy as it is, should cut memory span drastically. This prediction turns out to be correct.

Second, with visually presented items, concurrent articulation should eliminate the sound-alike errors. Roughly put, the relevant sequence of events is as follows: With visual presentation, items are initially seen, and registered by the central executive. The executive then launches the subvocalization of the to-be-remembered items, using the inner voice, and this loads a record of these items into the inner ear. It is here, in the inner ear, that the sound-alike errors arise. This sequence of events is blocked, however, by concurrent articulation: With the inner voice unavailable, there's no way for these items to reach the inner ear, and so no way for these errors to arise. If errors do occur, they'll be errors of some other sort—perhaps look-alike errors, rather than sound-alike errors. These predictions are, once again, correct: With concurrent articulation, sound-alike errors are largely eliminated.

Third, we can also test subjects' memory span using complex visual shapes. Subjects are shown these shapes, and then must echo the sequence back, by drawing what they have just seen. If we choose shapes that are not easily named, then the shapes cannot be rehearsed via the inner-voice / inner-ear combination. (What would one subvocalize to rehearse these?) With such stimuli, there should be no effect of concurrent articulation: If subjects aren't using the rehearsal loop, there is no cost attached to denying them use of the loop. This prediction is also correct.

Fourth, let's focus on the overlap between subvocalization and overt speech. We've already appealed to this overlap in explaining the effects of concurrent articulation. But the overlap has other implications as well. In particular, we might expect the inner voice to share certain traits with overt speech, and it does: For example, some words obviously take longer to pronounce than others (e.g., three-syllable words vs. one-syllable words), and we might expect that this would matter for the inner voice: If a word takes more time to vocalize, then it should also take more time to subvocalize, and so it should be more difficult to rehearse. Consistent with this observation, memory span turns out to be smaller for longer words: If we test your span with one-syllable words, we'll estimate your memory's capacity at 8 or 9 items. If we test your span with three-syllable words, our estimate will be closer to 4 or 5. This is often referred to as the **word-length effect**.

Handwritten margin notes:

eg.1
☺ visual item
↓
registered by executive
↓
subvocalization
↓
goes into inner ear

STOP!
—can't go into inner ear b/c inner voice is already busy in "tah, tah, tah"
(∴ few sound-alike errors, but maybe look alike)

eg 2
complex shape (supposed to reproduce later)
↓
subvocalize
STOP!!
what would you subvocalize to rehearse this?
∴ no effect of concurrent articulation b/c item never gets to inner ear.

word length effect matters for inner voice (takes longer to rehearse)

Fifth, we have shown that rehearsal is disrupted if we deny subjects use of the inner voice, via concurrent articulation. Rehearsal is also disrupted if we deny subjects use of the inner ear. The manipulation here exploits the fact that the inner ear draws on mechanisms ordinarily used for hearing. Therefore, if we ask subjects to memorize various items while sitting in a noisy environment, then these incoming noises will pre-empt use of the inner ear, and thus block use of the inner-voice/inner-ear partnership. (See Figure 1.3.)

Figure 1.3

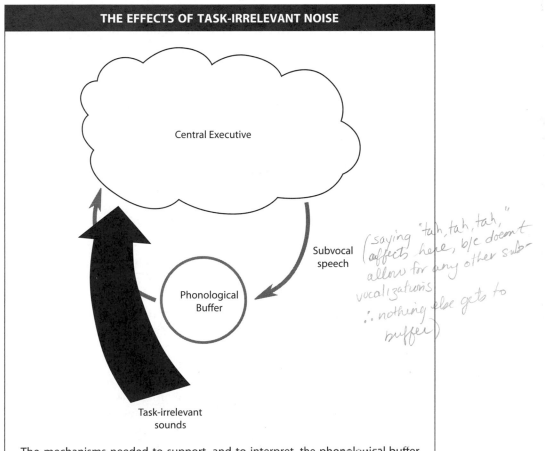

THE EFFECTS OF TASK-IRRELEVANT NOISE

Central Executive

Subvocal speech

Phonological Buffer

Task-irrelevant sounds

(saying "tah, tah, tah," affects here, b/c doesn't allow for any other sub-vocalizations ∴ nothing else gets to buffer)

The mechanisms needed to support, and to interpret, the phonological buffer (the "inner ear") overlap heavily with those needed for actual *hearing*. Therefore, if these mechanisms are in use for hearing, they are not available for rehearsal. Hence, many experiments show rehearsal to be disrupted by sounds presented to subjects, even though the sounds are irrelevant to the subjects' task.

The results confirm this: In a noisy environment, span is reduced (since subjects can't rely on the loop), the word-length effect is eliminated (since subjects aren't using the inner-voice), and the sound-alike confusions disappear from the data (since subjects aren't able to use the inner ear). All of this is exactly as predicted.

Finally, here is a different sort of prediction: We have claimed that the rehearsal loop is required only for storage; this slave system is incapable of any more sophisticated operations. Therefore, these other operations should not be compromised if the loop is unavailable. This turns out to be correct: Concurrent articulation blocks use of the loop, but has no effect on subjects' ability to read brief sentences, to do logic problems, and so on. Likewise, we can present subjects with a string of three or four letters and ask them to remember these while solving a simple problem. After they've solved the problem, they report back the original letters. It turns out that "half filling" working memory in this fashion has virtually no impact on problem-solving—performance is just as fast and just as accurate under these circumstances as it is without the memory load. That is because this memory load is accommodated within the rehearsal loop, placing no burden on the executive. And it is the executive, not the loop, that is needed for problem-solving, again in accord with the overall model.

The Nature of the Working-Memory Evidence

Let's highlight a few points about the evidence just catalogued. First, the results we have just surveyed, and many other findings as well, fit well with the Baddeley and Hitch conception of a working-memory system. Note, though, that no one has ever seen the "inner voice" or the "inner ear" directly. Instead, we propose that these entities exist because they play a key role in a well-supported account of the data. That is, we infer the existence of these entities because they seem required if we are to explain the evidence. In this sense, we *reconstruct* what the unobserved structures and processes must be.

Second, notice that in supporting our account, we have many forms of data available to us. We can manipulate subjects' activities, as we did with concurrent articulation, and look at how this changes the subjects' performance (i.e., the size of the measured memory span). We can also manipulate the stimuli themselves, as we did with the word-length effect, and see how this changes things. We can likewise change the setting in which subjects do our tasks (noisy environment vs. quiet). We can also look in detail at the nature of the performance, asking not just about the overall level of performance, but also at the specific errors (sound-alike vs. look-alike). We can also measure the speed of subjects' performance and ask how this is influenced by various manipulations. We did this, for example, in asking whether problem solving is compromised by a concurrent memory load. The obvious assumption here is that mental processes are very quick, but nonetheless do take a measurable amount of time. By timing how quickly subjects answer various questions, or perform various tasks, we can ask what factors speed up mental processes, and what factors slow them down.

Other sorts of data can also be brought into play. For example, what exactly is the nature of subvocalization? Does it literally involve covert speech and thus movements (perhaps tiny movements) of the tongue, the vocal chords, and so on? One way to find out would be to *paralyze* these various muscles. Would this disrupt use of the rehearsal loop? As it turns out, we don't have to perform this experiment; nature has performed it for us. Because of specific forms of neurological damage, some individuals have no ability to move these various muscles, and thus are quite unable to speak. These individuals are **anarthric**—i.e., without speech. Data indicate that these individuals show a word-length effect in their data, and also sound alike confusions, just as ordinary subjects do. Apparently, then, actual muscle movements are not needed for subvocalization. Instead, "inner speech" probably relies on the brain areas responsible for planning the muscle movements of speech. This is by itself an interesting fact, but, for present purposes, note the relevance of yet another type of data—observations from **neuropsychology**, concerned with how various forms of brain dysfunction influence observed performance.

We might also mention a sort of evidence we have *not* considered, namely, the subjects' own reports on what is going on in these tasks, or on what strategies they are using. As we discussed earlier, introspection is a research tool of uncertain value, and it seems entirely possible that subjects do not know exactly how they perform a memory span task. Subjects might well have the intuition that they are talking to themselves (i.e., subvocalizing) in this task, but the relation between the inner ear and actual hearing, or the relation between the rehearsal loop and the executive, are not intuitively obvious. Hence, subjects' testimonials play little role in our account.

Finally, it is crucial to note that we have built our argument with several lines of evidence: Our account had to be compatible with the initial observations, but the account also led us to predict other observations, predictions that, as it turns out, were all correct. This pattern is a common one in research: We start with data, construct an account of those data, then seek further results to confirm, or disconfirm, our account. In addition, it is important that no one line of evidence is by itself decisive. There are probably other ways to explain our initial observations about span, if those effects were all we had to go on. There are also other ways to explain the other individual results we have mentioned, if these likewise were considered in isolation. The key comes in finding an account that will fit with all of the available data.

When we have done our work well, there will be just one such account, and this will be our assurance that we have correctly reconstructed what is going on, invisible and never directly observed, in the mind. There is, in short, no other way to explain the data. This is what tells us we have the theory right.

Working Memory in a Broader Context

Having made all of these methodological points, let us round out this section with one final comment: Why should we care about the structure of working memory? Why is this interesting? The memory-span task itself seems quite unnatural—how often do we need to memorize a set of unrelated numbers or letters? For that matter, how often do we need to work on some problem while simultaneously saying "tah-tah-tah" over and over? In short, what does this task, and this procedure, have to do with things we care about?

The answer to these questions allows us to replay an issue we have already discussed: There is a vast number of circumstances in which we rely on working memory and so, if we understand working memory, we move toward an understanding of this far broader set of problems and issues. For example, bear in mind our initial comments about the role of working memory in reading, or in any other task in which you must store early "products," keeping them ready for integration with later products. One might imagine that many tasks have this character—reading, reasoning tasks, and problem-solving are a few. If you make effective use of working memory, therefore, you will have an advantage in all of these domains. Indeed, some scholars have suggested that "intelligence" in many domains amounts to nothing more than excess capacity in working memory. (See, for example, Kyllonen & Cristal, 1990.)

In a similar vein, the use of articulatory rehearsal seems a simple trick—a trick you use quite spontaneously, a trick in which you take no special pride. But it is a trick you had to learn, and young children, for example, often seem not to know the trick. There is some indication that this can be a problem for these children in learning to read: Without the option of relying on articulatory rehearsal, reading becomes much more difficult.

Here is a rather different example: Many individuals seem particularly vulnerable to depression. Sad memories and unhappy ideas spontaneously intrude into their thoughts, poisoning their mood and their subsequent thinking. This sequence of thoughts, it turns out, is recorded (where else?) in working memory, and so it seems possible to defeat these intrusive thoughts by seizing control of working memory and occupying it with other contents. In this way, there is at least some indication that the saddening thoughts, and so the depression, can be avoided. By understanding working memory, we understand how this dynamic might function. (For discussion, see Teasdale, Proctor, Lloyd & Baddeley, 1993.)

These examples can easily be multiplied but, by now, the point should be clear: Working memory and articulatory rehearsal are relevant to a wide range of mental activities, in adults and in children. Understanding working memory, therefore, may give us insight into a wide range of tasks. Similar claims can be made about many other cognitive resources: By understanding what it means to pay attention, we move toward an understanding of all the contexts in which attention plays a role. By understanding how we comprehend text, or how we use our knowledge to supplement our perceptions, we move toward an understanding of all the contexts in which these play a part. And in each case the number of such contexts is vast.

We end this section by echoing a comment we have already made: The machinery of cognition is essential to virtually all of our waking activities (and perhaps some of our sleeping activities, as well). We have given a few examples, including some that seem explicitly "intellectual" (reasoning, problem-solving) and some that seem not (depression). The scope of cognitive psychology is broad indeed, and the relevance of our research is wide.

2

Recognizing Objects in the World

A number of themes will emerge again and again in this text; for instance, it is enormously difficult to divide up cognitive functioning, to study its aspects one by one. This is because each aspect of cognition is inter-coordinated with, and often influenced by, other aspects. For example, how we learn new material is influenced by what we already know. What we know, in turn, has been shaped by what we paid attention to in the past. What we pay attention to is generally guided by what we expect. What we expect depends on what we have already learned. Around and around we go, with each strand tied to the others. These interconnections make for a fascinating story, as they reveal a surprising complexity in our mental lives—not just in overtly complicated tasks (like mastering a new field of study or solving complex equations) but even in seemingly simple activities (like recognizing the individual words on this page).

Pattern Recognition

These interconnections create a difficulty, though, for anyone—a teacher, a textbook writer—seeking to present this material: To understand virtually any topic in cognitive psychology, one first needs to know about several other topics as well. Of course, we need to cut into this network of complexities some place, and in this chapter, we will begin in a traditional fashion with the topic of "pattern recognition." In these opening pages, we seek to explain the reason for this starting point by making two broad points: Pattern recognition (which we'll define in a moment) is a crucial intellectual activity, and it is far more complicated than it looks.

We should be clear from the start, though, that this chapter presents only a "first pass" at the topic of pattern recognition. For a fuller account, we will need to incorporate concepts covered in later chapters. But this chapter will provide a base on which to build, and we will return to many of the ideas introduced here.

What Is Pattern Recognition?

You open your eyes, and you see around you a world filled with familiar objects—chairs and desks, windows and walls, telephones and pencils. As you read this page, you can see the individual letters printed here. They are letters that you know and can identify. The letters form words, and you can recognize the words—you could say them out loud if requested, you know what is being said, so that you easily understand these sentences.

How is any of this possible? How do you know that the chairs are chairs, or the telephones are telephones? How do you know that the letter "Q" is a Q and not an R or a Z or, for that matter, a map of Brazil? When you recognize these objects, you are identifying or categorizing the objects in your environment. The process of doing all this is broadly referred to as **pattern recognition**, and when it involves things that you can see, it is called *visual pattern recognition*. If you want, you can think of pattern recognition as object identification, or, indeed, as categorization.

Why Is Pattern Recognition Crucial?

Pattern recognition is, for several reasons, a good place to begin our inquiry. Virtually all use of knowledge depends on pattern recognition. To see this, think about a physician who might know how to *treat* diabetes, but who doesn't know how to *diagnose* diabetes. In this case, the physician's knowledge about treatment becomes useless, because the physician doesn't know when (or with which patients) to use the treatment. The same can be said for much of your knowledge. For example, you know a great deal about telephones, and you use that knowledge in many ways. But you could not do this if you couldn't recognize a telephone when you saw one. Without recognition, one cannot bring one's knowledge to bear on the world.

Likewise, pattern recognition and categorization are crucial for learning. In virtually all learning, one must combine new information with information learned previously. Otherwise, no accumulation of knowledge would be possible—each learning episode would stand separately, unintegrated with other learning episodes. But for this to happen, one must categorize things properly. Today you learn something about Solomon. Yesterday you learned something about Solomon. If you are to integrate the new knowledge with the old, you need to realize that the person before you today is the same person as the one you met yesterday. Without proper categorization, there is no way to combine and integrate information.

One way to drive all this home is to consider people who cannot recognize patterns. These people suffer from a condition called visual **agnosia**, generally because of some brain injury, often a stroke. A great deal is known about agnosia (e.g., Farah, 1990) but, for our purposes, let's consider a single case, "Dr. P.", described in an essay by Oliver Sacks.

> "What is this?" I asked, holding up a glove.
> "May I examine it?" he asked, and, taking it from me, he proceeded to examine it. "A continuous surface," he announced at last, "infolded in itself. It appears to have"—he hesitated—"five outpouchings, if this is the word."
> "Yes," I said cautiously. " . . . Now tell me what it is."

"A container of some sort?"

"Yes," I said, "and what would it contain?"

"It would contain its contents!" said Dr. P., with a laugh. "There are many possibilities. It could be a change purse, for example, for coins of five sizes. It could . . . ." (Sacks, 1985, pg. 14)

This agnosic is plainly quite intelligent but, needless to say, he has immense difficulties in acquiring knowledge or using what he knows. As Sacks describes, Dr. P. fails to put on his shoe, because he does not recognize it as a shoe. (At one point, Dr. P. is confused about which is his shoe and which is his foot.) At the end of his first meeting with Sacks, Dr. P. "reached out his hand and took hold of his wife's head, tried to lift it off, to put it on. He had apparently mistaken his wife for a hat!" (pg. 11).

Thus, visual pattern recognition may not be a glamorous skill, but it does seem to be a crucial one for even our most ordinary commerce with the world. Moreover, pattern recognition seems the essential base for learning and memory. For our purposes, therefore, we will start our inquiry where much of knowledge starts—with the recognition and identification of objects in the world.

The Recognition of Print

Our goal in this chapter is to convey an understanding of how we recognize the thousands of objects we encounter. For much of the chapter, however, our focus will be far narrower, and most of the evidence considered will be concerned with the recognition of a specific sort of pattern—namely, the letters and words that make up printed language. We will say far less about patterns in other modalities (sounds or odors we recognize); we will say only a little about visual patterns other than printed language.

This emphasis reflects the fact that more is known about the recognition of print than about recognition of any other sort. There are several reasons for this. For one, the research is easy to do—the stimuli to be shown to subjects can be produced by any typewriter. Second, and more important, the recognition of print is obviously a crucial part of *reading*, an activity that is of considerable importance for its own sake. How do we learn to read? Why do we sometimes make errors in reading (when, for example, you proofread one of your papers and fail to discover the typing errors)? Why do some people have difficulty in reading, or in learning to read? What is speed-reading all about? One might expect that an understanding of the recognition of print might move us toward understanding these other problems as well.

Finally, we present the study of print as a microcosm for pattern recognition in general. To be sure, some questions about pattern recognition can not be studied via print. (For example, the study of print, which is only two-dimensional, doesn't allow us to examine the recognition of three-dimensional objects.) Nonetheless, many of the lessons learned in studying word recognition will apply to a broader range of cases—how we recognize cabbages and kings, or auditory patterns like "C-major chords" or "sad melodies," or even abstract patterns like "injustices" or "schizophrenics." Indeed, many of the lessons learned here will apply far beyond the study of pattern recognition, so that, for example, our discussion of memory, in Chapter 7, will bring us back to the idea of "network processing" and the idea of knowledge "distributed across a net," ideas that will be introduced here, in the discussion of print.

We should note in passing that this strategy of "study the simple cases first, then build from there" is a common strategy in psychology, and a reasonably successful one as well. Just how successful the strategy has been will be discussed later in this chapter.

Recognition: Some Early Considerations

You are plainly able to recognize a huge number of different patterns. If we stay in the domain of print, then you are able to recognize tens of thousands of different words. Beyond print, though, you are also able to recognize objects (cows, trees, hats), actions (running, jumping, falling), events (crises, comedies), and so on.

Not only do you recognize all these different things, you also recognize many variations of each. You recognize cats standing up and cats sitting down, cats running and cats asleep. And of course the same is true for your recognition of pigs, chairs, and any other object in your recognition repertoire.

You also recognize objects even when your information is partial. For example, you can still recognize a cat even when it is hiding behind a tree, so that only its head and one paw are visible to you. You recognize a chair even when someone is sitting on it, despite the fact that this blocks much of the chair from view.

All of this is obviously true for print as well. You recognize the letter "A" whether it printed in large type, bold type, italic, etc. You also recognize lower-case A's. Further, you recognize handwritten A's, for which the variation from one to the next is huge.

To all of this, let's add a further complication: Your recognition of various objects is, in important ways, influenced by the *context* in which the objects are encountered. For example, a fire hydrant will be recognized more easily (more quickly, more accurately) in the context of a "street corner scene," compared to a fire hydrant presented with no context. Moreover, to obtain this effect, the objects must be shown in appropriate contexts, and in the correct *position* within the context. Thus, the context will not facilitate performance if the fire hydrant is shown on top of a mailbox (Biederman, Glass & Stacy, 1973; Boyce & Pollatsek, 1992).

Context can also have stronger effects—literally changing how something looks and, in many cases, changing how an object is categorized, changing what it is recognized *as*. Consider Figure 2.1 (after Selfridge, 1955). The middle character is the same in both words, but the character doesn't *look* the same. Instead, the character looks more like an "H" in the left word, and more like an "A" in the right. Likewise, one unhesitatingly reads the left word as "THE" and not "TAE"; the right word is read as "CAT" and not "CHT."

Context can even determine whether an object is recognized at all. Figure 2.2 provides some examples. The pattern labeled A contains the numeral "4", but you probably didn't notice this until it was pointed out. The pattern labeled B contains the pattern labeled C but, again, this isn't obvious until you search for the "hidden" form. In each case, one can perceive the embedded figure if one dissects the overall form into the appropriate pieces, that is, if one **parses** the overall form in the right way. But with other parsings, the embedded figure is, in effect, hidden from view. Thus, how one perceives and, more precisely, whether one detects a familiar pattern, depends on how one organizes the overall pattern.

How should we think about all this? What unseen mechanisms underlie all of these effects? In the pages to come, we develop a proposal for such a mechanism. First, we will suggest that patterns are often recognized by virtue of their parts: You know a square is a square because you can see the four straight lines and the four right angles. You recognize a right angle as such because you can see its parts—perhaps one horizontal line juxtaposed with one vertical line. In general, the idea is that you first recognize small pieces of a pattern, and then combine these to form the larger-scale, more complex whole.

Figure 2.1

CONTEXT INFLUENCES PERCEPTION

T A E   C A T

Pattern recognition is influenced by the fact that THE is a commonly observed sequence of letters; TAE is not. Likewise, CAT is often encountered; CHT is not. Given this knowledge, one is likely to read this sequence as THE CAT, reading the middle symbol as an "H" in one case and as an "A" in the other. [After Selfridge, 1955 © 1955 IRE (now, IEEE).]

Figure 2.2

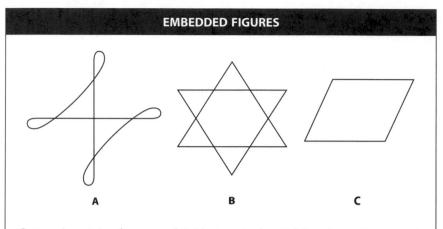

EMBEDDED FIGURES

A   B   C

Pattern A contains the numeral "4," but most subjects fail to detect the numeral. Likewise, Pattern B *contains* Pattern C, but this isn't obvious until you search for the "hidden" form. Thus, perception of forms depends on how one "dissects" the overall pattern.

We will then need to focus, though, on just how it is that these pieces are combined to form a larger pattern. In particular, we will need to address the context effects just mentioned. These effects might seem peculiar if one identifies larger-scale patterns by first identifying the patterns' parts. In this view, the parts come first, and the context second, and so the parts' identity shouldn't depend on the context. Yet context does influence the parts' identity, and this needs to be addressed as we assemble our account.

Evidence for Features

We have suggested that object recognition might begin with the recognition of object *parts* and then "build" from there. But what are the parts, and how are they recognized? One possibility is that object parts are in turn recognized via their parts (parts of parts). In the case of print, one would recognize words by first identifying the constituent letters; one would recognize the letters by first identifying their constituent **features**, such as vertical lines, curves, or loops. Having recognized two verticals and a horizontal line, one would identify an "H".

How are the features recognized? One possibility is that each of us has in memory a repertoire of specific patterns, one for each feature. These memory patterns are then compared to the pattern before your eyes. If some part of this input matches one of the patterns in your repertoire, then you know that the relevant feature is present. "That bit matches my 'corner' pattern, so I know a corner is present. That bit matches my 'curve' pattern, so I know a curve is present."

feature system →

Some advantages of a feature system are obvious immediately. First, features such as line segments and curves could serve as *general-purpose* building blocks. Not only would these features serve as the basis for recognizing letters, they could also serve as the basis for recognizing other more complex visual patterns (chairs, jackets, smiling faces), opening the possibility of a single pattern recognition system able to deal with patterns of many sorts.

Second, we have noted that we recognize many variations on the objects we encounter—cats in different positions, A's in different fonts or different handwritings. But while the various A's are different from each other in overall shape, they do have a great deal in common—two inwardly-sloping lines and a horizontal cross bar. Focusing on features might allow us to concentrate on what is common to the various A's, and so might allow us to recognize A's despite their apparent diversity.

Visual Search

The considerations just sketched indicate that features might be useful as a base for recognition. But can we find more direct evidence for the existence of features? One line of evidence comes from studies of **visual search**—studies in which subjects need to scan through a set of visual stimuli, searching for a particular target.

Some cases of visual search are easy; some are much more difficult. For example, it is generally easy to locate a target defined by a single feature—one red letter among a background of blue letters, or one round shape against a background of angular shapes. It is harder to search for a target defined via a *combination* of features—e.g., a red circle amidst a backdrop of red squares and blue circles (Treisman, 1986; Treisman & Gormican, 1988; for earlier studies of visual search, see Neisser, 1964). Note, then, that there appears to be something primitive and basic about feature perception: Targets that can be distinguished on the basis of feature perception "pop out" from the background. Targets that cannot be distinguished in this fashion, i.e., targets that require some higher-order analysis, do not pop out.

Data also indicate striking **search asymmetries**. For example, it is easy to find a tilted line against a background of vertical lines, but hard to do the reverse: to find a vertical line against a background of tilted lines (Figure 2.3). Likewise, it is easy to find an incomplete circle against a background of complete circles, but harder to find a complete circle against a background of

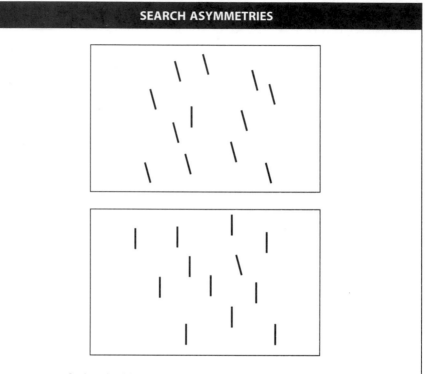

Figure 2.3

SEARCH ASYMMETRIES

It is easy to find a tilted line against a background of vertical lines, but hard to do the reverse: to find a vertical against a background of tilted lines. This implies that "tilt" is a feature detected by the visual system and so, in searching for tilt, one is searching for a single feature. "Absence of tilt" seems *not* to be a feature detected by the visual system.

incomplete circles (Figure 2.4). In some ways, these results seem peculiar, since the same discrimination is required (tilt vs. vertical, incomplete vs. complete) in both versions of the search. Researchers have interpreted these asymmetries, however, as implying that "gap" and "tilt" are features for the visual system and, in searching for these, one is simply searching for a single feature. As we've already seen, feature-based search is easy; targets defined in terms of a single feature pop out from the background. "Absence of gap" or "absence of tilt" (vertical), however, are not features, making it more difficult to search for these (Treisman & Gormican, 1988; Treisman & Souther, 1985).

Note that visual search data can be used to *identify* some of the specific features used by the visual system. That is, we could not tell from the outset whether "vertical" was a feature, or whether "tilt" was a feature, or whether

Figure 2.4

SEARCH ASYMMETRIES

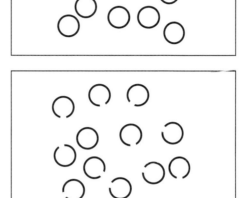

It is also easy to find an incomplete circle against a background of complete circles, but harder to find a complete circle against a background of incomplete circles, even though the discrimination is the same in both cases. This implies that the visual system treats "gap" as a single feature, but not "absence of gap."

both might be features. Search asymmetries can be used to explore these issues, since these data tell us that there is a priority to "tilt" that is not shared by "vertical." In this way, search data can literally tell us what is in the alphabet from which visual forms are assembled. More broadly, though, visual-search evidence indicates that patterns are easily distinguishable from each other if the patterns differ at the feature level. This is what one would expect if the process of pattern recognition began with features, and of course that is our main concern here.

Neurological Data

Further evidence for feature analysis comes from neurological data. Leaving aside many details, the idea is this: It is possible to record the activity of individual cells within the nervous system—literally, recording when a specific cell in the eye or the brain is activated. This technique is referred to as **single-cell recording**, and can be used to assess when individual neurons are firing. By determining *when* a neuron fires (that is, under what circumstances), we can figure out roughly what job that neuron does, within the broad context of the entire nervous system.

The technique of single-cell recording has been used with enormous success in the study of vision. In a typical study, the animal being studied is first immobilized. Then, electrodes are inserted into a single neuron in the animal's brain—for example, a neuron in the **visual cortex** (that is, the portion of the brain primarily responsible for vision). Next, a computer-screen is placed in front of the animal's eyes, and various patterns are flashed on the computer-screen—circles, lines at various angles, or squares of various sizes,

Figure 2.5

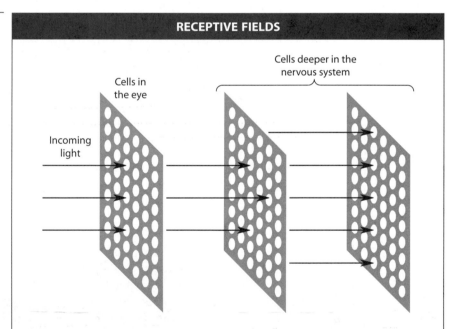

RECEPTIVE FIELDS

Cells deep within the nervous system are not triggered directly by incoming light. Instead, light causes cells in the eye to respond, and these cells trigger other cells, which in turn trigger other cells, deeper and deeper in the nervous system. Nonetheless, when we define a cell's "receptive field," we refer to the pattern in the light that, via these intermediate steps, causes the cell to fire. Receptive fields can be quite specific, so that a cell might fire only in the presence of a particular shape of a particular color in a particular position.

at various positions. Researchers can then ask: Which patterns "trigger" that neuron? For what visual inputs does that cell fire?

By analogy, we know that a smoke-detector is a smoke-detector because it "fires" (makes noise) when smoke is on the scene. We know that a motion-detector is a motion-detector because it "fires" when something moves nearby. But what kind of detector is the neuron? Is it responsive to *any* light in *any* position within the field of view? In that case we might call this cell a "light-detector." Or is it perhaps responsive only to certain shapes at certain positions (and therefore is a shape-detector)? Technically speaking, we are seeking to define the cell's **receptive field**, i.e., that portion of the visual field to which the cell is receptive. The shape, size, and position of the receptive field will define what kind of detector this cell is. (For more on receptive fields, see Figure 2.5.)

Simple Cells, Complex Cells, Hypercomplex Cells

Classic data from single-cell recording come from studies by David Hubel and Torsten Wiesel (1959; 1968), who obtained the Nobel prize for their work; many subsequent studies have elaborated and extended Hubel and Wiesel's findings. Much of the early work in this domain was done with cats, but more recent studies have observed similar patterns in several other species, including various species of monkeys. It seems a good bet, therefore, that cells in the *human* visual cortex would show the same profile.

Hubel and Wiesel documented the existence of several types of neurons within the visual system, with each type having a different kind of visual trigger, i.e., a different type of receptive field. Some neurons in the visual system can be described as "dot-detectors." These cells fire at their maximum rate when light is presented in a small, roughly circular area, in a specific position within the field of view. Presentations of light just outside of this area cause the cell to fire at *less* than its usual "resting" rate, so that the input must be precisely positioned to make this cell fire. Figure 2.6A depicts such a receptive field.

These cells are often called **center-surround cells**, to illustrate the fact that light presentations in the central region of the receptive field have one influence, but light presentations in the surrounding ring have the opposite influence. If *both* the center and surround are strongly stimulated, the cell will fire neither more nor less than usual; for this cell, a strong uniform stimulus is equivalent to no stimulus at all. In addition, many "compromises" are possible: Imagine, for example, that we present a stimulus as shown in Figure 2.6B. The entire center of the receptive field is being stimulated, but only a portion of the surround. In this case, the positive signal would outweigh the negative, and so the cell's firing rate would increase.

Figure 2.6

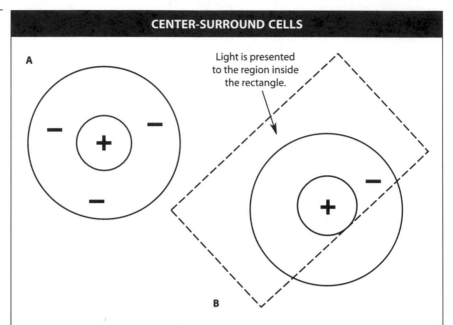

CENTER-SURROUND CELLS

A

Light is presented to the region inside the rectangle.

B

Some neurons function as "dot detectors," and have receptive fields with a *center-surround* organization. If light shines onto the central region, the cell increases its firing rate; this is why the center is marked "+". If light shines onto the peripheral region, the cell *decreases* its firing. If both regions are illuminated, the cell will not change its firing rate in either direction. Stimuli presented outside the periphery have no effect on the cell. If we present a stimulus as shown in B, the entire center is stimulated, but only a portion of the surround. Therefore, the positive signal outweighs the negative, and so the cell's firing rate would increase somewhat.

Other neurons, slightly "deeper" into the visual system, have been dubbed "simple cells." These cells seem responsive to lines and edges at a very specific orientation, and at a very specific position within the field of view. Again, presentations of light just outside this sensitive area cause a decrease, rather than an increase, of firing rate.

Still other neurons have been dubbed "complex cells" and others, "hypercomplex cells." Complex cells, like simple cells, fire maximally to lines or angles of a specific orientation, but position of the line within the field of view is not so critical. Hypercomplex cells are responsive, as their names implies, to still more complicated patterns—corners, notches, and angles.

Early Integration of the Components

It is easy to speculate about how these different neurons function together. However, we should emphasize that this is speculation, because it is impossible at present (for technical reasons) to trace how an individual neuron is functionally "connected" to other neurons. Nonetheless, the obvious suggestion is this: There is a huge number of center-surround cells, each with its receptive field in a specific portion of the field of view. Some of these receptive fields are illustrated in Figure 2.7. Region A in the incoming light pattern constitutes the receptive field, let us say, for cell A—that is, cell A will fire whenever light is present in the center of region A. Likewise, region B constitutes the receptive field for cell B, and so on. The figure shows just a few receptive fields but, of course, many, many more receptive fields (alongside of and overlapping the ones shown) would also be present, blanketing the entire field of vision.

These center-surround cells "pass" their information along to the simple cells. Thus, the *output* from cells A, B, C, and D might serve as the *input* to one simple cell, call it Simp1. That is, Simp1 would fire only when *all four* of these center-surround cells are firing. When will that be? If a line is in view, stretching across the receptive fields of cells A–D, as shown in the figure. Functionally, then, Simp1's receptive field overlaps with the receptive fields for these four center-surround cells. An appropriately positioned line will cause cells A–D to fire, and thus also Simp1.

Simp1 is not receiving any input from cells E or F, and so Simp1 would not respond when light is present elsewhere in the visual field. A different simple cell, though, call it Simp2, might receive, as *its* input, the output from cells C, E, and F. Simp2 will fire only when these three center-surround cells are firing, that is, when a line is in view stretching across the centers of these three fields. And so on for the many other center-surround receptive fields blanketing the field of view.

With a great enough number of center-surround cells, light can be detected at virtually any position in the visual field—with each position "covered" by a cell. With a great enough number of *simple* cells, line segments at any position and at any orientation can be detected. The output from these simple cells would then feed into the complex cells. There might be a complex cell, for example, that receives input from both Simp1 and Simp3 (which receives input from cells G, H, I, and J). Moreover, each of these simple cells might provide a strong trigger for the complex cell, so that the complex cell (Comp1) would fire when *either* Simp1 *or* Simp3 was firing. In this way, Comp1 would fire only when lines of a specific orientation (in the example, vertical lines) were present, but Comp1 would not be limited by the specific position of these lines.

Figure 2.7 INTEGRATION OF NEURAL INFORMATION

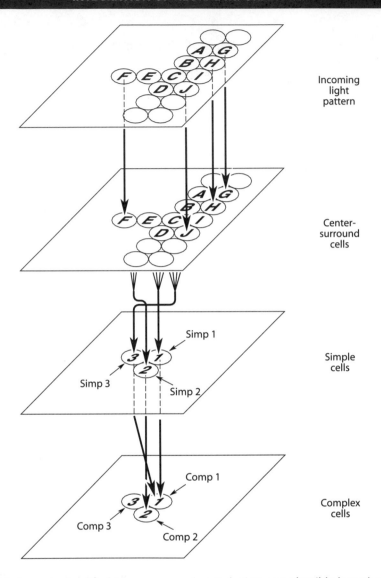

Incoming light pattern

Center-surround cells

Simple cells

Complex cells

This figure is simplified in many ways, but it depicts one plausible hypothesis about how cells in the visual system are interconnected. The suggestion is that simple cells are triggered by center-surround cells, as shown, and then complex cells are triggered by simple cells. For example, the simple cell "Simp1" might fire whenever cells A, B, C, *and* D are firing; in this case, Simp1 would fire whenever a line segment of the appropriate position and orientation was present in the environment. "Simp2" might fire whenever cells C, E, and F are firing, and so it would detect horizontal line segments. "Simp3" fires whenever G, H, I, and J are firing and so, like Simp1, Simp3 serves as a "vertical-line detector." Comp1 might fire whenever Simp1 *or* Simp3 are firing; in this case, Comp1 might respond to vertical lines independent of their exact position.

Let us emphasize, though, that the actual neural connections are likely to be more complex than this. Some of the complexity comes from the fact that there are several sets of neural processors: The neural mechanisms responding to pattern turn out to be different from the ones responding to *motion*, and these in turn are different from the mechanisms responding to *color*. These systems work in parallel with each other but also interact in ways not well understood at present. (Crick, 1994, provides a recent and accessible review of some of the relevant evidence.) It may also turn out that the detection of form itself is more complicated than we have just indicated (cf. Heeger, 1994). Even with these complexities, however, the conception sketched provides a reasonable start toward an account of how visual information is assembled in the perception of complex patterns.

Word Recognition

The single-cell data tell us that the visual system does indeed begin by detecting small elements of the input. And it is plausible that, at these early levels, the elements are simply added together, like tiles within a mosaic, to produce larger patterns. But this cannot be the whole story of recognition, given the various context effects described earlier. In these cases, one seems to recognize parts only by virtue of *first* understanding the larger pattern. To explain these context effects, we'll need some other account of how the features are combined.

Before developing a model, though, we need to be more precise about what these contexts effects are—*how* context influences recognition, and also what sorts of contexts have an effect. Let's look, therefore, at some studies of word recognition.

The Logic of Word-Recognition Studies

Pattern recognition is, in general, pretty easy. It requires no great effort to see that a telephone is a telephone; you have no difficulties in identifying the letters on this page. This facility reflects, in part, the degree to which the relevant skills are extremely well practiced. In addition, ordinary circumstances do little to challenge these recognition skills. Generally, the patterns you encounter are out in plain view, and you have plenty of time to inspect them. As a result, ordinary pattern recognition demands little of you and, consequently, may not tell us much about your abilities.

By analogy, think of a spelling test in which you are asked to spell words like "CAT" or "DOG." Surely you would do quite well on this test, but this wouldn't tell us how good a speller you are since most people, good spellers or bad, would do well on this easy test. Nor would it tell us whether some words are more difficult to spell than others, since all words on the test are very easy. Performance in this test will be at ceiling levels, and so the test will be insensitive, unable to discriminate good spellers from poor ones, or to discriminate easy words from hard. To make the test more sensitive, it has to be more difficult, so that it will challenge your abilities in a more serious way.

By the same logic, if we want to uncover how pattern recognition works, we need a test that challenges the subjects, to get performance away from ceiling levels. This can be done by presenting a degraded stimulus; in most procedures, this is accomplished simply by presenting the words to subjects very quickly, for fractions of a second. Older research did this by means of a device called a **tachistoscope**—a device that allows presentation of stimuli for precisely-controlled amounts of time, including very brief presentations. More modern research uses computers for this purpose, rather than tachistoscopes, but the brief presentations are still called *tachistoscopic* presentations.

In an ordinary procedure, the subject is shown a series of stimulus words on a computer screen, each for some brief duration—perhaps 20 or 30 msec (milliseconds). Each word is followed by a **post-stimulus mask**—often just a random jumble of letters, such as "XJDKEL." This mask serves to disrupt any "sensory memory" that subjects might have for the just-presented stimulus, allowing researchers to be certain that a stimulus presented for (say) 20 msec is visible to the subject for exactly 20 msec and no longer. This allows us to determine just how much subjects can discern in this brief presentation.

With such a procedure, subjects (after a bit of practice) can recognize words presented for only 20 or 30 milliseconds. Various factors, though, can increase or decrease the likelihood of recognizing a word and so, to study these factors, we need some means of measuring performance more precisely. One option is simply to ask how many subjects recognize a particular word, in a particular setting. A different option is to ask, for each subject, how many words were recognized, how many not. Either of these methods will generate data assessed in terms of "percent recognized." Alternatively, we can show a word briefly (say, 10 msec). If the subject fails to recognize the word, we re-show that word, for a slightly longer exposure, perhaps 15 msec. If the subject still fails to recognize the word, we re-show it, again for a slightly longer exposure. Eventually, we will show the word for enough time for the subject to recognize it and, in this way, we can determine how long the exposure has to be for recognition to happen. This duration is referred to as the **recognition threshold**.

The Word-Frequency Effect

One factor that distinguishes the easy-to-recognize words is simply their frequency in the language. This claim is based quite literally on counts of how often each word appears in newspapers, magazines, and books (Thorndike & Lorge, 1963; Kucera & Francis, 1967). These counts confirm that "smirk," "noodle," and "wart" are infrequent words, while "weather," "happy," and "marry" are frequent.

These counts turn out to be excellent predictors of tachistoscopic recognition. For example, Figure 2.8 shows the results of a classic study by Howes and Solomon (1951). As you can see, there is an orderly relationship between threshold and frequency: The more frequent the word, the lower the thresh-

Figure 2.8

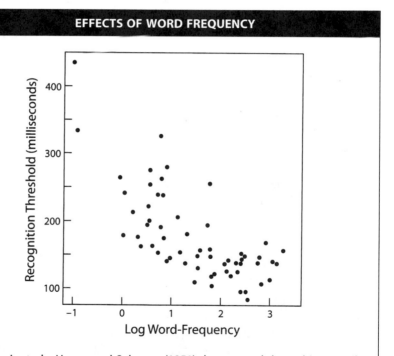

EFFECTS OF WORD FREQUENCY

In a classic study, Howes and Solomon (1951) documented that subjects easily recognize words that appear frequently in print; words that appear rarely are harder to recognize. Each dot in the figure represents the averaged data for one of their test words. "Recognition threshold" indicates the length of time for which a word had to be exposed in order for subjects to identify it. Thresholds were much higher (more time needed) for rare words (low frequency).

old. Words that appear in print frequently are easy to recognize in tachisto-scopic presentations; words that appear rarely are harder to recognize.

In a different experiment, Jacoby and Dallas (1981) showed their subjects words that were either very frequent (appearing more than 50 times in every million printed words) or infrequent (occurring only 1 to 5 times per million words of print). In one of their studies, subjects viewed these words for 35 msec, followed by a post-stimulus mask. On average, subjects recognized 65% of the frequent words under these conditions, but only 33% of the infrequent words—a striking 2 to 1 advantage for frequent words.

Repetition Priming

Another factor that makes words easier to recognize is recency-of-view. If subjects view a word and then, a little later, view it again, they will recognize the word much more readily the second time around. The first exposure primes the subject for the second exposure; more specifically, this is a case of repetition **priming**.

As an example, subjects in one study read a list of words aloud. The subjects were then shown a series of words in a tachistoscope. Some of the tachistoscopic words were from the earlier list, and so had been primed; others were not from the earlier list, and so were unprimed. For words that were high in frequency, 68% of the unprimed words were recognized, as compared to 84% of the primed words. For words low in frequency, 37% of the unprimed words were recognized, but 73% of the primed words (Jacoby & Dallas, 1981, Exp. 3). These are large effects, with repetition priming doubling the rate of recognition for low-frequency words.

The Word-Superiority Effect

The suggestion so far is that words frequent in the language are literally easier to perceive. Likewise, priming seems to facilitate perception. But here is a different way to think about the data: Imagine, for example, that a subject is shown a stimulus string, but, because of the brief exposure, is only able to discern the first two letters, "DA," or perhaps the first three, "DAR." The subject knows, however, that all of the exposures within the experiment involve *words*, and so the subject will probably try to guess what the rest of the word might have been. The subject's guess, of course, will depend on what "DA" words come to mind. Which will these be? Presumably, words frequently encountered in the past will come easily to mind, so will words recently encountered. Thus, the subject's guesses will tend toward frequently or recently-encountered words—perhaps guessing "DARK," or "DARE."

If the string presented was, in fact, "DARK," then guessing will be a useful strategy, since it is likely to produce the correct response. More generally, if guesses are guided by word frequency, then guessing will be helpful whenever the target actually was a frequent word. This same guessing strategy won't help, though, if the target was an infrequent word; in this case, the guesses won't even be "in the right ballpark." In these ways, then, the benefits of guessing will be correlated with frequency, and perhaps this is what lies behind the pattern shown in Figure 2.8 (and likewise for repetition priming).

It is possible, however, to rule out this guessing account, and thus to document that word frequency and priming are genuinely perceptual effects. Crucial data come from studies of the word-superiority effect. To understand this effect, consider two cases: In some trials, we tachistoscopically present a single letter, let's say K, followed by a post-stimulus mask, followed by the question, "Was there an E or a K in the display?" In other trials, we present a word, let's say "DARK," followed by a mask, followed by the question, "Was there an E or a K in the display?"

Note that the question is the same in the two cases, allowing a direct comparison of letter recognition and word recognition or, more precisely, a direct comparison of letter recognition when the letter is in isolation, with letter recognition when the letter is in context. Moreover, here we've dealt with the problem of guessing: Imagine that subjects have only seen the word's beginning, "DAR." This gives them no basis for choosing between the E and K alternatives, because either would create a common word (*dare* or *dark*). With no basis for *guessing*, subjects are forced to rely on what they have *perceived*, and therefore their responses will truly tell us how much they have gleaned from the stimulus itself—i.e., how well they have perceived the word.

Procedures like this show that subjects are reliably faster and more accurate in letter identification *if the letter appears within a word*. That is, performance is better in the "word" condition than in the "letter" condition (Reicher, 1969; Rumelhart & Siple, 1974; Wheeler, 1970) , and it is this advantage that is referred to as the word-superiority effect.

This is in some ways a peculiar result: The identity of a word is determined by the word's constituent letters. Thus, in order to identify a word, one must first identify its letters. Perceiving letters, therefore, is contained within the task of perceiving a word; presumably, then, perceiving letters is the "smaller" task and, one would think, the easier task. The reverse, however, is the case: It is easier to do the "larger" task, not the "smaller." In the same way, letter recognition requires only the identification of one letter. Word recognition, at least in this example, requires the identification of four letters. Therefore, one could argue that there is four times as much work to be done in recognizing a four-letter word as there is in recognizing a single letter. But it is the task with more "work" that's easier!

This effect still needs to be explained (and we'll say more about it later).

For now, though, notice that we have ruled out a contribution from guessing, making it look like context does indeed influence how a word is perceived. More broadly, the word-superiority effect plainly provides another case in which identification of elements is influenced by context. In earlier examples, we showed that context can bias perception in one way or another (Figure 2.1, p. 00), or that context can make elements more difficult to perceive (Figure 2.2, p. 00). We now see that context can also, in the right circumstances, actually facilitate perception of a pattern's parts.

Degrees of Well-Formedness

What creates the word-superiority effect? Will any context produce this effect? Imagine that we present a B within the context of "BWQX." Will this facilitate perception of the B, in comparison to a case in which the B is presented in isolation? Or is perception aided only by *familiar* contexts, or perhaps *meaningful* contexts?

It turns out that neither familiarity nor meaning is crucial for the word-superiority effect. For example, it is easier to recognize an E if it appears within the string "FIKE" than if it appears in isolation. But not all contexts provide an advantage: Recognition of the letter H is helped very little by contexts like "HGFD" or "HXXX."

Likewise, consider these two strings of letters: "JPSRW," and "GLAKE." Neither of these is a word, and neither is familiar. Strings like JPSRW are difficult to recognize if tachistoscopically presented. With exposures of 20 or 30 msec, subjects will identify one or two letters from a string like this, but no more. The non-word "GLAKE," however, is far easier to recognize in a tachistoscope, and will probably be read correctly with a 20 or 30 msec exposure.

The pattern of these data is straightforward: The word-superiority effect is obtained, and recognition is aided, if a letter appears within a context that is well-formed, according to the rules of the language. Moreover, this is a graded effect, not all-or-none: The more regular the context, the stronger the facilitation. For English-speakers, the more a string resembles English, the easier it is to recognize. This is a well-documented pattern, and has been known for a long time (e.g., Cattell, 1885).

How should we assess "resemblance to English"? One way is via pronounceability (e.g., "GLAKE" is easy to say; "JPSRW" is not) and, in general, pronounceable strings are more easily recognized with tachistoscopic presentations than unpronounceable strings. Alternatively, one can assess "resemblance to English" in statistical terms. One can count up, in English, how often the letter P follows the letter J, how often the letter S follows the letter

P, and so forth. In this way, one can ask which letter combinations are likely and which are rare. With this done, one can then evaluate any new string in terms of how likely its letter combinations are in English. Well-formedness measured in this way is also a good predictor of tachistoscopic performance (Gibson, Bishop, Schiff, & Smith, 1964; Miller, Bruner, & Postman, 1954).

Making Errors

Which is more common in the English language, words beginning with "TO" or words beginning with "TH"? Are there more words in English ending with a T or more words ending with an L? Surely you don't know the answers to these questions—most of us have little (or no) explicit knowledge about the spelling patterns of our language. Nonetheless, our perception of words is unmistakably influenced by these spelling patterns. Subjects have an easier time recognizing the more-probable sequences, a harder time with less-probable ones. The more-probable sequences have lower recognition thresholds, and it is these sequences that produce the word-superiority effect.

The influence of spelling rules also emerges in another way—namely, in the mistakes we make. With tachistoscopic exposures, word recognition is good, but not perfect, and the errors that occur are quite systematic: There is a strong tendency to misread less-common letter sequences as if they were more-common patterns; irregular patterns are misread as if they were regular patterns. Thus, for example, "TPUM" is likely to be misread as "TRUM" or even "DRUM." But the reverse errors are rare: "DRUM" is unlikely to be misread as "TRUM" or "TPUM."

These errors often involve the misreading of a feature or two (e.g., misperceiving the P as an R, or an O as a Q). But larger errors also occur (for example, a subject shown the four letters, "TPUM," might instead perceive "TRUMPET"). Both the large and the small errors show the pattern described: Misspelled words, partial words, or non-words, are read in a way that brings them into line with normal spelling. In effect, subjects perceive the input as being more regular than it actually is, and so these errors are referred to as **over-regularization errors**. This suggests once again that subjects' recognition is guided by (or, in this case, *mis*guided by) some knowledge of spelling patterns.

One more point about these errors should be emphasized. Subjects in these procedures usually do not realize when they have made an error (e.g., Pillsbury, 1897). From the subjects' point of view, they are reporting what they see, and thus the misspelled or mangled letter sequences actually *look correct* to the subjects. Errors occur, and the errors go undetected by the subjects. Subjects don't merely mis-identify the stimuli; they *mis-perceive*.

Feature Nets and Word Recognition

How can we explain this pattern of evidence? Key elements of the explanation derive from a theory of pattern recognition first published more than thirty years ago (Selfridge, 1959).

The Design of a Feature Net

Imagine that you wanted to design a system that would recognize the words of printed English. How would you do it? Let's imagine that one component of this system has the task of recognizing the word "CLOCK" whenever it is presented. This component is therefore the "CLOCK-detector." How might the CLOCK-detector work? Perhaps the CLOCK-detector is "wired" to a C-detector, an L-detector, an O-detector, and so on. Whenever these letter-detectors are all activated, this activates the word-detector. But what activates the letter-detectors? Perhaps the L-detector is "wired" to a horizontal-line detector, and also a vertical-line detector, and maybe also a corner-detector, as shown in Figure 2.9. When all of these feature-detectors are activated as a group, this activates the letter-detector.

The idea here is that there is a network of detectors, organized in layers, with each subsequent layer concerned with more complex, larger-scale patterns. The "bottom" layer is concerned with features, although this may, in truth, not be the bottom layer. One could imagine the feature-detectors as being connected to sub-feature detectors, and then to sub-sub-feature detectors, along the lines sketched in Figure 2.7 (p. 42). In general, networks of this sort, drawing on features, are referred to as **feature** nets.

This conception fits easily with the neurological data reviewed earlier in this chapter and, in fact, the neurological data suggest a refinement for the conception: Quite simply, some neurons are easier to activate than others. We can hold the reasons for this off to the side, but, with an eye on our model, let us suppose, in a parallel fashion, that some *detectors* are easier to activate than others. That is, some detectors require a very strong input to make them fire, while other detectors have a "hair trigger," and so will fire even with a weak input.

There are several ways to conceptualize this readiness to fire within our model. Here is one way, designed to stay as close as possible to what is known about neural functioning: At any point in time, each detector has a particular **activation level**. This level reflects how active that detector is at that moment. When a detector receives some input, this increases the activation level. A strong input will increase the activation level by a lot, as will a *series* of weaker

Figure 2.9

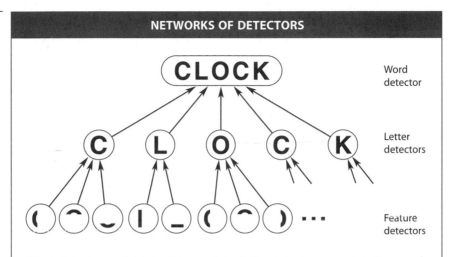

NETWORKS OF DETECTORS

Word-detectors might be triggered by letter detectors, so that the word-detector would fire whenever the appropriate letters were presented. The letter-detectors in turn might be triggered by feature-detectors, so the letter-detectors would fire whenever the features are on the scene.

inputs. In either case, the activation level eventually gets high enough to cause the detector to fire, that is, to send its signal to the other detectors to which it is connected. The detector's **response threshold** is the activation level at which this response occurs—that is, a detector fires when its activation level reaches the response threshold.

In addition, each detector has its own **baseline activation level**, or **resting level**. This is the detector's activation level prior to any inputs, its activation level when the detector is, so to speak, at rest. If a detector happens to have a high baseline level, then only a little input is needed to raise the activation level to threshold. This is why some detectors are relatively easy to activate. If another detector happens to have a low baseline level, then a strong input is needed to bring the detector to threshold; this detector will be relatively difficult to activate.

What determines a detector's baseline level? Detectors that have fired *recently* will have a higher baseline level. Detectors that have fired *frequently* in the past will gradually gain a higher and higher baseline level. Thus the baseline level is dependent on principles of *recency* and *frequency*.

We now can put this mechanism to work. Why are frequent words in the language easier to recognize with tachistoscopic exposures than rare words?

recency + frequency

Frequent words have, by definition, appeared often in the things you read. Therefore, the detectors needed for recognizing these words have been frequently used, and so they have relatively high levels of baseline activation. Thus, even a weak signal (e.g., a very brief presentation of the word) will bring these detectors to the response threshold, and so will be enough to make these detectors fire. Thus, the word will be recognized even with a weak or degraded input.

Repetition priming is explained in similar terms. Presenting a word once will cause the relevant detectors to fire. Once they have fired, baseline activation levels will be temporarily lifted, because of recency of use. Therefore only a weak signal will be needed to make these detectors fire again. As a result, the word will be more easily recognized the second time around.

The Feature Net and Well-Formedness

The net we've described so far, however, cannot explain all of the data. Consider the effects of well-formedness—for instance, the fact that subjects are quite efficient at reading strings like "PIRT" or "HICE," but are inefficient in reading strings like "ITPR" or "HCEI." None of these strings is a word, so word-detectors don't come into play here. Hence, we cannot explain this observation—the efficiency of recognizing regular strings, the inefficiency of recognizing irregular strings—in terms of differential priming in word-detectors. We also can't explain this observation in terms of the priming of letter-detectors, since, as it turns out, we have held constant the individual letters being used ("ITPR" is an anagram of "PIRT").

There are several ways we might accommodate these results: Let's add another layer to the net, a layer filled with detectors for letter combinations. In Figure 2.10, we have added a layer of **bigram**-detectors—detectors of letter pairs. These detectors, like all the rest, will each have a baseline activation level (again: their activation level when they're at rest), and then a moment-by-moment activation level, changing as new inputs arrive. As before, activation levels will be influenced by the frequency with which these detectors have fired in the past, and also the recency with which they have fired.

This turns out to be all the theory we need in explaining the influence of well-formedness. Why are English-like non-words more easily recognized than strings *not* resembling English ("RSFK" or "IUBE")? Well-formed words involve familiar letter combinations. You have never seen the sequence "HICE" before, but you have seen the letter pair "HI" (in *hit, high,* or *hill*) and the pair "CE" (*face, mace, pace*). The detectors for these letter groups, therefore, have high baseline activations and don't need much additional input to reach their threshold. As a result, these well-used detectors will fire

Figure 2.10

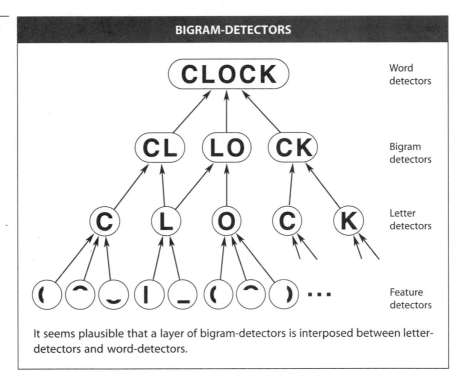

BIGRAM-DETECTORS

Word detectors

Bigram detectors

Letter detectors

Feature detectors

It seems plausible that a layer of bigram-detectors is interposed between letter-detectors and word-detectors.

easily, with only weak input. That will make the corresponding letter combinations easy to recognize, easing the recognition of strings like "HICE." None of this is true for "RSFK." None of these letter combinations is familiar, and so this string will receive no benefits from priming. A strong input will be needed to bring the relevant detectors to threshold, and the string will be recognized only with difficulty.

Recovery from Errors, and Being "Robust"

Human pattern recognition is remarkably robust. We can recognize patterns when the light levels are low. We can recognize patterns when we are tired. Even with tachistoscopic presentations, we recognize a great many stimuli. If a feature net serves as the basis for human pattern recognition, then the net needs to be similarly robust.

Imagine that we tachistoscopically present the word "CORN." With a brief presentation, the quantity of incoming information is small, and so the relevant detectors will fire only weakly. Figure 2.11 shows how this might play

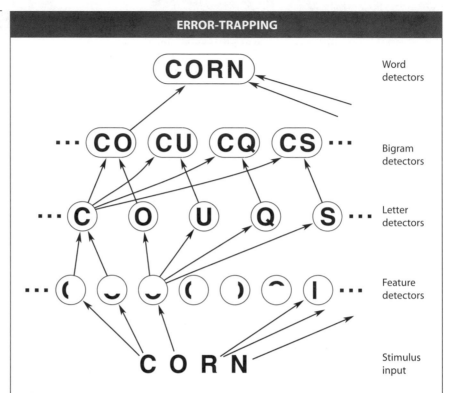

Figure 2.11

ERROR-TRAPPING

CORN — Word detectors

··· CO CU CQ CS ··· — Bigram detectors

··· C O U Q S ··· — Letter detectors

··· (⌣ ⌣ ( ) ⌢ I ··· — Feature detectors

C O R N — Stimulus input

If CORN is presented briefly, not all of its features will be detected. Imagine, for example, that only the bottom curve of the O is detected, and not the O's top or sides. This will (weakly) activate the O-detector, but will also activate various letters having a bottom curve, including U, Q, and S. This will, in turn, send weak activation to the appropriate bigram detectors. The CO-detector, however, is well primed, and so is likely to respond even though it is receiving only a weak input. The other bigram-detectors (for CQ or CS) are less well primed, and so will not respond to this weak input. Therefore, CORN will be correctly perceived, despite the confusion at the letter level caused by the weak signal.

[handwritten note in margin:] if presented too slow, not all appropriate feature detectors will be triggered ∴ C may seem like O or Q or S

out: The fast presentation of the O wasn't enough to trigger all of the feature-detectors appropriate for the O. As it turns out, only the "bottom-curve" detector is firing. This feature detector feeds into many letter detectors—for example, the O-detector, the U-detector, the Q-detector, and the S-detector. Thus, with only this single feature detector activated, each of these letter-detectors will be weakly activated.

But look what happens at the next level. The CO-, CU-, CQ-, and CS-bigram detectors will all receive the same signal. Each will receive a strong signal from the C-detector, and a weak signal about the second letter in the bigram. However, the CO-detector is well-primed (because this is a frequent pattern), and so this detector has a frequency advantage. Consequently, a weak signal will be enough to fire this detector. The CU-detector is less primed (since this is a less frequent pattern); the CQ- or CS-detectors, if these even exist, are not primed at all. The weak input will therefore not be enough to activate these detectors. Thus, at the letter level, there was confusion about the input letter's identity—several detectors were firing, and all were firing equally. At the bigram level, this confusion has been sorted out, and so an error has been avoided.

In this example, confusion at the letter level was straightened out at the bigram level. In the same way, uncertainty at the feature level can be sorted out at the letter level, and confusion at the bigram level can be straightened out at higher levels (e.g., the word-detectors). Psychologists refer to this sort of process as **error trapping**—procedures that detect and correct errors before the errors cause further confusion.

Ambiguous Inputs

The mechanism just described will also help in explaining some other evidence. Look again at Figure 2.1 (p. 33). The character in the middle of the left-hand string is the same as the character in the middle of the right-hand string. Yet the left-hand string is perceived as "THE," and the character as an H, and the right-hand string is perceived as "CAT," and the character as an A.

This observation is now easily explained. At the feature level, the ambiguous neither-A-nor-H has some features of an A and some features of an H. When the pattern is presented, the relevant feature-detectors will fire. But not all of the A features will fire (since not all are present), and ditto for the H features. So the A-detector only receives partial input, and will fire only weakly. Likewise for the H-detector. At this level, therefore, there is uncertainty about what the incoming letter is.

The uncertainty is resolved at subsequent levels. The TH-detector is enormously well primed; so is the THE-detector. If there were a TAE-detector, it would be barely primed, since this is a string rarely encountered. Thus the THE- and TAE-detectors might be receiving comparable input, since both the A-detector and H-detector are (weakly) firing. But this weak input is sufficient for the well-primed THE-detector, and so it will be activated. In this way, the net will recognize the ambiguous pattern as "THE," not "TAE."

(And likewise for the ambiguous pattern on the right, perceived as "CAT," not "CHT.")

A similar explanation will handle the word-superiority effect (see, for example, Rumelhart & Siple, 1974). To take a simple case, imagine that we present A in the context, "AT." If the presentation is brief enough, subjects may see very little of the A, perhaps just the horizontal cross-bar. This would not be enough to distinguish among A, F, or H, and so all these letter-detectors would fire weakly. If this were all the information subjects had, they'd be stuck. But let us imagine that the subjects did perceive the second letter in the display, the T. It seems likely that the AT bigram is far better primed than the FT or HT bigrams. (That is because you often encounter words like *cat* or *boat*; words like *soft* or *heft* are simply less frequent in the language.) Thus, the weak firing of the A-detector *would* be enough to fire the AT bigram-detector, while the weak firing for the F and H might not trigger their bigram-detectors. In this way, a "choice" would be made at the bigram level that the input was "AT" and not something else. Once this bigram has been detected, the question, "was there an A or an F in the display?" is easy. In this manner, the letter will be better detected in context than in isolation. This is not because context allows you to see more; instead, context allows you to make better use of what you see.

Recognition Errors

Note, though, that there is a downside to all this: Imagine that we present the string "CQRN" to subjects. If the presentation is brief enough, subjects will register only a subset of the string's features. Let's imagine, in line with an earlier example, that subjects only register the bottom bit of the string's second letter. This detection of the bottom-curve will weakly activate the Q-detector, and also the U-detector and the O-detector. The resulting pattern of network activation is shown in Figure 2.12, and you should notice that this figure is nearly identical to Figure 2.11.

We have already argued that the dynamic of network function in Figure 2.11 will lead to a response of "CORN." But, since the "grist" for the network is the same in Figure 2.12, then this pattern, too, will lead to "CORN." Hence, in the first case, the functional dynamic built into the net aids performance; in the second case, the same dynamic causes us to misread the stimulus.

Let's make three points about this observation. First, we now have a straightforward account of over-regularization errors: Because of the pattern of priming, the network's responses will tend toward frequent words, and also toward words recently viewed. If the input was, in fact, a frequent word, then the bias built into the network facilitates perception. If the input was an infrequent word, or an irregular word, then the network's bias will lead to

Figure 2.12

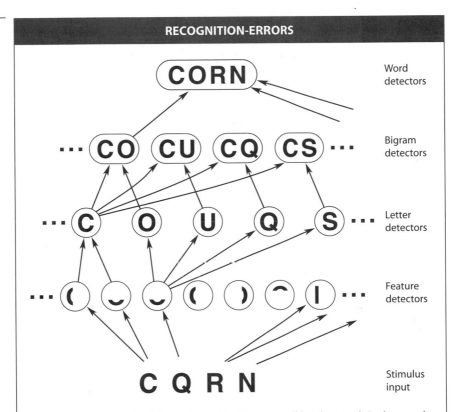

If CQRN is presented briefly, not all of its features will be detected. Perhaps only the bottom curve of the Q is detected, and this will (weakly) activate various letters having a bottom curve, including O, U, Q, and S. However, this is the same situation that would result from a brief presentation of CORN (as shown in Figure 2.11) and therefore, by the logic we have already discussed, this stimulus is likely to be *mis*perceived as CORN.

errors. Moreover, the network's mistakes will be systematic in their form: "CQRN" will be identified as "CORN," "TAE" as "THE," and so on.

Second, we've now seen that the net will reliably make certain errors. From our point of view, however, this is an advantage, not a problem. Humans make these errors. If our model provides a plausible account of the human achievements, then it is appropriate that the model should make errors as well.

Finally, note that these errors are usually unproblematic. Low frequency words are likely to be misperceived but, by definition, low frequency words aren't encountered that often. The network's bias facilitates perception of *frequent* words, and these (by definition) are the words you encounter most of the time. Hence, the network's bias aids recognition in the more frequent cases, and only hurts recognition in the rare cases. Necessarily, then, the network's bias helps perception more often than it hurts.

Why Aren't the Mistakes Noticed?

We mentioned earlier that subjects don't merely *misidentify* the input; they seem instead to *misperceive* it. When subjects in tachistoscopic procedures make errors, they often insist that they are reporting what they clearly saw. What produces this illusion?

Our answer to this question does little more than emphasize points we have already made: Consider the similarity between Figures 2.11 and 2.12. In Figure 2.11, the firing of the CO-detector is a legitimate detection. In Figure 2.12, the firing of this detector constitutes a false alarm, a detection even though the specified target is absent—there's no "CO" present! However, from the network's point of view, these cases are indistinguishable. Once the CO-detector fires, this will trigger subsequent detectors. The only information available to these subsequent detectors is the fact that the CO-detector is firing. There is no way for the subsequent detectors to know *why* the detector is firing—whether in response to a genuine signal, or as a false alarm. Thus, the distinction between false alarm and genuine detection is soon lost.

Let's complicate things somewhat: Imagine that we again present the string, "CQRN," as in Figure 2.12, but let's say that, this time, the subject detects a bit more information about the Q. Perhaps, for example, the subject also detects the Q's "tail." With this feature detected, we would expect a somewhat stronger response from the Q-detector. Therefore, in this scenario, the Q-detector will be firing at a moderate level, while the O-detector and the S-detectors, as before, are firing only weakly. None of this changes the fact that the CO-detector is well-primed, while the CQ-detector is not. As a result, the outcome from this case may be the same as before: We've already said that a weak response from the O-detector may be enough to trigger the well-primed CO-detector. In contrast, even a moderate response from the Q-detector may not be enough to trigger the (unprimed) CQ-detector. Thus it is the CO-detector that fires, and we are right back in the situation of Figure 2.12. In this case, the Q was initially perceived *correctly* but, in the chain of subsequent events, this information is "lost."

There's no way for the network to record the fact that a detector has been "over-ruled," as the Q-detector is, in the previous example. There is also, as we have seen, no way for the network to distinguish false alarms from detections. Remarkably, all of this guarantees that, for the network, mistakes will be indistinguishable from the "real thing." There will be no difference, as far as the net is concerned, between stimuli that actually occurred and stimuli that were merely inferred. In this particular domain, there is no clear distinction between reality and hallucination.

Parallel Processing and Distributed Knowledge

We are almost ready to leave our discussion of the feature net. In closing, though, we need to work through two last points—first, the nature of the "knowledge" built into the network and, second, the broader question of *why* the network should function as it does.

We've seen many indications that, somehow, knowledge of spelling patterns is "built into" the network. For example, knowledge that "CO" is a common bigram in English, while "CF" is not, is built into the network by virtue of the fact that the CO-detector has a higher baseline activation than the CF-detector. As a result, it's literally true that the system is better-prepared for one of these patterns than for the other. In a way, it seems as if the system "expects" one of these patterns ("CO") to appear often, but has no such expectation for the other ("CF"). However, this "expectation" is an entirely passive one—built into the activation levels (and therefore the preparedness) of the net.

The sense in which the net "knows" these facts about spelling is worth emphasizing, since we will return to this idea in later chapters. This knowledge is not explicitly stored anywhere. Nowhere within the net is there a sentence like "CO is a common bigram in English; CF is not." Instead, this memory, if we even want to call it that, is manifest only in the fact that the CO-detector happens to be more primed than the CF-detector. The CO-detector doesn't "know" anything about this relation, nor does the CF-detector. Each simply does its job. In the course of doing their jobs, occasions will arise which involve a "competition" between these detectors. (We considered such situations in our discussion of error trapping, or ambiguous inputs.) In these cases, the better-primed detector will be more likely to respond to weak inputs, and so the better-primed detector will be more likely to influence subsequent events.

In sum, the knowledge that "CO" is a common bigram is implicit knowledge, and implicit in a special sense: This knowledge does not reside in any particular place. Instead, the knowledge is manifest only by virtue of how the various elements of the net function relative to each other—which voices are influential, and which not—when all these detectors are doing their individual jobs. The knowledge is thus visible only if we take a "bird's-eye view," and consider how the entire system functions. The knowledge, therefore, is *not* **locally represented**, but is instead **distributed** across the pattern of network functioning.

The same can be said for all of the net's knowledge, and about the net's inferences. For example, if we present the stimulus "T-[smudge]-E," it is convenient to speak of the network "drawing the inference" that the input was "THE," rather than (say) "TAE." But of course, the net doesn't literally make an inference. Instead, the THE-detector is simply readier to fire than the TAE-detector and, once that happens, something like an inference has taken place. There is no "inference-maker"—the inference is not a local process. The inference is only manifest, once again, in how various detectors work in conjunction with each other, and so the inference is a distributed process.

What is perhaps most remarkable about the feature net, then, lies in how much can be accomplished with simple, mechanical elements, correctly connected to each other. The net appears to make inferences and appears to "know" the rules of English spelling. But the actual mechanics of the net involve neither inferences nor knowledge (at least not in any conventional sense). Information about spelling patterns is distributed across the net. You or I could discern this information about spelling patterns, by taking the bird's-eye view, and comparing the activation of one detector with the activation level of some other. But nothing in the net's functioning depends on a bird's-eye view. The activity of each detector is locally determined—influenced by just those detectors feeding into it. When all of these detectors work in conjunction with each other, that is, when they work in parallel, the net result is a process that acts as if it "knows the rules." But the rules themselves play no causal role in the network's moment-by-moment activities.

It is crucial, of course, that the network elements do work in parallel: Distributed knowledge is only possible if one local operation is played off against the others. Thus, parallel processes and distributed knowledge go hand in hand and, together, they allow the simple elements to act as if they know the rules of spelling.

Efficiency versus Accuracy

The net, just like humans, makes mistakes. Moreover, the same mechanisms lie behind the net's errors and the net's advantages. In a sense, then, you can view the recognition errors as simply the price one pays in order to obtain the benefits associated with the net. But why should anyone pay this price? Why couldn't evolution have provided a mechanism that was both robust and error-free? To tackle this question, we need to spell out some considerations about the network's *efficiency*.

Our world is in many ways a highly predictable place. When you look around a kitchen, it is extremely likely that you will find a stove and a refrigerator, far less likely that you will find a hippopotamus. When you attend a birthday party, it is likely that presents will be given and cake will be served, it is unlikely that wood will be chopped during the party, or floors will be scrubbed. Thus, it is redundant to say "I went to a birthday party, but we didn't scrub any floors," since the second claim is already implied by the first.[1]

Our language itself is also quite redundant, so that many of the letters of a wrd are completely predictable from contxt; the same often true for words within a sentence. In fact, we can push this quite far: It's am-z-ng, f-r -x-mple, h-w m-ny l-tt-rs we c-n r-m-v-, -nd st-ll h-v- a s-nt-nc- th-t's n-t d-ff-c-lt to r--d. Because of this redundancy, one does not need to scrutinize every letter on a page, or every word. Instead, one can selectively glance at the page, and let the net "fill in" the rest.

Why should we exploit this redundancy? Why should we opt for efficiency? Are we simply an impatient species? We can think this through by considering what the alternative is to "being efficient." If, for example, we wished for perfect accuracy, then we would want to make no inferences (since these might be mistaken), and no assumptions (since these might be unwarranted). To achieve this, we would need to spell out *everything*. But what does this mean?

Think back to the "Betsy and Jacob" story, discussed in Chapter 1. This story leaves a great deal unsaid, relying on the fact that listeners (or readers) can fill in the missing information. The savings for the storyteller are enormous: The story can be told with a few short sentences, rather than extending for many pages. The savings for the listener are comparable: The story can be digested in a matter of seconds, rather than requiring hours of study. If, instead, we insisted on "spelling out everything," this story would need to be intolerably long, and the telling of it impossibly slow. Moreover, the gains of "spelling out everything" would be tiny, since we'd be forced to include extraordinary quantities of information that, in truth, should be blindingly obvious (e.g., the fact that people need money to buy things). If we insist on greater efficiency, then, we are not being impatient, we are simply being reasonable.

These claims are also true of word recognition, and of reading in general. To maximize accuracy, we would, of course, want to scrutinize every character on the page. That way, if any character is missing or misprinted, we would

---

[1] The term *redundancy* has a technical meaning within psychology. Here we use the term only in its ordinary sense—so that "redundant" inputs are those that tell you nothing new, those that simply repeat information you already have.

be sure to detect it. But the cost associated with this strategy would be insufferable: Reading would be unspeakably slow. In contrast, one can make *inferences* about a page with remarkable speed, and this leads readers to adopt the obvious strategy: They read some of the letters, and make inferences about the rest. This does risk error but, if the inferences are well-guided, then the errors will be rare. Thus, in short, the efficient reader is not being careless, or hasty, or lazy. Given the redundancy of text, and given the slowness of letter-by-letter reading, the inferential strategy is the only strategy that makes sense.

It's not surprising, therefore, that we do exploit the redundancy of text in our ordinary reading—this is reflected, for example, in studies of eye movements made while reading. Indeed, one of the major differences between fast and slow readers, or between adults and children, is that fast, skilled readers genuinely look at fewer positions on the page (Crowder & Wagner, 1992; Rayner, 1993). Skilled readers, in other words, seem literally to *read less*, but *infer more*, than less-skilled readers. Thus, skill in reading hinges on the ability to make effective *use* of what you've seen on the page—supplementing what you see with inferences guided by the redundancy of the language. (Evidence suggests that this is also the central core of "speed-reading." This is why, for example, speed-reading courses often urge you to study a book's illustrations and its table of contents before starting to read; this provides a base for making inferences, helping you to get by with more inference and less reading.)

Proofreading

Consider the familiar task of proofreading, to correct spelling or grammatical errors. This is a task in which you *do* want to read letter-by-letter, even if this is quite slow, in order to catch the errors. As it turns out, though, this is rather difficult to do, underscoring the important role of inference in reading.

It is obvious that proofreading is hard. Despite careful and repeated readings of your own paper, you fail to spot some of the errors: you overlook words that are misspelled or omitted, you fail to detect inappropriate substitutions (*from* when you meant to type *form*). Inevitably, though, some other reader (for example, your professor!) does spot the errors, and returns your paper covered with red ink.

We need no new theory to explain this, since we have already discussed how misperceptions can occur. Ironically, these misperceptions may be *more* likely in reading your own papers than in reading anything else. In reading something that you wrote yourself, you are particularly well-primed for the words on the page. You know what you intended to write, and this knowledge will guide your inferences. In addition, odds are that you have read the page several times as you worked on successive drafts. With all of this priming, this is surely a case in which minimal input is needed to make the detectors fire. Hence, it is possible here for you to rely on maximal use of inference as you read down the page. And, like it or not, that is exactly what you do, reading efficiently, but not spotting the errors. For these reasons, it is a useful strategy to have a friend proofread for you, since he or she will be less well primed for the words on the page, and will therefore be less able to use the fully inferential strategy.

The difficulties of proofreading allow us to make one further point: It seems that you have little choice about adopting the efficient strategy of reading. In proofreading, you might prefer to read *less* efficiently, in order to make no recognition errors. You want to find your typing mistakes! Nonetheless, the strategy of using inference is so well-practiced, so automatic, that you use it even here. (For studies of proofreading, see Daneman & Stainton, 1991; Healy, Volbrecht & Nye, 1983; Healy, 1981.)

Descendants of the Feature Net

As we mentioned early on, we have been focusing on one of the simpler and older versions of the feature net. This has allowed us to get a number of important themes into view—such as the trade-off between efficiency and accuracy, and the notion of distributed knowledge built into a network's functioning. However, it should be said that many variations on the feature-net idea are possible, each differing somewhat from the specific proposal we have discussed, and each with its own advantages and disadvantages. In this section, we consider two other, more recent, versions of the network idea.

The McClelland and Rumelhart Model

An influential model of word recognition was proposed by McClelland and Rumelhart (1981). A portion of their model is illustrated in Figure 2.13. Once again, there is a feature-base, and a network of connections, as various detectors serve to influence each other. This net, like the one we have been discussing, is better able to identify well-formed strings than irregular strings, this net is also more efficient in identifying characters in context, as opposed to characters in isolation. However, several new features of this net make it possible to accomplish all this *without* bigram-detectors.

In the network proposal we have considered so far, activation of one detector serves to activate other detectors; these **excitatory connections** are

Figure 2.13

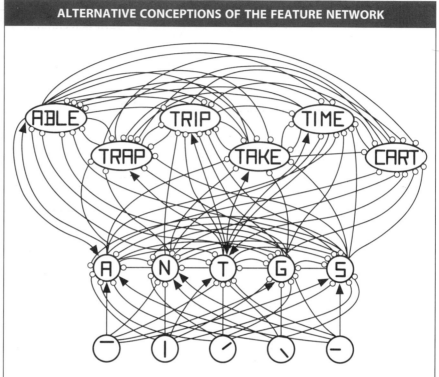

ALTERNATIVE CONCEPTIONS OF THE FEATURE NETWORK

McClelland and Rumelhart (1981) offered a pattern-recognition model with no detectors for letter combinations. Instead, letter-detectors directly activate word-detectors. This model includes both excitatory connections (indicated by arrows) and inhibitory connections (indicated by connections with round heads). Connections *within* a specific level are also possible so that, for example, activation of the TRIP detector will inhibit the detectors for TRAP, TAKE, or TIME.

shown in Figure 2.13 with arrows, so that detection of a T serves to "excite" the TRIP-detector. In the McClelland and Rumelhart model, however, detectors can also *inhibit* each other, so that detection of a G, for example, inhibits the TRIP-detector. These **inhibitory connections** are shown in the figure with dots. In addition, this model allows for more complicated signaling than we have employed so far. In our discussion, we have assumed that lower-level detectors trigger upper-level detectors, but not the reverse. The flow of information, it seemed, was a one-way street. In the McClelland and Rumelhart model, though, higher-level detectors (word-detectors) can influence the lower-lever detectors, and detectors at any level can also influence the other detectors at the same level (e.g., letter detectors inhibit other letter detectors; word detectors inhibit other word detectors).

To see how this would work, let's say that the word "TRIP" is briefly shown, allowing the subject to see enough features to identify, say, only the R, I, and P. Detectors for these letters will therefore fire, and this will in turn activate the detector for "TRIP." Activation of this word-detector will cause two further effects: First, it will inhibit the firing of all the other word-detectors (e.g., detectors for "ABLE," "TRAP," "TAKE," and so on). Second, activation of the TRIP-detector will excite the detectors for its component letters—i.e., will excite detectors for T, R, I, and P. The R-, I-, and P-detectors, we've supposed, were already firing, so this extra activation "from above" has little impact. But the T-detector, we've supposed, was not firing before. The relevant features were on the scene, but in a degraded form, thanks to the brief presentation. This weak input was insufficient to trigger an unprimed detector. But the excitation from the word detector now primes the T detector, making it more likely to fire, even with a weak input.

In essence, activation of the word-detector for TRIP implied that this was a context in which a T was quite likely; hence the network "prepared itself" for a T by priming the appropriate detector. Once the network was suitably prepared, detection was facilitated. In this way, the detection of a letter sequence made the network more sensitive to elements likely to occur within that sequence. That is exactly what we need for the network to be responsive to the regularities of spelling patterns. And, of course, there is ample evidence that humans are sensitive to (and exploit) these regularities.

There are several reasons why one might prefer this kind of net to the kind considered earlier, but they are beyond the scope of this book. Let us highlight, though, the crucial point—namely, the kinds of flexibility availability in how a feature net can be implemented.

Recognition by Components

We noted early on that our discussion would focus largely on the recognition of print. But what can we say about recognition of other things, including the recognition of three-dimensional objects? Can these also be recognized by a network?

In a series of studies, Biederman (1987; Biederman & Cooper, 1991) has presented a network theory of object recognition, dubbed the **recognition by components** (or **RBC**) model. The crucial innovation here is an intermediate level of detectors, sensitive to **geons**. Biederman's proposal is that geons (for "geometric ions") serve as the basic building blocks of all the objects we recognize; geons are, in essence, the "alphabet" from which all objects are constructed. Geons are simple shapes, such as cylinders, cones, and blocks

(Figure 2.14A). And only a small set of these shapes are needed: According to Biederman, we need (at most) three dozen different geons to describe every object in the world, just as 26 letters are all that are needed to produce all the words of English. These geons can then be combined in various ways—in a "top-of" relation, or a "side-connected" relation, and so on, to create all the objects we perceive (see Figure 2.14B).

The RBC model, like the network we have been discussing, utilizes a hierarchy of detectors. The lowest level detectors are feature-detectors, which respond to edges, curves, vertices, and so on. These detectors in turn activate the geon-detectors. Higher levels of detectors are then sensitive to combinations of geons. More precisely, geons are assembled into more complex ar-

---

Figure 2.14

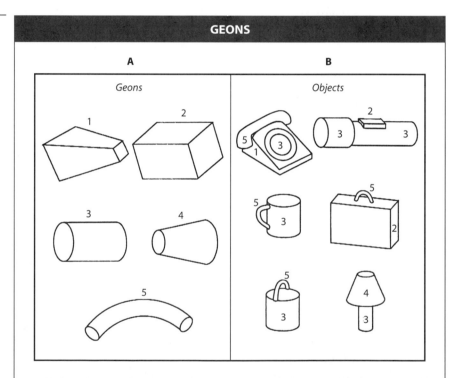

GEONS

A   **B**

Geons   *Objects*

Biederman (1987, 1990) has proposed that geons serve as the basic building blocks of all the objects we recognize. In other words, we recognize objects by first recognizing their component geons. Panel A shows five different geons; Panel B shows how these geons can be assembled into objects. The numbers in Panel B identify the specific geons, so that a bucket contains Geon 5 "top-connected" to Geon 3.

rangements called "geon assemblies," and these in turn activate the "object model," a representation of the complete, recognized, object.

The presence of the geon level, within this hierarchy, buys us several advantages. For one, we noted at the very start of this chapter that, quite obviously, we can recognize objects from many different angles. It is therefore an important attribute of geons that they can be identified from virtually any angle of view. Thus, no matter what your position, relative to a cat, you'll be able to identify its geons, and thus identify the cat. Moreover, it seems that most objects can be recognized from just a few geons (in the appropriate configuration). As a consequence, geon-based models like RBC can recognize objects even if many of the object's geons are hidden from view.

In addition, several further lines of evidence increase our confidence that geons do play a role in recognition. For example, recognition of simple objects is relatively easy if the geons are easy to discern; recognition is much more difficult if the geons are hard to identify (e.g., Biederman, 1985). As an example, consider the objects shown in Figure 2.15. In columns B and C, about two-thirds of the contour has been deleted from each drawing. In column B, this deletion has been carefully done so that the geons can still be identified and, as you can see, these objects can be recognized without much difficulty. In column C, the deletion has been done in a fashion that obscures geon identity, and now object recognition is much more difficult. Thus, it really does seem that the geons capture something crucial for identification of these objects.

A different line of evidence draws on a procedure we have already discussed, namely, repetition priming. In this procedure, a stimulus is presented and then, some time later, the same stimulus is presented again. Thanks to repetition priming, the stimulus will be easier to recognize the second time around. In general, repetition priming is maximal when the second stimulus is identical to the first (same size, same orientation, and so on). However, we can also observe repetition priming with non-identical stimuli. The trick, though, is that the two stimuli (the primer and the primed) must be related in the right way. More precisely, repetition priming is observed if the two stimuli employ the same geons.

To see how this works, note that the pictures in Figure 2.16 are in "complementary pairs"—if you literally superimpose picture A1 on picture A2, you'd get a complete drawing of a piano; superimposing B1 on B2 would yield a complete drawing of an elephant. But the two pairs are fragmented in different ways: A1 and A2 depict different features, but the *geons* included in A1 are the same as those shown in A2. That is because (for example) A1 might depict the left-hand side of the geon, while A2 depicts the right-hand side. In contrast, B1 and B2 do not share geons: If a geon is depicted in B1, it is not depicted in B2, and vice versa.

Figure 2.15

RECOGNIZING DEGRADED PICTURES

A   B   C

[handwritten annotations: "geon shape still here :: easier to identify", "geon shape not here :: harder to identify"]

In the middle column, one can still identify the objects' geons, and so the forms are easily recognized. In the right column, it is difficult to identify the geons, and correspondingly difficult to identify the objects. This adds strength to the claim that geon identification plays an important role in object recognition.

Figure 2.16

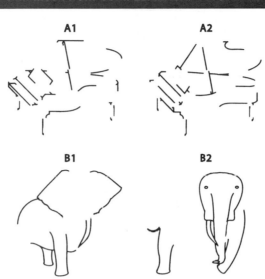

PRIMING FROM COMPLEMENTARY PICTURES

A1   A2

B1   B2

Superimposing A1 and A2 would yield a complete drawing of a piano; super-imposing B1 and B2 would yield a complete drawing of an elephant. But the drawings are fragmented in different ways: A1 and A2 depict different features, but the *geons* identifiable in A1 are the same as the geons shown in A2. Because of this "geon overlap," experience with A1 helps subjects in later recognizing A2. For the elephant picture, the geons identifiable in B1 are different from those identifiable in B2. With no geon overlap, experience with B1 does *not* help in later recognizing B2.

[handwritten margin notes: as lng as same geons are present in 2 diff. angles of a picture it should be recognized — *"geon overlap" facilitates later recognition]*

Biederman and Cooper (1991) used pictures like these in a repetition priming experiment. Subjects were initially shown one partial picture (for example, A1 or B1), and then were subsequently shown that picture's complement (A2 or B2). The question was whether repetition priming would be observed—that is, whether A1 would prime A2, and whether B1 would prime B2. Biederman and Cooper hypothesized that priming takes place largely at the geon level. Since A1 and A2 depict the same geons, each should prime the other. On the other hand, B1 and B2 do not share geons, and so should not prime each other. The geon-detectors needed for B1 are irrelevant to the perception of B2; therefore, "warming up" these detectors (by presenting B1) should have no effect on the perception of B2. All of this fits with the data: Complementary pictures did prime each other if the complements shared geons; complementary pictures without shared geons did not prime each other. This indicates that priming in this procedure is indeed taking place at the level of geon detection and, for our purposes, confirms the central point: that geons do play a role in object identification.

The RBC model does an impressive job of object recognition—recognizing a wide range of objects, across a wide range of variations in size, position, and so on. Thus, this seems like a promising approach to object recognition and confirms the claim that a network of hierarchically arranged detectors plays an important part in pattern recognition. (For some concerns about the RBC model, see Ullman, 1989. For other current research, see Biederman, 1987; Biederman & Gerhardstein, 1993; Hummel & Biederman, 1992.)

Different Objects, Different Recognition Systems?

The previous section shifted our focus away from print: A network can also be designed, it seems, to recognize three-dimensional objects. But how far can we travel on this path? Can other sorts of recognition—recognition of sounds, recognition of faces, recognition of smells—be approached in the same way?

These are, of course, questions to be settled by research, and in this section we will consider some of the relevant evidence, which is uneven. Many domains, rather distant from print, show effects similar to the ones we have reviewed, suggesting that similar mechanisms are in play. Other domains, however, reveal a different dynamic, implying that, for these domains, we will need a different sort of theory.

Recognition Errors in Hearing

The recognition of print provides an excellent case study for how recognition in general might proceed. And, in fact, many of the principles surveyed so far do generalize to other domains. For example, it seems true in general that more frequently viewed (or more frequently heard) patterns are easier to recognize. Likewise, repetition priming can be demonstrated in many domains. It is also true in general that regular or well-formed patterns are easier to recognize than ill-formed patterns. And, when recognition errors occur, these are, in general, in the direction of "regularizing" the input, just as in the case of print. All of this invites the conclusion that a uniform theoretical treatment will be possible, across diverse domains.

As an illustration of the relevant research, consider studies of the so-called

restoration effect. In these procedures, sounds are tape-recorded and then carefully modified. For example, the "s" sound in the word "legislature" might be removed, and replaced by a brief burst of noise. When subjects hear this degraded input, however, they do not detect the omission; instead, they report hearing the *complete* word, *legislature, accompanied by* a burst of noise. In effect, subjects supply the missing sound on their own. If subjects are asked exactly when the "accompanying" noise occurred (simultaneous with the first syllable? the second?), they often cannot tell (Repp, 1992; Samuel, 1987, 1991; for further discussion of the recognition of speech, see Chapter 9). Similar effects have been documented with musical stimuli. In this case, simple melodies or scales are recorded, and then single notes are replaced by bursts of noise. Once again, subjects report hearing the notes that are not there, and once again, subjects are inaccurate in judging when, within the sequence, the noise appeared (DeWitt & Samuel, 1990).

These restoration errors are plainly related to the errors we have described in print recognition—for example, proof-reading errors. In both cases, the perceiver goes beyond the information actually provided, filling in the information that should be there. In the case of print, we attributed this to well-primed detectors. Thanks to priming, these detectors will fire even in response to a weak input; that makes the network robust. Unfortunately, though, we can find circumstances in which the detectors fire in the *absence* of an input—producing what we called a false alarm response. Apparently, the same is true with auditory stimuli such as speech, or even with non-linguistic stimuli, such as musical phrases.

Faces

However, there is at least one category of input that seems to require a different sort of recognition system, namely, faces. Several pieces of evidence support the claim that face memory is served by specialized structures and mechanisms. One indication comes from individuals who have suffered brain strokes. Depending on where exactly in the brain these strokes occur, patients can develop a striking variety of very specific symptoms, and we mentioned one category of symptoms, namely, visual agnosia, at the beginning of this chapter. It turns out, though, that there are many subtypes of agnosia. In particular, patients who suffer brain damage sometimes develop a syndrome called **prosopagnosia:** They lose their ability to recognize faces, even though their other visual abilities seem to be relatively intact. This implies the existence of a special neural structure, involved almost exclusively in the recognition and discrimination of faces (Alexander & Albert, 1983; Burton, Young, Bruce, Johnston & Ellis, 1991; Damasio, Damasio & Van Hoesen, 1982; Damasio, Tranel & Damasio, 1990; De Renzi, Faglioni, Grossi & Nichelli, 1991; Ellis, 1989; Hecaen, 1981; Sergent & Poncet, 1990; Tranel, Damasio & Damasio, 1988).

A second distinguishing principle of face recognition is its strong dependency on orientation. It is generally more difficult to recognize things if they are presented at a novel orientation (e.g., upside-down), although, as we have noted, recognition of disoriented objects is still possible. However, the effects of disorientation are particularly pronounced with faces. In one study, for example, four categories of stimuli were considered: right-side up faces, upside-down faces, right-side up pictures of common objects other than faces, and upside-down pictures of common objects. As can be seen in Figure 2.17, performance suffered for all of the upside-down stimuli. However, this effect is much larger for faces than it is for other kinds of stimuli (Yin, 1969).

The same point can be made informally. Figure 2.18 shows two upside-down photographs of former British Prime Minister, Margaret Thatcher (from Thompson, 1980). You can probably detect that something is odd about these, but now try turning the book upside down, so that the faces are right-side up. As you can see, the difference between these faces is immense,

Figure 2.17

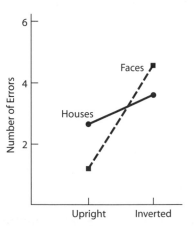

MEMORY FOR FACES PRESENTED UPRIGHT OR UPSIDE DOWN

Subjects' memory for faces is quite good, compared with memory for other pictures (in this case, pictures of houses). However, subjects' performance is very much disrupted when the pictures of faces are inverted. Performance with houses is also worse with inverted pictures, but the effect of inversion is far smaller. [After Yin, 1969.]

Figure 2.18

PERCEPTION OF UPSIDE-DOWN FACES

The left-hand picture looks somewhat odd, but the two pictures still look relatively similar to each other. Now try turning the book upside down (so that the faces are upright). In this position, the left-hand face (now on the right) looks ghoulish, and the two pictures look very different from each other. Perception of upside-down faces is apparently quite different from our perception of upright faces. [From Thompson, 1980.]

and yet this rather fiendish contrast is largely lost when the faces are upside down. Once again, it seems that the perception of faces is strikingly different when we view the faces upside down. (Also see Rhodes, Brake & Atkinson, 1993.)

All of this seems to imply that face recognition is different from recognition of other sorts—served by its own neural "apparatus" and particularly dependent on orientation. But is it just faces that show these patterns? Consider first the evidence of prosopagnosia. Our understanding of this syndrome has grown as a greater number of cases have been examined. For example, there is a well-documented report of a prosopagnosic farmer who not only lost the ability to recognize faces, he also lost the ability to recognize his individual cows. Likewise, there is a case of a prosopagnosic bird-watcher who has, it seems, lost both the ability to discriminate faces and also the ability to discriminate warblers (Bornstein, 1963; Bornstein, Sroka & Munitz, 1969). Still another patient has lost the ability to tell cars apart, and is only able to locate her car in a parking lot by reading all the license plates until she finds her own (Damasio et al., 1982). Thus, prosopagnosia is not strictly a disorder of face recognition.

Likewise, it appears that other categories of stimuli, and not just faces, show the "upside-down effect" we have already described. For example, similar data have been reported in a study of highly experienced judges from dog shows, that is, people who know a particular breed extremely well. Diamond and Carey (1986) compared how well these judges recognized right-side up and up-side down stimuli in each of two categories: faces and dogs in the familiar breed. Not surprisingly, performance was much worse with up-side down faces than with right-side up faces, replicating the pattern of Figure 2.17. The critical result, though, is that performance suffered just as much with upside-down pictures of dogs.

This overall pattern of evidence has led some authors to suggest that humans have a specialized recognition system, not just for faces, but for recognizing specific individuals within any highly familiar category (cf. Diamond & Carey, 1986). It is this system that is impaired in people with prosopagnosia, disrupting their recognition of faces, but also disrupting the recognition of warblers for someone highly familiar with birds, the recognition of cows for someone highly familiar with the herd, and so on. Likewise, it is this same system that is unable to operate when stimuli are presented upside-down. Again, this compromises the recognition of faces, but it will also compromise other forms of recognition *provided* that the viewer is trying to distinguish individuals and is also highly familiar with the category (for example, the category of dogs, for an expert dog-judge).

A related proposal has been offered by Farah (1992), who proposes that humans have two distinct pattern-recognition systems. One system is specialized for the recognition of simple parts, and then the assembly of those parts into larger wholes. This is presumably the system we have been discussing throughout this chapter. A second system is specialized for the recognition of larger configurations. This system is less able to analyze patterns into their parts, and less able to recognize these parts, but this system is more sensitive to larger-scale configurational properties. Presumably it is this system that is crucial for the recognition of faces and the other cases discussed in this section. In this view, prosopagnosia would involve damage to the second system, but not the first. Farah notes, though, that other forms of brain damage have the opposite effect—for example, disrupting the ability to recognize words, with no damage to the ability to recognize faces. These cases would result from damage to the first, more analytic system, while the second, more configurational system is spared.

Further work is needed to refine these distinctions and to specify how the configurational system functions. Nonetheless, the available evidence does indicate the need for a distinction of some sort. The feature-net approach we have discussed in this chapter seems very powerful, and applicable to a wide variety of patterns. More strongly, no one is arguing that we can do *without* the feature net. Quite the contrary: The feature net plays a critical role in the processes of pattern recognition. But the feature net can't do it all. Some patterns, including faces, seem to involve a different sort of pattern recognition. (For examples of other research on memory for faces, see Baddeley, 1982; Bower & Karlin, 1974; Burton et al. 1991; Etcoff & Magee, 1992; Hay, Young & Ellis, 1991; Young & Bruce, 1991.)

Top-down Influences on Pattern Recognition

The previous section had a two-part message: On the one side, we saw that the feature-net idea is applicable to a great many domains: It is not only useful for the recognition of print; it is also applicable to the recognition of common objects, speech sounds and, it seems, musical phrases. At the same time, though, there are limits on what the feature net can do so that, more specifically, there are domains for which the feature net is not well suited. The suggestion, then, is that we need multiple recognition systems. The feature net will be one of those systems, used for a broad class of targets (print, three-dimensional objects, and perhaps music). A different system (about which we know relatively little) will be used for other sorts of targets (faces).

In the present section, we explore a different limit on the feature net. Our concern here is with targets for which the feature net is useful—print, common objects, and so on. Even in this domain, it turns out that the feature net must be supplemented with some further mechanisms. This doesn't undermine the importance of the feature-net idea—the net is plainly needed, as part of our theoretical account. The key word, though, is *part*, since, as we'll see, we need to place the feature net in a larger context. The net is crucial, but can't do it all.

The Benefits of Larger Contexts

Let us begin with some evidence. We have already seen that letter recognition is improved by context, so that the letter V, for example, is easier to recognize in the context "VIMP" than it is if presented alone. It turns out that the same is true for *words*—these too are better recognized in context, in particular, in the context of a sentence.

In an early demonstration of this effect, subjects were asked to read a phrase, and then were briefly shown a word that completed the phrase (Tulving & Gold, 1963). The length of the phrase was varied: In some trials, the test word was accompanied by no context, so that subjects might read "[blank]," followed by the test word "airplane." In other trials, one context-word was given so that, for example, subjects might read, "the . . . ," followed by "airplane." In still other trials, eight context-words were given, so that the test word completed a nine-word sentence. Sometimes this context was appropriate for the test word, and sometimes the context was inappropriate. As an inappropriate context, subjects might read, "The governor planned soon to initiate the new . . . ," followed by the test word "birdhouse."

The results from this study are easy to describe: Word recognition was facilitated by context if the context was appropriate for that word. Larger contexts provided stronger effects, so that subjects were better able to recognize the test stimuli after eight-word (appropriate) contexts than after four-word or two-word contexts. The size of context also mattered for the "inappropriate" condition—recognition was *worse* after an eight-word inappropriate context than after a four-word or two-word context.

One might worry that subjects are simply *guessing* the target word, based on the context, so that context is not really aiding perception of the word itself. We can measure this guessing effect by presenting the context *without* the target stimulus, and asking subjects directly to guess that target's identity. In this condition, context does produce a benefit: Subjects are better able to guess the target if given a larger (appropriate) context. But the benefits of context in this guessing condition are relatively small (Tulving, Mandler & Baumal, 1964). The real benefit of context comes by the facilitation of perception, not by the support of guessing; to obtain this benefit, one needs to have something to perceive. (See also Rueckl & Oden, 1986.)

These effects obviously resemble the word-superiority effect, described on pages 46–48. In both cases, a target in context is easier to recognize than a target in isolation. In both cases, the effect is obtained with well-formed contexts, but not with ill-formed or inappropriate contexts (Potter, Moryadas, Abrams & Noel, 1993; Simpson, Peterson, Castell & Burgess, 1989). Despite these parallels, however, we probably need rather different accounts of how word context benefits letter recognition, and of how sentence context benefits word recognition.

To explain how word context benefits letters, we relied on bigram detectors, all primed in the right ways, allowing subjects to make maximal use of the incoming information and, in particular, allowing easier identification of well-formed strings. Thus, the detector for "TH" is better primed than the detector for "HT," allowing easier recognition of "THE" than of "HTE." Now let's extend this same argument to sentences: We know, for example, that subjects can easily read "THE BOY RAN"; they have more trouble with the (ill-formed) sentence "BOY THE RAN." By analogy with word recognition, we could explain this by supposing that there is a detector for "THE BOY," and another detector for "BOY THE." The former detector would be well primed, since the relevant word combination is often encountered; the latter detector would not be well primed. Hence, the former detector would fire more easily and more quickly, even with a weak input. This would "explain" the easier perception of the grammatical sentence.

But is this plausible? This explanation presumes that there are detectors for the various word combinations ("bi-word" detectors), all primed in the right way. How many of these detectors would we need? With a vocabulary of 25,000 words, the number of possible word pairs is huge (625 million, to be exact), and so one might need hundreds of millions of bi-word detectors. And that's just the beginning: As we've just seen, an eight-word context provides a greater recognition benefit than a four-word context. To account for this in terms of primed detectors, we would presumably need detectors sensitive to eight-word sequences. With a vocabulary of 25,000 words, the number of eight-word combinations is 152 billion trillion trillion. For comparison, realize that the number of neurons on the brain has been estimated at about 100 trillion. Thus, the word combinations outnumber the neurons by a billion trillion to one!

It is therefore absurd to claim we have detectors for each of these combinations. And with no detectors on the scene, we obviously can't appeal to detector *priming* in explaining the data.

How *should* we explain the benefits of phrase context? Some would argue that we simply cannot explain these effects in network terms. Others, however, have argued that a different *style* of network modeling will explain the data. We'll return to this debate in Chapter 7, and we will return, more broadly, to patterns of linguistic knowledge in Chapter 9. For now, though, our point is modest: We cannot explain these data by simply enlarging the model we so far have in place. This model is enormously useful, but to explain how we recognize complex, larger scale stimuli, we will need more than just a vast army of primed detectors.

Interactive Models

The same broad conclusion can be reached in another way: So far, our focus has largely been on **data-driven**, or bottom-up processing. That is, we have discussed how the incoming information (the "data") triggers a response by feature detectors, which in turn triggers a response by letter-detectors (or geon-detectors), and so on. The data take the initiative; the data get things going. However, there is reason to believe that there is more to pattern recognition than this. Pattern recognition is also influenced by a broad pattern

top-down +
bottom-up =
interactive
models

of knowledge and expectations. These influences are generally referred to as **concept-driven**, or top-down. Models that include both top-down and bottom-up components are described as **interactive models**.

The data in the previous section indicated some of the limits of self-contained, data-driven models; here is another way to make the same general point: We can tell subjects: "I am about to show you a word very briefly on a computer screen; the word is the name of something that you can eat." If we forced subjects to *guess* the word at this point, they would be unlikely to name the target word. But if we now tachistoscopically show the word, "ARTICHOKE," we are likely to observe a large priming effect—that is, subjects are more likely to recognize "ARTICHOKE" with this cue than they would have been without the cue.

Consider what this priming involves. First, the subject needs to understand all of the words in the instruction. If a subject did not understand the word "eat" (if, for example, the subject mistakenly thought we had said, "something that you can *beat*"), we would not get the priming. Second, the subject must understand the *syntax* of the instruction and, specifically, the relations among the words in the instruction. Again, if the subject mistakenly thought we said "something that *can eat you*," we would expect a very different sort of priming. Third, the subject has to know some facts about the world—namely, the kinds of things that can be eaten; without this knowledge, we would expect no priming.

sentence-based
priming is top-down

repetition priming/frequency
is bottom-up

Priming of this sort is plainly top-down, or concept-driven, since it depends on things the subject knows. The same is true for the "sentence-based" priming discussed in the previous section. Both of these stand in contrast to the other sorts of priming we have discussed. With repetition priming, for example, what mattered was not a subject's knowledge, but merely a subject's "stimulus history," i.e., what stimuli the subject had seen recently. The same was true for frequency-based priming. In an obvious way, therefore, these sorts of priming are data-driven, or perhaps we should say "stimulus-driven."

The existence of concept-based priming is a major argument in favor of some sort of interactive approach to pattern recognition. We need a model, in other words, that includes both data-driven and concept-driven processes. But this interactive approach indicates that pattern recognition cannot be viewed as a self-contained process: Knowledge that is external to pattern recognition (for example, knowledge about what is edible) is imported into the recognition process, and clearly influences that process. Put differently, the "ARTICHOKE" example, and all the studies described in the previous section, do not depend on stimulus history, at least not in any straightforward way. Instead, what is crucial for priming is what the subject knows, coming into the experiment, and also how this knowledge is used.

We have, therefore, come full circle. We began this chapter by noting that the various aspects of cognition are all interconnected, each dependent on the others. Nonetheless, we have tried, in this chapter, to examine pattern-recognition on its own—considering how a separate "pattern-recognition module" might function, with the module then handing its "product" (the patterns it had recognized) on to subsequent processes. We have made good progress in this attempt, and have described how a significant piece of pattern recognition might proceed. But in the end we have also run up against a problem, namely, concept-driven priming. This sort of priming depends on what is in memory, and on how that knowledge is accessed and used. Therefore, we really cannot tackle concept-driven priming until we have said a great deal more about memory, knowledge, and thought. These are precisely the interconnections among various domains, the interconnections among different aspects of cognition, promised at the very outset. We leave pattern recognition for now, in order to fill in some other pieces of the puzzle. We will have more to say about pattern recognition in later chapters, once we have some more theoretical machinery in place.

3

Paying Attention

In discussing pattern recognition, we began with a situation simplified in many ways. The experiments we described all took place in a quiet setting, so that no noise distracted subjects. The stimuli were presented briefly, but they were presented one at a time, in a known location, with nothing else on the computer screen. Subjects therefore had no difficulty in locating the target information, nor did they have to decide which bits of the input were crucial for the task, and which irrelevant. The subjects' task was difficult, since the stimuli were degraded, but subjects had exactly one task to do, so they could focus their full attention on this task.

One's ordinary commerce with the world takes place in a very different situation. Consider your circumstances right now. You are paying attention to this page, reading these words. However, think of the other inputs available to you, things you could pay attention to if you chose. You are concentrating on this line of print, but you can easily see that there are other lines of print on the page. You are paying attention to the meanings of these words, but you could choose instead to look at the shapes of the letters, or you could attend to the font in which the words are presented, rather than the words themselves. There are also many sounds in the room. Perhaps the radio is on, or perhaps you can hear someone at the next desk turning pages. There are also stimuli available to you from other modalities. You could, if you wished, pay attention to the weight of the book in your hands, or to the pressure of your chair against your body. Or, if you liked, you could pay attention to none of these things, and choose instead to think about what you did last weekend, or what you'll write in your term paper.

There are two crucial facts here, and explaining these facts will be the task of this chapter. First, you can choose to pay attention to any of the things just mentioned and, if you do, you will be virtually oblivious to the other things on the list. In fact, until you read the previous paragraph, you may not even have noticed these other stimuli. Second, there seems to be one thing you cannot easily do: pay attention to all of these things at once. If you start musing about your weekend, you are likely to lose track of what's on the page; if you start planning your paper, you won't finish the reading assignment. Of course, it is possible, in some circumstances, to divide your attention, to deal with two different inputs at once, or to perform two different tasks at once. You can, if you choose, hum a melody while reading these words. And, no matter how hard you concentrate on this page, surely you would notice if someone tapped you on the shoulder while you were reading. But where are the limits? When can you do two (or more) things at the same time, and when can't you? Can these limits be changed, so that, potentially, you could learn to do several things at once?

All these questions set the agenda for the present chapter. We will start with **selective attention**—the processes through which you somehow select one input and "tune out" the rest. We will then turn to questions about **divided attention**, examining when (and if) you can do multiple tasks at once. Selective and divided attention are clearly linked to each other (since one has to select when one cannot divide!), but it will be useful to start by treating them separately.

Selective Listening

Let's first look at some classic studies of attention. We will then turn to theoretical accounts that might help to explain these results.

Basic Findings from Selective Listening

Many early studies of attention employed a task called **shadowing**. In this task, subjects hear a tape-recording of someone speaking, and must echo this speech back, word for word, while they are listening to it. Shadowing is initially difficult, but becomes easy with just a few minutes practice. (You might try it, shadowing a voice on the radio or TV.)

In most experiments, the to-be-shadowed message, the **attended channel**, is presented through stereo headphones, so that subjects hear the attended channel through, say, the right earphone. Into the left earphone, the unattended channel, we play a different message. This set-up is referred to as **dichotic listening**.

Under these circumstances, subjects easily follow one message, and their shadowing performance is generally near perfect. At the same time, however, subjects hear remarkably little from the unattended message. If we ask them, after a minute or so of shadowing, to report what the unattended message was about, they cannot (e.g., Cherry, 1953). Subjects cannot even tell if the unattended channel contained a coherent message or just random words. In fact, in one study, subjects shadowed coherent prose in the attended channel, while, in the unattended channel, they heard a text in Czechoslovakian, read with English pronunciation. Thus, the individual sounds (the vowels, the consonants) resembled English, but the message itself was (for an English-speaker) gibberish. After a minute of shadowing, only four of thirty subjects detected the peculiar character of the unattended message (Treisman, 1964; for related findings with visual inputs, see Neisser & Becklen, 1975).

In a different study, the content of the unattended channel consisted merely of a list of seven words, repeated over and over. At the end of the shadowing, subjects were given a printed page and told, "Some of the words printed here were just presented in the unattended channel; others were not. Please mark the ones that you just heard in the unattended channel." Despite their having heard the repetitions 35 times, performance on this recognition test was effectively random (Moray, 1959).

However, subjects are not simply *deaf* to the unattended channel: They easily and accurately report whether the unattended channel contained human speech, musical instruments, or silence. If the unattended channel contains human speech, subjects can report whether the speaker was male or female, had a high or low voice, and so on. We can also arrange to change the apparent location of the unattended channel from one ear to the other (simply by adjusting the controls on the stereo running the study). Subjects easily note and can report the location of this voice. (For reviews of this early work, see Broadbent, 1958; Kahneman, 1973; Moray, 1969.)

Some Unattended Inputs Are Detected

So far the pattern of evidence shows that physical attributes of the unattended channel are easily heard: Subjects can describe the type of sound, the loudness, the pitch, and the direction. But subjects seem oblivious to the *semantic* content of the unattended channel—they can't even tell if the unattended channel contained English prose or gibberish.

However, some results do not fit this pattern. Some bits of the unattended input do leak through and are noticed. In one study, subjects shadowed one passage while ignoring a second passage. Embedded within the unattended channel, though, was a series of names, including the subject's own name. Overall, subjects heard very little of the unattended message, in keeping with the other studies mentioned. Nonetheless, about a third of them did hear their own name (Moray, 1959). As we commonly say, the name seemed to "catch" the subject's attention. Other contents will also catch attention, if one is suitably primed for them: Mention of a movie you just saw, or of your favorite restaurant, will often be noticed in the unattended channel. Likewise, words with some personal importance will also be noticed (e.g., Corteen & Dunn, 1974; Corteen & Wood, 1972; but also see Wardlaw & Kroll, 1976).

These results are often referred to under the banner of the cocktail party effect: There you are at a cocktail party, engaged in conversation. Many other conversations are taking place in the room but, somehow, you're able to "tune them out." You are aware that other people in the room are talking, but you don't have a clue what they're saying. All you "hear" is the single conversation you're attending, plus a "buzz" of background noise. But now imagine that someone a few steps away from you mentions your name, or mentions the name of a close friend of yours. Your attention is immediately caught by this, and you find yourself listening to that other conversation, and so you are (momentarily) oblivious to the conversation you had been engaged in.

A similar point emerges from an early study by Anne Treisman (1964). In this experiment, subjects were bilingual, fully fluent in English and in French. For these subjects, the attended channel contained a message in one of these languages; the unattended channel contained the same message, but translated into the other language. Nonetheless, 50% of the subjects still noticed the identity of these messages. Note that in this case the messages were "identical" in their semantic content, but not in their form, and not in their sounds. Thus, to notice the identity, subjects must have been sensitive to the *meaning* of both messages.

In short, therefore, the pattern of results is uneven: On the one hand, many studies document how little we hear from the unattended channel. Other studies, though, show that, in some circumstances, we *do* understand the unattended message. (See also Hirst, 1986; Johnston & Dark, 1986.) Our theory will plainly need to explain both sets of results—the general insensitivity to the unattended channel and also the cases in which the unattended channel "leaks through."

"Ignoring"

As we'll soon see, the explanation for these results has several parts, but one part is simply this: Subjects are, in these experiments, taking steps to *block* processing of the irrelevant inputs; they are, in other words, working to shut out or *ignore* the unwanted inputs. Moreover, the activity involved in ignoring is rather specific, "tuned" to the particular distractors being ignored.

This tuning is evident if subjects are given an opportunity to practice coping with distractors. If we choose distractors that are intrusive enough, they are initially quite disruptive to subjects' performance. With practice, though, the distractors bother the subjects less and less. However, the practice doesn't help if, a few minutes later, subjects are asked to cope with new distractors (e.g., Reisberg, Baron & Kemler, 1980). As an analogy, it is as if subjects learn how to study while the TV is on, playing one show, but then can not "transfer" this skill to studying while the TV is playing some other show. Subjects apparently learn to deal with distractors of a certain type, rather than learning to deal with distractors in general.

Evidence concerning negative priming makes the same point. In one study, subjects were shown two superimposed letters—for example, a green R superimposed on a red F. Subjects were asked to name, as rapidly as possible, the letter printed in green. On the next trial, subjects again had to name the letter in green, but this time they were shown a green F superimposed on a red J. Notice that, on the first trial, subjects had to *ignore* the F, while, on the second, they had to *focus* on the F. This sequence actually leads to a slower response to the F on the second trial, compared to a control sequence, in which subjects first ignore some other letter, and then focus on the F (Fox, 1994, 1995; Greenwald, 1972; May, Kane & Hasher, 1995; Neill, 1977; Neill & Terry, 1995; Tipper, 1985, 1992; Tipper & Driver, 1988).

Apparently, therefore, there is an "aftereffect" of ignoring: Having just ignored a stimulus, it is now a bit harder to pay attention to that stimulus. And this aftereffect is specific to the particular distractor: Having ignored an F makes it harder to pay attention to an F; having ignored a T makes it harder to pay attention to a T. This clearly implies that subjects are doing something with the specific distractors, taking some steps to avoid responding to them. This suggests that ignoring is an active mechanism, somehow blocking or inhibiting the response to unwanted stimulus inputs.

active ignoring = taking steps to block out unwanted stimuli

Perceiving and the Limits on Cognitive Capacity

The notion of "active ignoring"—steps taken to *block* processing of unwanted stimuli—was pivotal for early theories of attention (e.g., Broadbent, 1958; for more recent discussion of ignoring, see, for example, Kahneman & Treisman, 1984; Yantis & Johnston, 1990). However, theorists soon came to endorse a two-part theory of attention: Not only do we *block* the processing of distractors, we are also able to *promote* the processing of desired stimuli.

Selective Priming via Mental Resources

Broadly speaking, the proposal to be considered is this: We perceive most easily, and most effectively, when we are prepared for the upcoming stimulus. Therefore, to select an input, we prepare for it. With this preparation in place, the desired input will easily be perceived. We obviously won't take steps to get ourselves ready to perceive distractors, since we don't want to perceive these. As a result, because of this lack of preparedness, we won't perceive the distractors.

Notice, then, that we are describing a mechanism which is, in effect, the inverse of ignoring: To ignore, our action focuses on the distractor stimuli— we block them, while we don't block the desired input. Preparation, in con-

is b/c of lack of preparedness that we can ignore something, not b/c of active

trast, does the reverse: The action is focused on the desired inputs, not the distractors. We take steps to facilitate the perception of the former, while we don't take those steps for the distractors.

This preparation for an input can take several forms, but one possibility builds on mechanisms we have already described: In Chapter 2, we proposed that recognition of stimuli depends (in part) on a network of detectors, and these detectors fire most readily, and most quickly, if they are suitably primed. Preparation, therefore, can take the form of selective priming, which will pave the way for an anticipated stimulus. With this priming, the stimulus will be easily perceived, even if the input is somehow degraded. Without priming, a much stronger input will be required, and responding will be correspondingly slower.

This account, even in its skeletal form, allows us to explain some of the results we have already mentioned, including cases of "leakage" in selective attention. In general, you are not preparing yourself for the unattended channel, and so you won't perceive its contents. But what happens if the unattended channel happens to contain your name? The detectors for this stimulus will be well primed, since you are frequently exposed to your own name. Therefore, these (prepared) detectors will fire, and you will perceive your name, even if this input is contained in the unattended channel. The same is true for personally important words.

This notion of selective priming also allows us to explain some other results. For example, subjects have a relatively easy time in shadowing regular, predictable messages. It is more difficult to shadow less predictable messages—sequences of random words, or even text that you don't comprehend (e.g., Moray, 1959; also see Neisser & Becklen, 1975). This fits with the priming idea: With predictable messages, one can more easily anticipate what the upcoming signal will be, and therefore one can more readily prime just the right detectors. With unpredictable messages, you don't know what is coming, and so you can't prepare and attending is difficult.

Thus, several results can be explained in these terms: We attend by taking the steps of preparing for an upcoming stimulus, i.e., by priming the relevant pathways. Once we are prepared, perception is facilitated. By the same token, in many contexts, we ignore simply by doing nothing—that is, we don't prepare, and so the inputs fall, so to speak, on "untuned ears."

Once again, though, this raises new questions. For example, common sense tells us there are limits on our ability to pay attention. If you try to read a book while listening to a complex lecture, you are likely to understand the book, or the lecture, but not both. When attending to one channel, we have seen, you hear rather little from the other channel. What sets these limits? If we attend to stimuli by priming the relevant detectors, then why can't we prime two sets of detectors (one for each incoming message) at the same time?

Two Types of Priming

One hypothesis is that preparation for an input requires some mental resources, and these resources are in short supply. Thus, to perceive a message, one must commit the necessary resources. Once this is done, there might not be enough resources left over for the perception of a second message. As a different way of stating this, we could argue that the mind has a limited capacity for handling inputs or, for that matter, for dealing with any tasks. Perhaps the situations we have described (e.g., listening to two simultaneous messages, or reading and listening at the same time) exceed this capacity.

Of course, this does little more than rename the problem. Instead of talking about the observable limits on attention, we are now talking about hypothesized limits on some unspecified mental resources. What are these "resources?" Why is there a "limited capacity?" And, above all, can we get some direct evidence for these (allegedly) limited resources?

In a classic series of studies, Posner and Snyder (1975) gave subjects this simple task: A pair of letters was shown on a computer screen, and subjects had to decide, as swiftly as they could, whether the letters were the same or different. So a subject might see "A A" and answer "same," or might see "A B" and answer "different."

Before each pair, subjects saw a warning signal. In the neutral condition, the warning signal was a plus sign ("+"). This notified subjects that the stimuli were about to arrive but provided no other information. In a different condition, the warning signal was itself a letter, and actually matched the stimuli-to-come. So subjects might see the warning signal "C" followed by the pair "C C." In this case, the warning signal actually served to prime the subjects for the stimuli. In a third condition, though, the warning signal was *misleading*: The warning signal was again a letter, but it was a letter different from the stimuli-to-come. Subjects might see "C" followed by the pair "G G." Let's call these three conditions *neutral, primed*, and *misled*.

In each condition, Posner and Snyder recorded how swiftly subjects responded—that is, they measured response-times, or RTs. By comparing RTs in the primed and neutral condition, we can ask what benefit there is from the prime. In particular, we would expect faster responses, and so shorter response-times, in the primed condition. Likewise, by comparing RTs in the misled and neutral condition, we can ask what *cost* there is, if any, from being misled.

We need one further complication before we turn to the results: Posner and Snyder ran this procedure in two different versions. (The design is depicted in Figure 3.1.) In one version, the warning signal was an excellent predictor of the upcoming stimuli: For example, if the warning signal was an A, there was an 80% chance that the upcoming stimulus pair would contain A's. In Posner and Snyder's terms, the warning signal provided a "high validity" prime. In a different version of the procedure, the warning signal was

Figure 3.1

DESIGN OF POSNER AND SNYDER'S EXPERIMENT				

Low validity condition

| Type of trial | Typical sequence | | Provides repetition priming? | Provides basis for expectation? |
	Warning signal	Test Stimuli		
Neutral	+	AA	No	No
Primed	G	GG	Yes	No
Misled	H	GG	No	No

High validity condition

| Type of trial | Typical sequence | | Provides repetition priming? | Provides basis for expectation? |
	Warning signal	Test Stimuli		
Neutral	+	AA	No	No
Primed	G	GG	Yes	Prime leads to *correct* expectation
Misled	H	GG	No	Prime leads to *incorrect* expectation

The sequence of events was the same in the high-validity and low-validity conditions. What distinguished the conditions was *how often* the various events occurred. In the low-validity condition, "misled" trials occurred *four times as often* as "primed" trials (80% vs. 20%). Therefore, subjects had reason *not* to trust the primes, and correspondingly had no reason to generate an expectation based on the prime. In the high-validity condition, things were reversed: Now "primed" trials occurred four times as often as "misled" trials. Therefore, subjects had good reason to trust the primes, and good reason to generate an expectation. For most of the trials, this expectation will be correct. Note, though, that if subjects base their expectations on the prime, then they will generate the *wrong* expectation in the "misled" trials.

a poor predictor of the upcoming stimuli: If the warning signal was an A, there was only a 20% chance that the upcoming pair would contain A's. This is the "low validity" condition.

Let's consider the low-validity condition first, and let's focus on those rare occasions in which the prime *did* match the subsequent stimuli. That is, we are focusing on 20% of the trials, and ignoring the other 80%. In this condition, the subject can't use the prime as a basis for predicting the stimuli since, after all, the prime is a poor indicator of things-to-come. Therefore, the prime should *not* lead subjects to any specific expectations. Nonetheless, we do expect faster RTs in the primed condition than in the neutral condition: Thanks to the prime, the relevant detectors have just fired, and so the detectors should still be warmed up. When the target stimuli arrive, therefore, the detectors should fire more readily, allowing a faster response. This is, in effect, a case of repetition priming, as described in Chapter 2.

The results bear this out. RTs were reliably faster in the primed condition than in the neutral condition; Figure 3.2 shows this as a 30 msec *difference* between the primed and neutral conditions. Apparently, the detectors can be primed by mere exposure to a stimulus. Or, to put it differently, priming is observed even in the absence of expectations. This priming seems truly stimulus-based.

What about the misled condition? With a low-validity prime, misleading subjects had no effect: Performance in the misled condition was the *same* as performance in the neutral condition. Priming the "wrong" detector, it seems, takes nothing away from the other detectors—including the detectors actually needed for that trial. This fits with our discussion in Chapter 2: Each of the various detectors works independently of the others. Thus, if one detector is primed, this obviously influences the functioning of that specific detector, but this neither helps nor hinders the other detectors.

In sum, the low-validity primes document two things: First, priming can be produced by stimulus repetition alone, even in the absence of expectations. Second, the detectors work independently of each other, so that priming one detector takes nothing away from the other detectors.

What about the high-validity primes? In this case, subjects might see, for example, a "J" as the warning signal, and then the stimulus pair "J J". Presentation of the prime itself will fire the J-detectors, and so it should, once again, "warm-up" these detectors, just as the low-validity primes did. Thus, we expect a stimulus-driven benefit from the prime. However, the high-validity primes may also have a further influence. High-validity primes are excellent predictors of the stimulus-to-come. Subjects are told this at the outset, and they have lots of opportunity to see that it is true. High-validity primes will therefore produce a warm-up effect and also an expectation effect, whereas low-validity primes only produced the warm-up. Consequently, we

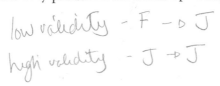

low validity - F → J

high validity - J → J

Figure 3.2

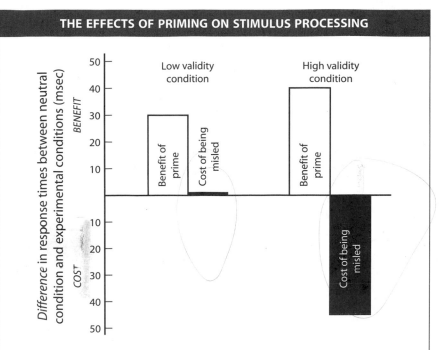

THE EFFECTS OF PRIMING ON STIMULUS PROCESSING

As one way of assessing the Posner and Snyder (1975) results, we can subtract the response times for the neutral condition from those for the primed condition; in this way, we measure the benefits of priming. Likewise, we can subtract the response times for the neutral condition from those for the *misled* condition; in this way, we measure the *costs* of being misled. In these terms, the low-validity condition shows a small benefit (from repetition priming) but zero cost from being misled. The high-validity condition, in contrast, shows a larger benefit, but also a substantial cost. The results shown here reflect trials with a 300 msec interval between the warning signal and the test stimuli; the results were somewhat different at other intervals.

can explore the influence of expectations by comparing the impact of high- and low-validity primes.

As Figure 3.2 shows, high-validity primes produced a *larger* benefit than low-validity primes. The combination of warm-up and expectations produces a larger benefit than warm-up alone. From the subjects' point of view, it pays to know what the upcoming stimulus might be.

The key finding, though, lies in the misled condition: With high-validity primes, responses in the misled condition were slower than responses in the neutral condition. That is, misleading subjects actually hurt performance: As

a concrete example, F-detection was *slower* if G was primed, compared to F-detection when the prime was simply the neutral warning signal ("+").

Explaining the Costs and Benefits

How should we think about all this? As we have already noted, there is nothing new for us in the data pattern from low-validity primes. When the prime matches the subsequent stimuli, we observe a benefit from "detector warm-up." However, warming up one detector takes nothing away from the other detectors. The detectors work independently of each other, and so there is no cost attached to warming-up the "wrong" detector.

The high-validity primes, though, do give us new information. First, note that the benefits of warm up *plus* expectations are larger than the benefits from warm up alone. Therefore, there is a form of priming that is different from (and larger than) repetition priming. It also turns out that this form of priming is somewhat slower: Priming based on warm up can be observed almost immediately; priming based on expectations takes time to develop. Concretely, expectation-based priming is only observed if there's a half-second or so in between the priming stimulus and the test stimulus (e.g., Neely, 1977).

These results—indicating the existence of two types of priming—strengthen the claims offered at the end of Chapter 2. There we distinguished between data-driven (or bottom-up) priming and concept-driven (or top-down) priming. This obviously parallels the distinction under scrutiny here, between stimulus-based and expectation-based primes. Data-driven priming, once again, is small in magnitude, depends only on stimulus presentation (not on expectations), and is relatively quick to appear. Concept-driven priming, in contrast, is larger, does depend on expectations, and is slower to appear.

Moreover, and crucial for our purposes here, consider the cost observed when a high-validity prime turns out to be misleading. In this condition, it looks as if priming the "wrong" detector takes something away from the other detectors. Once subjects were misled, the other detectors ended up less primed, less well prepared, than they would have been with no prime at all. And, of course, in the misled condition, it is one of these less well-prepared detectors that is needed.

What produces this pattern? As an analogy, think about being on a limited budget. Imagine, for example, that you have just $50 to spend on groceries. In that case, you can spend more on ice-cream if you wish but, if you do, you'll have that much less to spend on other foods. Any increase in the "ice-cream allotment" must be covered by a decrease somewhere else. This trade-off only arises, though, because of the limited budget. If you had unlimited

funds, you could spend more on ice cream and still have enough money for everything else.

Expectation-based priming shows the same pattern. If the Q-detector is primed, this takes something away from the other detectors. Getting prepared for one target seems to make subjects less prepared for other targets. But we just said that this sort of pattern implies a limited "budget." If an unlimited supply of activation were available, one could prime the Q-detector, and leave the other detectors just as they were. And that is the point: Expectation-based priming, by virtue of revealing costs when misled, reveals the presence of a limited-capacity system.

We can now put the pieces together: Ultimately, we need to explain the facts of selective attention, including the fact that, while listening to one message, one hears little content from other messages. To explain this, we have proposed that perceiving involves some work: One must *prepare* for upcoming stimuli, preparation that takes the form of priming the relevant processing path. This preparation, we supposed, draws on some limited mental resources. That is why you can't listen to two complex messages at the same time: This would require more resources than you have. And now, finally, we are seeing evidence for those limited resources: The Posner and Snyder research reveal the workings of a limited-capacity system, just as our hypothesis demands.

Chronometric Studies and Spatial Attention

The Posner and Snyder study provides important data, but it also introduces an important method, useful for studying attention and many other topics. The study draws on a **chronometric** analysis. Chronometric studies (literally, "time-measuring") exploit the simple fact that mental tasks take time. Of course, mental tasks do proceed swiftly—we are talking about decisions and identifications that take, at most, a fraction of a second. But, with suitable devices, one can measure precisely how long these tasks take. Then, with the appropriate logic, one can use these chronometric results to figure out exactly what the task involves, exactly what factors influence performance, and so on.

Chronometric studies have been used to address a number of questions. For example, what is the nature of subjects' expectations? How precise, or how vague, are those expectations? To see the point, imagine that subjects are told: "The next stimulus will be a 'T.'" In this case, subjects know exactly what to get ready for. But now imagine that subjects are told, "The next stimulus will be a letter," or "Here comes the next stimulus." Will these cues allow subjects to prepare themselves?

In these latter cases, subjects obviously can't prepare for the *content* of the upcoming message, because they have no basis for anticipating what that content will be. They can, however, prepare in a more general sense: They can prepare for a stimulus, for example, coming from a specific *position in space*, so that they will be ready for anything that appears in that location.

A number of studies have examined such "spatial anticipations." For example, Posner, Snyder and Davidson (1980) required subjects to detect letter presentations—subjects' task was to press a button as soon as a letter appeared. Subjects kept their eyes pointed at a central fixation mark, and letters could appear either to the left or to the right of this mark.

For some trials, a neutral warning signal was presented, so that subjects knew a trial was about to start, but had no information about stimulus location. For other trials, an *arrow* was used as the warning signal. Sometimes the arrow pointed left, sometimes right, and the arrow was generally an accurate predictor of stimulus-to-come's location—if the arrow pointed right, the stimulus would be on the right side of the computer screen. (In the terms we used earlier, this is a high-validity cue.) On 20% of the trials, however, the arrow *misled* subjects about location. By comparing correctly cued trials with misleading trials, we can again ask about the benefits of anticipating a stimulus, and also the (potential) costs of having incorrect expectations.

The results show a familiar pattern (Posner et al., 1980, Experiment 2): With high-validity priming, the data show a large *benefit* from cues that correctly signal where the upcoming target will appear. Concretely, with a neutral warning signal, subjects took 266 msec to detect the signal. With a correct prime, subjects were faster—249 msec. This isn't a huge difference, but keep the task in mind—all subjects had to do was detect the input. Even with the simplest of tasks, therefore, it pays to be prepared.

The data also show a *cost* when the cue misled subjects about the target's position. RTs in this condition averaged 297 msec, 31 msec slower (about 12%) than the neutral condition.

These results indicate that subjects can direct their attention to a position in space and, once this is done, they are more efficient in processing signals that appear in this position. Conversely, once subjects have focused their attention in this way, they are *less* efficient in processing signals that appear elsewhere—that is the cost of being misled, a cost, once again, that reveals some sort of limited-capacity system. It also should be said that these results involve movements of *attention*, and not movements of the eyes. Subjects were required, throughout these procedures, to keep their eyes in one position. In addition, we can rule out eye movements on grounds of speed. Eye movements are surprisingly slow, requiring 180 to 200 msec. Yet the benefits of primes can be detected within the first 150 msec after the warning signal is presented (e.g., Remington, 1980). Thus the benefits of attention occur prior to any eye movement and so cannot be a consequence of eye movements.

Given results like these, some psychologists have likened visual attention to a "search-light beam" that can "shine" anywhere in the visual field. The "beam" marks the region of space for which one is prepared, so that inputs within the beam are processed more efficiently and more swiftly. The beam can be wide or narrowly focused (Castiello & Umiltá, 1990; Eriksen & St. James, 1986; Eriksen & Yeh, 1985; Navon, 1977; Podgorny & Shepard, 1983; Shulman & Wilson, 1987), and can be moved about at will as one explores (attends to) one aspect of the visual field or another.

In addition, some stimuli seem to draw the search-light beam to themselves. We commonly speak of these stimuli as "eye-catching"—stimuli that "demand" your attention. (Most warning signals are designed to have this attention-summoning property.) Thus, we can distinguish cases in which the search-light beam is deliberately directed here or there, and cases in which the search-light is summoned to a particular location. (For reviews, see Briand & Klein, 1987; Jonides, 1981; Yantis, 1993.)

Evidence also suggests that it is difficult to split the attention beam: In one procedure, Posner et al. (1980, Experiment 5) presented subjects with targets that could appear in one of *four* positions. Just before each target, subjects were told which position was *most* likely for the upcoming target, and also which position was the *second* most likely. For some trials, these two positions were adjacent to each other; in other trials, they were not.

To no one's surprise, there was a large priming effect if the target did appear in the most-likely position. In other words, subjects moved their attention to this position and, as a result, were more efficient in processing targets in this position. The key results, however, concern the trials in which the target appeared in the second-most-likely position. If this position happened to be alongside of the most-likely position, priming was observed. In this case, subjects have the option of simply setting the beam to "wide," so that it takes in both positions. However, if the second-most-likely position was not adjacent to the primary position, no priming was observed. Apparently, subjects cannot split the beam to cover two separated locations at once. (For discussion of this issue, see Eriksen & Yeh, 1985; Castiello & Umiltá, 1992; Jonides, 1983.)

We note in passing, though, that this search-light metaphor must not be taken too literally. Imagine, for example, that you shine an actual search-light on a donut. The light will illuminate the donut, but it will also shine through the donut's hole, illuminating a small bit of the plate on which the donut sits. If attention were truly like a search-light, therefore, attention to the donut would entail attention to at least part of the plate. But this is not what the

tions in which there was a clear primary task and a clear primary input. If other tasks and other inputs were on the scene, these were mere distractors. Our focus, therefore, has been on how subjects manage to select just the desired information, while avoiding the distractors.

There are also circumstances, however, in which you *want* to do multiple things at once, in which you try to divide your attention among various tasks or various inputs. In some cases, we can do this, but our ability to perform concurrent tasks is clearly limited. Almost anyone can walk and chew gum simultaneously, but it is far harder to solve calculus problems while reading a history text. Most drivers can converse while navigating through traffic, but few people can write poetry while reading a novel. Therefore, we need to ask why some task combinations are difficult, while others are easy.

As a further question, we might wonder how rigid these limits on performance are. It would be rather useful if you *could* do calculus problems while reading a text; it would be terrific if you could complete your assignment for one course while also participating in another course. So the question is: Can you learn to do several things at once? Can you learn to divide attention more effectively? Or are there fixed and unchangeable boundaries on what humans can achieve?

Our initial answer to these questions is already in view. We have proposed that mental tasks require resources that are in short supply. This provides a straightforward account of divided attention: One can perform concurrent tasks only if the sum of the tasks' demands is within the "cognitive budget." To trace through one of our examples, solving calculus problems requires some mental resources, and so does reading a text. You have enough resources to do either one of these tasks by itself, but not enough for both; if you try to do both at the same time, you will fail.

What are these hypothesized mental resources? Do all tasks, no matter what they involve, draw on the *same* mental resources? This is a hypothesis of **general resources**. Or are mental resources somehow specialized, so that the resources required by a task will depend on the exact nature of the task? This is a hypothesis of **task-specific resources**. We turn now to the evaluation of these two hypotheses and, more broadly, to questions about what mental resources are, and how these resources should be characterized.

Testing Claims about Task Specificity

The hypotheses just sketched differ with regard to their predictions about when concurrent performance of tasks will be possible and, conversely, when task interference will be observed. Consider first the proposal that performance is limited by general resources. General resources, by definition, are relevant to all tasks, so all tasks, no matter what their nature, will compete for this limited pool of resources. Consequently, in asking whether concurrent performance will be possible, we do not need to worry about the nature of the task. All we need to worry about is the resource demand, the cost, of the individual tasks. If the combined demand from the simultaneous tasks is greater than the available resources, then task interference will be observed.

Contrast this with the hypothesis that performance is limited by task-specific resources. These resources, by definition, are needed for some tasks but not others; the nature of the task determines *which* resources will be needed. Moreover, two tasks will interfere with each other only if they make conflicting demands on the *same set* of resources. To make this concrete, let us say that Task 1 requires some sort of spatial reasoning, and therefore draws on resources pertinent to this reasoning. Task 2, let us say, is a verbal task, and so draws on "verbal resources." In this case, combining Task 1 and Task 2 should be easy, since the tasks make non-overlapping resource demands. It won't even matter if Task 1 requires *all* the "spatial reasoning resources" or if Task 2 requires all the "verbal resources." Even in this case, concurrent performance will not "break the budget."

In short, if resources are task-general, then the possibility of divided attention should depend only on the resource demands of the individual tasks, and not on the nature of the tasks being combined. If, on the other hand, resources are task-specific, then the nature of the tasks is critical: Interference will be observed only to the extent that the tasks draw on overlapping sets of resources. If the tasks are sufficiently different, divided attention should be easy, since the tasks will require different sets of (task-specific) resources, and so will not compete with each other.

Evidence for Task-Specific Resources

These predictions lend themselves easily to experimental test, and the results are clear: *Both* hypotheses capture an element of the truth. The nature of the tasks being combined does matter, consistent with the claim of task-specific resources, but interference can be observed even with extremely different tasks, consistent with the claim of task-general resources. Let us consider each of these claims in turn.

Many studies show that divided attention is difficult with similar tasks, and much easier with dissimilar tasks (Hirst, 1986; Hirst & Kalmar, 1987). As an example, consider an early study by Allport, Antonis and Reynolds (1972). Subjects heard a list of words, presented through headphones into one ear. Subjects' task was simply to shadow these words. At the same time, subjects were also presented with a second list. No immediate response was required to this second list, but later on memory was tested for these items. In one condition, these memory items consisted of words presented into the other ear, so that subjects were hearing (and shadowing) a list of words in one ear while simultaneously hearing the memory list in the other ear. In a second condition, the memory items were presented visually. That is, while subjects were shadowing one list of words, they were also seeing, on a screen before them, a different list of words. Finally, in a third condition the memory items consisted of pictures, also presented on a screen.

These three conditions have similar task requirements, namely shadowing one list while memorizing another. But the first condition (hear words + hear words) involves very similar tasks; the second condition (hear words + see words) involves less similar tasks; the third condition (hear words + see pictures), even less similar tasks. If performance is limited by task-specific resources, then it seems most likely that the first pair of tasks will compete with each other for resources, and least likely that the last pair will. Thus, in terms of task-specific resource, we would expect most interference in the first condition, least in the third. And that is what the data show.

As a different example, consider a study by Brooks (1968). In one condition, subjects were asked to memorize a sentence, such as "A bird in the hand is not in the bush." Then subjects had to scan through this sentence and indicate whether each word was a noun or not (and so the correct answers are "no, yes, no, no, yes . . . "). In a different condition, subjects were shown a block letter like the one in Figure 3.3. Based on memory, subjects had to scan around the outline of the letter and indicate whether each corner was at the extreme top or extreme bottom, or somewhere in between. (Thus, if "yes" indicates "extreme top or extreme bottom," the responses, starting at the star, would be "yes, yes, no . . . .")

Half of the subjects made their responses verbally, literally saying "yes" and "no." The remaining subjects made their responses by pointing—toward a "Y" or toward a "N." It turns out that the *verbal* mode of responding was rather difficult with the sentence task, but relatively easy with the block-letter task. The pattern reversed for the *pointing* response: This was easy for the sentence-task, but difficult with block letters.

What is going on here is a species of task-interference. More precisely, we are here seeing interference between elements of a single task, namely, the making of a judgment and the production of a response. The verbal response is largely incompatible with the verbal judgment, but easily combined with the spatial judgment. The spatial response interferes with the spatial judgment, but not the verbal one. Clearly, the degree of interference depends, in an orderly fashion, on the nature of the tasks being performed.

Evidence for Task-General Resources

We can easily find evidence for task-specific interference, and thus for task-specific resources. Other results favor claims about task-*general* resources. Specifically, task interference can be observed even with extremely dissimilar

Figure 3.3

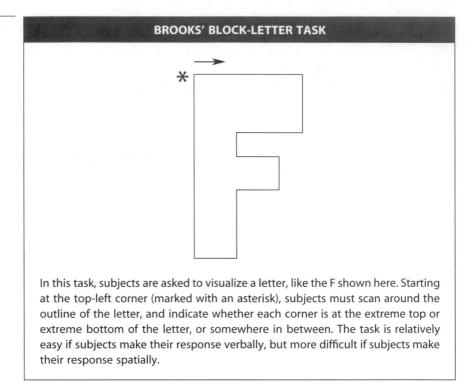

BROOKS' BLOCK-LETTER TASK

In this task, subjects are asked to visualize a letter, like the F shown here. Starting at the top-left corner (marked with an asterisk), subjects must scan around the outline of the letter, and indicate whether each corner is at the extreme top or extreme bottom of the letter, or somewhere in between. The task is relatively easy if subjects make their response verbally, but more difficult if subjects make their response spatially.

tasks, suggesting that, even when tasks have little in common, they still compete for resources. Indeed, some of the evidence is provided by common sense: As we mentioned early on, it is easy for most of us to drive a car while holding a conversation—apparently these two tasks (driving + conversing) can be combined. But what happens if the driver must navigate through a complicated intersection, or do a high-speed merge into traffic? When these complexities enter the scene, concurrent performance seems to be impossible: If you are the driver, you may suddenly realize that you don't know what your friend has been saying for the last minute or so. If it is your turn to talk, there are suddenly long pauses in the conversation, while you focus on the driving. (Of course, some drivers have different priorities and so, under these circumstances, the conversation continues but the quality of driving suffers. For purposes of theory, the point is the same, since we are still observing task interference.)

If interference is observed between driving and conversing, this suggests that these tasks overlap in their resource-demands. Presumably, routine driving through ordinary traffic makes light demands on mental resources, so does "routine" conversation. The combined demands are within your budget. But, if the complexity of either activity is increased, the resource requirements are correspondingly increased. As the demands of the individual tasks grow, so must the (combined) demands of concurrent performance. Eventually, the combined demands will exceed the resources available, resulting in interference.

Driving and talking are, of course, very different from each other—one is verbal, one not; one requires visual inputs, one not; one requires a spoken output, one does not. Therefore, any resource that is required by both of these activities must be a resource applicable to highly diverse tasks—that is, it must be a *general resource.*

A number of laboratory studies confirm this pattern, namely, that interference can be observed between very different tasks. If this interference is to be explained in terms of resource competition, the relevant resource must be a general one. In one study, subjects performed mental arithmetic while making judgments about visual patterns (specifically, whether the patterns depicted possible three-dimensional objects); interference was observed between these seemingly distinct activities (Reisberg, 1983; other similar examples can be found in Kahneman, 1973).

In summary, then, concurrent performance of tasks is easier if the tasks are distinct, but interference is still observed even with highly dissimilar tasks. The former result implies that performance is, in some cases, limited by task-specific resources; the latter result implies the existence of task-general resources. Apparently, then, there is more than one constraint on performance, with the consequence that divided attention will be possible only if *all* constraints are satisfied.

Finally, it should be said that task-specificity and task-generality are almost certainly a matter of *degree,* rather than distinct categories. Some resources will be needed for virtually all tasks; other resources will be needed for most (but not all) tasks; and so on, up to the opposite extreme, of resources needed only for a tiny number of tightly-defined tasks. It would probably be more accurate, therefore, to cease speaking of resources as being simply "general" and "specific," and instead to speak of resources as being "more general" or "more specific" in their application.

Unitary Resources, Divisible Resources

We have made some progress, but we have still said little about what exactly mental resources *are.* At the more task-specific end of things, the characterization of resources must be done task by task, as we ask what each individual mental task involves, what steps it requires. This means we cannot specify these resources until we have first analyzed the individual tasks. That enter-

must stop talking when difficult during conditions & evidence for task-general prise is underway for many tasks so that, just for some examples, we know a great deal about the processes involved in reading (e.g., Crowder & Wagner, 1992) or the processes involved in many motor activities (typing, walking, running, singing, and so on—Rosenbaum, 1991).

But what about the task-general resources? What can we say in characterizing those? This issue is still being debated and, therefore, we cannot in this domain provide a definitive account. Nonetheless, let's look at how some of the argument has unfolded.

Some theories liken mental resources to an energy supply, or a bank account, drawn on by all tasks, and we have obviously used this analogy in much of our discussion. For example, Kahneman (1973) hypothesized that mental tasks require the expenditure of mental effort (also see Eysenck, 1982). The term *effort* was meant rather literally here, so that mental tasks require effort in about the same fashion that physical tasks do.

Other authors, however, have offered a different view, conceiving of these resources more as "mental tools," rather than as some sort of mental "energy supply." Thus, there is a task-general resource needed for *planning*, another needed for *response-initiation*, and so on (Allport, 1989; Baddeley, 1986; Johnson-Laird, 1988; Norman & Shallice, 1986). Let's trace through the details of one of these proposals.

Pashler and Johnson (e.g., McCann & Johnston, 1992; Pashler, 1991, 1992) have proposed that a single mental mechanism is required for selecting and initiating responses, including both physical responses and mental ones (such as the beginning of a memory search, or the making of a decision). This "response-selector" will be needed for a wide range of tasks, and so it is certainly a task-general resource. Crucially, though, this mechanism can only initiate one response at a time, and so it is not possible to divide this resource in any literal sense. If two concurrent tasks each require the response-selector, then one of them must wait its turn while the selector deals with the other task.

This clearly stands in contrast to notions like "mental effort," which imply that mental resources are *divisible*, so that you could devote 90% of your effort to a task, leaving 10% available for other chores, or you could devote 23%, leaving 77% available, or any other split you chose.

If one rejects this notion of divisible resources—if one, instead, conceives of resources as unitary—then what does this imply for divided attention? Again, let's focus on the response selector. Most tasks, of course, do not require a constant stream of new actions: You select and then initiate an action, and then you spend some time *carrying out* that action. Only when the action is completed do you need to select the next step. It is this pattern that makes divided attention possible. If, for example, you are trying to divide your attention between Task A and Task B, you could first select and launch some action that is part of Task A. This will require the response-selector, and so the selector won't be available for Task B. However, while you are carrying out the just-selected step for A, you no longer need the response-selector for this task. Therefore, the response-selector is momentarily free to select and launch a step for Task B. Then, while that step is being carried out, you can use the response-selector to launch the next step of A. This kind of back-and-forth, turn-taking arrangement is referred to as **time-sharing**.

Evidence for the Response-Selector

Many computer systems appear to do multiple tasks at once but, in fact, the computers are time-sharing: quickly switching from one task to another, and actually doing just one thing at a time. If you are working on such a system, the machine appears to be devoting all its resources to you, but that is only because you fail to notice the very brief delays, as the machine hops from your task to some other task, and then back to you. You *would* detect the time-sharing if you were able to detect these very brief delays. And that is the point: One can detect time-sharing (as opposed to truly simultaneous processing) only by careful timing of the relevant activities.

Thus, to study time-sharing within human performance, we need a moment-by-moment analysis of how subjects are allocating attention. To make this analysis possible, we often need to study rather simple tasks. For example, we can present two signals (call them S1 and S2) to subjects, and subjects must respond with the appropriate button for each. Thus, S1 might be a number, "1" or "2", presented on a computer screen, and subjects must respond to indicate which of the numbers was presented. Let's call the response to this signal, R1. R1 might be a press of a red button if a "1" was presented, and a press of a green button if a "2" was presented. Likewise, S2 might be a letter, "A" or "B", and again subjects must respond to indicate which was shown. This second response we will call R2—a button on the left for "A", one on the right for "B."

Each of these tasks—R1 in response to S1; R2 in response to S2—is, by itself, rather easy. But *combining* them is surprisingly difficult. We can, for example, present S1 and then, 150 msec later, while the subject is still "working on" S1, we present S2. We are, in effect, asking subjects to deal with both stimuli at the same time.

In this set-up, responses to the second stimulus will be quite slow. The time that elapses between S2 and R2 will be much longer than the time that elapses between S1 and R1, often by several hundred milliseconds. In percentage terms, subjects are 30%–40% slower with the second signal than they are with the first. This delay is known as the psychological refractory period (PRP), and can be observed in a wide variety of procedures. (For reviews, see Pashler, 1991, 1992, 1994.)

How should we think about this result? An account in terms of *mental effort* would suggest that subjects must commit a certain amount of effort to processing the first signal, with little effort left over for the second. As a result, the second signal will be processed less efficiently. An account in terms of the *response selector*, in contrast, would propose that processing of the second signal is placed on hold until the selector has finished with the first signal. The delay, therefore, comes while the second signal waits its turn for processing.

These two hypotheses make different predictions about what will happen if we vary the procedure in certain ways. For example, what will happen if we make the signals difficult to perceive (perhaps dimmer or smaller)? What will happen if we make the selection of responses more complex, in the manner shown in Figure 3.4? According to the divisible effort hypothesis, either of these manipulations will increase the effort required for the task. This will simply widen the gap between "effort needed" and "effort available," and so will increase the size of the PRP.

The response-selector hypothesis makes different predictions and, in fact, makes rather fine-grained predictions: To choose the response for S1, one must perceive S1 in order to identify whether it's a "1" or a "2". Once the stimulus is identified, a response can be selected and initiated, and the actual execution of the response can begin. We can think of this as taking place in three steps: perceive, select a response, execute a response, as shown in Figure 3.5. What about S2? Let's hypothesize that the *perception* of S2 goes on in parallel with processing of S1, as shown in the figure. In other words, we are proposing that, for this task, perception is *not* where the bottleneck lies. Once S2 has been identified, though, we are ready for the next step—the selection and initiation of a response. This requires the selector, and our proposal is that the selector can't do two things at once. Therefore, what *can't* happen is shown in Figure 3.5A. In this scenario, the response-selector is working on two things at the same time and that, according to our hypothesis, is impossible. Instead, what happens is shown in Figure 3.5B: Processing of S2 is put on hold until the response selector has finished with S1; only then is the selector available to deal with S2. In essence, then, we have four steps: perceive, wait for your turn, select a response, execute a response.

Let's now think through what will happen, according to this view, if we slow the perception of S1 (e.g., by using a dimmer signal). If this bit of perceiving is slowed, this will delay the start of *response selection* for S1. (This is shown in Figure 3.5C.) This will in turn delay the *completion* of response selection for S1. This will cause a delay in the *start* of response selection for

Figure 3.4

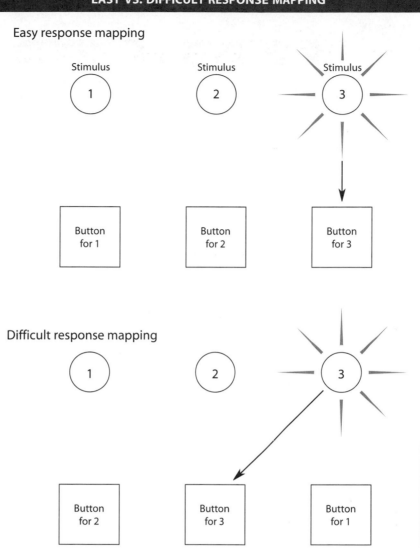

Imagine that we show subjects a "1", "2", or "3" on a computer screen, and require them to press one of three buttons, to indicate which signal they have just seen. With an easy response mapping, subjects might be told to press the key on the left for "1", the key in the middle for "2", and the key on the right for "3". This left-to-right, 1-2-3 pattern is easy for subjects to learn. With a more difficult response mapping, subjects might be told to press the key on the left for "2", the middle key for "3", and the key on the right for "1". With this mapping, subjects' responses are slower overall, and errors are common.

Figure 3.5   POSSIBLE SEQUENCES OF EVENTS IN INFORMATION PROCESSING

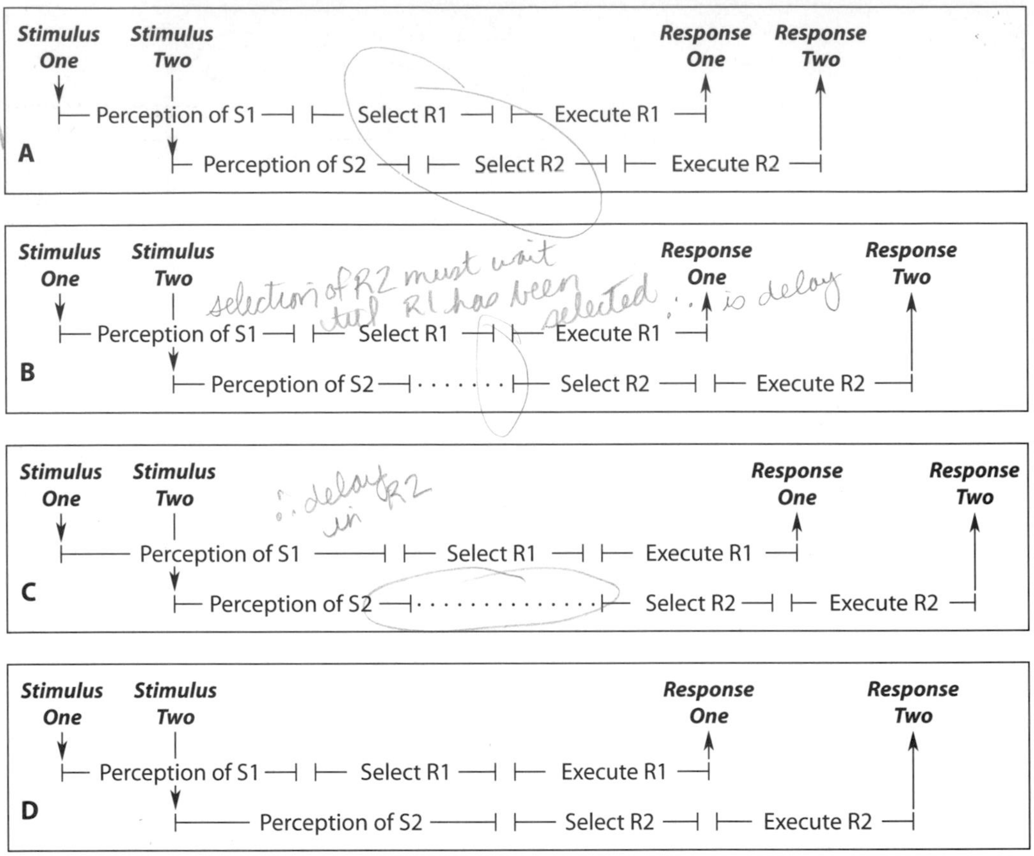

[handwritten annotations in margins:]
can't happen (response selector can't do 2 things at once)
dimmer switch on S1
if slow perception of S2 R2 will NOT be delayed
selection of R2 must wait until R1 has been selected ∴ is delay
∴ delay in R2

According to Pashler (1991, 1992), Panel A shows what *can't* happen: Notice that, in this case, the selection of Response 2 *overlaps* with the selection of Response 1. This would require the response-selector to do two things at once. What will happen instead is shown in Panel B: The selection of Response 2 must *wait* until the selection of Response 1 is completed, and this will cause a delay in the production of Response 2. Panel C shows what will happen if we slow the perception of S1 (for example, by using a dimmer signal). This leads to a delay in Response 2 (compare Panel C to Panel B). In contrast, Panel D shows what happens if we slow the perception of S2. This will *not* cause a delay in Response 2 (again, compare Panel D to Panel B).

S2, since S2's response selection can only begin after S1's response selection is completed. Ultimately this will lead to a delay in R2. In short, then, slowing the *perception* of S1 will delay R2.

Things will go differently, though, if we slow down the perception of S2, rather than S1. Recall the sequence of events for S2: perceive, wait for the selector, select a response, and then execute the response. Thus, there is some "slack" in the sequence of events for this signal, thanks to the moment of waiting for the selector. Whether S2 is perceived slowly or perceived quickly, the response selector is only ready when it is done with S1. In effect, then, slowing down the perception of S2 is just a way of "killing time" while waiting for the selector. Therefore slowing down S2's perception will not delay the start of response initiation, and so will not delay R2. (This sequence is shown in Figure 3.5D.)

These and other specific predictions have all been confirmed in the laboratory, indicating that the response-selector does indeed provide a bottleneck in the flow of mental events (McCann & Johnston, 1992; Pashler, 1991, 1992; Pashler & Johnston, 1989). Since the selector can only deal with one decision at a time, other decisions get stacked up, waiting for their turn at the selector. (For some complications, though, see De Jong, 1993; De Jong & Sweet, 1994; Pashler, 1994.)

Divided Attention: An Interim Summary

Once again, it may be useful to take stock of where we are. Our consideration of selective attention drove us toward a several-part account, and the same seems to be true here. On the one side, task-*specific* interference can easily be demonstrated: Interference between tasks plainly depends on the nature of the tasks, and the interference is greatest when the tasks overlap in their processing demands. This fits with the claim of task-specific limited resources. At the same time, though, task-*general* interference can also be demonstrated. That is, concurrent tasks can interfere with each other even if there is no detectable overlap in the tasks' processing demands. Thus, we also need to include task-general resources in our account.

Therefore, we need a complex account, but with a single unifying principle: Tasks will interfere with each other if they compete for resources. However, the nature of the "resource competition" will vary from case to case. If two tasks each require a complex series of responses, then the tasks will place heavy demands on the response selector. Since the response selector can only do one thing at a time, divided attention will be difficult. (Or, more precisely, divided attention will be possible only via time-sharing.) If, in contrast, one of the tasks requires few responses, or if the responses are easily predictable in advance, then there will be little competition for the response selector, but there may still be competition for some other, task-specific resource. This will be more likely if the two tasks being combined are similar to each other.

We emphasize, though, how many questions are still to be asked, particularly about task-general resources. For example, we have discussed one such resource, the response selector, but what other task-general resources might there be? Duncan (1994) has argued for the existence of a different general resource, needed for *planning* and the *setting of goals* (also see Allport, 1989). We won't pursue this argument here, since our point in mentioning this claim is merely this: A planning resource would surely be applicable to a wide variety of tasks and would, in our terms, be a task-general resource. Moreover, this resource would be separate from the mechanism that actually launches activities—that is, it would be separate from the response-selector. And, again, we would need to ask various questions about this resource—exactly which tasks need it, whether this resource is divisible or unitary, and so on. Thus, our catalog of task-general resources may not be complete and, for each proposed resource, there are obvious questions to ask. (Also see Allport, Styles & Hsieh, 1994.)

Practice

We have been discussing the possibility of doing "two tasks at the same time." But what exactly is a "task?" For example, we have talked about the case of driving while talking, and we described this as *two* simultaneous tasks. Is this realistic? After all, driving itself has several clearly distinguishable parts: You have to pay attention to the curve of the road in order to steer. You also have to pay attention to your speed, to the car in front of you, to the cars behind you, and to the oncoming traffic. Is it fair to call all of this "one task"? Or is driving all by itself an example of divided attention, an example of multiple simultaneous activities? Likewise, in talking, you must coordinate the movements of your teeth, tongue, and lips, the vibration of your vocal chords, and also the movement of air out of the lungs, not to mention the selection of what you are going to say, decisions about how you are going to phrase your thoughts, and so on.

As these examples suggest, virtually any complex task can be thought of as an assembly of specific subtasks. Indeed, when a complex task is first being mastered, it does feel like a problem in divided attention, and task interference can be observed: If the steering becomes complex, the novice driver may lose track of how fast he or she is going; if the novice is paying attention to the road, he or she may forget to shift gears. These components of driving seem truly separate for the novice, competing with each other for attention, and making concurrent performance difficult. Once the skill of driving is mastered, however, the skill seems to be run off as a single organized unit: A skilled driver handles all these components simultaneously, with no apparent interference among the subtasks.

All of this suggests that problems of divided attention may crop up fairly often. In essence, every time you seek to master a new task, you are called on, at least initially, to divide your attention among the task's components. With practice, though, the task's demands change, and you are able to perform the various elements of the task as a single, integrated package. It would seem, then, that if we are to understand divided attention, we need to understand *practice.*

Practice in Visual Search

At a very general level, there is an obvious way for our theory to accommodate the effects of practice: Practice decreases the resource-demand of a task. Various versions of this idea have been suggested (Kahneman, 1973; Norman & Bobrow, 1975), and the idea, general as it is, fits easily with the data. Early on, steering a car demands a lot of resources, and so doesn't leave enough resources available for other activities (for example, shifting gears); hence, interference is observed. With practice, steering requires fewer resources, so more is left over. As a result, driving can now be combined with shifting.

However, this plainly leaves a great deal unsaid. We have, for example, discussed a diversity of mental resources, some task-general, some task-specific. Which of these are needed less, as practice proceeds? Moreover, *why* does practice diminish a task's resource demand? Through what mechanism? Will any sort of practice diminish the resource demand? Or does the practice have to be of a special sort? Let's start with these latter questions, and then build from there.

In an influential pair of papers, Schneider and Shiffrin proposed that practice diminishes resource-demand only if it is practice of the right sort (Schneider & Shiffrin, 1977; Shiffrin & Schneider, 1977). In support of this claim, they reported data concerned with the effects of practice on a single task, visual search. Their subjects were shown a group of letters; let's call these the "targets." Subjects were then shown a different group of letters, and had to decide if any of the targets were present in this second group. The targets on a particular trial might be J and T, and now subjects have to decide if any targets are present in the group "P W D S J F" (see Figure 3.6). The answer in this case would be "yes" because a J was present.

Subjects were given much practice with the task, searching for a particular set of targets within a given field, and then searching for a new set of targets

Figure 3.6

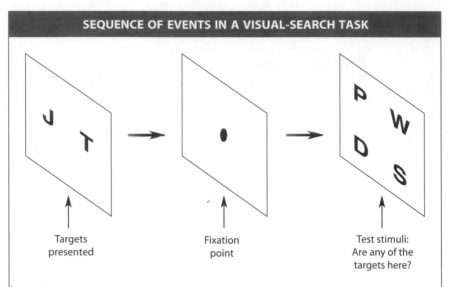

SEQUENCE OF EVENTS IN A VISUAL-SEARCH TASK

Targets
presented

Fixation
point

Test stimuli:
Are any of the
targets here?

Subjects are first shown a group of "targets"; the number of targets varies from trial to trial. Then subjects are shown a fixation point, to ensure that their eyes are pointed in the right direction. Finally, subjects are shown a group of test letters, and they must respond "yes" if *any* of the targets are present in this group.

within a new field. Importantly, there was no consistency in which letters appeared as targets, and which appeared as distractors. To make this concrete, the targets for trial 28 might be S and H, and the subject might have to search among this set: "A M S." In this case, a "yes" response would be correct, since one of the targets is present. The targets for trial 29 might then be F and C, and the target might have to search among this set: "P S R" (the response should be "no"). Notice that the appearance of the S in the first of these trials demanded a "yes" response, whereas the appearance of the S in the second of these trials does *not* demand a "yes" response. In other words, there is no consistent linkage between letters and responses, since the response appropriate for each letter will vary from trial to trial. Schneider and Shiffrin call this a **varied mapping** between inputs and responses.

In a different version of the procedure, the setup was different: Before starting the procedure, Schneider and Shiffrin selected a portion of the alphabet to be the "potential targets." For example, we identify A, E, I, M, Q, U, and Y as the potential targets. Every trial of the procedure involves different targets, but the targets are always drawn from this group. In addition, these potential target letters never appear as the distractor letters. Thus, a Q may or may not appear in any individual trial but, if it appears, it will appear as a target. In other words, if a Q appears, it demands a "yes" response. On no trial is Q one of the distractors, and so a Q never demands a "no" response. The letter F cannot be a target, because it is not in the set of potential targets. Therefore a "yes" response is never appropriate for the letter F. Overall then, this condition provides a **consistent mapping** between inputs and responses.

Schneider and Shiffrin found that practice with consistent mapping had very different consequences from practice with varied mapping. To understand this, we need one more fact about the Schneider and Shiffrin procedure. In some trials, only one target was presented so that, for example, the subject searched the display for the letter A, and responded "yes" only if an A was present. On other trials, multiple targets were presented so that, for example, subjects had to respond "yes" if an E or an X or a Z was in the display. How might this matter? As one possibility, subjects might search the display for the E, and then for X, and then for the Z. This one-at-a-time process is called a serial search (since the individual searches are lined up in a series). With a serial search, it would take longer to search for two targets than for one, longer to search for three than for two, and so on.

As a different possibility, subjects might be able to divide their attention and, in effect, do several searches at once—look for the E at the same time they are looking for the X at the same they are looking for the Z. With this parallel search, search time should not depend on the number of targets.

Schneider and Shiffrin's data indicate that subjects trained with a *varied* mapping always used a serial search. Even after much practice with the overall task, they still searched for one target, then the next, then another. Consequently, search times were slower for two targets than for one, slower still for three targets. In the early trials, subjects trained with a *consistent* mapping showed the same pattern. However, after some practice, these subjects were able to do a parallel search (and so needed the same time to search for multiple targets as they did to search for single targets).

A parallel search is just like a divided-attention procedure: Subjects are searching for the Z at the same time that they are searching for the L; they are, in short, doing two things at once. Yet the results indicate no interference between these concurrent searches: Subjects can do two simultaneous searches, or even three or four simultaneous searches, just as quickly, and just as efficiently, as they can do a single search. Apparently, then, the individual searches are not competing with each other for some limited resource; if they were, we would observe interference. And that is the point: Consistent-mapping practice makes possible "resource-free" searching.

Another aspect of the data is also quite striking: After giving subjects extensive practice in the consistent-mapping task, Schneider and Shiffrin *re-*

versed the categorization of targets and distractors. From this point forward, stimuli that had been in the set of possible targets were now *never* targets; stimuli that had never been targets now became the possible targets. This reversal was enormously difficult for subjects—their responses were now quite slow, they made many errors, and they reverted to a serial search, rather than a parallel one. In short, it appeared that the earlier consistent-mapping practice had created a new "reflex" for subjects: They had acquired immense skill in searching, but they had also, in a sense, lost control of their performance—they could not turn off their newly established skill, even when the procedure demanded it.

Automaticity

According to some theoretical accounts, visual search has, for the consistent-mapping subjects, become automatic. Early discussions suggested that **automaticity** has several interesting features: Automatized skills require few resources, and so are unlikely to compete for resources with other tasks. Hence, it should be easy to divide attention between an automatized task and virtually any other task. Likewise, many authors suggested that automatized skills are largely independent of *intention*; they should, in essence, be out of control. (Indeed, some authors speak of automatized skills as we just did, as "mental reflexes.") Finally, in many cases, automatized activities should go forward independent of *awareness*. We have said little about what awareness *is* but, at the least, one might expect that awareness will be intimately tied up with the control systems of attention (including the response selector). Since automatized activities are performed without these control systems, it seems likely that one can do automatized acts without thinking much about them—you can do them on "autopilot." (We return to this theme in Chapter 14.)

These claims certainly fit with the Shiffrin and Schneider data. We hasten to say, though, that these claims about automaticity need to be refined somewhat. For example, we have listed three traits of automatized behaviors—these behaviors are produced without intention, without awareness, and without requiring resources (and thus not disrupting, and not being disrupted by, other simultaneous activities). It turns out, however, that these traits need not cluster together—i.e., we can document cases of behaviors that are produced without intention, but that do require resources; behaviors that don't require resources, but do seem to be under the subjects' control, and so on. Therefore, we need a theory that accounts individually for these aspects of skilled behavior, rather than a theory that accounts for them as a group. (For discussion, see Bargh, 1989; Kahneman & Chajczyk, 1983; Logan, 1989; Paap & Ogden, 1981; Zbrodoff & Logan, 1986; for debate specifically focused on the Shiffrin and Schneider paradigm, see Cheng, 1985; Fisher, 1984; Logan &

Stadler, 1991; Ryan, 1983; Schneider & Shiffrin, 1985; Shiffrin & Schneider, 1984; Strayer & Kramer, 1994a, 1994b.)

Even with these complexities acknowledged, though, certain features of automaticity remain quite striking—particularly the reflex-like quality of automatized behaviors. Indeed, such reflexes are easily demonstrated with the classic experiment conducted by Stroop (1935). Stroop showed his subjects a series of words and asked them to name aloud the color of the ink used for each word. The trick, though, was that the words themselves were color names. So subjects might see the word "BLUE" printed in green ink, and would have to say "green" out loud.

This task turns out to be enormously difficult. There is a strong tendency to read the printed word itself, rather than naming the ink color, and subjects make many mistakes in this task. What is going on here? Word-recognition, especially for college-age adults, is enormously well-practiced and, as a consequence, word-recognition can proceed automatically. This is a condition, therefore, in which we expect great difficulties in *ignoring* a stimulus, great difficulties in not perceiving, and that is exactly what the **Stroop effect** shows. (For reviews of Stroop research, see MacLeod, 1991; Yee & Hunt, 1991. For older treatments, see LaBerge, 1975; Posner & Snyder, 1974.)

A wide range of related effects can also be observed. For example, subjects can be asked to judge how many items are in a row, with the to-be-counted items themselves numbers (Figure 3.7). Here, too, Stroop-like interference is observed, with subjects showing a strong tendency to name the digits shown, rather than counting them. Similar effects can also be demonstrated in hearing if, for example, subjects must judge whether a speaker is male or female, and they hear voices (male or female) pronouncing the words "male" or "girl" (Green & Barber, 1981; "girl" was used in this procedure rather than "female" so that both stimuli would be one-syllable words).

Response Selection and the "Reflex" Quality of Automaticity

Why does practice produce this reflex quality? To address this, let's again focus on Schneider and Shiffrin's visual-search task. Think back to the variable-mapping condition, in which a stimulus can be a target in one trial, but a distractor in the next trial. This condition, by its design, requires subjects to keep track, trial by trial, of the response appropriate for each stimulus. Hence, subjects must, throughout the experiment, monitor what response is appropriate for an S on *this* trial; what response is appropriate for a T on *this* trial. This certainly implies that this condition will make heavy use of the mental resource we earlier called the *response-selector*. Moreover, this is a fixed

Figure 3.7

STROOP INTERFERENCE	
How many items are in each row?	How about these rows?
# #	4 4
? ? ? ?	2 2 2 2
&	3
& &	3 3
/ / / /	1 1 1 1
#	4
? ?	2 2
/ / /	1 1 1
# # #	4 4 4
& & & &	3 3 3 3
?	2
/ /	1 1

Stroop's original demonstration involved color naming, but many variations on this effect can be demonstrated. For example, scan down the left column, saying out loud how many items are in each row. Now do the same with the right column. Here the task is more difficult, because of the strong tendency to *read* the numerals, rather than *counting* them.

feature of this condition; it is, after all, built into the definition of variable-mapping, and so will not be changed by practice. Thus, whatever the level of practice, this condition will continue to place a heavy demand on the selector.

Contrast this with consistent-mapping. Here, each stimulus is reliably associated with a specific response. If an S requires a "no" response on one trial, it will require a "no" response on all trials. With practice, therefore, response selection will become a matter of familiar routine: When you see the S, you don't have to ponder what the response should be; all you need to do is recall how you responded to a S the last time you saw one. And likewise for all the other stimuli so that, in this condition, the role of the response-selector soon becomes trivial. Consequently, the selector will cease to be a bottle-neck in the flow of events, allowing a move away from serial processing.

This reliance on routine can be enormously helpful: After some practice, subjects no longer need to make choices; they no longer need to weigh the factors favoring one response over another. Instead, all they have to do is ask: "What did I do the last time I was in this situation?" This "memory look-up" will usually be easier than working through the actual decision. Indeed, for more complicated tasks, a reliance on routine will allow subjects to replace a whole *series* of decisions (one for each of the task's steps) with a *single* memory look-up. ("What was the *sequence* of decisions I made last time?") Presumably, the selector will be needed to choose and launch this overall routine but, with that done, subjects can simply run off the routine, with no further need for the selector.

Note, though, that there is a price paid for this efficiency: By relying on routine, one sacrifices flexibility. If you always repeat what you did the last time around, you lose the option of changing your response; indeed, you lose the option of choosing to do *nothing* this time. That is why diminished use of the response-selector, and the increased use of routine, gives automatic actions their reflex character.

Let's be careful, though, about what is meant here by "reflex." In the account just sketched, a sequence of actions will run off automatically *once the routine has been launched*. Once you have decided to tie your shoes, you rely on the familiar routine of shoe-tying. Hence, you don't make decisions about the individual steps of this process and, correspondingly, you have little control over the details of this process. However, you did make the initial decision—to tie your shoes. Shoe-tying is automatic *once started*, but it is not a reflex in any literal sense. The same is true for Stroop interference: Once you have initiated the routine of uttering color names, you are vulnerable to this interference. But, of course, you don't say "RED" aloud every time you encounter the letters "r-e-d." Color naming is only automatic once the overall sequence has been launched. Thus, current researchers speak of contingent automaticity, rather than automaticity in general, to emphasize the fact that automaticity is contingent on the subject first being in the appropriate "response mode" (for discussion, see Bargh, 1989).

The "Limits" of Divided Attention

A key benefit of practice, therefore, is the establishment of a routine. With a routine in place, you no longer need to make decisions, step by step, about what to do next as you are performing the task. Instead, you can rely on the sequence of decisions you used last time around, with corresponding gains in speed, efficiency, and ease.

In fact, we may be able, in some circumstances, to obtain these advantages without practice. For example, even before subjects get any practice with a task, we might be able to explain the task to them in a way that makes clear the appropriate routine. If subjects are then able to remember this procedure, they will be able to rely on it when they *first* try the task. In other words, they will draw immediately on the routine, even without the benefit of any practice. This sort of "automaticity without practice" has in fact been documented, at least for some tasks (Logan, 1989; Logan & Klapp, 1991).

What are the limits of all this? Are there things that cannot be reduced to a routine? Or, with practice, can you automatize any activity? Likewise, given the link between routine and divided attention, could you learn, with enough practice, to divide attention between *any* two tasks? Or are some task combinations simply impossible?

In an extraordinary series of experiments, subjects were trained to read and write simultaneously (Spelke, Hirst & Neisser, 1976; Hirst, Spelke, Reaves, Caharack & Neisser, 1980). To understand the task, imagine sitting in a lecture, taking careful notes, *and simultaneously* reading the assignment for your next class. What a time-saver that would be!

In the actual experiments, subjects were given stories to read and, while they were reading, they listened to the experimenters dictating lists of words. Subjects were required to write down these dictated words, and they were also tested on the reading material, later on, to ensure that they comprehended what they were reading.

Initially, to no one's surprise, this combination of tasks was very difficult—subjects either read more slowly, or skipped lines, or missed some of the dictated words. After about six weeks of practice, however, subjects learned to combine the tasks, and could read while taking dictation just as well as they did when reading was their sole concern.

As we've noted, the comprehension tests confirm that subjects did understand what they were reading. Were they also comprehending what they *heard*—that is, the dictated materials? To find out, Hirst et al. (1980) changed what was being dictated to the subjects, so that the dictated material actually formed sentences, and the sentences formed miniature stories. For example, subjects, while reading one story, might hear these three sentences: "The dancers performed. They were excellent. The director bowed." Later on, subjects were given 30 more sentences in a recognition test and had to judge which of these had been presented earlier. Some of the test sentences were identical to the sentences contained within the dictation; some of the test sentences were different (e.g., "The dancers bowed"). Our main interest, though, is with a third category of test sentences. These sentences were *implied* by what was presented, but not literally said. A test sentence in this category might be, "Dancers were excellent."

If subjects say "yes" to this last category, this is an interesting error, implying that subjects understood the gist of the story that was dictated to them. A "yes" response would indicate that subjects not only understood the individual sentences, but also understood how the sentences were linked to each other. And, in fact, subjects did say "yes" to this third category of "implied" sentences, suggesting that they did indeed grasp the meaning of the dictated material—at the same time that they were reading other material, at their normal speed, and with their normal comprehension.

The Importance of "Combined" Practice

The Spelke, Hirst and Neisser experiments are for many people mind-boggling. At the least, one has to be impressed by what these subjects could accomplish. Moreover, one has to wonder what else could be accomplished by sufficient practice. Where are the limits? What *can't* we do, given sufficient practice? These are important questions, and clearly need further examination.

In addition, the Spelke, Hirst and Neisser data force us to enlarge our view of the relationship between practice and divided attention. After all, these subjects were well-practiced in reading, with at least 15 years of experience, prior to the experiment's start. Likewise, before the experiment began, the subjects all had extensive practice in note-taking. Therefore, if practice is the key to divided attention, why couldn't subjects combine these two well-practiced activities on the very first day they were tested?

The obvious suggestion is that subjects didn't need more practice in reading or in note-taking. Instead, they needed practice in *coordinating* these two activities. They were already skilled enough in the individual tasks; what they needed to learn was the complex of reading-while-taking-dictation. (For fuller discussion of this point, see Allport, 1989.)

Notice that this claim represents a real shift in focus for us: Up until now, we have been talking about divided attention by referring to the characteristics of the individual tasks being combined: Individual tasks require resources of certain sorts; individual tasks are automatized (or are not). If a task leaves resources available, then other tasks can be performed simultaneously. If a task is automatized, then it can easily be combined with other tasks, no matter what the other tasks are. All of this implies that combining tasks will be easy once you have practiced the *individual* tasks. The practice diminishes the resource demands of each task, and this is what allows divided attention.

The Spelke, Hirst and Neisser data, however, indicate that we need to enlarge this view: In some circumstances, it would seem, it is practice with the task *combination* that matters, rather than practice with the individual tasks. And if this is true, then our account of divided attention needs to pay attention to this combination, rather than to the individual tasks (e.g., the resource demands of each, the automaticity of each) by themselves.

[handwritten margin note: Combined practice of 2 tasks is what is important to do them simultaneously]

Channel Segregation and Divided Attention as a "Skill"

Why is "combined practice" so important? One possibility is that, in some cases, the limits to divided attention are not limits of resources. Instead, performance may be limited by problems in "bookkeeping," that is, the chore of keeping straight which task is which. Think about the game of rubbing your stomach with one hand while simultaneously tapping your head with the other hand. The difficulty of this task lies simply in keeping track of which hand is doing the rubbing, and which hand the tapping. This problem is technically known as **channel segregation**—it isn't easy to keep the "stomach-rubbing channel" separate from the "head-tapping channel." Said differently, one suffers from **crosstalk** between the two channels (Kinsbourne, 1981).

Channel segregation is probably relevant to several of the studies we have discussed. For example, consider the result reported by Allport et al. (1972): Their subjects had little trouble memorizing a series of pictures while simultaneously shadowing a series of words; it was difficult, though, to memorize a series of words heard through one ear while shadowing different words heard through the other ear. In this latter condition, the simultaneous inputs are obviously quite similar to each other, and so easily confused with each other. For example, subjects may know they have just heard the word "box" but may not be certain whether they heard it in the left ear or the right. As a result, they wouldn't know if this is a word to be shadowed or a word to be memorized. This sort of confusion is far less likely, though, with dissimilar tasks, like listening to words while viewing pictures. Now, if one hears the word "box," it could only have come from one source, making it easy to keep track of which input is which. With easy channel segregation, subjects won't become confused, and successful divided attention is more likely.

In addition, for a variety of reasons, some cases of channel segregation are, from the start, easier than others. To put it informally, some inputs seem to "belong" with some outputs, and not to belong with other outputs. We first encountered this idea in the context of the response-selector; there we noted that some input-output mappings are easy, while others are difficult. (See Figure 3.4.) Likewise, consider evidence reported by Shaffer (1975a; 1975b): His subjects were all well-practiced typists. They were shown printed material and asked to type a copy of this material. At the same time, subjects heard a verbal input through headphones and were asked to shadow this material. Remarkably, subjects were able to do this divided attention task, typing and talking simultaneously, confirming the Spelke, Hirst and Neisser findings. But Shaffer's subjects had great difficulty if the task was reversed—if they were asked to type what they heard through headphones, while reading the printed material aloud.

This result can be explained in terms of channel segregation, since there is an obvious compatibility between the visual input and typing, and the auditory input and shadowing. For example, in typing one produces words letter-by-letter. This letter-by-letter sequence is, of course, directly available with a visual input, but not with an auditory one. Likewise, in shadowing, one produces words sound-by-sound. This sequence of sounds is specified by an auditory input, but not a visual one. In a straightforward way, therefore, the visual input "belongs" with the typing output, and the auditory input belongs with the vocal output. Because of this relationship, it is easy to keep straight which input goes with which if the inputs and outputs are arranged in a compatible fashion, and far more difficult if they are arranged in an incompatible fashion. (For further discussion of this point and related studies, see Allport, 1989; Hirst & Kalmar, 1987.)

To connect all of this back to practice effects, we merely need to argue that channel segregation is a skill that can be improved with practice. This suggests that we might think of divided attention itself as a practiceable skill: When one learns to sing while riding a bicycle, one is not merely learning to sing, and not merely learning to ride a bicycle. Instead, one is specifically learning how to divide attention between these activities, and this may in turn depend largely on learning how to keep these two activities segregated.

How plausible is this? Channel segregation obviously depends on being able to discriminate the channels: If you can't tell your left ear from your right, you will never be able to segregate a left-ear message from a right-ear message. It also seems clear that the ability to discriminate among categories improves with practice: The novice bird-watcher may think that all small birds look alike. With a little experience, however, the bird-watcher learns to distinguish the warblers from the wrens and, eventually, to distinguish among the different warblers. If segregation depends on discrimination, and if discrimination improves with practice, then the ability to segregate should improve with practice. This is, of course, exactly the argument we need in order to explain the Spelke, Hirst and Neisser results in terms of channel segregation.

Divided Attention: A Reprise

Let us again summarize where we are: We have argued that there are multiple constraints, multiple limits, on divided attention. If two tasks make competing demands on task-specific resources, this will rule out concurrent performance of the tasks. If two tasks make competing demands on task-general resources (such as the response selector), this too will rule out concurrent performance. Finally, if two tasks cannot be segregated, this will also rule out concurrent performance, because of problems with crosstalk.

Do we really need *all* of these mechanisms? Or might a simpler theory of attention be possible? Some researchers have argued that considerations of channel segregation may be all we need to explain the limits of divided attention (Allport, 1989; Navon, 1984, 1985; Neisser, 1976), making any claims about "resources" superfluous. Despite these arguments, though, it does seem likely that we need a multi-part theory of attention, with performance limited by different factors in different occasions. For example, difficulties in divided attention can be documented even when channel segregation is easy, but there is competition for resources (e.g., Pashler & O'Brien, 1993). Thus, it does seem that interference between concurrent activities can arise for several different reasons.

What, then, is "attention"? It would seem that attention isn't just a skill, or a mechanism, or a capacity. Instead, attention is an *achievement*—an achievement of performing multiple activities simultaneously, or an achievement of successfully avoiding distraction, when you wish to focus on a single task. And, as we have now seen, this achievement rests on an intricate base, so that many skills, mechanisms, and capacities contribute to our ability to attend.

Moreover, we have argued for an intimate connection between divided attention and skilled performance: That is, any complex task—whether it is playing tennis, or driving a car, or even ordinary talking—can be thought of as an assembly of subtasks, and these must be done simultaneously (and coordinated with each other) to achieve task proficiency. The ability to divide attention among a task's components is an essential ingredient in the development of skill. The achievement of paying attention is therefore crucial in its own right, and is also a fundamental element of almost everything else we do.

4

The Acquisition of Memories

In Chapter 1, we argued that *memory* plays a pivotal role in our mental lives. Without memory, there would be no learning. Without memory, we would get no benefit from our prior experiences. And, of course, there are many questions to ask about memory: How does learning proceed? Are there more or less effective ways to learn? Why do we sometimes forget? And, finally, how much trust should we place in our memories—how accurate, and how complete, is our recollection of previous events? These questions will be our focus for the next three chapters.

Acquisition, Storage, and Retrieval

There is an obvious way to organize our inquiry into memory. Before there can be a memory, some learning must occur, that is, new information must be acquired. Therefore, acquisition should be our first topic for discussion. Then, once information has been acquired, it must be held in memory until it is needed. We refer to this as the storage phase. Finally, we *use* the information that is in memory; we remember. Information is somehow found in the vast warehouse that is memory, and brought into active use; this is called retrieval.

This organization probably strikes you as intuitively sensible; it fits, for example, with the way most "electronic memories" (e.g., computers) work. Information ("input") is provided to a computer (the acquisition phase). The information then resides in some dormant form, perhaps in the computer's memory, or perhaps on a magnetic disk (the storage phase). Finally, the information can be brought back from this dormant form, often via a search process that hunts through the memory or disk (the retrieval phase). Of course, there's nothing special about a computer here, since "low-tech" information storage works the same way. Think about a file-drawer: Information is acquired (i.e., filed), then rests in this or that folder, and then is retrieved.

This framework makes it sound like acquisition, storage, and retrieval are separate processes which happen in sequence. This in turn implies that these three elements of remembering can be discussed independently of each other. Consistent with this, we begin our inquiry by focusing on the acquisition of new memories, leaving discussion of storage and retrieval for later. As it turns out, though, we will soon find reasons for challenging this overall approach to memory. In discussing acquisition, for example, we might wish to ask: What is good learning? What guarantees that material is firmly recorded in memory? As we will see, the evidence indicates that what is good learning depends on how the memory is retrieved—good preparation for one kind of test can be poor preparation for a different kind of test. Claims about acquisition must be interwoven with claims about retrieval. These interconnections between acquisition and retrieval will be the central theme of Chapter 5.

In the same way, we cannot separate claims about memory acquisition from claims about memory storage. To put it simply, how you learn, and how well you learn, depend heavily on what you already know. That needs to be explored and explained, and will provide a recurrent theme both for this chapter and Chapter 6.

With these caveats in mind, we will begin by describing the acquisition process. Our approach will be roughly historical: We will start with a simple model, emphasizing data largely collected in the 1970s. We will then use this as the framework for examining more recent research, adding refinements to the model as we proceed.

The Route into Memory

Starting in the late 1950s, much theorizing in cognitive psychology was guided by a new way of thinking about mental events, a perspective known as **information processing**. This perspective borrowed heavily from developments in electronic information processing, including developments in computers (see Chapter 1). Leaving the details aside, the notion was that complex mental events such as learning, remembering, or deciding could be understood as being built up out of a large number of discrete steps. These steps occurred one-by-one, each with its own characteristics and its own job to do, and with each providing as its "output," the input to the next step in the sequence. Within this framework, theories could often be illustrated with charts such as the one in Figure 4.1. In this diagram, each enclosed shape represents a separate event or process, and the arrows represent the flow of information from one event to the next. The research goal was to make the charts more and more complete, by analyzing each box into still smaller boxes, continuing until the complex process under scrutiny could be described in terms of elementary information-processing components.

A great deal of information-processing theory focused on the processes through which information was detected, recognized, and entered into memory storage—that is, on the process of information acquisition. While there was disagreement about the details, there was reasonable consensus on the bold outline of events. An early version of this model was described by Waugh and Norman (1965); later refinements were added by Atkinson & Shiffrin (1968). The consensus model quickly came to be known as the **modal model**, and it is on this model that we will focus.

Figure 4.1

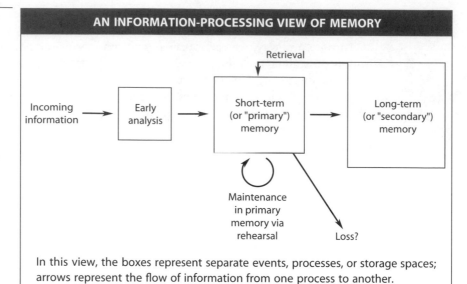

AN INFORMATION-PROCESSING VIEW OF MEMORY

In this view, the boxes represent separate events, processes, or storage spaces; arrows represent the flow of information from one process to another.

The Modal Model

According to the modal model, our information processing involves different kinds of memory, two of which are short-term memory and long-term memory. Short-term memory holds onto information currently "in use," much as your desk contains the papers or books with which you are currently working. Short-term memory is limited in how much it can hold but, most important, information in short-term memory is instantly and easily available to you.

We first mentioned short-term memory in Chapter 1, although there we used the more modern terminology, working memory, a term that emphasizes the function of this memory. As we noted in Chapter 1, virtually all mental tasks rely on working memory. To mention one of our earlier examples, as you read this sentence, your interpretation of the early words will depend on what comes later; therefore, you will need to store the early words for a second or two, until you have read the entire sentence. Those early words, presumably, would be stored in working memory. Or, if you are asked to multiply 23 by 12, you are likely to multiply 23 by 2, hang on to the result, then multiply 23 by 10, and finally add this result to the earlier one. These cases help to make it clear why this memory is referred to as working memory—it is where you store information while you are working on it. (In Chapter 1, we also emphasized the fact that working memory has different components—we spoke of a working-memory *system*. We will return to this point later in the chapter.)

If working memory provides a mental "desk space," then long-term memory is the mental "reference library." Long-term memory (or LTM) is a vast store, and contains all of the information you remember—your memories of what you did yesterday, how you spent your childhood, a vast number of facts about your favorite topic, the names and faces of a hundred acquaintances, and so on.

While there is a close association between working memory and the contents of your current thinking, there is no such association for long-term memory. At any point in time, much of the material in LTM lies dormant, neither influencing nor influenced by your current thoughts. Correspondingly, the process of retrieving information from LTM, and thus making the information available for use, is often effortful and slow.

Working Memory and Long-Term Memory: One Memory or Two?

Many pieces of evidence demand this distinction between working memory and LTM, but much of the evidence comes from a single task: Subjects are read a series of words, like "bicycle, artichoke, radio, chair, palace." The length of the list can vary, and so can the rate at which the words are presented. Typical experiments, though, use lists of about 30 words, presented at a rate of about one word per second. Immediately after the last word is read, subjects are asked to repeat back as many words as they can. Subjects are free to report the words in any order they choose, which is why this is referred to as a free recall procedure.

Subjects usually remember 12 to 15 words in such a test, in a consistent pattern: Subjects are extremely likely to remember the first few words on the list, something known as the **primacy effect**, and are also likely to remember the last five or six words on the list, a **recency effect**. Results of such a study are shown in Figure 4.2, with a U-shaped curve showing the relation between position within the series (or serial position) and likelihood of recall (Baddeley & Hitch, 1977; Deese & Kaufman, 1957; Glanzer & Cunitz, 1966; Murdock, 1962; Postman & Phillips, 1965).

This **serial position curve** is easily explained by the modal model. At any point in time, according to our model, working memory contains the material you are "working on" at that moment. During the list presentation, subjects are obviously thinking about the words they are hearing, and so it is these words that are in working memory. Working memory, though, is limited in its size, capable of holding only five or six words. Therefore, as subjects try

Figure 4.2

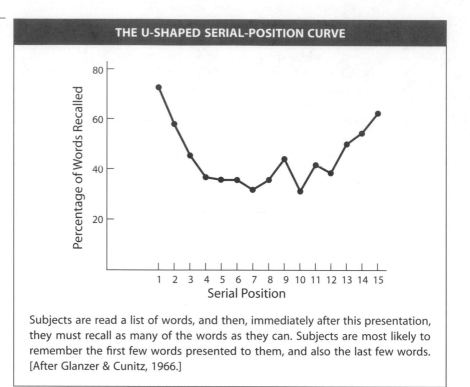

THE U-SHAPED SERIAL-POSITION CURVE

Subjects are read a list of words, and then, immediately after this presentation, they must recall as many of the words as they can. Subjects are most likely to remember the first few words presented to them, and also the last few words. [After Glanzer & Cunitz, 1966.]

to keep up with the list presentation, they will be placing the "just heard" words into working memory, and this will bump the previous words out of this memory. Consequently, as subjects proceed through the list, their working memories will, at each moment, contain just the half-dozen words that arrived most recently.

On this account, the only words that don't get "bumped" out of working memory are the last few words on the list, since obviously no further input arrives to displace these words. Hence, when the list presentation ends, these few words are still in working memory. Moreover, our hypothesis is that materials in working memory are readily available—easily and quickly retrieved. When the time comes for recall, we expect accurate and complete recall for these last few words. This is the source of the recency effect.

The primacy effect comes from a different source. According to the modal model, the transfer of material from working memory to LTM depends on processes that require time and attention. Let's examine how subjects allocate their attention to the list items. As subjects hear the list, they do their best to be good memorizers. When they hear the first word, they repeat it over and over to themselves ("bicycle, bicycle, bicycle"), a process referred to as **memory rehearsal**. When the second word arrives, they rehease it, too ("bicycle, artichoke, bicycle, artichoke"). Likewise for the third ("bicycle, artichoke, radio, bicycle, artichoke, radio . . ."), and so on through the list. Note that the first few items on the list are *privileged*: For a brief moment, "bicycle" was the only word subjects had to worry about, and so it had 100% of the subjects' attention lavished on it; no other word received this privilege. For a brief moment, "artichoke" had 50% of the subject's attention, more attention than any word except the first. When "radio" arrived, it only received 33% of the subjects' attention.

Thus, only the first few words on the list receive subjects' focused attention; all of the other words receive just a fraction of subjects' efforts. In fact, evidence indicates that subjects can only rehearse five or six words at a time. This follows from our claims about working memory's size but, in any case, we can confirm this by simply asking subjects to rehearse out loud (cf. Rundus, 1971). Hence, words in the middle of the list share subjects' attention with four or five other words and so receive only a small part of the subjects' attention.

This easily provides an explanation of the primacy effect, that is, the observed memory advantage for the early list items. These early words didn't have to "share" attention with lots of other words. Therefore, more attention, and more time, was devoted to these early words than to other words on the list, and long-term retention, we propose, depends on processes that require attention. It is the early words that are most likely to reach LTM, and so it is these words that are most likely to be remembered after a delay.

This account of the serial-position curve leads to many further predictions. First, note that the model claims that the recency portion of the curve is coming from working memory, while the other items on the list are being recalled from LTM. Therefore, any manipulation of working memory should affect recall of the recency items, but not recall of the other items on the list. To see how this works, consider a modification of our procedure: In the standard procedure, we allow subjects to recite what they remember immediately after the list's end. In place of this, we can delay subjects' recall by asking them to perform some other task prior to the recall. For example, we can ask subjects, immediately after hearing the list, to count backwards by three's, starting from 201. Subjects do this for just 30 seconds, and then they try to recall the list.

This counting activity will itself draw on working memory (to keep track of where one is in the sequence), and so it will bump the recency items out of working memory. Therefore, this activity should eliminate the recency effect, but have *no* effect on recall of items earlier on the list, since these items are being recalled from long-term memory, not working memory, and LTM is not dependent on current activity. Figure 4.3 shows that these predictions are correct: An activity interpolated between the list and recall essentially eliminates the recency effect, but has no influence elsewhere in the list (Baddeley & Hitch, 1977; Glanzer & Cunitz, 1966; Postman & Phillips, 1965; other influential data were reported early on by Brown, 1958; Peterson & Peterson, 1959). Note that merely delaying the recall (with no interpolated activity) has no impact. In this case, subjects can continue, during the delay, to maintain the recency items—no new materials are coming in, and so nothing displaces these items from working memory.

The modal model also predicts that manipulations of long-term memory should affect all performance *except* for recency. For example, what happens

Figure 4.3

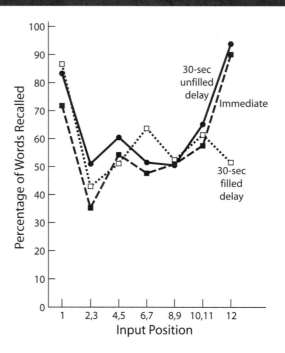

THE IMPACT OF INTERPOLATED ACTIVITY ON THE RECENCY EFFECT

With immediate recall, or if recall is delayed by 30 seconds with no activity during this delay, a strong recency effect is detected. In contrast, if subjects spend 30 seconds on some other activity, between hearing the list and the subsequent memory test, the recency effect is eliminated. This interpolated activity has no impact on the pre-recency portion of the curve.

if we slow down the presentation of the list? Now, subjects will have more time to spend on *all* of the list items, increasing the likelihood of transfer into more permanent storage. This should improve recall for all items coming from LTM. Working memory, in contrast, is limited by its *size*, not by ease of entry or ease of access. Therefore, the slower list presentation should have no influence on working memory performance. As predicted, Figure 4.4 shows that slowing list presentation improves retention of all the pre-recency items, but does not improve the recency effect. Other variables that influence entry into long-term memory have comparable effects. Using more familiar or more common words, for example, would be expected to ease entry into long-term memory, and does improve pre-recency retention, but has no effect on recency (e.g., Sumby, 1963).

Over and over, therefore, the recency and pre-recency portions of the curve are open to separate sets of influences, and obey different principles. This strongly indicates that these portions of the curve are the products of different mechanisms.

Figure 4.4

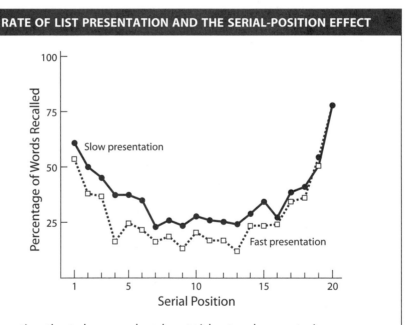

RATE OF LIST PRESENTATION AND THE SERIAL-POSITION EFFECT

Presenting the to-be-remembered materials at a slower rate improves pre-recency performance, but has no effect on recency. The slow rate in this case was 9 seconds per item; the fast rate was 3 seconds per item.

Recency Revisited

For many years, the recency effect was considered the "signature" of working memory: If a recency effect appeared in the data, it was because the last-presented items were still in working memory, and because items in working memory were easily recalled. It turns out, however, that recency effects can also be created in other ways. This doesn't mean our account so far is wrong. Instead, it's simply the case that recency effects cannot be attributed to just one mechanism. Several different mechanisms can each produce a recency effect, and, ironically, these various mechanisms may all be working in concert in the experiments just described.

For example, we have just described a procedure in which subjects hear a series of to-be-remembered words, and then must perform a distractor task for some brief period (e.g., thirty seconds). As we have seen, this procedure largely eliminates the recency effect. In a variation of this design, subjects have been asked to perform the distractor task *after every item*. That is, subjects hear the first item, and then must perform a distractor task for 20 seconds; they then hear the second item, and again perform the distractor task for 20 seconds, and so on until the last item on the list, which, like all the others, is followed by the distractor task (Bjork & Whitten, 1974; Thapar & Greene, 1993). What should we expect here? Subjects in this new procedure obviously do the distractor task after hearing the final items. This should displace the last-heard items from working memory and so, if retrieval from working memory is the source of the recency effect, then that effect should not be observed here. However, that is not what the data show: This "continuous-distractor paradigm" *does* yield a reliable recency effect.

A related puzzle is posed by these cases: Take a blank piece of paper and write down as many U.S. presidents as you can. Or list every vacation you have ever taken. Tests like these yield a pattern of results quite similar to the serial-position data we have already described. For example, Figure 4.5 shows data from a study in which subjects were asked to recall U.S. presidents (after Crowder, 1993). Notice that the curve looks much like the U-shaped curves we've been considering, with a clear primacy effect (that is, accurate memory for Washington, Adams, and Jefferson) and a clear recency effect (Carter, Reagan, Bush). Subjects were less likely to remember the presidents in the middle of the series, with the exception of highly-memorable Abraham Lincoln.

Similar results have been obtained with a variety of other ordered material, for example rugby players recalling the teams they've played against that season; here, too, a recency effect was observed, with memory performance best for the most recent games (Baddeley, 1963; Baddeley & Hitch, 1977; Bjork & Whitten, 1974). In the same vein, subjects who had visited a laboratory

get primacy & recency effects for personal memories too!

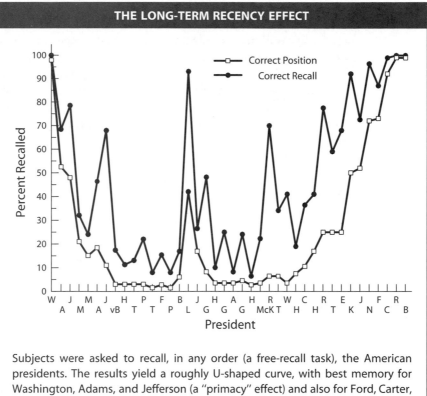

Figure 4.5

THE LONG-TERM RECENCY EFFECT

Subjects were asked to recall, in any order (a free-recall task), the American presidents. The results yield a roughly U-shaped curve, with best memory for Washington, Adams, and Jefferson (a "primacy" effect) and also for Ford, Carter, Reagan, and Bush (a "recency" effect in this 1993 study). The conspicuous exception to this pattern, though, comes from the presidents whose names are associated with the Civil War. [After Crowder, 1993.]

many times were asked to recall where exactly they had parked on each occasion; again, a recency effect was observed in their recall (da Costa Pinto & Baddeley, 1991).

For convenience, let's generate some terminology: we will call the recency effect that results from list-learning experiments (i.e., the recency effect we had been discussing prior to this section) the "standard recency" effect. In standard recency, one is recalling material learned just moments ago. For contrast, we will call these new effects, in which one is recalling material learned some time ago, **long-term recency** effects.

How should we think about long-term recency? Standard recency, we have proposed, comes from the fact that the last few items heard are still "on your mind," are still in working memory, and the retrieval of items from working memory is easy. Moreover, the reason these items are in working memory is because you have just heard them and you haven't heard anything else since. Within this frame, consider what happens if you are asked, with no warning, to name the American presidents. Prior to the request, you were surely thinking about something *other than* presidents' names. Therefore, prior to the question, presidents' names were not in your working memory. Thus you have to dredge up the names from long-term memory, not from working memory, and so our account of standard recency *does not apply* to your recall. Obviously, then, we will need some different explanation for the long-term recency effect.

Recency Is Multiply-Determined

Let's be clear, though, that what is at stake here is the status of the recency effect, and not the status of our overall model. This is because a variety of other evidence, some of which we will present later, also supports the model and, in particular, demands a distinction between working memory and long-term memory. (For some of the evidence, see Vallar & Shallice, 1990. For discussion of this issue, see Crowder, 1993, or Pashler & Carrier, in press.) Thus, we need to continue thinking in terms of a two-memory system, with a long-term memory vast in size, which serves as the repository for all of our knowledge, and a working memory small in size, which holds only that information which is currently "active."

What does need to change, however, is our account of recency. Specifically, we cannot "read" the recency effect as the unique signature of "working memory in action." The evidence suggests instead that the recency effect is multiply-determined—the product of several different mechanisms all working in parallel. One mechanism is the one we have already described—the easy retrieval of items still in working memory. What are the other mechanisms? We can only sketch an account here, since the proposal draws on themes not yet presented. In essence, though, the account rests on the simple claim that memory is, for several reasons, easier for *distinctive* items, items that are readily discriminated from the vast background of all the other information in long-term storage. There are many ways for an item to become distinctive—e.g., a word spelled in capital letters when all the other words to be remembered are in lower-case; a frightening event when the other events to be recalled are emotionally neutral; a bizarre image when the other images to be recalled are mundane. One way to be distinctive, though, is via position—being the first in a series, or the last. And now we have (at least the bare bones of) our account: Items late in a to be remembered list are distinctive *because* they are late in the list; this distinctiveness makes the items easier to recall. (For further discussion of these points, including why and how distinctiveness aids memory, see Chapters 5, 6, and 7.)

With this said, the position we are moving toward is that on the one side, evidence indicates (a) that we need to distinguish working memory from long-term memory, (b) that items just heard are likely to be still in working memory, and (c) that items in working memory are easily and accurately retrieved. This provides one source of recency effects. In addition, other evidence indicates (d) that distinctive items are easier to recall, and (e) that items at the end of a series are distinctive, by virtue of their position. This provides a second source of recency effects. Thus, at least two different mechanisms are simultaneously operative in creating the standard recency advantage. (For elaborations of this argument, including distinctiveness-based accounts of recency, see Baddeley & Hitch, 1993; Thapar & Greene, 1993. For further discussion of the claim that multiple mechanisms contribute to the standard recency effects, see Cowan, Wood & Borne, 1994. For evidence that some forms of brain damage eliminate one of these recency mechanisms, while leaving the other mechanism intact, see Vallar, Papagno & Baddeley, 1991.)

A Closer Look at Working Memory

There is still a great deal to be said about memory acquisition and, in particular, about how materials are "entered" into long-term memory. Before turning to these matters, though, we should pause to consider working memory more fully. This will allow us to fill in some details about this store, and will also allow us to say more about this memory's function.

The Function of Working Memory

As we noted in Chapter 1, virtually all mental activities require the coordination of several pieces of information or several inputs. We often need to start by working on these ideas or inputs one at a time, and only then integrating them into a full package. We earlier mentioned the example of reading a sentence: One first must decipher the sentence's early words, then place these words on "hold" while working on the sentence's later words. Then, once these have been identified, one can integrate all the words to understand the full phrase. Likewise, consider a simple plan: One must first choose one's goal, but then must put this choice on hold in order to concentrate on the early steps needed to reach this goal. Then, once these early steps are taken, one must think about the goal again, in order to select one's next steps.

These examples underscore the important interplay between thought and memory: In order to devote attention to one aspect of a problem, one must set other aspects to the side. But these other aspects, while set to the side, must remain easily available, so that they can be coordinated into a full package. (If, in thinking about a plan's early steps, you forgot the goal, then you wouldn't know what to do after the early steps.)

As we have already noted, the memory making this possible is working memory. When information is currently in use, or likely to be needed soon, it is stored in working memory. This clearly implies that working memory will be involved in a wide range of tasks, and this suggestion has been confirmed in many studies. Some of the studies exploit the fact that working memory's capacity varies somewhat from one individual to the next. One can therefore ask about this memory's function by asking what tasks are facilitated by a slightly larger working memory, and what tasks are compromised by a smaller memory. For example, research on reading reveals a crucial role for working memory, with strong correlations observed between working memory's capacity and various measures of reading comprehension and reading speed. That is, a subject with a larger-capacity working memory is likely also to be a more efficient reader (Baddeley, Logie, Nimmo-Smith & Brereton, 1985; Daneman & Carpenter, 1980; Just & Carpenter, 1992). Similar results have been obtained with assessments of reasoning skills, with positive correlations reported between working-memory capacity and overall performance (Carpenter, Just & Shell, 1990; Kyllonen & Cristal, 1990).

The Holding Capacity of Working Memory

The research just mentioned relies on measurements of working memory's holding capacity, but where do these estimates come from? We've already said that the capacity is relatively small and, indeed, one could argue that it *has to be* small: Given working memory's function, information in this store must be quickly and readily available. This by itself implies that working memory is limited in capacity. To make this clear, recall our analogy between working memory and your desk: If there is information you use all the time, it makes sense to keep that information on your desk, rather than in your file drawer or on your book shelf. That way, the information will be quickly available when you need it. But you will lose this advantage if there is too much on your desk—then it will take time and effort to sort through the desk's contents, to locate any particular bit of information. Thus, there is a trade-off between accessibility and amount stored; as one of these increases, the other decreases. To serve its function as an efficient workplace, then, working memory must be small.

But just how big is this memory? For many years, working memory's capacity was measured with a **digit-span task**. In this task, subjects are read a series of digits (e.g., "8 3 4") and must immediately repeat them back. If subjects do this successfully, they are given a slightly longer list (e.g., "9 2 4 0"), and so forth. The list is gradually increased until subjects start to make errors. This task, it would appear, draws directly on working memory; the errors should appear when we put more on the list than this memory can hold. As it turns out, with seven or eight items on the list, subject perform quite well. With eight or nine items, subjects begin to make errors. With lists longer than this, many errors will occur, primarily in the middle of the list— that is, we will get a serial position curve, with the by-now familiar primacy and recency effects.

Procedures such as this imply that working memory's capacity is around seven items or, more cautiously, at least five items, and probably not more than nine items. These estimates are often summarized by the statement that this memory holds "7 plus-or-minus 2" items (Chi, 1976; Dempster, 1981; Miller, 1956; Watkins, 1977).

However, these "measurements" of working memory may be misleading. We've said that working memory can hold 7 plus-or-minus 2 items, but what exactly is an "item"? Can we remember seven sentences as easily as seven words? Seven letters as easily as seven equations? In a classic paper, George Miller proposed that working memory holds 7 plus-or-minus 2 **chunks** (Miller, 1956). The term "chunk" is a deliberately unscientific-sounding term, in order to remind us that a chunk does not hold a fixed quantity of information. Instead, Miller proposed, working memory holds 7 plus-or-minus 2 packages, and what those packages contain is largely up to the subject.

The effects of chunking are easily visible in a digit-span test, since performance in this task turns out to depend enormously on how the subjects think about or organize the items. A subject might, for example, hear a list like "H, O, P, T, R, A, E, G," etc. If the subject thinks of these as individual letters, then he or she will remember 7 of them, more or less. If the same subject instead thinks of the list as composed of syllables, "ho, pit, rah, egg," then he or she will remember approximately 7 syllables, or 14 letters. If the subject happens to form three-letter syllables, ("hop, tra, . . ."), the subject may remember close to 21 letters, and so on (Postman, 1975; Simon, 1974).

This chunking process, however, does have a cost attached to it. Working memory seems able to hold 7 plus-or-minus 2 digits or letters, but slightly fewer syllables, and slightly fewer words, and even fewer sentences. There are probably several reasons for this, but here is one: All we need to assume is

[handwritten margin note: greater amount of repackaging = fewer items retained]

that attention is required to "re-package" the materials (assembling the letters into syllables, or the syllables into words). With some amount of attention spent in this way, less attention is available for maintaining these items in working memory. Hence, the greater the amount of re-packaging, the fewer items that can be retained. (Simon, 1974, offers a slightly different explanation of this finding.)

Even with these costs of re-packaging, though, we should not understate the flexibility of the chunking strategy and, consequently, the flexibility of what working memory can hold. Consider a subject studied by Chase and Ericsson (Chase & Ericsson, 1978, 1979, 1982; Ericsson, Chase & Faloon, 1980). This subject happens to be a fan of track events and, when he hears numbers, he thinks of them as finishing times for races. ("3, 4, 9, 2," for example, becomes "3 minutes and 49 point 2 seconds, near world-record mile time.") The subject can then retain seven finishing times in memory, and that can involve 20 or 30 digits! He also associates numbers with people's ages and with historical dates. These chunks are then grouped into larger chunks, and then these into even larger chunks. For example, finishing times for individual racers can be chunked together into heats within a track meet. With strategies like this and with a considerable amount of practice, this subject has increased his apparent memory span from the "normal" seven digits to 79 digits.

[handwritten margin note: With practice, can improve chunking skills & ∴ increase what goes into working memory but you cannot increase actual size of working memory]

However, let's emphasize that what has changed through practice is merely the subject's chunking strategy, and not the size of working memory itself. For example, after three months of practice, the subject was tested with sequences of letters, rather than digits. With letters, the subject's memory span dropped back to a normal six consonants. Thus the seven-chunk limit is still in place, although, given the great flexibility of grouping, it seems odd to call this a "limit" for this remarkable subject.

What Is Working Memory?

Our discussion of chunking calls attention to a crucial issue—namely, how we should conceptualize working memory. The language of the modal model implies that working memory is something like a box in which information is stored or, continuing our earlier desk analogy, something like a location in which information can be displayed. On this view, learning would be a matter of transferring information from one position (working memory) to another (long-term memory), as though working memory were the "loading dock" just outside the large "memory warehouse." Likewise, memory *retrieval* would also be a matter of transfer—in this case, copying information from the long-term memory box into the working-memory box (out of the warehouse, back onto the dock).

However, contemporary authors regard this conception as far too static. As one concern, working memory might not be a "place" at all. Instead, working memory might refer to just those memories, *within* long-term storage, which are currently activated. By analogy, think of a huge choir, with most of the singers quiet, but with just a few singing out. Each member of the choir would represent a memory. The full set of singers would represent the broad contents of long-term memory. The group of singers currently active would then represent working memory. In this way, "working memory" wouldn't refer to those items in a specific *place*; it would instead refer to those items, within a broader set, which happen to be in a specific *state* (in our analogy: in the "state" of singing).

This conception is fully consistent with the data we have reviewed so far: The data indicate that working memory and long-term memory are qualitatively distinct from each other, with each following its own rules. That assertion would, of course, still be true within the active/dormant distinction just described.

The box conception of working memory may also be misleading in other ways: Our discussion of chunking indicates that some amount of "re-packaging" is taking place on the memory "loading dock." Indeed, we'll consider cases later in this chapter in which the re-packaging involves sophisticated analysis of the to-be-remembered materials, and often involves the finding of *connections* between the incoming information and other information already in storage. Given these points, the notion of a loading platform may be simplistic, as is the notion of mechanical transfer between one position and another. If working memory is a place at all, it's not a mere box. It is instead more like the office of a busy librarian, who is energetically categorizing, cataloging, and cross-referencing new material.

Moreover, our discussion of chunking also mentioned the *cost* of chunking, as though attention was required to re-package the to-be-remembered items. With attention spent in this way, less is available for maintaining items within working memory, and so there is a decrease in the total number of items that can be held. (As we said earlier, the greater the amount of re-packaging, the fewer items that can be retained.) Quite clearly, this implies that items in working memory don't just sit there; instead, they must be actively maintained, and this maintenance requires attention. This is just what one might expect if working memory were some sort of dynamic store, and *not* what you would expect if working memory were a passive "memory box."

This emphasis on the active, dynamic nature of working memory also raises questions about how we should measure working memory's capacity. In the previous section, we noted that this capacity has traditionally been measured by the "span" test. However, this test places too much emphasis on the number of slots in working memory, and not enough emphasis on working memory's capacity to *do things* with these slots. This concern has led researchers to develop more dynamic measures of working memory (see Figure 4.6), and these measures are far more effective in predicting subjects' ability to *use* working memory, than the more static digit-span measure (Cantor & Engle, 1993; Carpenter, Just & Shell, 1990; Daneman & Carpenter, 1980; Engle, Cantor & Carullo, 1992; Just & Carpenter, 1992).

The Diversity of Working Memory's Contents

The dynamic nature of working memory is also reflected in the considerations raised in Chapter 1, and it may be useful, in this context, to review some of those claims briefly. This will underscore our points about the active nature of working memory, but will also highlight the architectural design of working memory.

Some of the earliest theorizing about working memory came from Wil-

Figure 4.6

DYNAMIC MEASURES OF WORKING MEMORY

$(7 \times 7) + 1 = 50;$ dog
$(10 / 2) + 6 = 10;$ gas
$(4 \times 2) + 1 = 9;$ nose
$(3 / 1) + 1 = 4;$ beat
$(5 / 5) + 1 = 2;$ tree
$(8 \times 2) - 4 = 13;$ help
$(6 / 2) - 3 = 2;$ stay

The capacity of working memory has traditionally been measured by the digit-span task. In recent years, however, researchers have argued for more dynamic measures of working memory—measures that reflect the *efficiency* of working memory and not just its "holding capacity." Thus, subjects might see a series of items like the ones shown here. For each, subjects must announce out loud whether the equation is true or false, and then must read the associated word aloud. (For the first item, the subject would say: "True; dog.") After a series of such items, a cue appears, at which point subjects write down as many of the *words* as they can. This task seems peculiar, but does provide an accurate assessment of working memory's capacity. Performance in this task turns out to be well-correlated with many other measures, including, for example, verbal SAT scores.

liam James, at the end of the last century. James's (1890) term for this memory was "primary memory," and he argued that primary memory was inseparable from the current stream of thought. To put it loosely, James's proposal was that whatever you are thinking about right now, and whatever you are attending to, are represented in primary memory. This is certainly consistent with modern discussions of this memory, which have emphasized its role as the "workplace" for cognitive functioning.

This view of working memory's function leads to certain claims about this memory's contents or, at least, its potential contents. One can obviously think about, or attend to, a vast variety of events or stimuli or ideas—pictures and words and smells and abstract ideas, to mention just a few. If we take the proposal in the previous paragraph at face value, then working memory must be capable of holding this diversity of contents. Indeed, it is an important fact that we can think about *combinations* of pictures and words, abstract ideas and concrete ones, and so forth. Therefore, there must be somewhere in the mind that all these contents can be brought together "under one roof"; how else could we think about these combinations?

All of this demands considerable flexibility from working memory, specifically with regard to what information it can represent. These theoretical claims, however, seem not to fit with evidence showing a strong linkage between short-term remembering and a single type of information, namely, speech. For example, we mentioned in Chapter 1 that, when subjects make mistakes on working-memory tasks, they often make "sound alike" confusions and not "look alike" confusions—remembering D instead of B, but not F in place of E (Baddeley, 1966; Coltheart, 1993; Conrad, 1964; Conrad & Hull, 1964; Sperling, 1960; Sperling & Speelman, 1970). This is true even if subjects saw the list initially, rather than hearing it. This implies that the memory, even for a visually-presented list, draws on processes akin to hearing, and is vulnerable to the same confusions as hearing. This clearly points to a working memory reliance on some sort of speech-based code.

Chapter 1 also mentioned a related observation, the so-called **word-length effect**. This effect is observed when subjects' memory-span is measured, using lists of words. The measured span (whether 5 or 6 or 7) turns out to depend on how quickly the individual words can be pronounced (Baddeley, Thomson & Buchanan, 1975; Ellis & Henneley, 1980). And it is literally the pronunciation time that matters, and not the length of the word in number of letters or number of syllables. For example, subjects can remember slightly more words with lists like "tip, pack, cat"; these happen to be words that can be pronounced very quickly, in comparison to lists like "fine, wish, lob," all of which take slightly longer to say. This is true even if the words are *seen* initially, indicating once more that *saying the words* has a key role in working memory. Again, this implies that working memory often relies on a speech-like mode of representation. (For other evidence on this point, see Baddeley, 1966; Baddeley & Dale, 1966; Dale & Baddeley, 1969.)

The Working-Memory System

If working memory is to serve as the workplace of cognition, then it must be capable of storing all of the diverse contents that we can contemplate and attend. But there is some tension between this claim and working memory's strong inclination toward a single kind of content, one drawing on a speech-like code. That is, speech seems implicated in a wide range of working-memory tasks, and this has led many psychologists to argue that working memory is, at its essence, a "phonological" storage system.

In Chapter 1, we considered how these observations might be reconciled, namely, the proposal that working memory is not a single entity, but is instead a *system* built out of several components (Baddeley, 1986, 1992; Baddeley & Hitch, 1974; Salame & Baddeley, 1982). At the center of the system is the central executive, which is served by a number of specialized slave systems. One of the slave systems is the visuospatial buffer, used for storing "visual" materials, such as mental images (see Chapter 10). Another slave system is the rehearsal loop, crucial for subvocalized rehearsal.

The central executive of working memory is a multi-purpose processor, capable of running many different operations on many different types of material. The central executive is closely associated with the processes of attention: When one focuses attention on some task, this turns out to mean (among other things) that the central executive is engaged with that task. Thus, the executive is needed for many aspects of cognitive processing. (One might speculate that the central executive is closely related to the response-selector described in Chapter 3, but little evidence is available for evaluating this claim. For discussion, see Baddeley, 1993.)

If one has to work on some bit of information—think about or analyze the information, transform the information in some way—this requires the executive. But if one merely needs to "hold on" to some information, this can be done by the slave systems, which frees up the executive for other, more demanding, tasks. Roughly speaking, the executive is where the "real work" happens in working memory; the slave systems serve as internal scratch pads, storing information you will soon need, but don't need right now.

The advantages of this set-up are clear: It allows the executive to focus on more demanding tasks, turning mere storage over to the slaves. To get a sense of how this works, try reading the next few sentences while "holding onto" this list of numbers: "1, 4, 6, 4, 9." Got them? Now read on. You are probably repeating the numbers over and over to yourself, rehearsing them with your

[handwritten margin note: say 14649 while continuing to read q.b Why?]

inner voice. But this turns out to require very little effort, so that you can continue reading while doing this rehearsal. And, of course, the moment you need to recall the numbers (what were they?), they are available to you. The claim, of course, is that the numbers were maintained by one of the slave systems, namely, the rehearsal loop. While the slave system provided this maintenance, the central executive was free to continue reading.

The Rehearsal Loop

In Chapter 1, we also argued that the slave systems themselves involve multiple components. To reiterate the claims made there, the rehearsal loop appears to be comprised of two parts, sometimes referred to as the inner ear and the inner voice (Baddeley, 1986). To remember a list of numbers, for example, the executive uses the "inner voice" to pronounce the numbers. The activity of speaking is immensely well practiced and so, in the terms used in Chapter 3, most of the components of speaking are highly automatized. Hence, minimal attention is required to direct the inner voice, and this is what allows the executive to launch the inner speech, but then deal with other matters.

The inner voice pronounces the materials, and this causes a trace of this pronunciation to be loaded into the inner ear. In essence, an auditory image is created. This image will gradually fade away and, when it does, the cycle must be restarted: One again pronounces the material, using the inner voice, and so the image is "refreshed." The executive will be needed periodically, to restart each cycle. But, while the cycle is going on, the inner voice and inner ear can carry out their functions without supervision.

All of this provides a ready account for why speech-like effects are observed in working memory. The central executive can deal with any sort of material—concrete or abstract, visual or verbal, but the rehearsal loop is specialized for dealing with *verbal* material. So in this sense the rehearsal loop is limited in its function. Nonetheless, many tasks can be treated as verbal tasks and, moreover, the rehearsal loop is a highly-efficient, well-practiced aid for the executive. Consequently, the executive will rely on the loop in a wide range of tasks.

The use of this loop will, in turn, shape memory performance. Since, for example, the inner ear literally draws on mechanisms used for ordinary hearing, the traits of the inner ear will resemble those of actual audition. Consequently, inputs that can be confused with each other will also be confusable in the inner ear. It is no surprise, therefore, that errors in short-term remembering reflect perceptual confusions. Likewise, the inner voice literally draws on mechanisms ordinarily used for speech. Words that can be said more quickly with overt speech can also be more readily pronounced by the inner voice. This provides our account of the word-length effect: The inner voice is more efficient in rehearsing quickly-pronounceable words and so, when the rehearsal loop is used, quickly-pronounceable words are more easily remembered.

As we discussed in Chapter 1, various experiments have tested this proposal. For example, since the inner voice draws on the mechanisms of speech, subjects cannot speak and use the inner voice at the same time. Thus a concurrent articulation task (e.g., repeating "tah-tah-tah" over and over) should block use of the inner voice. Since we have hypothesized that it is use of the inner voice that produces the word-length effect, concurrent articulation should eliminate the word-length effect. This is the case (Vallar & Baddeley, 1982).

Concurrent articulation should also eliminate the sound-alike confusions (with visually-presented materials) because now, with the inner voice unavailable, there is no way for the memory items to "reach" the inner ear. This, too, is correct. Moreover, either concurrent articulation or the presentation of irrelevant sounds (disrupting the inner ear) should diminish working-memory capacity, because either of these manipulations will block use of the rehearsal loop. Thus, with either of these manipulations in place, measured memory capacity will equal the capacity of the total system minus the capacity of the loop. Again, this prediction is correct.

Finally, the effects of irrelevant sounds and of concurrent articulation should be redundant with each other: Both the inner voice and the inner ear are required for the rehearsal loop's function, and so blocking the use of either one should prevent use of the loop. We would expect no further "harm" from blocking *both* the inner voice and the inner ear: A loop that is unavailable for two reasons is the same as a loop that is unavailable for a single reason. This prediction, too, has been confirmed. (For an expansion of these points, see Chapter 1; for a detailed discussion of the evidence, see Baddeley, 1986; Richardson, 1984.)

In summary, the notion of a working-memory system seems well-supported by the data. We should reiterate, though, that the rehearsal loop we have described is only one of the slave systems within the working memory system. We have already mentioned the "visuospatial sketch pad," presumably used to rehearse visual or spatial materials, much as the phonological loop is used to rehearse verbal materials (Baddeley, 1986, 1990; Smyth & Scholey, 1994). It also appears that the deaf use a *manual* rehearsal loop (Bellugi, Klima & Siple, 1975; Shand, 1982), and there is evidence that the hearing population can be taught to use a different manual system to perform rehearsal (Reisberg, Rappaport & O'Shaughnessy, 1984; for other evidence of haptic short-term remembering, see Bowers, Mollenhauer, & Luxford, 1990; Murray, Ward & Hockley, 1975).

Finally, many studies have sought to detail the functions of these various slave systems. Some of the evidence derives from neuropsychological patients who have lost use of one or more loops (e.g., Vallar & Shallice, 1990). Other evidence derives from studies in which use of the loops is experimentally prevented. As an example of this evidence, it now appears that use of the phonological loop is crucial in the acquisition of new language skills, including the acquisition of new vocabulary. This has been documented in the acquisition of words from a foreign language (Baddeley, Papagno & Vallar, 1988; Papagno, Valentine & Baddeley, 1991), and also in young children's acquisition of new words in their own language (Gathercole & Baddeley, 1989, 1990).

The Differences between Working Memory and Long-Term Memory

Let's pause to take stock. As we have already noted, we are starting to change the tone of our discussion in important ways. Working memory seems not to be a box or a storage container. Instead, working memory may simply be the name we have given to an organized set of activities—the activities of the inner voice and inner ear, and, above all, the activities of the central executive. In essence, to say that items are "in working memory" may be equivalent to saying those items are "being worked on by the central executive." And, of course, the executive can do many different things with these items—linking memories to each other, interconnecting ideas, drawing inferences, and so on. All of this implies that an understanding of the central executive may be elusive—we will need to understand a great deal about the ongoing nature of thought. But, for our purposes, this emphasizes the activity inherent in this aspect of the working-memory system, and, with that, the active nature of working memory.

Despite this change in tone, though, we can't lose track of the already-established facts. Thus, our discussion of the working-memory system still leaves us thinking about working memory as limited in its storage capacity, but easily accessed. We are also still conceiving of working memory as playing a pivotal role in the sequence of thoughts, since materials currently being thought about are represented in this memory. This has the consequence, however, of making this store somewhat fragile: Every shift in attention will cause new items to be placed in working memory, and these newly-arriving materials will displace early items from storage.

Last but not least, there are many entrance paths to working memory: Working memory may contain representations of the last few items noticed in the environment, or it may contain items retrieved from long-term memory, or it may contain the products of one's current thoughts. Working memory can also be filled by "recycling" the items currently in this memory—this is, in effect, what memory rehearsal is all about.

We are still thinking about long-term memory, in contrast, as vast in size, since this is the repository in which we carry around all the things that we know. It also seems not so easy to enter information in long-term memory: Items must be attended and contemplated for some time before they can be entered into long-term memory; this played a key role in our account of the primacy effect. Likewise, it is often difficult to locate information within this warehouse—memory retrieval can take some time and, for that matter, may sometimes fail altogether. (We will have more to say about cases of retrieval failure in Chapters 5 and 6.)

Finally, while much of the evidence we have mentioned comes from human studies, there is no reason to believe that this description is unique to humans. Other species might need to keep some information activated and immediately available, while leaving other information in storage. Given this, it is no surprise that several of the procedures we have described yield parallel results in other species. For example, it seems that active rehearsal is needed to maintain information in pigeons' working memories, or to transfer information into long-term memory (Wagner, 1979, 1981). In addition, research has shown that pigeons show approximately the same primacy and recency effects as humans do, if asked to learn about series of stimuli (Olton, 1978; Roberts, 1981).

Entering Long-Term Storage: The Role of the Intent to Learn

We have by now said a great deal about the nature of working memory, and about the relationship between working memory and long-term memory. But we still need to explain how material enters long-term memory in the first place. We have provided a number of important suggestions about this issue in our discussion of primacy. But the time has come to tackle this topic directly.

Two Types of Rehearsal

In our earlier discussion, we suggested that the more an item was rehearsed, the more likely it is to be remembered. But we have to complicate this claim in an important way, because a great deal depends on how an item is rehearsed. It turns out that subjects have at least two different forms of rehearsal available to them. Both forms involve continued attention to the items being rehearsed, with the consequence that the rehearsed items remain available in working memory. But the two forms of rehearsal are in all other ways rather different from each other.

As one option, subjects can engage in item-specific rehearsal, also referred to as **maintenance rehearsal**. In this case, the subjects simply focus on the to-be-remembered items themselves, with little thought about what the items mean, or how they are related to other bits of knowledge. You can think of this as a rote, mechanical process, recycling items in working memory simply by repeating them over and over. Evidence indicates that this form of rehearsal requires relatively little effort, but is also quite limited in what it accomplishes. Specifically, maintenance rehearsal is effective in holding onto materials for a short time but, if you want to recall the material later on, maintenance rehearsal is of little use.

Contrast this with relational, or **elaborative rehearsal**. Roughly speaking, this form of rehearsal involves thinking about what the to-be-remembered items mean, and how they are related to each other, or to other things in the surroundings, or to other things you already know. This form of rehearsal often requires more effort than mere maintenance, but also pays off in the long run, since items rehearsed in this fashion will be easier to recall later on.

The choice between these rehearsal types is largely up to the memorizer, as suggested by this example: Imagine that you want to telephone a friend, but don't know the number. You might call directory assistance, or look up the number in the telephone book. Once you've learned the number, you recite it over and over to yourself, while finding a quarter for the phone, and then dialing. But then it turns out that the line is busy, so you wait a minute or so, and try again. You then discover that you don't have a clue what the number is, even though you knew it just moments earlier, even though you had the number in memory long enough to dial it the first time. The number was initially rehearsed via mere maintenance. There was no reason to use the more effortful elaborative rehearsal, because you anticipated that you would only need to remember the number for a few seconds—long enough to dial it. But when that expectation turns out to be wrong, the limitations of maintenance rehearsal become clear.

A more formal demonstration of this effect was provided in a study by Craik and Watkins (1973). Subjects were asked to listen to a series of word lists, and to monitor each list for words beginning with the letter "B". Subjects were told that, at the end of each list, their task was to report the *most recent word* on the list that began with a "B". Thus, if the subject heard "basket, spoon, telephone, cub, lamp, fish, hair, plant, lake, book, chair, foot, baby, hill, tree," the subject was to report "baby." Then subjects heard a new list, and again had to report the most recent "B-word." Things proceeded in this fashion until the end of the session when, to subjects' surprise, they were asked to write down *all* of the "B-words" they had heard, during the entire session. Up until that moment, subjects had no idea their memories were being tested, and no idea that they had reason to remember "B-words" other than the most recent one.

Consider this task from the subjects' point of view. While listening to the list, subjects are presumably keeping track of just one word—namely, the most recent "B-word." To continue with the example from before, when subjects hear "basket," they should try to remember it, on the chance that the list will contain no other "B-words"—in that case, "basket" would be the word to be reported. The moment subjects hear "book," they can cease thinking about "basket," since they now know that "basket" won't be the last "B-word" on the list.

In this set-up, subjects are quite likely to rely on maintenance rehearsal. Bear in mind that this form of rehearsal is easier, and so subjects will use it whenever they can "get away with it." And subjects believe that they *can* get away with it in this task: They anticipate no memory test, so don't need to take steps to promote long-term retention. Moreover, during the list presentations subjects only need to keep track of one word at a time, and so nothing will interrupt their continued maintenance of this single item.

Let's now add one further complication. The stimuli in this experiment were actually devised with a scheme in mind. Sometimes the "B-words" were positioned very closely together on the list (like "book" and "baby," with just two words in between). Other words (like "basket" in our example) were followed by several words not beginning with "B." How should this matter for memory? Words like "book" were presumably kept in working memory for only a short time, since this word was quickly followed by (and so displaced by) another "B-word." Consequently, "book" was only rehearsed a few times. Words like "basket" were kept in working memory for a longer period, and so were rehearsed many times.

If subjects are only doing maintenance rehearsal, then memory performance in this procedure should be very poor. In addition, it should not matter how much of this rehearsal subjects did: If maintenance rehearsal is an ineffective preparation for the memory test, then it is irrelevant whether subjects did a lot, or a little, of this ineffective activity. Therefore, we should expect similar results if a "B-word" was quickly followed by another (and so rehearsed only briefly) or if a "B-word" was followed by another only after a long interval. All of this is exactly what the data show (Figure 4.7).

Another study makes the same point: There are certain objects, and certain scenes, that we encounter day after day after day. Each day, you pass the

Figure 4.7

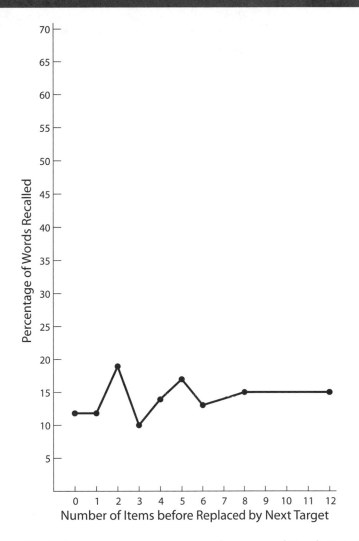

"MAINTENANCE" REHEARSAL DOES NOT LEAD TO BETTER RECALL

When subjects do not expect a memory test, there is no relation between the amount of rehearsal and likelihood of recall. The number of rehearsals was manipulated in this study by varying the position of target words within the presentation list. Targets that were soon "replaced" by another target were presumably rehearsed only a few times; targets that were followed by another target only after many intervening items were presumably rehearsed many times. [After Craik & Watkins, 1973.]

same houses on your way to school. Each day, you see the same forks in the cafeteria, the same furniture in your home. But the Craik and Watkins result implies that these countless exposures may not be enough to lay down useful memory traces. Instead, recallable memories will be created only if you do elaborative rehearsal, that is, only if you engage the materials in an active fashion. This implies that you may have poor memory for these items in your surround, despite the fact that you have seen these items literally tens of thousands of times.

In fact, evidence suggests that you do not remember the familiar objects in your world very well. For example, try drawing a picture of a Lincoln penny. Obviously, Lincoln's head is on the "heads" side, but what else is? Is Lincoln facing to the left, or to the right, on the penny? Most people do very poorly with these questions; indeed, they often don't have a clue which way Lincoln is facing (Nickerson & Adams, 1979). Even though you encounter the penny day after day after day, you seem unable to recall what it looks like. Mere exposure is plainly limited in its memory effects.

It should be said, though, that maintenance, or item-specific, rehearsal *does* have a lasting impact if memory is tested in just the right way. (For a review, see Wixted, 1991; we will return to this issue in Chapter 5.) However, this doesn't touch the point we are trying to make here: Quite plainly, maintenance rehearsal is distinct from elaborative rehearsal, and, more important, maintenance rehearsal is a poor preparation for many forms of memory testing.

One final point should also be mentioned about maintenance rehearsal: We have spoken as if subjects make a strategic choice between maintenance and elaborative rehearsal—as though they know about both forms of rehearsal, know the advantages and disadvantages of each, and so make a deliberate choice about which is appropriate for their present circumstances. All of this does seem true, but with an important proviso: Subjects are generally aware of none of this. Subjects' choice between rehearsal strategies is sensibly influenced by various factors in the task setting, implying that subjects are sensitive to the circumstances that permit maintenance, and the factors that demand elaboration (Watkins & Watkins, 1974; Wixted, 1991). But subjects make these decisions without realizing they are doing so. Apparently, the choice is sensibly tuned to the task setting but also is quite automatic.

Incidental Learning, Intentional Learning, and Depth of Processing

What about elaborative, or relational, rehearsal? How does it function? We have also implied that subjects shift to this more effortful form of rehearsal when they anticipate an upcoming memory test, i.e., when they intend to memorize. But can we be more precise about what this intention to remember actually contributes?

The evidence suggests that the effects of intention are actually *indirect*. That is, when subjects are trying to memorize, they approach the material in a certain way, and it is the approach, rather than the intent itself, that has consequences for memory. As an illustration, consider the following procedure. The experiment is a bit complicated, so we have illustrated the design in Figure 4.8. (Actually, this experiment represents a composite of many procedures, all of which converge on the same conclusion. An early procedure

Figure 4.8

Type of processing	"Incidental learning"	"Intentional learning"
STUDYING THE EFFECTS OF INTENTION AND THE EFFECTS OF LEVELS OF PROCESSING ON MEMORY		
"Shallow"	Are these words in the same typeface? "HOUSE—trick"	Are these words in the same typeface? "HOUSE—trick" *and,* in addition, you'll have to remember these words later on!
"Medium"	Do these words rhyme? "BALL—TALL"	Do these words rhyme? "BALL—TALL" *and,* in addition, you'll have to remember these words later on!
"Deep"	Are these words synonyms? "CAR—AUTOMOBILE"	Are these words synonyms? "CAR—AUTOMOBILE" *and,* in addition, you'll have to remember these words later on!

(handwritten annotations: "poorly" next to "Shallow"; "quite well" below "Deep")

Illustrated here is a composite of many procedures examining how memory performance is shaped by the intention to memorize, and also by how one approaches the to-be-remembered material at the time of learning.

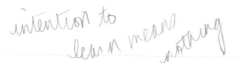
(handwritten note: intention to learn means nothing)

by Hyde & Jenkins, 1969, is quite close to the one we're about to describe, but related data have been reported by Bobrow & Bower, 1969; Craik & Lockhart, 1972; Hyde & Jenkins, 1973; Jacoby, 1978; Lockhart, Craik & Jacoby, 1976; Parkin, 1984; Slamecka & Graf, 1978, and others.)

Subjects in a lab are told that we are studying how quickly they can make judgments about letters. No indication is given that we are actually interested in memory. Subjects are shown a series of word pairs on a computer screen. For each pair, they decide as quickly as possible whether the two words are typed in the same case (both capitalized or both not) or typed in different cases. Let's refer to this as shallow processing, since subjects are engaging the information in a relatively superficial fashion. (Other examples of shallow processing would be a decision about whether the words are printed in red or in green, high or low on the screen, and so on.) At the end of this sequence, the subjects are surprised to learn that their memories are being tested, and they are asked to write down as many of the words as they can remember. This is the top-left cell in the design shown in Figure 4.8. This sort of procedure assesses incidental learning, that is, learning in the absence of any intention to learn.

A second group of subjects is given the same instructions, but with one change. Like the first group, these subjects are told that we want them to make judgments about word pairs, specifically, whether the words in each pair are in the same case or in different cases. This group, however, is also told that their memories will be tested, so that when the memory test arrives, it comes as no surprise. These subjects, therefore, have been led to do shallow processing, but they are doing this processing in the context of the intention to learn. This is the top-right cell in Figure 4.8, and examines intentional learning.

A third group of subjects is brought into the lab, and they are told that we are studying how quickly people can make judgments about rhyme. If the two words shown on the computer screen rhyme, they press one button; if not, they press a different button. Again, a surprise memory test follows this presentation. These subjects are doing what we might call medium processing.

A fourth group is given the same rhyme task, but is warned about the upcoming memory test. This group is doing medium processing *with* the intention to memorize the words they are viewing.

The fifth and sixth groups (the bottom row in the design) are led to do deep processing—that is, to think about the meaning of the items. Subjects in the fifth group are shown pairs of words on a computer screen, with the instruction that they should press one button if the words on the screen are synonymous, another button if they are not. No warning is given about a memory test, and therefore, these subjects presumably have no intention to memorize the words. Subjects in the sixth group are given the same task but are warned about the memory test, so this group is doing deep processing *with* the intention to learn.

Let's frame the results in terms of Figure 4.8. When the time comes for recall, subjects from the bottom-left cell (deep processing with *no* intention to learn) perform quite well, while subjects from the top-left cell (shallow processing) do rather poorly. In other words, attention to meaning really pays off for recall, while attention to surface characteristics produces little memory benefit. Moderate levels of processing (attention to sound) produce a moderate level of recall performance.

What about the right column of the table? Here the result is quite straightforward: There is no difference between the left and right columns of the table. That is, the intention to learn seems to add nothing. For purposes of memorizing, there is *no difference* between shallow processing with the intention to learn, and shallow processing without this intention. Likewise, there is no difference between deep processing with the intention to learn, and deep processing without this intention.

The Intention to Learn

In the design just sketched, incidental learning and intentional learning yielded identical patterns, indicating little role for the intention to learn. But let's take a closer look at the importance of intentions, by considering one last group of subjects: This group is told that they are about to be shown words on a computer screen, and they are asked to memorize these words. No further instructions are given, so subjects are free to approach this memorization in any way they choose. These subjects are then shown a sequence just like the ones described in the previous section.

When subjects are instructed to memorize, each subject will use the strategy that he or she thinks best. And, in fact, different subjects have different beliefs about the "best way" to memorize. Some subjects, for example, have discovered that thinking about meaning is an effective strategy and so, if asked to memorize, they spontaneously draw on deep processing. Other subjects seem to believe that the best way to memorize is by listening to the sound of the word over and over. These latter subjects will end up indistinguishable from the subjects in the middle-right-hand cell in Figure 4.8, while the subjects who spontaneously employ deep processing will end up equivalent to subjects in the lower-right-hand cell. Of course, the subjects we were discussing before had been *instructed* to use a particular form of processing, while the subjects we are now considering have self-instructed. But, as it turns out, this difference, between instruction and self-instruction, is irrelevant to performance.

All of this leads to the expectation that results from this "just memorize"

If subjects tell themselves to use deep processing

condition will be rather variable, depending on *how* subjects self-instruct, i.e., on what strategy they choose. If subjects have figured out, on their own, that attention to meaning aids memory, then they perform quite well. More precisely, they perform as well as—but no better than—subjects specifically told to do deep processing. If subjects select a less-than-optimal strategy, then they perform at a lower level. And, in fact, it turns out that subjects do often have peculiar beliefs about what "works" in placing material into memory; if these subjects choose their memorizing strategy based on these (faulty) beliefs, their performance will be poor. (For studies of subjects' spontaneous strategies, see Anderson & Bower, 1972; Brown, 1979; Hyde & Jenkins, 1969; Nelson, 1976; Postman, 1964.)

As an example, consider a case reported by John Anderson (1985, pp. 112–113), a researcher whose work we will discuss extensively in Chapter 7. Anderson reports that he himself served as a subject in a memory experiment during his sophomore year of college. He was determined to perform well and, therefore, applied his personal theory of memorizing: that the best strategy was to say the items out loud, over and over, preferably as loudly and as quickly as possible. Needless to say, this "loud and fast" theory stands in contrast to the true means of improving memory and, to Anderson's embarrassment, his performance was the worst in his class.

What, therefore, should we conclude about the role of intention in guiding the learning process? Clearly, intention does matter: A subject who has no intention to learn may end up doing maintenance processing, rather than elaborative processing, and this obviously will affect what is remembered. Likewise, a subject who intends to learn will select the strategy he or she thinks best and, as we have seen, this choice of strategy will also affect the quality of memory. But these effects of intention are all *indirect*. The intention to learn leads subjects to approach the materials in a certain fashion, and it is the *approach*, not the intention, that matters for memory. If we can lead subjects to approach the materials in the same way without the intention, we get the same memory results.

The Role of Meaning and Memory Connections

We've now seen that memory is strongly influenced by how subjects engage the materials at the time of learning. But what does this "engagement" amount to? Attention to *meaning*, it seems, leads to good recall, but why is this? And what about other study techniques? Are there other, more effective ways to learn?

Making Memories Findable

A great many studies have shown that attention to meaning does indeed promote subsequent recall (e.g., Elias & Perfetti, 1973; Jacoby & Craik, 1979; Till & Jenkins, 1973). What lies behind this effect, and what exactly does attention to meaning accomplish? Our understanding of these issues has evolved over the years (for an early view, see Craik & Lockhart, 1972; Lockhart et al., 1976; for more recent developments, see Baddeley, 1978; Craik & Tulving, 1975; Nelson, Walling & McEvoy, 1979; Postman, Thompkins & Gray, 1978). From a modern perspective, though, it seems that several factors are relevant. A pivotal one is that the benefits of deep processing may not lie in the learning process per se. Instead, deep processing may influence *subsequent* events. More precisely, attention to meaning may promote recall by virtue of facilitating *retrieval* of the memory, later on.

Consider what happens when a library acquires a new book. It would be no good at all if the book were merely tossed on a shelf somewhere. In that case, users of the library might never be able to locate the book when they wanted it. Indeed, unless the book was properly entered into the catalogue, users of the library might not even realize the book was in the building. Obviously, then, the library must place the book on the shelf and also arrange for appropriate cataloguing, so that the book can be located by users. And, of course, cataloguing doesn't in any sense influence the book's "arrival" into the library—the book isn't "more firmly" or "more strongly" in the library, thanks to the cataloguing. Instead, cataloguing has its effects on events subsequent to the book's arrival—that is, it influences the subsequent retrieval of the book.

Likewise for the vast library that is our memory: The task of "learning" is not merely a matter of placing information into long-term memory. Learning also needs to establish some appropriate indexing; it must, in effect, pave a path to the newly acquired information, so that this information can be retrieved at some future point. In essence, then, one of the main chores of memory *acquisition* is to lay the groundwork for memory *retrieval*.

We now need to ask what it is that facilitates memory retrieval. There are, in fact, several ways to search through memory, but a great deal depends on memory *connections*. Connections allow one memory to trigger another, and then that to trigger another, so that, like a series of dominoes falling, one is "led" to the sought-after information. If remembering the experimenter's shirt reminds you of materials you learned during the experiment, this will help you to locate these materials in memory. In this case, there must have been some connection in your thoughts between the shirt and the target materials, and this is what triggered the reminding. Likewise, if remembering the third word on a list reminds you of the fourth and fifth, this too will improve memory performance, because of connections among the items.

This line of reasoning easily accounts for why attention to meaning promotes memory. Attention to meaning is likely to lead to understanding and, at least in part, understanding is a matter of "seeing connections." When you understand the meaning of a story, you understand how the pieces of the story fit together, you understand the resemblances between this story and other stories you've read, you know what the story's implications are. Each of these connections, each of these relationships, will serve as a potential reminder, and so will help you to remember the story later on. Likewise for attention to the meaning of a picture, or a sentence, or even a list of words.

These are broad claims and, in fact, it will take us several chapters to work through all the evidence for these claims. One bit of evidence, though, is immediately accessible: On the hypotheses just sketched, attention to meaning should not be the only way to improve memory. Other strategies should have similar effects, provided that these strategies help the memorizer to establish memory connections.

As an example, consider a study by Craik and Tulving (1975). Subjects were shown a word, and then were shown a sentence with one word left out. The subjects' task was to decide whether the word fit into the sentence. For example, subjects might see the word, "chicken," then the sentence, "She cooked the _____ ." Subjects' response would be "yes," since the word does fit in this sentence. After a series of these trials, there was a surprise memory test, with subjects asked to remember all the words they had seen.

This experiment was arranged so that some of the sentences shown to subjects were simple, while others were more elaborate. For example, "She cooked the _____" would be a simple sentence, while a more complex sentence might be "The great bird swooped down and carried off the struggling _____ ." The data showed that words were more likely to be remembered if they appeared with these rich, elaborate sentences.

The decision about whether each word fits with its sentence depends, in large part, on the word's meaning. Consequently, subjects had to think about the meaning of *every* word presented to them. If this were all that matters for memory, then all of the words should be remembered equally. But that's not what the data show. Instead, "deep and elaborate" processing led to better recall than deep processing alone.

These data fit well, though, with our claims about the importance of memory connections. The elaborate sentences offer the potential for many connections. Perhaps the "great bird swooped" sentence calls to mind a barnyard scene, with the hawk carrying a chicken away. In this way, the richness of the sentence can call other thoughts to mind, each of which provides a potential connection, and thus a potential **retrieval path**. All of this seems less likely for the impoverished sentences. These will evoke fewer connections and will establish a narrower set of retrieval paths. Consequently, they'll be less likely to be recalled later on.

Organizing and Memorizing

We have just suggested that memory connections are crucial for recall, since these connections provide a means of locating material, within memory, later on. Sometimes, these connections link the to-be-remembered material to other material already in memory. In other cases, these connections will link one aspect of the material to some other aspect. This will ensure that, if any *part* of the material is recalled, then all will be recalled.

How does one go about discovering (or creating) these connections? Over fifty years ago, a German psychologist, George Katona, argued that the key lies in *organization* (Katona, 1940). Katona's central argument was that the two processes—organization and memorization—are inseparable: We memorize well when we discover the order within the material. Said differently, if we find (or impose) an organization on the material, we will easily remember it.

These suggestions are fully compatible with the conception we are developing, since what organization provides is, once again, memory connections. Some of these connections will be within the material being learned (as, for example, when you see why the left-hand side of a painting "makes sense" in relation to the right-hand side). In many cases, the organization will also require connections between the newly acquired information and things you already know. (When you see how the painting "makes sense," it is probably because you understand the pattern of the painting with reference to other beliefs you have—perhaps beliefs about that style of painting, or beliefs about the objects being depicted in the painting.) In either case, Katona's claim about the utility of organization merges nicely with our argument about the importance of connections, and so we can take the evidence for his claim as further support for our proposal. In the next sections, we consider that evidence.

Mnemonics

For thousands of years, people have wished for "better" memories—they have wished to learn more quickly, and to remember more accurately. Motivated by these wishes, a number of techniques have been designed to "improve" memory, techniques known as **mnemonic strategies**. Some of these mnemonics are modern inventions, but most are very old, dating back to ancient Greece.

There are actually many different mnemonic strategies, but most of them involve a straightforward and familiar principle, namely, that organization helps. If an organization can be found within the materials, then locating this organization will lead to good memory. If an organization cannot be found, then often an "external" organization can be imposed on the material, with the same memory benefit.

Let us take a concrete case. You want to remember a list of largely unrelated items, perhaps the entries on your shopping list, or a list of questions you want to ask when you next see your advisor. You might try to remember this list using one of the so-called **peg-word systems**. Peg-word systems begin with a well-organized structure, such as this one:

One is a bun.
Two is a shoe.
Three is a tree.
Four is a door.
Five is a hive.
Six are sticks.
Seven is heaven.
Eight is a gate.
Nine is a line.
Ten is a hen.

Not great poetry, but highly memorable, since you already know the numbers, and the rhyme scheme makes the sentences easy to reconstruct. The rhymes provide ten "peg-words"—"bun, shoe, tree," and so on—and, in memorizing something, you can "hang" the to-be-remembered materials on these "pegs." Let's imagine, therefore, that you are trying to memorize the list of topics you want to discuss with your advisor. If you want to discuss your unhappiness with your chemistry class, you might form an association between chemistry and the first peg, *bun*. You might, for example, form a mental image of a hamburger bun floating in an Erlenmeyer flask. If you also want to discuss possible graduate school plans, form an association between some aspect of those plans and the next peg, *shoe*—perhaps you might think about how you hope to avoid paying your way in graduate school by selling shoes. If you continue in this fashion, then, when the time comes to meet with your advisor, all you have to do is think through that silly rhyme again. When you think of "one is a bun," it is highly likely that the image of the flask (and therefore of chemistry lab) will come to mind.

Hundreds of variations on this strategy are possible, some taught in self-help courses (you've probably seen the ads—"How to Improve Your Memory!"), some presented by corporations as part of management training, and on and on. Some mnemonic strategies rely heavily on visualization (for example, we mentioned that you might form an image of the bun floating in the flask), others do not. (For further discussion of imagery and visualization, see Chapter 10.) But all employ the same basic scheme. To remember a list with no apparent organization, impose an organization on it, by employing a skeleton or scaffold that is itself tightly organized. The number-rhymes provides one such scaffold, but other scaffolds are easily located.

For example, the ancient Greeks used a system called the **method of loci**, to remember speeches they were to give in the Forum. In this method, the memory pegs are not words, but places. To use this technique to memorize a speech, you might think about a walk you often take, and then associate the various topics within the speech with conspicuous locations along that walk. Thus, you might form an association between your first topic and your front door. (Imagine, for example, that you wanted to start your speech by talking about your childhood. You might, in that case, think about some favorite childhood toy dangling from the door knob.) Next, you might form some association between your second topic and the sidewalk just outside your house. When the time comes to remember, you would simply think about the familiar routine of locking your door, walking down the sidewalk, and so on, and, at each position along the route, the relevant association is available.

In later chapters, we will consider why these systems work. Our point for now is simply that these systems *do* work (Bower, 1970, 1972; Bower & Reitman, 1972; Christen & Bjork, 1976; Higbee, 1977; Roediger, 1980; Ross & Lawrence, 1968; Yates, 1966), not only helping you to remember individual items, but also helping you to remember those items in a specific sequence. All of this confirms our central claims: Organizing improves recall. Mnemonics work by imposing an organization on the to-be-remembered materials, by establishing connections between the material and some other easily-remembered structure.

Recall and Clustering

Mnemonic techniques can dramatically improve memory by imposing order on the to-be-remembered material. But you might object: These techniques are based on tricks and unusual strategies one might employ, if you were especially motivated to remember. What do these have to do with "ordinary" remembering?

It is easy to show, however, that subjects spontaneously use organizing schemes to help them remember, without special instruction to do so, and without extraordinary motivation. A lot of the evidence comes from experiments similar to those discussed earlier in this chapter. Subjects are given lists of 25 to 35 words to learn. They hear the words once, and repeat them back immediately. It turns out that subjects' recall performance is considerably better if the words are not chosen at random, but fall into categories. Subjects will perform quite well, for example, with this list: "Apple, plum, cherry, pear, shoe, pants, shirt, belt, sofa, chair."

For that matter, we don't have to present the list category by category. If we take the same items, and scramble the sequence, the availability of a categorization scheme still seems to help subjects. In fact, if the items are scrambled together in presentation, they will be "unscrambled" when the subject reports them back. That is, we can present subjects with this list: "apple, shoe, sofa, plum, cherry, chair, belt." In the recall test, subjects are likely to report back one category of items (perhaps the furniture), then pause, then report back one of the other categories, and so on. This highly reliable pattern is referred to as **clustering** in free recall. The recall is "free" since we have allowed the subjects to report back the items in any sequence they choose. Nonetheless, the sequence they do choose consistently shows the pattern just described (Bousfield, 1953; Bower, Clark, Lesgold & Winzenz, 1969; Cofer, Bruce & Reicher, 1966).

You might still object that these are artificial materials, since they fall so neatly into categories. Perhaps this by itself is what triggers a clustering strategy. That objection also quickly falls, through experiments on subjective organization. There are actually several ways to run these experiments (Buschke, 1977; Tulving, 1962). In one, Tulving presented subjects with a list to learn, as described already. In this experiment, though, there were no obvious categories of material in the list; the list was instead randomly chosen, with no apparent structure or order. Subjects were tested on this list three times. First, they were asked to report back the items immediately after the presentation, as is normal in these experiments. Some time later, they were tested a second time, and had to recall as much as they could about the earlier-presented list. Then, after another delay, subjects were tested a third time on this same list.

Tulving reasoned that subjects were probably spontaneously organizing the list of randomly-chosen words. With no obvious order in the list, the organization subjects would choose would be idiosyncratic, with each subject finding his or her own pattern. We could nonetheless find out how successful subjects had been in finding an organization by comparing the results of the first and second tests. We look at the sequence of report, and ask what items were reported close together, what items were not. If a subject has tightly organized the list, we might expect an absolutely identical order of report in the first two tests. If the subject has found no organization, there is no reason to expect the order-of-report on the second testing to match that of the first.

Tulving used a statistical assessment of match-between-the-orderings as a measurement of the degree of "subjective organization" that had been imposed on the list by the subject. If organization is critical for remembering, then we make the following prediction: The more agreement between the first order-of-report and the second, i.e., the greater the degree of inferred subjective organization, the better subjects will do on the third, and final test. In short, the earlier stability of organization should pay off in better remembering. This is what the data show. With no coaching, with no special instructions, and with materials that are randomly chosen, subjects spontaneously rely on an organizational strategy, and the better they can organize, the better they can recall (cf. Bower et al., 1969; Mandler & Pearlstone, 1966).

Understanding and Memorizing

So far, we have been focusing on memory for rather impoverished stimulus materials—for example, lists of randomly selected words. This allowed us to argue that subjects' recall is improved by organization even when there is nothing, within the materials to encourage that organization. In our day-to-day lives, though, we typically want to remember more meaningful, and more complicated, material—we wish to remember the episodes of our lives, the details of rich scenes we have observed, the plots of movies we have seen, or the many-step arguments we have read in a book. Do the same principles apply to these cases?

The answer to this question is clearly "yes." Our memory for events, or pictures, or complex bodies of knowledge is enormously dependent on our being able to organize the to-be-remembered material. We remember best what we have organized best; we remember poorly when we can neither find nor create an organizing scheme. With these more complicated materials, though, our best bet for organization is not some arbitrary skeleton, like those used in peg-word systems. Instead, the optimal organization of these complex materials is generally dependent on *understanding*. That is, we remember best what we understand best.

There are many ways to show that this is true. For example, one can give subjects a sentence or paragraph to read, and test their comprehension by asking questions about the material, or asking them to paraphrase the material. Some time later, we can test subjects' memory for this material. Moreover, we can use memory materials difficult enough so that understanding is not guaranteed and, in this way, we can look at different degrees of success in understanding, and ask how these influence memory.

The results are straightforward: If subjects understand a sentence or a paragraph, they will better remember it. If their paraphrase was more accurate or more complete, so will be their report from memory, whether we give the memory test ten minutes later or ten days later. If subjects could accurately answer questions immediately after reading the material, they will probably be able to remember the material after a delay. (For reviews of the relevant research, see Baddeley, 1976; Bransford, 1979. For some complications, see Kintsch, 1994; we'll return to these complications in Chapters 5 and 6.)

As a different way of making this point, it is also possible to *manipulate* whether subjects will understand the material or not. For example, in an often-quoted experiment by Bransford and Johnson (1972), subjects read this passage:

> The procedure is actually quite simple. First you arrange items into different groups. Of course one pile may be sufficient depending on how much there is to do. If you have to go somewhere else due to lack of facilities that is the next step; otherwise you are pretty well set. It is important not to overdo things. That is, it is better to do too few things at once than too many. In the short run, this may not seem important but complications can easily arise. A mistake can be expensive as well. At first, the whole procedure will seem complicated. Soon, however, it will become just another facet of life. It is difficult to foresee any end to the necessity for this task in the immediate future, but then, one never can tell. After the procedure is completed one arranges the materials into different groups again. Then they can be put into their appropriate places. Eventually they will be used once more and the whole cycle will then have to be repeated. However, that is part of life.

You are probably puzzled by this passage; so are most subjects. The story is easy to understand, though, if we give it a title: "Doing the Laundry." In the experiment, some subjects were given the title before reading the passage; others were not. The first group easily understood the passage, and was able to remember it after a delay. The second group, reading the same words, was not confronting a meaningful passage, and did poorly on the memory test.

These effects, with a memory benefit when subjects understand verbal materials, have been widely documented (Bransford & Franks, 1971; Sulin & Dooling, 1974). Similar effects can be documented with nonverbal materials. Consider, for example, the picture shown in Figure 4.9. This picture at first looks like a bunch of meaningless blotches; with some study, though, you may discover that a familiar object is depicted. Wiseman and Neisser (1974)

Figure 4.9

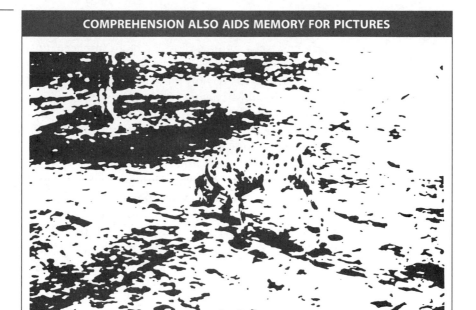

COMPREHENSION ALSO AIDS MEMORY FOR PICTURES

Subjects who perceive this picture as a pattern of meaningless blotches are unlikely to remember the picture. Subjects who perceive the "hidden" form do remember the picture. [After Wiseman & Neisser, 1974.]

tested subjects' memory for this picture. Consistent with what we have seen so far, subjects' memory was good if they understood the picture, and bad otherwise. (Also see Bower, Karlin & Dueck, 1975; Mandler & Ritchey, 1977; Rubin & Kontis, 1983.)

Chunking and Entry into Long-Term Memory

One might still object to these examples, however, on the grounds that they involve a trick: In the "laundry" study, we are not really testing subjects' memory *for the passage*. All subjects need to remember is the passage's *title*. Given their prior knowledge about how one washes clothes, that would be enough to allow them to *reconstruct* the passage at the time of test. Likewise for pictorial materials: To do well on a memory test, subjects don't need to remember the complex pattern of blotches in Figure 4.9. Instead, remembering a one-word summary (e.g., "Dalmatian") might be enough. In either case, it is no surprise that understanding aids memory, because understanding might literally reduce the amount of information to be remembered—a title instead of a passage, a summary instead of a complicated pattern.

This suggestion, that understanding reduces the load on memory, turns out to be well-founded. The only bit of confusion in the preceding paragraph lies in the idea that this is some sort of memory "trick." Instead, what is at stake here is an important principle of memory, a principle with wide application. As we have already noted, understanding a story depends in part on the discovery of various connections—among the various elements of the story, between the story and other things you know, and so on. We have argued that one function of these connections is to render the story *findable* in memory later on. But an equally important function of the connections is to *unify* the elements of the story, so that we think of them, not as individual elements, but as constituents in an interconnected whole. It is then this "whole" that enters memory, rather than the separate items—one unit rather than many.

You should note that this suggestion parallels the earlier claims we made about "chunking." We noted that more information could be "packed" into working memory if the information was "chunked." Rather than trying to remember a list of letters, one could instead think of the list as containing three-letter syllables. By assembling the material into more complex packages, one reduces the total number of packages—one is thinking about seven syllables, rather than 21 letters. By integrating and unifying the materials, one ends up with less to remember. We earlier made these points with regard to short-term remembering, but all of this obviously resembles our current point with longer-term remembering: Understanding serves to integrate and unify materials, reducing the load on memory.

There are a great many illustrations of this point, but a classic example was devised by Katona, whose work we have already mentioned. Katona asked his subjects to learn the following string of digits:

1 4 9 1 6 2 5 3 6 4 9 6 4 8 1 1 0 0 1 2 1

The data follow a familiar pattern. Subjects remember well the first two or three digits (a primacy effect) and the last few (recency), but cannot easily remember the full list. We then point out to the subjects that the list follows a simple pattern. To help them seen the pattern, we add some punctuation:

1, 4, 9, 16, 25, 36 . . .

In this form, you probably recognize the series as being 1^2, 2^2, 3^2, 4^2, 5^2, 6^2 . . . 11^2. Once subjects see this, the results are rather different. Subjects can now remember the entire list perfectly and, in fact, can remember the list even if we extend it (. . . 1 4 4 1 6 9).

When subjects find the connections that unify this list, they turn the 21 separate digits into a single whole. In effect, subjects are translating the number series into a rule or a sentence ("The list consists of the squares of the integers from 1 to 11"), and the sentence is appreciably easier to remember than the original series was. In a sense, this "translation" from a number series to a sentence actually increases the sophistication and complexity of what is being remembered: Grasping the number series merely required that one recognize the various digits. In contrast, the summary sentence requires comprehension of English syntax, and of the mathematical terms "squares" and "integers." But this is not what is crucial for memory. The number of "memory packages" is more important than the internal complexity of these packages, and so there is considerable gain from translating 21 packages into one.

The Study of "Memory Acquisition"

This chapter has ostensibly been about "memory acquisition." How do we acquire new memories? How is new information, new knowledge, established in long-term memory? Or, in more pragmatic terms, what is the best, most effective, most efficient way to learn?

The Contribution of the Memorizer

In some ways, the answer to the questions just posed is straightforward: Over and over, we have seen that memory is facilitated by *organizing* and *understanding* the to-be-remembered materials. Hand in hand with this, it appears that memories are not established by sheer contact with these items. If subjects are merely exposed to the items, without giving those items any thought, then subsequent recall of those items will be poor.

Note how large a role is played by the subject. If we wish to predict whether this or that event will be recalled, it is not enough to know that the subjects were exposed to the materials. Likewise, if we wish to predict memory performance, it is not enough to describe the memory "equipment" possessed by each of us—e.g., a working memory with various components, a long-term memory with a specific structure. Instead, if we wish to predict recall performance, then we need to pay attention to what the subject was *doing* at the time of learning. We need to examine the strategies and activities of the memorizer. Did she elect to do mere maintenance rehearsal, or did she engage the material in some other way? If the latter, *how* did the subject choose to think about the material: Did she pay attention to the appearance of the words or to their meaning? If the latter, was she able to grasp the meaning? Did she think about the words as isolated words or as constituents in a sentence or story? Did she think about the implications of the story and how the story fits with other beliefs? It is these considerations that are crucial for predicting the success of memory.

The contribution of the individual subject is also visible in another way: We have argued that learning depends on the subject making *connections*, but connections to what? If the subjects wants to connect the to-be-remembered material to other knowledge, to other memories, then the subject needs to have that other knowledge, she needs to have other (potentially relevant) memories. Thus, what subjects contribute to learning also includes their own prior knowledge. If the subject happens to enter the learning situation with a great deal of relevant knowledge, then he or she arrives with a considerable advantage—a rich framework onto which the new materials can be "hooked." If the subject enters the learning situation with little relevant background, then there is no framework, there is nothing to connect to, and learning will be correspondingly more difficult. Thus, if we wish to predict the success of memorizing, we also need to consider what other knowledge the individual brings into the situation.

The Links among Acquisition, Retrieval, and Storage

These points lead us to another theme of immense importance. Our emphasis in this chapter was on memory *acquisition*, but we have now seen several indications that claims about acquisition cannot be separated from claims about memory storage and memory retrieval. For example, why is recall improved by organization and understanding? We have suggested that organization provides *retrieval paths*, making the memories "findable" later on, when the time comes for memory retrieval. Therefore, our claims about acquisition rest on assumptions about memory retrieval, and the utility of memory connections within retrieval.

Likewise, we have just noted that a subject's ability to learn new material depends, in part, on the subject having a framework of prior knowledge to which the new materials can be tied. In this way, claims about memory acquisition must be coordinated with claims about the nature of what is already in storage.

The same can be said about chunking, both in working memory and in long-term storage. In most cases, chunking depends on understanding, and understanding rests on things you already know. The number series, "1 4 9 1 6 . . ." can only be chunked as the squares of the digits if you already know what the squares of the digits are. The passage about laundry is understood only by virtue of your prior knowledge about how clothing gets washed. In both of these cases, therefore, chunking at the time of memory acquisition is completely tied up with knowledge you already have, and so again we see the interdependency of memory acquisition and knowledge already in storage.

We close this chapter then with a two-sided message. We have offered several claims about memory acquisition, and about how memories are established. In particular, we have offered claims about the importance of memory connections, organization, and understanding. At the same time, though, these claims cannot stand by themselves. At the level of theory, our account of acquisition has already made references to the role of prior knowledge, and to the nature of memory retrieval. At the level of data, we will soon see that these interactions among acquisition, knowledge, and retrieval have important implications—for learning, for forgetting, and for memory accuracy. We turn next to some of those implications.

5

Interconnections between Acquisition and Retrieval

Putting information into long-term memory helps us only if we can retrieve it later on. Otherwise, it would be like putting money into a savings
account from which no withdrawals are possible, or like writing books
that could never be read. And it is equally clear that there are different ways
to retrieve information from memory. We can try to *recall* the information
("What was the name of your tenth-grade homeroom teacher?") or to *recognize* it ("Was the name perhaps 'Miller'?"). If we try to recall the information, a variety of cues may or may not be available (we might be told, as
a hint, that the name began with an "M," or rhymed with "tiller").

In Chapter 4, we largely ignored these variations in retrieval. We talked
as if material was well established in memory or was not, with no regard to
how the material would be retrieved from memory. We spoke about certain
principles as promoting memory, as though these claims held true independent of how the memory will be used.

There is every reason to believe, however, that we cannot ignore these
variations in retrieval. Imagine that you knew an upcoming German vocabulary test would be in multiple-choice format ("Which of the following is the
German word for 'backpack'?"). Would you study differently than you would
if the vocabulary test were fill-in ("What is the word for 'backpack'?")? Moreover, what would happen if you studied anticipating one sort of test, and you
instead received a different sort of test? Would this affect your performance?

In a study by Tversky (1973), subjects were asked to study a series of
pictures for an upcoming test. Half the subjects were told that they would
have to **recall** the names of the objects shown in the pictures. A recall test is
defined as one in which the tester names a context ("the series of pictures
you saw earlier"), and the subject must come up with the target materials. A
recall procedure is similar to an essay test, or a fill-in-the-blank test. The
remaining subjects were told they would be given a **recognition** test. They
were told that, after seeing the to-be-remembered pictures, they would be
shown test pictures, some of which were from the earlier group, some of
which were new. Their task would be to discriminate which of the test pictures
they had seen before, and which they had not. This is similar to a multiple-
choice or true-false test.

When the time came for the test, half of each group got what they expected, but half did not. Hence, we end up with four groups: subjects who
expected recall and got it; ones who expected recognition and got it; some
who expected recall but got recognition; and some who expected recognition
but got recall. The results (Figure 5.1) show a clear interaction between type
of preparation and type of test. That is, subjects who got the recall test did
better if they had prepared for a recall test than if they had prepared for
recognition (62% vs. 40%). Subjects who got the recognition test did better
if that is what they were expecting (87% vs. 67%).

Figure 5.1

MEMORY PERFORMANCE WITH TWO DIFFERENT TYPES OF TESTS AND TWO DIFFERENT TYPES OF EXPECTATIONS		

	Test Used:	
	Recall	Recognition
Subjects Expect: Recall	62%	67%
Recognition	40%	87%

Half of the subjects in this study were led to expect a recall test; half expected a recognition test. Half of each group got the test they expected; half did not. In the left-hand column of data, we see that subjects did better with a recall test if this is what they expected (62% vs. 40%). Likewise, in the right-hand column, subjects did better with a recognition test if this is what they had been led to expect (87% vs. 67%). [After Tversky, 1973.]

Is it better, therefore, to prepare for the recognition test or to prepare for recall? Which of these produces "better learning"? Tversky's data indicate that these are the wrong questions to ask. In these results, which of the learning strategies is "better" depends on how memory is tested. We will not try to draw strong conclusions from this study by itself but, as we will see, this interdependency between learning and retrieval is indeed the pattern of things: Learning prepares us for using our memories in a particular way. Learning that is effective preparation for one test may be less effective with other tests.

Retrieval Hints and Cues

Why should there be a connection between the particular form of learning and the particular form of memory retrieval? Imagine that you hear a history lecture, and think about it in the context of other lectures you have heard from that same professor. These thoughts will establish a memory connection between this lecture and others you have heard, and this connection can in turn serve as a retrieval path. Thus, if asked, later on, "What did Professor Jones say about such and such?" your retrieval path will lead you to the sought-after material.

But now imagine that we try to locate this same memory via a *different* retrieval path: "Does the current political situation remind you of anything you have learned recently?" Under these circumstances, what you need is some memory connection between "current political situation" and the target memory. That connection would lead you from your starting point to your goal. It is of little use, though, that you've established a connection between "Professor Jones" and the target memory, since that is not the connection you need. Therefore, for this memory search, your earlier learning may be irrelevant. By analogy, if you're trying to reach Chicago from the south, it doesn't matter that there's a good highway going into Chicago from the west. Likewise, if a memory search begins at a particular starting-point, you need a path from that starting-point to your target; it is irrelevant that paths from *other* starting points might eventually lead to your goal.

To put this broadly, establishing a particular retrieval path may be of little use if you later on need some *other* path! In general, your learning will serve you best if, at the time of retrieval, you approach the material in the same way (with the same focus, with the same connections) as you did at the time of learning. Then the connections you need will match the ones that are already available in memory.

Of course, we should say from the start that there is a way to defeat these concerns: If you initially thought about Jones's lecture in conjunction with other lectures *and* in conjunction with political concerns and in conjunction with some other ideas, then each of these would establish a retrieval path, and so the memory could be retrieved from each of these perspectives. This multi-perspective approach, therefore, might provide something close to an "optimal learning strategy." But the fact is that we usually don't adopt this multi-perspective approach. Hence, our memories are typically bound to the particular perspective we had in mind at the time of learning. As a result, the memory is most likely to be retrieved if that perspective is reinstated at the time of retrieval.

State-Dependent Learning

What is the evidence for these claims? As one path toward the evidence, let's ask a slightly different question: If your perspective on the to-be-learned material is so crucial, then what determines, or influences, that perspective? Many factors are surely relevant, but one influence is your circumstances.

Consider a broad class of studies on state-dependent learning (Eich, 1980; Overton, 1985). In these studies, there are typically two different learning situations, and two different tests. One of the test formats is matched to one of the learning situations, and one to the other learning situation. Hence, we end up with what psychologists call a "2 × 2" design.

One such design is illustrated in Figure 5.2. Godden and Baddeley (1975) asked deep-sea divers to learn various materials. Some of the divers learned the material while sitting by the edge of the water, not wearing their diving masks. Others learned the material while approximately 20 feet underwater, hearing the material via a special communication set. Within each group, half of the subjects were then tested while above water, and half were tested below. The test required subject to write down the materials they had heard earlier. (The writing was done on a Formica board, so that subjects tested underwater could record their responses.)

Being underwater clearly changes one's perspective in many ways, and so we would expect subjects' thoughts to be rather different from those while

Figure 5.2

THE DESIGN OF A STATE-DEPENDENT LEARNING EXPERIMENT

		Test while	
		On land	Underwater
Learn while	On land	Learning and test circumstances "match"	
	Underwater		Learning and test circumstances "match"

Half of the divers learned the test material while underwater; half learned while sitting on land. Likewise, half were tested while underwater; half were tested on land. We expect a retrieval advantage if the learning and test circumstances "match." Hence, we expect better performance in the top-left and bottom-right cells.

on land. By the logic previously described, therefore, we would expect subjects who learned material while wet to remember the material best if tested while wet; likewise, for subjects on land. That is exactly what the data show (Figure 5.3).

Related results have been obtained with odors present or absent during learning (Cann & Ross, 1989; Schab, 1990)—memory is best if the olfactory "environment" is the same during memory retrieval as it was during the initial learning. Similar data have been obtained using manipulations of background music (Balch, Bowman & Mohler, 1992; Smith, 1985). Smith, Glenberg and Bjork (1978) report the same pattern if learning and testing simply take place in different rooms—recall is best if done in the room in which the initial learning took place. Here, though, there is an interesting twist: In one procedure, subjects learned materials in one room and were tested in a dif-

Figure 5.3

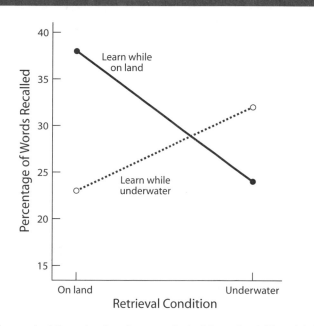

STATE-DEPENDENCY FROM A CHANGE IN PHYSICAL CIRCUMSTANCES

Materials learned while on land are best recalled while on land. Materials learned while underwater are best recalled while underwater. The change in circumstances doesn't obliterate the benefits of learning (in all conditions, performance is considerably better than 0%); nonetheless, the differences between conditions are substantial.

ferent room. Just before testing, however, the subjects were urged to think about the room in which they had learned—what it looked like, how it made them feel, and so on. When tested, these subjects performed as well as those subjects for whom there was no room change (Smith, 1979). What seems to matter, therefore, is not so much the physical context, but the psychological context, consistent with our account of this effect.

Other studies of state-dependent learning have manipulated subjects' internal states, rather than their external circumstances. For example, Eich, Weingartner, Stillman and Gillin (1975) had subjects learn a list of words either after smoking marijuana, or after smoking a cigarette without marijuana. Four hours later, subjects were tested either under the influence of marijuana or in control conditions. As Table 5.1 shows, performance was better, overall, if subjects were tested while not under the influence of the drug. This emerges, in the table, as better performance, on average, in the left-hand column. Superimposed on this, however, is a state-dependency effect: Subjects did better if learning and test took place in the same state; worse if learning and test took place in different states. Similar data have been reported with other procedures and other species, using such drugs as alcohol, amphetamines, and caffeine (Bliss, Sledjeski & Leiman, 1971; MacArdy & Riccio, 1991; Overton, 1964; Sachs, Weingarten & Klein, 1966; Weingartner, Adefris, Eich & Murphy, 1976). In each case, there is a performance boost if the physiological state at the time of test matches the state at the time of learning.

Similar studies have examined the memory effects of subjects' moods. There are many ways to run such studies, including hypnotic procedures for placing subjects in a happy mood or a sad one, or procedures that involve the subject reading a series of statements, designed to lift or depress their

Table 5.1	PERCENTAGE OF WORDS RECALLED IN A MEMORY TEST DESIGNED TO SHOW STATE-DEPENDENCY EFFECTS FROM MARIJUANA		
		Retrieval Condition	
	Encoding Condition	**Placebo**	**Marijuana**
	Placebo	25	14
	Marijuana	20	22
	Overall	22.5	18
	[After Eich, Weingartner, Stillman, & Gillin, 1975.]		

spirits. The design, though, is a by now familiar one: Subjects learn the experimental materials either while happy or while sad; they are later tested either while happy or sad. And once again, memory is best if the mood state at test matches the mood state in learning (see Figure 5.4, after Bower, 1981).

This effect of mood on memory has a number of interesting implications. Among them, it serves to keep our moods stable: When we are happy, we are better able to think of experiences and events we learned about while happy, and this helps to keep us happy. Unfortunately, the same pattern holds when we are depressed. It is worth saying, though, that, unlike other state-dependency effects, these mood effects have proven somewhat unreliable. That is, several experiments have sought to reproduce the findings just described, but with no success. Other studies, however, have confirmed state-dependency effects with moods. It remains unclear why this particular variety of state dependency sometimes does appear in the results and sometimes does not. (For reviews, see Blaney, 1986; Brewin, Andrews & Gotlib, 1993; Eich, 1995; Eich & Metcalfe, 1989; Ellis & Ashbrook, 1989; Kwiatkowski & Parkinson, 1994; Singer & Salovey, 1988.) One possibility, though, is quite interesting: Subjects may, in many cases, use their memories to influence their moods—

Figure 5.4

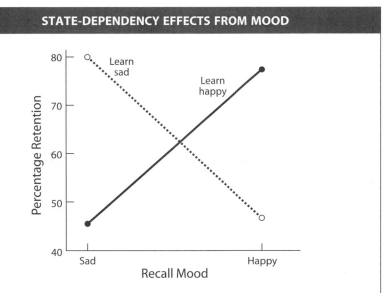

STATE-DEPENDENCY EFFECTS FROM MOOD

Half of the subjects in this study learned a word list while in a happy mood; half learned it while sad. Half of each group was tested while in a happy mood, half while sad. Being in the same mood during the learning and during the test improved memory performance. [After Bower, 1981.]

if you are feeling blue, you may seek out happy memories to cheer yourself up (Parrott & Sabini, 1990; Wegner, 1994). Therefore, this may be a circumstance in which memory influences mood at the same time that mood influences memory. No wonder, therefore, that mood and memory studies yield a complex pattern of results.

If we set aside the mood and memory data, however, the evidence is quite clear. Recall performance is best if subjects' state (internal or external) at the time of test matches their state at the time of learning. This is because one's state influences one's mental perspective, and perspective influences both the retrieval paths that are established and then, later on, the retrieval paths that are needed. If your perspective is the same, at learning and retrieval, you'll be able to use the memory connections established earlier. If your perspective changes, these retrieval paths may not be useful for you.

Changes in Subjects' Approach to the Memory Materials

Subjects' state, we have argued, influences how they approach to-be-remembered materials, and this is what matters for memory. What happens if we manipulate subjects' thinking directly?

Fisher and Craik (1977) presented their subjects with a series of word pairs. Subjects were instructed to learn the *second* word in each pair, and to use the first word in each pair only "as an aid to remembering the target words." For half of the pairs, the "context word" was semantically associated with the target word; for example, if subjects were shown "cat," they were also shown the context word "dog." This should encourage subjects to think about the words' meanings. For the other pairs, the context word was one that rhymed with the target (e.g., if shown "cat," they were also shown the context word "hat"). This should encourage subjects to think about the target word's sound.

When the time came for test, subjects were tested in one of two ways. Subjects were given either a hint concerning meaning ("Was there a word on the list associated with 'dog' "?) or a hint concerning sound ("Was there a word on the list associated with 'hat' "?). Table 5.2 shows the results. Note, first, the column all the way to the right (averaging together trials with meaning hints and trials with sound hints). Consistent with the data in Chapter 4, thinking about meaning generally leads to better memory, in this case with an impressive 30.5 to 21.5 advantage. That is, subjects who thought about meaning at the time of learning remembered about 50% more than subjects who thought about sound. But now look at the table's other two columns. If subjects thought about meaning at the time of learning, they do considerably better in the test if the cues provided by the experimenter concern meaning.

Table 5.2

	PERCENTAGE OF WORDS RECALLED ON TESTING AFTER PRIOR ASSOCIATION WITH EITHER MEANING OR SOUND		
	Type of Hint		
	Meaning	**Sound**	**Both Combined**
Type of processing at time of learning			
Meaning	44%	17%	30.5%
Sound	17%	26%	21.5%

[After Fisher & Craik, 1977.]

[handwritten margin note: learning by meaning produces best recall unless subject was taught to learn by sound (then recall by sound will be better)]

Likewise for sound: If subjects thought about sound at the time of learning, then they do better with a cue concerning the word's sound.

In fact, the table shows two separate influences on memory working at the same time: an advantage for thinking about meaning (overall, performance is better in the top row) and an advantage for "matched" learning and test conditions (overall, performance is best in the "main diagonal" of the table). In the table's top left cell, these effects combine, and here performance is better than in any other condition. These effects clash in the column showing the results of the sound cue. The advantage from thinking about meaning favors the top cell in this column; the advantage from "matched" learning and test favors the bottom cell. As it turns out, the "match" effect wins over the levels-of-processing effect: "Deep but unmatched" (17%) is inferior to "not so deep, but matched" (26%). Thus, the advantage for deep processing is simply overturned in this situation.

Encoding Specificity

We are starting to accumulate a broad set of cases in which memory performance depends on a "match" between subjects' mental state at the time of learning, and their mental state at the time of retrieval. As a result, learning that is effective for one sort of test may be ineffective with some other test.

Let's be clear, though, about what is going on in these experiments. Subjects who are currently sad haven't, in any sense, lost their memories of happier days. The problem is that subjects in the "wrong state" have a hard time *locating* these memories. Once the subject's state changes those memories will readily come to mind.

Moreover, we have emphasized that it is not just subjects' *state* that matters. What is crucial is subjects' *thoughts* about the to-be-remembered items, and how they approach those items, both at the time of learning and at the time of retrieval. A further set of results will help to illustrate this point. We ask a group of subjects to memorize a list of words. Midway down the list is the word "jam" and, by manipulating the context, we arrange things so that subjects understand this word as indicating the stuff one makes from berries or grapes. (This can be done in various ways; e.g., we can precede the word "jam" with a word like "jelly" or "fruit." In this situation, the context "primes" subjects to understand "jam" as we intend. We will discuss how this priming works in Chapter 7.) Some time later, we test memory by presenting various items and asking whether or not these appeared on the previous list. "Jam" is presented, but now we arrange context so that "jam" is understood as in "traffic jam." Under these circumstances, subjects typically will say that the word was not on the previous list, even though their memory for the list seems to be quite good. That is, subjects are quite likely to remember most of the other words on the list, even though they don't recall our test word.

This kind of demonstration is often referred to as **encoding specificity**, and has been reported in numerous forms by Endel Tulving (Tulving, 1983; also see Hunt & Ellis, 1974; Light & Carter-Sobell, 1970). The notion of encoding specificity, roughly, is that one learns more than just the word; one learns the word together with its context. In this case, the context would include what one thinks and understands about the word. When subjects are later presented with the word in some other context, they ask themselves, "Does this match anything I learned previously?" and answer *correctly*, "no." And we emphasize that their answer is indeed correct. It is as if subjects learned the word, "other" and were later asked whether they had been shown the word "the." In fact, "the" does appear as part of "other" or, more precisely, the letters T H E do appear within the word "other." But it is the whole that subjects learn, not the parts. Therefore, if you've seen "other," it's entirely sensible to deny that you have seen "the" or, for that matter, "he" or "her," even though all these letter combinations are contained within "other." (See also Figure 2.2, p. 34.)

Learning a list of words works in much the same way. The letters "J A M" were contained in what subjects learned, just as "T H E" is contained in "other." In both cases, however, what was learned was the broader, integrated experience, the word as the perceiver organized it, the word as the perceiver understood it.

In fact, a great many results fit with these assertions. For example, we can show subjects the pattern shown in Figure 5.5, and arrange things so that subjects perceive the pattern as a vase on a black background. (As before, we can use a priming procedure, perhaps previously showing subjects pictures of other vases, or other white figures on black backgrounds.) A few minutes later, we show the picture again, but this time we prime subjects so that they see two profiles, against a white background. We now ask subjects whether they have ever seen this figure before. This should be an extremely easy task since, after all, subjects have just seen this pattern. Nonetheless, subjects will often assert that they have not seen the figure before (Kanizsa, 1979; Rock, 1983). Apparently, what matters for figure memory is, just as with words, the "stimulus-as-understood," not the geometrically-defined picture itself.

Encoding specificity also can be demonstrated with ordinary, nonambiguous stimuli. In fact, these effects can be observed even with relatively subtle changes in meaning. For example, Tulving and Thomson (1973; also Watkins & Tulving, 1975; Flexser & Tulving, 1978) showed subjects a list of words, with each word accompanied by a context word. Subjects might see "grasp-baby," with "baby" being the to-be-remembered item. In the next step of the procedure, subjects were shown a new list of words, and asked to write down

Figure 5.5

THE AMBIGUOUS "VASE/PROFILES" FIGURE

This figure can be perceived either as a white vase against a black background or as two black profiles against a white background.

what these new words called to mind. Subjects were shown "infant" and, not surprisingly, many subjects wrote down "baby" in response. Finally, subjects were asked to look over their own responses, and to circle any of their responses that they recognized as having occurred in the previously seen input list. In many cases, subjects did not recognize "baby" as a list word. Simply by virtue of the change in context, memory seems to have been significantly disrupted. (For related results, see Bransford, Franks, Morris & Stein, 1979; Morris, Bransford & Franks, 1977; Tulving & Osler, 1968.)

Once again, therefore, we are led to some familiar themes. What happens during learning is the establishment of a memory that can be retrieved in a certain way, from a certain perspective. If the perspective changes—if, in particular, your understanding of the test item changes—then the original memory will not be retrieved. It seems, once more, like we cannot speak of "good learning" (or "less good learning") *in general*. What counts as good learning depends on later events: Whether it is better to learn underwater or on land depends on where one will be tested. Whether it is better to learn while listening to jazz or while sitting in a quiet room depends on the music background of the memory test. Even whether it is best to attend to meaning depends on whether meaning will be prominent when the time comes for memory retrieval. And, finally, devoting energy and time to memorizing a stimulus may be of no use if your understanding of the stimulus is changed in some significant way at the time of test.

Different Forms of Memory Testing

In the studies described so far, we've tested memory in some cases via a *recall* test and in other cases via recognition. Recall and recognition testing differ in many ways, but they also have an important attribute in common: In a recall test, we ask subjects what words they can remember from a prior presentation. We are not interested in what words subjects encountered yesterday, or in the morning paper; we instead want them to recall the words from the list we gave them. Thus, we are asking subjects to do more than simply recall some words; we are, in fact, asking them to recall an *episode* (namely, the episode in which the words were learned).

The same is true for a recognition test: In this procedure, subjects are shown test words (for example), and must decide whether each had or had not appeared on a previously-shown list. It will not be enough for subjects to decide which of the test words seem familiar, or which ones they have seen before. *All* of the test words are familiar (i.e., all are in the subjects' vocabulary), and all of the test words have been encountered *somewhere* before. Therefore, subjects must do more than register the familiarity of the test items; they must in addition identify the context in which they last encountered the item; in essence, they must say, "The last time I met this word was on the previous list." Thus, once again, subjects are required to remember an episode, and not just a list of words.

Against this backdrop, consider the following common experience: You are walking down the street, or perhaps you turn on the television, and you see a familiar face. Immediately, you know the face is familiar, but you are unable to say just *why* the face is familiar. Is it someone you saw in a movie last month? Is it the driver of the bus you often take? You are at a loss to answer these questions; all you know is that the face is familiar.

In cases like this, you cannot "place" the memory, you cannot identify the episode in which the face was last encountered. But, as we have just seen, it is precisely this identification of an episode that is required by recall and recognition measures. Thus, if we assess your memory via these measures, you are failing to remember. It is as if you said to the experimenter, "Yes, the test word is familiar to me, but I haven't a clue where I last saw it, and I haven't a clue whether it was on that list you showed me." If we require you to remember the connection between an item and the context of a previous encounter, then you have failed.

But this seems too harsh, since you clearly are remembering something. You know that the face is familiar; you probably also know that the face is usually encountered in a context sharply different from the current one. We therefore need to say something about this sort of memory and, in general, about the feeling of familiarity.

Remembering Source versus Familiarity Alone

Familiarity has been extensively investigated, with a great deal of the early work done by George Mandler (Mandler, 1980; Graf & Mandler, 1984; Mandler, Graf & Kraft, 1986). Mandler's proposal starts by formalizing the distinction introduced in the last section. That is, we need to distinguish **source memory** from familiarity. Source memory refers to the recollection of the *source* of one's current knowledge. That is, one remembers the episode in which the learning took place; one remembers the time and place in which a stimulus was encountered. Familiarity, in contrast, refers only to a feeling one has—a specific picture before your eyes "seems familiar" or a tune "sounds familiar."

Mandler proposes that source memory and familiarity derive from different memory processes, with each set of processes being fully independent of the other. That's what makes it possible for us to have familiarity without source memory. Presumably one can also have source memory without any feeling of familiarity (although examples of this are more difficult to find).

Source memory and familiarity influence us in different ways. To see this, consider the relation between recall and recognition testing. By definition, a recall test is one in which we name a prior episode, and require subjects to generate the items learned in this episode. The episode might be "the list presented earlier," in which case subjects must generate the items on the list. Or the episode might be "the last big party you attended," with you being asked to generate what happened at the party, or who was there. In either case, your memory search begins with the episode, and moves from there to the associated items. Thus, by its very nature, a recall test requires memory for the initial episode; it requires source memory.

The situation is more complicated, though, with recognition. Let's say that you are taking a recognition test. The fourth word on the test is "loon." You might say to yourself, "Yes, I remember seeing this word on the previous list. In fact, I'm certain that this word was on the list, because I remember the image that came to mind when I encountered this word." This line of reasoning draws on a memory for a particular episode, i.e., a source memory, and this would of course guide your response on the recognition test. But now let's say that the fifth word on the test is "butler." In response to this word, you might say to yourself, "I don't specifically remember seeing this word on the list, but this word feels extraordinarily familiar. If the word *wasn't* on the list, then it wouldn't seem so familiar. Therefore, it must have been on the list." In this case, there is no source memory. Instead, you are being guided by a sense of familiarity *plus* an inference about where that familiarity came from. And, thanks to the inference, you will probably respond "yes" on the recognition test.

In sum, recall tests provide a relatively "pure" assessment of source memory. But responses on a recognition test can be guided *either* by source memory or by the combination of familiarity and inference. If you remember the episode of seeing a word on the prior list, that can guide your response. If, on the other hand, a word seems extremely familiar, you are likely to infer that you saw it on the list, even if you cannot remember the actual encounter (Atkinson & Juola, 1974; Glucksberg & McCloskey, 1981; Jacoby & Brooks, 1984; Rajaram, 1993).

Finally, it also seems likely that different kinds of learning set the basis for source memory and for familiarity. Thus, when subjects anticipate a memory test, they are likely to do what we earlier called "relational" or "elaborative" rehearsal. In this form of rehearsal, subjects pay attention to the meaning of the material; perhaps they also form images of the material. Crucially, this form of rehearsal is also likely to include attention to the context of the material. Subjects may think about how the material is related to other items on the list, or to other bits of knowledge already in memory, or to other things they happen to be thinking about at the time. All of this will aid subjects in remembering the context in which they encountered the materials. All of this will provide good preparation for any task that requires memory for this context, that is, for source memory.

If subjects anticipate no memory test, though, they will probably elect to do the (easier) "maintenance" or "item-specific" rehearsal. No connections to the context will be sought, nor will any be made. The context of the items will not be encoded, and so this form of rehearsal will be poor preparation for tasks requiring source memory (e.g., recall). However, maintenance rehearsal does have an effect: In doing this rote, non-associative rehearsal, subjects will be exposed to the material over and over. As a result, the material will become more and more familiar to the subjects. Thus, maintenance rehearsal should benefit tasks that depend on familiarity.

The Hybrid Nature of Recognition

A wide range of evidence fits with the conception we have just sketched. For example, we noted in Chapter 4 that subjects' ability to recall an earlier-presented list is much improved if the list is organized; it turns out, however, that the effects of organization are far weaker with recognition testing (Mandler, 1981). This is sensible if we claim that recall depends on source memory, which in turn depends on memorial connections. In contrast, recognition can be based on familiarity, which does not depend on memory connections.

The results are different, though, if we delay testing. If subjects learn a list on one occasion, and are tested some weeks later, then organization has the same effect on recognition as it does on recall—that is, organization will then have a large benefit for both forms of testing. This can easily be explained if we make one further assumption: Recognition testing is more likely to be based on familiarity when the items are still "fresh" in one's mind. To see why, let's return to our earlier example, and imagine a subject who has just encountered the word "butler" on a recognition test. The subject might realize the word is familiar, but wonder why this is: "Perhaps it's familiar because I encountered it on the experimenter's list. Or perhaps it's familiar because I heard it in a conversation yesterday. Or perhaps it's familiar because I read something about butlers the day before yesterday. . . ." With numerous sources possible for the familiarity, subjects will be wary about attributing the familiarity to the earlier-presented list. The familiarity is clear, but the interpretation of the familiarity is uncertain. Under these circumstances, subjects might hesitate to offer a judgment based on familiarity alone; instead, they will only respond if they can locate a source memory. In this case, recognition should be influenced by memory connections, just as recall is, and this is precisely what the data show.

By the same token, our description of *state-dependent learning* emphasized the role of memory connections, in this case, connections between the to-be-remembered items and other thoughts triggered by your current state or circumstances. We should expect these effects to be stronger with recall testing (dependent on memory connections) than with recognition (sometimes dependent on familiarity). This is correct: state-dependent learning is more readily demonstrated if memory is tested via recall, than if it is tested via recognition (Murname & Phelps, 1994).

This perspective also leads to the claim that recognition will be more difficult with common words than with relatively rare words. Common words, by definition, are encountered in many contexts. If a common word seems familiar, therefore, subjects might be certain they have recently encountered it, but quite uncertain *where* they encountered it. For obvious reasons, this ambiguity is less severe with uncommon words. Consistent with this, recognition testing does yield poorer results with familiar words than with unfamiliar ones (Glanzer & Adams, 1985).

Finally, pertinent evidence also comes from studies that manipulate how subjects *approach* the materials in their initial learning. We can, in particular, structure a task so that subjects do *maintenance* rehearsal for some of the items, and *elaborative* rehearsal for other items. (There are several ways to arrange this. Just as an example, the Craik and Watkins, 1973, "B-word" experiment, described in Chapter 4, illustrates one way to lure subjects into maintenance rehearsal.) The hypothesis we are considering indicates that elaborative rehearsal, which promotes source memory, will serve as good preparation for either recall or recognition testing. Maintenance rehearsal, in contrast, is good preparation for recognition testing, but should be largely ineffective for recall. This also turns out to be correct (Bartz, 1976; Glenberg & Adams, 1978; Glenberg, Smith & Green, 1977; Woodward, Bjork & Jongeward, 1973).

The Complexity of Recall

These results fit well with the conception we are developing and also highlight the complex nature of recognition—sometimes based on familiarity, sometimes based on the recollection of a specific episode. Moreover, when recognition depends on familiarity, it does so in a complicated way: You notice that a test word seems familiar, and then you make an *inference* about the origins of this familiarity. If you decide the word is familiar because it appeared on the prior list, that will lead to one response; if you decide the word is familiar for some other reason, that will lead to the opposite response. Note, then, that the recognition response depends as much on the inference as it does on the familiarity itself.

What about recall? First, recall clearly depends on a memory search. In recognition testing, the experimenter provides the sought-after items: "Was this picture in the earlier series?" (or "this word?" or "this sentence?") In recall testing, the subject has to come up with the specific items on her own; the experimenter merely supplies the *category* of sought-after items ("a story you heard in childhood" or "the faces you saw at yesterday's meeting"). Coming up with these items will require *locating* them in memory, and that's where the memory search enters. It is this search that is facilitated by memory connections, and that is why connections matter so much for recall.

However, the task of recalling items does not end once the sought-after items are brought to mind. The subject needs to ask, "*Why* did this item come to mind? Is it a memory, or just some chance association? If a memory, is it drawn from the right source? Did the word 'loon' come to mind because it was on the experimenter's list, or because I was reminded of loons by something on the experimenter's list?" These are, of course, parallel to the questions demanded by recognition testing. In recognition, a test item might seem familiar to the subject, and the subject must decide why this is. In recall, a potential response comes to mind, and again the subject must decide why this is. In both cases, an *attribution* step is required, and whether the subject will respond one way or another is determined by this attribution. Evidence suggests that this attribution step is far from trivial, and attribution errors can occur. (For a fuller discussion of this attribution step, see Johnson, Hashtroudi & Lindsay, 1993.)

In summary, then, recall and recognition are both surprisingly complex. Recall clearly depends on a memory search and is therefore influenced mightily by the presence or absence of relevant memory connections. Recognition turns out to be something of a hybrid and can be based either on source memory (in which case it is just like recall) or on familiarity. In any event, both recognition and recall require a step of inference, as one attributes familiarity (in the case of recognition) or the retrieval of a particular memory (in recall) to some specific source.

Implicit Memory

We have emphasized that recognition, in many circumstances, relies on familiarity plus an inference. But what is this inference all about? And when subjects attribute a "feeling of familiarity," deciding that the feeling comes from a particular source, what sort of "feeling" are we talking about?

Memory without Awareness

In a study by Jacoby (1983; also Jacoby & Dallas, 1981; Winnick & Daniel, 1970), subjects were initially shown a series of words and then, later on, their memory for the words was tested. During the learning phase of the experiment, however, subjects experienced the words in one of three ways. In the "no context" condition, subjects were shown each word without any context. For example, subjects saw "XXXX, DARK" on the computer screen, and their task was to read "dark" aloud. In the "context" condition, subjects saw each word along with its antonym. For example, subjects were shown "HOT, COLD" and had to read "cold" aloud. Finally, in the "generate" condition, subjects saw the antonym only ("LOW, ???") and had to say out loud what the target word was.

In this experiment, the "generate" condition involves the most conceptual activity from the subject, since the subject must attend to the cue-word's meaning and come up with the antonym. In contrast, the "no context" condition provides neither reason nor encouragement to think about the word's meaning; it seems likely that subjects in this condition will read the word without thinking much about it. The "context" condition will probably involve an intermediate level of activity, since this condition does draw attention to meaning (via the antonym), but does not require the subjects to do anything with the antonym.

In Chapter 4, we argued that *attention to meaning* is often an effective way to memorize; mere exposure, in contrast, seems to provide little memory benefit. Based on this, we would expect subjects to remember words encountered in the "generate" condition, but probably not those encountered in the "no context" condition. That is exactly what the data show: Half of the subjects were tested via a conventional recognition procedure and, for these subjects, performance was best for words presented in the "generate" condition, worse if the words had appeared in the "context" condition, and worst of all in the "no context" condition (Figure 5.6).

So far, then, this looks just like studies we have already seen. The twist, though, comes from the other half of the subjects, tested in a rather different fashion. They were seated in front of a tachistoscope and shown a series of briefly-presented words. Subjects' task was simply to say what the words were—that is, to read them out loud. Some of the words presented had also been presented during the learning phase, and some of the words were novel—i.e., had not been recently viewed.

As we saw in Chapter 2, word recognition can be difficult, especially if

Figure 5.6

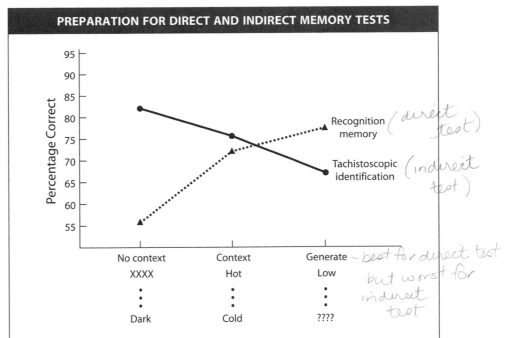

PREPARATION FOR DIRECT AND INDIRECT MEMORY TESTS

Recognition memory *(direct test)*

Tachistoscopic identification *(indirect test)*

best for direct test but worst for indirect test

Subjects in the "no context" condition saw words and read them aloud; subjects in the "generate" condition had to generate the words (antonyms) on their own (and did not see them). Subjects in the "context" condition saw the words, but had a meaningful context (antonyms) and so only had to glance at the words in order to identify them. The "generate" condition was the best preparation for a direct test ("Are these the words you saw before?") but worst for an indirect test (tachistoscopic identification). [After Jacoby, 1983.] *prob. had to also think of the words they generated*

the presentations are quite brief. Crucially, though, repetition helps. For example, let's say that the tenth word presented to subjects was "boat." If the fourteenth word in the series is also "boat," subjects will recognize the word more easily the second time around. In Chapter 2, we referred to this as repetition priming. Of course, priming involves some sort of memory since, obviously, a previous event is influencing current performance. This is only possible if the subject preserves some record, some memory, of that previous event. But what kind of memory is this? And what *creates* this memory? This brings us back to the Jacoby study.

Figure 5.6 shows the data. With tachistoscopic testing, performance was best if subjects had encountered the words in the "no context" condition, worst if subjects had encountered the words in the "generate" condition. This is, of course, exactly the opposite of the results from the standard recognition test. In that condition, performance was, it seems, dependent on "conceptual work"—thinking about the meaning of the words. The more conceptual work you had done, the better your recognition memory. In contrast, tachistoscopic performance seems dependent on *perceptual* "work," that is, on literally seeing the items. Subjects obviously see the words in the "no context" condition, and this condition produces strong priming. They don't see the word in the "generate" condition, and this condition produces negligible priming. The "context" condition again takes an intermediate position: Given the context, subjects do not need to look at the word with any great care. Having seen "hot," a quick glance will confirm what the next word ("cold") must be. Hence, there will be some "perceptual contact" with the stimulus, but it will be slight. It makes sense, therefore, that this condition produces an intermediate level of priming.

At the very least, it appears that we are seeing two different types of memory here. One type seems relevant to the standard recognition test and is promoted by conceptual engagement with the materials. We reveal this type of memory if we test subjects *directly*, asking them explicitly what they remember. The other type of memory seems relevant to the tachistoscopic test and is promoted by perceptually working with the materials. To reveal this sort of memory, we must test subjects *indirectly*, asking not what they remember, but how their current performance is influenced by recent events.

Similar results have been obtained with other tasks. For example, in a lexical-decision task, subjects are shown strings of letters (STAR, LAMB, HIRL); the task is to indicate (by pressing one button or another) whether the string of letters is a word in English or not. Lexical decisions are appreciably quicker if subjects have recently seen the test word; that is, lexical decision shows its own version of repetition priming. This priming is observed even when subjects have no explicit memory for having encountered the stimulus words before (e.g., Oliphant, 1983). Thus, if we ask subjects directly whether they have seen these words before, we will discover that the subjects have forgotten the words; according to the lexical-decision results, however, they have *not* forgotten.

The same pattern has been observed with a task called **word-stem completion**. In this task, subjects are given the first few letters of a word, and must produce a word with this beginning. For example, subjects might be asked to name a word that begins "CLA." In some versions of this task, an obscure word is required to complete the word-stem. In this situation, subjects are more likely to come up with the word if they have encountered it recently. In other versions of this task, more than one word provides a plausible ending to the stem (e.g., CLAM, CLASS, CLATTER), and the question of interest is *which* of these a subject produces. If one of these words has been

[handwritten margin note: don't need to have distinct memory for word you use in word-stem completions]

seen recently, subjects are likely to produce it, rather than a legitimate alternative, as the completion to the word stem. Once again, though, these priming effects are observed even if subjects, when tested directly, show no memory of having seen the word recently (e.g., Graf, Mandler & Haden, 1982). Apparently, therefore, the type of memory needed for word-stem completion is distinct from the type of memory needed for ordinary recollection.

Thus it seems that, in a range of settings, subjects are influenced by a previous encounter even if they have no conscious recollection of the encounter. (For reviews, see Richardson-Klavehn & Bjork, 1988; Schacter, 1987.) Results like these have led psychologists to distinguish two types of memories. **Explicit memories** are those revealed by *direct* memory testing and are typically accompanied by the conviction that one is remembering a specific prior episode. Recall is a direct memory test; so is the standard recognition test. **Implicit memories** are those revealed by *indirect* testing and so are often manifest as *priming* effects. In this form of testing, one's current behavior or current judgments are demonstrably influenced by a prior event, but one may be quite unaware of this. Tachistoscopic recognition, lexical-decision, word-stem completion, and many other tasks, provide indirect means of assessing memory.

The Breadth of Implicit Memory

The effects of implicit memory can also be demonstrated in many other circumstances. To describe the evidence, though, we first need to say more about how implicit memory *feels* from the subject's point of view. This will then lead us back into our discussion of familiarity and source memory.

Let us say that we show subjects a stimulus and then, sometime later, show them the same stimulus again. Let us say further that we arrange things so that subjects have no explicit memory for the previous encounter, but they do have an implicit memory. (There are many ways to do this; we can, for example, simply allow some time to pass between the initial exposure and the subsequent test.) The evidence indicates that subjects' reaction to the stimulus, in the second encounter, will depend a great deal on the context. Thanks to the implicit memory, the stimulus is likely to feel in some ways "special." We have several expressions in English that seem to capture this specialness: We sometimes say that something "rings a bell," or that it "strikes a chord." But exactly what this means, and exactly how this feels, seems to depend on your circumstances.

Several experiments will help to illustrate this point. Jacoby, Kelley, Brown and Jasechko (1989) presented subjects with a list of names to read out loud. Subjects were told nothing about a memory test; they thought the experiment was concerned with how they pronounced the names. Some time later, though, subjects were given the second step of the procedure: They were shown a new list of names, and asked to rate each person named on the list according to how famous they are. This list included some real, very famous people, some real but not-so-famous people, and also some fictional names. Crucially, the fictional names were of two types: Some were names that had occurred on the prior list, and some of them were simply new names.

Let's focus on the names that were fictional but familiar—that is, names taken from the prior list. How subjects responded to these names depended on *how much time had elapsed* between presentation of the two lists. To understand this, imagine yourself in the role of a subject. If you see the "famous" list right after the "pronounce" list, you might decide "This name rings a bell, but that's because I just saw it on the previous list." In the terms we have been using, you have a feeling of familiarity for the name, but you also remember the source of this familiarity. If, however, the two lists are presented 24 hours apart, things are different. At this delay, the familiarity still remains, but memory for the source of the familiarity has faded. In taking the test, therefore, you might say "This name rings a bell, and I have no idea why. I guess this must be a famous person." And this is indeed the pattern of the data: When the two lists are presented back-to-back, subjects do not rate the made-up names as being the names of famous people. But, when the lists are presented one day apart, subjects rate the made-up names as being famous. Apparently, the subjects correctly note that some names on the list seem familiar, but then they misinterpret this feeling of familiarity. And, critically, this misinterpretation is only possible once memory for the actual source has become less prominent; in this particular procedure, this is accomplished by the 24-hour delay. Without the 24-hour delay, we get no effect. Hence, Jacoby et al. refer to their study as the "how to become famous overnight" experiment.

Note that the sense of familiarity seems to outlast source memory. To be fair, we should say that the fast-fade of source memory was encouraged by the set-up of this study; other studies show greater longevity for source memory. Nonetheless, it is true in general that familiarity's effects seem more long-lasting than source memory (e.g., Jacoby & Dallas, 1981; Tulving, Schacter & Stark, 1982).

Moreover, note how subjects reacted to their sense of familiarity. They were not merely ignorant or uncertain about why some names on the list "rang a bell." Instead, subjects reached a conclusion about why these names seemed familiar and that conclusion was wrong. The subjects, in other words, forgot the *real* source of the familiarity (inclusion in the previous list), and then filled in a bogus source (fame). Of course, it's not hard to see why subjects made this particular misattribution. After all, the experiment was described to them as being about fame, and other names on the list were

[handwritten margin note: sense of familiarity seems to outlast source memory]

indeed those of famous people. From the subjects' point of view, therefore, it is a reasonable inference under these circumstances that any name that "rings a bell" belongs to a famous person. With this acknowledged, though, the fact remains that subjects' reaction to their implicit memory depended critically on how they *interpreted* that memory.

Implicit Memory and the "Illusion of Truth"

A different example is somewhat frightening. Subjects in one study heard a series of statements and had to judge how interesting each statement was (Begg, Anas & Farinacci, 1992). As an example, one sentence was "The average person in Switzerland eats about 25 pounds of cheese each year." (This is false; the average is closer to 18 pounds.) Another was, "Henry Ford forgot to put a reverse gear in his first automobile." (This is true.) After hearing these sentences, subjects were presented with some more sentences, but now had to judge the *credibility* of these, rating them on a scale from "certainly true" to "certainly false." Needless to say, some of the sentences in this "truth test" were repeats from the earlier presentation; the question of course is how sentence credibility is influenced by sentence familiarity.

The result was a propagandist's dream: Sentences heard before were more likely to be accepted as true: Familiarity increased credibility (Begg, Armour & Kerr, 1985; Brown & Halliday, 1990; Hasher, Goldstein & Toppino, 1977). To make this worse, this effect emerged even when subjects were explicitly warned in advance not to believe the sentences in the first list. In one procedure, subjects were told that half of the statements had been made by men, and half by women. The women's statements, they were told, were always true; the men's always false. (Half the subjects were told the reverse.) Then subjects rated how interesting the sentences were, with each sentence attributed either to a man or a woman. "Frank Foster says that house mice can run an average of four miles per hour" or "Gail Logan says that crocodiles sleep with their eyes open." Finally, subjects were presented with new sentences and had to judge their truth, including of course these assertions about mice and crocodiles and so forth.

Let's focus on the sentences initially identified as being false—in our example, Frank's claim about mice. If a subject explicitly remembers this sentence ("Oh yes—Frank said such and such.") then the subject should judge the assertion to be *false* ("After all, the experimenter said that all the men's statements were lies."). But what about a subject without this explicit memory? Such a subject might still have an implicit memory ("Gee, that statement rings a bell."), and this might increase the credibility of the statement. ("I'm sure I've heard that somewhere before; I guess it must be true.") This is exactly the pattern of the data: Statements plainly identified as false when they were first heard still created the so-called illusion of truth—that is, these statements were subsequently judged to be more credible than sentences never heard before.

The relevance of this to the political arena, or to advertising, should be clear. A newspaper headline inquires: "Is Mayor Wilson a crook?" Or perhaps the headline declares: "Known criminal claims Wilson is a crook!" In either case, the assertion that Wilson is a crook has now become familiar. The Begg et al. data indicate that this familiarity will, by itself, increase the likelihood that you'll later believe in Wilson's dishonesty. This will be true even if the paper merely raised the question; it will be true even if the allegation came from a disreputable source. Malicious innuendo does in fact work its nasty effects (e.g., Wegner, Wenzlaff, Kerker & Beattie, 1981).

Attributing Implicit Memories to the Wrong Stimulus

In all these experiments, subjects seem not to realize that they are being influenced by a specific prior experience. In the illusion-of-truth experiments, subjects are convinced that they are drawing on some sort of general knowledge, not on memory for specific episodes. From their perspective, they are relying on what they *know*, rather than on what they *remember*. (For discussion of when subjects say they "know" something, and when they say they "remember," see Gardiner & Java, 1991; LeCompte, 1995; Rajaram, 1993.)

This observation is consistent with our earlier assertion that implicit memories often don't feel like memories. Instead, implicit memories leave us only with a vague sense that a stimulus is "special." Of course, we don't leave things in this vague state; instead, we try to attribute the sense of "specialness" to some source. Sometimes, we attribute this feeling to a previous encounter, in which case the implicit memory may be registered as a feeling of subjective familiarity. But in many other cases, we *misattribute* this feeling of specialness, and it is this misattribution that leads to judgments of fame or to the illusion of truth.

Indeed, in some cases, we are completely off in our attributions: In one experiment, subjects were presented with bursts of noise and asked to judge how loud each noise was (Jacoby, Allan, Collins & Larwill, 1988). Embedded within each burst of noise, though, was a sentence. Some of the sentences were new to subjects but, crucially, some of the sentences had been presented to subjects earlier on. In this set-up, therefore, we are asking about subjects' memory *for the sentences*.

In this study, memory appeared in an odd way: If a sentence was one of the familiar ones, subjects had an easier time hearing it against the backdrop of noise. This is just another case of repetition priming, and so is consistent with results already described. But then subjects seemed to reason in this fashion: "Well, that sentence was easy to hear. I guess, therefore, the noise couldn't have been so loud." Likewise, for the *unfamiliar* sentences, subjects seemed to reason: "Gee, that noise must have been loud, since it really drowned out the sentence." And, in fact, noise containing familiar sentences was (mis)perceived as being softer than it actually was; noise containing novel sentences was (mis)perceived as being loud.

In this experiment, therefore, the (objectively) familiar sentences do stand out from the rest and, presumably, subjects register the fact that these sentences are easier to discern against the background of noise than the (objectively) unfamiliar sentences. However, subjects seem to attribute none of this to the sentences themselves. Instead, they attribute the "specialness" to the noise, so that memory is here producing a "loudness illusion." It is the *sentences* that are familiar, but it is the *noise judgment* that is influenced. This makes plain the role of an attribution process and illustrates how far this process can go astray.

Attributing Implicit Memory to the Wrong Source

Many times, though, subjects *do* attribute the familiarity of a stimulus to a specific prior episode: They correctly realize that they have encountered the familiar stimulus once before, at a particular time and place. Even here, however, there is a possibility for error, namely, that the memory will be attributed to the *wrong* episode! This sort of error is referred to as **source confusion**.

[margin handwritten note: why courts reject mugshot identifications ⇒]

Does this kind of confusion really occur? In a study by Brown, Deffenbacher and Sturgill (1977), subjects witnessed a staged event. Two or three days later, subjects were shown "mug shots" of individuals who supposedly had participated in the event. Of course, the people in the photos were different from the people who were actually on the scene. Finally, after four or five more days, subjects were shown a line-up of four persons, and asked to select the individuals seen in step one—namely, the original event. The data show massive source confusion, with 29% of the subjects "indicting" individuals they had only seen in the mug shots. Apparently, therefore, subjects were correctly noting that these individuals seemed familiar, but they were confused about *why* they were familiar. Thus, the Supreme Court is correct in rejecting identifications done in this way (*Simmons et al. v. United States*, 1968; Gorenstein & Ellsworth, 1980; but also see Egeth, 1993).

Theoretical Treatments of Implicit Memory

These implicit-memory results are far-reaching in their implications and have provoked a rich theoretical debate. For example, consider what these results may be telling us about learning and memory in other species: When we speak of animals learning or remembering the past, what we often mean is that the animals' current behavior reveals the influence of past experiences. In humans, this is close to what we are now calling implicit memory. It is conceivable, therefore, that explicit memory—being able to comment on the past or to describe a specific past event—is a uniquely human form of re-membering or at least a form of remembering found only in complex organ-isms (primates and perhaps dolphins).

Likewise, subjects in implicit-memory studies often have no idea they are displaying an influence of past exposures—to use Jacoby and Witherspoon's (1982) term, they are displaying "memory without awareness." Conversely, explicit memory might be defined as "memory with awareness," and may include the possibility of consciously "reliving" the prior event. This implies a connection between explicit memory and awareness of one's self, and aware-ness of the sources of one's thoughts and actions. This too may provide a signal that this is a very special form of memory, perhaps unique to humans. (For relevant discussion, see Fivush, 1988; Nelson, 1988; Oakley, 1983; Reber, 1992; Squire & Zola-Morgan, 1991.)

But what exactly is an implicit memory? What is the content of these memories? And what is this feeling of "specialness" all about? It is to these questions that we now turn.

Implicit Memory: A Hypothesis

We have already noted (e.g., in Chapter 2) that perceptual processes are im-proved by practice. Having once perceived a stimulus, it will be easier to perceive that same stimulus in the future, because the relevant processes will now run more smoothly and efficiently. That is what repetition priming is all about.

Presumably, though, the same can be said for other bits of intellectual performance: Just as perceiving a word leads to fluency in perceiving, perhaps contemplating a word's meaning leads to fluency of a parallel sort. The next time one contemplated the same word's meaning, one might be a little quicker or more efficient.

We would expect these practice effects to be rather specific. Exercising your legs makes your legs stronger, not your arms. In the same way, practice at perceiving Gladys will help you when next you see Gladys; the practice will not improve your ability to perceive Sally or Lola. More generally, practice in perceiving a stimulus will improve your ability to perceive *that* stimulus; similarly, practice in thinking through a specific chain of associations will make it easier to retrace *those* mental steps, and not some others.

With this as backdrop, here is a hypothesis: Implicit memory is simply the name we give to these practice effects and to the resulting increase in **processing fluency**. For some tasks, this increase in processing fluency is by itself enough to influence performance. Consider, for example, implicit memory's effect on tachistoscopic identification or on lexical decision. These tasks require little more than the identification of the presented stimuli, and so these tasks would benefit directly from anything that speeds up processing. Thus, the claim of implicit memory here simply summarizes the fact that, once a stimulus has been perceived, it will be easier to perceive the next time around.

To explain other implicit-memory effects, though, we need a further assumption, namely, that subjects are sensitive to the degree of processing fluency. That is, subjects know when they have perceived easily and when they have perceived only by expending more effort. They likewise know when a sequence of thoughts was particularly fluent and when the sequence was labored. Note that we are *not* claiming that subjects experience the fluency as fluency. When a stimulus is easy to perceive, subjects usually do not experience a feeling of "ease." Instead, they merely register that vague sense of specialness. They feel like the stimulus "rings a bell." No matter how it is described, though, our hypothesis is that the sense of specialness has a simple cause—namely, ease in processing, brought on by fluency, which in turn was created by practice.

We still need one more step in our hypothesis, but it is a step we have already introduced: When a stimulus feels special, subjects typically want to know *why*. Thus, it is the feeling of specialness (again: produced by fluency) that triggers the attribution process, as subjects seek to attribute the specialness to some source. As we have seen, though, what happens next depends enormously on how the attribution goes. In some circumstances, the specialness will be (correctly) interpreted as "familiarity." In other situations, subjects may attribute the fluency to other sources, often incorrectly. As we have seen, this can lead to a variety of consequences beyond the "sense of familiarity"—including the false-fame effect, the illusion of truth, and so on.

It also seems likely that we can detect *decreases* in perceptual fluency, as well as increases. Consider what happens when someone you know well changes her hairstyle, or gets new eyeglasses. In such cases, you often have the uncomfortable feeling that something in your friend's appearance has changed, but you can't figure out what it is. In our terms, your friend's face was a stimulus that you had seen often, and therefore a stimulus you were fluent in perceiving. Once the stimulus is changed, though, your well-practiced steps of perceiving don't run as smoothly as they have in the past, and so the perception is less fluent than it had previously been. This lack of fluency is detected and produces the "something is new" feeling. But then the attribution step fails—you cannot identify what produced this feeling. This case provides the mirror-image of the cases we have been considering, in which familiarity leads to an *increase* in fluency, so that something "rings a bell," but one cannot say why.

In summary, then, the suggestion is that we should think of implicit memory as being more of a "skill" than a memory per se—a skill, as it turns out, in doing mental work (perceiving, or thinking about an idea, or whatever). This skill, and its concomitant fluency, will facilitate processing the next time the relevant mental steps are taken, and so the steps will go more easily and quickly the next time around. The subject will then detect the skill and seek to interpret it.

Implicit Memories Are Activity-Based

If this proposal is correct, then, in an important sense, implicit memories are *activity-based*. In other words, an implicit memory isn't simply a record of a stimulus you have encountered, or an event you have experienced. Instead, the implicit memory preserves a record of what you *did* in response to the stimulus or in response to the event. More precisely, the implicit memory is nothing other than the residual *skill*, created by your prior activity. It is this skill, "practiced" during the initial exposure, that produces fluency on the subsequent exposures.

The nature of an implicit memory, therefore, will depend crucially on what you did, what activities you engaged in, during the initial learning. Thus, imagine that you look at the word "hot." This doesn't create a broad implicit memory of this word. Instead, what is created is an implicit memory of *perceiving* this stimulus. This memory, this newly-created skill, will serve you well if, later on, you have occasion to perceive this same stimulus again. In that case, the fluency will pay off with greater ease, in perceiving the second time around. But this skill won't help if, later on, you want to *think about* this same stimulus, or contemplate its meaning; that is a different sort of activity, requiring a different sort of skill.

Likewise, an experimenter tells you: "Think about the opposite of 'cold.'" You will obviously think about the word, "hot" but, again, this won't create a broad implicit memory for the word itself. Instead, it will create a memory of *thinking about* "hot," and this will lead to greater fluency the next time you think about this concept. You haven't, in this set-up, practiced perceiving "hot," and so this exposure won't help you when next you try to perceive this word.

These claims turn out to be correct, as can be seen in a study by Blaxton (1989; Roediger & Blaxton, 1987a, 1987b). In the first step of this procedure, subjects read some words without any context, while other words were accompanied by a semantically related word. For still other words, subjects were shown *only* the semantic-associate and had to generate the word themselves.

Note that these three conditions are identical to those used by Jacoby (1983; see Figure 5.6); in describing the Jacoby study, we referred to the conditions as "no context," "context," and "generate." And, as before, we are assuming that these conditions can be understood in either of two ways: If we focus on how much *perceptual* work subjects must do, then the most work is required by the "no context" condition, and the least by the "generate" condition. If we focus on *conceptual* work, the ordering is reversed: Subjects must think about the word's meaning in the "generate" condition; there is nothing to encourage attention to meaning in the "no context" condition.

The "no context" condition, therefore, provides subjects with an opportunity to perceive the test words, and this should create some fluency in perceiving these words. Blaxton assessed this fluency with a word-fragment completion task ("What's the first word that comes to mind beginning with the letters c-o-p?"). This task obviously provides subjects with a perceptual cue: The letters "C O P" are there on the page, for subjects to look at. Therefore, if subjects are fluent in *perceiving* this word, they will have an advantage in this task. However, subjects won't be helped in this task by fluency of other sorts, by example, fluency in thinking about "copper." This is, of course, the kind of fluency created by the "generate" condition, but it is not the kind subjects need in this task. Hence, we predict little benefit for word-fragment completion from experience in the "generate" condition.

Other subjects were tested with a general-knowledge test ("What metal makes up 10% of yellow gold?"). For this task, there is no perceptual cue, and so prior practice at *perceiving* "copper" should provide no advantage. Hence, the "no context" condition should be poor preparation for this test. However, practice in the relevant conceptual operations should be helpful in this task and so, if subjects have recently thought about the *meaning* of "copper," this should produce priming. Therefore, we predict a benefit for this task from the "generate" condition.

Table 5.3 shows the data, fully in accord with these predictions. Practice in perceiving does seem to create an implicit memory of perceiving, and this influences performance with perceptual tasks, but not with meaning-based tasks. In contrast, practice in thinking about meaning creates an implicit memory for this activity, with the opposite pattern of benefits—aiding performance in meaning-based tasks but not in perceptual tasks. In short, the implicit memory does preserve a record of one's earlier activities, just as our hypothesis implies.

Perceptual Memories Are Stimulus-Specific

Implicit memories, therefore, appear to be rather specific: Practice in perceiving produces fluency in perceiving, and this leads to a benefit in subse-

Table 5.3

SUMMARY OF BLAXTON'S RESULTS: PERCENTAGE OF WORDS CORRECTLY IDENTIFIED ON TEST			
	Study Condition		
Type of Test	**Generate**	**Context**	**No Context**
General knowledge	50	38	33
Word-fragment completion	46	62	75
[After Blaxton, 1989.]			

quent perceptual tasks but not in tasks of other sorts. Likewise, practice in thinking about meaning produces its own fluency. This, too, leads to a benefit in some tasks but has no impact on perceptual tasks.

Implicit memories are also specific in another sense: To put this broadly, implicit-memory effects seem to emerge only when you "retrace your steps," and engage in mental operations that have been recently exercised. If these mental operations were largely *perceptual*, then you are most likely to "retrace your steps" if you are later on asked to perceive the exact same stimulus. As we said earlier, practice in perceiving Gladys will help you to recognize Gladys later on; it won't help you to recognize Lola. To achieve skill recognizing Lola, you need to practice recognizing Lola. Hence, perceptual skills are likely to be specific to the particular stimulus you have practiced perceiving.

What about other sorts of fluency? If you have thought about a stimulus's meaning in a certain way, this will create its own fluency—fluency in thinking about the meaning in that same way. Therefore, when you later return to these same thoughts, you will be more efficient, and swifter, the second time around. However, if you later try to think about that stimulus's meaning *from some other perspective*, there may be no benefit from this earlier-established fluency. Here too, it seems, fluency is observed when you "retrace your steps" and so, in this case, the fluency would be specific to a line of thinking, specific to a particular perspective.

These predictions are easy to confirm. For example, we have already discussed the priming effect in lexical-decision tasks. In the standard version of this procedure, subjects first see a list of words, and then they see the (visually-presented) lexical-decision test items. In an alternate version of this procedure, subjects first *hear* a tape-recorded list of words, and then see the test items. This shift in modality much reduces the priming effect. Apparently, therefore, perceptual practice with an *auditory* presentation of a word doesn't help you if you later need perceptual skill with a *visual* presentation of the same word (Jacoby & Witherspoon, 1982; Kirsner, Milech & Standen, 1983; Roediger & Blaxton, 1987a).

In the same vein, considerable priming is observed if subjects complete word-fragments (What is this word: "_L_P_A_T"?) and then are subsequently re-tested with the *same fragments*. However, virtually no priming is observed if subjects initially see one fragment ("_L_P_A_T") and are then tested with a *different* fragment of the *same word* ("E_E_H_N_"). Apparently, the initial exposure doesn't prime the *solution* to this fragment ("elephant"). If it did, then the initial exposure would help with the subsequent test. Instead, the initial exposure seems to be creating skill in working with one particular stimulus, and so this skill comes into view only if the same fragment is re-encountered later on.

Indeed, in some studies, even tiny changes in the stimulus—changes in type style—seem crucial. That is, priming effects are reduced if we present the to-be-remembered words in capital letters but then present the test items in lower case (Jacoby & Hayman, 1987; Jacoby & Witherspoon, 1982). Let us note, though, that other studies have not observed this pattern, leaving some question about whether implicit memories are specific to this rather extreme degree. (For discussion, see Biederman & Cooper, 1992; Cooper & Schacter, 1992; Cooper, Schacter, Ballesteros & Moore, 1992; Graf & Ryan, 1990.)

Fluency Dependent on a Stimulus's Meaning

In many cases, therefore, exposure to a stimulus produces fluency in dealing with just that stimulus. The fluency seems inapplicable to other stimuli, including stimuli closely related to those seen in practice. These data need to be contrasted, though, with data from other procedures and, in particular, with data from tasks requiring other forms of processing fluency.

We have already discussed the "illusion of truth," in which prior exposure to a sentence increases subsequent ratings of how credible that sentence is. In the "illusion of truth" procedures, the stimuli are clearly presented and with no time pressure so, in this situation, perceiving the stimuli should be easy. We would expect virtually no benefit, and virtually no influence, from perceptual fluency. Therefore, if we interpret the "illusion of truth" in terms of fluency, it is probably not perceptual fluency that is crucial. Instead, the key must be *conceptual* fluency—fluency in thinking about an idea's meaning or an idea's implications. This implies that we *shouldn't*, in this situation, observe stimulus specificity, and this turns out to be correct: The "illusion of truth" effect is still observed even if the sentences are *heard* the first time around and then *seen* in the test (Brown, Anas & Farinacci, 1992). This effect is therefore largely independent of stimulus format. (For related data, see

Brown, Neblett, Jones & Mitchell, 1991; Craik, Moscovitch & McDown, 1994; Srinivas, 1993; Weldon, 1993.)

This obviously fits with our claims: Perceptual fluency is fluency in dealing with a particular stimulus. Therefore, if perceptual fluency is crucial for a task, then the form of the stimulus should matter a great deal. If other forms of fluency are crucial, then the form of the stimulus should not matter.

These other forms of fluency, however, should be quite specific in other ways. As we have already mentioned, practice in thinking about a stimulus *from a certain perspective* will create fluency in thinking about the stimulus from just that perspective. This fluency will show up if you later on return to this line of thought, but this fluency won't benefit you if you later on think about the same topic, but from some other perspective.

To see this in action, consider a study by Bainbridge, Lewandowsky and Kirsner (1993). Their subjects were asked to do a lexical-decision task, judging whether strings of letters were English words or not. In addition, each stimulus string was shown with a context, so that subjects might see, "The policeman pulled him over and gave him a *tucket*." In this case, the correct response would be "no."

In some trials, the entire complex of context and string was identical to one presented in an earlier trial and, in these trials, a strong repetition priming effect was observed: Subjects were appreciably faster in their responses for these repeated items, in comparison to control items. In other trials, the *target string* was a repetition of an earlier-presented item but appeared with a *new context*, such as, "At the door to the cinema she collected a *ticket*." This change in context dramatically reduced the repetition priming effect.

This reduction in priming was most pronounced, however, when the change in context altered the meaning of the target item, e.g., from *ticket* as a "traffic citation," to *ticket* as an "entrance coupon." Once again, therefore, the priming effect is quite specific, but this time it is specific to a particular meaning. If the meaning changes, and if, accordingly, subjects think about the stimulus in a new fashion, then the earlier exposure to the stimulus (and the fluency it created) is largely irrelevant. (See Bainbridge, Lewandowsky & Kirsner, 1993, for a review of related findings.)

Thus, we can maintain our claim that, in general, fluency effects are quite specific. Whether they are specific to the *stimulus* or to *meaning*, however, depends on the sort of fluency relevant to the experiment in question. (For further discussion of these points, see Jacoby, Levy & Steinbach, 1992; Weldon, 1993.)

Illusions of Familiarity

A different line of results provides further support for the fluency claim. Let's start by reviewing the key hypotheses: Exposure to a task, we have suggested, provides practice in running the mental operations needed for that task. This practice, in turn, creates fluency, the next time the task is encountered. Finally, it is this fluency that produces the implicit-memory effects, including, in many cases, a sense of familiarity. This chain of events is depicted in Figure 5.7.

The idea, therefore, is that *fluency* is the direct trigger for the feeling that a stimulus is "special." Notice what will happen, therefore, if we make a stimulus easy to perceive *without* a prior exposure. In these cases, we will have externally produced a situation in which processing is fluent. By the logic of Figure 5.10, this may create an "illusion of familiarity."

In one study, subjects were shown a rapidly-presented series of seven words and then a test word. In half of the trials, the test word was identical to one of the just-presented seven words; in half of the trials, the test word was new. Subjects' task was to announce, in each trial, whether the test word was "old" (one of the previous seven) or "new" (Whittlesea, Jacoby & Girard, 1990).

This experiment also manipulated how easy the test word was to perceive. The test word in each trial, presented on a computer screen, was obscured

Figure 5.7

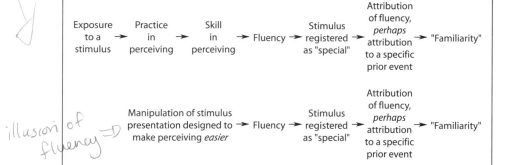

THE CHAIN OF EVENTS LEADING TO THE SENSE OF "FAMILIARITY"

The top line in the figure illustrates the chain of events leading to the sense that a stimulus is "familiar." Practice in perceiving leads to fluency. Once the fluency is detected, the subject may try to figure out what is *causing* this fluency. In many cases, the subject is likely to attribute the fluency to some specific prior encounter and, if so, the stimulus will "feel familiar." The *bottom* line in the figure, however, indicates that fluency can be created in other ways: A stimulus may be fluently perceived because the stimulus is presented more clearly, or presented for a longer exposure. Once this fluency is detected, though, it can set off a series of steps identical to those in the top row. Hence, an "illusion of familiarity" can be created.

by a swarm of constantly moving dots, as though the word were viewed through a snow storm. In some trials, the swarm of dots was relatively dense, making the word difficult to perceive. In other trials, the test word was obscured by fewer dots and so was easier to perceive. On some trials, therefore, the test word was easier to perceive because it was objectively familiar—presented just a moment ago, leading to an increase in perceptual fluency. We expect subjects to detect this increase in perceptual ease and, as a consequence, they should regard the stimulus as familiar. In other trials, though, the test word was easier to perceive, not because it was familiar, but because it was, in fact, more clearly presented. Subjects should again detect this increase in perceptual ease and, in this context, are likely to attribute the ease to familiarity. Thus, the more clearly presented stimuli should seem familiar, even when they are not.

Consistent with these claims, subjects in this study were often fooled: Clarity of presentation created an illusion of familiarity. In a follow-up experiment, subjects showed the reverse illusion: Subjects were explicitly asked to judge whether a stimulus was clearly presented or not. The data show these judgments to be heavily influenced by familiarity: When a word was a repetition of an earlier-presented stimulus, it seemed clearer; when the word was novel, it seemed less clear.

In short, subjects seem unable to distinguish perceptual ease created by familiarity from perceptual ease created by stimulus clarity. When asked to judge the former, they are inadvertently influenced by the latter; when asked to judge the latter, they are unwittingly influenced by the former. All of this is striking confirmation of the fluency notion and, in particular, of the claim that the feeling of familiarity derives in large measure from ease of processing.

Proceduralism

We have now gotten considerable mileage out of the claim that implicit memory involves some sort of *processing fluency*: Practice in a mental task leads to increased skill in that task, and this leads to fluency the next time the task is performed. Can we be more precise, though, in characterizing this fluency? If the fluency is the result of exercising mental skills, what *sort* of skills are they?

One answer to these questions is already in view: In our discussion so far, we have distinguished between two broad categories of mental skills: *perceptual* skills and *conceptual* skills. The former class of skills depends on exercise with perceptual processes, with this exercise leading to perceptual fluency. In this case, the skill will be stimulus-specific. The latter class depends on exercise with *conceptual* processes, leading to fluency in that domain, with the resulting skill being meaning-specific.

perceptual skills = stimulus specific

conceptual skills = meaning specific

Imagine, therefore, that you have had an opportunity to practice a word-fragment completion task. On the view just sketched, this practice will lead to perceptual skill, and this skill will then help you in other perceptual tasks—for example, tachistoscopic recognition. As an alternative, though, perhaps our mental skills are more fine-grained than this. Perhaps word-fragment completion requires its own specialized set of steps, its own profile of specialized operations. On this view, practice in word-fragment completion might lead to a skill that is highly specific—namely, skill in word-fragment completion. This skill will not transfer to tachistoscopic recognition—this task requires its own sort of skill. Instead, the skill of word-fragment completion will come fully into play only if you later re-use the skill—that is, only if you later on do more word-fragment completion.

On this view, we shouldn't be speaking of "perceptual skill" or "conceptual skill." Instead, we need to distinguish skills much more finely, so that there is a "word-fragment completion skill," a separate "tachistoscopic recognition skill," and so on. Indeed, there may be an infinite variety of these skills—one for each task you can perform. Is this plausible? When you perform a word-fragment completion test, you obviously go through some set of mental steps. Perhaps what is recorded in memory, therefore, is literally a record of these steps, a record of the *procedures* you used in performing the task. To make full use of this memory, therefore, you need to *retrace these steps*. Thus, it is word-fragment completion that you have practiced, and word-fragment completion that you remember.

This view of memory is sometimes referred to as "proceduralism," to highlight the claim that what memories contain, in general, may be a record of *mental procedures* that we have used in the past and that we are ready to use again, if the situation is appropriate (see, for example, Kolers & Smythe, 1984; Kolers & Roediger, 1984). From this perspective, one would expect that each task will yield its own highly specialized implicit memory, its own "procedure." This is because, in effect, our memories are largely records of what we have thought on some prior occasion. If thoughts differ from each other—in their contents, in their focus—then so will the corresponding memory. (For a closely related view, known as *transfer-appropriate processing*, or TAP, see Graf & Ryan, 1990; Masson & MacLeod, 1992; Morris et al., 1977; Roediger, Srinivas & Weldon, 1989.)

We are left with two broad options. One option describes our mental skills in general terms—a skill of perceiving relevant to all perceptual tasks, or a skill of doing conceptual work relevant to all meaning-based tasks. A different option is to cast the skills in a narrower fashion: One gains practice in a particular perceptual task, rather than practice at perceiving in general, and this practice will help you the next time you do that particular task. At present, there is no basis for choosing between these options. Let us note,

∴ not perceptual/conceptual skill, but word-fragment completion skill, etc

though, that both of these options are fully compatible with the fluency claim we have here been developing. What is at stake, therefore, is exactly how the fluency notion should be understood.

The Class of Implicit Memories

Let's pause to take stock. Throughout this chapter, we have argued that it is a mistake to describe learning as "effective" or "ineffective." Instead, it seems that learning that is effective for one sort of test may be ineffective with other tests. Therefore, to describe learning, we must take into account how the new memories are to be used later on.

Consistent with these themes, we have now seen that some forms of learning prepare you for implicit-memory tests, but not for explicit tests. Even *within* the domain of implicit memory, it seems that perceptual work prepares you for perceptual tasks, with the consequence that the learning is specific to a particular stimulus. Conceptual work prepares you for conceptual tasks, with the consequence that the learning is specific to a particular line of thought or a particular meaning. Again and again, it seems that the effectiveness of learning depends on how that learning will be used at some subsequent point.

Of course, all of this parallels precisely our earlier comments about *explicit* memory so that, for both implicit and explicit memory, we observe interactions between learning and memory retrieval. For both classes, the likelihood of accessing a memory depends on the concordance between your current perspective and your perspective when you first acquired the memory: The greater the "match" between these perspectives, the greater the chance that you will access the memory.

Given these parallels, though, how exactly should we conceive of the relation between explicit and implicit memory? How exactly are they alike? How are they different? As a related matter, we have emphasized the diversity inside the domain of implicit memories, with some of these memories stimulus-specific, some not, and with some of these memories meaning-specific and some not. This diversity leads us to ask: Exactly what properties do implicit memories have in common? What defines the *class* of implicit memories?

As it turns out, these are controversial questions. Most authors agree that there are two broad categories of memory; the disagreement, though, lies in how these categories should be defined. For example, some have argued that the key difference between implicit and explicit remembering lies in whether one is *trying* to remember. Hence, implicit memories represent "automatic" uses of memory, independent of intention, whereas explicit memories represent "deliberate, intentional" memory retrieval (e.g., Graf & Schacter, 1985; Jacoby, 1991; Richardson-Klavehn, Lee, Joubran & Bjork, 1994). Other authors have argued that this distinction is not critical; instead, we should focus on the "experience" of remembering—whether one does or does not have the conscious conviction of "remembering" the past. This conviction is presumably absent in implicit memory, present in explicit (e.g., Graf & Komatsu, 1994). Still others urge that we should focus neither on intention nor on the subjects' experience. Instead, what matters is the nature of the cues used to trigger these memories, whether perceptual or conceptual (e.g., Blaxton, 1989; Challis, Chiu, Kerr, Law, Schneider, Yonelinas & Tulving, 1993; Roediger, Weldon & Challis, 1989).

Still other authors have suggested that, in fact, we need to divide the domain differently, distinguishing between **declarative memories** and **procedural memories**, rather than implicit and explicit. Declarative memories are memories that such and such took place; these are memories that, in most cases, can be described in terms of specific propositions. Procedural memories, in contrast, are memories for how to do something. These are skills, not easily described in propositions. (From this perspective, the memories we have called "explicit" are generally declarative memories; the memories we have called "implicit" are generally procedural.) Moreover, the claim continues, each of these classes has its own profile, its own set of characteristics. Among others, each of these classes is represented in the brain in a certain fashion so that, for example, some forms of brain damage will damage the declarative system, but not the procedural. (We will return to these claims about brain damage in a moment. For discussion and extensions of this proposal, see Cooper & Schacter, 1992; Schacter, 1992; Tulving, Hayman & MacDonald, 1991.)

It seems that we are confronting a terminological Noah's ark, with terms marching two by two across the conceptual landscape—procedural and declarative; automatic and intentional; unconscious and conscious; perceptual and conceptual. (The "Noah's ark" image is Lockhart's, 1989.) In addition, we also have the claim of proceduralism, which suggests that all of these categorization schemes may be misguided, and that we should instead be talking about individual memories, rather than memory systems. (For a glimpse of some of the research attempting to choose among these options, see, e.g., Challis & Brodbeck, 1992; Jacoby & Kelley, 1992; Jacoby, Toth & Yonelinas, 1993; Joordens & Merikle, 1993; Schwartz & Hashtroudi, 1991; Srinivas, 1993; Tenpenny & Shoben, 1992; Thapar & Greene, 1994; Weldon, 1993; to name just a few.) This remains an area of active research, and it is simply too soon to know how this debate will be resolved. It does seem clear that there is a distinction to be drawn here: The memories we have called "implicit" look different in crucial ways from the memories we have called "explicit." However, there is still work to be done in finding the best, most precise way, to characterize this distinction.

Amnesia

We have been caught up in controversy in the last few sections, so it may be helpful to take a step back, to emphasize what is uncontroversial. At the very least, it is clear that we are often influenced by the past without our being aware of that influence. We often respond differently to familiar stimuli, even if we have no subjective feeling of familiarity. Thus, our conscious recollection seriously underestimates what is in our memories. Moreover, it is clear that some attribution step plays a crucial role in determining *how* we are influenced by our own implicit memories, with that attribution step often going astray. And, above all, it seems certain that we have only begun to document the many unconscious influences of memory on what we do, what we say, and what we think.

In addition, it seems clear that there are at least two different kinds of memory—one typically conscious, deliberate, and concerned with conceptual knowledge; one typically unconscious, automatic, and concerned with procedures. As we have seen, there is disagreement about how exactly we should *define* these two types of memory, but there is no disagreement about the need for some distinction, some categorization scheme.

In fact, two further lines of evidence also speak to the need to distinguish these categories of memory. One, which we'll simply mention, involves the attempt to "chart" memory performance across the life-span. Many studies are pertinent to this point but, in general, the pattern is that *implicit* memory can be documented at all ages, from very early childhood to very old age. Indeed, what is remarkable is the *similarity* in implicit memory performance by subjects at very different ages. Performance on explicit memory tasks, on the other hand, is strongly age-dependent, with children and the aged both out-performed by those in their middle years (e.g., Graf, 1990; Graf & Masson, 1993). These two different patterns add to the evidence that a distinction is needed here, with the memory systems distinguishable *developmentally* as well as *functionally*.

The distinction is also demanded by clinical evidence, in particular, evidence from cases of brain damage.

The Classic View of Amnesia

A variety of injuries or illnesses can lead to a loss of memory or **amnesia**. Some forms of amnesia are **retrograde**, that is, they disrupt memory for things learned prior to the event that initiated the amnesia. Retrograde amnesia is often caused, for example, by blows to the head; often one is unable to recall events occurring just prior to the blow. Other forms of amnesia have the reverse effect, causing disruption of memory for experiences *after* the onset of amnesia; these are cases of **anterograde amnesia**. (We should note that many cases of amnesia have both retrograde and anterograde memory loss.) Far more is known about anterograde amnesia than about retrograde, and it is anterograde amnesia that will be our focus here.

We discussed a famous case of anterograde amnesia in Chapter 1—the patient, H.M. (For a review of H.M.'s case, see Milner, 1966, 1970.) H.M. suffered from profound epilepsy, and a variety of attempts at cure had all failed. As a last resort, doctors sought to contain H.M.'s disease by brain surgery, specifically by removing portions of the brain that seemed to be the source of the seizures. The surgery did improve the epilepsy but at an incredible cost: H.M. seems unable to learn anything new. H.M. can function normally in many regards and can, for example, hold a coherent and consistent conversation. Within the conversation, H.M. may even talk about prior events in his life, since he seems fully able to recall events that took place prior to the surgery. However, he can't recall events that have taken place subsequent to his surgery. The severity of the problem is visible in many ways, but the problem becomes instantly clear if a conversation with H.M. is interrupted for some reason: If you leave the room, for example, and come back three or four minutes later, H.M. seems to have totally forgotten the conversation. Thus, thoughts currently in mind can be kept there by H.M.; thoughts out of mind seem lost forever.

H.M.'s specific case is unique, but a similar amnesia can be found in patients who have been long-time alcoholics. The problem is not the alcohol itself; the problem instead is that alcoholics tend to have inadequate diets, getting most of their nutrition from whatever they are drinking. As it turns out, though, most alcoholic beverages are missing several key nutrients, including vitamin B1 (thiamine). As a result, long-time alcoholics are vulnerable to a number of problems caused by thiamine deficiency, including a syndrome called **Korsakoff's syndrome** (Rao, Larkin & Derr, 1986; Ritchie, 1985).

A Korsakoff's patient seems in many ways similar to H.M. There is no problem in remembering events that took place before the alcoholism's onset. Current topics can be maintained in mind as long as there is no interruption. New information, though, if displaced from mind, is seemingly lost forever. Korsakoff's patients who have been in the hospital for decades will casually mention that they arrived only a week ago; if asked the name of the current president or events in the news they unhesitatingly give answers appropriate for two or three decades back, whenever the disease began (Marslen-Wilson & Teuber, 1975; Seltzer & Benson, 1974).

These cases can teach us a great deal about memory. For many years, these clinical amnesias were taken as striking confirmation of the memory model we first met in Chapter 4: In those terms, these amnesics seem to have intact long-term memories; that is why they remember events from before the amnesia's start. Likewise, the amnesic patient seems to have an intact working memory; that is how they remember events as they think about them. Information can be recycled and therefore maintained in working memory indefinitely, just like in a normal individual. What seemed to be wrong, though, is that the path from working memory to long-term memory is disrupted, so that no new information can enter permanent storage. Hence, if something is displaced from working memory, it vanishes without a trace.

Another Look at Amnesia: What Kind of Memory Is Disrupted?

More recent findings, however, have led to significant refinements in this account of amnesia. As it turns out, though, some of the relevant evidence has been available for a long time: In 1911, Edouard Claparède (1911/1951) reported the following incident: He was introduced to a young woman suffering from Korsakoff's amnesia, and he reached out to shake the patient's hand. However, Claparède had secretly positioned a pin in his own hand so that, when they clasped hands, the patient received a painful pin prick. (Respect for patient's rights would prevent any modern physician from doing this experiment, but ethical standards for physicians were rather different in 1911.) The next day, Claparède returned and reached to shake hands with the patient. Not surprisingly for a Korsakoff's amnesic, the patient initially gave no indication that she recognized Claparède or remembered anything about the prior encounter. Nevertheless, when the time came to clasp hands, the patient at the last moment abruptly withdrew her hand and would not shake hands with Claparède. Claparède asked her why this was and, after some confusion, the patient simply said vaguely that "sometimes pins are hidden in people's hands."

This patient seems to have no explicit memory of the prior encounter with Claparède. She does not mention the encounter in explaining her refusal to shake hands; if questioned closely about the prior encounter, she indicates no knowledge of it. Nonetheless, some sort of memory is retained. The patient knows something about the previous day's mishap but cannot report on the knowledge.

This peculiar kind of remembering can be demonstrated with Korsakoff's patients in many other ways. In one experiment, Korsakoff patients were asked a series of trivia questions (Schacter, Tulving & Wang, 1981). For each question, possible answers were offered in a multiple-choice format, and the patient had to choose which was the right answer. If the patient did not know the answer, he or she was told it, and then (unbeknownst to the patient) the question was replaced in the stack. Sometime later, therefore, as the game continued, the question came up again, and this time the patient was quite likely to get it right. Apparently, the patient had "learned" the answer in the previous encounter and "remembered" the relevant information. Consistent with their diagnosis, though, the patients had no recollection of the learning—they were consistently unable to explain why their answers were correct. They did not say "I know this bit of trivia because the same question came up just five minutes ago." Instead, they were likely to say things like, "I read about it somewhere," or "My sister once told me about it."

A different experiment makes a similar point: In a procedure by Johnson, Kim and Risse (1985), Korsakoff's amnesics heard a series of brief melodies. Sometime later, they were presented with a new series and told that some of the tunes in the second batch were repeats from the earlier presentation. The amnesics' assignment was to tell which were the repeats, and which they were hearing for the first time. As expected, the amnesics did poorly on this task; indeed, their memory responses were close to random. This is, of course, consistent with their clinical diagnosis. Remarkably, though, when asked which melodies they *preferred*, the amnesics uniformly preferred the familiar ones. The patients had no (explicit) memory for these tunes, but a memory did emerge with indirect testing—emerged, in this case, as a preference.

A great many results show this pattern, with amnesics showing profound memory loss on some measures but looking perfectly normal on other measures (Cohen & Squire, 1980; Graf & Schacter, 1985; Moscovitch, 1982; Schacter & Tulving, 1982; Squire & McKee, 1993). Thus, on the one side, these patients seem completely incapable of recalling episodes or events. In the terms we have been using, these patients seem to have no *explicit* memory; in Tulving's terms, they have no episodic memory.

At the same time, though, these patients do learn and do remember; in other words, they seem to have intact *implicit* memories. Indeed, in most tests of implicit memory, amnesic patients seem indistinguishable from ordinary individuals. The amnesics seem perfectly capable of perceptual learning, and of learning new skills. In fact, the range of skills that can be learned by amnesics is quite broad—with practice, amnesics can learn to solve math problems they have never seen before, they can learn to play difficult pieces of piano music, they can even learn to program a computer (Glisky, Schacter & Tulving, 1986). In some experiments, the amnesics also seem capable of acquiring new semantic information (Tulving, Hayman & Macdonald, 1991). All of this stands alongside the fact that, in each case, the amnesic has no memory for where or when the new skill was acquired or the new information learned. Any test that requires source memory reveals the profound amnesia. But, in tests not requiring source memory, amnesics seem remarkably ordinary.

These results have many implications, both for amnesia and more broadly for memory theory. For our purposes, the amnesia data draw attention once again to the importance of distinguishing different types of memory and different types of remembering. As we have seen, many experiments indicate that these types of memory can be distinguished on *functional* grounds, with the different types of memory created by different sorts of learning and evoked by different sorts of test. The amnesia data indicate that types of memory can also be distinguished on *neurological* grounds—with specific forms of brain damage disrupting some sorts of memory but not others.

The amnesia data thus draw us back to the issues with which this chapter began. It would be a mistake to claim that amnesics are "bad learners." Instead, their learning seems fine provided that memory is tested in the right way. Likewise, amnesics are not "poor rememberers." What they remember seems quite normal, given the appropriate kind of test and the appropriate preparation. All of this echoes some by now familiar themes: We cannot speak of learning and memory in global terms; instead we need to make finer distinctions. And it looks like we cannot discuss the processing of "loading" memory (encoding) without also paying attention to how the memory will be used or retrieved.

6

Memory Errors, Memory Gaps

In Chapter 4, we emphasized the role of *memory connections* in the learning of new materials. These connections, we argued, promote learning by tying the newly-acquired information to things you already know. These connections can then serve as *retrieval paths*, helping you to locate the newly-acquired material within long-term storage.

However, these same memory connections can also serve as a source of memory error. By virtue of interweaving the new information with your prior knowledge, you create the potential for confusion, as you can easily lose track of which elements are which—that is, which of these interconnected elements were actually contained within the episode you are trying to recall and which elements were supplied by *you*.

A study by Owens, Bower and Black (1979) puts these points nicely in view. Half of the subjects in their experiment read the following passage.

> Nancy arrived at the cocktail party. She looked around the room to see who was there. She went to talk with her professor. She felt she had to talk to him but was a little nervous about just what to say. A group of people started to play charades. Nancy went over and had some refreshments. The hors d'oeuvres were good but she wasn't interested in talking to the rest of the people at the party. After a while she decided she'd had enough and left the party.

Other subjects read the same passage, but with a prologue that set the stage:

> Nancy woke up feeling sick again and she wondered if she really were pregnant. How would she tell the professor she had been seeing? And the money was another problem.

All subjects were then given a recall test, in which they were asked to remember the sentences as exactly as they could. As can be seen in Table 6.1,

Table 6.1

NUMBER OF PROPOSITIONS REMEMBERED BY SUBJECTS		
	Theme Condition	Neutral Condition
Studied propositions (those in story)	29.2	20.2
Inferred propositions (those not in story)	15.2	3.7
[After Owens, Bower, & Black, 1979.]		

subjects who had read the prologue recalled considerably more of the original story. This is consistent with the claims made in Chapter 4: The prologue provided a meaningful context for the remainder of the story and thus helped understanding. Understanding, in turn, promoted recall.

At the same time, however, the story's prologue also led subjects to include many things in their recall which were not mentioned in the original episode. These are referred to as **intrusion errors**. In fact, subjects who had seen the prologue made *four times* as many intrusion errors as did subjects who did not see the prologue. For example, subjects might recall, "The professor had gotten Nancy pregnant." This is certainly implied by the story, and so will probably be part of subjects' understanding of the story. It is then this understanding (including the imported element) that is remembered. In this fashion, the story's prologue both helped memory and hurt memory: The prologue supported memory for the story's gist, but at the cost of a large number of intrusion errors.

As we will see in this chapter, intrusion errors are extremely easy to document. What we expect to see, or what we typically see, often becomes confused in memory with what we actually saw. This is in many ways troubling, since these memory errors raise the possibility that the objective past may be rather different from the past as we remember it. This in turn has implications for how we should think about our past, and for how much faith we should put in our own memories. These memory errors also have pragmatic implications, for example, for the legal system: Eyewitness testimony is taken very seriously by the courts, but of course this testimony relies on what the witness remembers. It is no surprise, therefore, that much research on memory accuracy has been applied directly to the situation of the eyewitness. We will examine some of this research in this chapter, as part of our broader discussion of the accuracy and completeness of memory.

Distortions and Intrusions

In the pages to come, we will argue that memory errors can, in some circumstances, be rather large and, in many cases, are undetectable: "Memories" that happen to be fictional are often just as vivid, and recalled with just as much confidence, as memories that happen to be correct. But we will also present some more reassuring data indicating that, in most cases, memory is quite accurate. Against this backdrop, we will then need to ask *when* the memory errors occur, and whether they can be avoided or corrected.

Distortions in Memory for Prose

Frederick Bartlett's book, *Remembering*, was published in 1932, but is in many ways still current. Bartlett presented his subjects with various passages to remember—for example, stories taken from the folklore of Native Americans. Subjects did reasonably well in recalling the *gist* of the stories but made many errors in recalling the particulars. Often, details of the original story were simply omitted from subjects' recall; other details were either added to the original, or changed. The pattern of errors, though, was quite systematic: The details omitted tended to be details that made little sense to Bartlett's British subjects. Likewise, aspects of the story that were unfamiliar were changed into aspects more familiar; steps of the story that seemed inexplicable were supplemented to make the story seem more logical, more coherent. In general, memory "cleaned up" the story—making it more coherent, and more sensible, than it actually was.

Many other studies show the same pattern. For example, consider a classic experiment by Bransford and Johnson (1972, 1973). Subjects were asked to read the following passage, entitled "Watching a Peace March from the Fortieth Floor."

> The view was breathtaking. From the window one could see the crowd below. Everything looked extremely small from such a distance, but the colorful costumes could still be seen. Everyone seemed to be moving in one direction in an orderly fashion, and there seemed to be little children as well as adults. The landing was gentle, and luckily the atmosphere was such that no special suits had to be worn. At first there was a great deal of activity. Later, when the speeches started, the crowd quieted down. The man with the television camera took many shots of the setting and the crowd. Everyone was very friendly and seemed glad when the music started.

As you read this story, one sentence ("The landing was gentle . . . ") probably seemed out of place. Subjects reacted the same way. When asked to recall the story later on, subjects did reasonably well, but were likely to forget this sentence altogether. If subjects did remember this peculiar sentence, they were likely to remember it in a transformed manner: Perhaps they might remember reading "In the relaxed mood, no special clothing was required" (and omit the puzzling "landing").

Things were different if subjects read the same story but with a different title, namely "Space Trip to an Inhabited Planet." In this situation, subjects were not jarred by the "landing" sentence, were likely to remember it, and were unlikely to transform it as just described.

Quite clearly, the pattern of recall here is guided by subjects' understanding of the story. What fits with subjects' understanding is likely to be remembered. What does not fit is likely to be lost or transformed. If we change subjects' understanding of the story, we will change what they remember.

Remembering Things that Never Took Place

Perhaps the most striking aspect of this pattern is the intrusion errors. Subjects in these experiments confidently claim to remember things that never happened, provided that the item in question fits with their understanding of the material. Here is another example, from a study by Johnson, Bransford and Solomon (1973): Half the subjects heard the following sentences:

> John was trying to fix the birdhouse.
> He was pounding the nail when his father came out to watch him and to help him do the work.

Other subjects heard these sentences:

> John was trying to fix the birdhouse.
> He was looking for the nail when his father came out to watch him and to help him do the work.

Sometime later, subjects were asked whether the following was among the sentences they heard:

> John was using the hammer to fix the bird house when his father came out to watch him and to help him do the work.

If the subjects were in the first group ("pounding the nail"), they were likely to say (incorrectly, but often confidently) that they had heard this sentence earlier. If the subjects were in the second group ("looking for the nail"), they were less likely to recall having heard the test sentence. In the "pounding" case, the initial sentences had invited subjects to assume a hammer was part of the scene; after all, John had to have been using something to "pound the nail." This (implied) hammer seems then to have become part of the remembered material. (See also Bower, Black & Turner, 1979.)

You might object, though, that this is a small error—with just a few words misremembered. However, much larger intrusion errors can also be documented. In a study by Brewer and Treyens (1981), subjects were asked to wait briefly in the experimenter's office (Figure 6.1), prior to the procedure's start. After 35 seconds, subjects were taken out of this office and told that there

Figure 6.1

THE OFFICE USED IN THE BREWER AND TREYENS STUDY

No books were in view in this office, but subjects, biased by their expectations for what *should be* in a scholar's office, often remembered seeing books! [After Brewer & Treyens, 1981.]

was no experimental procedure. Instead, the study was concerned with their memory for the room in which they had just been sitting.

Subjects' recollection of the office was plainly influenced by their prior knowledge—in this case, their knowledge about what an academic office typically contains. Some aspects of the office were consistent with subjects' expectations, and these aspects were well remembered. For example, 29 of 30 subjects correctly remembered that the office contained a desk and chair. For other aspects of the office, subjects probably had no expectations one way or the other, and these aspects were less well remembered. For example, only 8 of 30 subjects remembered the bulletin board. Still other aspects of the office, though, were quite different from what subjects might have expected. For example, subjects would surely expect an academic office to contain shelves filled with books, yet in this particular office no books were in view. Nonetheless, subjects' recall was in line with their expectations and not with reality: Almost one-third of the subjects (9 of 30) remembered seeing books in the office when, in fact, there were none. (But see also Pezdek, Whetstone, Reynolds, Askari & Dougherty, 1989.)

Remembering Actual Phrasing versus Remembering Gist

What is the nature of these memory errors? One possibility is that subjects confidently recall the office's desk, but are guessing about the books. If simply asked "yes or no" about each of these, subjects would say yes to both. If asked in a more sensitive fashion, though, subjects might be able to tell us which aspects of the office they remember in detail and for which aspects they are guessing.

Some memory errors do have this character, with the rememberer able to distinguish between recalled facts and inferred facts, objects observed and objects assumed. In many cases, though, the error is deeper than this. In a number of experiments, subjects' memories have been tested in a fashion that should discriminate between high-confidence memories and mere guesses, or between detailed recollections and mere assumptions. For example, some studies have asked subjects how *confident* they are in each of their responses. Other studies have urged subjects to be extremely careful, responding "Yes, this is familiar," only if they are quite certain about their judgments. Still other studies have tried timing subjects' responses, with the idea that responses based on inference or assumption might involve a moment of hesitation, and so should be somewhat slower than responses based on clear, detailed memory.

In these studies, the data are clear and somewhat dismaying: Subjects' responses are indistinguishable for the original materials—that is, the materials presented initially—and for paraphrases of those materials or inferences from those initial materials. The likelihood of subjects responding "Yes, this is familiar" is the same for both. Subjects' confidence in their responses is the same for both. The speed of responding is the same for both. (See, for examples of this broad pattern, Begg & Wickelgren, 1974; Bransford, Barclay & Franks, 1972; Bransford & Franks, 1971; Brewer, 1977; Paris & Lindauer, 1976; Sachs, 1967; Sulin & Dooling, 1974; Thorndyke, 1976.)

In these studies, therefore, subjects' memories seem to record only their understanding of an event, and so subjects endorse as familiar anything compatible with that understanding. No memory privilege is observed for the "objective" event itself. Thus, in these cases, what seems to be preserved in memory is the past-as-understood, with no advantage for the event as it actually unfolded.

Memory Accuracy and Memory Confidence

We have not said that memory errors happen all the time. As we will see in later sections, the evidence suggests that, more often than not, our memories do record the past accurately. Nonetheless, the data surveyed so far point toward several strong claims. First, when memory errors occur, they are likely to be errors of a certain sort—bringing the remembered past into line with our other knowledge and beliefs. In effect, we remember the past as being more "regular" than it actually was. Second, memory errors can be large. We have already considered a case of remembering books that weren't there; later on we will consider memories for entire *events* that, in fact, never occurred.

Third, when memory errors occur, they are often undetectable. We have just described cases in which subjects *do* recall the gist of an earlier event, that is, they do recall their own understanding of the event. But subjects seem not to have a clue about how exactly the event unfolded. In effect, they don't remember the "facts" that led them to a particular interpretation, they just remember the interpretation. If it turns out that the interpretation is wrong, or incomplete, there will be no way to think back to the facts to correct things. If the interpretation is *in conflict* with the facts, this will go undetected, because the facts aren't preserved in memory as a way of "checking" the interpretation.

These claims are strengthened by various other results. Let's focus specifically on memory *confidence*: Sometimes we are certain about the past ("I distinctly remember his yellow jacket"), and sometimes we are not ("Gee, I think he was wearing blue, but I'm not sure"). Common sense tells us that memories of the first sort are likely to be correct, and we tend to trust confident recollection. Conversely, we put little faith in less-confident recollections, and we are not surprised if these turn out to be mistaken.

However, this bit of common sense is almost certainly *wrong*. As we have just seen, subjects in many studies are equally confident in their accurate recollections and in their false recollections. In these studies, memory confidence seems no indication of memory accuracy. In fact, a large number of studies have documented this pattern. In these studies, subjects are asked to recall a number of items, and then are asked to assess their confidence in each one of their recollections. This allows the researcher to examine in detail the relationship between memory accuracy and memory confidence. Using this approach, study after study has observed low or even zero correlations between accuracy and confidence; some studies have even documented negative correlations, with subjects more confident in their wrong answers than in their right ones! (See, for example, Chandler, 1994; Loftus, 1979; or Bothwell, Deffenbacher & Brigham, 1987; Wells, Luus & Windschitl, 1994.)

How could this be? How could we be so far off in assessing our own memories? Several factors contribute to this. In many cases, our judgments of memory confidence probably hinge on the *familiarity* of the face, assertion, or event, being remembered. Yet, as we saw in Chapter 5, familiarity is itself a tricky notion. In addition, it also seems that familiarity with the general themes being remembered may, in some cases, lead to the illusion that the details are remembered as well (cf. Chandler, 1994). Finally, even when subjects do realize they are uncertain about their recall, they seem genuinely unable to gauge their *degree* of uncertainty (e.g., Schneider & Laurion, 1993). For all these reasons, confidence ends up being (at best) a poor index of memory accuracy. Worse still, in some cases subjects seem absolutely certain their memories are correct when in fact their memories contain large-scale errors (e.g., Neisser & Harsch, 1992).

At a theoretical level, this poor correspondence between memory accuracy and confidence obviously speaks to the difficulty of *detecting* false memories when they occur. At a more personal level, these findings are potentially rather troubling, since they invite the concern that some of our most cherished, most confident recollections of the past may turn out to be mistaken.

These findings also have important pragmatic implications: In accord with common sense, evidence indicates that eyewitnesses are more persuasive to a jury when their testimony is delivered with confidence, as opposed to when testimony is hedged or hesitant (Brigham & Wolfskiel, 1983; Cutler, Penrod & Stuve, 1988; Loftus, 1979; Wells, Lindsay & Ferguson, 1979). But this seems to be a domain in which juries are acting unwisely. There is no reason to grant more credibility to a confident witness; even testimony offered with enormous conviction may turn out to be false.

A number of researchers have suggested, though, that there may be circumstances in which confidence is predictive of memory accuracy. Studies of eyewitnesses indicate that confidence expressed *after* a line-up selection ("Are you sure that was the thief?") is more closely associated with accuracy than confidence expressed prior to the line-up ("Are you sure that you'll recognize the thief when you see him?"; Cutler & Penrod, 1989). Likewise, an eyewitness's confidence is more closely associated with accuracy if the suspect happens to be distinctive in appearance (Brigham, 1990; for other, related, studies, see Cutler & Penrod, 1989; Deffenbacher, 1980; Fleet, Brigham & Bothwell, 1987; Kassin, 1985). It should be emphasized, though, that even in circumstances favoring an accuracy-confidence correlation, this correlation is never a strong one. (The correlation values rarely exceed .30 or .40.) Under no circumstances, then, is memory confidence a reliable indicator of memory veracity.

Accurate Memory

Throughout the 1970s, psychologists documented case after case in which subjects' memories were heavily biased by their prior knowledge: If some fact didn't fit with subjects' understanding of the world, they failed to recall that fact. Intrusion errors occurred in study after study, with subjects recalling items that "should have been present," even though they weren't. Memory distortions were repeatedly demonstrated, with subjects "altering the past" to bring it into line with their beliefs.

This paints a grim picture of memory accuracy, making it important to balance this picture by acknowledging the many studies that reveal complete and accurate remembering. In this section, we will present some data from the other side—data showing accurate memory, which is not influenced by subjects' prior knowledge. We will also consider some cases in which subjects *do* seem able to discriminate which elements of their recollection are based on genuine recall and which on inference.

For example, we have considered several studies showing subjects' poor recall for stories they did not understand (Bartlett, 1932; Bransford & Johnson, 1972; Dooling & Lachman, 1971). It turns out, however, that subjects do seem to remember these very same materials if memory is tested via a recognition procedure, instead of by recall (Alba, Alexander, Hasher & Caniglia, 1981). In this procedure, the original materials do seem to be preserved in memory, independent of their "fit" with subjects' understanding. (For a wide range of related data, see Alba & Hasher, 1983.)

Even with recall testing, though, some studies show that memory errors can be avoided, if subjects are suitably instructed. For example, Hasher and Griffin (1978) presented subjects with a story about a man walking through the woods. Some of the subjects read the story together with an appropriate title ("Going Hunting"), and then were given this same title at the time of the recall test. Hasher and Griffin expected that this would encourage subjects to rely on the title itself in reconstructing the story. This, they predicted, would lead to many errors: Elements not consistent with the overall gist should drop out of the recollection; intrusion errors consistent with the gist should also be observed. The data confirm these predictions. When subjects have reason to believe their understanding of the story's gist is correct, they rely on this gist and use it to reconstruct the story.

Other subjects read the story with the same title, but then, at the time of the test, these subjects were told that an error had occurred and that they had inadvertently been given the wrong title for the story. They were given a new title ("An Escaped Convict") that was, in fact, also consistent with the story's contents. Hasher and Griffin reasoned that these subjects, now convinced that their prior understanding of the story was incorrect, would try to set aside this understanding, and to recall the exact story as it actually was presented. On this basis, Hasher and Griffin predicted that subjects in this group would recall the story without interpretation and without intrusions. That is exactly what the results show.

It seems that, at least in some circumstances, subjects can control whether they will reconstruct a story based on remembered gist, or try to reproduce it faithfully by digging through memory for the actual sentences. It seems that subjects did the former in the experiment's first condition, and so produced many errors and intrusions. But subjects did the latter in the experiment's second condition and thus avoided these errors.

A different study makes roughly the same points: In an experiment by Anderson and Pichert (1978), subjects read a story about two boys playing in one of their homes. Half of the subjects were told to read the story and the description of the home pretending that they were potential home-buyers; half read the passage from the perspective of a potential burglar. The story had been constructed so that it included information particularly relevant to a burglar, as well as information particularly useful for a potential buyer. When subjects' memories were tested, those reading from the "burglar" perspective recalled more of the burglar information; those reading from a "buyer" perspective recalled more of the information useful to a home-buyer. By leading subjects to employ one perspective or another, we influence how they understand the story and, correspondingly, what they notice and what they remember.

The twist, though, comes from the next step of the procedure. After a brief delay, subjects were again asked to recall the story, but this time they were encouraged to change perspective—from that of a burglar to that of a buyer or vice versa. With this change in perspective, subjects were able to remember things that they had earlier "forgotten" and, in particular, were able to remember things relevant to their new perspective. Once again, it seems that subjects do remember items external to their initial understanding and can recover these items if their understanding changes.

Misleading Eyewitnesses

The pattern of data, therefore, is clearly mixed. Earlier in this chapter, we described studies in which subjects showed no indication of remembering the actual materials they had experienced. Instead, all they seemed to remember was their *interpretation* of these materials. Now, though, we have introduced some studies with a different outcome: In these studies, subjects, in their initial attempt at recall, relied heavily on their understanding of the past. When this is discouraged, however, the subjects can recall the original facts.

The implication of all this is that memory errors arise through different mechanisms, with some mechanisms leading to "reversible" errors and some not. We will pursue this point later but, in the meantime, let's look at a further line of evidence, which speaks to the same general theme—namely, the variety of mechanisms potentially leading to memory error.

So far, our discussion has concerned errors caused by generic knowledge, knowledge acquired long before subjects encountered the target event. But what about the reverse error? Are there cases in which "new" knowledge gets confused with "old"?

Imagine that you are witness to a crime. Sometime later, you read an account of this crime in the newspaper, and this account *differs* from your own recollection. Perhaps the newspaper's version includes details you didn't notice, or perhaps it contains elements flatly contradicting what you remember. How will this affect your memory? Will your recollection by influenced by this experience?

Many studies address these questions, with procedures modeled closely after the situation of the eyewitness. The subjects witness an event and are then exposed to some new information about the event. Sometimes this post-event information is presented as an alternative account of the event. (This would be similar to the example just described, in which a witness to a crime reads a newspaper report about the same crime.) In other procedures, the post-event information is delivered in a subtler fashion, via leading questions. For example, Loftus and Palmer (1974) showed subjects a series of projected slides depicting an automobile collision. Some time later, some subjects were asked, "How fast were the cars going when they hit each other?" Other subjects were asked, "How fast were the cars going when they smashed into each other?" The difference between these questions (*hit* vs. *smashed*) is slight, but it is enough to bias subjects' estimates of speed. Subjects in the first group estimated the speed to have been 34 mph; subjects in the second group estimated 41 mph. But what is critical comes next: One week later, subjects were asked whether they had seen any broken glass in the slides. Subjects who had initially been asked the "hit" question tended to remember (correctly) that no glass was visible; only 14% said they had seen glass. Subjects asked the "smashed" question, though, were reasonably likely to remember glass: 32% asserted that glass was visible. It seems, therefore, that the change of just one word within the initial question can have a large effect—in this case, more than doubling the likelihood of memory error.

Loftus has reported a number of variations on this experiment, offering many refinements and extensions to the basic finding (Loftus, 1975, 1979; Loftus, Miller & Burns, 1978). In one experiment, Loftus showed subjects a slide sequence in which a car ran past a stop sign, and then subsequently misled them by asking them about the car's speed when it passed a *yield* sign. When later asked about the scene, subjects remembered quite clearly having seen the (fictitious) yield sign, choosing it when given the options of a stop sign, a yield sign, and a one-way sign. Loftus then told subjects directly that their response was incorrect and asked them to choose their answer from the remaining two. Now, subjects were equally likely to choose the (correct) stop sign and the (out-of-nowhere) one-way sign. Even given this "second-guess" option, subjects showed no sign of remembering the original event.

Similar effects can be documented if the original event is viewed on a videotape or even "live." Likewise, a wide range of memories can be changed in this fashion. Thus, with different versions of the misinformation procedure, psychologists have arranged things so that screwdrivers originally seen are remembered as hammers and blue sedans are remembered as brown pick-up trucks. In still other studies, misinformation has been used, after the fact, to alter how people remember the age, body size, or facial characteristics of actors within an event (Christiaansen, Sweeney & Ochalek, 1983; Loftus & Greene, 1980).

We have offered examples directly pertinent to the legal system, with subjects witnessing auto collisions and the like. But related effects can be observed with memories of a more mundane sort. This speaks to the breadth of these effects and also suggests that these memory effects may reach into a great deal of our day-to-day recollection. For example, Spiro (1977) presented subjects with descriptions like this one: "Bob and Margie are engaged to be married. Bob strongly desires not to have children." Half of the subjects were told that Margie shares this desire; the other subjects were told that Margie very much wants to have children. Near the end of the experiment, half of the subjects in each group were told that Margie and Bob did get married and are still happily together. The remaining subjects were told that Bob and Margie subsequently broke off their engagement. Thus, we have some subjects for whom the initial account fits with the later information: neither partner wants children and they stay together, or there is a conflict over children and they break up. For other subjects, the initial account does not fit so well with the later information (e.g., conflicting desires, but stay together anyway).

Later on, subjects were asked to recall the description of Bob and Margie, as accurately as they could. The data show that subjects' memories for the original materials were influenced by knowing Bob and Margie's current status. For those subjects believing that Bob and Margie stayed together, the conflict over children was remembered as being relatively minor. For those subjects believing that Bob and Margie eventually broke up, the conflict was remembered as being serious. Knowing the story's end, subjects seem to mis-remember the story's beginning, to bring it better into line with the story's end. (For related data, see Fischhoff, 1975, 1977.)

The Controversy over Updating

Apparently, then, memories can be altered, or even "planted," after the fact, by suitable suggestions or questioning. Are there limits on the "memories" that can be created in this fashion? Or can any sort of "memory" be planted— by a police investigator, a lawyer, or a therapist? No one has a firm answer to these questions. It does seem more difficult to create *large* memory errors than small ones but, nonetheless, large errors can be created. For example, researchers have been able to plant entire events in subjects' recollection, so that subjects end up recalling an episode that never took place. Subjects have been led to recall an occasion in which they hurt their hand in a mousetrap and had to be taken to the hospital, even though this event never occurred (Ceci, Huffman, & Smith, 1994). Other subjects have been led to remember a particular birthday in which a clown entertained everyone, even though, once again, this event was a bit of fiction (Hyman, Husband, & Billings, 1995; also see Loftus, 1993; Ofshe, 1992; Wright, 1993). Thus, *if* there are limits on the creation of false memories, we have not yet discovered them.

In addition, we should note that there has been considerable argument among researchers about why these errors occur. There is no question about the basic finding: Subjects' descriptions of an event, after a delay, can be strongly influenced by post-event misinformation. The **misinformation effect**, as it is often called, is well-established. But what lies behind this effect?

Consider a concrete case. An eyewitness observes a workman steal a calculator, pick up his hammer, and then leave the room. Later, the witness reads a printed account of the crime, but the account mentions that the worker picked up a *wrench* before leaving. Finally, the witness is asked, "In the original event, did you see the worker pick up a hammer or a wrench?" As we have seen, the witness is likely to report (incorrectly) seeing a wrench, that is, he will report the misleading information, not the original.

One interpretation of this result is that the post-event misinformation replaces or "overwrites" the original memory. Thus, subjects initially remembered the hammer, but this memory was overwritten by a newly-created memory of the wrench. This is referred to as a process of "destructive updating," since the new memory is presumed to destroy the old.

However, other explanations are possible. For example, perhaps subjects didn't notice the hammer in the first place, or perhaps they did notice it but forgot about it for reasons quite separate from the misleading information. Either of these would leave a gap in the memory record. When the misleading information arrives, therefore, there is nothing in memory to contradict it, and so it is accepted as true. In this case, no memory updating has taken place, since there was no memory to be updated.

As a different account, perhaps subjects remember both the hammer and the wrench. When the test arrives, they reason this way, "I remember seeing a hammer, but I know I just read about a wrench. I guess my memory must be wrong." Again, in this case, there has been no destruction of the hammer memory; subjects are simply electing to respond on the basis of a different memory.

Which of these accounts is correct? Debate about this issue is still ongoing, but the evidence seems to indicate that all of these mechanisms are active, and all contribute to the basic misinformation result. Most controversial, though, within this debate, has been the idea of destructive updating—the idea that a new memory can literally supplant an already-established memory. The best evidence is that updating does occur. That is, in some procedures, subjects' memory for the original information does seem to be genuinely weakened by the later-presented misinformation (e.g., Belli, Lindsay, Gales & McCarthy, 1994). It is not yet clear, however, whether the original memory is actually erased by the misinformation or simply rendered inaccessible. (For an early account of this controversy, see McCloskey & Zaragoza, 1985. For subsequent findings, see Belli, 1989; Belli, Windschitl, McCarthy & Winfrey, 1992; Lindsay, 1993; Loftus, 1992; Tversky & Tuchin, 1989; Weingardt, Loftus & Lindsay, 1995; Zaragoza & Lane, 1994.)

With this controversy acknowledged, let's not lose sight of one crucial point: Whatever the cause, subjects in these experiments truly believe that they are reporting the original event accurately. For example, subjects' confidence in their incorrect responses, responses plainly influenced by the misleading information, is often quite high. Likewise, when asked directly, "Did you *see* this, as part of the event, or was it something you *read* afterwards?" subjects will insist that the misinformation was part of the original episode. Thus, at a theoretical level, we may be uncertain about whether misinformation "erases" the earlier input, or whether it works through some other means. At the pragmatic level, though, what subjects report about an event is clearly influenced by the misleading information, with subjects utterly convinced by their own false memories. We can debate the mechanisms through which misinformation has its effect, but there is no doubt that misinformation does have a strong impact on how the past is described and, it seems, on how the past is remembered.

The Sources of Memory Errors

We have now described a number of memory errors, some small or subtle, but some rather large (as when subjects remember an entire fictional event). These errors can easily be documented in the laboratory, but they can also be documented when we are remembering actual events in our own lives (e.g., Neisser & Harsch, 1992). For that matter, these memory errors can even be documented when we are trying to remember events important to us professionally (Vicente & Brewer, 1993). To explain all these results, though, we need no new theory. Let's start by reviewing some claims made in earlier chapters and consider what these claims imply for memory accuracy.

Knowledge Guides Perception

In Chapters 1 and 2, we celebrated the fact that our moment-by-moment contact with the world is often *supplemented* by our background knowledge.

Among its other advantages, this allows communication to be vastly more efficient.

Our background knowledge also allows us to deal with degraded or ambiguous inputs. Several examples were described in Chapter 2, but here is one more. Consider the following sentences:

A. John wanted to take Bill to the movies, but he didn't have enough money.
B. Sally put the vase on the table, and it broke.

In *A*, who didn't have enough money? In *B*, what broke? You probably answered "John" and "the vase," for a simple reason: You bring to these sentences a wealth of prior knowledge, including knowledge about who pays for whom in our culture when you take someone to the movies, and knowledge about which is more easily broken, a vase or a table. Let's note that a number of other principles also govern the interpretation of these pronouns; we will have more to say about this in Chapter 9. But our point for now is that the interpretation is clearly influenced by knowledge you supply, and in this way your knowledge helps you to deal with the ambiguity in these sentences.

We should also note that there is nothing rigid about these interpretations: things will go differently if we precede the sentences with a bit of context. For example,

B. Sally has just gone to the cellar seeking a hammer and nails; she had put the vase on the table, and it broke.

In this case, you will draw a different inference, making it clear that there is nothing automatic about the interpretation of these pronouns, nothing within the main sentence that demands one interpretation or another. Instead, the interpretation is determined by your knowledge, and so your knowledge directly influences how the sentences are understood.

Schematic Knowledge

Psychologists have offered several different ways of thinking about how our prior knowledge influences us. Some have proposed, for example, that expectations and knowledge interact with our experience from the very start. Others have suggested that we are, at least initially, "neutral" and "objective" about our experiences but, moments later, we rely on our knowledge to interpret what we have seen or heard. On either view, however, it is clear that we are immensely influenced by our knowledge and, indeed, *helped* by our knowledge, in all aspects of our intellectual commerce with the world.

Here is one way to describe this use of knowledge: In trying to comprehend new material, we seek to "fit" this material into a familiar conceptual scheme. Traditionally these conceptual schemes are referred to with the Greek word **schema** (plural: schemata). Schemata derive from the fact that there is considerable redundancy in our world: Rather predictably, one gets food, not gasoline, in a restaurant. Rather predictably, academic offices contain many books, but no washing machine. Schemata summarize this redundancy, and so represent our **generic knowledge** about various situations—that is, our knowledge about how those situations unfold in *general*. Our schematic knowledge includes knowledge about places and things, and also about how events unfold. (Many psychologists use the term *script* to refer to this dynamic knowledge about events and reserve the term *schema* for more static knowledge about places and things. For discussion of schemata and scripts, see Abelson, 1981; Brewer, 1987; Friedman, 1979; Mandler, 1984; Rumelhart & Ortony, 1977; Schank, 1982; Schank & Abelson, 1977.)

Hence, we might have a kitchen schema that specifies that a refrigerator is almost certain to be present, as is a stove; a coffee-maker is likely to be present; a dishwasher might be, but cannot be counted on; a sofa, on the other hand, is quite unlikely. Given all this, the next time you walk into a kitchen, you need only to glance at the refrigerator. This is enough to tell you that you are indeed in a kitchen and, based on this glance, you already know a great deal about the room. It is this kind of knowledge that would be helpful to you in understanding a description of a kitchen or in reading a story about a kitchen.

When we *understand* something, therefore, what we are doing is fitting the new information into a schema and, once this is done, our understanding consists of the new information *plus* this schematic context. This obviously parallels claims we have already made: In Chapter 4, we argued that the process of understanding depends, in part, on your finding connections between the new information and things you already understand. All we are doing now is filling in a bit of that claim: The connections involved in understanding are usually connections to schematic knowledge, connections to knowledge about the "general case."

Schematic Influences on Memory

All of this has profound implications for memory. In some cases, your knowledge will literally shape your experience and thereby shape what there is to remember. Think about witnessing some action. If your prior knowledge leads you to perceive the action as generous, then you can remember the fact that you witnessed a generous act. If your prior knowledge leads you to some other perception, then there is no fact of generosity to be remembered. In an important way, prior knowledge colors events, shapes events, even creates events, and thereby colors and shapes the input to memory.

In addition, schemata also influence memory retrieval, since information *info~*

that is connected to a schematic frame will, in general, be easier to retrieve. (Once again, this is because the connections serve as retrieval paths.) As a result, you will be better able to retrieve those elements of an event that did fit with the frame (i.e., for which you could make connections), and you will be less able to retrieve elements that did not fit with the frame. Thus, prior knowledge plays a *selective* role, making it likely that you will remember some details, and less likely that you will remember others.

Connections to memory schemata will also allow intrusions of various sorts. In Chapter 5, we mentioned the possibility of **source confusion**, a type of error in which one simply loses track of *which* materials were learned on *which* occasion. Applied to the present concerns, source confusion provides a likely origin for intrusion errors.

Finally, schematic knowledge can also play a role when the time comes to retrieve information from memory. If, for any reason, your memory record is incomplete, the gaps can be filled with schema-based **reconstruction**. If you don't remember how you spent last Tuesday, you might be able to reconstruct the day's activities based on your schematic knowledge about how, in general, your Tuesdays proceed.

In each of these cases, the schemata serve us well, helping us to locate information within memory, helping us to fill in gaps in what we recall. These mechanisms make us more efficient perceivers and more efficient rememberers. But these same mechanisms also create the possibility of error. If your perception is guided by inference or assumption, there is a chance that your inference may be mistaken, or your assumptions inappropriate. If you rely on prior knowledge to fill in gaps, there is a chance that you will fill in the gaps in the wrong way. Moreover, these various mechanisms will all produce errors of the same general sort—errors in which the world is perceived, and remembered, as being more regular than it actually is.

There are also important differences among these mechanisms. If an event was "schematized" during the initial memory encoding, then this effect may be irreversible. Even if subjects are told that their initial impression of an event was wrong, they can't return to the "raw data" and reinterpret the event. This is because, in this scenario, there are no "raw data" in memory to be returned to. In contrast, if an event was "schematized" in the process of memory retrieval, then this effect may be reversible: It may be possible to dissuade subjects from reconstructing the event, encouraging them instead to take the trouble to dig through memory, to find the "original records" unshaded by their schematic knowledge.

Indeed, we have seen indications that both of these cases do occur. We have cited studies in which subjects seem able to reverse their "schematizing" of an event, but we have also considered cases in which subjects seem to have no recollection of how an event actually unfolded. The implication is that, in the former case, subjects initially found it easier to reconstruct the past rather than to remember it. It was only when reconstruction was specifically ruled out that subjects took the trouble to recall the facts. In the latter case, though, subjects seem not to have the option—the past-as-understood is the only memory they have.

These different data profiles underscore the simple point that memory errors can occur for various reasons, and the nature of each error will depend, to some extent, on why the error has occurred. This obviously invites several questions: What triggers these various mechanisms? When do these memory errors occur?

Blurring of Similar Episodes

It should be no surprise that multiple factors influence when memory errors will be observed and when memory will be accurate. After all, we have just argued that multiple mechanisms contribute to these errors, and each mechanism is likely to be influenced by its own set of factors. (Stangor & McMillan, 1992, provide a wide review of the evidence; also see Stern, Dahlgren & Gaffney, 1991.) Some of these factors are concerned with how memory is tested, so that schematic errors are more likely with recall testing than with recognition. Other factors are internal to the subjects themselves. For example, intrusions from prior knowledge require that you *have* the prior knowledge. Hence, ignorance about the to-be-remembered material can actually protect you from intrusion errors. This point echoes the example we presented at the very start of this chapter, in which subjects' knowledge helped them by promoting memory for gist, but also hurt them by serving as a source of intrusions.

This also explains why memory errors are less likely when subjects are remembering some unique event, as opposed to one episode within a series of similar episodes (e.g., Brewer, 1988). In the latter case, subjects obviously have some knowledge about how, in general, these events unfolded, and it is this knowledge that serves as a source of intrusions. In effect, the episodes in the series "blur" together, making accurate memory less likely and reconstruction more likely.

A compelling example of this blurring comes, oddly enough, from the Watergate scandal that ended the Nixon presidency. As the scandal unfolded, it became clear that Nixon's advisors had committed a series of illegal acts. There was uncertainty, however, about Nixon's own role in the planning or the cover-up of these crimes. A Senate committee carefully interrogated John Dean, former counsel to Nixon, about conversations that had taken place in the Oval Office, prior to and after the illegal acts.

It later came to light that Nixon had tape-recorded all Oval Office conversations, and so we can check the accuracy of Dean's testimony against these tapes. The tapes indicate that Dean's testimony was quite accurate in its gist (consistent with the evidence we have reviewed) but often wrong on the details. However, the errors were far from random. Instead, Dean often reported snippets of conversation as having taken place in one context when, in fact, they took place in a different context. In other words, the individual episodes were, indeed, being blurred together. Neisser (1981) argues that this is extremely likely when one remembers repeated and related episodes and proposes the name "repisodes" for our memories of these *repeated episodes*. Other evidence confirms this pattern (Jobe, Tourangeau & Smith, 1993; Reinitz, Lammers & Cochran, 1992): Memory for detail is likely to suffer when episodes are similar, as details get exchanged from one episode to another.

All of this fits well with our claim, in Chapter 5, that we often know that a stimulus is familiar without remembering why it is familiar; likewise, we are far better in recalling that something happened than we are in recalling *when* it happened (e.g., Jobe et al., 1993). This pattern obviously contributes to "repisodic" blurring.

The Role of Attention

Memory errors are also influenced by how subjects deploy their attention during the learning episode: If a particular aspect of the episode receives a great deal of thought, this will establish a rich memory record for this aspect and make errors less likely. Conversely, if an aspect of the episode is ignored, this will lead to an incomplete memory, since you cannot remember what you did not notice. The resulting gap in the memory will then encourage schema-based errors, as you rely on generic knowledge to fill in what you can't recall.

Of course, many factors influence how we deploy our attention. In some cases, it is the task itself that guides us. For example, subjects in one study were asked to read a series of sentences, some of which had complicated syntax, some of which were simple. Subjects had to spend considerable effort to understand the complicated sentences, and this led to a well-established memory. Hence, subjects were able to remember these sentences in detail later on, including their word-by-word phrasing. In contrast, subjects failed to remember the phrasing of the simple sentences; for these, they only remembered the gist (McDaniel, 1981).

We also—quite obviously—pay attention to things we find interesting or noteworthy. This point is nicely illustrated in an experiment by Keenan, MacWhinney and Mayhew (1977). They began their study by tape-recording a discussion by a group of psychology researchers. (The participants in the discussion knew they were being tape-recorded but were not aware of the purpose.) A day later, subjects were given a recognition test for sentences uttered during this discussion; subjects had to choose between sentences actually spoken and close paraphrases of these sentences.

The sentences from the conversation had been categorized in terms of their "interactional content," i.e., whether the sentence had been phrased in a way that was itself important for the conversation. A "high interactional content" sentence is one in which the exact phrasing conveys information about the speaker's intentions or his/her relations to the listener. Such a sentence might be particularly rude, for example, or witty, or elegant.

With the low-interactional sentences, subjects could not distinguish actually-spoken sentences from paraphrases—that is, subjects remembered only the gist. With the high-interactional content sentences, subjects did remember the exact phrasing, and they rejected the paraphrases as unfamiliar. Thus, subjects remembered exact phrasing when the phrasing caught their attention, when the sentence was said in a noteworthy way.

Attention can also be influenced by instructions. In some misinformation studies, subjects observe an initial event but then, before they are exposed to the misinformation, they are warned: "In the account you are about to read, some of the claims made about the video are false." Then memory is tested. Presumably, once subjects have been put on guard in this way, they will pay closer attention to the (attempted) misinformation and, indeed, this procedure does reduce the magnitude of misinformation effects (Greene, Flynn & Loftus, 1982; Tousignant, Hall & Loftus, 1986; for other data showing schema effects promoted by inattention, see Bartlett, Till & Levy, 1980; Loftus & Kallman, 1979; Murphy & Shapiro, 1994; Nakamura, Graesser, Zimmerman & Riha, 1985).

Memory, Attention, and Typicality

Apparently, inattention leads to gaps in the memory record, and this invites schema-based inferences and intrusions. Hence, *attention* helps determine the memorial role for *schemata*. But the reverse is also true: Schemata guide attention. As you sit in a restaurant, you are unlikely to be thinking, "Holy cow! They have menus!" Of course, a restaurant has menus, and so you probably won't give this fact much thought. You will instead pay attention to more interesting things, including what is *distinctive* about this restaurant, what is *atypical*. Now, bear in mind that schematic knowledge, by definition, summarizes what is typical; hence it is your schematic knowledge that tells you, by contrast, what is atypical and, therefore, what is worth attending.

Imagine that there is a small pig walking through the restaurant. This detail, clearly at odds with your restaurant schema, seems likely to seize your attention. Because of this extra attention, this detail is then quite likely to be remembered later on. In short, highly atypical aspects of an event are likely to be recalled.

Notice, then, that we are led to a paradoxical claim: We have argued in other sections that schematic knowledge helps you to remember the typical aspects of an event. We are now suggesting that your schematic knowledge also helps you to remember the highly *atypical*. Let's walk through the logic of this: We have just noted that the *typical* aspects of a scene generally won't draw your attention. Unattended, these typical aspects are unlikely to be encoded into memory. Nonetheless, these typical aspects will be remembered later on, thanks to subsequent *reconstruction* based on generic knowledge. Thus, even if you failed to notice the menus, you will remember them—or, more precisely, you will be able to infer their presence. Of course, this process can go astray: Even if there were no menus (if the food offerings were listed on a blackboard), you may remember them anyhow.

Atypical aspects will also be recalled but for a different reason: These aspects will draw your attention, and so they will be encoded into memory. In this case, we wouldn't expect intrusion errors (since you are not relying on inference), and we might expect some memory for detail (since you did pay attention to the target information). Hence, even though you recall both the typical and the atypical aspects, you remember them in different ways.

This is a complicated picture, but one that flows naturally from our claims so far. In addition and, indeed, more important, each of these claims is well-supported by data. (For example, Friedman, 1979, reports data on the interrelation among typicality, attention, and *picture* memory; we will return to this study in Chapter 10. Work by Graesser and his colleagues provides a rich description of how we remember the atypical—see, for example, Smith & Graesser, 1981; Graesser, Woll, Kowalski & Smith, 1980.)

The "Goal" of Remembering

Another factor relevant to memory errors influences the event of retrieval, rather than the event of encoding. To put this briefly, our *reasons* for trying to remember differ from one occasion to the next. Sometimes we have one goal in mind in trying to remember the past, and sometimes we have a different goal. And, as these reasons and goals change, so do our strategies, with important implications for memory error.

Sometimes, we are simply trying to remember the gist of some prior occasion and don't much care about the details. Sometimes, we do care about the details but can't be bothered to spend much effort in trying to recall them. On still other occasions, we are immensely motivated to recall the details and spend great effort in this recall.

These differences matter for memory accuracy, since evidence indicates that, to some extent, we can control whether we *reconstruct* the past or try to *recall* it. (See, for example, the studies reviewed by Alba & Hasher, 1983.) Moreover, it seems to be easier to reconstruct than to recall so that reconstruction can be used as a "memory short-cut." (See, for discussion, Reder, 1982; Reder & Ross, 1983.) Hence, we are more likely to reconstruct the past when we have no great stake in remembering the particulars and, indeed, in this circumstance, schema-based errors are more likely.

It also seems likely that, on many occasions, an emphasis on *accurate* recall will also lead to *incomplete* recall. After all, in trying to be accurate, one should avoid "filling in" memory gaps with inference and surmise. This too leads to a prediction that memory accuracy will be dependent on one's goals in trying to remember. For some goals (e.g., telling a good tale), memory incompleteness will be a nuisance while, for other goals, it will be inconsequential. Thus, we are led to the prediction that remembering in a social setting, where one often seeks to give a full, coherent report, may be less accurate than remembering in other circumstances. (For broader discussion of the "goals" of remembering, see Baddeley, 1988; Bruce, 1989; Pillemer, 1992; Ross, 1989; Ross & Buehler, 1994; Winograd, 1994.)

The Passage of Time

Yet another factor relevant to memory errors is unsurprising: Errors are more likely when we recall events from long ago. Presumably, the passage of time leads to some forgetting, which creates gaps in the memorial record. This, once again, invites inferences and intrusions, eroding memory accuracy.

As an example, consider a study by Belli, Windschitl, McCarthy and Winfrey (1992). Their subjects viewed a series of slides depicting an event, then read a narrative ostensibly describing that event but including items of misinformation. Finally, subjects' memories for the slides were tested. Crucially, **retention interval** was also varied—that is, the amount of time between the initial learning and the subsequent test. In this study, the misinformation influenced performance only at longer retention intervals (five to seven days). At these intervals, large-scale effects were observed, with subjects misremembering items that had been quite conspicuous in the initial slides. No such effects were observed with shorter testing intervals. Other researchers have reported broadly similar findings (Anderson & Pichert, 1978; Ceci & Bruck, 1993; Dooling & Christiaansen, 1977; Spiro, 1977).

Of course, we need to ask *why* the passage of time is relevant. One hypothesis is **decay**. With the passage of time, memories may fade or erode. Perhaps this is because the relevant brain cells gradually die off. Perhaps the connections among memories need to be constantly refreshed; if not, the connections may gradually weaken. In any event, it is largely the passage of time that triggers these events.

A different possibility is **retrieval failure**. We have noted in several contexts that the retrieval of information from memory is far from guaranteed; we also argued, in Chapter 5, that retrieval is most likely if your perspective (mental, emotional, and physical) at the time of retrieval matches that in place at the time of learning. If we now assume that your perspective is likely to change more and more as time goes by, we have a prediction about forgetting: The greater the retention interval, the greater the likelihood that your perspective has changed, and therefore the greater the likelihood of retrieval failure.

A third hypothesis is that new learning somehow works against, or *interferes* with, older learning. On this **interference** account, less is remembered about older events because more learning has come between older events and the present time than between newer events and the present. Hence, older events suffer from more interference.

We have ample reason to believe that retrieval failure and interference both occur. Many of the studies in Chapter 5 speak to retrieval failure: If subjects are tested in one way, they are able to remember. Hence, a memory is present. If subjects are tested in a different way, they fail to remember. Since we know that the memory is present, this must be a case of retrieval failure. Likewise, many of the studies in this chapter speak to interference. The effects of post-event misinformation, for example, are interference effects; technically, they are **retroactive interference**, since new learning is interfering with old. By the same token, intrusions from prior knowledge can also be thought of as interference effects, although in this case they are **proactive interference**, with old learning compromising new. (There is, in fact, a large literature on interference effects, much of it drawing on techniques no longer prominent in the literature. For reviews of this early literature, see Crowder, 1982; Hulse, Egeth & Deese, 1980; Postman & Underwood, 1973. For more recent discussion of interference, see Bower, Thomson-Schill & Tulving, 1994; Murname & Shiffrin, 1991.)

What about decay? If no interfering material is present, and if one's perspective does not change, do memories still decay with the passage of time? In principle, it should be easy to answer this question: All we need to do is teach subjects something, then have them spend some time without learning anything new (so there is no interference) and without thinking any new thoughts (so that we minimize the chance of a change in perspective, and thus minimize the chance of retrieval failure). Then, after a time spent in this fashion, we test their memories.

Of course, this experiment would be rather difficult to implement, but similar experiments have been carried out, mostly with other species. These procedures take advantage of the fact that many animals do spend long periods of time seemingly doing nothing or close to it. This allows us to test the decay claim.

Experiments with cockroaches exploit the fact that roaches, once they enter a warm, dark, dry place, will lie still for many minutes. We can therefore teach the cockroach a simple response, then provide a warm, dry place, and wait. If we wait a short time, then, on the decay hypothesis, little forgetting will take place. If we wait a longer interval, forgetting should be correspondingly greater. These predictions turn out to be wrong: In studies like these the passage of time is a poor predictor of forgetting (e.g., Minami & Dallenbach, 1946). Forgetting does occur, however, if we allow the cockroaches to crawl about in the interval between learning and test. In other words, the data favor an interference account, not decay.

We do not have exactly comparable data from humans, but we have something close: Many studies have looked at learning just before sleep in comparison with learning just before a day's activities. There is unquestionably mental activity during sleep, but there is surely less during sleep than during the day. Therefore, in this study we are comparing "less interference" with "more" rather than "no interference" with "interference."

In a study by Jenkins and Dallenbach (1924), two groups of subjects learned lists of nonsense syllables, like "BIV" or "ZAR." The subjects were then tested after retention intervals of one, two, four, or eight hours. Critically, subjects sometimes slept during the retention interval and sometimes were awake. Figure 6.2 shows the data. In both conditions, performance dropped as the interval between learning and test increased. However, this drop was much more pronounced if subjects were awake during the retention interval. That is, one hour with much interference produced more forgetting than one hour with minimal interference; likewise for two hours or four or eight. (See also Ekstrand, 1967, 1972; Hockey, Davies & Gray, 1972.) Thus, time seems not to be the crucial factor, and these data again favor an interference account.

Baddeley and Hitch (1977) offer yet another way of getting at this question. They asked rugby players to recall the names of the teams they had played against over the course of a rugby season. Not all players made it to all games, because of illness, injuries, or schedule conflicts. This allows us to compare players for whom "two games back" means two weeks ago, to players for whom "two games back" means four weeks ago. Thus, we can look at the effects of retention interval (two weeks vs. four) with number of intervening games held constant. Likewise, we can compare players for whom the game a month ago was "three games back" with players for whom a month means "one game back." Now we have the retention interval held constant, and we can look at the effects of intervening events. In this setting, Baddeley and

Figure 6.2

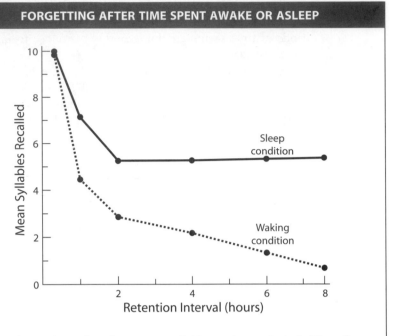

FORGETTING AFTER TIME SPENT AWAKE OR ASLEEP

Subjects learned a series of nonsense syllables and were tested either after a period of time spent asleep or after a period of time spent awake. Forgetting was greater after time awake, presumably because during that time subjects were thinking about and learning new things, leading to memory interference. [After Jenkins & Dallenbach, 1924.]

Hitch report that the mere passage of time accounts for very little; what really matters is the number of intervening events (Figure 6.3).

None of these tests is perfect. One might worry about extrapolating from cockroach memory to that of other species; one might worry about what other things were going on in the lives of Baddeley and Hitch's rugby players. For example, a player for whom the previous game was long ago is obviously a player who missed many games. Why is this? Frequent illness? A schedule filled with other things? Could these influence the pattern of data? With these questions unanswered, we must be cautious in interpreting the Baddeley and Hitch data.

Nevertheless, there is a consistent message emerging from these studies: There is a strong relationship between forgetting and the arrival of new information and new events; this is consistent both with the claim of interfer-

Figure 6.3

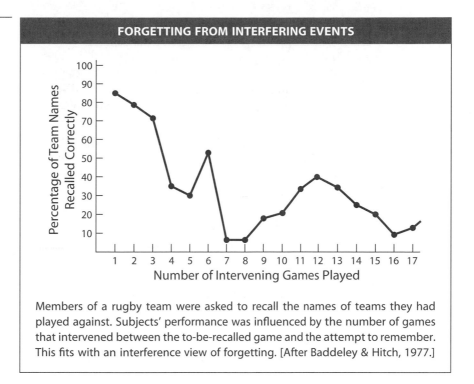

FORGETTING FROM INTERFERING EVENTS

Members of a rugby team were asked to recall the names of teams they had played against. Subjects' performance was influenced by the number of games that intervened between the to-be-recalled game and the attempt to remember. This fits with an interference view of forgetting. [After Baddeley & Hitch, 1977.]

ence and with the claim of retrieval failure. However, we have no firm evidence in favor of the decay claim. As we will see later in this chapter, there are at least some cases of excellent memory even with extremely long delays; this is plainly contrary to decay claims. Our best summary of the data seems to be that <u>little forgetting is attributable to decay.</u>

Exotic Strategies for Undoing Forgetting

Earlier in this chapter, we mentioned the possibility of reversing *some* memory errors by encouraging subjects to re-think an earlier episode in one fashion or another. We need to revisit this theme, however, in the context of our discussion of forgetting: Extravagant claims have been made about a number of techniques alleged to "undo" forgetting, and these claims need examination.

For example, a great deal has been asserted about the value of hypnosis in helping people to remember. Indeed, the suggestion is sometimes made that, under hypnosis, witnesses to an earlier event can remember everything about the event, including aspects they did not even notice (much less think about and interpret) at the time.

Many studies have examined these claims, and the evidence is clear: Hypnotized subjects who are instructed to remember do their very best to comply, and this means that they will give a full and detailed reporting of the target event. However, it is not the case that the hypnotized subjects remember *more*. Instead, they simply *say* more, in order to be cooperative. By saying more things, subjects will (just by chance) say some things that happen to be true. But *most* of the memory report by hypnotized subjects turns out not to be true and, worse, the hypnotized subjects cannot tell you which of the reported details are correct, and which are made up or are guesses. In other words, hypnosis does not improve memory; it just changes the willingness to talk (Dinges, Whitehouse, Orne, Powell, Orne & Erdelyi, 1992; Dywan & Bowers, 1983; Hilgard, 1968; Smith, 1982).

In fact, there is reason to believe hypnosis may actually *compromise* memory accuracy rather than improving it. Bear in mind that someone hypnotized will be quite compliant, quite cooperative. Therefore, suggestions made to someone who is hypnotized will be taken very seriously. Now, combine this with our earlier comments about post-event misinformation: We know, in general, that this misinformation can shape the way earlier events are recalled. There is every reason to believe these effects will be even stronger if the misinformation is delivered under hypnosis. Because of all these considerations, researchers tend to be quite skeptical about memories "recovered" under hypnosis.

Strong claims have also been made about cases of people receiving stimulation directly to the brain, often as part of brain surgery. The oft-quoted report is that, when the brain is suitably prodded or poked, one suddenly remembers scenes from long ago, often in clear and remarkable detail. Is this the way to defeat forgetting and to recover one's "lost past"?

These observations depend on the fact that brain surgery is usually done under local anesthesia, so that the reports of the awake patient can be used to map the brain. (As different parts of the brain are stimulated, subjects will see light flashes, or show bits of movement, and so on. These responses are then used as a means of guiding the surgery.) It is from surgery of this type that the relevant data are obtained (e.g., Penfield & Roberts, 1959).

Only a small number of patients, however, report recollections in response to this stimulation of the brain. But the memories evoked in this fashion are extraordinary—clear, detailed, as though the subjects were reliving the earlier experience. Unfortunately, though, we have no way of knowing whether these are *memories*. These experiences might, for example, be hallucinations of some sort. Or these experiences might be very vivid reconstructions. Because this evidence comes from an extreme circumstance, it has been difficult to track down the historical facts to confirm (or disconfirm) these patients' recollections. Until this is done, we have no evidence that they are remembering, much less remembering accurately. Hence, we have no basis for claiming that this technique promotes memory retrieval. (See Sacks, 1985, for similar cases, also without documentation about whether the remembering is bonafide.)

Techniques for Maximizing Recall

There are, however, some techniques that do promote the recovery of "lost" memories. The techniques are not exotic but simply capitalize on the fact that a great deal of forgetting involves retrieval failure. As a consequence, it is often possible for a "lost" memory to be recovered once the appropriate retrieval cues are on the scene.

How should one seek "appropriate cues"? One possibility is simply to try out a variety of *different* cues. In practice, this amounts to little more than trying to remember, with the efforts spread out over a period of time and a variety of circumstances. This does work, and less and less "forgetting" is observed as recall efforts continue. The technical term for this process is **hypermnesia**, sometimes referred to as "unforgetting."

Hypermnesia is alleged to occur as part of the process of psychotherapy, as the patient recalls more and more of the forgotten past. However, hypermnesia in this setting is hard to interpret, largely because we often have no way of checking whether the patient's reports are true. There is also some concern here about the possibility of memories being *suggested* by a therapist or mutually "constructed" by the therapist and client. Finally, memories "recovered" in therapy often involve events that should have been memorable in the first place—significant events in the patient's life or events for which many retrieval cues have long been available. The fact that these events *weren't* recalled prior to the therapy is often difficult to understand, and this adds to the suspicion that some of the memories recovered in therapy aren't memories at all. (For discussion, see Erdelyi & Goldberg, 1979, but, for a critical view of these issues, see Holmes, 1991; Loftus, 1993. For discussion of hypermnesia in forensic settings, see Turtle & Yuille, 1994.)

Nonetheless, it is clear that hypermnesia does exist, at least in some contexts. For example, subjects in one study were asked to recall pictures that they had earlier seen (Erdelyi & Kleinbard, 1978). Subjects then continued trying to recall the pictures, over a period of several days. As you can see in Figure 6.4, subjects' early recall indicated much forgetting. However, this forgetting steadily dissipated as subjects continued their recall efforts. (See also Bahrick & Hall, 1993; Erdelyi & Becker, 1974; Erdelyi, Buschke & Finkelstein, 1977; Erdelyi, Finkelstein, Herrell, Miller & Thomas, 1976; Roediger

Figure 6.4

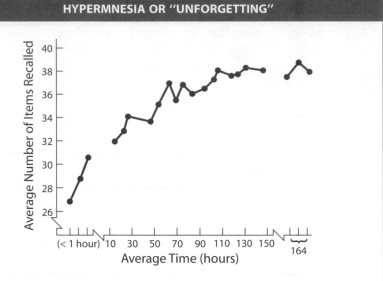

HYPERMNESIA OR "UNFORGETTING"

Subjects in this experiment continued, over the period of one week, to try remembering materials they had learned. As the figure shows, subjects' efforts were rewarded: With more time and effort spent on trying to remember, subjects actually remembered more and more. [After Erdelyi & Kleinbard, 1978.]

& Payne, 1982, 1985; Roediger & Thorpe, 1978; Roediger & Wheeler, 1993).

Is there anything one can do to promote hypermnesia? A promising approach has been developed by Fisher, Geiselman and their colleagues (Fisher, Geiselman & Amador, 1989; Fisher, Geiselman, Raymond & Jurkevich, 1987; Geiselman, 1984). Their so-called "Cognitive Interview" is often used in questioning eyewitnesses to crimes, in order to maximize what they recall. This technique employs several different strategies. For example, witnesses are encouraged to recount the event in more than one sequence (e.g., from first to last and from last to first) and from more than one perspective. Witnesses are also led to reconstruct the environmental and personal context of the witnessed event. In short, the technique tries to generate a large number, and a large variety, of retrieval cues, and this does seem to promote recall with adults and with children (Geiselman & Padilla, 1988; Fisher & Geiselman, 1992; Fisher & McCauley, 1994). However, there is no surprise here: We have argued that much forgetting involves retrieval failure; retrieval failure is less likely when appropriate memory cues are provided. It is exactly these claims that are confirmed by the success of the Cognitive Interview.

Emotion

Another factor that seems enormously important for memory, and for forgetting, is *emotion*. In Chapter 5, we mentioned that emotion can produce *state-dependent learning*, so that materials learned while happy are best recalled while happy; materials learned while angry are best recalled while angry. It turns out, though, that emotion also influences memory in other ways, and it is to these other effects that we now turn.

Emotional events are, in general, recalled with extraordinary vividness. This is reflected in studies that have asked subjects how clearly they remember various episodes in their lives (death of a favorite pet, getting a driver's license). These studies find a strong positive correlation (around .90) between subjects' assessments of how *vivid* each memory is and their assessments of how *emotional* the event was at the time it occurred. Thus, the greater the emotion, the greater the vividness. It does not seem to matter what the emotion was, and so the same data pattern is observed with happy events and sad ones, events that made subjects angry and events that made them afraid (Bohannon, 1988; Brown & Kulik, 1977; Christianson & Loftus, 1990; Pillemer, 1984; Reisberg, Heuer, McLean & O'Shaughnessy, 1988; Rubin & Kozin, 1984; White, 1989). We should mention that, on *some* measures, there is a memory advantage for emotionally positive events relative to negative events (Isen, 1985, 1987). However, for memory vividness and level of detail, it seems to be strength of emotion that matters and not the quality of emotion.

As we have seen, however, the vividness of a memory provides surprisingly little information about whether that memory is accurate or not. Therefore, we still need to ask how memory accuracy and, indeed, how forgetting, are influenced by emotion.

Studying Emotion in the Laboratory

A number of authors have argued that emotion changes how we pay attention during an event. For example, Easterbrook (1959) proposed that arousal, including the arousal caused by emotion, leads to a "narrowing" of attention so that, in an emotional event, all of one's attention will be focused on just a few aspects of the event. These aspects therefore receive "concentrated" attention and so will be firmly placed into memory. However, the rest of the event will be excluded from this "narrowed" focus and so won't be remembered later on. As a result, subjects will have good memory for the event's "center" but poor memory for the event's "periphery."

As a related claim, it is often asserted that eyewitnesses to a crime are likely to show a pattern called **weapon-focus**. The idea is that the witness will "zoom in" on some critical detail, such as the weapon, to the exclusion of much else. As a result, the witness will remember the perpetrator's gun or knife with great clarity but will remember little else about the crime.

Many laboratory studies have attempted to test these claims. For example, Burke, Heuer and Reisberg (1992) showed subjects a story, conveyed by a series of slides and accompanying narration. For some subjects, the episode was emotionally bland; for others, the story was emotionally arousing. Some time later (one week in one experiment, two weeks in another), subjects were given an unexpected memory test, examining memory for the story's plot and also memory for tiny details about the story and the pictures. Consistent with the claims just sketched, the results showed that emotion improved memory for details at the story's "center"—that is, details associated with the story's main characters. Subjects who saw the emotional version of the story remembered more of these details than did subjects who saw the neutral version. The situation reverses, though, for details associated with the story's background. Here, emotion *impaired* memory, and better performance was observed for subjects who had seen the neutral version of the tale. (For a review of related research, focusing specifically on the weapon-focus phenomenon, see Steblay, 1992; also see Christianson, 1992.)

These results, with improved memory for central details, impaired memory for the periphery, fit well with the Easterbrook claim or with claims about weapon-focus. At the same time, however, the results also reveal several other patterns. For one, emotion seemed to slow the process of forgetting—probably by diminishing the likelihood of subsequent retrieval failure. Emotional events are eventually forgotten, but the evidence suggests that they are forgotten more slowly than otherwise comparable neutral events. (For other studies showing this pattern, see Bohannon, 1993; Pillemer, 1984; Yuille & Tollestrup, 1992. For discussion of physiological mechanisms that may contribute to this slowed forgetting, see Cahill, Prins, Weber & McGaugh, 1994; Gold, 1987, 1995; White, 1991.)

In addition, evidence suggests that subjects *think about* emotional events, both during the event and afterwards, in ways quite different from how they think about neutral events—different associations come to mind, and different aspects of the event are contemplated (Christianson & Loftus, 1991; Heuer & Reisberg, 1992; Hockey, 1978). This pattern of thinking is then reflected in how subjects remember the event later on.

As an example, subjects in one study witnessed an emotional event and then, two weeks later, were asked to recall the event (Heuer & Reisberg, 1990). For our purposes, the interesting result concerns the *intrusion errors* in subjects' recall: Subjects who saw the neutral story made many errors about plot, as if they were trying to fill gaps in the sequence of what they remembered.

Arousal subjects, in contrast, made few plot errors. Instead, they tended to make up things about the motives or reactions of the story's protagonists. Subjects often exaggerated what the story had said about these, and sometimes falsified what the story had said. For example, subjects reported vivid recollections of hearing that one of the characters in the story was upset, although there was no indication of this in the presentation. It would appear that subjects were largely projecting their own emotions into the memory.

Flashbulb Memories

Overall, emotion seems to have multiple effects on memory—narrowing attention, slowing forgetting, changing how an event is thought about and, consequently, changing the pattern of subsequent intrusion errors. One might well ask, however, how much faith we can place in these laboratory studies of emotional remembering. Concretely, is the emotion experienced in these studies comparable to the emotion one feels in "real life"? After all, the laboratory subjects know they are in an artificial situation and, in any case, they are not directly involved in the emotional event. Is it fair, therefore, to make claims about emotional remembering based on these studies?

One way to address this question is by "checking" the laboratory data against cases of "real world" emotion: Are the memory patterns the same? In several ways, they are. For example, the "narrowing" of attention, evident in the laboratory studies, obviously echoes the "real life" phenomenon of weapon-focus. Likewise, the slowed forgetting documented in the laboratory also seems to have "real life" parallels. For example, Yuille and Cutshall (1986) interviewed 13 witnesses to an actual crime, four to five months after the event. The crime was clearly an emotional one—it involved a shooting, in which one person was killed and another wounded—and subjects' memory for this crime was impressively accurate: Months after the event, subjects were 83% correct in the details reported about the event itself, 76% correct about descriptions of people, 90% correct in their descriptions of objects on the scene. (Also see Fisher, Geiselman & Amador, 1989; Yuille & Kim, 1987.)

The accuracy of these reports, despite the passage of time, is certainly congruent with the claim that emotion leads to slower forgetting. This claim also seems to fit with reports of so-called **flashbulb memories**—memories of extraordinary clarity, typically for highly-emotional events, retained despite the passage of many years. When Brown and Kulik (1977) introduced the term "flashbulbs," they pointed as a paradigm case to the memories people have of first hearing the news of John Kennedy's assassination. Their subjects, interviewed more than a decade after this event, remembered it "as though it were yesterday," remembering details of where they were at the time, what they were doing, and who they were with. Many subjects were able to recall the clothing worn by people around them, the exact words uttered, and the like. Memories of comparable clarity have been reported for other, more recent, events, such as the space-shuttle disaster in 1986, or the 1981 assassination attempt on Ronald Reagan (Pillemer, 1984; Rubin & Kozin, 1984; see also Weaver, 1993; Winograd & Neisser, 1993).

There are many questions to be asked about flashbulb memories, but one crucial question concerns the *accuracy* of these memories. As we have seen repeatedly in this chapter, their accuracy surely cannot be assumed and, in some cases, these memories do seem to contain large-scale errors. For example, Neisser and Harsch (1992) interviewed subjects one day after the space-shuttle explosion, asking them how they first heard about the explosion, what they were doing at the time, and so on. They then re-interviewed these subjects three years later, asking the same questions about the shuttle explosion. The results show *remarkably little agreement* between the immediate and delayed reports, even with regard to major facts such as who delivered the news or where the subject was when the news arrived. It appears, then, that the three-year reports are mostly false, although it should be said that subjects were highly confident about the accuracy of these reports. (For similar data, see Christianson, 1989; Linton, 1975, pp. 386–387; Wagenaar & Groeneweg, 1990.)

There is no question, therefore, that subjects can make conspicuous errors in remembering emotional events. Let's emphasize, however, that subjects also retain a great deal about these events. For example, McCloskey, Wible and Cohen (1988) also examined subjects' recollection of the space-shuttle disaster, assessing memory accuracy by comparing reports collected immediately after the event with reports collected nine months later. Like Neisser and Harsch, they observed many errors in subjects' recall, but we can equally well focus on how much their subjects did remember. Nine months after the disaster, 81% of their subjects still remembered where they were when they first learned about the explosion; 70% of their subjects remembered who had told them the news.

What should we make of this? Why did the Neisser and Harsch subjects remember so little, while the McCloskey et al. subjects remembered a great deal? One predictor of memory accuracy seems to be the *consequentiality* of the flashbulb event. If the event matters directly for the subject's life, it seems, then the event will be well-remembered. If the event is largely inconsequential for the subject, then memory accuracy will be poor. Several results point toward this claim. For example, one study examined how accurately subjects remembered the 1989 San Francisco earthquake. For subjects who lived in Georgia, thousands of miles from the earthquake's epicenter, memory accuracy was quite low. For subjects who lived in Santa Clara (at the epicenter), the earthquake was remembered accurately and in detail (Neisser, Winograd

& Weldon, 1991; Palmer, Schreiber & Fox, 1991). Similarly, another study examined subjects' memories for the abrupt and unexpected resignation of British Prime Minister Margaret Thatcher. Subjects differed widely in the accuracy of their recall for this event, but this accuracy was closely linked to subjects' assessments of how important the event was for them: If it was important for you, you remember it, so that, again, consequentiality predicted accurate recollection (Conway, Anderson, Larsen, Donnelly, McDaniel, McClelland, Rawles & Logie, 1994).

In summary, some flashbulb memories do turn out to be marvelously accurate, while others turn out to be filled with error. From the subjects' point of view, however, there is no difference between these accurate memories and the inaccurate ones—both are recalled with great detail, both are recalled with enormous confidence. This adds strength to our earlier claim that memory errors can occur even in the midst of our strongest, most confident recollection. In addition, the pattern of flashbulb memories fits reasonably well with the pattern of laboratory evidence: In both cases, there is a selective pattern to what is remembered, with some details (presumably: the event's "center") remembered well, while other aspects (the "periphery") are remembered poorly. And in both cases, the longevity of these memories confirms the claim that, indeed, emotion does slow the process of forgetting.

Long, Long-Term Remembering

In many flashbulb memories, subjects claim to have vivid recollection for an event that took place decades earlier. Are flashbulb memories unique in this regard, or is this longevity found with other memories as well? What is the fate of memory accuracy over long spans of time?

Testing Memory after Long Intervals

A number of studies have examined how well subjects remember events from very long ago. Of course, if an episode is remembered, we will first need to verify that the memory is correct. If it is, we will also need to ensure that the episode has not been re-encountered in the meantime. If I remember my second birthday, this might be because I have heard the event discussed in the family or because I have seen the photos in the album. We need to rule out these possibilities in order to claim I truly remember the original event.

A number of studies, however, have satisfied these requirements. For example, Bahrick, Bahrick and Wittlinger (1975) tracked down the graduates of a particular high school—people who had graduated last year, and the year before, and the year before that and, ultimately, people who had graduated fifty years before. All of these alumni were shown photographs from their own high school yearbook. For each photo, they were given a group of names and had to choose the name of the person shown in the picture. The data show remarkably little forgetting—performance was approximately 90% correct if tested three months after graduation, the same after seven years, and the same after 14 years. In some versions of the test, performance was still excellent after 34 years (Figure 6.5).

Recall performance in this study was slightly worse but still impressive. When asked to come up with the names on their own, rather than choosing the correct name from a list, subjects were able to name 70% of the faces when tested three months after graduation, and 60% after nine months. Remarkably, subjects were still able to name 60% of their classmates after seven years.

As a different example, what about the material you are learning right now? You are presumably reading this textbook as part of a course on Cognitive Psychology. Five years from now, will you still remember things you have learned in this course? How about a decade from now? Conway, Cohen and Stanhope (1991) explored precisely these questions, testing subjects' retention of a Cognitive Psychology course taken years earlier. The results broadly echo the pattern we have already seen: Some forgetting of names and specific concepts was observed during the first three years after the course. After the third year, however, performance stabilized, so that subjects tested after ten years still remembered a fair amount and, indeed, remembered just as much as did subjects tested after three years. Memory for more general facts and memory for research methods showed even less forgetting.

Some loss of memories is observed in these studies, but what is remarkable is how much subjects do remember, and for how long. In study after a study, there is an initial period of forgetting, generally for the first three or four years. After that, performance remains impressively consistent, despite the passage of several decades. In other words, if you learn the material well enough to retain it for three years, odds are that you will remember it for the rest of your life. Indeed, Bahrick (1984) has claimed that memories can achieve a state of permastore (for "permanent storage"), although he argues that only some memories achieve this status. Permastore is more likely, for example, if the material is extremely well-learned in the first place (Bahrick, 1984; Bahrick & Hall, 1991; Conway et al., 1991; Conway, Cohen & Stanhope, 1992). Permastore is also more likely if the subject continues to learn new materials in that domain. Thus, students who take calculus courses in college are likely to remember their high school algebra even fifty years after high school (Bahrick & Hall, 1991). Some learning strategies also seem more likely to produce permastore (Bahrick, Bahrick, Bahrick & Bahrick, 1993).

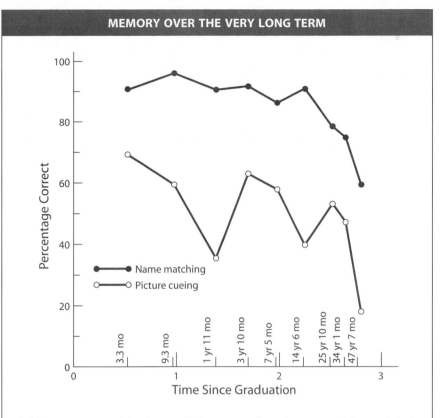

Subjects were tested for how well they remembered names and faces of their high school classmates. In one version, subjects were given a group of names and had to select which name belonged to the face shown. In this task ("name matching"), subjects were 90% correct even 14 years after graduation. In a different version, subjects were shown the pictures and had to come up with the names on their own ("picture cueing"). In this test, subjects were still 60% accurate after 7 years. The data do show a drop-off after 47 years, but it is unclear whether this reflects an erosion of memory, or a more general drop-off in performance caused by the normal process of aging. [After Bahrick, Bahrick & Wittlinger, 1975.]

Very long-term retention is also helped by one further factor: rehearsal. For many years, Linton (1975, 1978, 1982, 1986; also Wagenaar, 1986) has kept careful notes on the events that fill each of her days, sort of like keeping a detailed diary. After certain intervals, she selects events from the diary and tests her own memory for what transpired; this memory can then be checked against the written record. Linton reports impressive memory accuracy for these mundane events—over 65% remembered after three years, roughly the same after four years. In addition, Linton often retests her memory for a given event. This way, we can ask about the effects of rehearsing these memories since, after all, the experience of testing memory constitutes a re-en-

Figure 6.6

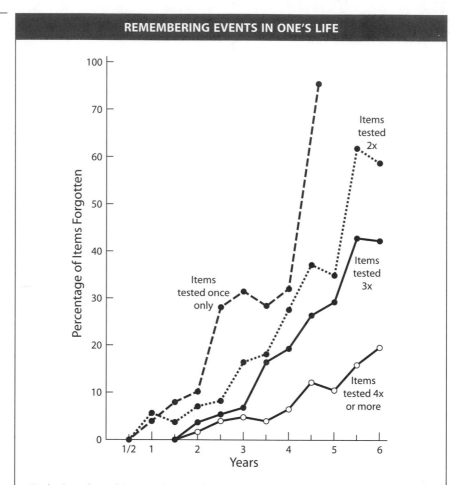

REMEMBERING EVENTS IN ONE'S LIFE

Each day, the subject in this study recorded what had happened during that day. At various later times she tested her memory for different events. Some events were tested only once; two-thirds of these were still remembered after 3 or 4 years. Other items were tested multiple times; each test served to remind the subject of the event, and so "refreshed" the memory. Even a single "refresher" can markedly decrease forgetting. [After Linton, 1978.]

counter with the original episode. (Thus, the *first* test provides a rehearsal that may then benefit the *second* test.) This rehearsal turns out to have enormous impact. For those events previously tested (rehearsed), forgetting after three years was cut in half, from 32% forgotten with no rehearsals, to 16% with one rehearsal (Figure 6.6).

Of course, we might worry that Linton is an unusual subject. After all, she has elected to do this self-study and has continued the effort over many years. We might suppose, therefore, that she is particularly motivated to remember. Even with these concerns, though, Linton's data seem to indicate that we remember our past remarkably well. There is surprisingly little forgetting, and the forgetting is much reduced by even a single rehearsal.

Childhood Amnesia

There is one aspect of our past, however, that we do not remember well, namely, the first few years of our lives. Many writers have noted how difficult it is to remember events that took place before one's third or fourth birthday, a phenomenon referred to as **childhood amnesia** (Dudycha & Dudycha, 1941; Loftus, 1993; Meudell, 1983; Nelson, 1988; Wetzler & Sweeney, 1986; White & Pillemer, 1979; Winograd & Killinger, 1983; Usher & Neisser, 1993). As an illustration, Waldfogel (1948) asked college students to write down a list of all their memories dating from before their eighth birthday. As can be seen in Figure 6.7, subjects remembered little from before their fourth birthday. Likewise, when college students are asked to describe their earliest remembered experience, the average age of these experiences is about 3.5 years (Dudycha & Dudycha, 1941). When these very early memories can be verified, they often turn out to be reasonably accurate (Howes, Siegel & Brown, 1993), adding to the evidence in the previous section: The passage of time does far less to erode our recollection than one might initially suppose. Nonetheless, the fact remains that memories earlier than this, from the first 20 or 30 months of life, are quite rare, and this needs to be explained.

One explanation of this pattern was suggested by Sigmund Freud. Freud argued that childhood is filled with many painful events, but memory of this pain is prevented by a number of psychological defense mechanisms. A key defense is **repression**, a process through which anxiety-provoking thoughts are denied access to the conscious mind. Thus, we forget our childhood years because, in large measure, these memories have been repressed.

Many contemporary psychologists, though, are deeply skeptical about this claim. As one consideration, evidence indicates that, in general, our memories for painful events are just as accurate, just as complete, as our memories for more up-beat episodes. There does not seem to be what Hollingworth (1910) called an "oblivescence of the disagreeable." There is, without question, some

Figure 6.7

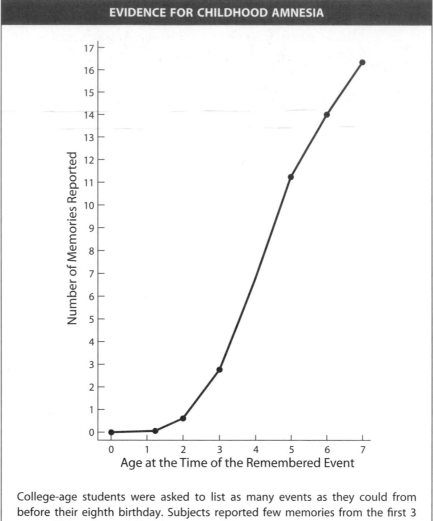

EVIDENCE FOR CHILDHOOD AMNESIA

College-age students were asked to list as many events as they could from before their eighth birthday. Subjects reported few memories from the first 3 years of life. [After Waldfogel, 1948.]

memory privilege (e.g., easier access) for positive events (Isen, 1985, 1987), but this doesn't undermine the fact that negative events are, overall, well remembered.

Moreover, the evidence offered in support of the repression construct is in several ways unpersuasive. Attempts to document this phenomenon in the laboratory have generally been unsuccessful (Erdelyi & Goldberg, 1979, provide a review). Outside of the laboratory, clinicians often interpret dreams, or symptom patterns, in terms of repressed wishes or memories; they then use these interpretations as evidence for repression. However, this argument rests on a system of "symbol interpretation" that is itself controversial. Many would argue that this system rests on assumptions that are untenable; others suggest that the system of interpretation is so loose as to be unusable. Finally, some have suggested that the possibility of *recovering* a memory within a clinical setting, is proof that the memory must have been *repressed* prior to the recovery. However, we have already noted that these cases of clinical hypermnesia are difficult to interpret, and the recovered memories may turn out to be reconstructions or outright fabrications. (For reviews of the repression debate, see Erdelyi, 1985; Erdelyi & Goldberg, 1979; Holmes, 1991; Loewenstein, 1993; Loftus, 1993. For a discussion of Freud's own evidence, see Schwartz & Reisberg, 1991.)

We have put these claims strongly, and so it should be emphasized that this is, without question, controversial territory. One way or another, though, most memory researchers find the repression claims uncompelling, and so we are motivated to look for some alternative account of childhood amnesia. The first few years of life are obviously years of enormous intellectual growth. The child is learning new facts about the world and new ways to conceptualize and organize these facts. These observations provide the core of several proposals about childhood amnesia (e.g., Nelson, 1988; Schactel, 1947; White & Pillemer, 1979). On these views, the child lacks the schematic framework that guides and structures adult memory. As a result, we would expect the child to store poorly organized or poorly integrated memories. Alternatively, the child may employ a schematic framework rather different from the adults', and so will store memories in a different fashion. Because of this, the adult has little access to these early memories.

Notice that these suggestions simply build on lines of argument we have already put in place, here and in Chapters 4 and 5. For example, we have reviewed much evidence, in this chapter and in Chapter 4, showing that one's current knowledge influences how one learns and how one remembers. We also saw, in Chapter 5, that forgetting is more likely if one's *perspective* changes between the time of learning and the time of recall. Thus, the elements of our account of childhood amnesia are already in place. In addition, several studies have looked directly at how young children organize and remember the events of their day-to-day lives (e.g., Nelson, 1988). Not surprisingly, these studies document that, before age three, children's understanding of life events is often rather different from that of adults, as we would expect on this account of childhood amnesia.

This account also leads to the prediction that childhood amnesia will be *least* severe for those children who had an "adult-like" schematic framework and who therefore understood and organized the events of their childhood in an adult-like manner. Which children will these be? One hypothesis is that if children spend a lot of time conversing with their parents about life events, they will soon realize how their parents organize those events. If children spend little time in such conversations, then they will presumably take longer to achieve an adult-like organization. We should therefore predict that children who converse more with their parents will, many years later, have less severe childhood amnesia. The evidence suggests that this is the case (e.g., Mullen, 1994). This adds even more strength to the concept of childhood amnesia offered here. (For a different view of childhood amnesia, though, see Jacobs & Nadel, 1985; Nadel & Zola-Morgan, 1984; Nelson, 1993.)

The Accuracy and Adequacy of Human Memory

We have covered a spectrum of topics in this chapter, and so it may be useful to reiterate some key points. As we have seen over and over, memory mistakes do occur, and these can sometimes be large. Moreover, these mistakes seem virtually undetectable, since false "memories" are recalled with just as much clarity and just as much conviction as genuine memories.

Just as important is the fact that our memories, overall, seem to be extraordinarily accurate. We mentioned earlier a study by Yuille and Cutshall (1986), showing high accuracy rates in eyewitness memory, even months after the observed event; we also mentioned a study by Howes, Siegel and Brown (1993), which documented the veracity of many memories from early childhood. Similarly, Brewin, Andrews and Gotlib (1993) summarize a number of studies showing that our autobiographical recollection is for the most part quite accurate. In short, it does seem safe to argue that our memories are correct more often than not. In addition, if something has been learned well enough, we seem able to remember it, with virtually no loss, for many decades.

We might also mention a number of case studies testifying to the power of human memory. As Neisser (1982) has noted, memory performance in non-laboratory settings is often remarkable, both for the completeness and the longevity of the memory record. For example, there are performers in Yugoslavia who recite long poems from memory. Some of these poems take all night to recite, and an individual performer might know as many as 30 of these poems (Lord, 1960). In the same vein, the anthropologist Gregory Bateson (1958) has described masters of totemic knowledge in New Guinea, who are able to recall the names of thousands of significant totems. Closer to home, the conductor Toscanini apparently had memorized the complete scores of a huge number of works of music and could remember details of each score with ease (Marek, 1975).

Memory Errors as the Price for Other Gains

Clearly, there is much to praise about human memory. Indeed, even the memory *errors* have a positive side. Explaining this will allow us to review several key themes from this chapter.

As we have repeatedly noted, the quantity of information in long-term storage is vast, and this creates a problem: Within this huge repository, it is often difficult to locate any specific memory. We have argued, though, that search through memory is facilitated by memory *connections*, with each connection serving as a retrieval path. Thus, to make memories *retrievable*, we often need the connections. Yet these same connections serve as a source for many memory errors and serve, in particular, as a source for intrusion errors. The connections interweave our memories, and interweave the records of specific episodes with more generic knowledge. All of this, in turn, allows bits to be exchanged from one memory to another, or between general knowledge and the memory of a specific case.

It would seem that these errors may be the price we have to pay for effective memory retrieval: To avoid the errors, we would need to restrict the connections. If we did that, we would lose the ability to locate our own memories within long-term storage.

Other memory errors need to be understood in a different way: We noted, in this chapter and in Chapter 2, that the information provided to us by the world is often ambiguous and often incomplete. In addition, and perhaps more important, the world often presents us with far more information than we can use. This point is illustrated in Figure 6.8. The figure is silly, but it makes a profound point: Our environments provide us with a vast number of things that we *might* notice. If we notice the wrong things, or if we try to notice everything, we will be overwhelmed by foolish irrelevancies. We therefore need to make some intelligent choices so that we focus on useful information and not on trivia.

It is these facts that force us to rely on inference and assumption in our intellectual commerce with the world. In particular, we rely on the regularities of our past experience in interpreting the information provided to us by the world and, indeed, in interpreting the (sometimes ambiguous, sometimes incomplete) information provided to us by our own memories. We rely on the same regularities in order to discern what is important and what is worth attending, and that is how we escape the disaster depicted in Figure 6.8.

However, while the world is generally a uniform place, it isn't entirely so.

Figure 6.8

THE IMPORTANCE OF SCHEMATA IN GUIDING OUR ATTENTION

Our world is rich with information, far more information than we could use. Worse, much of this information is not useful for many of our purposes. We therefore need some means of making intelligent selections from the overall information available to us. Guidance of this sort seems to be exactly what this corporate spy is missing.

Therefore, our assumptions will often be correct, but not always, and this is another source of memory error. But we simply have no choice about this: We need to make the assumptions, in order to make possible our moment-by-moment interactions with the world. If this strategy sometimes leads to mistakes, that is just the price we must pay.

One might argue that this price is relatively low: In many contexts, it doesn't matter if we get the details right. In many contexts, the knowledge that we need is simply generic knowledge or the gist of our experiences. If reliance on prior knowledge helps us, therefore, to get the gist, then we have done well. If this same reliance leads to errors concerning the *details*, often that will not matter.

The Advantages of Forgetting

This argument can, in fact, be carried one step further: It may turn out that memory errors are not merely the "price we pay" in order to achieve some gain. Instead, the errors may sometimes be *desirable*, and likewise for forgetting. There may be times when it is literally to our advantage to remember less, and to forget more.

In an extraordinary short story entitled "Funes the Memorious," Jorge Luis Borges describes a character named Funes, who has a perfect memory. Funes never forgets anything but, rather than being pleased or proud of this capacity, he is immensely distressed by his memorial prowess. "My memory, sir, is like a garbage heap," he complains. Funes's problem was that he was "almost incapable of ideas of a general, Platonic sort. Not only was it difficult for him to comprehend that the generic symbol *dog* embraces so many unlike individuals of diverse size and form; it bothered him that the dog at 3:14 (seen from the side) should have the same name as the dog at 3:15 (seen from the front)" (Borges, 1964).

This story is a work of fiction, but Funes is remarkably similar to an actual person. Luria (1968) describes a case of a man, identified only as "S," who, like Funes, never forgets anything. "S," just like Funes, is not well served by his extraordinary memory. In tests of intelligence, "S" does not do well; he is often distracted, it would seem, by the rich detail of his own recollections. Like Funes, "S" finds it difficult to think in abstract terms.

These remarkable cases imply a positive side to forgetting: To think abstractly, one must overlook many concrete details; forgetting seems to help make this possible. In order to generalize, one must ignore the points of difference between various episodes, focusing instead on what the episodes have in common; again, forgetting facilitates this. "S," the real character, complains about his "perfect" memory, just as Funes did. Apparently, a perfect memory, with no forgetting, is far from desirable. (For other discussion of the *advantages* of forgetting, see Johnson et al., 1993; Riccio, Rabinowitz & Axelrod, 1994.)

We close this chapter on a positive note. We have, to be sure, discussed a wide range of memory errors—often in domains where we would prefer to avoid error. Worse, we have argued that the errors, once made, are often undetectable, so that one never realizes that the past is incorrectly recalled. We have also emphasized, though, that these errors are the exception rather than the rule so that, in general, our memories preserve the past with impressive fidelity. In addition, we have now suggested that, even in making errors, even in forgetting, human memory functions in a fashion that serves us extraordinarily well.

7

Associative Theories of Long-Term Memory

At the close of Chapter 6, we remarked once again on the vastness of memory's contents. In fact, throughout the last few chapters, we have talked about memories for episodes and also memories for mundane facts, memories for verbal passages as well as for pictures. Our memories contain schemata, scripts, and an immense quantity of commonsense information about a diversity of objects, actions, and events. The scope of memory seems even greater when we include the unconscious, "implicit" memories described in Chapter 5.

We have also noted a problem created by this informational wealth—the problem of retrieval difficulty. How do we ever find anything in the huge warehouse of long-term storage? Indeed, we emphasized in Chapter 6 how "seamlessly" we combine remembered information with current environmental input, so that we are often not aware that we have supplemented the actual input with information supplied from memory. Apparently, then, we don't merely succeed in retrieving information from memory; we succeed swiftly, effortlessly, and unwittingly.

We have also suggested that memory search is aided by *connections* between the to-be-learned materials and things one already knows, or connections between the material and aspects of the learning context. We have claimed that these connections provide *retrieval paths*, routes that one can take when searching for some particular memory. But what are these connections? Who or what does the "traveling" on these retrieval paths? We turn now to these questions, and more broadly to the questions of how information is stored in long-term memory, and how that information is located when needed.

The Network Notion

Much of this chapter will be devoted to exploring a single idea. The idea is that memory connections provide the basic building blocks through which our knowledge is represented in memory. For example, you obviously know your mother's name; this fact is recorded in your memory. The proposal to be considered is that this memory is literally represented by a memory connection, in this case a connection between some memory content representing your mother and some memory content representing the sound pattern of her name. That connection isn't some appendage to the memory. Instead, the connection is the memory. Likewise for all the other facts you know (the opposite of "hot"; how you spent last Thanksgiving; the color of rubies), so that all of knowledge is represented via a sprawling network of these connections, a vast set of **associations**.

The notion that memory contains a network of associations is hardly new. The idea has been discussed, both in philosophy and in psychology, for several centuries. Modern conceptions of the network, however, differ from their predecessors in important ways; we will discuss some of these differences as we proceed. Our initial focus, though, will not be on the modern conceptions *per se.* Instead, we will be concerned with broader themes: What motivates this approach to memory? Why should we think that memory has an "associative" base? Then, once we have discussed those issues, we will turn to some of the specific ways an associative theory might be implemented. We will first consider a form of theorizing patterned after the work of Collins and Loftus (1975) and Anderson (1976, 1980; Anderson & Bower, 1973). Later in the chapter, we will turn to the most recent version of associative theorizing, a sophisticated treatment known as "connectionism."

How Might the Network Work?

The essence of a memory network is straightforward. First, we need some means of representing individual ideas; these representations will be the **nodes** within the net, just like the knots within a fisherman's net. (In fact, the word "node" is derived from the Latin word for knot, "nodus.") These nodes are then tied to each other via connections that we will call **associations** or associative links. If you like, you can think of the nodes as being akin to cities on a map, and associations as being the highways that link the cities. Learning, within this metaphor, would be similar to building a highway between two cities, or perhaps improving an existing highway, so that it is more easily and quickly traveled.

On this view, what it means to "search" through memory is to begin at one node (one "city") and to travel via the connections until the target information is reached. Critically, not all associations are of equal strength. Some "cities" are linked by superhighways, others only by country roads. Other "cities" are not linked to each other at all, but you can get from one to the next by traveling via some intermediate cities. This will immediately provide part of our account for why some memories are easily called up, while others are not: For example, if asked, "When is your birthday?" you answer quickly and easily. Presumably, this is because there is a strong connection between the BIRTHDAY node and the node representing a specific date. This connection has been established by the fact that this date and the idea of birthdays have frequently been thought about in conjunction with each other, creating an easily-traveled path from one to the other. (Throughout this chapter, we will use small capital letters when we are referring to a NODE in memory; we will use normal type when referring to the word or stimulus represented by that node.)

Even at this early stage of presentation, though, we reach a point in which modern versions of the network differ from older versions. According to philosophers like Locke or Berkeley, associations among ideas are largely "stamped in" by the environment. If you heard the word "birthday" and then heard a date, this would be enough to create a mental association. As we have seen, however, this claim is not correct: Memory connections are not established in this passive manner. (See our discussion of maintenance rehearsal and elaborative rehearsal in Chapter 4.)

Modern network theories therefore require a more active role for the learner. Thus, memory connections will be established only if the learner pays attention to the to-be-remembered items during the learning episode. Likewise, a great deal depends on *how* the learner engages the items. For example, if the learner chooses to think about the material in several different ways, this will create multiple connections, each of which can later be used as a retrieval path. The learner will also be helped if he or she thinks about the material in distinctive ways. For example, if you establish an association between "THE LIST I STUDIED EARLIER" and "SOME CAPITALIZED WORDS," this connection isn't very informative, and probably won't help you later on to remember the to-be-remembered words. In contrast, an association between "THE LIST I STUDIED EARLIER" and, say, "THE OPPOSITE OF LOVE" *is* distinctive and will help you to remember.

Spreading Activation

Theorists speak of a node becoming **activated** when it has received a strong enough input signal, sort of like a lightbulb being turned on by incoming electricity. This implies that what travels through the associative links is akin to energy or fuel, and the associative links themselves can be thought of as "activation carriers"—hoses carrying the fuel or wires carrying electricity. Then, once a node has been activated, it can in turn activate other nodes: Energy will spread out from the just-activated node, via its associations, and this will activate nodes connected to the just-activated node.

To put all of this more precisely, the **activation level** of each node depends on how much activation that node has received and how recently the activation arrived. Eventually, though, the activation level will reach the node's **response threshold**, and this triggers several other events, including an *outward* spread of activation from that node. Activation of a node will also serve to summon attention to that node; this is what it means to "find" a node within the network.

Activation levels below the response threshold, so-called **subthreshold**

activation, also have an important role to play: Activation is assumed to accumulate, so that two subthreshold inputs may add together, or **summate**, and bring the node to threshold. Likewise, if a node has been partially activated recently, it is, in effect, already "warmed up," and so even a weak further input may be sufficient to bring the node to threshold. (This idea should sound familiar: We offered similar claims in Chapter 2, when we described *repetition priming* in terms of "detector warm up." Indeed, our discussion throughout this section parallels claims made in Chapter 2; we will return to these parallels later in the chapter.)

In short, activation travels from node to node via the associative links. As each node becomes activated, it serves as a source for further activation, spreading onward through the network. This process, known as **spreading activation**, allows us to deal with a key issue. How does one navigate through the maze of associations? If you start a search at one node, how do you decide where to go from there? Our initial proposal is that you do not "choose" or "decide" which paths to travel. Instead, activation spreads out from its starting point in all directions simultaneously, flowing through whatever connections are in place. Think of fuel flowing through hoses: If two hoses radiate out from a starting point, the fuel does not "choose" the left hose or the right. If there are two hoses in place, the fuel will flow through both.

This is not to say, however, that all pathways are equally effective in carrying the activation. Some associative links, thanks to recent or frequent use, are particularly effective, others are less so. (To push the metaphor a bit further, some of the hoses are tiny, and so can only carry a small amount of activation; other hoses are much larger.) For that matter, perhaps some associations are "built in," that is, are innately strong. In any event, the stronger or better-established links will carry activation more efficiently and so will be more successful at activating subsequent nodes.

Evidence Favoring the Network Approach

This provides us with a preliminary description of how an associative network functions: *Spreading activation* causes differing *activation levels* of the network's nodes. The activation may not reach *threshold* immediately, but *subthreshold activation* can accumulate. When a node's activation level does reach threshold levels, this summons attention. In addition, once a node is activated to threshold levels, it will serve as a source for further spreading activation, exciting other nodes.

This sketch of the network leaves a great deal unspecified, but that is deliberate: Associative nets can be implemented in various ways, and we are not ready yet to talk about the details of this or that implementation. We first need to ask whether we are even on the right track. Is this a sensible approach at all? What can be explained in these terms?

Hints

Why do hints help us to remember? Why is a free recall procedure ("What was on the list?") more difficult than cued recall ("Was there a word on the list that rhymed with *glove*?")?

Any effort at recall starts with some designation of what it is you are trying to recall: Who was at the party last week? What do you know about Shakespeare's sonnets? What is the capital of South Dakota? These designations then provide the starting point for your memory search: Mention of South Dakota will activate the nodes in memory that represent your knowledge about this state. Activation can then spread outward from these nodes, eventually reaching nodes that represent the capital city's name.

It is possible, though, that there is only a weak connection between the SOUTH DAKOTA nodes and the nodes representing "Pierre." Perhaps you are not very familiar with South Dakota, or perhaps you haven't thought about this state, or its capital, for some time. In these cases, insufficient activation will flow into the PIERRE nodes, and so these nodes won't reach threshold and won't be "found."

Things will go differently if a hint is available. If you were told "South Dakota's capital is also a man's name," this will cause activation of the MAN'S NAME node, and so activation will spread out from this source at the same time that activation is spreading out from the SOUTH DAKOTA nodes. Therefore, the nodes for "Pierre" will now receive activation from two sources simultaneously, and this combined activation is much more likely to raise the target node to threshold levels (for an alternate example, see Figure 7.1).

Mnemonics

In Chapter 4, we saw that mnemonic devices such as the method of loci clearly improve memory. These mnemonics take advantage of the fact that activation can spread more efficiently through well-established indirect connections than it will via direct, but less well-established, connections. Thus, it is often in the memorizer's interest to let new connections be "parasitic" on old ones, linking materials together by hanging them onto an already well-connected frame. In the method of loci, for example, you exploit the fact that strong associations already exist in memory, binding together your knowledge of a series of familiar sites. These strong, already-existing associations then provide

Figure 7.1

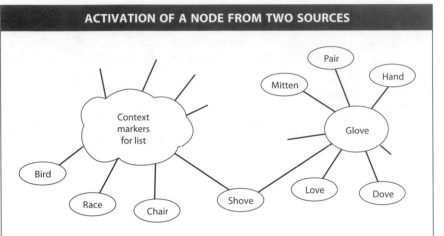

ACTIVATION OF A NODE FROM TWO SOURCES

A subject is asked, "Was there a word on the list that rhymed with 'glove'?" This activates nodes representing context markers for the list, and also the GLOVE node. The context markers are linked with various nodes, including nodes representing the words on the list. The GLOVE node is linked to various nodes, including words with similar sounds. If activation spreads from both GLOVE and the context markers, then the sought-after word ("shove") will receive activation from both sources, so this node is likely to be activated. In this sketch, words within ellipses represent individual nodes; no attempt has been made here to depict the propositions represented in the network.

the glue that holds the items together. When the time comes to retrieve these items all you have to do is find any piece of the mnemonic. Once the first piece is found, the strong connections among the mnemonic's parts will guarantee that the rest of the mnemonic (and the material it is carrying) will be found as well (Figure 7.2).

We note in passing, though, an untoward consequence of mnemonic use and, indeed, a consequence of some importance for students. To use a mnemonic, you focus your efforts on the creation of a few memory connections. As a consequence, you are likely to neglect other (potential) connections, and this can be problematic later on. Thus, if you were using the mnemonic illustrated in Figure 7.2, you would concentrate on the link between *shoe* and *firewood* and the link between *tree* and *picture*. No thought is given to the connection between *firewood* and *picture* or between *firewood* and *ashtray*.

The links thus established will serve you well if you are later asked: "What was the second word on the list?" or "What word was linked to *shoe*?" How-

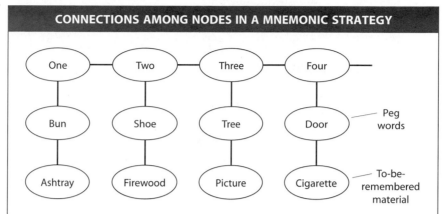

Figure 7.2

CONNECTIONS AMONG NODES IN A MNEMONIC STRATEGY

A subject memorizes a series of words ("ashtray," "firewood," "picture") using a mnemonic strategy. The mnemonic is based on the rhyme "one is a bun, two is a shoe, three is a tree." The rhyme is easily learned, given the links already in place between ONE and TWO, TWO and THREE, and so on, and also the strong connections between the rhymes ("one" and "bun," "two" and "shoe," etc.). In learning the word list, subjects make connections between each word and its *peg*—for example, between "bun" (the peg) and "ashtray." (The subject might think of a hamburger bun filled with ashes and cigarette butts.) With these connections, subjects easily remember which word was in each place on the list, or which was associated with "tree" and so on. Subjects will perform less well if asked what word followed "picture" on the list, since there is no connection between picture and its successor (cigarette).

ever, these links will be poor preparation if you are later asked: "What was the next word on the list after *firewood*?" In fact, if we ask you this question, you will need to think through, slowly and laboriously, the fact that *firewood* was associated with *shoe*, which rhymes with *two*, and therefore *firewood* was second on the list. Therefore, the next word must have been the third, and this will lead you to think of *three*, and then *tree*, and eventually *picture*. You will reach the goal, but only with considerable effort.

This point is consistent with claims made in Chapter 5: A particular learning strategy can create memories that are highly accessible from one perspective but not from others. In addition, we now see the "down-side" to mnemonic use: Mnemonics make the target material easily retrievable but in a narrow, rigid manner. In contrast, a student's knowledge, one would hope, is more fluidly retrieved, making that knowledge available in, and useful for, more than one context. In this way, most mnemonics provide a poor way for students to learn; students are far better off with memory strategies that lead to a richer network of retrieval paths, such as the network that results from trying to *understand* the to-be-remembered material.

State Dependency

We also saw in Chapter 5 that, if one learns materials while sad or while underwater, one is more likely to remember these materials while sad or while underwater. Why is this? The hypothesis is that these various states have a particular set of nodes connected to them. Perhaps there is literally a SAD node that is activated when you are sad; perhaps, instead, there is a set of thoughts that often occur when you are sad, and so the nodes representing these thoughts will be activated whenever you are in a sad state. In either case, if these nodes were active during learning, associations may have been formed between them and the nodes for the to-be-remembered material (cf. Gilligan & Bower, 1984; Bower, 1981).

At the time of test, these "state-marker" nodes would work the same way that hints do: Let us assume that you were sad during learning, and so memory connections have been established between the nodes affiliated with sad-

Figure 7.3

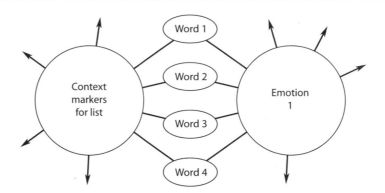

A NETWORK REPRESENTATION OF STATE-DEPENDENT RETRIEVAL

A subject learns a word list while in a specific context (a particular room, a particular time of day) and also while in a specific mood. Associations are therefore strengthened between the nodes representing the words and the nodes representing the context, *and also* between nodes representing the words and nodes representing the emotion. If the subject is in the same mood during the memory test, then the word nodes will be receiving activation from this mood source as well, making it more likely that the sought-after nodes will be activated. [Adapted from Bower, 1981.]

ness and the nodes representing the to-be-remembered material. If you are once again sad, at the time of the test, then the nodes affiliated with sadness will be activated. Activation will therefore spread out from these nodes, and, thanks to the connections established during learning, some of this activation will reach the nodes for the material. This will combine with the activation arriving at these nodes from other sources, making it likely that these sought-after nodes will reach threshold levels (Figure 7.3).

More Direct Tests of the Network Claims

It seems, therefore, that the network provides a natural way to bring together the evidence presented in the last few chapters. This by itself suggests that the network notion is a coherent and useful way to think about memory—a single framework into which we can bring many different claims and findings. But, in addition, the network approach makes its own predictions about memory, allowing a more direct test of the claim that memory does indeed have an associative base.

Spread of Activation and Priming

A key idea of the associative network is the idea that activation spreads through links to activate nodes, and that subthreshold activation can "accumulate" if, for example, activation reaches a node from more than one source. Evidence that directly supports this claim comes from several paradigms, one of which is the lexical-decision task.

In a lexical-decision experiment, subjects are shown a series of letter sequences on a computer screen. Some of the sequences spell words; other sequences are **pseudowords**, that is, letter strings that look like words, but aren't (e.g., "blar" or "plome" or "tuke"). Subjects' task is to hit a "yes" button if the sequence spells a word and a "no" button otherwise. Presumably, subjects perform this task by "looking up" these letter strings in their "mental dictionary," and they base their response on whether they find the string in the dictionary or not. We can therefore use subjects' speed of response in this task as an index of how quickly they can locate the word in their memories. (We have already encountered this task in Chapter 5.)

Meyer and Schvaneveldt (1971; Meyer, Schvaneveldt & Ruddy, 1974) presented subjects with pairs of letter strings like those shown in Table 7.1; subjects had to decide whether each letter string was a word or not. Notice that the procedure contains several different kinds of pairs—sometimes both are words, sometimes both are not. Sometimes the first string is a word, but

Table 7.1

STIMULI AND RESULTS FROM A PRIMING EXPERIMENT				
Positive Pairs		**Negative Pairs**		
Unrelated	**Related**	**Nonword First**	**Nonword Second**	**Both Nonwords**
Nurse	Bread	Plame	Wine	Plame
Butter	Butter	Wine	Plame	Reab
940 msec	855 msec	904 msec	1087 msec	884 msec

Note: Subjects must respond "yes" if both stimuli in the pair are words ("positive" pairs); subjects respond "no" if either stimulus in the pair is not a word ("negative" pairs). Within the positive pairs, some pairs are semantically related ("bread," "butter"), while others are not ("nurse," "butter"). Thanks to the spread of activation, responses are quickest for the related pairs.
[After Meyer & Schvaneveldt, 1971.]

[Handwritten margin note: is fastest RT b/c "bread" has already partially activated "butter" node b/c they are related]

not the second; sometimes the reverse is true. Our main interest, though, is with the first two types of pairs: For these, both strings are words, but in one case the words are semantically related, while in the other case they are not.

Consider a trial in which subjects see a *related* pair, for example "bread, butter." Subjects first respond "yes" to "bread." Presumably, they have located the BREAD node in memory, which is equivalent to saying that this node has been activated. This triggers a spread of activation outward from the BREAD node, bringing activation to other, nearby nodes. It seems likely that the association from "bread" to "butter" is a strong one and, therefore, once BREAD is activated, activation should also spread to the BUTTER node.

The subject now turns his or her attention to the second word in the pair, "butter." To select a response, the subject must locate "butter" in memory. But of course the process of activating this node has already begun, thanks to the activation received from BREAD. This should accelerate the process of bringing this node to threshold, and so it will require less time to activate. Hence, we expect quicker responses to "butter" in this context, compared to a context in which "butter" was preceded by some unrelated word, or by a non-word.

As the figure shows, this priming result is in fact what occurs. Subjects' lexical-decision responses are faster if the present stimulus word was preceded by a semantically related word. Priming effects are easy to demonstrate and can be used as a way to "map" the network. That is, we can discover how closely associated two nodes are by assessing the degree to which activation of one primes the other. By repeating this for many pairs of nodes, we can begin to outline the patterns and organizations of memory. (For reviews, including some alternative conceptions of priming, see McKoon & Ratcliff, 1992; McNamara, 1992a, 1992b, 1994; Neely, 1991; for a somewhat different perspective, see Smith, Besner & Miyoshi, 1994.)

Sentence Verification

When one searches through the network, activation spreads from node to node to node. Search through the network, therefore, is like travel, and so the further one must travel, the longer it should take to reach one's destination. In a classic experiment, Collins and Quillian (1969) tested this claim using a sentence verification task. Subjects were shown sentences on a computer screen like, "A robin is a bird," or "A robin is an animal," or "Cats have claws," or "Cats have hearts." Mixed together with these obviously true sentences was a variety of false sentences ("A cat is a bird") and subjects had to hit a "true" or "false" button as quickly as they could.

Collins and Quillian reasoned as follows: Subjects perform this task by "traveling" through the network from the ROBIN node to the BIRD node. This travel allows the subject to confirm that there is, in fact, an associative path between these two nodes, and this tells the subject that the sentence about these two concepts is *true*. This "travel" will require little time, of course, if the two nodes are directly linked by an association, as ROBIN and BIRD probably are. In this case, subjects should answer "true" rather quickly. The travel will require more time, however, if the two nodes are connected only indirectly (like ROBIN and ANIMAL), and so we should expect slower responses to sentences that require a "two-step" connection than to sentences that exploit a single connection.

In addition, Collins and Quillian noted that there is no point in storing in memory the fact that cats have hearts and the fact that dogs have hearts and the fact that squirrels have hearts. Instead, they proposed, it would be more efficient just to store the fact that these various creatures are animals, and then the separate fact that animals have hearts. Hence the property "has a heart" would be associated with the ANIMAL node, rather than the nodes for each individual animal, and likewise for all the other properties of animals, as shown in Figure 7.4. On this logic, we should expect relatively slow responses to sentences like "Cats have hearts," since, to choose a response, a subject must locate the linkage from CAT to ANIMAL and then a second linkage from ANIMAL to HEART. We would expect a quicker response to "Cats have claws," because here there would be a direct connection between CAT and the node representing this property: While all cats have claws, other animals do not, and so this information could not be entered at the higher level.

As Figure 7.5 shows, these predictions are all borne out. Responses to

Figure 7.4

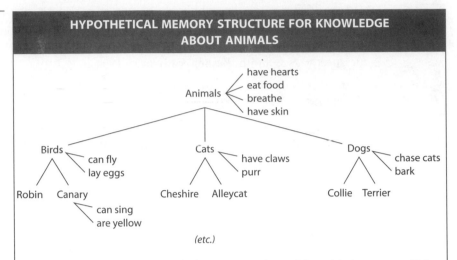

HYPOTHETICAL MEMORY STRUCTURE FOR KNOWLEDGE ABOUT ANIMALS

Collins and Quillian proposed that memory has a hierarchical structure. This system avoids redundant storage of connections between CATS and HAVE HEARTS, and between DOGS and HAVE HEARTS, and so on for all the other animals. Instead, HAVE HEARTS is stored as a property of *all* animals. To confirm that cats have hearts, therefore, one must traverse two links: from CATS to ANIMALS, and from ANIMALS to HAVE HEARTS. This should take more time than it would to confirm that cats have claws and that cats purr, which require traversing only one link. [After Collins & Quillian, 1969.]

sentences like "A canary is a canary" take approximately 1000 msec (one second). This is presumably the time it takes just to the read the sentence, and to move one's finger on the response button. Sentences like "A canary can sing" require an additional step of traversing one link in memory, and yield slower responses. Sentences like "A canary can fly" require the traversing of two links, from CANARY to BIRD and then from BIRD to CAN FLY, and are correspondingly slower.

The picture presented in the Collins and Quillian data is remarkably clear-cut: To predict response times, all we need to do is count the number of associative steps that must be traversed to support a response. In addition, the evidence seems to fit nicely with the claim that material is not stored redundantly in memory. Instead, information is stored as high as possible in the hierarchy, so that what we remember is properties of *classes* not properties of individuals.

However, these claims have not gone unchallenged (McCloskey & Glucksberg, 1978; Rips, Shoben & Smith, 1973; Smith, Rips & Shoben, 1974). Collins

Figure 7.5

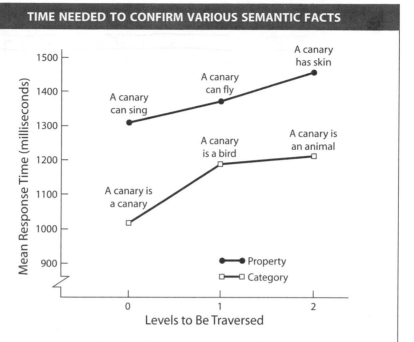

TIME NEEDED TO CONFIRM VARIOUS SEMANTIC FACTS

Subjects must answer "true" or "false" to sentences such as "A canary is a bird." The graph shows the relation between the type of sentence and how long it took subjects to respond to each sentence (response time, or RT). Subjects were fastest when no links in the network had to be traversed, slower when the necessary ideas were separated by one link, and slower still if the ideas were separated by two links. [After Collins & Quillian, 1969.]

and Quillian are surely correct that response times are influenced by the number of associative steps traversed, but this turns out not to be the whole story. For example, consider the fact that subjects are much quicker to assent to "A robin is a bird" than to "A peacock is a bird" (Rosch, 1973, 1975; Smith et al., 1974). If we were simply to count nodes, these are both one-step connections and so should yield similar response times. In general, though, the more "typical" the exemplar, the faster the response times, and so these **typicality effects** must be accommodated with our theorizing. (We will say a great deal more about typicality in Chapter 8.)

The evidence also suggests that the principle of non-redundancy envisioned by Collins and Quillian does not always hold. For example, from the standpoint of economy, the property of "having feathers" should be associated with the BIRD node rather than (redundantly) with the ROBIN node and the EAGLE node and so forth. Therefore responses will be relatively slow to sentences like, "Pigeons have feathers," since verifying this sentence requires a two-step connection, from PIGEON to BIRD and then from BIRD to HAS FEATHERS. However, subjects respond very quickly to a sentence like "Peacocks have feathers." This is because, in observing peacocks or speaking of peacocks, one often thinks about their prominent tail feathers (cf. Conrad, 1972). Even though it is informationally redundant, a strong association between PEACOCK and FEATHERS is likely to be established.

Finally, there is also reason to be skeptical about the proposal that our knowledge, in general, can be represented via neat hierarchies like the one shown in Figure 7.5. This is because, to put it simply, most things can be classified in more than one way, yielding a complex pattern of multiple, overlapping hierarchies. For example, the concept *personal computer* might be represented within the hierarchy of *electronic devices*, and so would be represented along with radar, ignition coils, and stereo amplifiers. However, *personal computers* can also be represented within the hierarchy of *office equipment*, and so would now be joined by staplers, pencils, and file cabinets. For that matter, *personal computers* can also be represented within the hierarchy of *modern inventions*, with yet a different set of conceptual cousins. This complexity obviously speaks against a strict hierarchical organization, such as the one depicted in Figure 7.5.

For these reasons, psychologists have moved away from the model proposed by Collins and Quillian. However, let's not lose sight of the contribution here: It does seem that, all other things being equal, we can predict memory access by counting the number of nodes subjects must traverse in answering a question. This by itself strengthens the claim that associative links play an important role in memory representation. But we also cannot neglect the phrase "all other things being equal." Speed of memory access also depends on several other factors, including the efficiency of individual associations, the existence of special connections, and also something referred to as the "degree of fan."

Degree of Fan

Imagine a sentence verification task in which a subject confronts (on separate trials) the following two sentences: "A robin has wings," and "An aardvark has legs." The associations between ROBIN and its properties are likely to be stronger than those between AARDVARK and its properties, simply because subjects in these experiments have probably encountered many more robins than aardvarks. In addition, though, there are probably many more associations radiating out from ROBIN than there are from AARDVARK. As illustrated in Figure 7.6, this implies that the ROBIN node will look like the hub of a

Figure 7.6

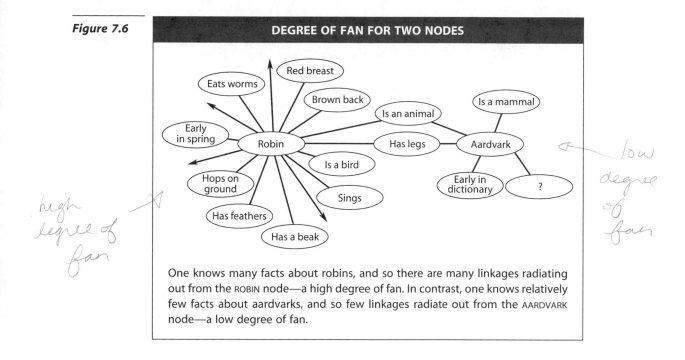

DEGREE OF FAN FOR TWO NODES

high degree of fan

low degree of fan

One knows many facts about robins, and so there are many linkages radiating out from the ROBIN node—a high degree of fan. In contrast, one knows relatively few facts about aardvarks, and so few linkages radiate out from the AARDVARK node—a low degree of fan.

many-spoked wheel, while the AARDVARK node will not. In the standard terminology, ROBIN has a "high degree of fan" (many things fanning out from it), AARDVARK has a low degree of fan.

The notion of "fan" has been extensively explored by Anderson and his associates (Anderson, 1974, 1976; Lewis & Anderson, 1976; also see Peterson & Potts, 1982; Thorndyke & Bower, 1974). Why should degree of fan matter? Recall that, once a node is activated, the links radiating out from this node will all receive activation energy simultaneously—the links will be activated in parallel with each other, rather than in some serial order. In addition, it seems sensible to assume that the quantity of activation is limited. Therefore, the more the activation is divided, the less will go to each recipient. Activation spreading outward from AARDVARK will only be divided five ways, and so each link will receive 20% of the total. The activation spreading outward from ROBIN will be much more thinly divided, and so each link will receive a smaller share of the whole.

Does degree of fan matter for memory retrieval? This question is difficult to ask with "robin" and "aardvark," because these concepts differ both in degree of fan and in strength of association. Imagine that we asked subjects to verify the sentences, "Aardvarks have legs," and "Robins have wings." The prediction is that the ROBIN node has a greater degree of fan, and this will slow down verification of the "robin" sentence. At the same time, the links radiating out from ROBIN are likely to be more efficient, thanks to frequency of use, and this will speed up verification of the "robin" sentence. Hence, we have two effects on the scene, working in opposite directions, and potentially canceling each other out.

To ask whether degree of fan matters, we need to find a case in which two nodes differ *only* in degree of fan. One way to do this is to start, so to speak, from scratch. For example, Anderson (1974) taught subjects a set of sentences about people in locations. "The doctor is in the bank." "The fireman is in the park." "The lawyer is in the church." "The lawyer is in the park." And so on. In the full set of sentences, some of the actors (e.g., the doctor) appeared in only one location (the bank); others (the lawyer) appeared in two locations. Likewise, some locations (the church) only contained one person; other locations (the park) contained two. In this way, Anderson controlled the degree of fan from the nodes representing each of these terms—there was greater fan for PARK than for CHURCH, greater fan for LAWYER than for DOCTOR.

At the same time, all of these were new facts for the subjects, since Anderson had just made them up. Therefore, the strength of the association for these sentences started out at zero. Then, by controlling the learning process, Anderson controlled the growth of association strength and, in particular, made certain that association strength was the same for all of the sentences.

Table 7.2

INFLUENCE OF DEGREE OF FAN ON DECISION TIME		
Number of Sentences Using a Specific Location	**Number of Sentences about a Specific Person**	
	1 Sentence	**2 Sentences**
1 Sentence	1.11 sec	1.17 sec
2 Sentences	1.17 sec	1.22 sec

Note: Subjects were slower in recognizing sentences that involved nodes with a higher degree of fan and faster with sentences that involved a lower degree of fan. The sentences were of the form "The lawyer is in the park." Fan was manipulated by varying how many facts the subjects knew about the lawyer (that is, whether the lawyer appeared in only one of the sentences that had been learned or in two), and also how many facts the subjects knew about the park (that is, whether the park had been mentioned in one of the sentences or in two). The effect observed in this experiment is not large (for example, a 0.06-second difference in the left-hand column), but this is probably because we are considering only small differences in degree of fan (1 versus 2).

[After Anderson, 1974.]

In this way, Anderson ended up with a set of nodes that differed in degree of fan, but not in the strength of their connections to other nodes.

Once subjects had memorized these sentences, they were given a recognition test, in which they had to decide as quickly as possible whether each of the test sentences had been presented as part of the learning set. As Table 7.2 shows, speed of response was influenced by degree of fan: Response times were fastest when only one sentence mentioned a specific person or a specific place, response times were slowest when multiple sentences named a specific person or place. This is exactly what we would expect if activation were a fixed quantity and so, the more ways divided, the less to each recipient. The less to each recipient, the longer it takes for the target node to be fully activated and so, finally, the longer for the response to be chosen. (For a somewhat different account of the fan effect, see Radvansky & Zacks, 1991.)

Is There a Cost to Knowing "Too Much"?

Note an odd consequence of the experiment just described, and of the notion of fan. In a sense, there is sometimes a cost attached to knowing "too much." If you know just one fact about aardvarks, then this fact will be easily remembered whenever you think about aardvarks. That is because, with such a low degree of fan, all the activation from the AARDVARK node will spread down this single association. However, as you learn more and more about aardvarks, the degree of fan is increasing, and so less and less activation will spread down any particular association.

Consider the bit of network shown in Figure 7.7. At an early stage of learning (Situation 1 in the figure), there is just a single association radiating out from Node A; therefore, all of A's activation will be channeled to Node B. In this situation, activation of A is almost certain to activate B.

At a later stage of learning (Situation 2), more has been learned about A, and so the degree of fan from Node A has increased. Now Node B receives only one-tenth of A's activation and, as a consequence, thinking about A is *less* likely to remind you of B in Situation 2 than it is in Situation 1. In effect, the increase in fan will lead to a case of *retrieval failure*. Node B is still on the scene, but it may not be activated by a memory search originating with Node A.

The suggestion, then, is that new knowledge about a topic leads, among other things, to an increase in fan at the relevant nodes, and this, by itself, can cause a species of memory interference—in this case, interference mediated by retrieval failure. One way or the other, though, this seems to be a case in which you are better off early in learning than late.

Let's be very careful, though, not to overstate this point. It is true that, in some cases, there is a cost to knowing too much. But this is most definitely

Figure 7.7

DEGREE OF FAN VERSUS THE NUMBER OF RETRIEVAL PATHS

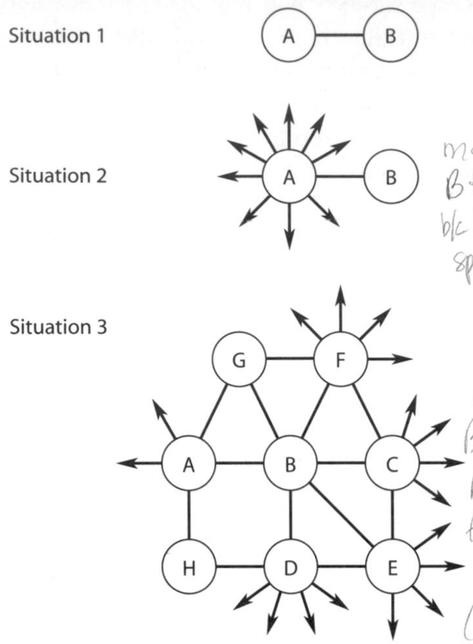

Situation 1

Situation 2

more difficult to activate B than in Situation 1 b/c less of A's activation spreads there

Situation 3

less of A's is going to B, but that's OK b/c B is getting activation from many new sources (∴ B is easier to activate than in Situation 1)

Early in learning (Situation 1), a subject may know only a single fact about A, namely, that it is associated with B. Later in learning (Situation 2), the subject may have learned more about A. Thanks to the increased fan, less of A's activation spreads to B. This makes it more difficult to activate Node B in Situation 2 than in Situation 1. As an alternative, the subject may learn a rich network of interconnected facts (Situation 3). In this case, A's degree of fan is increasing, so that less of A's activation spreads to B. At the same time, B is receiving activation from many new sources. As a result, B will be *easier* to activate in this case than in Situation 1.

not the general case. To see why, think about what is depicted in Situation 2. This is a case in which someone has learned a list of separate, individual facts, all about the same topic, but with the facts not connected to each other. In contrast, consider the learning you are doing right now, as you read this chapter. You are not (I hope) simply learning a list of individual facts, each associated with the concept "associative networks." Instead, you are learning a set of *interrelated* facts, so that you are acquiring a whole network of new connections, more closely modeled by Situation 3 than by Situation 2. In

Situation 3, A's degree of fan has once again increased, relative to Situation 1, and so, here too, B receives less input from A than it did initially. At the same time, however, B can now receive input from many other sources and, as a result, Node B will be *easier* to activate in Situation 3 than in the other situations—receiving less input from A, but receiving more input overall. Hence, the fan effect gave an advantage to Situation 1, but Situation 3 has a greater advantage: the advantage created by the existence of multiple retrieval paths. It is in this fashion, therefore, that, <u>even with the fan effect, learning new facts can *aid* retrieval.</u>

Retrieving Information from a Network

So far, things look good for the network model. We have easily encompassed a large set of prior findings; likewise, the data confirm our claims about spreading activation and fan. In addition, the network idea offers us one further benefit—it holds the promise of explaining how we search through memory so quickly and easily.

Searching through the Network via Associative Links

Think about how an encyclopedia is organized. There is obviously a vast amount of information contained within the encyclopedia, neatly compartmentalized into individual entries. Therefore, if you want to learn about *dogs*, you turn to the entry on that topic; if you want to learn about *glaciers*, you turn to that topic, and so on.

Imagine, though, that your dog is ill, and you are trying to figure out what the problem is. You read the entry about dogs, but you find nothing useful. It is possible that the information you need is present in the encyclopedia, but is contained within a different entry. Perhaps the entry on *veterinary medicine* talks about particular diseases, their symptoms and their cures. But you won't find this information as long as you are focusing on the "dog" entry. Indeed, perhaps the information you seek is quite close to the "dog" entry, in an entry 10 pages further along, or 12 pages back. (Perhaps your dog has an illness called, "doffinitis." Given the encyclopedia's alphabetic organization, this [fictional] disease might be described in an entry just a few pages away from the "dog" entry.) Even in this case, though, you might not find the target information, since few of us adopt a strategy of "exploring the neighborhood" when looking for information in an encyclopedia.

Editors of encyclopedias, however, have anticipated these situations, and they have done something to help you out: At the end of many entries, you will find a series of "pointers," saying "For related information, see the entry on X or the entry on Y." If the right pointers are in place, you will be led to the entry containing the information you want. In some cases, you may need to repeat this process (perhaps the entry on "dogs" leads you to the entry on "veterinary medicine," and, from there, a new series of pointers leads you to the entry talking about "doffinitis"). Indeed, with enough of these pointers in place, one could imagine leading a reader through a succession of entries, allowing a broad range of "access paths." Plausibly, therefore, you could find out about "doffinitis" by starting with the "dog" entry, or by starting with the "pet" entry, or even by starting with the "disease" entry. The "disease" entry might have pointers leading you to the "medicine" entry, which would have its own pointers, including one that led to "veterinary medicine," which would lead you to the desired information.

Of course, all depends on having the right pointers and, indeed, on having a lot of pointers—otherwise, bridges between related topics may be omitted. However, the system won't work if you have too many pointers. Imagine that, at the end of an entry, you find the message, "For related information, see all of the rest of this encyclopedia." This obviously would provide no guidance whatsoever; as Nillson (1971) remarked, "A point in every direction is the same as no point at all." Presumably, though, an appropriate middle number of pointers, neither too few nor too many, can be found.

All of this is easily translated into network terms. Associative links can guide search through memory, just as the pointers guide search through an encyclopedia. Let's imagine that, at some prior point, you have thought about the relationship between *disease* and *medicine*, and the relationship between *medicine* and *veterinary medicine*. Therefore, the corresponding nodes will be linked, and so activating the DISEASE node will cause activation to spread to the MEDICINE node. Activation of that node will in turn activate the VETERINARY MEDICINE node, and so on, leading eventually to the material you seek.

Recall also that spreading activation can proceed from more than one source simultaneously; we relied on this claim in our discussion of hints and state-dependency. This is actually better than what you do with an encyclopedia. It is the equivalent of looking up one encyclopedia entry and finding its list of pointers, and then looking up a different entry, with its own list of pointers, and then, finally, asking which pointers appear on *both* lists. Obviously, this could narrow your search considerably but, with the encyclopedia, it would be a cumbersome process. In the associative net, however, this process is achieved automatically: Activation will simply spread out from both of the entry points and, with no intervention and no guidance, will "converge" on the sought-after node.

Finding Entry Nodes

We have now seen how associative links might guide a search from an "entry point" in the network to some sought-after information. But what starts this process? How does one get to the entry point in the first place? There are surely many options here. Sometimes our memory searches begin with an idea or with some other memory. This obviously happens whenever one idea, or one thought, triggers another. Sometimes, though, the search begins with a perceptual cue: You smell an aroma and are reminded of your childhood; you hear a song and find yourself thinking about the last time you heard that song. Let's consider these cases in turn.

You are thinking about your favorite restaurant, and this calls to mind various other memories, perhaps memories for particular meals you have had at that restaurant. You are contemplating what a friend said to you last weekend, and you are reminded of related comments you've heard from other friends. In cases like these, entry into the associative net is easy: Some number of nodes within the network represent your knowledge about your favorite restaurant; in thinking about the restaurant, these nodes are activated. Likewise, your recollection of last weekend's conversation is also represented via some number of nodes, and these are activated when you think about the conversation. In either case, activation can then spread out from these nodes, representing your initial idea, to other nodes, representing other, related, ideas. Thus, it is no problem for a memory search to be launched by a thought or by a memory. This will simply involve more spreading activation along the lines we have already described.

What about memory searches triggered by a perceptual cue? In most cases, the perceptual cue will bring some ideas to mind, and this will initiate the search in exactly the fashion just described. But how does the cue manage to trigger an idea in the first place? One option is simply to link the network directly to the mechanisms of perception, so that some nodes within the net are *input nodes*. In their functioning, these nodes will be like any others: They will receive activation via associative links; once triggered, they will send activation to other nodes. What is special about these input nodes is that they receive most of their input activation from appropriate detectors, with these in turn connected to the eyes, ears, and so on.

Consider, for example, the portion of the network shown in Figure 7.8. Notice that this bit of network includes ties between the node for APPLE and nodes corresponding to certain colors. These color nodes are tied in the appropriate way to the visual system, so that the presence of the specified colors would lead to the activation of these nodes, which in turn would lead to the activation of the APPLE node. Needless to say, this leaves out a great deal, since

Figure 7.8

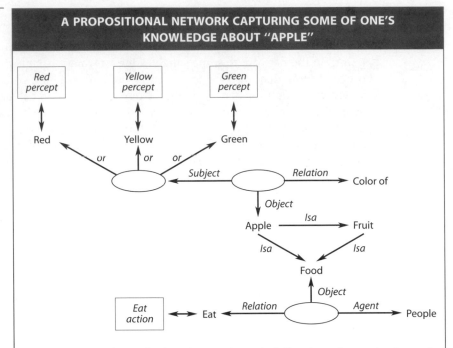

A PROPOSITIONAL NETWORK CAPTURING SOME OF ONE'S KNOWLEDGE ABOUT "APPLE"

Some of the nodes in this bit of network are tied directly to the mechanisms of perception, so that the presence of a red stimulus, or a yellow one, or a green one will contribute activation to nodes within the network. In this way, perceptual processes can directly activate nodes. The actual network would be much more complicated than this, since apples are not merely a certain color, they are also a certain size, shape, and so on. [After Anderson, 1980.]

apples are not merely a certain color, they are also a certain shape and size and so on. However, these other attributes could be similarly tied, on the one side, to the APPLE node and, on the other side, to the mechanisms of vision.

In fact, we have already considered more complicated cases than this. In Chapter 2, we discussed how you recognize words. We suggested that detectors for words might be triggered by detectors for the appropriate letter combinations. These in turn would be triggered by letter detectors, which are themselves triggered by feature detectors. All we need to do now is notice that these various detectors are actually nodes within a network, functioning just like any other nodes—accumulating activation, eventually reaching threshold, and then sending activation to other nodes. And, since they are nodes, there is no problem with these perceptually driven "input nodes" (the detectors) sending their activation to the long-term memory nodes we are describing in this chapter.

However, we do need to be cautious here: We argued in Chapter 2 that this sort of "data-driven" network cannot, by itself, explain all of pattern recognition, and by the same token it cannot provide our full account for how search within the memory network is initiated. As an example, notice that you would respond differently to these two memory questions: "Tell me what you ate for dinner yesterday" and "Tell me what ate you for dinner yesterday." Therefore, you must have a means of discriminating between these two requests, but the process we have so far sketched, in terms of simple detectors, does not provide a ready means of making this discrimination. (See Chapter 2 for further discussion of this point, and also Chapter 9.)

Our point for the moment, then, is a modest one. How do we begin a search through memory? In most cases, it is a thought or idea that triggers a memory search and, for these, "entry" into the system is easy. For perceptual cues, we can hope to initiate memory searches by allowing direct connections between the network and the mechanisms of perception. This will surely work for simple stimuli but, for more complex stimuli, we will need a more elaborate process, and we will say more about this later in the chapter. In either case, though, the key idea is that perceiving and identifying an input will involve, among other steps, the locating and activating of that input's node in the network. Perceiving itself will launch memory search.

Unpacking the Nodes

We have so far spoken of nodes as representing "ideas" or "memories." But what does this mean? Could a node contain, for example, "my full memory of last semester's courses"? A node such as this would create two problems. First, this node would encompass a great deal of information. We would then need to figure out how one searches through the information *inside* of a node, in addition to the problem of how one finds nodes in the first place. Second, if we build a lot of information into a single node, we invite a worry about how one "interprets" or "reads" the information in a node. If each node contained a book-length description of an event or episode, we would need to incorporate into our theorizing some device capable of reading and interpreting this corpus of material. Conversely, the simpler we keep each node's informational content, the less we have to rely on some interpretive device.

These claims apply to any network model, to any model seeking to describe memory in terms of a pattern of associations. To say more than this, however, we need to start distinguishing among the various types of associative model and, in particular, we need to distinguish the most recent versions of associative theory from earlier versions. Let's start with the older perspective; we will consider the more recent innovations later on.

The proposal is that nodes represent single concepts, and nothing more complicated than that. This is consistent with the examples we have used so far, in which nodes have stood for concepts such as *chair* or *doctor*. This still leaves many questions: *How* does a node represent a concept? Does the DOG node contain a brief definition of the concept "dog"? A small picture of a dog? Perhaps the node contains a list of the *perceptual* features that characterize dogs, so that you could use this list to help you in recognizing a dog the next time you encounter one. It turns out that none of these proposals is satisfactory, and we will need most of Chapter 8 to work through the problem of *how* concepts are represented in the mind.

In the meantime, though, we can use the network notion to help us with a related problem, namely, how we might represent more complex ideas, such as "George Washington was the first president," or "My favorite movie is *Casablanca*." For that matter, how do we represent an idea as complicated as "My understanding of Darwin's theory of evolution," or a memory as complicated as "How I spent last summer"?

These complex ideas are represented, oddly enough, with more network. As a first approximation, an associative link may exist between "George Washington" and "first president," and a set of links may tie together "movie" and "favorite" and "*Casablanca*." But this is too simple. How, for example, would one represent the contrast between "Sam has a dog," and "Sam is a dog"? If all we have is an association between SAM and DOG, we won't be able to tell these two ideas apart. Early theorizing sought to deal with this problem by introducing different *types* of associative links, with some links representing equivalence (or partial equivalence) relations and other links representing possessive relations. These links were termed "**isa**" **links**, as in "Sam isa dog," and "**hasa**" **links**, as in "A bird hasa head," or "Sam hasa dog" (Norman, Rumelhart & Group, 1975).

Propositional Networks and ACT

There are clear limits, however, on what we can accomplish with these labeled associations. The problem is that we are able to remember, and to think about, a wide range of relationships, not just equivalence and possession. We can, for example, consider the relationship "is the opposite of," or the relationship "is analogous to," and a thousand others as well. If each type of relationship is represented by a specific type of associative link, then we risk losing the simplicity of the network idea and thereby render the whole proposal less attractive.

Researchers have sought other mechanisms through which network models might represent complex ideas. Their proposals share certain assumptions but differ in many ways, so once again we cannot talk about network models in general; we are forced instead to consider a specific model. Let's therefore look at a model developed by John Anderson (1976, 1980, 1993; Anderson & Bower, 1973), bearing in mind as we do that this is simply one way a network *might be* implemented; other implementations are possible.

Central to Anderson's conception is the idea of *propositions*; these are defined as the smallest unit of knowledge that can be either true or false. For example, "Children love candy" is a proposition but "Children" is not; "Susan likes blue cars" is a proposition but "blue cars" is not. Propositions are easily represented as sentences, but this is merely a convenience. In fact, the same proposition can be represented in a variety of different sentences: "Children love candy," "Candy is loved by children," and "Kinder lieben bonbons" all express the same proposition. For that matter, this same proposition can also be represented in various non-linguistic forms, including a structure of nodes and linkages, and that is exactly what Anderson's model does.

Anderson's theory is embodied in a computer program known as ACT (and, in later versions, as ACT-R—see Anderson, 1993). Within ACT, propositions are represented as shown in Figure 7.9. The ellipse identifies the proposition itself; associations connect the ellipse to the ideas that are the proposition's constituents. The associations are labeled, but only in general terms. That is, the associations are identified in terms of their syntactic role within the proposition. This allows us to distinguish the proposition "Dogs chase cats" from the proposition "Cats chase dogs."

This simple network can be expanded to represent more complex bits of knowledge (although see Rumelhart & McClelland, 1986b; Smith, Adams & Schorr, 1978; Wexler, 1978). Figure 7.10 shows the proposition, "Dogs chew bones" in the context of other propositions about dogs; the overall structure represents (part of) our knowledge about what a dog is and how it behaves. Figure 7.8 (p. 000) shows a portion of the network representing our knowledge about apples.

As a different example, Figure 7.11 shows how propositions can be interconnected to represent more complex relationships. This figure depicts the propositional representation of the sentence, "Children who are slow eat bread that is cold." Sentences like these have been used to test one aspect of the propositional network. Weisberg (1969) had subjects memorize sentences like this one. Later, subjects were given a single word from the sentence and

Figure 7.9

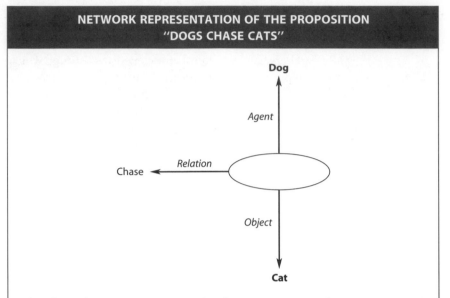

NETWORK REPRESENTATION OF THE PROPOSITION "DOGS CHASE CATS"

The ellipse denotes a proposition; the ellipse is, in essence, the "meeting point" for the various elements of the proposition. Three nodes are involved in this proposition: "dog," "cat," and the action, "chase." Arrows indicate associations among the nodes; labels on the arrows specify the nature of the association. [After Anderson, 1980.]

asked to respond with the first word from the sentence that came to mind. Subjects' responses were in line with the propositional structure of the sentence (as shown in the figure). That is, if cued with the word "slow," subjects were more likely to respond with words close to "slow" in the propositional representation, rather than with words close to "slow" in the original sentence ("eat," "bread"). These data indicate that subjects' memory representation for this sentence does correspond to the propositional representation.

How does ACT represent more specific memories? Our examples so far have centered on *semantic* or *generic* knowledge rather than *episodic* knowledge. Likewise, we have provided no means for ACT to distinguish between knowledge about, say, dogs in general (as in Figure 7.10) and knowledge about a specific dog, say, Leo's dog, Merlin.

To represent specific episodes, or a specific being, ACT makes a distinction between **type** nodes and **token** nodes. "Type" refers to a general category, and type nodes are embedded in propositions true for the entire category. A "token" is a specific instance of a category, and token nodes are therefore

Figure 7.10

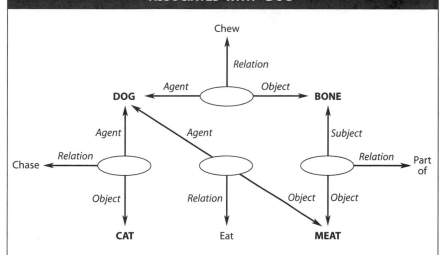

NETWORK REPRESENTATION OF SOME OF THE CONCEPTS ASSOCIATED WITH "DOG"

One's understanding of dogs—what dogs are, what they are likely to do—is represented by an interconnected network of propositions, with each proposition indicated by an ellipse. Thus, one's understanding involves the propositions "Dogs chase cats," "Dogs eat meat," and "Dogs chew bones," and so on. A complete representation of knowledge about dogs would of course include a far greater number of propositions. [After Anderson, 1980.]

Figure 7.11

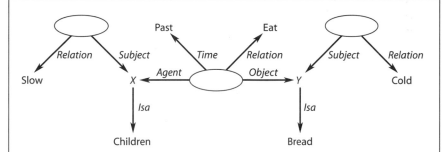

PROPOSITIONAL NETWORK REPRESENTATION OF "CHILDREN WHO ARE SLOW EAT BREAD THAT IS COLD"

Ideas that are closely linked in this representation turn out to be closely linked in subjects' memories, even if these ideas were not positioned closely together in the original sentence. [After Anderson, 1985.]

found in propositions concerned with specific events and individuals. Note that type and token nodes are typically connected to each other, as shown in Figure 7.12.

In addition, the ACT model distinguishes between timeless truths, like "Jacob feeds the pigeons" and more specific statements, like "Last spring, Jacob fed the pigeons in Trafalgar Square." ACT does this by incorporating time and location nodes as part of propositions, and in this fashion can mark when and where the proposition was true. This allows ACT to represent facts about specific episodes (Figure 7.13).

The ACT model shares many claims with other network models: Nodes are connected by associative links. Some of these links are stronger than others, with the strength of the link depending on how frequently and recently the link has been used. Once a node is activated, the process of spreading activation causes the nearby nodes to become activated as well. ACT is distinctive, however, in its attempt to represent knowledge in terms of propositions, and the promise of this approach has attracted the support of many researchers in this area.

Figure 7.12

NETWORKS CONTAIN INFORMATION ABOUT CATEGORIES AND ABOUT INDIVIDUALS

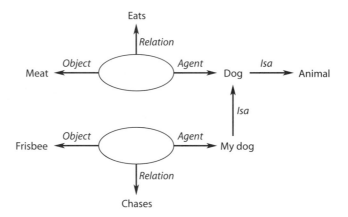

This fragment of a network contains a "type node," representing dogs in general, and a "token node," representing a specific dog ("my dog"). The type node is linked to propositions true for all dogs; the token node is linked to propositions true only for "my dog." That is, all dogs eat meat. Not all dogs chase Frisbees, although "my dog" does. The type node and token node are linked to each other, indicating that "my dog" is a member of the category "dogs."

[handwritten margin note: type node = all dogs eat; token node = my dog chases frisbees]

Figure 7.13

REPRESENTING EPISODES WITHIN A PROPOSITIONAL NETWORK

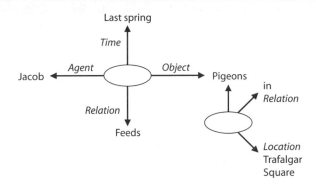

In order to represent episodes, the propositional network includes time and location nodes. This fragment of a network represents two propositions—the proposition that Jacob last spring fed pigeons, and the proposition that the pigeons are in Trafalgar Square. Note that no time node is associated with the proposition about pigeons being in Trafalgar Square. Therefore, what is represented is that the feeding of the pigeons took place last spring, but the pigeons are generally in the square.

Evaluating Network Models

Associative theories of memory have generated much excitement and much research and strike many as our best hypothesis about how knowledge is represented in the mind. These models have attempted to characterize both our generic knowledge and also our knowledge about specific episodes.

At the same time, these models have been controversial. In this section, we will review some of the concerns that have arisen about network models in an attempt to ask whether these models do represent the optimal way to theorize about memory.

How to Test Network Models?

The evidence we have considered confirms many of the network claims. Mechanisms such as spreading activation and subthreshold priming do seem to play a role in memory search. However, the data presented so far do not speak to a larger and more interesting issue: The network claim is not merely that these mechanisms are involved in memory search. The claim instead is that these mechanisms, by themselves, can provide our entire account of memory retrieval, that these mechanisms are enough "to get the job done."

Can the network deliver on this promise? Bear in mind just how vast our memories are. This leads one to ask: Will spreading activation by itself support a search through a huge number of nodes, each with a very high degree of fan? Or will we need to add other mechanisms to support and perhaps guide the search?

Perhaps the best way to address these questions might be simply to give networks a serious try. If one has a theory of memory and memory organization, a powerful test of the theory would be to build a "working model," based on the theoretical claims, and to examine how well the model performed as an information storage and retrieval device. In fact, many psychologists are seeking to construct these models, usually implemented as a computer system that functions according to the rules and procedures specified by the theory. (We mentioned earlier, for example, that Anderson's ACT model is embodied in such a system.) This allows us to see how well the computer does in "learning," that is, in storing new information and then in retrieving facts, based on some cue or hint. If the computer fails in these tasks, or does less well than humans do, we know that something is missing (or wrong) in the theory. What if the computer succeeds? This would indicate that the processes and strategies programmed into the computer are sufficient to accomplish the tasks of learning and remembering. This would not by itself show that humans use the same processes and strategies. It would, however, be a strong argument that the theory must be taken seriously as an account of human performance.

It would take us rather far afield to evaluate these modeling efforts in any detail. To make a long story short, though, it is not currently possible to point to a working model of an associative network as a successful simulation of human memory prowess. All of this is "work in progress." The available models do work reasonably well, but all have various limitations and bugs and work only on a scale far more modest than "all of knowledge." How should we think about this? The limitations of current models may reflect deep inadequacies in the network approach. But it is also possible that the limitations merely reflect the early state of the models' evolution. With further work and refinements, perhaps these weaknesses will be overcome.

For present purposes, then, the moral is a simple one: Computer implementation of psychological models provides a potentially powerful tool for testing the models. The evidence so far indicates limits on what these models can accomplish, but there is room for disagreement about what these limits are telling us (see Charniak & McDermott, 1987; Johnson-Laird, Herrmann & Chaffin, 1984; Winston, 1984).

In considering why this might be so, our plan is not to look at the models themselves. Instead, we will look at some of the potential "trouble spots" for this modeling effort. We will first present the concerns and then circle back to ask how we might address these concerns.

Retrieval Blocks and Partial Retrievals

One attractive feature of the associative net is that activation spreads out indiscriminately through all of the available connections. We need no means of "directing" the activation or supervising the search. Instead, one simply allows the activation to travel wherever the connections lead.

This approach keeps our theorizing simple, but do things always work in a fashion consistent with this "automatic" view? Try to think of the word that means a type of carving done on whale bone, often depicting whaling ships, or pictures of whales. Try to think of the name of the navigational device used by sailors to determine the positions of stars. Try to think of the name of the Russian sled drawn by three horses. Chances are that, in at least one of these cases, you found yourself in a frustrated state—certain you knew the word but unable to come up with it. The word was, as they say, right on the "tip of your tongue" and, following this lead, psychologists refer to this as the **T.O.T. phenomenon**. Subjects in the T.O.T. state often know correctly that the word is somewhere in their vocabulary, they often correctly remember what letter the word begins with, how many syllables it has, and approximately what it sounds like. Thus a subject might remember, "It's something like Sanskrit" in trying to remember "scrimshaw," or "something like secant" in trying to remember "sextant" (Brown, 1991; Brown & McNeill, 1966; James, 1890; Read & Bruce, 1982; Reason & Lucas, 1984). Similar results have been obtained when subjects try to recall specific names: Who played the nervous man with the knife in the shower scene in Hitchcock's *Psycho*? What was the name of the Greek orator who taught himself to speak clearly by practicing speeches with pebbles in his mouth? With clues like these, subjects are often able to recall the number of syllables in the name and the name's initial letter, but not the name itself (Brennen, Baguley, Bright & Bruce, 1990; Yarmey, 1973). (The orator was Demosthenes, and Anthony Perkins was the nervous man with the knife. The Russian sled is a troika.)

These findings do not easily fit with the network view, at least as it has been described so far. It seems clear that a subject in the T.O.T. state has reached the memory vicinity of the sought-after word. After all, the subject is able to come up with the correct starting letter and the correct number of syllables. In addition, the nodes in this area of memory are presumably receiving a great deal of activation, given the time and effort one spends in trying to find the word. But this activation seems not to spread to the sought-after node or, if it does, the activation of this node is not being recognized or acknowledged. In short, then, you are in the right neighborhood; there is lots of activation on the scene, but the activation does not reach the target. All of this is peculiar if we conceive of spreading activation as a purely mechanical process whose success is guaranteed once one is in the correct memory vicinity. It would seem, therefore, that we are going to need some other mechanism to explain this result—a mechanism that somehow *undermines* memory search. (For a fuller discussion of these "retrieval blocks," see Roediger & Neely, 1982.)

Finding More Distant Connections

A different concern is, in a sense, the mirror image of the points just raised. In the T.O.T. state, we fail to locate a target memory, despite our being in the right memory vicinity with plenty of activation. Here is the inverse case: How do we *succeed* in locating memories when there are no close connections between our starting point and our target?

The crux of the issue here is part psychology, part arithmetic. Consider first the range of jobs we want associative links to do for us—they tie together episodic memories, they tie together generic memories, they tie together aspects of our concepts (e.g., the "possession of feathers" is presumably part of, or closely tied to, our concept of "bird," and the linkage between these is, once again, a memory association). Given all this, it becomes clear that the number of associative links radiating out from any individual concept—that is, the realistic degree of fan—will be very high indeed.

We have already said that only some of the links radiating out from a node will be efficient—namely, those used frequently or recently. But, realistically, what is the number of these likely to be? How many strong associations does one have to "water"? Is 100 a halfway plausible number? We suspect that this is a gross underestimate, but it will serve for the moment. Using this estimate, think about what happens when activation spreads outward from the WATER node. One hundred new nodes each receive some activation (Figure 7.14). If the sought-for information is directly associated with the WATER node, things will now go well: One only has to choose which among these hundred is the node one seeks.

But what if the sought-for node is *not* directly tied to WATER? What if it is tied by means of one intermediate step? We have already said that 100 nodes receive activation directly from WATER; now, activation spreads out from these. If each of these 100 is connected to 100 more nodes, we end up with activation reaching 10,000 nodes. And, of course, if the sought-for node is still one more step removed, we need to let activation spread once again, so that now activation reaches a million.

It would seem, then, that we will create problems if we let the spreading

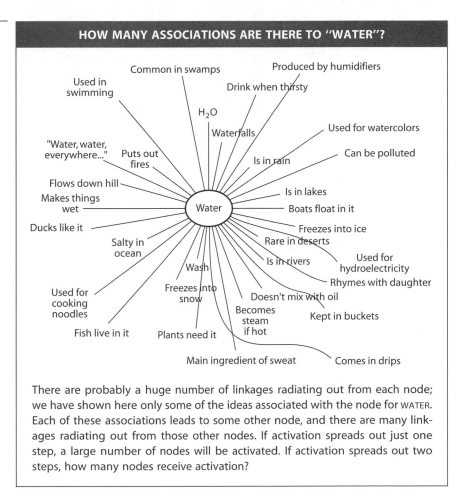

Figure 7.14

HOW MANY ASSOCIATIONS ARE THERE TO "WATER"?

There are probably a huge number of linkages radiating out from each node; we have shown here only some of the ideas associated with the node for WATER. Each of these associations leads to some other node, and there are many linkages radiating out from those other nodes. If activation spreads out just one step, a large number of nodes will be activated. If activation spreads out two steps, how many nodes receive activation?

activation spread too far. Even if the spread is only three or four steps, we will end up with far too many nodes activated, and so we will lose the selective guidance we hoped for in the first place. We can avoid this danger, of course, if we place limits on how far the spreading activation can spread or, alternatively, if we arrange things so that the spreading activation gets weaker and weaker as it moves outward from its source. In either of these cases, we will avoid the risk of activating too many nodes, but we also risk not finding the node we seek.

The same tension can be framed differently, in terms of degree of fan: If each node is connected to every other node, that is, if there is a very high fan, we lose the selective guidance that linkages were supposed to provide. As we remarked earlier, a point in every direction is the same as no point at all. If, on the other hand, we decrease the fan at each node, then it becomes likely that our entry and target nodes will be connected only indirectly. In this case, we are forced to rely on more steps from entry to target, inviting the multiplication of nodes: Each time we let the activation go another step, we multiply again the number of nodes reached. Too high a degree of fan is problematic and so is too low a degree of fan. Whether there is a middle value that escapes these concerns simply remains to be seen.

The Homunculus

This worry, about the multiplication of nodes, is created by the fact that activation spreads within the network in a mechanical and automatic fashion, flowing wherever the connections lead. By the same token, our puzzlement over the T.O.T. effect arose because, in this case, the activation seems *not* to be spreading as mechanically and as automatically as it should. Perhaps we should be seeking a model in which things are a little *less* mechanical. That might allow us to avoid a sequence in which too many nodes become activated; it might also help us in explaining what goes wrong in the T.O.T. state.

To make this concrete, imagine that you are trying to remember the chemical formula for water. In this situation, there is no point in thinking about all the memory associates for water, since most of these would be irrelevant to your goal. You would prefer *not* to be reminded of Coleridge's line, "Water, water, everywhere," or all the words that rhyme with water, or your vacation last summer on the lake. Thus, it would be handy if you could somehow "shut down" these various associations and let activation spread only in the productive directions, or at least in those directions that have some reasonable likelihood of being productive. In this way, you would activate nodes much more selectively, much more *intelligently*, and so not risk activating a vast number of nodes.

A related point has been suggested by Tulving (1983). Tulving notes that we live our lives in a world filled with retrieval cues, stimuli that, in the past, have been strongly associated with one event or another. Using these stimuli as our cues, we are capable of remembering a great deal if we try. Yet, despite the presence of these cues, most of us spend relatively little time in spontaneous reminiscing. As Tulving puts it (p. 46), "if you meet a friend unexpectedly, your likely reaction to the encounter will consist of wonderment why the friend . . . should be in that particular place at that particular time. The sight of the friend is less likely to immediately trigger the memory of any particular previous occasion where you met him or her."

Tulving's observation, then, suggests that we are usually *not* victims of a reflex-like, automatic process of memory retrieval. Yet some sort of reflexive process is what one might expect if presentation of a cue (and so activation of the corresponding node) led inevitably to activation of its near associates. Tulving proposes instead that our episodic memories become available only if we are in a special state, which he dubs "retrieval mode." Whatever one makes of this proposal, the fact remains that, once again, it seems that memory retrieval is controlled and directed rather than passive and automatic. (For related discussion, see Henik, Friedrich, Tzelgov & Tramer, 1994.)

But if the flow of activation is guided through the net, who guides it? If someone or something "chooses" which nodes to pursue, then who is it? In explaining the overall efficiency of memory search, it is tempting to say that some efficient process or mechanism must guide this search. More broadly, in explaining the intelligence of behavior, it is tempting to say that there must be some processes in the mind that are themselves intelligent, strategic, and foresightful. But this simply postpones an explanation. It is like saying that we act intelligently because we are guided by an intelligent little "man in the head." This explains nothing, because the little man or **homunculus** (as he is classically called) would itself need to be explained. (We first met this term in Chapter 1, also in the context of discussing memory search.)

The problem with "homunculus" explanations, then, is that they are not really explanations. Instead, they are "I.O.U.s," a promise of an explanation to come. But this is not a disaster if one is prepared to provide an explanation of how the homunculus functions (cf. Rozin, 1976).

Where, then, does this leave us? Spread of activation, as we have seen, allows us to explain a great deal and, of course, this process requires no appeal to mysterious Directors or unexplained Guides; it involves no I.O.U.s. At the same time, however, several considerations do point toward the idea that the spread of activation, in some circumstances, is not mechanical, not automatic. In short, it looks like we may need a homunculus of some sort. The key, though, is not to accept this assertion as our final account. If there is a Director, we need to explain how it works.

Theories about the "memory executive," about the "Search Director," have been proposed, but they have typically been proposed within the context of specific (and often highly technical) computer models. Examination of these theories would therefore carry us rather far from our main agenda. Nonetheless, let us at least be clear about where the evidence has brought us so far: Associations and spreading activation do play a role in memory. We have also seen a plausible proposal that knowledge can be represented in terms of propositions and that propositions can then be represented in terms of a network. All of this invited us to ask if these terms might be all we need to account for the full range of memory successes and memory failures. At present, our best way to tackle this question is via computer modeling, but so far these models are limited in what they can do.

It may turn out that these limits reflect the need for a rather different approach—an approach involving processes more complex than mere spreading activation. In particular, we may need to add some mechanism capable of "directing" the flow of activation, so that it flows only in "promising" directions, directions likely to lead to the target.

Alternatively, maybe we *don't* need this homunculus. Maybe the limits of extant models can be escaped in another way. Perhaps we can preserve the associative base, with no need for complicated, sophisticated Directors or Guides. A number of researchers are currently pursuing this claim, and it is to their work that we now turn.

The Newest Chapter: Connectionism

In the last dozen years or so, an important descendant of the network idea has appeared on the intellectual scene, and has generated enormous excitement in psychology as well as in computer science and philosophy. This development seeks to address (among other things) exactly the worries we have just been considering. Rather than adding a more intelligent component to the network (i.e., a homunculus), this new approach goes in the opposite direction and tries to show just how much we can accomplish with network and more network.

Distributed Processing, Distributed Representations

Connectionism = parallel distributed processing (PDP)

A small number of important innovations has spurred this new wave of theorizing, a wave referred to as Connectionism, or parallel distributed processing (PDP). (For detailed descriptions of PDP proposals, see Ackley, Hinton & Sejnowski, 1985; Hinton & Anderson, 1981; McClelland & Rumelhart, 1986; Rumelhart & McClelland, 1986b; for somewhat broader perspectives, and excellent introductions to this domain, see Churchland, 1989; Flanagan, 1991.)

In the networks we have considered so far, what it means to "think about" or "remember" a particular idea is to activate the node for that idea. This assumes a system of **local representations**, with one idea per node, or one content per location. (We first met this terminology, by the way, in Chapter 2.) Within a PDP network, however, there are no local representations. There is no BIRTHDAY node, no GRANDMOTHER node, no node at all to which we can attach a single label.

In a PDP system, contents are represented by widespread patterns of activation. The suggestion, roughly, is that thoughts about birthdays would correspond to the simultaneous activation of node #1,432 and node #27,456 and node #24,478 and a thousand others that we would have to specify. This combination would uniquely correspond to (and thus represent) ideas about birthdays. These same nodes, in different combinations, will also be part of the patterns representing other contents. In other words, the activation of node #1,432 has no intrinsic meaning by itself; we can only learn what is being represented by looking at many other nodes simultaneously to find out what *pattern* of activation currently exists across the entire network.

In Chapter 2, we referred to representations of this sort as **distributed representations**, rather than a local representation, and we now have the "DP" in PDP: The PDP networks employ distributed processing to represent, and to act on, mental contents. This is in some ways a radical idea, and so it is worth spending a moment to make it clear.

Think about a complicated spy novel, in which the Master Spy has a plan involving many operatives. Each operative receives her instructions, and this puts the plan into motion, piece by piece. Let's emphasize that each operative knows only about her small part of the operation; each has no idea about how her actions will fit into the overall scheme. (This is desirable from the perspective of the Master Spy, since it makes detection of the plan difficult.) The plan itself is known only to the Master Spy.

Now imagine that the Master Spy is killed in an accident, immediately after giving the last operative her instructions. Has the plan ceased to exist? Up until the Master Spy's death, there had been a "local representation" of the plan in the mind of the Master Spy. After the Master Spy's death, however, there is no one place where the plan exists and is represented in a unitary form. Nonetheless, the plan does continue to exist in a larger sense—in the collective actions of the full set of operatives. Even without the Master Spy, the plan is still in motion and is there to be perceived if only we could get a broad enough view—if only we could take a large step back and view the actions of all the operatives and if we could see how these actions are inter-related. The plan still exists, then, in a "distributed" mode and would be detected if we viewed the actions at the aggregate level, not at the level of the parts.

Notice, though, that it is crucial that all of the operatives go about following their instructions simultaneously, since it is only in their collective actions that the plan takes form. All of the operatives must work in parallel, and we now meet the final part of the PDP label. What is critical for PDP theorizing is *parallel* distributed processing.

Notice also that if the Master Spy's plan is well-devised then it has to be *flexible*. Steps late in the plan may depend on how earlier steps have unfolded; at various points, adjustments may be needed because of new information coming in. If the plan is truly distributed, however, these adjustments can't require the intervention of some centralized authority. Instead, the adjustments will all be made at the local level by the individual operatives. Thus the adjustments, too, must be distributed. Recall, though, that each operative has no sense of how her actions fit into the overall scheme; indeed she doesn't even know there *is* an overall scheme. Hence, there is no way for an operative to make decisions about how well this or that action fits into the full pattern. If the operatives are making adjustments, these must be based entirely on each operative's understanding of just her part of the operation and based just on information locally available to her. Nonetheless, if we set this up right, these local adjustments, each based on local information, will as a package add up to a plan that is, overall, coherent, flexible, and sensibly responsive to large-scale changes.

It would, without question, require a clever novelist indeed to invent such a scheme; in real life, it would take an extraordinary Master Spy to set up this kind of operation. Of course, designing such an operation would be easier if we envisioned someone continuing to supervise the plan, so that this authority could coordinate the operations, making certain that the actions of one spy complement the actions of the others. But that would defeat the purpose, if we are after a *distributed* process. That is why, in our metaphor, we "killed off" the Master Spy as soon as the plan was set up. That way, we could be sure of no centralized, localized, authority.

In fact, one could argue that our metaphor is limited in its value, because it is not distributed enough. The operatives are themselves individuals with knowledge and intelligence. Even if each is ignorant about the overall plan, each is able to contemplate ideas and meanings in her own actions and her own decision making. Compared to the nodes within a PDP network, this is far too much processing going on at the local level.

To make our metaphor more accurate, we would need to replace our crew of spies with something less sophisticated, less intelligent. In effect, the Master Spy would need to recruit a vast army of morons. This would require that the tasks assigned to each operative be extremely simple, so that the tasks would be within the morons' very limited competence. But that is precisely the proposal of PDP. With enough morons connected together in the right ways, and with each doing the appropriate, very simple task, the aggregate activity of the network will reproduce the full intelligence of which the mind is capable.

How plausible is this? Is it possible that the complexity of our mental lives depends entirely on such simple components? It is important to bear in mind here how much depends on one's *point of view*. Think back to Chapter 2, where we discussed how a feature-net could act as if it knew the rules of

English spelling and could act as if it were making "inferences" to fill in missing information. This kind of description, in terms of "knowing rules" and "making inferences," describes what the feature-net is doing *on aggregate*. On a more local level, though, the detectors within the net don't make inferences, and they don't know anything. The detectors simply have a certain firing threshold and fire whenever they receive the appropriate inputs. Thus, if one takes a close look at mechanism, one finds interactions and processes that are extremely simple, and entirely driven by local concerns. Things look much more sophisticated and intelligent, however, if we consider what an organism "equipped" with this mechanism will accomplish. Clearly, one's point of view is crucial: whether one is looking at the mechanism, which is quite simple, or at what the mechanism accomplishes, which is complex. Indeed, this is a consistent message of connectionism: Behaviors that look complicated from the outside can be produced by the combined actions of many very simple mechanisms.

In addition, consider the brain. Individual neurons within the brain are structurally and biochemically complicated, but their function is not: Inputs reach the neuron; activation accumulates; when the activation gets to a high enough level, the neuron fires. A simple plan; in fact, idiotically simple. Yet many millions of these "idiots," when connected together in the right ways, do produce the full intelligence of which the mind is capable. Advocates of the PDP approach have in fact argued that PDP networks work in a fashion closely akin to the brain's functioning and, because of this analogy, connectionist nets are often referred to as neural nets. In the eyes of many scholars, this analogy between PDP nets and the brain is a further point in favor of taking this approach seriously (see many of the contributions to McClelland & Rumelhart, 1986; Rumelhart & McClelland, 1986b; but also see Crick, 1989; Grossberg, 1988).

Who Runs the Show?

In our metaphoric presentation of the PDP idea, a Master Spy served the important function of setting up the network in the first place, by giving each of the operatives her specific instructions. Likewise, one might imagine a comparable Master Spy from the enemy country, who is then in a position to *perceive* the entire plan or, more likely, to perceive the consequences of the entire plan (and then to make responses to the plan). Who plays these parts in actual PDP networks? Who sets up the pattern at the start? And then who is it, in the end, that perceives the aggregate pattern?

The problem of "reading" the network is formidable. After all, with a distributed representation, any memory content is represented only via the simultaneous activation of a large number of nodes. Therefore, to "read" the net, one needs to do far more than locate a single node. Instead, one must survey the entire network to discern the overall pattern.

But this frames things in the wrong way. The idea of "reading" the net, or "surveying" the net's activities, implies that the distributed representation is being examined by some centralized authority, so that the pattern can then be summarized in some way. That is, a local representation will be generated as the product of reading the broad distributed pattern. But is this sensible? What exactly do we gain by this translation from a distributed representation into a local one?

Think back to our discussion of how one enters a network. The idea was that some nodes are connected directly to perceptual inputs. When the relevant stimulus is presented, this leads directly to activation of these nodes, presumably via steps similar to those described in Chapter 2. Hence, there is no question of *first* understanding or identifying a stimulus, and then finding its node within the network. That is, we do not use the process depicted in the top of Figure 7.15. Instead, the processes of identification and look-up are one and the same: The process of understanding a word is the process of looking it up, as shown in the bottom of the figure.

The answer to reading a PDP network is analogous. The idea we are rejecting is shown in the top of Figure 7.16. In this conception, the net is first read, yielding some local representation summarizing the net's activity, and then this local representation is used as the basis for action. In place of this, why not connect the network directly to "output" nodes, just as we connected it, at the other end, to "input" nodes? Output nodes receive their signals from the network via the same spreading activation as any other nodes. When the right configuration of activations is on the scene, this will bring the output nodes to some threshold level of activation, and this will in turn trigger a response.

As an example, we might ask subjects, "What does one call the offspring of a dog?" In the ways we have described, this input will trigger the appropriate feature detectors, which activate other nodes leading eventually to the activation of the many nodes that comprise the distributed representation of "dog" and those that comprise the distributed representation of "offspring." Activation will spread from these nodes to many other nodes, namely those that represent the various ideas associated with "dog" and "offspring." One set of nodes, though, will receive activation from both of these sources: That is, the nodes that comprise the distributed representation of "puppy" will receive activation both from the dog nodes and from the offspring nodes. As a result, the many nodes representing puppy will themselves become strongly activated. Each of these nodes will in turn send activation to output nodes.

Figure 7.15

TWO VIEWS OF ENTRY INTO THE MEMORY NETWORK

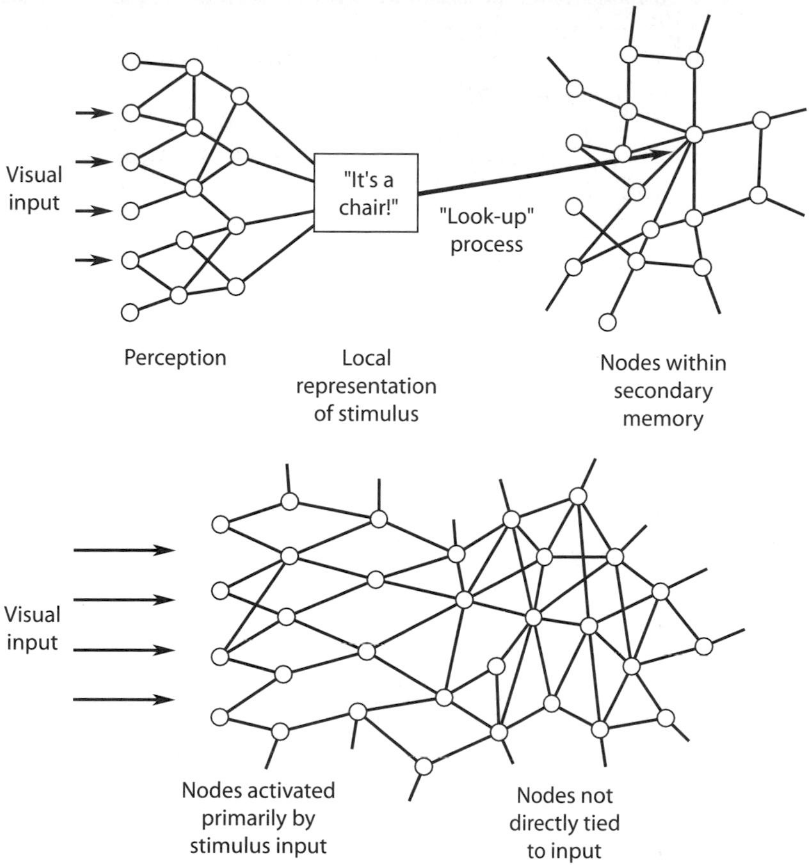

Visual input →

"It's a chair!"

"Look-up" process

Perception

Local representation of stimulus

Nodes within secondary memory

Visual input →

Nodes activated primarily by stimulus input

Nodes not directly tied to input

In the top panel, the processes involved in perception lead to a local representation of the stimulus. That representation identifies what the stimulus is, specifies its size, shape, and so on. A further process would be needed to find the memory representation corresponding to this stimulus. Many network theorists, however, would reject this conception in favor of that shown in the bottom panel. In this view, the memory network is directly connected to the processes of perception (as indicated in Figure 7.8, p. 278). There is no local representation of the input, and no separate process of "look-up." Instead, stimulus identification and "network look-up" are simply different names for the same process.

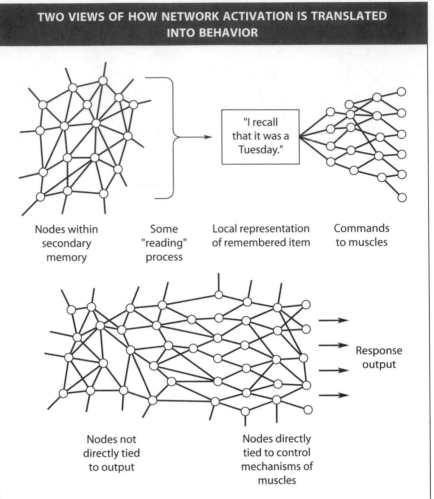

Figure 7.16

TWO VIEWS OF HOW NETWORK ACTIVATION IS TRANSLATED INTO BEHAVIOR

"I recall that it was a Tuesday."

Nodes within secondary memory

Some "reading" process

Local representation of remembered item

Commands to muscles

Response output

Nodes not directly tied to output

Nodes directly tied to control mechanisms of muscles

In the top panel, the broad pattern of activation within the network is "read," leading to a summary of the network's status (that is, a local representation). This is then translated into commands to the muscles, causing the actual response. Most network theorists, however, prefer the conception in the bottom panel. No summary of the network is "read" from the pattern of activations. Instead, the nodes within the network are directly tied to control mechanisms for the muscles. When sufficient activation accumulates in the appropriate pattern, a response is produced.

Once enough activation reaches the output nodes, they will send activation to the control system for the muscles, causing the subject to utter a response.

Thus, connectionism may be the ultimate "grass-roots" enterprise. In our "puppy" example, there is a distributed recognition of the input, leading to a distributed selection of an answer, leading to a distributed production of the actual response. Nowhere in this process does a light-bulb come on indicating "puppy." Nowhere is there a local summary of the input, used as the basis for "looking" here or there in the system. The distributed pattern is never summarized in some central place, and so no Master Spy is needed in reading the network pattern. The system is start-to-finish concerned with distributed representations; there is no reader, no executive, no supervisor.

Learning as the Setting of "Connection Weights"

Obviously, all of this distributed processing depends on having the appropriate connections in place, so that activation will spread to the desired target rather than in some other direction. But how are the connections set up in the first place? How, on a connectionist account, does *learning* take place?

Let us first be clear about what it means, in network terms, to "know something." In any associative network, connectionist or otherwise, knowledge is literally contained within the connections themselves. We already took a step in this direction when we discussed the "unpacking" of the nodes—that what it means to know "George Washington was a President" is to have a connection between a node for GEORGE WASHINGTON and a node for PRESIDENT.

This is, of course, phrased in terms of *local* representations, with individual nodes having specific assigned referents. The basic idea, however, is the same in a distributed system. What it means to know this fact about Washington is to have a pattern of connections between the many nodes that together represent "Washington," and the many nodes that together represent "President." Once these connections are in place, activation of either of these patterns will lead to the activation of the other.

Notice, then, that knowledge refers to a *potential* rather than to a *state*. If you know that Washington was a President, then the connections are in place so that *if* the "Washington" pattern of activations happens to occur, this will lead to the "President" pattern of activations. And, of course, this state of "readiness" will remain even if you happen not to be thinking about Washington right now. Thus "thinking about" something, in network terms, corresponds to which nodes are active right now, with no comment about where that activation will spread next. "Knowing" something, in contrast, corresponds to how the activation will flow if there is activation on the scene.

This conception of "knowing" has obvious implications for the nature of

PDP learning is adjusting connection weights so that activation will flow the right way.

"learning." Bear in mind that connections within the network can be strong or weak; PDP shares this idea with other versions of network theorizing and refers to the strength of each connection as its **connection weight**. Learning, therefore, is simply a process of adjusting connection weights in order that activation will "flow" in the right way, so that activating the "Washington" pattern will lead to the "President" pattern and not to the "Queen of England" pattern. More generally, learning involves an adjustment in connection weights so that a specific input will, via the flow of activation, eventually lead to the appropriate output.

Consistent with other aspects of PDP theorizing, the adjustment of connection weights is not done via some executive's intervention. Instead, the changes at each node are governed entirely by what is happening in the node's immediate vicinity. In other words, learning, like all other events in this scheme, is a distributed process. Overall, therefore, any instance of learning literally involves hundred of thousands of microscopic changes, taking place all over the network, with no attempt at, indeed, with no mechanism for, overall coordination.

This is, to be sure, an amazing proposal. In order to achieve any distributed learning, the various bits of local learning must be coordinated so that coherent action can emerge from the aggregate activity of the network. At the same time, though, there is no explicit mechanism in place to achieve this coordination. How is this possible? Here we arrive at one of the most important intellectual innovations driving connectionism forward. Connectionists have offered a number of powerful computing schemes, "learning algorithms," that seek to accomplish learning within the PDP set-up. The learning typically requires a large number of learning trials and some sort of feedback about the correctness or appropriateness of the response. But given this, connectionists have offered schemes, with names like the "delta rule" and "back propagation," that accomplish learning on the local level, without an executive, and that seem to make the entire system grow gradually and impressively smarter.

These learning algorithms cause connection weights to increase or decrease whenever specific, locally described configurations are present. As a simple example, we might set things up so that the connection weight between two nodes will increase whenever the two nodes are both activated or both not activated; the connection weight will decrease when either is activated but the other is not. With this rule in place, the connection weight will be determined by the correlation between the activation levels of the two nodes. If the correlation is strong, that is, if Node A tends to be activated whenever Node B is activated, the connection weight will often be incremented and will end up fairly strong. If the correlation is weak, that is, if A is often activated without B, or B without A, the connection weight will often be decremented and will end up weak.

As a different example, we can "teach" the network new information by allowing it to produce an output and then comparing this output to the desired output. (This is analogous to saying, "No, the answer isn't X; it is Y.") If the network has, in fact, produced the desired response, then there is no difference between the output produced and that desired; hence, there is no error. If the network has gone wildly astray, there will be a large difference between the output produced and that desired. It is then possible to feed this information about error back into the network. Locally, each node will receive an **error signal**, a flow of activation *proportional* to the *magnitude* of error (i.e., proportional to the difference between output produced and output desired). Each node can then compare the error signal to its own pattern of connection weights. If there is a weak error signal (i.e., if little or no error was made), then there is no reason to make adjustments. If there is a strong error signal, then a large adjustment in connection weights will be made. It is as if each node were saying, "I made an error, so my inputs must have led me astray. Therefore, let me ask *which* inputs favored this (incorrect) response and then adjust things, so that I will be less influenced by these inputs in the future." If this process is repeated at all the other nodes and repeated over many trials, eventually the connections will be adjusted so as to minimize error, which is just what we want.

We have left the details of connectionism's learning algorithms to the side, both because they are mathematically complex and also because, when we talk about the state-of-the-art, anything we say will be quickly out of date. We emphasize, though, that in all of these algorithms, the adjustment of connection weights depends entirely on local conditions. Moreover, individual nodes are extremely simple in their processing capacities. In making use of an error signal, for example, a node does nothing more than compare one activation level to another level and make specific adjustments on this basis. The interesting question, therefore, lies in whether the accumulation of such simple mechanisms can be used as the basis for much more complex, much more sophisticated cognition. This question is at the heart of current controversy.

Possible Limits on PDP Networks

Psychologists are clearly divided in their assessments of PDP models—some view these models as an important step forward; others argue that the models are woefully inadequate and that we should be pursuing other approaches. (For advocates of the PDP approach, see many of the contributions to Rumelhart & McClelland, 1986b; for more critical views, see Fodor & Pylyshyn, 1988; Holyoak, 1987; Lachter & Bever, 1988; Pinker & Prince, 1988.)

What arguments might incline us for or against the PDP approach? First, as we have already noted, many argue that connectionist models make biological sense—these models fit well, they claim, with what we know about the nervous system. Second, there seems little doubt that connectionist models do offer a powerful means of information storage. Third, we need to take these models seriously simply because of what they can accomplish. Connectionist models have so far learned to recognize patterns, and can generalize what they have learned in appropriate ways. Connectionist models can, it is claimed, learn the rules of English grammar, can learn how to read, and can even learn how to play strategic games such as backgammon. (Many of these accomplishments are summarized in Rumelhart & McClelland, 1986b.) All of this has led to considerable enthusiasm for connectionist approaches.

Others, however, have expressed considerable skepticism about these claims. There is, first of all, room for debate about the biological realism of connectionist models. Some aspects of these models (distributed processing, parallel activities) surely do make biological sense, but other aspects may not. (For example, it is not clear how some of the learning algorithms, particularly those involving "back propagation" of error signals, are to be translated into neural terms.) Second, some have argued that connectionist models can learn only when the programmers "stack the deck" in the right way. Since the models often learn by inspecting examples, it is possible to "help" the models enormously by providing just the right examples, in just the right sequence. Perhaps, then, connectionist models can't learn as we learn or, more precisely, perhaps they can learn what we learn only if we give them a great deal of help. (For discussion of the "psychological realism" of connectionist learning, see McCloskey & Cohen, 1989; Pinker & Prince, 1988.) Third, the existing PDP models are fairly specific in their focus, modeling one or another well-defined task. But humans are capable of a huge variety of tasks, raising questions about how (or whether) PDP models might rise from the miniature to the grand scale.

The state-of-the-art, therefore, resembles what we saw with networks in general. There have been, to be sure, some conspicuous successes for connectionist theory, with seemingly complex mental activities successfully modeled. However, the range of these successes is still small, and important questions have been raised about whether this learning matches the learning that humans do.

As a result of all this, controversy remains, and many in the field have adopted a wait-and-see attitude about what PDP modeling will eventually accomplish. (For discussion, see Gluck & Rumelhart, 1990; Ramsey, Stich & Rumelhart, 1991.) Others are ready to predict that PDP will meet only with limited success—providing an excellent account of some phenomena but unable to explain other phenomena (see, for example, Fodor & Pylyshyn, 1988.) Let's emphasize, though, that these reservations do not make the PDP program of research less interesting. The reservations simply state that PDP will not be the answer to all of psychology's mysteries.

We leave this chapter with some very obvious loose ends. There is surely widespread agreement that memory does draw on associative processes and spreading activation. There is likewise no doubt that network theorizing can encompass an enormous range of memory data. But there is considerable uncertainly about whether network theorizing, either in a traditional version or in PDP, can explain all of mental functioning. This is still "work-in-progress" on an immensely complex and subtle topic—merely the task of describing All of Knowledge. Moreover, we can take considerable comfort from the fact that, unsolved mysteries or no, we have at least a part of the puzzle under control. Our theorizing is allowing us to handle a lot of data and is leading us to new discoveries. This is, on anybody's account, a positive and promising sign.

8

Concepts and Generic Knowledge

In Chapter 6, we made a distinction between *episodic* memories and *generic* memories. Episodic memories record specific events—the party you went to last weekend, or the lecture you heard last Tuesday, or the adventure you had last summer. In each case, the memory records an *episode* tied to a particular time and place.

Generic memories, in contrast, are not tied to any particular episode; instead, these memories record *facts* and *beliefs*. Over the last few chapters, we have appealed to generic memory as the source of our knowledge about what various words mean, or about what things break more or less easily, or about what is kept in piggy banks. These memories often contain knowledge of a commonplace sort, knowledge about low-level, unsophisticated facts: What is a dog? What is "jumping"? What appliances does one usually find in a kitchen? These cases seem neither glamorous nor complicated. Nonetheless, the *importance* of this knowledge within our mental lives is extraordinary. We saw in Chapters 4 and 6 that generic knowledge plays a huge role in our day-to-day commerce with the world. Indeed, we argued in Chapter 6 that, without our reliance on generic knowledge, our ordinary functioning would be much less efficient, much more difficult. Thus, while this knowledge seems commonplace, it is an ingredient without which cognition cannot proceed.

In this chapter, we will examine generic knowledge. What is this knowledge? How is it represented in the mind? Our initial focus will be on cases that seem relatively simple—the knowledge each of us has about concepts like "dog" or "chair" or "tree." As we will soon see, however, describing these concepts is more difficult than one might initially guess. In addition, it is clear that each of us understands a great *diversity* of concepts—not just concepts of things ("cat," "movie star," "sitting Supreme Court Justice"), but also concepts concerned with actions ("walking," "wanting," "waltzing"), events ("birthday party," "trips to the zoo," "taking an examination"), complex systems ("free-market capitalism," "automobile industry") and so on. It is not obvious at the outset whether one theory, or one form of representation, will serve for this broad range of concepts. Nonetheless, we will proceed on the assumption that one theory will do the job; we will see how far we can get with this assumption.

Definitions: What Do We Know When We Know What a Dog Is?

We all know what a dog is. If someone sends us to the pet shop to buy a dog, we are sure to succeed. If someone tells us that a particular disease is common among dogs, we know that our pet terrier is at risk and so are the wolves in the zoo. Clearly, our store of knowledge about dogs will support these not-very-exciting achievements. But what is that knowledge?

One possibility is that we know something akin to a dictionary definition. That is, what we know is of the form: "A dog is a creature that is (a) mammalian, (b) has four legs, (c) barks, (d) wags its tail. . . . " This definition would presumably serve us well. When asked whether a candidate creature is a dog, we could use our definition as a check-list, scrutinizing the candidate for the various defining features. When told that "A dog is an animal," we would know that we had not learned anything new, since this information is already contained, presumably, within our mental definition. If we were asked what dogs, cats, and horses have in common, we could scan our definition of each looking for common elements.

The difficulty with this proposal, however, comes when we try to spell out just how these terms are defined. The relevant argument here comes not from a psychologist, but from an important twentieth-century philosopher, Ludwig Wittgenstein. Wittgenstein (1953) noted that philosophers had been trying for thousands of years to define terms like "virtue" or "knowledge." There had been some success, inasmuch as various features had been identified as important aspects of these terms. However, even after thousands of years of careful thought, these terms were still without accepted, full definitions.

Perhaps this is unsurprising, since these are subtle, philosophically rich terms, embedded in a complex web of human activities and so naturally resistant to definition. However, Wittgenstein wondered if this really was the problem. He wondered whether we could find definitions even for simple, ordinary terms, for example, the word, "game."

What is a game? Consider, for example, the game of hide-and-seek. What makes hide-and-seek a game? Hide-and-seek (a) is an activity most often found in children, (b) is engaged in for fun, (c) has certain rules, (d) involves multiple people, (e) is in some ways competitive, (f) is played during periods of leisure. All these are plausible attributes of games, and so we seem well on our way to defining "game." But are these attributes really part of the definition of "game"? Consider (a) and (b): What about the Olympic games? The competitors in these games are not children, and runners in marathon races do not look like they are having a great deal of fun. Consider (d) and (e): What about card games played by one person? These are played alone, without competition. Consider (f): What about professional golfers?

For each clause of the definition, one can find an exception: an activity that we call a game but that does not have the relevant characteristic. And the same is true for most any concept: We might define "shoe" as an item of apparel made out of leather, designed to be worn on the foot. But what about wooden shoes? What about a shoe, designed by a Master Shoemaker, intended only for display, and never for use? What about a shoe filled with cement, which therefore cannot be worn? Similarly, we might define "dog" in a way that includes four-leggedness, but what about a dog who has lost a limb in some accident? We might specify "communicates by barking" as part of the definition of dog, but what about the Egyptian Basenji, which has no bark? Quite consistently, our most common terms, terms denoting concepts that we use easily and often, resist being defined. When we do come up with a definition, it is all too easy to find exceptions to it.

To put this more precisely, we cannot equate "knowing a term" or "knowing a concept" with "knowing a definition." To be sure, each of us can fully and correctly define *some* of the terms we know (e.g., "triangle") but, it seems, we are unable to define many other terms that we commonly use. Of course, many of the concepts we use can be defined by the relevant experts. A botanist, for example, might be able to define "elm tree" fully, with a definition that distinguishes between an elm and a beech. Similarly, a biologist might be able to define "dog" in terms of a particular genetic pattern. But these technical definitions are unknown to most of the people who know and use these concepts. If asked to define "dog," these concept-holders are unlikely to spell out the correct genetic pattern. Instead, they will list plausible dog features but, once again, we can easily find exceptions to their proposed definitions.

Family Resemblance

If asked to define commonplace terms, we do not name foolish or inappropriate features. If asked to define "dog," for example, we do not say, "A dog is a creature who lives in Brooklyn and has green hair." Instead, we name plausible "dog features." It might be that not all dogs have these features, but many dogs do.

Given all of this, perhaps what concept-holders have is not a firm, "works every time" definition but instead something less rigid: It looks like we cannot say, "A creature with features X, Y, and Z is a dog." But we can say, "A creature with these features is *probably* a dog, and a creature without these features *probably* isn't." This probabilistic phrasing preserves what is good within definitions—e.g., the fact that definitions do name sensible, relevant features. But this phrasing also allows some degree of uncertainty, some number of exceptions to the rule.

Wittgenstein's proposal was roughly along these lines. His notion was that members of a category have a **family resemblance** to each other. Consider the ways that members of a family resemble each other: Some features are common in the family (a particular hair color, a particular shape of nose),

Figure 8.1

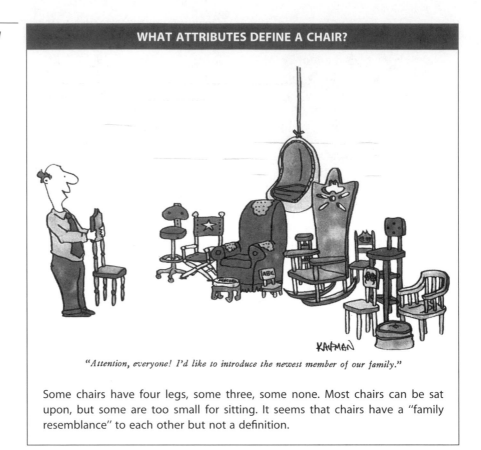

WHAT ATTRIBUTES DEFINE A CHAIR?

"Attention, everyone! I'd like to introduce the newest member of our family."

Some chairs have four legs, some three, some none. Most chairs can be sat upon, but some are too small for sitting. It seems that chairs have a "family resemblance" to each other but not a definition.

but this does not mean that everyone in the family has these features. You might resemble your mother because you both have the same high cheekbones. You might resemble your sister because you both have the same eyeshape and the same strong chin (neither of which your mother shares). You might resemble your brother because of yet some other features. In these ways, if we take members of the family two or even three at a time, we will find considerable feature overlap. However, if we consider *all* of the members of the family, we may find no features that they all share. Nevertheless, because of the feature overlap, family members do resemble each other.

Family resemblance will give us something like a probabilistic definition. A "definition" of a family's appearance ("What it *means* to 'look like a Smith' is brown hair, green eyes. . . . ") won't be possible, since there may be no features shared by all family members. Nonetheless, there will be characteristic features for each family, so that someone who has these features will probably be perceived as being a member of the family. Moreover, the more of these features someone has, the more likely we are to believe they are in the family. Family resemblance is a matter of degree, not all-or-none.

In the same fashion, there may be no definition of categories like dog, because there may be no attributes that consistently distinguish dogs from non-dogs. More precisely, there may be no **necessary conditions** of being a dog—i.e., attributes you must have in order to be a dog.[1] Likewise, there may be no **sufficient conditions**—i.e., attributes that, if you have them, are sufficient to qualify you as a dog. However, this does not mean that the category of "all dogs" is a random assembly. Instead, any two or three dogs we might consider are likely to have a great deal in common, just as you and your brother have a great deal in common, or your brother and your father. *What* they have in common may shift from case to case, just as the features you and your brother share may be different from the features shared by your brother and your father. Nonetheless there will be resemblance among the members of the category, even though we cannot specify anything that all members of the category have in common (Figure 8.1).

There are several ways we might translate all of this into a psychological theory, but the most influential translation was proposed by Eleanor Rosch, in the mid-1970s (Rosch, 1973, 1978; Rosch & Mervis, 1975; Rosch, Mervis, Gray, Johnson & Boyes-Braem, 1976).

Prototypes and "Typicality" Effects

One way to think about definitions is that they set the "boundaries" for a category: If a test case has certain attributes, then it is "inside" the category. If the test case does not have the defining attributes, then it is "outside" the category. (For discussion of this "classical" view, see Smith, 1988; Margolis, 1994; Smith & Medin, 1981.)

Prototype theory begins with a different tactic: Perhaps the best way to identify a category, to characterize a concept, is to specify the "center" of the category rather than the "boundaries." Perhaps the concept of "dog," for example, is represented in the mind by some representation of the "ideal"

---

[1] As a subtle point, note that there are some necessary conditions for being a dog: For example, it is necessary that an entity be a physical object in order to be a dog. It is likewise necessary that an entity consist of more than one molecule in order to be a dog. But these conditions, while necessary for "dogdom," obviously won't distinguish dogs from cats or even fire hydrants. Hence, this condition is not distinctive for dogs, and is therefore not necessary for being counted as a dog *as opposed to* being counted as a member of one of these other categories.

dog, the *prototype* dog. In this view, all judgments about dogs are made with reference to this ideal. Categorization, for example, would involve some sort of comparison between a test case (the furry creature currently before your eyes) and the prototype. If there is no similarity between these, then the creature before you is probably not in the category; if there is considerable similarity, then you draw the opposite conclusion.

What is a prototype? For most purposes, we can think of a prototype as an "average" of the various category members one has encountered. The prototype will be of average color, age, size, and so forth. When averaging is not appropriate, the prototype's attributes will match the most frequent attributes in the category. The prototype for "family" will be of average age, average education level, and average income, but will have one child, not (the average of) 1.19! In still other cases, a prototype *may* represent an "ideal" for the category rather than an average. (The prototype diet soft drink, for example, might have zero calories, yet taste great, even if no actual soft drinks reach this ideal.)

Likewise, it seems plausible that different people will have different prototypes. If a prototype reflects the ideal for a category, then people may disagree about what that ideal would involve. If a prototype reflects the average of the cases you have encountered, then an American's prototype for "house" might have one form, while for someone living in Japan, the prototype "house" might be rather different.

Thus we will need to allow some flexibility in how we characterize prototypes. (For some further complexities here, see Armstrong, Gleitman & Gleitman, 1983; Barsalou, 1987; Neuman, 1977.) Nonetheless, in all these cases, the prototype will serve as the "anchor," the "benchmark," for our conceptual knowledge. When we reason about a concept, or use our conceptual knowledge, our reasoning is done with reference to the prototype.

Fuzzy Boundaries and Graded Membership

Our hypothesis is that what it means to "know" a concept, to represent a concept in the mind, is to represent a prototype for that concept. Consider the simple task of categorization: As we sketched before, one might categorize objects by comparing them to prototypes stored in memory. If the dog now before your eyes has many attributes in common with the dog prototype, it will easily and quickly be recognized as a dog. Dogs that have fewer attributes in common with the prototype will probably cause you uncertainty about their identity. Similarly, in deciding that a particular ceramic vessel is a cup and not a bowl, you might compare the vessel to both your cup prototype and your bowl prototype. By discovering that the vessel is more similar to one than to the other, a decision is reached.

This sounds plausible enough, but there is an odd implication here. Imagine a range of vessels, each one further and further removed from the cup prototype. The first might, for example, be the shape and size of a teacup, and white in color. The second might be the same shape and size, but shocking pink in color. The third might be shocking pink, and twice the size of a normal teacup; the next might be all these things, and also made of lead. According to a definition view (the "classical" view), our cup definition would tell us that some of these cases do count as cups and others do not. That is all. The category of cups has a boundary somewhere, and each test case is either on one side of the boundary or the other. Moreover, all of the cups inside the boundary are "equal citizens," each one fully and legitimately entitled to be called a cup. All of the non-cups are also "equal citizens," each one fully and equivalently not a cup. You are a cup, or you are not a cup. End of story.

The prototype view would allow us to say none of this. We could certainly say that some of the vessels under consideration are closer to the prototype than others, and that the ones closer to the prototype are more likely to be cups, the ones further from it are less likely. But at no point is there a boundary between "inside" the category and "outside." Instead, the category of cup has a **fuzzy boundary**, with no clear specification of membership and non-membership.

Hand in hand with this, not all cups are equal. Instead, some are "cupier" than others, namely the ones near the prototype. To put this more generally, prototype-based categories not only have fuzzy boundaries, they also have **graded membership**. Thus, some dogs are "better" dogs than others, according to how close they are to the prototype. The graded membership notion, therefore, is a striking and important implication of the prototype view.

Testing the Prototype Notion

Consider the sentence verification task, which we first met in Chapter 7. In this task, subjects are presented with a succession of sentences; their task is to indicate (by pressing the appropriate button) whether each sentence is true or false. The sentences are simple in form: "A sparrow is a bird. A chair is furniture. A collie is a cat."

Subjects' speed in this task depends on several factors. As we have seen, response speed depends on the number of "steps" subjects must traverse to confirm the sentence (see Chapter 7). Subjects also respond faster for true sentences than for false, and faster for familiar categories. Most important for our purposes, though, the speed of response varies from item to item within a category. For example, response times are longer for sentences like "A penguin is a bird" than for "A robin is a bird"; longer for "An Afghan hound is a dog" than for "A German shepherd is a dog" (e.g., Smith, Rips & Shoben, 1974).

Why should this be? According to a prototype perspective, subjects make these judgments by comparing the thing mentioned (penguin, for example) to their prototype for that category (their bird prototype). When there is much similarity between the test case and the prototype, subjects can make their decisions quickly; judgments about items more distant from the prototype take more time. Given the results, it seems that penguins and Afghans are more distant from their respective prototypes than are robins and German shepherds.

There are several different ways to flesh out this proposal, and, in particular, different ways to unpack this idea of being "more distant" or "less distant" from the prototype. Let's hold these points to the side, though, because we first need to deal with a problem in the argument just offered: Why does "robin" yield fast responses, while "penguin" doesn't? Because robins are closer to the prototype than penguins. How do we know that robins are closer to the prototype? Because they yield faster responses. This is plainly circular: We are using proximity to the prototype as a basis for predicting fast responses, but we are then turning around and arguing the reverse: fast responses as a basis for claiming proximity to the prototype.

However, the escape from this circle is easy to find. What we cannot do is make "double-use" of the same results: We can't use a set of data to determine which cases are close to the prototype, and which distant, and then use those same data to support the prototype perspective. What we can do, though, is make predictions from one data set to a *different* data set. For example, we can use experiments like the sentence verification task to identify which category members seem to be close to the prototype. We can then use this information to predict the results of other studies. As one option, we can ask subjects to name as many birds as they can (cf. Mervis, Catlin & Rosch, 1976). According to a prototype view, subjects will do this production task by first locating their bird or dog prototype in memory and then asking themselves what resembles this prototype. In essence, they will start with the center of the category (the prototype) and work their way outward from there. Thus, birds close to the prototype should be mentioned first, birds further from the prototype later on. More concretely, the first birds to be mentioned in this task should be the birds that yielded fast response times in the verification task; the birds mentioned later in production should have yielded slower response times in verification. This is exactly what happens.

This sets the pattern of evidence for prototype theory: Over and over, in category after category, members of a category that are "privileged" on one task (e.g., yield the fastest response times) turn out also to be privileged on other tasks (e.g., are most likely to be mentioned). That is, various tasks

converge in the sense that each task yields the same answer, i.e., picks out the same category members as special. (For some examples of these "privileged" category members, see Table 8.1.)

This notion of **converging evidence** provides two benefits. First, it allows us to escape the problem of circular arguments. Second, and perhaps more important, consider what it *means* to study concepts: Presumably, concepts constitute the knowledge we draw on for a variety of purposes—we use our "fish" concept to identify fish, to talk about fish, to draw inferences about fish. In other words, a variety of tasks are based on the same underlying conceptual knowledge. Thus, if we are trying to study the concept of "fish," we are less interested in how subjects do this or that particular task, and more interested in what these various tasks have in common; we are less interested in the processes or strategies involved in the task, and more interested in the

Table 8.1

SUBJECTS' TYPICALITY RATINGS FOR THE CATEGORY "FRUIT" AND THE CATEGORY "BIRD"			
Fruit	**Rating**	**Bird**	**Rating**
Apple	6.25	Robin	6.89
Peach	5.81	Bluebird	6.42
Pear	5.25	Seagull	6.26
Grape	5.13	Swallow	6.16
Strawberry	5.00	Falcon	5.74
Lemon	4.86	Mockingbird	5.47
Blueberry	4.56	Starling	5.16
Watermelon	4.06	Owl	5.00
Raisin	3.75	Vulture	4.84
Fig	3.38	Sandpiper	4.47
Coconut	3.06	Chicken	3.95
Pomegranate	2.50	Flamingo	3.37
Avocado	2.38	Albatross	3.32
Pumpkin	2.31	Penguin	2.63
Olive	2.25	Bat	1.53

Note: Ratings were made on a 7-point scale, 7 corresponding to the highest typicality. [After Malt & Smith, 1984.]

knowledge that supports the task. Given this, the idea that we are getting data from a spectrum of tasks, and that these data are converging on the same answer, gives us reason to believe that we are not "merely" studying how subjects do a particular task. Instead, this gives us reason to believe that we are studying knowledge of a broadly useful, fundamental sort, exactly the kind of knowledge that we would expect concepts to provide.

The Converging Evidence for Prototypes

We have mentioned two lines of experiments with converging data patterns, but there are many more. We list six of these here, to give you a sense of the evidence:

1. *Sentence verification.* As indicated, items close to the prototype are more quickly identified as category members. This presumably reflects the fact that category membership is determined by assessing the similarity to the prototype (Rosch, Simpson & Miller, 1976; although, for some complications in the sentence verification procedure, see Glass, Holyoak & Kiger, 1979; McCloskey & Glucksberg, 1979; Smith, 1978; Smith et al., 1974).

2. *Production.* As indicated, items close to the prototype are the earliest and the most likely to be mentioned in a production task. This presumably reflects the fact that the memory search supporting this task begins with the prototype and "works outward" (Barsalou, 1983, 1985; Barsalou & Sewell, 1985; Mervis et al., 1976).

3. *Picture identification.* This task is similar to the sentence verification task. Subjects are told that they are about to see a picture that may or may not be a dog; they are asked to hit a "yes" or "no" button as quickly as they can. Pictures of dogs similar to the prototype (e.g., German shepherd or collie) are more quickly identified, pictures of dogs less similar to the prototype (for example, chihuahua or dachshund) are more slowly identified (Figure 8.2) (Rosch, Mervis et al., 1976; Smith, Balzano & Walker, 1978).

4. *Explicit judgments of category membership.* Rosch (1975; also Malt & Smith, 1984) explicitly asked subjects to judge how typical various category members were for the category. In these **typicality** studies, subjects are given instructions like these: "We all know that some birds are 'birdier' than others; some dogs are 'doggier' than others, and so on. I'm going to present you with a list of birds or of dogs, and I want you to rate each one on the basis of how 'birdy' or 'doggy' it is." Subjects are easily able to render these judgments. Quite consistently, subjects rate items as being very "birdy" or "doggy" when these instances are close to the prototype (as determined in the other tasks). Subjects rate items as being less "birdy" or "doggy" when these are further from the prototype. This suggests that subjects perform this task by comparing the test item to the prototype.

Figure 8.2

TYPICALITY ALSO INFLUENCES THE IDENTIFICATION PICTURES

American subjects are quicker in identifying pictures of German shepherds or collies as dogs than they are in identifying pictures of chihuahuas or dachshunds. This is what one would expect if subjects make these identifications by comparing each picture to their mental prototype for the category "dog."

5. *Induction.* An interesting result involves subjects' willingness to extrapolate from current information. In one study, subjects were told a new fact about robins and were willing to infer that the new fact would also be true for ducks; if subjects were told a new fact about ducks, they would not extrapolate to robins (Rips, 1975). Apparently, subjects will make inferences from the typical to the whole category but will not make inferences from the atypical to the category.

6. *Tasks asking subjects to "think about" categories.* The procedure here has three steps (after Rosch, 1977a). First, we ask subjects to make up sentences about a category. If the category were "birds," subjects might make up sentences as, "I saw two birds in a tree," or "I like to feed birds in the park." Next, the experimenters rewrite these sentences, substituting for the category name either the name of a prototypical member of the category (e.g., robin) or a not-so-prototypical member (e.g., penguin). In our example, we would

get "I like to feed robins in the park," and "I like to feed penguins in the park." Finally, we take these new, edited sentences to a different group of subjects and ask this group to rate how silly or implausible the sentences seem.

The hypothesis is that, when we ask subjects to think about a category, they are in fact thinking about the prototype for that category. Therefore, in making up their sentences, subjects will come up with statements appropriate for the prototype. It follows from this that the sentence's sensibility will be pretty much unchanged if we substitute a prototypical category-member for the category name, since that will be close to what the subject had in mind in the first place. Substituting a non-prototypical member, on the other hand, may yield a peculiar, even ridiculous, proposition. This is fully in line with the data. When the new group of subjects rates these sentences, they rate as quite ordinary the sentences into which we have placed a prototypical case ("I saw two robins in a tree") and reject as silly the sentences into which we have placed a non-prototypical case ("I saw two penguins in a tree").

Basic-Level Categories

Much of the research just reviewed derives from Eleanor Rosch's theorizing about the nature and function of mental prototypes. We should mention, though, that Rosch's work also contains a further theme. As a way of introducing this point, consider the following task: I show you a picture of a chair, and I ask, "What is this?" What you are likely to say is that the picture shows a chair. You are far less likely to offer a more specific response ("It's a Windsor chair") or a more general response ("It's an item of furniture"), although these responses would also be correct. Likewise, how do people get to work? In responding, you are unlikely to say, "Some people drive Fords; some drive Chevies." Instead, your answer is likely to use more general terms, such as cars and trains and buses.

In keeping with these observations, Rosch has argued that there is a "natural" level of categorization, neither too specific nor too general, that we tend to use in our conversations and in our reasoning. She refers to this level as providing **basic-level** categorization. Basic-level categories are usually represented in our language via a single word, while more specific categories are identified only via a phrase. Thus, "chair" is a basic-level category and so is "apple." The subcategories of "arm chair" or "wooden chair" are not basic level; nor is "red apple" or "Delicious apple." If asked to describe an object, we are likely spontaneously to use the basic-level term. If asked to explain what members of a category have in common with each other, we have an easy time with basic-level categories (what do all chairs have in common?)

but some difficulty with more encompassing categories (what does all furniture have in common?).

There has been some debate about these claims. Do all categorization schemes have a basic level? How "stable" is the designation of the basic level? Do novices and experts agree, for example, in defining the basic level? (People in general might regard "plant" as basic level; a gardener might regard "annual" or "perennial" as basic levels; and a botanist might regard "monocots" and "dicots" as basic-level.) Likewise, is the designation of basic level stable from one task to the next or from one context to the next? The evidence is mixed on these various questions.

Even with these complexities, basic-level categorization is important for a variety of purposes, for at least some concepts. For example, in studies of children learning how to talk, there are some indications that basic-level terms are acquired earlier than either the more specific subcategories, or the more general, more encompassing categories. Thus, basic-level categories do seem to reflect a natural way to categorize some of the objects in our world (Rosch, Mervis et al., 1976; for more recent work, see Corter & Gluck, 1992).

Exemplars

Let's return, though, to our main agenda. As we have seen, a broad spectrum of tasks reflect the "graded membership" of mental categories. Some members of the categories are "better" than others, and the "better" members are recognized more readily, mentioned more often, judged more typical, and so on. Thus, subjects give fast responses to sentences like, "An apple is a fruit" and slower responses to "An olive is a fruit." If asked to name fruits, subjects are likely to name apple fairly quickly; if they name olive at all, it will be much later. If asked to rate how "fruity" apples and olives are, they will give a higher rating for the former.

Likewise, it seems plain that typicality does guide many of our category judgments: In diagnosing diseases, for example, physicians often seem to function as if asking themselves: "How much does this case resemble a typical case of disease X? How closely does it resemble a typical case of disease Y?" The greater the resemblance to this or that diagnostic prototype, the more likely the diagnosis will be of that disease. (See, e.g., Klayman & Brown, 1993.)

All of this is obviously in accord with prototype theory: Our conceptual knowledge is represented via a prototype, and we categorize by making comparisons to that prototype. It turns out, though, that prototype theory isn't the only way one can think about these data. Another perspective is available, providing a different way to explain typicality effects and the graded membership of categories. In this section, we examine this alternate view.

Analogies from Remembered Exemplars

Imagine that we place a wooden object in front of you and ask, "Is this a chair?" According to the prototype view, you would answer this question by calling up your chair prototype from memory and then comparing the candidate to that prototype. If the resemblance is great, you announce, "Yes, this is a chair."

But you might make this decision in a different way: You might notice that this object is very similar to an object in your Uncle Jack's living room, and you know that the object in Uncle Jack's living room is a chair. After all, you've seen Uncle Jack sitting in the thing, reading his newspaper. If Jack's possession is a chair, and if the new object resembles Jack's, then it is a safe bet that the new object is a chair, too.

The idea here is that, in some cases, categorization can draw on knowledge about specific category members rather than more general information about the overall category. In our example, the categorization is supported by memories of a specific chair, rather than remembered knowledge about chairs in general. This is referred to as an **exemplar-based** approach, with an exemplar defined as a specific remembered instance—in essence, an example.

This approach overlaps with the prototype view in several regards. According to both of these views, you categorize objects by comparing them to a mentally represented "standard." For prototype theory, this standard is the prototype; for exemplar theory, the standard is provided by whatever example of the category comes to mind. In either case, though, the process is then the same: You assess the similarity between a candidate object and this standard. If the resemblance is great, you judge the candidate as being within the relevant category; if the resemblance is minimal, you seek some alternative categorization.

It should be emphasized, though, that these two views diverge on some key points. For one, the prototype view implies that reasoning will always draw on the same standard, namely the prototype itself. According to the exemplar view, however, this need not be true—it is quite possible that different examples will come to mind on different occasions, and this will influence our performance. An illustration will help show how this matters and will also show us how far an exemplar approach might be extended.

You are reading along, and encounter the novel word "tave." How should you pronounce this letter string? You might call to mind the rules of English spelling, which tell you that this pattern of consonant–vowel–consonant–"e" demands a long vowel. Therefore, the word is pronounced as though it rhymes with "save" or "cave."

Alternatively, you might look at the word "tave" and be reminded, not of a rule, but of other words, such as "save" or "cave." By analogy with these, you would pronounce "tave" with a long vowel. In this way, you would arrive at the same decision as you would have via the rule. But this process of find-an-instance, draw-an-analogy, leaves open another possibility: "Tave" might also remind you of "have" and, in this case, the analogy would lead you to a short-vowel pronunciation. And, interestingly enough, college students, asked to pronounce this letter string, do on occasion come up with the short-vowel pronunciation, a peculiar finding if they are using the rule, but easily explained if they are using instances plus analogies (Baron, 1977).

Our confidence that this is what is going on is increased by the fact that we can prime subjects in a simple way: Subjects read down a list of words, some of which are real words, some of which are made-up. Word number 23 on this list might be "have." Word number 26 is the test word, "tave." It turns out that this recent activation of "have" makes the short-vowel pronunciation much more likely, just as we would expect on an instance-plus-analogy account: If the instance "have" is made more likely to come to mind, it is more likely that it (and not *save* or *cave* or *rave*) will be the basis for the analogy, and so, by manipulating memory availability of "have," we influence how the analogy will turn out.

We should emphasize, though, that subjects' reliance on exemplars is typically unwitting. If we ask them directly why they pronounced the letter string as they did, subjects generally don't mention the earlier-presented word. But the data tell us that subjects are, in fact, being influenced by this earlier presentation. This obviously resembles the pattern we encountered again and again in Chapter 5: There we distinguished between "explicit" memories, of which the subject is aware, and "implicit" memories, which influence us without any awareness. It seems likely that exemplars are remembered in the latter way—*implicitly*, with subjects plainly being influenced by remembered exemplars without realizing it. (For discussion, see Brooks, 1990; Knowlton & Squire, 1993.)

Explaining Typicality Data with an Exemplar Model

The proposal to be considered, then, is that judgments about concepts are often made via analogies based on specific remembered instances. Many authors have endorsed this proposal, albeit with some variations in the particulars of how these analogies are selected or created (Brooks, 1978, 1987; Estes, 1976, 1993; Hintzman, 1986; Medin, 1975, 1976; Medin & Schaffer, 1978; Nosofsky, 1986; Reed, 1972; Shin & Nosofsky, 1992).

It seems undeniable that we do have knowledge about particular cases: Not only do we know about birds, we also know about penguins and emus and ospreys. Not only do we know about dogs, we also know about Fido and Spot and Rover. In some cases, this specific knowledge conflicts with our conceptual knowledge and, when this happens, the specific knowledge dominates. (For a discussion of this point, see, e.g., Brooks, 1990.) Thus we know that, in general, birds fly, but we overrule this knowledge when we are considering a specific bird that we know to be flightless.

In addition, it turns out that exemplar-based approaches can also explain the graded-membership pattern so often seen in concept tasks. For example, consider a task in which we show subjects a series of pictures and ask them to decide whether each picture shows a fruit or not. We already know that subjects will respond more quickly for typical fruits than for less typical fruits. We have seen how this result is handled by a prototype account. How could an exemplar model explain this finding?

According to an exemplar theory, subjects make their judgments in this task by comparing the pictures to specific mentally-represented examples. Let's pause, though, to ask *which* examples are going to come to mind. It seems likely that, as you go through your days, you encounter apples more often than olives, oranges more often than dates. This simply reflects the fact that apples and oranges are indeed common fruits: often seen, often eaten, often mentioned. If you then remember what you have encountered, you will end up with more apple and orange memories than olive and date memories. Consequently, if you reach into memory for a fruit exemplar, you are more likely to find a memory of an apple or an orange than a memory for a date. This isn't because of prototyping; it is simply a result of memory's reflecting what is in your surround.

Given this assumption about what is in memory, the typicality result is easily explained. The exemplars coming to mind are likely to be exemplars of typical fruits. Therefore, if one is judging an apple or an orange, there is obviously a great resemblance between the candidate and the remembered exemplars, supporting a fast response. Dates and honeydews will be judged more slowly, because the exemplars coming to mind are likely not to be dates and honeydews. Hence there is less resemblance between the candidate and the remembered exemplars, and so a slower response.

Exemplars Preserve Information about Variability

As we have just seen, exemplar-based views can explain typicality effects—largely by appealing to a "typicality bias" in subjects' memories: It is typical exemplars that are likely to come to mind not atypical ones. As a consequence of this, the graded-membership pattern, which we have seen over and over, favors neither the exemplar view nor the prototype view—both positions are compatible with the evidence. Other results, however, do favor the exemplar view.

For example, we have noted that a prototype can be thought of as the *average* for a category and, as such, it provides a summary of what is typical or frequent for that category. But much information is lost in an average. For example, an average, by itself, doesn't tell you how *variable* a set is, and sometimes information about variability is rather useful (after Rips, 1989a; Rips & Collins, 1993). The average size of a pizza is twelve inches. The average size of a ruler is, of course, also twelve inches. Now let's imagine that I hand you a new object that is 19 inches across. Is it more likely that this new object is a pizza or a ruler? If you make this decision by comparing the test case to the averages, then you have no basis for a judgment—the test case departs from both averages by 7 inches. But of course you know that pizzas vary in size enormously, and so a pizza could easily be 19 inches across. Rulers do not vary, and so the test case is almost certainly not a ruler.

In this situation, your judgment is plainly influenced by knowledge about variability. This knowledge would not be reflected in a prototype (which is just like an average), but *could* be reflected via exemplars. If you remember both a 7-inch pizza and one that was 30 inches across, this tells you in an instant that a pizza can vary in its size (at least) from 7 to 30 inches. For that matter, if you reflect on the full set of pizzas you have seen, you can make a reasonable assessment of how variable the set has been.

In short, a set of exemplars preserves information about variability; a prototype does not. Since subjects do seem sensitive to variability information, this seems a strike against prototype theory and in favor of exemplars. (For further discussion of subjects' sensitivity to variability, see Fried & Holyoak, 1984; Nisbett, Krantz, Jepson & Kunda, 1983.)

Exemplars Preserve Information about Correlated Features

Here is a different type of information that would be preserved in a set of exemplars but lost in a prototype: Consider two hypothetical softball teams. Both the Blue Team and the Red Team include some members who are tall, and some who are short, some who are thin and some who are fat. (See Figure 8.3.) In fact, the average height of a Blue Team member is the same as the average for the Red Team, and likewise for average weight. It turns out, though, that all of the Red Team members who are tall are also fat. All on this team who are short are also thin. In sum, there is a correlation between these two traits. No such correlation exists for the Blue Team.

Let us now imagine that a new team player, Alice, appears in the field, and she happens to be 6 foot, 2 inches tall, and is also quite slender. Is Alice

Figure 8.3

USING CORRELATED FEATURES IN CATEGORIZATION					
BLUE TEAM			**RED TEAM**		
	Height	Weight		Height	Weight
George	6'3"	120	Fred	6'4"	250 lb.
Tina	4'1"	240	Sam	4'1"	110 lb.
Lee	6'4"	250	Susan	6'3"	240 lb.
Alyson	4'2"	110	Jane	4'3"	90 lb.
Tom	4'3"	160	Chris	6'2"	240 lb.
Mary	6'2"	170	Jeff	4'2"	120 lb.
Average	**5'2½"**	**175 lb.**	**Average**	**5'2½"**	**175 lb.**

A new player, Alice, has arrived on the field. Alice is 6'2" tall, and quite slender. Is she more likely to be a Red Team member or a Blue Team member? Note that the two teams are, *on average*, the same height and the same weight. Therefore, if we try to categorize Alice by comparing her to these averages, then we have no basis for categorization. However, Alice does resemble some of the *individuals* on the Blue Team (e.g., George, who happens, like Alice, to be tall and thin). She resembles none of the individuals on the Red Team. (No Red Team members are both tall and thin.) Therefore, if we categorize by comparing Alice to the individuals, she is more likely to be on the Blue Team than on the Red.

a Blue Team member or a Red Team member? If we compare her to the prototype for each team, we have no basis for judgment since, you will recall, the averages for the two teams (and so the prototypes) were identical. We will do better, though, if we compare Alice to specific team members. Alice resembles none of the Red Team players. Members of that team who happened to be 6 foot 2 were also quite fat; members of that team who were slender were also short. But Alice may resemble some of the Blue Team players. For Blue, there was no correlation between height and weight, and so there might well have been some players who were both tall and slender. Hence, resemblance to exemplars provides a basis for categorization; resemblance to the prototype does not.

Are subjects sensitive to these patterns and, in particular, to correlations among features? In one study, subjects learned about a fictitious disease, "burlosis," by examining a series of case studies (Medin, Altom, Edelson & Freko, 1982; also see Wattenmaker, 1991). In these case studies, there was a pattern of correlation among the symptoms: If a patient had discolored gums, he or she was certain to have nosebleeds, and vice versa (see Table 8.2). Other

Table 8.2

TRAINING AND TEST CASES FOR DIAGNOSIS OF "BURLOSIS"			
Symptoms			
Swollen Eyelids (A)	Splotches on Ears (B)	Discolored Gums (C)	Nosebleed (D)
Training Cases: All of these cases have burlosis.			
R.C. Yes	Yes	Yes	Yes
R.M. Yes	Yes	Yes	Yes
J.J. —	Yes	—	—
L.F. Yes	Yes	Yes	Yes
A.M. Yes	—	Yes	Yes
J.S. Yes	Yes	—	—
S.T. —	Yes	Yes	Yes
S.E. Yes	—	—	—
E.M. —	—	Yes	Yes
Test Cases: Within each pair, which case is *more* likely to have burlosis?			
Pair 1: A (Jack) Yes	—	Yes	Yes
B (Jill) Yes	Yes	—	Yes
Pair 2: X —	—	—	Yes
Y —	Yes	—	—

Note: Subjects learned about the disease "burlosis" by examining the nine case studies. Each of the symptoms occurs in 6 of 9 training cases; therefore, these symptoms are all indications of burlosis. The prototypical burlosis sufferer, therefore, would probably have all of these symptoms. In additon, discolored gums and nosebleeds are correlated symptoms: If a patient has one of these symptoms, he or she has both. In the test cases, which patient in each of the pairs is more likely to have burlosis? The number of symptoms is the same for both members of each pair; however, one patient in each pair has the symptoms in the correlated pattern and the other does not. Subjects typically choose the patients with correlated symptoms, evidence of an exemplar approach.

[After Medin, Altom, Edelson, & Freko, 1982.]

symptoms, though, were uncorrelated: A patient with burlosis might have swollen eyelids and also nosebleeds, or one of these symptoms without the other, or neither.

Subjects were subsequently asked to diagnose several test cases, some of which had symptoms in line with this correlated pattern, and some of which did not. For example, we might present subjects with two patients—Jack, who has swollen eyelids, discolored gums, and nosebleeds, and Jill, who has nosebleeds, swollen eyelids, and splotches on her ears, but normal gums. Which of these is more likely to have burlosis? Jack's symptoms are consistent with the correlation in the training cases, but Jill's are not. Therefore, even though these patients have the same number of burlosis symptoms, Jack is more likely to have the disease.

Subjects in this study were clearly influenced by the correlation pattern. That is, they tended to choose the case that preserved the correlation among symptoms over the case that broke the correlation. This would be peculiar if subjects were basing their diagnosis on a burlosis prototype, since, as we have seen, the prototype will not preserve information about this correlation. The result is sensible, though, if subjects are basing their diagnosis on exemplars: Jack resembles several individuals known to have burlosis, since his symptoms are in the same configuration as theirs. This is not true for Jill—none of the studied patients had her configuration of symptoms. Jack therefore resembles the exemplars more than Jill does. Thus, once again, the results favor the exemplar view.

The Pliability of Mental Categories

Here's a different line of evidence favoring the exemplar perspective: One might think that the concept of giraffe that I have today is the same as the concept I had yesterday (assuming that I haven't learned any new facts about giraffes). Likewise, the concept that I use in identifying giraffes is presumably the same concept I use when talking about giraffes or drawing inferences about them. There is every reason to believe, however, that our concepts are more pliable, more flexible, than these cases suggest. This pliability is easily accommodated by the exemplar view but not by prototype theory.

What are the objects in Figure 8.4? Are they cups, bowls, or vases? In a study by Labov (1973), subjects categorized the wider objects as cups if they appeared in someone's hands; they were categorized as *bowls* if they were filled with mashed potatoes. Likewise for the other shapes; categorization of these depended heavily on the context. Apparently, then, context can determine what counts as a "cup" or as a "bowl."

More strongly, context can even determine what counts as a "typical" cup or "typical" bowl. Consider the effects of perspective: We have already sup-

Figure 8.4

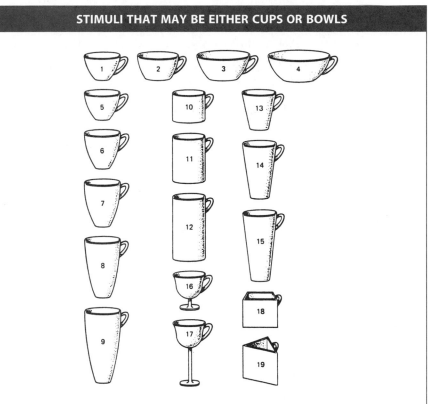

STIMULI THAT MAY BE EITHER CUPS OR BOWLS

Subjects' identification of these figures as "cups," "bowls," or "vases" was influenced by the context. Object 1 was likely to be called a cup no matter what its context. Object 4 was more likely to be called a cup if subjects imagined the object in someone's hands. However, Object 4 was likely to be called a bowl if subjects thought about it as sitting on a table, filled with mashed potatoes. [After Labov, 1973.]

posed that typicality is, in large measure, a reflection of our experience. What counts as a "typical animal," for example, will depend on the animals you have seen, and this will be different for a pet-store owner than it is for a zookeeper. Likewise, your idea of a "typical gift" will depend on the gifts you have given and received; this will be different for a college student than it would be for a professor.

What is striking, though, is that each of us can adopt the other's perspective, and our judgments of typicality change accordingly. To demonstrate this, we repeat the standard typicality demonstrations (e.g., the sentence verification tasks mentioned earlier, or the explicit judgments of typicality), but this time we instruct subjects to respond on these tasks from a specific point of view. When this is done, subjects easily shift perspective and give rather different answers as their vantage point changes. For instance, subjects instructed to take an American point of view rate robin and eagle as highly typical birds; the same subjects taking a Chinese point of view rate robin and eagle much lower, and now rate swan and peacock as being more typical (Barsalou, 1988; Barsalou & Sewell, 1985).

One could, in principle, explain these results in terms of conceptual prototypes. Perhaps subjects just have a great many prototypes and draw on each as appropriate. That is, subjects might arrive in the laboratory with a prototype for "Chinese bird," and also a prototype for "American bird"; a student-gift prototype, and also a faculty-gift prototype, and so on. On this view, the procedures just described are simply urging subjects to move from one concept to another as they do the various tasks.

However, some further evidence speaks against this proposal: So far, almost all of the categories we have considered involve the meanings of single words (e.g., *bird* or *gift*). But Barsalou (1988) notes that there are also (in his terms) *goal-derived* categories and completely *ad hoc* categories. In the first of these, we might include "things to eat on a diet" or "things to carry out of your house in case of a fire"; in the latter group we might include "things that could fall on your head" or "things you might see while in Paris." Interestingly, these categories also turn out to have a graded membership: Subjects identify some category members as being more typical than others; they more quickly recognize the typical ones in a sentence verification task. If we interpret *graded membership* as indicating *reliance on a prototype* then, it seems, subjects must have a prototype for these categories—a prototypical thing to see in Paris, a prototypical thing that could fall on your head.

Of course, we can proliferate categories like these endlessly. (There is, for example, the category of "gifts to give one's former high-school friend who has just had her second baby.") We surely don't want to argue that subjects arrive in the laboratory with a ready-made prototype for each of these; that would be tantamount to assuming an infinite stockpile of prototypes. If categories like these do have prototypes, subjects must be making them up on the spot, in response to the experimenter's questions.

All of this implies that subjects' conceptual knowledge must include more than prototypes. For example, subjects seem, in addition, to have knowledge useful for creating these ad hoc prototypes. Prototype theory, by itself, tells us nothing about what this other knowledge might be. Moreover, we have just argued that subjects create these ad hoc prototypes *on the spot*, as needed to perform the experimental task. Having made this argument, though, what stops us from arguing in the same way for *other* prototypes—for example,

ad hoc – evidence against prototype theory

the "bird" prototype, or "dog" or "fruit"? Perhaps these, too, are created on the spot, as needed. That would certainly fit with the fact that subjects are easily able to "adjust" these prototypes to fit a new context or a new perspective. If this is right, however, then prototypes wouldn't characterize our conceptual knowledge at all. Instead, prototypes would be a form of representation that can be *created from* our conceptual knowledge.

Things look better, though, if we adopt an exemplar-based view. On this view, category judgments depend on the specific exemplars that come to mind, and we have already noted that different exemplars may come to mind on different occasions. This is because the search for remembered exemplars, like any memory search, can be influenced by various forms of cueing or priming. Thus, the set of exemplars evoked by the cue "Chinese bird" may well be different from the set evoked by the cue "bird." With different exemplars coming to mind, different judgments will be rendered. Therefore, it is certainly no surprise that typicality judgments are influenced by context.

With this view there is also no problem with ad hoc categories. In making judgments about these categories, subjects are relying on specific remembered cases (or, perhaps, specific *imagined* cases). Since there is no reliance here on prototypes, there is no issue of creating ad hoc prototypes on the spot. Indeed, using the exemplar-based view, there is no difference between how subjects judge familiar categories and how they judge ad hoc categories: In both cases, they draw on a remembered (or imagined) instance and base their judgment on that instance. It is sensible, on this account, that subjects behave similarly with familiar and unfamiliar categories.

Exemplar Use with Highly Familiar Categories

A variety of results, then, indicate that we do rely on exemplars in making category judgments. It seems certain, for a start, that we remember various exemplars we have encountered. Moreover, exemplar storage provides an easy way of talking about our knowledge of variability within a category and category pliability, as well as our sensitivity to patterns of correlation among a category's features.

In addition to these general considerations, consider the acquisition of *new* concepts. Consider, for example, a child's first trip to the zoo, and thus the child's first sight of a camel. Immediately after this encounter, the child has knowledge about a specific camel but no information about the camel category. Concretely, the child has no way of knowing whether the camel just seen was a common type or a rare type. Likewise, the child has no way of knowing which of the camel's features will be shared by others of the breed, and which features will not be shared. At least for the moment, this remembered exemplar represents the full breadth of the child's camel knowledge.

After the child has seen *several* camels, though, she can take the next step—"averaging" these together, potentially creating a camel prototype.

This example implies that novice category users are especially likely to rely on exemplars. Indeed, exemplars may be all they have, all they know about. More expert category users, however, have the option of "pooling" the various examples they have encountered, to create a prototype. We might expect that prototype use would be unlikely for novices (someone who is just learning about a category) but more likely for experts.

Several lines of evidence are consistent with this claim. The relevant studies begin with novel categories, to ensure that subjects are unfamiliar with the category at the experiment's start. For example, subjects in an experiment might learn about some category of fictional animal or perhaps some abstract category, e.g., a category of *shapes*. Subjects are then allowed to memorize instances of the category and, as their learning proceeds, subjects are periodically tested: They are presented with a novel case and asked whether the case belongs inside the category they are studying.

We can test subjects with two kinds of cases: Sometimes, we present a case that is not typical for the category, but which happens to be rather similar to an instance already studied. Stimuli of this sort will obviously resemble the studied exemplars but won't resemble the category's prototype. Therefore, subjects will do quite well with these stimuli if comparing them to exemplars; they will have more difficulty, though, if comparing them to the prototype.

Other test stimuli have these attributes reversed. These stimuli are close, in their appearance, to the category's average, and thus are typical for the category. However, these cases are carefully selected such that they don't resemble any single case that has been studied. These stimuli *do* resemble the prototype, but not the exemplars. As a consequence, these stimuli will be easily judged if compared to the prototype but not if compared to the exemplars.

Evidence suggests that subjects who are just starting to learn the category do better with stimuli resembling instances rather than the category average. With increasing expertise, however, this pattern reverses: Now subjects do better with stimuli resembling the category average, even if the stimuli bear little resemble to specific cases they have studied. This obviously fits with the sequence of learning we just sketched—exemplars early on, and then a prototype emerging as category experience increases. (For discussion and relevant data, see Homa, Sterling & Trepel, 1981; Homa, Dunbar & Nohre, 1991.)

Notice, then, that we are on the verge of a great compromise: Which is the better theory, one based on prototypes, or one based on exemplars? The answer may be that *both* theories capture an element of the truth, with subjects shifting from exemplar-based to prototype-based knowledge as they gather more and more familiarity with a concept or category.

Let us be careful, though, in what is being claimed here. As we accumulate experience with a category, we are able to abstract the prototype and to use it in making various judgments. However, this does not mean we *cease* relying on exemplar information. Instead, the evidence suggests that, with familiar categories, we use *both* sorts of information, prototypes *and* exemplars.

For example, Brooks, Norman and Allen (1991; also Brooks, 1990) have studied how expert dermatologists achieve their diagnoses. These physicians have viewed an enormous number of patients, and so they certainly have a basis for deriving a prototype for each diagnostic category. In addition, dermatologists are explicitly trained in the use of rules and definitions in achieving their diagnosis. Therefore, this seems a group highly likely to rely on abstract information in their categorization and unlikely to rely on exemplars. Nonetheless, the dermatologists show clear evidence of relying on exemplars: A correct diagnosis is more likely if the physicians have recently seen a specific case that resembles the one currently under scrutiny. Apparently, this prior case is still "fresh" in the doctors' memories and so comes readily to mind. Therefore, this prior case serves as a likely basis for analogy (and so a likely basis for *diagnosis*) for the new case now in view. Even the experts, in other words, rely on exemplars.

The Difficulties with Categorizing via Resemblance

Where are we so far? It seems clear that typicality plays a large role in our thinking about concepts and in our use of concepts. In many cases, this reflects our reliance on a prototype abstracted from our experiences with the category's members. In other cases, typicality arises from our use of specific exemplars, drawn from memory. Exemplar use is particularly likely, we have suggested, early in our learning about a category. Later on, though, we have both kinds of knowledge available to us, and we probably use both in a largely opportunistic fashion. In other words, if an object before your eyes happens to remind you of a specific prior experience, you can reason via an exemplar. If, instead, the object before you calls up some prototype knowledge, you will use that knowledge in your reasoning. In short, you will rely on whichever sort of information comes to mind more readily. (For a discussion of the principles governing how these different species of conceptual knowledge are triggered, see Whittlesea, Brooks & Westcott, 1994.) In either case, though, the process will be substantially the same, with a judgment based simply on the *resemblance* between this conceptual information, supplied by memory, and the novel case currently before you.

All of this seems straightforward enough. However, there are some observations and some results, which do not fit easily into this picture. The time has come to broaden our conception of concepts.

Odd Number, Even Number

On the views we have been developing, judgments of typicality and judgments of category membership both derive from the same source—resemblance to an exemplar or to a prototype. If the resemblance is great, then a test case will be judged to be typical and will swiftly be judged to be a category member. If the resemblance is small, then the test case will be judged atypical and probably not a category member. Thus, typicality and category membership should go hand in hand.

As we have seen, much evidence fits with this claim. It turns out, however, that we can also find situations in which there is *no relation* between typicality and category membership, and this is surely inconsistent with our claims so far. For example, Rips and Collins (1993) have shown that the factors that influence typicality judgments are often different from the factors that influence judgments of category membership. As a striking example of this pattern, consider a study by Armstrong, Gleitman and Gleitman (1983). These researchers asked their subjects to do several of the concept tasks we have been discussing—for example, sentence verification, or explicit judgments about whether individuals were typical or not for their category. The twist, though, is that Armstrong et al. used categories for which there clearly is a definition, for example, the category "odd number." As a subject, therefore, you might be told, "We all know that some numbers are odder than others. What I want you to do is to rate each of the numbers on this list for how good an example it is for the category 'odd'." Subjects felt that this was a rather silly task but, nevertheless, they were able to render these judgments and, interestingly, were just as consistent with each other using these stimuli as they were with categories like "dog" or "bird" or "fruit" (see Table 8.3).

The obvious response to this experiment is that subjects knew the definition of odd number but were somehow "playing along" in response to the experimenters' peculiar request. Even with this point acknowledged, however, the fact still remains that subjects' judgments about typicality were, in this case, "disconnected" from their judgments about category membership: They knew that all the test numbers were in the category of "odd number," but they still judged some to be more "typical" than others. Apparently, then, there is no necessary linkage between typicality and membership.

In addition, these results suggest limits on what we should conclude when we observe a typicality effect. In particular, the *presence* of a graded-membership pattern cannot imply the *absence* of other conceptual knowledge. In

Table 8.3

SUBJECTS' TYPICALITY RATINGS FOR WELL-DEFINED CATEGORIES			
Even Number		Odd Number	
Stimulus	Typicality Rating	Stimulus	Typicality Rating
4	5.9	3	5.4
8	5.5	7	5.1
10	5.3	23	4.6
18	4.4	57	4.4
34	3.6	501	3.5
106	3.1	447	3.3

Note: Subjects rated each item for how "good an example" it was for its category. Ratings were on a 0 to 7 scale, with 7 meaning the item is a "very good example." Subjects rated some even numbers as being "better examples" of even numbers than others, although, mathematically, this is absurd: Either a number is even (divisible by 2 without a remainder) or it is not.

[After Armstrong, Gleitman, & Gleitman, 1983.]

the Armstrong et al. study, we have both—graded membership *and* a definition. This is an important fact to remember when considering the many other results revealing the graded-membership pattern. These results *do* indicate that typicality is prominent in subjects' judgments, but we shouldn't conclude from this that typicality is *all* subjects know about the category.

At the same time, these results also convey a different message: Subjects in this experiment were able to judge the typicality of odd numbers with ease and consistency, effortlessly overruling what they really knew about oddness. This is important, since it suggests that thinking in terms of typicality is quite "natural" for subjects, even when this thinking is not practiced and (in this case) not even legitimate. This "naturalness" needs to be explained, and we will return to this point later in the chapter.

Lemons, Counterfeits, and the Role of History

Many results echo the messages just described: On the one side, subjects find it easy and "natural" to judge typicality. At the same time, though, subjects often find some basis for judging category membership that is independent of typicality—so that a test case can be a category member without being typical or can be typical without being a category member. This is, to be sure, peculiar if both these judgments derive from the same source.

For example, it is true that robins strike us as closer to the typical bird than penguins do. Nonetheless, most of us are quite certain that both robins and penguins are birds. Likewise, Moby Dick was definitely not a typical whale, but he certainly was a whale; Abraham Lincoln was not a typical American, but he was an American. These informal observations are easily confirmed in the laboratory. For example, subjects judge whales to be more typical of the concept "fish" than sea lampreys are. These same subjects, though, know perfectly well that sea lampreys *are* fish and whales are *not* (McCloskey & Glucksberg, 1978).

It seems, therefore, that category judgments are often *not* based on typicality. What *are* they based on? As a way of approaching the problem, let's think through some examples. Consider a lemon. Paint the lemon with red and white stripes. Is it still a lemon? Most people believe that it is. Now inject the lemon with sugar water, so that it has a sweet taste. Then run over the lemon with a truck, so that it is flat as a pancake. What have we got at this point? Do we have a striped, artificially sweet, flattened lemon? Or do we have a non-lemon? Most people still accept this poor, abused fruit as a lemon, but consider what this entails: We have taken steps to make this object more and more distant from the prototype and also very different from any specific lemon you have ever encountered (and thus very different from any remembered exemplars). But this seems not to shake our faith that the object remains a lemon. To be sure, we have a not-easily-recognized lemon, an exceptional lemon, but it is still a lemon. Apparently, one can be a lemon with virtually *no resemblance* to other lemons. (For discussion of a similar case, with category members transformed by exposure to toxic waste, see Rips, 1989a.)

Here is the opposite case. Consider a really perfect counterfeit $10 bill. This bill will be enormously similar to the prototype for a real $10 bill and highly similar to any remembered exemplar of a $10 bill. Yet we still consider it to be counterfeit, not real. Apparently, resemblance to other cases is not enough to qualify this bill for membership in the category of real money. In fact, think about the *category* "perfect counterfeit." One can certainly imagine a prototype for this category and, of course, the prototype would have to be very similar to the prototype for the category of real money. But despite this resemblance, you have no trouble keeping the categories distinct from each other: You know many things that are true for one category but not for the other, and you clearly understand, despite the near-identical prototypes, that counterfeit money is not the same thing as real money. We might be *perceptually* confused between a real bill and a counterfeit, but we are not confused about the concepts, and we certainly know when we are thinking about one and when we are thinking about the other.

These examples underscore the distinction between typicality and category membership. In the case of the lemon, we see category membership even though the test case bears no resemblance to the prototype and, indeed, no resemblance to any of the other members of the lemon category. Conversely, one can have close resemblance to category members, and high typicality, without category membership (the counterfeit bill). If we take these cases at face value, then category membership cannot rest on typicality.

But can we take these cases at face value? Perhaps these cases are too playful. Perhaps subjects think about mutilated lemons in some artificial way, differently from how they think about more conventional concepts. Similarly, perhaps the Armstrong, Gleitman and Gleitman subjects realized they were doing something bizarre in judging the odd numbers and treated the task as a game, somehow different from their customary way of thinking about concepts. So again one might ask whether the data pattern would be different with more typical concepts, in more typical settings.

Relevant evidence for this point comes from work by Keil (1986). Keil was particularly interested in how children come to have concepts, and what children's concepts do or do not include. For our purposes, this is ideal, since it allows us to ask about concept holders who are relatively untutored and relatively naive. These pre-school children have not yet learned technical definitions for their concepts, nor have they been trained to reflect on, or manipulate, their mental categories. Thus, we can use the data from children as a way of asking about concepts "uncontaminated" by education or training.

In one of Keil's studies, pre-school children were asked what it is that makes something a "coffeepot" or a "raccoon," and so on. In one aspect of the procedure, the children were asked whether it would be possible to turn a toaster into a coffeepot. Children often acknowledged that this would be possible. One would have to widen the holes in the top of the toaster and fix things so that the water would not leak out of the bottom. One would need to design a place to put the coffee grounds, and so on. But the children saw no obstacles to these various manipulations, and they were quite certain that, with these adjustments in place, one would have created a bonafide coffeepot.

Things were quite different, though, when the children were asked a parallel question, namely, whether one could, with suitable adjustments, turn a skunk into a raccoon. The children understood that we could dye the skunk's fur, teach it to climb trees, and that we could teach it to behave in a raccoonly fashion. Even with these provisions, though, the children steadfastly denied that we would have created a raccoon. A skunk who looks, sounds, and acts just like a raccoon might be a very peculiar skunk, but it is a skunk nonetheless. (For related data, see Gelman & Wellman, 1991. Walker, 1993, offers an interesting extension of Keil's findings, including data on how people from other cultures make these judgments.)

What lies behind all these judgments? If people are asked why the abused lemon still counts as a lemon, they are likely to mention the fact that it grew on a lemon tree, is genetically a lemon, and so on. It is these "deep" features that matter and not the lemon's current properties. Likewise, counterfeit money is defined as such, not because of its current attributes, but because of its history—real money was printed by the government, in special circumstances; counterfeit money was not. And so, too, for raccoons: On the child's view, being a raccoon is not merely a function of having the relevant features; there is something deeper to raccoonhood than that. What is this "something deeper"? In the eyes of the child, the key to being a raccoon involves (among other things) having a raccoon mommy and a raccoon daddy. Thus, a raccoon, just like lemons and counterfeit money, is defined in ways that refer to the creature's history.

These claims seem straightforward enough: Some properties are *essential* for being a lemon or being a raccoon and, if an object has these essential properties, it doesn't matter what the object looks like. Note, though, that these claims give rise to a further complication: These appeals to an object's *essence* depend on a web of other beliefs—beliefs about cause and effect, and beliefs about how things come to be as they are. It is not the case, for example, that you always worry about parentage in thinking about an object's categorization. For example, whether someone is a thief or not is quite independent of whether they have a thief mommy and a thief daddy. Thus, concern with a *raccoon's* parentage comes into play only because you have certain beliefs about how biological species are created and the role of inheritance in biological species. (You presumably have different beliefs about the category *thief*.) Likewise, the circumstances of printing are relevant to counterfeit bills only by virtue of other beliefs—beliefs in this case about ownership, and authenticity, and monetary systems. If a bunch of thieves printed a hundred copies of the Bible, we wouldn't refer to this as "counterfeiting." Printing circumstances matter enormously for money and matter considerably less for other publications.

Here's a different way to make the same general point: One might argue that the abused lemon doesn't resemble the lemon prototype *perceptually*, but it does resemble the lemon prototype in *the ways that matter*. For example, the abused lemon has a DNA pattern that resembles the DNA of the prototype. Likewise, the abused lemon has seeds inside it which, if planted, would grow into lemon trees; this, too, is a property of the prototype. Therefore, if we could focus on these "essential" properties, and ignore the "superficial" attributes, then we could preserve the claim that category membership depends on properties shared with the prototype or shared with exemplars. In this way, we could preserve the claim that category membership depends on resemblance.

The trick, though, lies in explaining what we mean by "resembling the prototype in the ways that matter." How is it that we manage to isolate some

properties of the prototype as essential, while disparaging other properties as superficial and pliable? To make this distinction, it seems that we would need a theory, for each concept, about how the concept's traits "bundle" together, how the traits came to be and, above all, why some traits *matter*, while others do not. In other words, we would need a web of beliefs about each concept in order to "guide" our judgments of resemblance. This simply brings us back to where we were, with categorization dependent on a widespread fabric of beliefs. With those beliefs in place, it might be possible to preserve the idea of "categorization via resemblance." Without those beliefs, categorization via resemblance just won't work.

The Complexity of Similarity

Let's take stock of where we are. Both the prototype and exemplar views depend, at their base, on judgments of resemblance—resemblance to the prototype or to some remembered instance. And there is no doubt that resemblance does have a strong influence on category judgments. Yet, as we have now seen, we can't base category membership on resemblance alone. At the least, we need some basis for "guiding" our judgments of resemblance, so that we are influenced by attributes "that really matter" but are not distracted by "superficial" attributes.

We have made this argument by appealing to some peculiar cases—mutilated lemons and transformed skunks. Even with more conventional cases, though, it turns out that categorization-via-resemblance is a problematic idea because, when closely examined, *resemblance* is a problematic idea. For example, subjects judge *snake* and *raccoon* to be rather dissimilar from each other. However, if both are put in the context of "pet," then their perceived similarity increases appreciably (e.g., Barsalou, 1982). Both are perceived as atypical but possible pets and, in the process, their similarity to each other goes up. Likewise for *Italy* and *Switzerland*: These countries are judged to be rather different from each other, but their similarity goes up if we make it a three-way comparison, among, let's say, *Italy*, *Switzerland*, and *Brazil*. This third country calls attention to the attribute shared by the first two, "in Europe." This attribute initially contributed little to the perceived similarity between Italy and Switzerland but, given the appropriate context, it can play a large role (Tversky, 1977).

Apparently, then, we can't rely on similarity as a stable and solid base on which to build category judgments. Instead, similarity seems quite flexible, and certainly context-dependent. In the same vein, consider *plums* and *lawn mowers*. How similar are these to each other? Actually, these two have a great deal in common: Both weigh less than a ton, both are found on earth, both cannot hear well, both have an odor, both are used by people, both can be

dropped, both cost less than a thousand dollars, and so on. (For discussion, see Goodman, 1972; Medin & Ortony, 1989; Medin, Goldstone & Gentner, 1993.) Of course, we ignore most of these shared features in judging these two entities and so, as a result, we regard plums and lawn mowers as rather different from each other. But that brings us back to a familiar question: How do we decide which features to ignore, when assessing similarity, and which features to consider? How do we decide which features are essential, and which superficial, which attributes are important, and which trivial?

Of course, we have already suggested an answer to these questions: A decision about which features are trivial, and which are crucial, depends, at least in part, on your *beliefs* about the concept in question. We know, for example, that what matters for being a lawn mower is suitability for getting a particular job done. Costing less than a thousand dollars is irrelevant to this function. (Imagine a lawn mower covered with diamonds.) Therefore, cost is an unimportant feature for lawn mowers.

Cost is a critical attribute, however, for other categories (consider the category "luxury item"). Similarly, we were unimpressed by the fact that plums and lawn mowers both weigh less than a ton: Weight is not critical for either of these categories. But weight is crucial in other settings (imagine a paper-weight made out of gaseous helium). Apparently, then, the importance of an attribute—cost, or weight, or whatever—varies from category to category, and varies, in particular, according to your beliefs about what matters for that category. Likewise, the attributes that matter, for judging similarity, will vary from category to category.

To tie this back to issues of categorization, imagine that a furry creature stands before you, and you reason, "This creature reminds me of the animal I saw in the zoo yesterday. The sign at the zoo indicated that the animal was a gnu, so this must be one, too." This sounds like a simple case of categorization via exemplars. But, of course, the creature before your eyes is not a "perfect match" for the gnu in the zoo, and so you might reason this way, "The gnu in the zoo was a different color, and slightly smaller. But I bet that does not matter. Despite the new hue, this is a gnu, too."

In this case, you have decided that color isn't a critical feature, and you categorize despite the contrast on this dimension. Things will go differently, though, in this case: "This stone in my hand reminds me of the ruby I saw yesterday. Therefore, I bet this is a ruby, too. Of course, the ruby I saw yesterday was red, and this stone is green, but. . . ." You surely would *not* draw this analogy because, in this case, you know that it is wrong to ignore hue. Rubies are red. If a stone isn't red, it isn't a ruby. Color might not matter for gnus, but it does matter here, and our category judgments respect this fact.

The Mutual Dependence of Categorization and Resemblance

Let's put all these pieces together: For cases like the mutilated lemon or the disguised raccoon, subjects seem to make their categorization judgments on some basis *other than* resemblance (again, either resemblance to the prototype or resemblance to exemplars). Instead, subjects seem guided by a web of interconnected beliefs, beliefs that somehow specify the "essence" of being a lemon or the "essence" of being a raccoon. Or, to put this differently, we can *preserve* the claim that subjects categorize according to resemblance *if* we can somehow discriminate between the attributes that "matter" and the attributes that don't. But here, too, we need a web of interconnected beliefs, specifying what is "essential" for each concept.

One might be skeptical about these peculiar examples but, as we have now seen, the same concerns emerge when we consider entirely mundane examples. *Any* judgment of resemblance, it seems, depends on a decision about which attributes matter and which don't. That is why plums and lawn mowers seem so different from each other, despite their shared attributes. And that is why, in categorizing gnus, we decide that color doesn't matter, whereas, in categorizing rubies, we make the opposite decision. Once again, it seems, we rely on a web of beliefs, specifying what is "essential" for these concepts and what's not.

We obviously need to say more about what these beliefs are and what they involve. Before that, though, two points: First, notice that we risk a contradiction in the argument being developed: Categorization, in many circumstances, depends on a comparison between a test candidate and some representation in memory. If there is resemblance between these, then we count the candidate as a member of the relevant category. Hence, categorization depends on resemblance. We have now argued, though, that to judge resemblance one first needs to decide which features are important and which are not, and this decision, in turn, depends on the particular categories being evaluated. (Color is crucial for rubies, not for gnus; cost is crucial for the category "luxury item," but not for plums.)

However, there may be no contradiction here. It may turn out that a preliminary assessment of similarity is made, in categorizing objects, which allows a tentative categorization. This, in turn, allows a determination of which features are crucial and which not, which leads to a more accurate assessment of similarity and thus to a final categorization. (For further discussion of similarity, see Goldstone, 1994; Goldstone & Medin, 1994; Heit & Rubinstein, 1994; Keil, 1979; Komatsu, 1992.)

Second, we have emphasized the role of beliefs *in our initial categoriza-*

tion—when we are deciding, for example, whether an animal is a gnu, whether a stone is a ruby. The same considerations arise, though, when we use our conceptual knowledge in other ways. For example, if we encounter a single gnu, and discover it likes to eat oats, we are willing to extrapolate this property to other gnus. If we discover, in addition, that this particular gnu has a red-haired keeper, we are likely *not* to extrapolate this property. Here, too, we seem guided by other knowledge, other beliefs—in this case, beliefs about which features are directly derived from gnu-hood, and which features are likely to be accidental. And this is knowledge, once again, not captured within prototypes or exemplars.

Concepts as "Implicit Theories"

How should we characterize these other beliefs about concepts, and the other conceptual knowledge, which has repeatedly entered our discussion? And, within this broader context, what role is played by prototypes and exemplars?

Identification Heuristics

In earlier chapters, we noted that the world provides us with a vast quantity of information. At any point in time, many stimuli are in view; moreover, there are many aspects of each stimulus that we could focus on if we so choose. All of this is compounded by the rich quantity of information available to us from memory, again providing us with a large number of things we could think about and a large number of things we could attend.

This informational wealth can easily create information *overload*, since we do not have correspondingly large quantities of time, attention, or working memory. These resources are in short supply, creating a strong pressure toward **cognitive economy**. That is, we are amply motivated to preserve our resources by using short-cuts whenever possible and by using strategies that are maximally efficient.

These short-cuts are often called **heuristics**. For now, heuristics can be defined as strategies that are reasonably efficient and work most of the time. Note the implied trade-off here: If you want a strategy that will always work, a strategy that will never lead you astray, you may need a strategy that is relatively laborious, relatively inefficient. Thus, a heuristic strategy tolerates occasional error, in order to gain efficiency overall. This trade-off, between efficiency and accuracy, should look familiar to you, since it was a prominent feature in Chapters 2 and 4. Indeed, this trade-off is an important feature of our mental lives and will come up again in several other contexts.

Returning to present concerns, our proposal should be obvious: The use of typicality in judging concepts is one of the mental short-cuts we often rely on. Why is this efficient? First, judgments about typicality draw on only *part* of our conceptual knowledge, so there is less information to retrieve from memory and less information to consider. Second, it seems plausible that typicality is often judged on the basis of relatively superficial features rather than on the basis of more abstract knowledge about a category. This emphasis on superficial characteristics is precisely what we want for a categorization heuristic: These traits can generally be judged swiftly, allowing comparisons to be made quickly and efficiently.

Like any heuristic, however, the use of typicality will occasionally lead to error: If you rely on the bird prototype to categorize flying creatures, you may misidentify a bat. That is the price one pays for heuristic use. If the heuristic is well-chosen, though, these errors will be relatively rare; otherwise, the efficiency is purchased at too high a price. But here, too, a reliance on typicality seems sensible. Prototypes, by their very nature, represent the most common features of a category, and so prototypes will be representative of most category members. Categorization via prototypes will usually be accurate—most members of the category *do* resemble the prototype, even though some members do not. The same considerations apply to a reliance on exemplars: As we have seen, the exemplars coming to mind will usually be examples of *typical* category members and so, more often than not, will resemble the new category members you encounter.

This view of things, therefore, preserves a central insight of both the prototype and exemplar views: As we have seen again and again, we cannot equate "goodness of example" with "membership in a category." An individual (e.g., the abused lemon) can be a member of a category even if it is a poor example of the category; likewise, an individual can closely resemble a category's ideal but not be in the category (e.g., a perfect counterfeit). At the same time, though, "membership" and "exemplariness" are clearly related to each other, and this is critical for the heuristic idea. Creatures closely resembling a robin are not guaranteed to be birds, but they are highly likely to be birds, and it is this which allows us to use typicality as a fast and efficient basis for judging membership.

Mental Models, Implicit Theories

The previous section gives us a picture of what role prototypes and exemplars serve, and therefore why they are so important: These representations provide us with an "identification heuristic," useful for efficient recognition of category members. Over and over, though, we have argued that there is more to category knowledge than this. What is the "more"?

We have already seen a broad set of hints about this issue: Subjects' understanding of a concept seems to depend on a network of interwoven beliefs, and these beliefs, in turn, draw on a number of other concepts: To understand what counterfeit is, one needs to know what money is, and probably what a government is, and what crime is. To understand what a raccoon is, one needs to understand what parents are and, with that, one needs to know some facts about life cycles, and heredity, and the like.

Perhaps, therefore, we need a different approach. We have been trying, throughout this chapter, to characterize concepts one by one, as though each concept could be characterized independently of other concepts. We talked about the prototype for *bird*, for example, without any thought about how this prototype is related to the *animal* prototype or to the *egg* prototype. Perhaps, though, we need a more holistic approach, so that we will characterize each concept by characterizing a wide network of beliefs in which that concept is embedded.

Consider the concept "blood pressure." It would be surprising if this concept could be characterized in isolation from a set of other terms, terms such as "circulation" or "heart" or "arteries." To understand blood pressure, one must understand these other terms, and one needs a web of beliefs about how these various terms are interrelated (Banks, Thompson, Henry & Weissmann, 1986; Carey, 1985). This set of beliefs is surely less sophisticated, and probably less accurate, than a medically correct, scientific model of blood pressure. Nonetheless, our beliefs serve the same function as a scientific model: These beliefs unify our understanding of these various terms and provide a global cause-and-effect account that corresponds to our understanding of the processes involved.

There have been several proposals for how this web of beliefs should be characterized. Neisser (1987) has proposed that these beliefs can be thought of as an implicit "theory" about the relevant subject matter, a theory that the individual holds about how the various terms are interconnected. Lakoff (1987) has offered a related notion defined as an "idealized cognitive model." Several psychologists have explored the idea of a "mental model" (Gentner & Stevens, 1983), with this model embodying our set of beliefs about the terms in question. (Also see Johnson-Laird, 1987; Keil, 1989; Komatsu, 1992; Medin & Ortony, 1989; Rips & Collins, 1993; for some of the philosophical roots of these arguments, see Kripke, 1972; Putnam, 1975.)

Implicit theories seem essential for describing complex concepts such as blood pressure. It may turn out, though, that we also need implicit theories to describe seemingly simpler concepts. Our discussion so far in this chapter has clearly pointed in this direction. As a different example, consider the concept "drunk" (after Medin & Ortony, 1989). Jumping into a pool with your clothes on is surely not a defining feature of being drunk; it is probably not even a typical feature. Nonetheless, this behavior is certainly indicative of being drunk, thanks to a variety of other causal beliefs we have about how drunks behave. In effect, each of us has a "theory" about drunkenness—what being drunk will cause you do, what it will cause you *not* to do—and we rely on this theory in identifying someone who is drunk, and in reasoning about their behavior.

A different example is the term "bachelor." This noun is a particularly interesting example, since the term seems to be easily defined: A bachelor is an unmarried adult male. However, it turns out that here, too, we seem to need some sort of implicit theory, since being a bachelor can, in fact, only be understood in the context of certain expectations about marriage and marriageable age (cf. Fillmore, 1982). The examples in Figure 8.5 will help make this clear. As you read these examples, your judgments about each case are guided by a rich understanding of who is eligible to marry and who is likely to marry. Thus, understanding even a term like bachelor may depend on a mental model, in this case a model that encompasses your understanding of matrimonial customs in our culture. (For related examples, see Lakoff, 1987; Neisser, 1987.)

Implicit Theories and Schemata

So far, we have said little about what an implicit theory *is*. How is our network of beliefs about, say, blood pressure or drunkenness represented in the mind? Researchers have offered a variety of proposals, and there is no clear consensus on which of these is best. In what follows, therefore, we will describe one way these claims *might* be fleshed out; we emphasize that this is only an illustration, and other conceptions are possible.

In Chapter 6, we emphasized that each of us has a great deal of generic knowledge, which we use to guide and supplement our interactions with the world. This knowledge, we suggested, was encoded in mental "schemata" (or, in the case of knowledge about *events*, encoded in "scripts"). Schemata often specify the interrelations among diverse concepts, and this implies that the contents of a schema may not be very different from the contents of what we are now calling, in this chapter, an implicit theory. In fact, our suggestion is that schemata and implicit theories are roughly the same thing. More precisely, schemata provide the means through which these theories are represented in the mind.

Let's be a little more specific about how schemata function. Within the schema view, one understands new information by virtue of fitting that in-

Figure 8.5

WHAT MAKES SOMEONE A BACHELOR?

VARIOUS POTENTIAL BACHELORS

Alfred is an unmarried adult male, but he has been living with his girlfriend for the last 23 years. Their relationship is happy and stable. Is Alfred a bachelor?

Bernard is an unmarried adult male and does not have a partner. But Bernard is a monk, living in a monastery. Is Bernard a bachelor?

Charles is a married adult male, but he has not seen his wife for many years; Charles is earnestly dating, hoping to find a new partner. Is Charles a bachelor?

Donald is a married adult male, but he lives in a culture that encourages males to take two wives. Donald is earnestly dating, hoping to find a new partner. Is Donald a bachelor?

The term "bachelor" is often considered to have a firm definition: A bachelor is an unmarried adult male. However, this noun can be understood only in the context of certain expectations about marriage and marriageable age. As you read the examples shown here, think about what it is that guides your judgments. [After Fillmore, 1982.]

formation into a schematic frame. This implies that the schema has slots or openings into which the new information can be placed. Many theorists implement this idea by defining the schema in terms of *variables*, not fixed information (see Rumelhart & Ortony, 1977). In the case of the kitchen schema, for example, there is no representation of a specific stove. Instead, there is a "marker" standing for some to-be-specified stove. Likewise, there is a marker standing for some to-be-specified countertop appliance, a marker standing for some to-be-specified kitchen table, and so on. When we are thinking about, or looking at, a specific kitchen, these variables are filled in to reflect the particular kitchen under scrutiny. When we are thinking about kitchens in general, these variables will be left open.

Moreover, the variables within a schema do not have equal status. Some (for example, the stove) are designated as "obligatory"—they are more or less necessary and so must be filled in when we are thinking about a particular kitchen. Presumably, these "obligatory" variables play an important part in giving the schema its identity. This is why we would say that kitchen-without-a-toaster is still a kitchen; it is, so to speak, only a minor variation on "kitchenhood." Kitchen-without-a-place-to-prepare-food, however, is a contradiction in terms. Note, however, that we cannot be rigid when we speak of these variables as "obligatory." Just as definitions are hard to find, because one can routinely find exceptions, so also are "obligatory" features. Hence, "obligatory" here needs to be toned down to "extremely likely."

Other variables, such as the countertop appliance, are "optional"—they may or may not be filled in when we are thinking about a specific kitchen or exploring a new kitchen. These variables usually have **default values**—values we automatically fill in unless we have some reason to the contrary. For example, it is a good bet that a kitchen table is present, although not all kitchens have tables. Hence, the default here is to assume a kitchen table of standard size, unless otherwise informed.

How is all of this information represented in the mind? In Chapter 7, we suggested that much of our knowledge can be represented via a network of associations, and this idea will serve us well here: The network allows us to interconnect various elements of our knowledge, for example, to interconnect the various aspects of the kitchen schema. In this way, we can start building our way toward a fabric of interconnections among concepts, just as we need. We also saw in Chapter 7 that propositions can be represented within the network, allowing us to represent beliefs.

Notice, then, where we are going: To represent concepts, we have suggested, we need to represent the interconnections among related concepts. A network representation of schematic knowledge surely provides these interconnections. Likewise, to represent concepts, we need to represent certain beliefs—e.g., our belief that "raccoonhood" is an inherited trait. This, too, can be done in network terms, if (for example) we represent the belief as a proposition.

Prototypes, Exemplars, and Schematic Knowledge

The claim before us is that a network of associations provides a plausible way to represent these implicit theories. Various beliefs within the theory can be described in terms of propositions, and these can be represented, as we saw in Chapter 7, in terms of labeled associations. By using *variables* within this network, we can allow the associations to represent generic knowledge rather than specific cases. When we encounter a specific case, or when we wish to think about a specific case, we can replace the variables with particular values—a particular stove, a particular sink—and in this fashion we can link our general knowledge to a specific instance.

Recall also that variables within a schematic frame have a "default" value, a value taken if no other information is available. Default values presumably represent the typical way a variable is filled in. Thus, by setting the variables to the default value, we are describing the typical form for the schema or script. In short, one can use a schema, with its default values, to represent a prototype.

This approach easily allows us to explain how subjects can adjust their prototypes to fit one situation or another, or to change perspective. If prototypes are generated by replacing the variables with specific values, then adjustments are possible simply by choosing different values rather than the defaults. Thus, the flexibility of prototypes derives from the fact that conceptual knowledge is framed in terms of variables, allowing us to shift the prototype into other forms as the situation demands. (For further discussion of the relation between concepts and schemata, see Komatsu, 1992.)

Is this the right way to think about conceptual knowledge and about implicit theories? We noted early on that there is disagreement about these points, and perhaps this is inevitable since, as we saw in Chapter 7, there is disagreement in the field about whether networks provide an adequate way to describe *any* knowledge. More specifically, there is surely room for debate about whether schemata are rich enough and precise enough to do the job of representing implicit theories. For example, notions like *mechanism* or *explanation* or *causality* are presumably crucial for our implicit theories, and it is not obvious how (or whether) these notions might be represented in schematic terms.

For now, therefore, let's keep our claims modest. We need some way of distinguishing a concept's essential features from its trivial features; otherwise, we fail to explain even simple cases of categorization with perfectly ordinary concepts. Implicit theories, linking the concept to other concepts, would help us with this crucial issue. Likewise, we need some way of explaining how subjects *reason* about their concepts, and what inferences they draw about specific cases. Here, too, implicit theories seem to be involved. This is reflected both in the inferences subjects draw about category members (e.g., what features they generalize, what features they don't), and also in how subjects *talk* about their concepts, when they are asked to reason out loud.

What are these implicit theories? At the very least, these theories specify a network of interconnected beliefs about how certain concepts are related to each other. These theories also specify cause-and-effect relations, such as how one comes to be a raccoon, or how one comes to be "counterfeit." These cause-and-effect relations would also explain why you are certain that an airplane made out of fine porcelain would be a bad idea and likewise a fireplace sculpted out of ice.

What is less clear, though, is exactly how these theories are represented in the mind. We have provided one illustration of how this representation might go, but we have acknowledged problems for this proposal, and other approaches may turn out to be more promising. Against this backdrop, though, let us not lose sight of one very important claim: Even for the simplest cases, the simplest examples, human generic knowledge is impressively complex. To put it bluntly, none of the questions we might ask about generic knowledge receives a simple, one-part answer. Considering that our use of this knowledge seems effortless and ubiquitous, this gives us both an indication of the complexity of cognitive processes and of the remarkable complexity of our species.

9

Language

One type of knowledge seems worth singling out for special consideration—our knowledge of language. What does it mean to "know a language"? Obviously, one has to know the vocabulary and how to assemble the vocabulary items into coherent sentences. One also needs to know how to decipher sentences produced by others. But what does all of this involve?

Scholars have long been intrigued by language, and it's not hard to see why. Virtually every human being knows and uses a language; some of us know and use several languages. Indeed, to find a human *without* language, we need to seek out people in extraordinary circumstances—people who have suffered serious brain damage or people who have grown up completely isolated from other humans. In sharp contrast, no other species has and uses a language comparable to ours in complexity, sophistication, or communicative power (cf. Demers, 1989). In a real sense, knowing a language is a key part of being a human: a near-universal achievement in our species, yet unknown, in its full-blown form, in any other species.

Language seems no less central if we consider how language is *used* and what language makes possible. We use language to convey our ideas to each other, and our wishes, and our needs. Without language, our social interactions would be grossly impoverished, and cooperative endeavors would be a thousand times more difficult. Without language, the transmission of information, and the acquisition of knowledge, would be enormously impaired. (How much have you learned by listening to others or by reading?) Without language, there would be no science and no culture. Language is at the heart of, and essential for, a huge range of human activities and achievements.

What is this tool, therefore, that is universal for our species, unique to our species, and crucial for much of what our species does? We actually know an enormous amount about language and, indeed, the study of language constitutes an important and distinct academic discipline, **linguistics**. At the boundary between linguistics and psychology stands a separate area of study, called **psycholinguistics**, which is concerned with how linguistic knowledge is acquired, represented, and used by the human mind. In this chapter, we will provide a broad overview of psycholinguistic research. We begin with a consideration of the *sounds* of language—the domain of **phonology**.

Phonology

It is convenient to think of language as having a hierarchical structure (Figure 9.1). At the top of the hierarchy, there are sentences—coherent sequences of words that express the intended meaning of a speaker. Sentences are com-

Figure 9.1

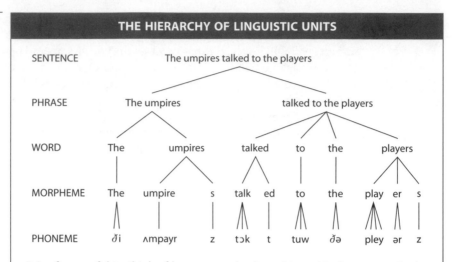

THE HIERARCHY OF LINGUISTIC UNITS

It is often useful to think of language as having a hierarchical structure. At the top of the hierarchy, there are sentences. These are composed of phrases, which are themselves composed of words. The words are composed of morphemes, the smallest language units that carry meaning. When the morphemes are pronounced, the units of sound are called phonemes. In describing phonemes, the symbols correspond to the actual sounds produced, independent of how these sounds are expressed in ordinary writing.

posed of phrases, which are in turn composed of words. Words are composed of **morphemes**, the smallest language units that carry meaning. Meaning is largely carried by **content morphemes**, such as "umpire" or "talk" in the figure. However, **function morphemes** also add information crucial for interpretation, signaling the relations among words and also providing information about a word's grammatical role within a sentence. Examples of function morphemes are the past-tense morpheme "ed" or the plural morpheme "s".

In spoken language, morphemes are conveyed by sounds called **phonemes**. Some phonemes are easily represented by letters of the alphabet, but others are not, and that is why the symbols look strange in the figure's bottom row—the symbols correspond to the actual sounds produced, independent of how those sounds are expressed in our (or any) alphabet.

The Production of Speech

How are phonemes produced? In ordinary breathing, air flows quietly out of the lungs, through the larynx, and up through the nose and mouth (Figure

9.2). However, noises are produced if this passageway is constricted in a fashion that impedes or interrupts the airflow. There are many forms of this constriction, allowing humans to produce a wide range of different sounds. It is this variety of sounds that makes speech possible.

For example, within the larynx there are two flaps of muscular tissue called the "vocal folds." (These structures are also called the "vocal cords," although they are not cords at all.) The vocal folds can be rapidly opened and closed, producing a buzzing sort of vibration known as **voicing**. You can feel this vibration by putting your palm on your throat while you produce a [z] sound. You will feel no vibration, though, if you hiss like a snake, producing a sustained [s] sound. The [z] sound is voiced, the [s] is not.

Sound can also be produced by narrowing the air passageway within the mouth itself. For example, hiss like a snake again, and pay attention to your tongue's position. To produce this sound, you have placed your tongue's tip

Figure 9.2

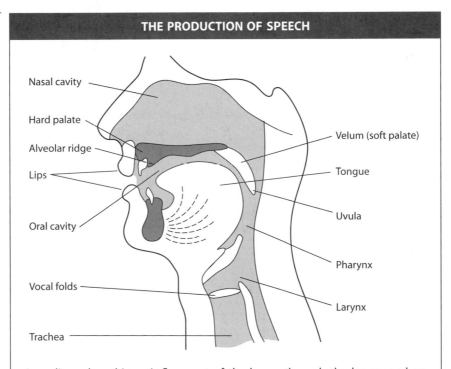

THE PRODUCTION OF SPEECH

Nasal cavity

Hard palate

Alveolar ridge

Lips

Oral cavity

Vocal folds

Trachea

Velum (soft palate)

Tongue

Uvula

Pharynx

Larynx

In ordinary breathing, air flows out of the lungs, through the larynx, and up through the nose and mouth. To produce speech, this passageway must be constricted in a fashion that impedes or interrupts the airflow. For example, the uvula can be closed, to block air from moving into the nasal cavity. Likewise, the tongue and lips control the movement of air through the oral cavity.

near the roof of your mouth, just behind your teeth. The [s] sound is the sound of the air rushing through the narrow gap you have created.

If the gap is elsewhere, a different sound results. For example, to produce the "sh" sound (as in "shoot" or "shine"), the tongue is positioned so that it creates a narrow gap a bit further back in the mouth; air rushing through this gap causes the desired sound. Alternatively, the narrow gap can be more toward the front. Pronounce an [f] sound; in this case, the sound is produced by air rushing between your bottom lip and your top teeth.

Other sounds are produced by air moving through the nose rather than the mouth. Try humming an [m] sound while opening and closing your lips. This will cause some changes in the quality of the sound, but there is no interruption in the sound when your lips close. But now try humming an [m] sound and, while humming, pinch your nose shut. With air unable to move through your nose, the sound ceases.

All these aspects of speech production allow us to *categorize* the various speech sounds. Thus, linguists distinguish, first, between sounds that are *voiced*—produced with the vocal folds vibrating—and those that are not. The sounds of [v], [z], and [n] (to name a few) are voiced; [f], [s], [t], and [k] are unvoiced. (You can confirm this by running the hand-on-throat test while producing each of these sounds.) Second, sounds can be categorized according to *where* the airflow is restricted; this is referred to as **place of articulation**. Thus, you close your lips to produce "bilabial" sounds, like [p] or [b]; you place your top teeth close to your bottom lip to produce "labiodental" sounds, like [f] or [v]; and you place your tongue just behind your upper teeth to produce "alveolar" sounds, like [t] or [d].

Sounds can also be categorized according to *how* the airflow is restricted. This is referred to as **manner of production**. Thus, as we have seen, air is allowed to move through the nose for some speech sounds but not for others. Similarly, for some speech sounds, the flow of air is fully stopped for a moment—for example, [p], [b], and [t]. For other sounds, the air passage is restricted, but some air continues to flow (e.g., [f], [z], and [r]).

This categorization scheme allows us to describe any speech sound in terms of a few simple features. For example, the [p] sound is produced (1) without voicing, (2) with air moving through the mouth (not the nose), and with a full interruption to the flow of air, and (3) with a bilabial place of articulation. If any of these features change—voicing, manner of production, or place of articulation—so does the sound's identity.

Put differently, these few features, in varying combinations, allow us to make all the sounds our language needs. In English, these features are combined and re-combined to produce 40 or so different phonemes. Other languages use as few as a dozen phonemes; still others, many more. (For example, there are 141 different phonemes in the language of Khoisan, spoken by the

"Bushmen"—Halle, 1990.) In all cases, though, the phonemes are created by simple combinations of the features just described.

The Complexity of Speech Perception

These features of speech production also correspond to what listeners *hear* when they are listening to speech. Thus, phonemes that differ only in one production feature sound similar to each other; phonemes that differ in multiple features sound more distinct. This is reflected in the pattern of *errors* subjects make, when they try to understand speech in a noisy environment. Subjects' misperceptions are usually off by just one feature, so that [p] is confused with [b] (a difference only in voicing), [p] with [t] (a difference only in place of articulation), and so on (Miller & Nicely, 1955; Wang & Bilger, 1973).

This makes it seem like the perception of speech may be a straightforward matter: A small number of features is sufficient to characterize any particular speech sound. All the perceiver needs to do, therefore, is detect these features and, with this done, the speech sounds are identified.

As it turns out, though, speech perception is far more complicated than this. For one problem, consider Figure 9.3, which shows the moment-by-moment sound amplitudes produced by a speaker uttering a brief greeting.

Figure 9.3

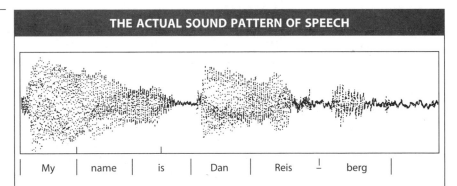

THE ACTUAL SOUND PATTERN OF SPEECH

| My | name | is | Dan | Reis | berg |

This figure shows the moment-by-moment sound amplitudes produced by a speaker uttering a greeting. Notice that there is no gap between the sounds carrying the word "my" and the sounds carrying "name." Nor is there a gap between the sounds carrying "name" and the sounds carrying "is." Therefore, the listener needs to figure out where one sound stops and the next begins, a process known as segmentation.

It is these amplitudes, in the form of air-pressure changes, that reach the ear and so, in an important sense, the figure shows the pattern of input with which "real" speech perception begins.

Notice that, within this stream of speech, there are no markers to indicate where one phoneme ends and the next begins. Likewise, there are often no gaps, or signals of any sort, to indicate the boundaries between successive syllables or successive words. Thus, as a first step *prior* to phoneme identification, you need to "slice" this stream into the appropriate segments—a step known as **speech segmentation**.

For many people, this pattern comes as a surprise. As perceivers of speech, we are usually convinced that there are pauses between words, marking the word boundaries. This turns out to be an illusion, and we are "hearing" pauses that, in truth, aren't there. The illusion is revealed when we physically measure the speech stream (as we did, in order to create Figure 9.3) or when we listen to speech we can't understand—for example, speech in a foreign language. In this latter circumstance, we lack the skill needed to segment the stream, and thus we are unable to "supply" the word boundaries. As a consequence, we hear what is really there—a continuous, uninterrupted flow of sound. That is why speech in a foreign language often sounds so fast.

Speech perception is further complicated by a phenomenon known as **coarticulation** (Liberman, 1970; also Daniloff & Hammarberg, 1973). This term refers to the fact that, in producing speech, one does not utter one phoneme at a time. Instead, the phonemes "overlap." Thus, while you are producing the [s] sound in "soup," your mouth is already getting ready to say the vowel. While uttering the vowel, you are already starting to move your tongue and lips and teeth into position for producing the [p].

This overlap in production allows speech to be faster and considerably more fluent. But this overlap also has important consequences for the sounds produced, and so the [s] produced while getting ready for one upcoming vowel is actually different from the [s] produced while getting ready for a different vowel. As a result, we can't point to a specific acoustical pattern and say, "This is the pattern of an [s] sound." Instead, the acoustical pattern is different in different contexts. Speech perception therefore has to "read past" these context differences, in order to identify the phonemes produced.

Speech sounds also vary in many other ways: For example, each of us has our own individual speech habits; and each of us has a slightly different shaped mouth, and slightly different shaped tongue. As a result, there is some variation, from one speaker to the next, in how each word is pronounced. However, this change in acoustical properties does not change the identities of the phonemes involved. Hence, this variation must be ignored in the process of identifying phonemes and in the process of recognizing speech.

Aids to Speech Perception

These complications—the need for segmentation in a continuous speech stream; the variations caused by coarticulation; and the variations from speaker to speaker or from occasion to occasion—render speech perception surprisingly complex. As one measure of this complexity, note that speech recognition *by machine* is still relatively primitive. Speech recognition programs do exist but are quite limited. Some of these programs "understand" a wide range of speech but only from a single speaker. (That is, the programs have great difficulty with speaker-to-speaker variation.) Other programs can "understand" many different speakers but can only handle a limited vocabulary.

Obviously, though, humans manage quite well to perceive speech. How do we do it? Several mechanisms contribute. For one, we are generally able to supplement what we hear with expectations and knowledge, and this guides our interpretation of difficult-to-perceive speech. Note the similarity between this claim and our arguments about reading, in Chapter 2: There we noted that reading typically involves a considerable amount of inference, with "top-down" processes working to fill in information about letters you have barely glanced at. In the same fashion, top-down processes in speech perception allow you to identify phonemes that are unclear in the sound-stream.

In Chapter 2, we pointed to proofreading errors as one manifestation of this inferential process: In proofreading, one "sees" what one expects to see and thus misses the misspelled word, or the misformed phrase. A parallel phenomenon is evident in speech perception, and this phenomenon was also discussed in Chapter 2: In the so-called restoration effect, subjects "hear" speech sounds that were not presented. This provides clear evidence for inference and extrapolation in speech perception.

In many cases, the inferences used to guide speech perception rely on knowledge external to language. For example, if you hear me say, "He put mustard on his [cough] dog," you easily infer what the missing word is, thanks to your knowledge of the popular foods of our culture. In other cases, though, the inferences are guided by redundancies inside of language—that is, the fact that many phonemes are predictable, given the surrounding phonemes and the vocabulary (and structure) of English.

We will provide some examples of these redundancies later on when we consider how phonemes are (and are not) combined. In the meantime, though, we can ask how much we are helped by these redundancies and by context overall. Pollack and Pickett (1964) tape-recorded a number of naturally occurring conversations. From these recordings, they spliced out individual words and presented these, now in isolation, to their subjects. Remarkably, subjects were unable to identify half of these words. If restored to their context, though, these same stimuli were easy to identify.

Our chore of recognizing speech is also helped by the fact that the speech we encounter, from day to day, tends to be rather limited in its range. Each of us knows tens of thousands of different words, but most of these words are rarely used. In fact, it has been estimated that the 50 most commonly used words in English make up more than half of the words we actually utter. (After Miller, 1951. For discussion of other top-down effects in speech perception, see Cole & Jakimik, 1980; Garnes & Bond, 1976; Samuel, 1986.)

Categorical Perception

Apparently, then, the incoming speech signal is predictable in important ways: A relatively small number of words, it seems, get used over and over. The structure of the language adds further predictability and so does the meaningful context. All of this can then be exploited by speech perception via inferential processes that supplement the information actually reaching the ear.

However, let's not put too much weight on these inferential processes. Humans are, in addition, exquisitely talented in deriving information from the speech signal. Indeed, there is every indication that we have evolved highly specialized mechanisms for this purpose and, more broadly, specialized mechanisms for the perception, acquisition, and use of language. (We will describe some of these specializations later in the chapter.)

The power of our speech recognition abilities is well revealed in the phenomenon of **categorical perception**. This refers to our tendency to hear speech sounds "merely" as members of a category—the category of [z] sounds or the category of [p] sounds. More precisely, we are quite adept at hearing differences *between* categories, but we are relatively *insensitive* to variations *within* the category. Thus, we easily hear the difference between a [p] and a [b], but we are rather inept in distinguishing one [p] from the next or one [z] from the next. Of course, this insensitivity is precisely what we want, since it allows us to separate the wheat from the chaff: We easily detect what category a sound belongs in, but we are virtually oblivious to the inconsequential (and potentially distracting) background variations.

Let's examine categorical perception in terms of an example. Consider the consonants [p] and [b]. Both of these are "bilabial" consonants (that is the "place of articulation"), and both are "stops" (that is the "manner of production"). In other words, both involve a complete interruption of the flow of air, caused by closing the lips. These consonants differ, though, on the feature of voicing—[b] is voiced, [p] is not. But let's be more precise about what that means: Place your hand flat on your throat, and pronounce the word "pit." If you pay close attention, you will notice that the sound of the word begins slightly *before* you feel the vibration in your throat. In fact, there is (approximately) a 60 msec gap between the word's start (i.e., when you release your lips, which is when the air starts moving) and the onset of voicing. In other words, there is a 60 msec **voice-onset time**, or **VOT**.

Place your hand on your throat again, and now pronounce the word "bit." This time, you will detect no gap between the word's start and onset of voicing. For the phoneme [b], the VOT is essentially zero. (We note in passing that English uses only these two VOTs—one of 60 msec or so, and one of zero. Other languages use other VOTs. Many Asian languages, for example, use *negative* VOTs, so that the vocal folds start vibrating slightly *before* the air is released.)

What about "compromise" VOTs? With the aid of a computer, we can create synthetic speech with any specifications we like. Thus we can ask: How will (English-speaking) subjects perceive a bilabial stop with a 30 msec voice-onset time? Acoustically, this stimulus is midway between an ordinary [b] and an ordinary [p]. Will subjects perceive it as midway between these syllables? Will they perceive it as a sort-of-p, sort-of-b? Or will they perhaps be uncertain about what the sound is? Likewise, how will subjects perceive a "compromise" between a [t] and [d]? (Again, these two consonants differ only in VOT.) Or between [f] and [v]?

To address these questions, let's consider a *series* of compromise sounds, created via synthetic speech. Thus, one of our stimuli might be a bilabial stop with a zero VOT. (This is an ordinary [b] sound.) Another stimulus might be a bilabial stop with a 10 msec VOT (this is a [b] with the voicing just slightly delayed). Another stimulus might have a 20 msec VOT; one might have a 30 msec VOT (that is our balanced compromise between [b] and [p]); and so on, up to a bilabial stop with a 60 msec VOT (that is, an ordinary [p]). We can now attach a vowel to each of these synthetic consonants and ask subjects to identify the resulting syllables. More precisely, we might add an "a" sound, and then ask subjects whether each stimulus is the syllable "ba" or the syllable "pa."

The top panel of Figure 9.4 shows the pattern we might expect. After all, our stimuli are gradually shading from a clear "ba" to a clear "pa." Therefore, as we move through the series, one might expect subjects to be less and less likely to identify each stimulus as a "ba," and correspondingly more and more likely to identify each as a "pa." In the terms we used in Chapter 8, this would be a "graded membership" pattern: Test cases close to the "ba prototype" should be reliably identified as "ba." As we move away from this prototype, though, cases should be harder and harder to categorize.

The graded membership pattern emerged again and again in Chapter 8, but it doesn't show up here. The actual data are shown in the bottom of

Figure 9.4

Hypothetical identification data

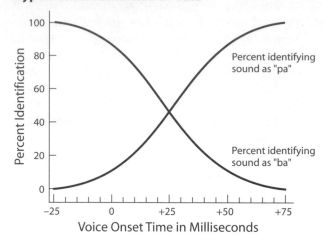

Percent identifying sound as "pa"

Percent identifying sound as "ba"

Actual identification data

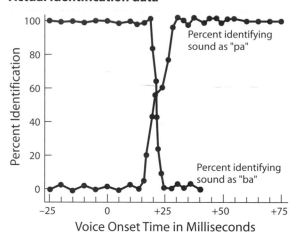

Percent identifying sound as "pa"

Percent identifying sound as "ba"

In ordinary speech, the syllable "ba" is pronounced with a zero voice onset time (VOT). That is, *voicing* begins at the same time as the air begins to flow. The syllable "pa" is pronounced with a 60 or 70 msec VOT—that is, voicing begins approximately 60 or 70 msec after the air begins to flow. With computer speech, we can produce a variety of compromises between these two sounds, and the top panel shows a plausible prediction about how these sounds will be perceived: As the sound becomes less and less like an ordinary "ba," subjects should be less and less likely to perceive it as a "ba." The bottom panel, however, shows the actual data: Subjects seem indifferent to small variations on the "ba" sound, and categorize a sound with a 10 or 15 msec VOT in exactly the same way that they categorize a sound with a 0 VOT. Subjects' categorizations also show an abrupt categorical "boundary" between "pa" and "ba," although there is no corresponding abrupt change in the stimuli themselves.

Figure 9.4. As you can see, all of the sounds with short VOTs are perceived as "ba." Moreover, in terms of their categorizations, subjects seem indifferent to whether the syllable resembles the "ba prototype" (with a 0 msec VOT) or not (e.g., a 20 msec VOT). Likewise, all of the long-VOT sounds are perceived as "pa." And, again, subjects seem indifferent to the contrast between a prototypical "pa" (e.g., 60 msec VOT) or a lousy exemplar (40 msec VOT). We might mention that the steep cut-off, visible in Figure 9.4, occurs at slightly different points for different subjects; nonetheless, every subject shows the pattern of a well-defined category boundary. (For the classic presentation of this pattern, see Liberman, Harris, Hoffman & Griffith, 1957; for reviews, see Handel, 1989; Yeni-Komshian, 1993. For studies of this pattern in children, see Werker & Desjardins, 1995.)

In a variation of this procedure, we can present these stimuli two by two. This time, the subjects are asked whether the two stimuli they hear are the *same* or *different*. If the first stimulus in a pair has a VOT of 20 msec, then how different (in terms of VOT) does the second stimulus in the pair have to be in order for subjects reliably to hear the difference? Likewise, if the first stimulus in a pair has a 30 msec VOT, how different does the second have to be for subjects to hear the difference?

In this discrimination task, subjects have great difficulty in hearing the difference between a stimulus with a 10 msec VOT and one with a 30 msec VOT. To put it bluntly, all "ba's" sound alike. Likewise, subjects have difficulty in hearing the difference between a stimulus with a 40 msec VOT and one with a 60 msec VOT. Apparently, all "pa's" sound alike. But the problem is *not* that subjects are insensitive to these 20 msec differences. Subjects do quite well, in fact, in hearing the difference between a 20 msec VOT and a 40 msec VOT. Discriminations across the category boundary are relatively easy.

The identification data (Figure 9.4) indicate that subjects are reasonably tolerant in their categorization: Stimuli at some distance from a "classic ba" are still counted as a "ba," and likewise for stimuli at some distance from a "classic pa." But this isn't because subjects hear the stimulus-to-stimulus variation but then elect to ignore it. Instead, subjects seem genuinely insensitive to differences within each category. Thus, in a real sense, subjects hear these sounds only as *exemplars* of their respective categories. What is perceived, in other words, is only the fact of a stimulus being in this or that category and, hence, the term "categorical perception."

Combining Phonemes

What about more complicated sounds? We have already noted that speech production involves relatively few production features but, from these, English speakers fashion 40 different phonemes. Those 40 phonemes, in turn, can be combined and recombined to form tens of thousands of different morphemes, which can themselves be combined to create word after word after word.

These combinations don't happen, however, in a helter-skelter fashion. Instead, there is a pattern to the combinations—some combinations seem common, others are rare; others seem prohibited outright. For example, Gleitman (1995) invites us to imagine an advertising executive trying to name a new breakfast cereal. One possibility is "Pritos." Another is "Glitos." But here is an option that seems a non-starter: "Tlitos." In English, words simply don't begin with the tl combination. This restriction isn't shared by all languages (there is, for example, a Northwest Indian language called "Tlingit"), but it is a restriction learned by, and honored by, all speakers of English.

Other principles govern the pattern of *change* that must occur when two morphemes are married together. For example, consider the "s" ending that marks the English plural—as in *books, cats, tapes*, and so on. In the cases just listed, the plural is pronounced as an [s]. In other contexts, though, the plural ending is pronounced differently. Say these words out loud: *bags, duds, pills*. If you listen carefully, you will realize that these words actually end with a [z] sound, not an [s]. The choice between these—a [z] pronunciation or an [s]—depends on how the base noun ends. If it ends with a *voiced* sound, then the [z] ending is used to make the plural. If the base noun ends with an *unvoiced* sound, then the plural is created with an [s].

It should be said that there is nothing inevitable about this pattern. The human voice can, for example, easily create the sound of "pills" with an [s] on the end, instead of a [z]. Nonetheless, it is the [z] pronunciation that we always use, suggesting that English speakers have internalized something equivalent to a "rule" for how this word (and every other plural) should be pronounced. These phonological rules thus provide part of the knowledge one must acquire if one is "to know English." (For a classic treatment of these issues, see Chomsky & Halle, 1968; for a more recent discussion, see Halle, 1990.)

Words

The average American high-school graduate knows about 45,000 different words (cf. Miller, 1991). For college students, the estimates are larger—between 75,000 and 100,000 words in their speaking vocabulary (Oldfield, 1963). For each of these, the speaker must know the *meaning* that corresponds to the word's *sound* and so, in general, our word knowledge allows us to tie together a phonological representation with a **semantic** representation—that is, a representation of the word's meaning.

There is an obvious connection between semantic knowledge and the conceptual knowledge we discussed in Chapter 8. To be sure, some concepts are difficult to express in words; other concepts can only be expressed via many words. Nonetheless, many words do express single concepts and, more generally, one can only understand a word's meaning if one understands the relevant concepts. It is no surprise, therefore, that the issues discussed in Chapter 8 also emerge in discussions of word meaning. Thus, some have proposed that, to know a word, one must know the word's *definition*. Others have argued that, to know a word, one must know a *prototype* for the concept named by that word. These are, of course, exactly the hypotheses we examined in the previous chapter.

Sense and Reference

One further distinction, though, is worth making explicit: Words are generally used to name objects or events in the world around us. The word "page," for example, refers to the sort of thing you are looking at right now; the word "reading" refers to the activity you are now engaged in, and so on. What a word refers to is called the word's **referent**.

However, it is crucial not to confuse a word's reference with the word's meaning. There are several reasons for this. For one, a word's reference is often a matter of accident or coincidence. Thus, the reference of the phrase "President of the United States" changes at regular intervals, but the meaning of the phrase is surely more stable than that.

In addition, we can often find two phrases that refer to the same objects in the world but that mean different things. These cases of "same reference, different meaning" make it clear that there must be more to meaning than reference. We refer to this "more" as the **sense** of a word, distinct from its referent (cf. Frege, 1892).

For example, consider the phrase "creature with a heart" and also the phrase "creature with a kidney." As it turns out, these phrases refer to the same creatures: In the biology of our planet, all of the creatures that have hearts also have kidneys, and all of the creatures that have kidneys also have hearts. Thus, these two phrases have the same referent. Nonetheless, these two phrases mean different things. (For example, we could imagine a planet in which "creatures with kidneys" were distinct from the "creatures with hearts." This wouldn't be possible if the two phrases *meant* the same thing.)

The phrase "creature with a heart" allows us to pick out a set of creatures in the world, and this set constitutes the referent for this phrase. But this phrase also *identifies* these creatures *in a specific way*—by virtue of their having hearts. This means of identifying the creatures (as opposed to the creatures being identified) provides the *sense* of the term, and the sense matters in a number of important ways. Thus, for example, by virtue of having identified these creatures via their heart possession, we also know some other things about them (e.g., that they have blood of some sort). This implication might not be conveyed by some other sense, even if that sense picked out exactly the same creatures.

Notice the parallels between these points and issues that we raised in Chapter 8. Prototypes and exemplars, for example, provide a reasonable way to categorize many of the objects in the world around us: We can categorize, in effect, by comparing the objects (or events) we encounter to these mental representations. Thus, prototypes and exemplars provide one way to capture the *referent* of a term. However, we have just argued that there is more to meaning than this, and that is entirely consonant with the message of Chapter 8. There we argued that concepts must contain more than prototypes and exemplars, in order to guide our judgments and reasoning about concepts. In effect, then, the latter half of Chapter 8 provides one way we might think about a term's sense.

Building New Words

We have mentioned the average vocabulary size for a high-school student or a college-student. But these counts are difficult to nail down, since one can easily create *new* words as needed. This happens, for example, whenever a new style of music or new style of clothing, demands a correspondingly new descriptive vocabulary. Likewise for the world of computers—so that "cyberspace" is a recent arrival in the language as is "geek" or "kludge." In many cases, these novel words are made up from scratch ("kludge"). More often, though, new words are "built" out of other morphemes. Thus, as Pinker (1994) points out, some foods are "unmicrowaveable"—a vocabulary item of recent vintage.

Scholars often speak of the **generativity** of language, to capture this idea that one can combine and recombine the units to create (or "generate") new linguistic entities. This generativity may, in fact, be limitless. For example, as a child, I was told that "antidisestablishmentarianism" is the longest word in the English language. Notice, though, that most of this word's length comes from the concatenation of various morphemes—from establish to *dis*establish, from there to disestablish*ment*, from there to disestablishment*arian*, and so on. The same thing happens routinely at more modest levels: Thus there are trucks and hand-trucks; grandmothers, great-grandmothers, and great-great-grandmothers; leftists, rightists and centrists; street-sweepers and minesweepers. In each case, the language is effortlessly enhanced by the combination of existing elements.

This ability to combine and recombine morphemes also provides another advantage: You don't need to memorize, as separate vocabulary items, the word "hat" and its plural "hats," or "cow" and "cows." Instead, all you need is the base noun in each case, plus the plural morpheme, "s". With these ingredients, you can create the plural, when needed. You can then generalize this procedure for other nouns, including nouns you are meeting for the first time. (I have one "grattiff." If I get another, I'll have two . . . ?) Likewise, once you know the past tense morpheme "ed" you can create the past tense of most verbs.

This generativity therefore lightens the load of anyone seeking to learn the vocabulary of a language and also allows us to deal with novel cases as they arise. Imagine that you have just heard the word "hack" for the very first time. You know immediately that someone who likes to hack is a *hacker*, the activity is called *hacking*, and you understand someone who says "I've been *hacked*." Once again, though, these combinations are not done in a helter-skelter fashion. Instead, a number of rules govern the combinations of morphemes. For example, you are now reasonably familiar with the Reisberg writing style; we might call this style "Reisbergian." And perhaps there are many who write in this style; we might call them all "Reisbergians." So there is no problem in the sequence of "Reisberg" + "ian" + "s." But things can't go the other way around: What if there are many Reisbergs who write in this style? In that case, what would we call someone else who writes in the style of (many) Reisbergs? The word, "Reisbergsian," sounds awkward, and terms like this one virtually never appear in spontaneous speech. Apparently, then, something prohibits the sequence composed of "base word" + "s" + "ian."

Prescriptive Rules, Descriptive Rules

In what sense, though, are these combinations of morphemes "prohibited"? Prohibited by whom? Likewise, we earlier noted that there is a "rule" governing the construction of plurals, so that "bugs" is pronounced with a [z] sound, while "bucks" is pronounced with an [s]. What sort of rule is this?

Let's first be clear about what these rules and prohibitions are *not*. We were all taught, at some stage of our education, how to talk and write "properly." We were all taught never to say "ain't." Many of us were scolded for writing in the passive voice; others were reprimanded for splitting infinitives. Many of us were counseled to say "For whom are you looking?" rather than "Who are you looking for?"; "It is I!" rather than "It's me."

The rules at stake in these cases are called **prescriptive rules**, rules describing how language is "supposed" to be. Often these rules seek to preserve a pattern of usage or a pattern of speaking that was common in some prior period, for some prior generation. Often these rules are intended to mark the difference between social classes, so that "upper class" people speak in one way, while "lower class" people don't talk so good. Thus, if one wishes to avoid being stigmatized, or if one wishes for membership in the elite, one tries to use the rules and to speak "proper" English.

One might well be skeptical about these prescriptive rules. As one concern, these rules often rest on misconceptions about language (cf. Pinker, 1994). As a different concern, it should be noted that all languages change with the passage of time and, therefore, what is considered "proper usage" in one time period may be different from what is proper a generation later. Hence, the prescriptive rules try, in a sense, to "stop the clock" on language change, and it is not obvious *why* the clock should be stopped: Do we have reason to believe that the English of 1928 is better than the English of 1992 or 1996? If not, then why should the English of 1996 conform to the pattern that was deemed acceptable in the earlier time?

The rules we are concerned with, though, are rules of a different sort—not prescriptive rules but **descriptive**, i.e., characterizing the language as it is ordinarily used by fluent speakers and listeners. There are strong regularities in the way English is used, and the rules we are discussing describe these patterns. No value judgment is offered (nor should one be) about whether these patterns constitute "proper" or "good" English. These patterns simply describe *how* English *is* or, perhaps we should say, *what* English is.

Notice also how we go about discovering these regularities. In some cases, it is important to track what is said, and what is not said in ordinary language usage. However, for many purposes, this provides evidence of a limited sort. For one consideration, the *absence* of a word or construction from ordinary usage is difficult to interpret: If Leo never uses the word "boustrephedon," is this because he doesn't know the word or because he simply has no interest in talking about boustrephedon? If Miriam never uses the word "unmicrowaveable," is this because she regards the word as illegitimate or merely because she is in the habit of using some other term to convey this idea?

In addition, the pattern of spontaneous speech is filled with performance errors. Sometimes, you start a sentence with one idea in mind, but then change your idea as you are speaking. You might end up saying something like, "He went my father went yesterday," even though you realize, as you are uttering it, that the sentence contains an error. In other occasions, you slip in your production, and so end up saying something different than you had intended. You might say, "They were I mean weren't fine," even though (again) you regret the slip the moment you produce it.

These slips are of considerable importance if we are studying the pattern of speech production. However, these slips are a nuisance if we are trying to study linguistic knowledge: In most cases, you would agree that you had, in fact, made an error. In many cases, you even know how to "repair" the error, in order to produce a "correct" sentence. Clearly, therefore, your original performance, with its errors, doesn't reflect the full extent of your linguistic knowledge.

Because of considerations like these, we sometimes need to examine language **competence** rather than language performance, with competence defined as the pattern of skills and knowledge that might be revealed under optimal circumstances (after Chomsky, 1957, 1965). One way to reveal this competence is via linguistic *judgments*: Subjects are asked to reflect on one structure or another and to tell us whether they find the structure acceptable or not. Note that we are not asking subjects whether they find the structure to be clumsy, or pleasing to the ear, or useful. Instead, we are asking subjects whether the structure is something that one *could* say, if one wished. Thus, to use an earlier example, "Reisbergians" seems acceptable but "Reisbergsian" does not. Likewise, "There's the big blue house" seems fine, but "There's house blue big the" does not. Or, to return to an earlier example, you might slip and say, "He went my father went yesterday," but you certainly know there is something wrong with this sequence.

It should be said that these judgments do involve a peculiar use of language: Normally, we use language to communicate about some (nonlinguistic) object or event; language is the medium of expression and not by itself the topic of discussion. In the judgments we are considering, though, language *is* the topic of scrutiny, and so subjects are (for example) asked to make a judgment *about* language rather than simply *using* language. Judgments like these are called **metalinguistic judgments**, and these in turn are members of a broader category: **metacognitive judgments**. Metacognitive judgments are in general defined as judgments in which one must stand back from a particular mental activity, and comment on the activity rather than participating in it.

The "Psychological Reality" of Linguistic Rules

Metalinguistic judgments reveal a number of strong patterns: Certain combinations of phonemes are reliably regarded as acceptable, others are not. Likewise, certain combinations of morphemes are regarded as acceptable, others are not. In most cases, it is convenient to describe these patterns in terms of a rule: If a word's final phoneme is voiced, then the plural ending must be voiced as well (and so a [z] rather than an [s]). If a noun has an *irregular* plural, then it can be combined with other morphemes in the plural form. (Thus a beaver can leave "teethmarks," and a house can be "mice-infested.") If a noun has a *regular* plural, though, it is combined with other morphemes only in the *singular* form. (A house might be a "rat-infested," but not "rats-infested." A porcupine leaves "claw-marks," not "claws-marks.")

What is the nature of these rules? One possibility is that the rules are consciously known and deliberately followed, just as most people know the spelling rule "*i* before *e* except after *c*." (Never mind that this rule has many exceptions—like "either" or "neither." What matters is that people know the rule, can report the rule, and try explicitly to apply the rule.)

However, we can swiftly rule out this claim: Linguistic rules are surely not conscious. Indeed, before reading these paragraphs, you probably didn't realize there was a relation between regularity-of-plurals and how a word combines with other words. Nonetheless, you have followed this rule for most of your life—at least since you were three or four years old (Gordon, 1986).

A different possibility is that you know the rules *unconsciously* and apply them without realizing you are doing so. Evidence for this claim comes from studies of children learning language. For example, English-speaking children seem initially to learn the past-tense in a word-by-word fashion, and so they memorize the fact that the past tense of "play" is "played," that the past tense of "climb" is "climbed," and so on. By age two or three, however, children realize that there is a pattern here, so that one doesn't have to memorize each word's past tense as a separate vocabulary item. Instead, they realize, you can produce the past tense by manipulating morphemes—that is, by adding the "ed" ending onto a word. Once children make this discovery, they are able to apply this principle to many new verbs, including verbs they have never encountered before. Thus, Berko (1958) showed children a picture and told them, "Here is a man who likes to rick. Yesterday, he did the same thing. Yesterday, he . . . . " Prompted in this way, three-year-olds unhesitatingly supply the past-tense: "ricked."

However, children seem to get carried away with this pattern and so, at this age, children's spontaneous speech contains many **over-regularization errors**: Children say things like, "Yesterday, we goed," or "Yesterday, I run-ned." The same thing happens with other morphemes, and so children of this age also over-generalize in their use of the plural ending ("foots," "tooths") and contractions. (For example, they over-generalize the pattern of "You aren't" to produce "I amn't," meaning, of course, "I am not.") Remarkably, these same children were *correctly* using the irregular forms (*feet, teeth, went, ran*) just a few months earlier and so, to the casual viewer, it seems that the child's linguistic development is going backward—first using correct forms, and then later using incorrect ones. Moreover, it is clear that the child *still remembers* the irregular past tense. A child of this age will often use the correct forms "went," "ran," "did," "sang," and so on, but will interweave with these the over-regularized "goed," "runned," and the like. One can even hear these children voicing such peculiarities as "He wented." (For a review, see Marcus, Pinker, Ullman, Hollander, Rosen & Xu, 1992.)

This pattern makes it clear that language learning is not a matter of *imitation*, since these over-regularizations are never produced by adults. Nor is language acquisition a matter of explicit instruction, since no adult would encourage children to make these errors. Instead, in describing these data, it is tempting simply to say that the child has induced a rule about how the past tense is formed and is then applying (and, indeed, over-applying) that rule. (And likewise for plurals.) In this fashion, the child generates the over-regularized forms, even though he or she has never heard them spoken by anyone else. On this view, therefore, the rules are literally in place (although unconsciously) in the child's mind and are governing the child's linguistic productions.

It should be said, though, that there is controversy over this point. For example, Rumelhart and McClelland (1986a) have argued that these over-regularization errors could also emerge from a connectionist PDP model, involving (as all PDP models do) nothing more than a number of simple associations—that is, without the use of any rules. (For discussion of PDP modeling, see Chapter 7.) Others, however, have argued that PDP models will produce this pattern only if they receive exactly the right pattern of input—and, in fact, a pattern of input different from what the child receives (e.g., Pinker, 1991; for a response to this point, see MacWhinney & Leinbach, 1991).

It is unclear how this controversy will be resolved. (For some interesting complications, see Kim, Pinker, Prince & Prasada, 1991; also Smith, Langston & Nisbett, 1992.) In the meantime, several points are certain: Our linguistic behavior is, on anyone's account, highly creative (in the sense that new forms can always be generated) but also highly constrained (in the sense that many of the possible combinations of units are deemed unacceptable by speakers/ hearers of the language). These constraints fall into patterns that are well described by rules, and in large measure it is the business of linguistics to discover these rules. However, whether the rules are literally represented in the mind, and thus govern our linguistic practices, remains to be seen.

Syntax

We have already mentioned that a few production features are all you need to create dozens of phonemes, and these phonemes then allow you to create tens of thousands of words. But now let's consider what you can do with those words: If you have 40,000 words in your vocabulary, or 60,000, or 80,000, how many *sentences* can you build from those words? How many sentences are you able to understand or to produce?

Sentences can range in length from the very brief ("Go!" or "I do.") to the absurdly long. (According to the Guinness Book of World Records, the longest sentence ever printed contains 1,300 words.) Most sentences, though, contain 20 words or fewer. With this "length limit," it has been estimated that there are 100,000,000,000,000,000,000 possible sentences in English (that's 10^{20}; after Pinker, 1994). For comparison, this is 100 million times larger than the number of neurons in your brain.

Do we need obscure or complicated sentences to produce this absurdly large number? It turns out that we don't. Think of how many ways you can complete this sentence: "I can see the. . . ." Or imagine endings to this sentence, "I detest Coco-Puffs because. . . ." If you press ahead in this exercise, you will realize that even commonplace, easily generated sentences are vast in their numbers.

Of course, some sequences of words *aren't* sentences: Thus, in English, one could say, "The boy hit the ball," but couldn't say "The boy hit ball the." Likewise, one could say, "The bird squashed the car," but couldn't say "The bird the car," or "The bird squashed the," or just "squashed the car." These sequences are (more or less) interpretable, but virtually any speaker of the language would agree these sequences have something wrong in them. They are unacceptable; they are not sentences. Once again, therefore, it is tempting to appeal to *rules*—rules that permit endless numbers of word combinations, but which *prohibit* other combinations. These rules, governing the sequences and combinations of words in the formation of phrases and sentences, are called rules of **syntax**. Syntactic rules determine whether a sequence of words is **grammatical**—i.e., conforms to the patterns acceptable within the language.

One might think that grammatical acceptability is a matter of *meaning*: Sentences are meaningful, but non-sentences aren't. This suggestion, though, is plainly wrong. To see this, consider these two sentences (which are surely the two most-widely-quoted bits of gibberish ever composed):

'Twas brillig, and the slithey toves did gyre and gimble in the wabe.
Colorless green ideas sleep furiously.

(The first of these is part of Lewis Carroll's famous poem, "Jabberwocky"; the second was penned by the important linguist, Noam Chomsky.) These sentences are, of course, without meaning—colorless things aren't green; ideas don't sleep; toves aren't slithey. Nonetheless, these sequences are sentences: Speakers of English, perhaps after a moment's reflection, do regard these sequences as grammatically acceptable, in a way that "Furiously sleep ideas green colorless" is not. It seems that we need principles of syntax that are largely independent of semantics and sensibility.

Phrase Structure

We have already noted that syntactic rules "prohibit" some sequences of words or, more precisely, the rules designate these sequences as "ungrammatical." In addition, the rules of syntax specify the "role" of each word within the sentence. To put it rather crudely, the rules specify which word within the sentence identifies the doer of the action, and which identifies the recipient of the action. This is one of the reasons why grammar is important: If a sequence isn't grammatical, then often we can't decipher the role of each word or phrase, blocking interpretation of the sequence.

These roles are specified, in part, by the phrase structure of the sentence, a structure often illustrated via an (upside-down) tree, such as the one shown in Figure 9.5. If you read this structure from bottom to top, the structure specifies how the words in the sentence are grouped together: The first three words constitute one phrase and, in particular, constitute a "noun phrase" (abbreviated "NP"). The last three words in the sentence form another NP. This last NP joins with the word "chased" to constitute a larger phrase—a "verb phrase" (or "VP").

Figure 9.5

A PHRASE-STRUCTURE TREE

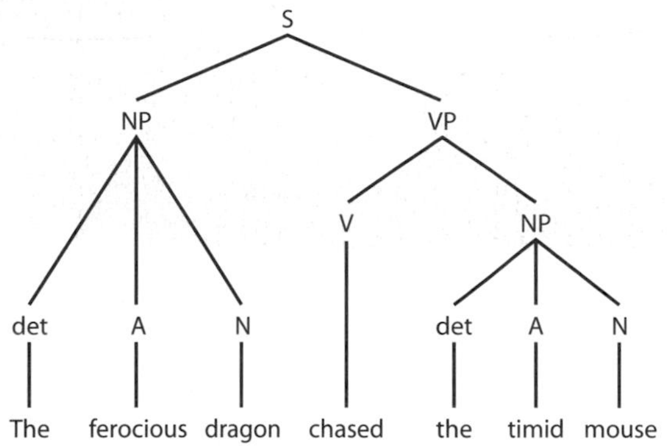

The syntax of a sentence is often depicted via a "tree" diagram. The diagram shows that the overall sentence itself (S) consists of a noun phrase (NP) followed by a verb phrase (VP). The noun phrase is composed of a determiner, followed by an adjective and a noun. The verb phrase is composed of a verb followed by a noun phrase.

Of course, there are constraints on the pattern of branching in a phrase-structure tree, and these constraints are specified by **phrase-structure rules**. Thus, a *sentence* (S) always consists of a noun phrase (NP) followed by a verb phrase (VP). Therefore, every phrase-structure tree starts with the branching of NP + VP visible at the top of Figure 9.5. This rule is often written in this fashion:

$$S \rightarrow NP \quad VP$$

Expressed this way, the rule is referred to as a **rewrite rule**, such that whenever you find a sentence in a tree structure, you can rewrite it as a noun phrase followed by a verb phrase. Equivalently: Whenever there is a sentence in a tree structure, it can "branch out" into a noun phrase plus a verb phrase.

Likewise, the rule

$$NP \rightarrow (det) \quad A \quad * \quad N$$

means there can be a # of adjectives

means that, whenever you find a noun phrase in a tree structure, you can rewrite it as a *determiner* (like "a" or "one" or "the"), followed by an *adjective* (A), followed by a *noun* (N). Notice that you need not have a determiner—there is none in this sentence: "Trees like sunlight." This is why the symbol "det" is in parentheses, connoting that this term is optional. Likewise, there can be any number of adjectives, including none; this is indicated by the asterisk. Other rewrite rules are listed in Figure 9.6.

These rewrite rules also have another interesting feature, called **recursion**. A rule system is recursive if a symbol can appear both on the left side of a definition (the part being defined) and on the right side (the part providing the definition). Thus, a sentence always includes a noun phrase and a verb phrase (remember: S → NP VP; here it is the S that is being defined). The verb phrase, in turn can be unpacked in several different ways, including

$$VP \rightarrow V \quad NP$$

or:

$$VP \rightarrow V \quad S$$

Notice that, in this last rule, S appears *as part of the definition*. This allows us to create sentences like this one:

I believe she is the thief.

Figure 9.6

SYNTACTIC REWRITE RULES

$$S \longrightarrow NP \; VP$$
$$NP \longrightarrow (det) \; A* \; N$$

$$VP \longrightarrow V \; (NP)$$
$$VP \longrightarrow V \; S$$
$$VP \longrightarrow V \; PP$$
$$VP \longrightarrow V \; AP$$
$$AP \longrightarrow A \; A$$

Most syntactic rules can be captured in terms of "rewrite rules." The top rule indicates that a sentence can consist of a noun phrase followed by a verb phrase. A verb phrase, however, can take several different forms—a verb by itself, or a verb followed by a noun phrase, or a verb followed by a prepositional phrase, and so on. Note that these rules are *recursive:* A sentence can contain a verb phrase, which can contain a sentence.

Here, there is a sentence ("She is the thief.") within the sentence. (The relevant phrase structure is shown in Figure 9.7; notice that we begin, as always, with an S node at the top, but then unpack the S node in a fashion that leads to another S node, in the middle of the tree.) We can then repeat this cycle, if we wish, with sentences including verb phrases including sentences including verb phrases including sentences, as in

I fear that you believe Sam told her I am the thief.

Recursion provides an easy way to accommodate this pattern. In addition, recursion is one of the features of language supporting vast generativity, since one can, quite literally, use recursion to create an infinite number of sentences.

The Function of Phrase Structure

Phrase-structure rules carry us closer toward understanding why some sequences of words are rejected as ungrammatical or as "non-sentences." As we have noted, these rules specify what must be included within a sentence, and they often specify an *order* for the sentence. Sequences that break these rules, therefore, can't be sentences.

Figure 9.7

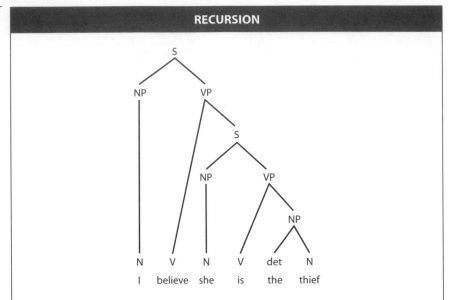

RECURSION

Shown here is the phrase-structure tree for a sentence that makes use of recursion. Recursion refers to the possibility for an element to appear as part of its own definition. Thus, sentences are defined as including verb phrases, but verb phrases can include sentences, leading to the possibility of sentences within sentences.

Phrase structure rules are also reflected in many other aspects of language use. For example, the *groups* of words identified by these rules (e.g., the noun phrase, the verb phrase, and so on) really do seem to "hang together" as a group. In other words, the phrase-structure rules capture the "natural" groupings of words within each sentence. As a concrete case, imagine that you wanted to turn this sentence into a question: "The rocket is ready to launch." You would obviously say: "Is the rocket ready to launch?" Now, what principle guided your response? You might think that you simply searched for the auxiliary verb "is" and moved it to the "front" of the sentence. But this isn't quite right. To see this, turn this sentence into a question: "The rocket that is on the far pad is ready to launch." In this case, you wouldn't move the first "is" to the front. In other words, you wouldn't say, "Is the rocket that on the far pad is ready to launch?" Instead, the "is" you would move is the one just after the sentence's first noun phrase. In other words, you "respect" the integrity of the noun phrase, and look for the auxiliary verb *after* this unit, rather than one within the unit.

In the same way, notice that the phrase-structure rules define the sequence of a noun phrase *no matter where* that phrase appears within a sentence. In other words, the rules define a noun phrase "module" that can be "plugged in" wherever a noun phrase is appropriate. Therefore, you don't have to memorize the constructions possible for a sentence's *subject* and also the constructions possible for a sentence's object and also the constructions for the object of a preposition. Instead, you simply learn the constructions for a noun phrase and "plug in" one of those constructions whenever it is needed.

You only need to learn one rule in order to know that each of these sentences is ill-formed: "The ball big rolled away," "He chased the ball big," and "The ant was squashed under the ball big." Likewise, one rule tells you that if a "module" can be plugged into one of the noun-phrase positions, then it can be plugged into *any* of the noun-phrase positions. Thus, if this sentence is legitimate: "I kissed a girl who is allergic to coconuts," then so is this one: "A girl who is allergic to coconuts was chased by the moose," as is: "He hid the flowers behind a girl who is allergic to coconuts."

Once again, therefore, it looks like "noun phrase" really does correspond to a natural grouping of words within our sentences: In producing speech, or in making judgments about speech, we recognize a noun phrase whenever it occurs, and we apply our "noun-phrase knowledge" to that phrase. This leads, as we have seen, to regular patterns that occur whenever (and wherever) a noun phrase is used and also to regular patterns that *don't* occur.

Note also that this "modular" scheme appreciably lightens the load for anyone seeking to *learn* a language: You only need to learn one noun-phrase rule, rather than many, and this single rule will govern the construction of noun phrases no matter where they appear within the sentence. The same is true for verb phrases and prepositional phrases; for these, also, we will only need a single rule, rather than many.

In addition to all of this, phrase-structure rules also seem to guide our interpretation of a sentence: The rule S → NP VP divides a sentence into the "doer" (the NP) and some information about that doer (the VP)—in other words, the rule divides the sentence into the subject and the predicate. If the verb phrase is rewritten VP → V NP, then the initial verb indicates the action described by the sentence, and the NP specifies the recipient of that action. In these ways, then, the phrase structure of a sentence provides an initial "roadmap" useful in understanding the sentence, as shown in Figure 9.8.

Interestingly, sometimes more than one phrase structure, more than one roadmap, is compatible with a sentence. If the phrase structure guides interpretation then, in these cases, there should be more than one way to interpret the sentence. There should, in other words, be a **phrase-structure ambiguity**. (This is in contrast to other forms of ambiguity—e.g., the ambiguity of an individual word, like "bank" or "ball" or "hood.") Some examples of phrase-

Figure 9.8

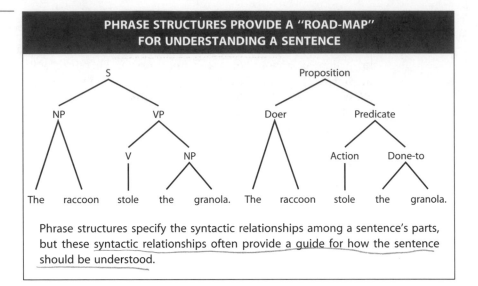

**PHRASE STRUCTURES PROVIDE A "ROAD-MAP"
FOR UNDERSTANDING A SENTENCE**

Phrase structures specify the syntactic relationships among a sentence's parts, but these syntactic relationships often provide a guide for how the sentence should be understood.

structure ambiguity are shown in Figure 9.9 and, for the first of these, we have illustrated the two alternative phrase structures consistent with the sequence of words. In short, then, ambiguity is predicted, on the basis of the phrase-structure rules, and the ambiguity is (often humorously) observed.

Finally, phrase structure rules are also evident in subjects' *memories* for sentences. For example, subjects in one study heard a tape-recorded passage that was interrupted at various points. Whenever an interruption occurred, this was a signal to subjects to report back as much as they could of the passage up to that point. In this task, the data show high levels of verbatim recall for the phrase that had actually been underway, at the moment of the interruption. Recall accuracy was at a much lower level for words prior to the current phrase (Jarvella, 1970, 1971).

One plausible interpretation of these data rests on the idea that subjects can't interpret the words within a phrase until they have heard (or read) the entire phrase; only then can they see how the words fit together to express the speaker's (or author's) intent. Thus, while listening to a phrase, subjects must remember its individual words and so, if tested, memory for these words will be good. Once the phrase ends, though, subjects can "distill" these words down to their essence and, at this point, they no longer need to hang on to the individual words. Therefore, they cease maintaining the words in working

Figure 9.9

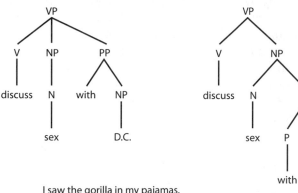

PHRASE-STRUCTURE AMBIGUITY

He wants to discuss sex with Dick Cavett.

I saw the gorilla in my pajamas.
The shooting of the hunters was terrible.
They are roasting chickens.
Visiting relatives can be awful.
Two computers were reported stolen by the TV announcer.

Often, the words of a sentence are compatible with more than one phrase struc-ture; in this case, the sentence will be ambiguous. Thus, one can understand the first sentence as describing a *discussion* with Cavett, or as describing *sex* with Cavett; both analyses of the verb phrase are shown. Can you find both inter-pretations for the remaining sentences?

memory, and ability to recall the individual words drops accordingly. (For related data, see Sachs, 1967; Wingfield & Butterworth, 1984.)

Transformations

We have now seen several influences of phrase-structure rules. First, these rules play an important part in determining which sequences of words are sentences and which are not. Second, these rules identify sections within a sentence that really do seem to provide natural groupings: Any phrase ac-ceptable as a subject noun-phrase, for example, also seems acceptable as an object noun-phase, implying that the unit "noun phrase" really does capture an operative unit within our linguistic knowledge. (And likewise for the other units identified by the phrase-structure rules.) Third, phrase-structure rules seem to guide interpretation of a sentence and, correspondingly, a sentence will be ambiguous if more than one phrase-structure analysis can be computed. Fourth, phrase structure shapes subjects' memory for sentences in various ways. In particular, the memory pattern implies that subjects listen to a sentence in a "phrase by phrase" manner, using the end of a phrase as an opportunity to compile what they have heard so far.

It turns out, though, that some aspects of syntax cannot be explained in terms of phrase-structure rules. Instead, we need a two-part system: Phrase-structure rules allow us to "grow" a sentence tree, but then a separate set of rules allows us to "reshape" the tree by exchanging the positions of some of the tree's branches. More precisely, the phrase-structure rules allow us to generate an abstract representation of the sentence to-be-expressed. This representation is called the sentence's **underlying structure**, or d-structure. (Older texts refer to this structure as "deep structure.") It is this structure that provides the starting point for semantic analysis, since it is this structure that makes clear who did what to whom.

Generally, though, one wants to move around the elements of a sentence's underlying structure—perhaps for stylistic reasons or perhaps to draw the listener's (or reader's) attention to one or another element of the proposition. These movements are, once again, governed by rules, which allow the creation of a **surface structure** (or s-structure) for the sentence. It is then the surface structure that is expressed in speech. (The movement rules are, in many texts, referred to as "transformation rules." We should also note that most of the theorizing in this domain was launched by Chomsky, about 40 years ago, and work in this area continues to be shaped heavily by his ideas. See, for example, Chomsky, 1957, 1965; for reviews of how the theory has evolved, see Cook, 1988; Riemsdijk & Williams, 1986.)

The movement rules allow us to capture a number of regularities. For example, it turns out that different verbs require different sorts of *verb phrases.* "Devour," for example, demands a direct object, while "dine" insists on having no object (cf. Grimshaw, 1990; Pinker, 1989). You would say "He devoured the pie," but not "He dined the pie." You could say "He dined at 8:00," but not "He devoured at 8:00." "Put" demands an object and a place (see Figure 9.10). "Believe" accepts a sentence as its direct object ("I believe he is tall"), but will also take a simple noun phrase ("I believe him"). And so on for other verbs, each having its own requirements.

Notice, though, that each of these requirements can be satisfied in different ways. Thus, for example, you can say "He devoured a pie" or "All the pies were devoured" or "It was pies that were devoured" or "What did he devour?" (but not "When did he devour?"). It seems, therefore, that "devour" does require a direct object, but this direct object doesn't have to appear in the "direct-object position" for the sentence that is articulated.

Figure 9.10

DIFFERENT VERBS HAVE DIFFERENT SYNTACTIC REQUIREMENTS

dine—demands only a subject

| So you could say: | "We dined at nine." |
| But you wouldn't say: | "We dined the chicken." |

eat—*can* have an object

| So you could say: | "We ate at nine." |
| or | "We ate the chicken." |

devour—*must* have an object

| So you could say: | "We devoured the chicken." |
| But you wouldn't say: | "We devoured at nine." |

put—must have an object *and* a location

So you could say:	"We put the loot in a safe hiding place."
But you wouldn't say:	"We put the loot."
or	"We put in a safe hiding place."

Some verbs cannot take an object; other verbs must have an object. These requirements, however, can be met in many ways, and this makes it useful to represent each sentence in two different fashions: One representation specifies the thematic relations of who-did-what-to-whom, and this level allows us to determine if the verb's requirements have been met. The second representation corresponds to the sentence as it is actually pronounced.

One could imagine, of course, that one simply memorizes the full range of sentence types that satisfy the "devour" requirements and also the range of sentence types that satisfy the "dine" requirements, the "put" requirements, and so on. Needless to say, however, this would place an enormous burden on the language learner, and it would also leave us with a rather messy description of the language.

A more economical way to capture this pattern is by claiming that each sentence has two representations: One representation determines the thematic relations of who did what to whom. This level allows you easily to determine whether the verb's requirements have been satisfied. The second representation, then, would be created by swapping around these parts, and this would lead to the sentence as it is actually spoken.

This is, of course, exactly the proposal we are considering: The underlying structure, generated by the phrase-structure rules, ensures, from the start, that the verb's requirements will be met. Differently put, the verb places strong requirements on the form of the phrase-structure tree. Once this is done, however, these pieces are then "free to move," allowing the speaker to highlight just those pieces of the sentence that seem, within the conversation, worth emphasizing.

Trace Theory

A sentence's underlying structure cannot be observed directly. Instead, this structure is *inferred* from various patterns in the surface structure. To see how this works, let's consider an example.

Linguists generally argue that questions are formed by moving an element out of a sentence's underlying structure and replacing that element with the appropriate "wh-" word. The question "What did he give?" is derived from an underlying structure that looks something like: "He did give X." In other words, in the surface structure, "what," has replaced a "place holder" that used to reside in the position appropriate for the sentence's direct object. Similarly, the proposition: "He will go to X" is the basis for: "Where will he go?" In this case, "where" has replaced a place holder that used to reside in the position appropriate for the object of the preposition "to."

Figure 9.11 illustrates how this swapping of elements takes place. What is shown on the left is a representation of the sentence's underlying structure, created in accordance with the phrase-structure rules. The movement rules then govern how these elements are shifted around to create the surface structure shown on the right.

This claim has a number of interesting consequences. For example, since we are moving elements from one position to another, there is no way an element could end up in both places at once. Hence, we will never end up with strings such as:

What will she see an animal?

or:

Who will he speak to some guy?

In these, an element has both moved out of its initial position and remained in its initial position. Since these strings are obviously ungrammatical, it is

Figure 9.11

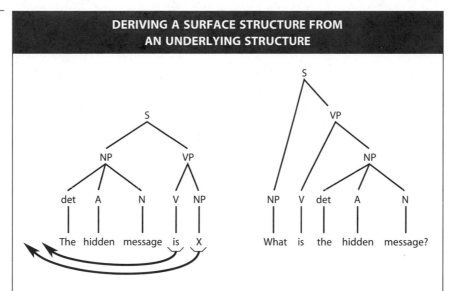

**DERIVING A SURFACE STRUCTURE FROM
AN UNDERLYING STRUCTURE**

The panel on the right shows the phrase structure for the surface form of the question. This surface structure was derived, however, from the phrase structure shown on the left. The arrows indicate how the elements of this underlying structure have been moved around, in order to create the surface structure.

entirely appropriate that they can't be produced by our transformational scheme.

In addition, when an element vacates a position to move somewhere else, it doesn't depart cleanly. Instead, it leaves a **trace** behind—much as a burglar sometimes leaves footprints, indicating where he has been. The trace isn't expressed out loud, but it is evident in the speech pattern. As one way to demonstrate this, we can exploit the fact that speech is often filled with contractions—such as:

I wanna go to bed.

instead of:

I want to go to bed.

This contraction—from "want to" to "wanna"—is only possible if the word "want" appears in the sentence right alongside of the word "to." You can't contract "want to" in this sentence, because the two crucial words *aren't* adjacent:

I want Jacob to go to bed.

This sentence can't become: "I wanna Jacob go to bed." The contraction, in other words, is blocked if anything appears between the "want" and the "to." With that said, we are ready for traces.

Consider the sentence:

I want Sol to have the next turn.

From this, we can create the question:

Who do you want to have the next turn? *say this*

Notice that in this question "want" and "to" *seem* adjacent to each other, and so contraction should be possible. But it isn't. If you read this question out loud, you are likely to pronounce "want" with a clear /t/ on the end. You won't pronounce it this way:

Who do you wanna have the next turn? *not this (b/c of the trace of Sol left)*

Why is this? In the base sentence, "Sol" appeared between "want" and "to." When this word was removed, to create the question, it left a trace behind. Therefore, in the question, "want" and "to" *aren't* adjacent, even though they seem to be. Instead, there is a trace in between them, and this blocks the contraction.

Traces can also be detected in a variety of other ways. For example, if we measure the electrical activity of the brain, moment by moment, we discover a shift in the electrical pattern the moment a listener reaches the trace—as if the listener were saying: "Aha—*here* is where the moved element belongs!" (For this and related evidence, see Chomsky, 1981; Kluender & Kutas, 1993; MacDonald, 1989; Nicol & Swinney, 1989.)

Traces thus allow us to document that elements in a sentence have been moved around and, more important, they show us where the elements have been moved from. This in turns establishes the point we are after: Questions are not formed simply by running through the appropriate phrase-structure rules. Instead, questions are formed by moving elements around in a tree structure—all in accord with the movement rules.

Questions are formed by moving elements around in a tree structure

Linguistic Universals

Let's pause to take stock. We have slowly climbed up the linguistic hierarchy—from subphonemic features (like voicing or place of articulation) to phonemes, from there to morphemes, then to words and, finally, to full sentences. At each step, we have seen how linguistic elements can be combined to create larger and more sophisticated linguistic units. In the process, we have seen how a relatively small number of elements can be used to create a vast (and, at some levels, infinite) number of combinations.

We have argued, though, that these combinations are rule-governed, with the rules visible in a number of ways. Thus, some combinations of elements are permitted by the rules; others are not. In addition, the rules often impose a *structure* on our linguistic products; this was evident, for example, in our discussion of phrase-structure rules. In still other cases, we detect the operation of the rules by virtue of the "traces" the rules' operation leaves behind. In one fashion or another, though, the rules do leave their mark, and in this way we can discover the rules.

It seems unquestionable that these rules capture some striking regularities—in the patterns of language we accept and the patterns we reject. Some of these regularities are obvious from the start (for example, the fact that every sentence needs a noun phrase and a verb phrase). In other cases, the regularities are quite subtle (e.g., the pattern of when a contraction is possible and when it is not). In all cases, though, the rules seem to be extremely strong, tolerating *no* exceptions. Thus, sentence after sentence seems to conform to the rules. Indeed, many of these regularities hold up even if we consider other languages, including languages distant from our own—Japanese and Turkish, Mayan, Walbiri, and Kivunjo. To describe these other languages, we need to adjust the rules in small ways, by shifting a "parameter" or two. With that done, though, the rules do seem to hold. Thus, some have argued that these rules constitute **linguistic universals**—that is, they are applicable to every human language (after Chomsky, 1965, 1975, 1986; see also Comrie, 1981; Cook, 1988; Greenberg, Ferguson & Moravcsik, 1978; Hawkins, 1988).

The proposed universals are of various sorts. Some are framed in terms of probabilities. Thus, in all the world's languages, some sequences of words are quite common, while other sequences are quite rare. As an example, it is possible in English to put a sentence's object *before* the sentence's subject ("A bear he shot."), but this isn't the normal pattern for English—the normal pattern, instead, is subject then verb then object. And it is not only English that shows this pattern: The subject of a sentence tends to precede the object in roughly 98% of the world's languages. The sequence of subject-before-verb is preferred in roughly 80% of the world's languages. (Cf. Crystal, 1987.)

Most universals, though, concern linguistic features that seem to come and go together. Thus, for example, if a language's preferred word order is subject-object-verb, the language is likely to form its questions by adding some words at the *end* of the question. If, in contrast, a language's preferred sequence is subject-verb-object (as in English), then the language will place its question words at the *beginning* of the question (as in: *Where* did he . . . ? *When* did they . . . ?).

The existence of these linguistic universals opens an intriguing possibility: Consider the fact that every human child learns how to speak and, indeed, children acquire language rather rapidly: A two-year-old's linguistic skills are quite limited; a four-year-old, in contrast, speaks perfectly well. Hence, the learning process is somehow compressed into a period lasting just a couple of years. Moreover, what is learned seems quite complex—with rules governing the combinations of phonemes and different rules governing the combinations of morphemes, and phrase-structure rules and movement rules. Finally, bear in mind that we have already considered evidence that language is not learned via simple imitation or via instruction by the parents. (Many considerations rule out these possibilities, including the over-regularization errors we considered earlier in the chapter.) How, then, is language learning possible?

A number of scholars have argued that language learning is possible only because the child enters this process with an enormous head start: a biological heritage that (somehow) stipulates the broad outline of human language. In this view, the child might begin the process already knowing the universal rules of language. The process of language learning would therefore be a process of figuring out exactly how the rules are realized within the language community in which the child is raised. The child might actually begin with some complex "language machinery," so that the process of learning is a process of adjusting the "switches" on this machinery so that the child ends up speaking Portuguese instead of Urdu, or Swedish instead of Mandarin. This seems a plausible account of language learning, with the plausibility deriving from the fact that many of the rules we have discussed do seem, with the appropriate adjustments of parameters, universal. (For further discussion of these suggestions, see Bloom, 1994; Hyams, 1986.)

Sentence Parsing

What about linguistic *performance*? So far we have focused on linguistic *judgments*, but how do we actually manage to comprehend the speech (or printed language) that we encounter?

The Difficulty of Sentence Parsing

As we have discussed, a sentence's phrase structure conveys crucial information about who did what to whom. Thus, once you know the phrase structure, you are well on your way to understanding the sentence. But how do you figure out the phrase structure in the first place? Likewise, we know that subjects *use* the phrase structure as a guide to interpretation as they proceed through a sentence. This was evident in the memory result, discussed earlier, showing that subjects are quite accurate in remembering the exact words of the phrase they are currently working on. Once the phrase ends, though, subjects seem to pause and "compile" what they have heard so far. With that done, there is no further need to remember the exact wording of the phrase, and memory performance suffers accordingly.

A similar point emerges from several other studies. For example, we can show sentences to subjects, one word at a time. The subject might see the word "The" on a computer screen then, a moment later, "Chinese," then "who," and so forth through the sentence. Crucially, though, we allow the subjects to set the pace of the presentation, pressing a key as soon as they are ready for the next word. Figure 9.12 shows the pattern of subjects' key presses: Subjects look at "The" for 800 msec or so before requesting the next word; they look at "Chinese" for about a full second before requesting the next word, and so on. Note that the pattern of "scallops" corresponds reasonably well to the sentence's phrase structure, with the longest responses positioned at the ends of phrases. This suggests that readers need more time at the end of each phrase in order to integrate what they have read so far (Stine, 1990; also Aaronson & Scarborough, 1977).

Thus, listeners and readers *use* phrase endings as they proceed through a sentence. In order to do this, though, they need to *recognize* phrase endings when they occur. This would be a simple matter if sentences were uniform in their structure: "The boy hit the ball. The girl chased the cat. The elephant trampled the geraniums." But, of course, sentences are vastly more variable than this, and this makes the identification of phrase endings appreciably more difficult.

To put this more broadly, in order to *understand* a sentence, you first need to **parse** the sentence—that is, you need to figure out each word's syntactic role. This will lead you directly to the sentence's phrase structure, which, as we have seen, can then guide your interpretation. (For broad reviews of the processes involved in parsing, see Abney & Johnson, 1991; Clifton, Speer & Abney, 1991.)

Parsing turns out to be a surprisingly complex process. One source of complexity is the *variety* of sentence forms you encounter. Another complication is *ambiguity*: You routinely encounter sentences that are ambiguous

Figure 9.12

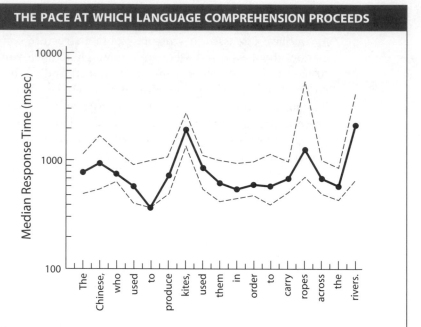

THE PACE AT WHICH LANGUAGE COMPREHENSION PROCEEDS

Subjects were shown the sentence, "The Chinese, who used to produce kites …," one word at a time. The pace of presentation, however, was controlled by the subjects, with subjects pressing a key, as they read, each time they felt ready for the next word. The key presses come quickly when subjects are in the middle of the phrase; the key presses are slower at the phrase boundaries (e.g., just after the word "kites"). This probably reflects the fact that, at the phrase boundaries, subjects are pausing to "assemble" the words they have heard so far, and request the next word only after they have finished this "assembly."

in their structure, requiring you to make decisions about how the sentence should be parsed. Several examples were provided in Figure 9.9, but let's note that even common sentences can be ambiguous if one is open-minded (or perverse) enough:

> Mary had a little lamb. (But I was quite hungry, so I had the lamb and also a bowl of soup.)
> Time flies like an arrow. (But fruit flies, in contrast, like a banana.)

Temporary ambiguity is also common *inside* a sentence. More precisely, the early part of a sentence is often open to multiple interpretations, but then the later part of the sentence clears things up:

> The old man the ships.

In this sentence, one tends to read the initial phrase as a three-word noun phrase—"the old man." However, this interpretation leaves the sentence with no verb. A different interpretation is demanded by the rest of the sentence, with the subject of the sentence being "the old" and with "man" as the verb. Likewise:

The secretary applauded for his efforts was soon promoted.

Here one tends to read "applauded" as the sentence's main verb but, of course, it isn't. Instead, this sentence is just a shorthand way of answering the question: "Which secretary was soon promoted?" (Answer: "The one who was applauded for his efforts.")

These last two examples are referred to as **garden-path sentences**: You are initially led to one interpretation (you are, as they say, "led down the garden path"), but this interpretation then turns out to be *wrong*. Hence, you need to reject your initial construal and seek an alternative. Here are two more examples:

Fat people eat accumulates.
Because he ran the second mile went quickly.

Garden-path sentences are interesting for several reasons. First, these sentences highlight the fact that parsing is often a complex business—to understand these sentences, one obviously needs to resolve the ambiguity. Second, it is interesting that one does a "double take" midway through these sentences. Apparently, therefore, you don't remain "neutral" as you read or listen to a sentence. Instead, you commit yourself fairly early to one interpretation or another and then try to "fit" subsequent words, as they arrive, into that interpretation. This strategy is probably an efficient one more often than not, but it does lead to the "double take" reaction, when the late-arriving information forces you to abandon your interpretive efforts so far. (This interpret-as-you-go tendency is also reflected, of course, in Figure 9.11; also see Just & Carpenter, 1987, 1992; Marslen-Wilson & Tyler, 1987; Morton, 1969, 1970.)

Finally, we can also use garden-path sentences as a research tool: What is it that leads us down the garden path? Why do we initially choose one interpretation, one parsing, rather than another? As we will see in a moment, garden-path sentences provide us with a useful means of addressing these questions.

Syntax as a Guide to Parsing

Evidence suggests that we use a bundle of different strategies in parsing the sentences we encounter. For one, we tend to assume, in general, that we will be hearing or reading *active* sentences rather than *passive,* and so we tend to interpret a sentence's initial noun phrase as the "doer" of the action not the recipient. As it happens, English speakers do use the active form more often than the passive (Svartik, 1966), and so this assumption is correct more often than not. However, this assumption works against us whenever we do encounter a passive sentence and, as a result, active sentences are somewhat easier to understand than are passive sentences (e.g., Hornby, 1974; Slobin, 1966).

Let's pause briefly, though, to add a note of caution to this claim: Some style books offer a blanket injunction against passive sentences, arguing that the passive should always be avoided. This is bad advice. The assumption of active voice is only *one* of the factors that guides parsing. In some contexts, therefore, with other factors on the scene, passive sentences can be *easier* to understand, not harder. (For discussion, see Pinker, 1994.)

What are the other factors guiding parsing? It is not surprising that parsing is also influenced by the little function words that appear in a sentence and also by the various morphemes that signal syntactic role (cf. Bever, 1970). One quickly grasps the structure of "He gliply rivitched the flidget." That's because the "-ly" ending indicates that "glip" is an adverb; the "-ed" ending identifies "rivitch" as a verb; and "the" signals that "flidget" is a noun—all excellent cues to the sentence's structure.

In addition, parsing seems to be guided by a number of other strategies, including an assumption of so-called **minimal attachment**. Roughly, this means that the listener or reader proceeds through a sentence seeking the simplest possible phrase structure that will accommodate the words heard so far. Consider the earlier sentence, "The secretary applauded for his efforts was soon promoted." As you read "The secretary applauded," you had the option of interpreting this as a noun phrase plus the beginning of a separate clause, modifying "secretary." This is, of course, the *correct* construal and is demanded by the way the sentence ends. However, the principle of minimal attachment led you to ignore this possibility, at least initially, and to proceed instead with a simpler interpretation—of a noun phrase + verb, with no idea of a separate embedded clause.

The "secretary" sentence also capitalizes on some other factors. The embedded clause is in the passive voice (the secretary was applauded by someone else); your tendency to assume active voice, therefore, worked against the correct interpretation of this sentence. Likewise, this sentence deliberately omits the helpful function words. Notice that we *didn't* say, "The secretary *who was* applauded. . . ." With all these factors stacked against you, no wonder you were led to the incorrect construal. Indeed, with all these factors in place, garden-path sentences can sometimes be enormously difficult to comprehend. For example, spend a moment puzzling over this (fully grammatical) sequence:

The horse raced past the barn fell.

(If you get stuck with this sentence, try adding commas after "horse" and after "barn.")

Semantics as a Guide to Parsing

The "secretary" sentence was also complicated by one further factor: The sentence said, "The secretary applauded for *his* efforts. . . ." Many people assume, in reading this sentence, that the secretary is a woman, hence "his" must refer to someone else. The suggestion, therefore, is that parsing is also guided by *semantic* factors, and not just syntax, and this turns out to be correct.

For example, we have already noted that, in general, it is easier to understand active sentences than it is to understand the corresponding passive sentence. However, this is only true if the sentence is "reversible," such as "The dog chased the cat." (or its passive: "The cat was chased by dog."). In this case, either the dog or the cat could plausibly be the chaser, and either could be the "chasee." But now consider this sentence "The elephant squashed the peanut." This sentence isn't reversible: Elephants can certainly squash peanuts, but peanuts can't squash elephants. In this case, therefore, you almost don't need the syntax to figure out who was the squasher and who was the squashed. And, indeed, for sentences like this, there is no processing advantage for the active form, relative to the passive (Slobin, 1966).

Semantic factors also influence us in another way: We have already mentioned the fact that different verbs seem to demand different sentence contexts, so that some verbs ("devour") demand a direct object, while other verbs insist that there be *no* direct object ("dine," "sleep"). Some demand a direct object *and* an indirect object ("give") and so on. (See Figure 9.10.) These patterns are presumably recorded in our "mental dictionary," and so, for each verb, the "dictionary" specifies the meaning of the verb and also the sorts of context in which that verb can appear.

There is every indication that these verb-based patterns are exploited by sentence parsing. Of course, you first need to locate the sentence's verb and look it up in your mental dictionary. Once that is done, though, you have a ready guide for interpreting key aspects of the sentence's structure (Trueswell,

Tanenhaus & Kello, 1995; but see also Ferreira & Henderson, 1990; Ford, Bresnan & Kaplan, 1982; Frazier, 1989).

Finally, listeners and readers also seem sensitive to certain statistical properties in the language. If a word has several meanings, we tend to assume its most frequent meaning, whenever we encounter the word. You therefore tend to assume that "train" means the thing on tracks rather than the activity one engages in to teach tricks to a dog. Likewise, you tend to assume that "tree" refers to a type of plant, rather than an activity (as in "The hounds want to tree the raccoon"). Similarly, we tend to assume that adjectives, when they occur, will be followed by nouns. This isn't an obligatory pattern, but it is certainly a frequent pattern, and so the assumption seems safe.

Once again, we can see these factors in action in some of the garden-path sentences: The assumption of adjective-noun gets us in trouble when we encounter "Fat people eat accumulates." Likewise, our reliance on frequent meanings is part of our problem in understanding sentences like "The old man ships," or "The new train quickly, but the old train more slowly."

Interactions between Syntax and Semantics

We have now seen that several different syntactic and semantic factors contribute to parsing. But how do all these factors combine? One possibility is that all of your knowledge is simultaneously brought to bear on a sentence. This might be a powerful procedure, since you would have a variety of resources to draw on as you parsed any bit of language. Semantic considerations might guide syntactic analyses, and syntactic considerations might guide semantic analyses. This position is referred to as an **interactionist** view (cf. Tyler & Marslen-Wilson, 1977).

A different possibility is that one uses different sources of information at different points in parsing a sentence. One might first attempt to analyze the sentence's syntax, uninfluenced by semantic considerations. With that done, one then brings semantic knowledge to bear. In this **modular** scheme, each individual stage seems less powerful, but stages might end up more streamlined, with less information to juggle, and so the stages might function more swiftly (cf. Fodor, 1983, 1985; Garfield, 1987).

The choice between these two approaches has been a matter of considerable research, and much of the research has, again, relied on garden-path sentences. Consider this example:

The defendant examined by the lawyer turned out to be unreliable.

In reading this sentence, subjects initially interpret "examined" as a verb in the active voice, with the defendant doing the examining. When they reach the word "by," though, they realize their error, and recompute. (This is evident either in subjects' reading speed or in their eye movements.)

But now consider this sentence:

The evidence examined by the lawyer turned out to be unreliable.

The syntax of this sentence is identical to that of the "defendant" sentence. But now common sense tells us that "examined" can't be in the active voice, since "evidence" isn't capable of examining anything. And, in fact, common sense prevents the garden-path misreading from occurring: Subjects march smoothly past the word "by," apparently having assumed from the start that "examined" was a past participle not an active verb. Thus, it seems, that, moment-by-moment, word-by-word, parsing *is* influenced by semantics. (Cf. Tanenhaus, Spivey-Knowlton, Eberhard & Sedivy, 1995. But also see McElree & Griffith, 1995; Mecklinger, Schriefers, Steinhauer, & Friderici, 1995; Trueswell, Tanenhaus & Kello, 1995.)

It does appear that the interactionist perspective provides a better fit with the facts, since the syntactic analysis of a sentence does seem to be guided by semantic considerations. The picture is different, though, if we consider the process of *word identification*. According to the interactionist view, the process of interpreting the individual words in a sentence should be interwoven with the process of integrating the various words to form coherent phrases. According to a modular view, however, these two processes—identifying individual words and then integrating them—should be separate and independent. It turns out that the modular view is closer to the truth.

For example, the word "bug" can mean a sort of insect, or it can mean a hidden microphone. Only one of these meanings is plausible, though, in this context:

Rumor had it that, for years, the government building had been plagued with problems. The man was not surprised when he found several spiders, roaches, and other bugs in the corner of his room.

Do listeners use this context, as they go, to identify the meaning of "bug"? Or are they initially neutral, or uncertain, about what this word means? The first outcome would be consistent with the interactionist perspective; the second outcome would favor a modular view.

Swinney (1979) probed these issues with a lexical-decision task. (We first encountered this task in Chapter 7.) Subjects heard tape-recorded sentences like the "Rumor had it . . . " sentence just quoted. Right after the word "bug," though, a computer flashed a string of letters on a screen, and subjects had to report, as quickly as they could, whether the string was a legitimate word or not. In some trials, the string "ant" was presented, and subjects' responses to this string were quite fast. Apparently, then, the sentences they were hearing had served to *prime* the idea of bug-as-type-of-insect, and this priming had spread to the word "ant." Priming was also observed, though, for the word "spy," and so responses to this word were reliably faster than responses to an independent control word (like "sew"). It would seem, therefore, that the presentation of "bug" had also activated the idea of bug-as-hidden-microphone, despite the fact that this interpretation of bug is ruled out by the context.

Things were different, though, if the lexical-decision task was delayed slightly. Thus, for example, subjects might again hear the "Rumor had it . . . " sentence, but this time the test word was presented right after subjects heard "corner"—i.e., just a few syllables *after* "bug." In this condition, priming *was* observed for "ant" (as before) but was *not* observed for "spy."

What is happening here? When the word "bug" is heard, it seems to call to mind *both* the (appropriate) idea of bug-as-type-of-insect *and* the (inappropriate) idea of bug-as-hidden-microphone. Hence, the initial activation is insensitive to the context, and so we are here seeing evidence for a modular process, with the processes of word identification *not* influenced by subjects' understanding of the surrounding words. A moment later, though, subjects have had a chance to "digest" the surrounding context and to integrate this context with their "bug" thoughts. The inappropriate idea, bug-as-hidden-microphone, is somehow "turned off," and so it ceases the priming of the related idea, "spy." In effect, the word-identification process is initially quite "open-minded" but, a moment later, it makes its selection and "shuts down" all ideas but one. (For related data, see Onifer & Swinney, 1981; Seidenberg, Tanenhaus, Leiman & Bienkowski, 1982; Simpson, 1984. For discussion of related phenomena, see May, Kane & Hasher 1995.)

The Use of Language: What Is Left Unsaid

Earlier in this chapter, we argued that a rich set of rules is needed to explain why some sound combinations, some words, and some sentences, seem acceptable to speakers of a language, while others do not. These rules must be acquired by anyone who wishes to learn a language; indeed, these rules are a part of what it means "to know a language."

As we have now seen, we need a further set of principles to account for how the language is perceived and understood—either by the listener or by the reader. Several different syntactic principles seem relevant, as do several different semantic principles. These factors then interact in an intricate fashion—with some bits of semantic knowledge penetrating into syntactic processing, but with other aspects of processing proceeding in a modular fashion.

Note, though, that this brief overview surely *understates* the complexity of sentence parsing. For one, we have said nothing about how one deals with *pronouns*, as in:

Fred went swimming; Sam played tennis; later he napped.

Who napped? Here, a principle of "recency" seems crucial, and most people believe that it is Sam who napped. In other cases, though, other principles come into play:

Susan waved at Maria, but then she insulted her.

Who insulted whom? Here it is grammatical role that seems to matter, so that "she," the subject of the second phrase, seems to refer to "Susan," the subject of the first phrase. In short, then, we will need still other principles to deal with pronouns. (For a fuller treatment of pronouns, see Gordon & Scearce, 1995; Just and Carpenter, 1987).

We have also not mentioned a further source of information useful in parsing: the rise and fall of speech intonation and the pattern of pauses. These rhythm and pitch cues are together called **prosody** and play an important role in speech perception. Prosody can reveal the mood of a speaker; it can also direct the listener's attention by, in effect, specifying the focus or theme of a sentence (Jackendoff, 1972). Prosody can also render unambiguous a sentence that would otherwise be entirely confusing (Beach, 1991). (Thus, garden-path sentences and ambiguous sentences are much more effective in print, where prosody provides no information.)

Finally, we have not even touched on several related puzzles. For one, how is language *produced*? How does one turn ideas, intentions, and queries into actual sentences? How does one turn the sentences into sequences of sounds? These are important issues but, for brevity's sake, we have held them to the side here. (For a tutorial review of these issues, see Fromkin, 1993.)

Likewise, what happens *after* one has parsed and understood an individual sentence? How is the sentence integrated with earlier sentences or subsequent sentences? Here, too, more theory is needed to explain the inferences we routinely make in ordinary conversation. If you are asked, "Do you know the time?" you understand this as a request that you *tell* the time—despite the fact that the question, understood literally, is a yes/no question about the extent of your temporal knowledge. In the same vein, consider this bit of conversation (after Pinker, 1994):

Woman: "I'm leaving you."
Man: "Who is he?"

We easily provide the soap-opera script that lies behind this exchange, but we do so by drawing on a rich set of further knowledge, including knowledge of **pragmatics** (that is, knowledge of how language is ordinarily used) and, in this case, also knowledge about the vicissitudes of romance. (For discussion, see Austin, 1962; Ervin-Tripp, 1993; Grice, 1975; Hilton, 1995; Kumon-Nakamura, Glucksberg & Brown, 1995.)

If you are intrigued by the topic of language, then these topics—pronouns, prosody, production, and pragmatics—certainly warrant further exploration. For our purposes, though, this fast mention of these topics at least serves to lend emphasis to a central message of this chapter: Each of us uses language all the time—to learn, to gossip, to instruct, to persuade, to express affection. We use this tool as easily as we breathe; we probably spend more effort in choosing our dinner menu than in choosing the words we will utter in the sentences we speak. Yet, despite this ease of use, and this centrality of use, and the universality of use for human language, language is a remarkably complicated tool, and we are all exquisitely skilled in its use.

The Biology of Language

How is all of this possible? How is it that ordinary human beings—indeed, ordinary two-and-a-half-year-olds—manage the extraordinary task of mastering and fluently using language? We have already suggested part of the answer: Humans are equipped with extremely sophisticated neural machinery, specialized for learning, and then using, language. In this final section, therefore, we will give a quick overview of this neural machinery.

Aphasias

Much of what we know about the neural basis for language comes from the study of brain damage. As we have seen in other chapters, brain damage can cause a variety of effects, depending on where and how widespread the damage is. For a number of brain sites, damage causes disruption of language—a disruption known as **aphasia**.

Aphasias take many different forms and are often quite specialized. The specific symptoms observed in any case of aphasia depend on the locus of the brain damage. It should be said, however, that this correspondence between brain location and type of aphasia is somewhat rough, since two patients with similar brain damage will sometimes show very different forms of aphasia. This probably reflects the fact that the hunk of brain tissue supporting any particular function is anatomically quite small; moreover, the bits of brain tissue needed for a function may be anatomically interlaced with brain tissue involved in some other function. Therefore, if the zone of damage extends just a few neurons further on one patient than it does on another, this may have a large impact on the pattern of damage observed. This is why it is often difficult to discern a precise relation between site of damage and nature of symptoms.

Nonetheless, the study of aphasias has allowed us to locate many brain regions crucially involved in the production and comprehension of language. For example, damage to the left frontal lobe of the brain (Figure 9.13) produces a pattern known as **Broca's aphasia**, in which patients show relatively good language *comprehension* but disrupted *production*. Moreover, the speech they produce is "agrammatic": They produce strings of nouns and (to a lesser

Figure 9.13

BRAIN AREAS CRUCIAL FOR THE PERCEPTION AND PRODUCTION OF LANGUAGE

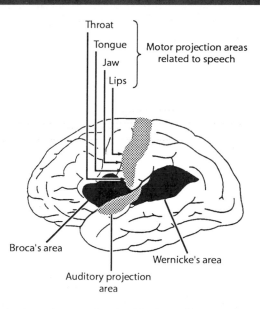

Many different brain regions are involved in the ordinary understanding or production of language. Many of these regions, however, are positioned close together; for most individuals, these regions are in the left cerebral hemisphere (as shown here). Broca's area is heavily involved in language production; Wernicke's area plays a crucial role in language comprehension.

extent) verbs, but with none of the function words ("of," "to," "by"), and with no inflections (e.g., no marking of plural, no marking of verb tense).

In contrast, damage in another area produces **Wernicke's aphasia**. Patients with this disorder seem largely unable to *comprehend* speech, but the speech that they produce sounds effortless and fluent, with the function words and the appropriate suffixes all correctly in place. As it turns out, though, their speech makes no sense. Here is a quotation from a patient with Wernicke's aphasia (after Gardner, 1974):

> Oh sure, go ahead, any old think you want. If I could I would. Oh I'm taking the word the wrong way to say, all of the barbers here whenever they stop you it's going around and around, if you know what I mean, that is tying and tying for repucer, repuceration, well, we were trying the best that we could while another time it was with the beds over there the same thing . . .

Still other aphasics show a pattern called **echolalia**: They turn into virtual echo-boxes, able to repeat back anything they hear. However, these patients show no sign of understanding the speech they are echoing, nor do they produce speech on their own. Other patients show yet another pattern, with brain damage causing disruption to their "mental dictionary." These patients suffer from **anomia** and lose the ability to *name* various objects. Anomias can be extraordinarily specific: Some patients can use concrete nouns but not abstract nouns; some can name animate objects but not inanimate ones; some patients lose the ability to name colors. Still other patients show a pattern called "pure word deafness." These patients can speak, write, and read normally, and they can hear perfectly well, but they can't make any sense out of the language they hear. (For descriptions of the various aphasias, see Caplan, 1987, 1992; Dingwall, 1993; Hillis & Caramazza, 1991.)

The specificity of these disorders seems to imply that separate "processing units" are responsible for this or that particular chore, within the larger scheme of producing and understanding language. By close examination of these patients, researchers hope that they will be able to characterize each "processing unit" and then, eventually, understand how the units work together for intact language use. In addition, the technology of brain-mapping is steadily improving and, as it does, there is reason to believe that we will be able to clarify the linkage between specific language disorders and specific brain regions. In that way, there is real hope that we will also understand at a *neural* level how these "processing units" function and interact.

Language Function in the Intact Brain

The biological roots of language use are also visible in subjects with no neurological damage. For example, all humans have a number of anatomical specializations, apparently provided by evolution for purposes of supporting speech. Thus, virtually all mammals can manage the trick of eating and breathing at the same time. (This is handy if you want to sniff the air for predators while you are eating lunch.) Human infants can do this as well (and so babies can breathe and nurse simultaneously). However, adults cannot do this, thanks to the arrangement of our throat (and, in particular, the shape of the human larynx).

The adult human larynx not only blocks us from breathing while eating, it also dramatically increases the risk of death by choking, since it is all too easy for humans to end up with food going down the larynx, rather than the esophagus. Why, then, did evolution burden us with this arrangement? Because the arrangement allows us considerably more control over the flow of air through the vocal tract, which in turn is crucial for the production of speech. The obvious suggestion, then, is that the evolutionary value of speech outweighed the cost associated with this throat arrangement, and that is why all modern humans have a throat arrangement that supports the vocal output of language.

Biological specializations for language can also be observed in the brains of all humans. We have discussed the fact that *damage* to certain brain sites causes a disruption of language, indicating that these sites are crucial for language use. This claim is confirmed by brain-imaging studies, using the PET or MRI techniques introduced in Chapter 3. For example, damage to Wernicke's area produces an inability to comprehend speech. Conversely, if we examine intact brains, we discover that Wernicke's area is particularly activated when subjects are asked to make simple judgments about words (e.g., Peterson, Fox, Posner, Mintern & Raichle, 1989; Peterson, Fox, Snyder & Raichle, 1990). Similarly, we have noted that the speech of Broca's aphasics is highly agrammatic. This lines up nicely with the finding that Broca's area, in an intact brain, is particularly activated by tasks that require grammatical processing—e.g., telling a story or understanding complicated sentences (e.g., Caplan, 1992).

In short, then, we have ample evidence that specific sections of the brain are, indeed, specialized for one or another aspect of language use. This is clearly the message of the aphasia evidence; it is plainly reflected in studies recording the activity of intact, healthy brains. We can close this chapter, then, by circling back to a theme that was prominent at the chapter's start: We argued early on that language is something central to our species, and is crucial for many of the activities our species engages in. As we have now seen, it is likewise clear that specializations for language are very much evident in the biology of our species, making it certain that, in an important sense, we are indeed linguistic creatures.

10

Visual Knowledge

In Chapter 9, we focused entirely on knowledge about language. In Chapters 7 and 8, we weren't focusing on language, but, as it turns out, we were largely concerned with knowledge we might call "verbal"—knowledge that can be expressed in words. Of course, this knowledge probably *isn't* represented in the mind via words; we argued, in fact, for a different, more abstract, mental code. Nonetheless, the knowledge we were describing could be readily translated into mental propositions with a "subject-predicate" format.

What about knowledge of other sorts? You know what ammonia smells like, as well as apple pie and strawberries. Knowledge of this sort is not readily verbalizable, and is not in any obvious way translatable into propositions. How is this "smell knowledge" represented in the mind? Likewise, you remember the sound of a guitar or a fire-engine's siren; you know what Judy's voice sounds like, and you can recall how it contrasts with Barbara's. What can we say about this auditory knowledge? You also have visual memories, and memories for pains and for tastes. In each case, how is this nonverbal knowledge encoded in memory?

Psychologists have examined many of these types of knowledge—memory for odors (Algom & Cain, 1991; Lyman & McDaniel, 1990; Schab, 1990, 1991); for familiar voices (Van Lancker, Kreiman & Wickens, 1985; Van Lancker, Kreiman & Emmorey, 1985; Nairn & Pusen, 1984); for movements (Engelkamp, Zimmer, Mohr & Sellen, 1994); and for pain (Algom & Lubel, 1994; Eich, Reeves, Jaeger & Graff-Radford, 1985; Kahneman, Fredrickson, Schreiber & Redelmeier, 1993; Kent, 1985; Linton & Melin, 1982; Rachman & Eyrl, 1989), to name just a few.

In this chapter, we will explore this nonverbal knowledge, with our main emphasis on visual knowledge. We will ask how this knowledge is recorded in memory, and also how this knowledge is used. Several factors motivate this focus on visual knowledge, but the main consideration is straightforward: Far more is known about visual knowledge than about knowledge in any other modality. As we proceed, though, you should try to read this chapter on two different levels. At a concrete level, we will be surveying what is known about visual knowledge and visual imagery. At the same time, we will also be pursuing a broader agenda, as we seek to illustrate more generally how one can do research on nonverbal knowledge and what questions need to be asked about such knowledge.

Visual Imagery

How many windows are there in your house or your apartment? Who has bushier eyebrows, Sylvester Stallone or Bill Clinton? For most people, questions like these seem to elicit "mental pictures." You know what Clinton and Stallone look like, and you call a "picture" of each before your "mind's eye" in order to make the comparison. Likewise, you call to mind a "map" of your apartment, and count the windows by inspecting this "map." Many people even trace the "map" in the air, by moving their finger around, following the imagined map's contours.

Various practical problems also seem to evoke images. There you are in the store, trying on a new sweater. Will the sweater look good with your blue pants? To decide, you will probably try to visualize the blue of the pants, thus using your "mind's eye" to ask how they will look with the sweater. Equivalently, there you are in the hardware store, hoping to fix your leaky faucet. Is this washer the right size? You will probably try to visualize what the old washer looked like, comparing it to the one in your hand. Or, as a different example: "Where did I leave my keys? Did I leave them on my desk?" I may try to decide by visualizing what my desk looked like when I left my office—were the keys in view?

These examples illustrate the common, everyday use of visual images—as a basis for making decisions, as an aid to remembering. But what are these images? Surely there is no tiny eye, somewhere deep in your brain; thus the phrase "mind's eye" cannot be taken literally. Likewise, mental "pictures" cannot be actual pictures—with no eye deep inside the brain, who or what would inspect such pictures?

Introspections about Images

Mental images have been described and discussed for thousands of years. However, it is only within the last century or so that psychologists have begun to gather systematic data about imagery. Among the earliest researchers was Francis Galton, who asked various people to describe their images and to rate them for vividness (Galton, 1883). In essence, Galton asked his subjects to introspect, and to report on their own mental contents. The self-report data he obtained fit well with common sense: The subjects reported that they could "inspect" their images much as they would inspect a picture. In their images, scenes were represented as if viewed from a certain position and a certain distance. Subjects also reported that they could "read off" from the image details of color and of texture. All of this implies a mode of representation that is in many ways picture-like, and is of course quite consistent with our informal manner of describing mental images as "pictures in the head," to be inspected with the "mind's eye."

There was also another side of Galton's data: Galton's subjects differed widely from each other. Many described images of photographic clarity, rich in detail, almost as if they were *seeing* the imaged scene, rather than visualizing it. Other subjects, however, reported very sketchy images, or no images at all. They were certainly able to think about the scenes or objects Galton named for them, but in no sense were they "seeing" these scenes. Their self-reports rarely included mention of color or size or viewing perspective; indeed, their reports were largely devoid of visual qualities.

These observations are in themselves interesting—do individuals really differ in the nature of their mental imagery? If so, what consequences does this have? Are there tasks that the "visualizers" can do better than the "non-visualizers" (or vice versa)? If so, this could provide crucial information about how visual imagery is used, and what it is good for.

Before we can answer these questions, though, we must address a methodological question raised by Galton's data, a question which we have met before: Can we take these self-reports at face value? Perhaps all of Galton's subjects had the same imagery skill, but some were cautious in how they chose to describe their imagery, while others were more extravagant. In this way, Galton's data might reveal differences in how people *talk* about their imagery, rather than differences in the imagery per se. (For further discussion of this issue, see Chapters 1 and 14.)

These concerns highlight the difficulties inherent in self-report data. These data, by their nature, are always filtered through a subject's verbal habits. What is revealed in the data, therefore, is not *imagery*. Instead, what is revealed is "imagery as the subject elects to describe it." And there is always a danger that these descriptions will be misleading in some way, or incomplete, or perhaps just imprecise. What seems required is a more *objective* means of assessing imagery, which does not rely on the subjectivity inherent in self-reports. With this more objective approach, we could assess the differences, from one individual to the next, evident in Galton's data. Indeed, with this more objective approach, we could hope to find out exactly what images *are*.

Chronometric Studies of Imagery

One useful strategy would be to ask subjects to *do* something with their images—to read information off of them, or to manipulate them in some way—allowing us to measure how well they do. This more objective approach has characterized the last twenty-five years of imagery research, with much of this research drawing on a straightforward claim: Mental processes are relatively quick, but they do take some measurable amount of time. Even the simplest of decisions requires a quarter of a second or so (250 msec), and more complex decisions take correspondingly longer. This opens up an interesting research strategy for us: We can ask what factors slow down a task, or speed it up; likewise, we can ask which variations of a task require slightly more time, and which require slightly less. We can then use this information to develop a theory about the mental processes and representations needed for task performance.

What information is available in a mental image? What can subjects "read" from their images easily, and what can they read only with difficulty? These questions can provide important clues about the nature of imagery representation but, to understand the data, we need a bit of background: Think about how pictures themselves are different from verbal descriptions. Concretely, consider what would happen if you were asked to write a paragraph describing a cat. It seems likely that you would mention the distinctive features of cats—their claws, their whiskers, and so on. You probably would not include the fact that cats have heads, since this is too obvious to be worth mentioning. Now consider, in contrast, what would happen if we asked you to draw a sketch of a cat. In this format, the cat's head would be prominent, for the simple reason that the head is relatively large and up front. The claws and whiskers might be less salient, because these features are small, and so would not take up much space in the drawing.

The point here is that the pattern of what information is included, and what information is prominent, depends on the mode of presentation. For a *description* of a cat, size or position won't matter for prominence, but these factors will matter for a *depiction* of a cat. Conversely, distinctiveness and strength of association will heavily influence what is mentioned in a description; these factors matter less for a depiction.

Against this backdrop, let's now ask what information is available in a visual image. Is it the pictorially prominent features, which would imply a depictive mode of representation, or verbally prominent ones, implying a descriptive mode? Self-reports about imagery surely indicate a picture-like representation; is this confirmed by the data?

In a study by Kosslyn (1976), subjects were asked to form a series of mental images, and to answer yes/no questions about each. For example, subjects were asked to form a mental image of a cat, and then asked: Does the cat have a head? Does the cat have claws? Subjects responded to these questions quickly but, strikingly, responses to the head question were quicker than those to the claws question. This suggests that information quickly available in the image follows the rules for pictures, not paragraphs. In contrast, a different group of subjects was asked merely to think about cats (with no mention of imagery). These subjects, asked the same questions, gave quicker responses to claws than to head, the *reverse* pattern of before. Thus, it seems that subjects have the option of thinking about cats via imagery, and also the option of thinking about cats without imagery and, as the mode of representation changes, so does the pattern of information availability.

Here is a different experiment, making a related point (Kosslyn, Ball & Reiser, 1978). Subjects were asked to memorize the fictional map shown in

Figure 10.1 and, in particular, to memorize the locations of the various landmarks: the well, the straw hut, and so on. The experimenters made sure subjects had the map memorized by asking them to draw a replica of the map from memory; once they could do this, the main experiment began. Subjects were asked to form an image of the island, and to point their "mind's eye" at a specific landmark, let us say the well. Another landmark was then mentioned, perhaps the straw hut, and subjects were asked to imagine a black speck moving in a straight line from the first landmark to the second. When the speck "reached" the target, subjects pressed a button, stopping a clock. This provides a measure of how long it takes to scan from the well to the hut. The same was done for the well and the palm tree, the hut and the rock, and so on, so that we end up with "scanning times" for each of the various pairs of landmarks.

Figure 10.2 shows the results. The data clearly suggest that subjects scan across their image at a constant rate, so that doubling the scanning "distance" doubles the time required, tripling the distance triples the time required. This in turn implies that the image somehow preserves the various distance relationships that were present in the original map: Points that were close together on the map are somehow close together in the image; points that were further apart on the map are further apart in the image. Thus, in a very real sense,

Figure 10.1

MAP OF A FICTIONAL ISLAND USED IN IMAGE-SCANNING EXPERIMENTS

Subjects in the study first memorized this map, including the various landmarks (the hut, the well, the patch of grass, and so on). Subjects then formed a mental image of this map for the scanning procedure. [After Kosslyn, 1983.]

Figure 10.2

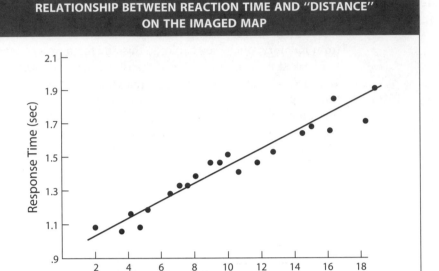

RELATIONSHIP BETWEEN REACTION TIME AND "DISTANCE" ON THE IMAGED MAP

Subjects had to "scan" from one point on their mental image to another point; they pressed a button to indicate when their "mind's eye" had arrived at its destination. Response times in this task were closely related to the "distance" subjects had to scan across on the image, implying that mental images are similar to actual pictures in how they represent positions and distance. [After Kosslyn, 1983.]

the image preserves the spatial lay-out of the original map. The image *depicts* *in your mind* the map, rather than describing it.

Similar results are obtained if subjects are given a task that requires them to "zoom in" on their images (for example, a task that requires them to inspect the image for some small detail), or a task that requires them to "zoom back" (e.g., a task that requires a more global judgment). In these studies, response times are directly proportional to the amount of "zoom" required, suggesting once again that travel in the imaged world resembles travel in the actual world, at least with regard to timing. Subjects in one study were asked to imagine a mouse standing next to an elephant, and were then asked to confirm, by inspecting their image, that the mouse has whiskers. This task yields relatively slow response times, since subjects need some time to zoom in, in order to "see" the whiskers. Response times are faster if subjects are initially asked to imagine the mouse standing next to a paper clip. For this image, subjects can start with a "close-up" view and so, in this set-up, no zooming is needed.

Physical Distance, Functional Distance

The data pattern in these experiments is just what we would expect if subjects were literally zooming in on, or scanning across, actual pictures. If subjects were scanning across an actual map, for example, using some sort of pointer that moved at a constant rate, then it follows from simple algebra that scanning times will be directly proportional to scanning distance. No one is suggesting, though, that images are actually laid out the way pictures or maps are. Instead, what the scanning data tell us is that points close together on the map are *functionally* close together on the image. This does not require that these points be *physically* close together on the image (and similarly for the "zooming" data).

To understand this distinction between physical and functional proximity, consider Figure 10.3. Imagine that the list shown in the figure is recorded in some computer's memory. Imagine further that the process of scanning down the list is extremely fast—so fast, in fact, that even a brief scan will move you *five* positions down the list: If you launch a scan, you will move five positions before you have a chance to stop. Consequently, there is no way you can move *fewer than* five positions in any one scan. Now let's think about a specific scan: If you read the list's first entry (A), and then do the briefest possible scan, the next entry you encounter will be F. If you scan again, the next entry you encounter will be *C* (thanks to the loop-back feature we've included in the list). Therefore, A and F are *physically separated*, but *functionally close*. Physically, they are five steps apart but, functionally, they are merely one scanning-step apart. A and B, in contrast, are physically close, but functionally distant (five scanning-steps apart).

Of course, functional proximity depends both on physical locations and also on how one "travels" or scans through physical locations. A and F are close together only by virtue of this five-step scan. With different travel modes, different sets of points would be functionally close. For example, if the briefest possible scan carried you only *three* steps, then A and D would be just one step apart; A and F would, with this scan, be *seven* scans apart, instead of one.

Returning to the image-scanning data, we know that subjects can scan quickly from the imaged hut to the imaged well. But this does not mean that some brain activity, corresponding to the imaged hut, is physically side by side with brain activity corresponding to the imaged well. In our computer-list example, subjects could scan quickly from A to F, even though these were physically separated in the computer's memory. The same may be true for

Figure 10.3

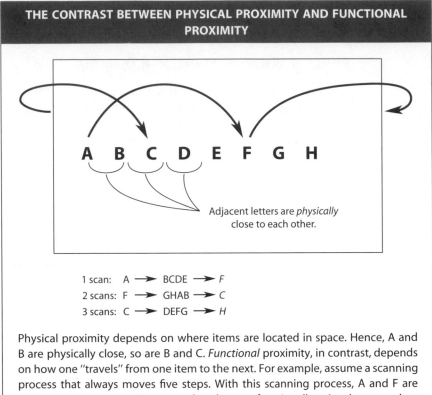

THE CONTRAST BETWEEN PHYSICAL PROXIMITY AND FUNCTIONAL PROXIMITY

Adjacent letters are *physically* close to each other.

1 scan: A → BCDE → F
2 scans: F → GHAB → C
3 scans: C → DEFG → H

Physical proximity depends on where items are located in space. Hence, A and B are physically close, so are B and C. *Functional* proximity, in contrast, depends on how one "travels" from one item to the next. For example, assume a scanning process that always moves five steps. With this scanning process, A and F are just one "scanning step" apart, and so they are *functionally* quite close together, even though they are *physically* distant from each other. A and C are two "scanning steps" apart (thanks to the "loop-back" feature we have built into the scan). A and B are actually five scanning steps apart—hence, physically close, but functionally far from each other.

the imaged hut and well: We know that these two are functionally close—this is just another way of saying that each is quickly reached starting from the other. But this does not entail that they are physically close. Perhaps they are, and perhaps they are not. The scanning data don't tell us that.

Let's be clear, then, that the chronometric studies of imagery don't tell us how images are physically manifested in the brain. In terms of their *physical* lay-out, we simply don't know if images are picture-like or not. But what the scanning data do tell us is of enormous importance. Images preserve distance relationships, so that *functional proximity* in the image directly reflects *physical proximity* in the imaged scene. As a direct consequence of this, the image also preserves information about shapes and sizes within the imaged scene, and also many of the spatial relations present in the scene (relations such as one point being *between* two other points, or *aligned with* other points, and so on). It is in this fashion that images preserve the geometry of the depicted scene and, indeed, it is in this way that images *depict* spatial lay-out.

Mental Rotation

So far, we have seen impressive correspondence between the time needed to travel within a mental image and the time needed to move relative to an actual picture—in both cases, greater "distances" require greater "travel-time." Other results make a similar point with regard to the *transformation* of mental images.

Consider the display shown in Figure 10.4A. In a series of experiments by Shepard, Cooper, and Metzler, subjects were asked to decide whether displays like this one showed two different shapes, or just one shape viewed from two different perspectives. In other words, is it possible to "rotate" the form shown on the left in Figure 10.4A, so that it will end up looking just like the form on the right? What about the two shapes shown in Figure 10.4B, or the two in 10.4C?

To perform this task, subjects seem first to imagine one of the forms rotating into "alignment" with the other. Then, once the forms are oriented in the same way, subjects can make their judgment. This step of imagined rotation takes some time, and, in fact, the amount of time it takes depends on how much rotation is needed. Figure 10.5 shows the data pattern, with subjects' response times clearly influenced by how far apart the two forms were, in their initial orientations. Thus, once again, imagined "movement" resembles actual movement—the further a form has to be rotated, the longer it takes (Cooper & Shepard, 1973; Shepard & Metzler, 1971).

The mental-rotation task can be used to answer a number of questions about imagery. For example, notice that the two forms in Figure 10.4A are identical except for a "picture-plane" rotation. In other words, if you were to cut out the left-hand drawing, and spin it around (while leaving it flat on the table), you could align it with the drawing on the right. The relevant rotation, therefore, is a rotation that leaves the pictures within the two-dimensional plane in which they are drawn. In contrast, the two forms shown in Figure 10.4B are identical except for a rotation *in depth*. No matter how you spin the *picture* on the left, it will not line up with the picture on the right. You can align these forms, but to do so you need to spin them around a vertical axis, in essence lifting them off the page.

Subjects have no trouble with depth rotation. They make very few errors (with accuracy levels around 95%), and the data resemble those obtained

Figure 10.4

STIMULI FOR A MENTAL ROTATION EXPERIMENT

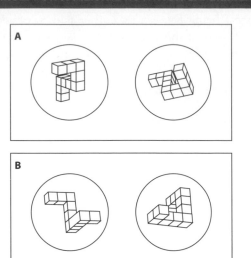

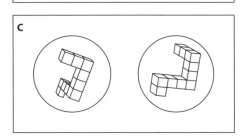

Subjects had to judge whether the two stimuli shown in Panel A are the same as each other, but viewed from different perspectives; likewise for the pairs shown in B and C. Subjects seem to make these judgments by imagining one of the forms rotating until its position matches that of the other form. [After Shepard & Metzler, 1971.]

with picture-plane rotation. Figure 10.5A shows data from picture-plane rotation; Figure 10.5B shows data from pairs requiring depth rotation. In both cases, there is a clear relation between angle of rotation and response times, and the speed of rotation seems similar for both. Apparently, then, subjects can represent three-dimensional forms in their images, and they can imagine these forms moving in depth. In some circumstances, therefore, visual images are not mental pictures—they are more like mental sculptures. (For a review,

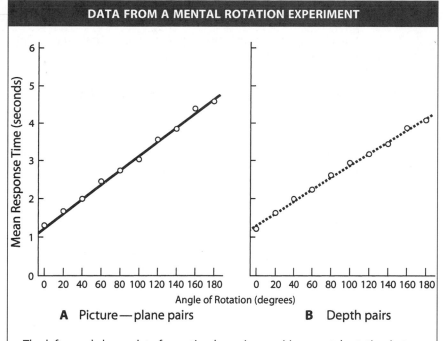

Figure 10.5

DATA FROM A MENTAL ROTATION EXPERIMENT

A   Picture—plane pairs

B   Depth pairs

The left panel shows data from stimulus pairs requiring mental rotation in two dimensions—such that the imaged forms stay "within" the imagined picture-plane. The right panel shows data from pairs requiring an imagined rotation in depth. The data are obviously similar, indicating that subjects can imagine three-dimensional rotations as easily, and as swiftly, as they can imagine two-dimensional rotations. In both cases, the greater the degree of rotation required, the longer the response times. [After Shepard & Metzler, 1971.]

see Shepard & Cooper, 1982. For data on image *scanning* in three-dimensions, see Pinker & Finke, 1980; Pinker, 1980.)

We should mention in passing that there has been some controversy about the exact relationship between response-time and degree of rotation. In Figure 10.5, this relationship is linear, with the implication that subjects imagine these forms rotating at a constant velocity (around 60 msec for every degree of rotation). Other studies have suggested that, in some circumstances, the speed of mental rotation is *not* constant, particularly if subjects are imagining familiar forms rotating, rather than the made-up forms illustrated in Figure 10.4. (See, for example, Parsons, 1995.)

However, let's not allow this complication to distract us from the main finding: Across procedures, response times reliably increase as the angle of rotation increases. Thus, in mental rotation, just as in mental scanning, "distance" relations are functionally preserved so that, in all cases, the further the imagined "travel," the longer it takes.

Interactions between Imagery and Perception

We have now observed a number of correspondences between visual images and actual visual stimuli, and this leads to a question: If images are so much like pictures, then are the processes used to inspect images similar to those used to inspect stimuli? To put it more broadly, what is the relation between imaging and perceiving?

In a study by Segal and Fusella (1970, 1971), subjects were asked to detect very faint signals—either dim visual stimuli, or soft tones. On each trial, the subjects' task was merely to indicate whether a signal had been presented or not. Subjects did this in either of two conditions: either while forming a visual image before their "mind's eye," or while forming an auditory image before their "mind's ear." Thus we have a 2 × 2 design—two types of signals to be detected, and two types of imagery.

Let's hypothesize that there is some overlap between imaging and perceiving. That is, there are some mental structures, or mental processes, used by both activities. Therefore, if these processes or structures are occupied with imaging, they are not available for perceiving, and vice versa. We should expect competition if subjects try to do both activities at once. That is exactly what Segal and Fusella observed: Their results, shown in Figure 10.6, indicate that forming a visual image interferes with seeing, and that forming an auditory image interferes with hearing (see also Farah & Smith, 1983).

Notice, though, that the Segal and Fusella subjects were trying to visualize one thing while perceiving something altogether different. What happens if subjects are trying to image a stimulus *related to* the one they are trying to perceive? Can visualizing a stimulus "pave the way" for perception? Farah (1985) had subjects visualize a form (either an "H" or a "T"). A moment later, either an "H" or a "T" was actually presented, although at a very low contrast, making the letter difficult to perceive. Perception was facilitated if subjects had just been visualizing the target form and, again, the effect was quite specific—visualizing an "H" made it easier to perceive an "H", visualizing a "T" made it easier to perceive a "T". This provides further confirmation of the claim that visualizing and perceiving draw on similar mechanisms, so that one of these activities can serve to prime the other. (For further discussion, see Farah, 1989; Heil, Rösler & Hennighausen, 1993; also see McDermott & Roediger, 1994.)

Similar conclusions can be drawn from biological evidence. For example,

Figure 10.6

CAN ONE VISUALIZE AND SEE AT THE SAME TIME?

	Percentage Detections			Percentage False Alarms	
	Visual signal	Auditory signal		Visual signal	Auditory signal
While visualizing	61%	67%	While visualizing	7.8%	3.7%
While maintaining an auditory image	63%	61%	While maintaining an auditory image	3.6%	6.7%

Subjects were less successful in detecting a weak visual signal if they were simultaneously maintaining a visual image than if they were maintaining an auditory image. (The effect is small, but highly reliable.) The reverse is true with weak auditory signals: Subjects were less successful in this detection if maintaining an auditory image than if visualizing. In addition, visual images often led to "false alarms" for subjects trying to detect visual signals; auditory images led to false alarms for auditory signals. [After Segal & Fusella, 1970.]

we know a great deal about the specific brain structures required for vision; it turns out that many of the same structures are crucial for imagery. This can be documented in several ways, including techniques, described in Chapter 3, that map the moment-by-moment pattern of activity in the brain. These techniques can tell us which brain regions are heavily activated during a particular task and which are not. Thus, we know that when subjects are visualizing, activity levels are high in various parts of the occipital cortex—the brain area central for visual perception (Farah, 1988; also Isha & Sagi, 1995; Miyashita, 1995).

Likewise, consider studies of brain damage, usually damage resulting from stroke. We mentioned in Chapters 1 and 2 that this damage can, in some cases, disrupt subjects' ability to perceive; in Chapter 3, we saw that other forms of brain damage can disrupt the ability to pay attention to visual inputs. It turns out that these same forms of brain damage disrupt the ability to image, so that patients often have "parallel" gaps in their perception and their imagery: Patients who, because of a stroke, lose the ability to perceive color often seem to lose the ability to imagine scenes in color; patients who lose the ability to perceive fine detail seem also to lose the ability to visualize fine detail, and so on (Farah, 1988; Farah, Soso & Dasheiff, 1992; for some contrasting data, however, see Behrmann, Moscovitch & Winocur, 1994).

In one striking case, a patient had suffered a stroke and, as a result, had developed the "neglect syndrome" we described in Chapter 3: If this patient was shown a picture, he seemed to see only the right side of it; if asked to read a word, he only read the right half. The same pattern of neglect was evident in the patient's imagery: In one test, the patient was urged to visualize a familiar plaza in his city, and to list the buildings "in view" in the image. If the patient imagined himself standing at the southern edge of the plaza, he listed all the buildings on the plaza's west side, but none on the east. If the patient imagined himself standing on the *northern* edge of the plaza, he listed all the sights on the plaza's *east* side, but none on the west. In both cases, therefore, the subject "neglected" the right half of the imaged scene, just as he did with perceived scenes (Bisiach & Luzzatti, 1978; Bisiach, Luzzatti & Perani, 1979).

"Sensory" Effects in Imagery

Clearly, the neural "machinery" needed for imagery overlaps with that needed for perception. If the machinery is occupied with one of these functions, it is not available for the other. If the machinery is damaged, then both activities are compromised. If we scrutinize activation patterns, we find that, to a large extent, the same brain structures are involved in visualizing and in vision. All of this indicates an intimate relationship between imagery and perception.

Against this backdrop, we would expect imagery and perception to share many traits, and research indicates that this is the case. For example, consider **visual acuity**, that is, the ability to see fine detail. In vision, acuity is much greater at the center of the visual field than it is in the visual periphery. Can we find a comparable pattern in imagery? Is it easier to discern detail at the image's center than at its periphery?

There are many ways to measure acuity, one of which is an assessment of "two-point acuity." In this test, subjects are shown two dots. If the dots are 5 mm apart, can the subjects see that there are two separate dots, or do the dots seem to "fuse" into one? How about a 4 mm separation? By determining the point at which the dots do fuse together, we can assess subjects' ability to discern the small gap that actually separates the dots.

In vision, two-point acuity is greatest when subjects are looking directly at the dots; under these circumstances, even minuscule gaps can be detected. However, if we position the dots 10 degrees away from subjects' line of vision, acuity is far worse. What about imagery? In one study, subjects were first shown two dots of the appropriate size. The dots were then removed, but subjects were asked to imagine the dots as still being present. Subjects then moved their eyes away from the imaged dots' position and, as they looked further and further away, they had to judge whether they could still "see" that the dots were separate. In this way, "two-point acuity" was measured with imaginary stimuli (Finke & Kosslyn, 1980).

The data show a remarkable correspondence between subjects' performance with actually perceived dots and their performance with imagined dots. In both cases, acuity fell off abruptly if the dots were not in the center of vision and, indeed, the pattern of fall-off was virtually the same in perception and in imagery. Moreover, in vision, acuity falls off more rapidly if subjects look *above* or *below* the two dots, rather than to the left or right. This pattern was also observed in the imagery condition. Thus, qualitatively and quantitatively, the imagery data match the perceptual data. (For a variety of related data, see Finke, 1989. We should note, though, that there has been some controversy about these data and so, for alternative views, see Harris, 1982; Intons-Peterson & White, 1981; Kolers, 1983; Kunen & May, 1981.)

Spatial Images and Visual Images

We are building an impressive case, therefore, for a close relationship between imagery and perception. Indeed, the evidence implies that we can truly speak of imagery as being *visual* imagery, drawing on the same mechanisms, and having the same traits, as actual vision. Other results, however, add some complications.

A number of studies have examined imagery in subjects blind since birth (Carpenter & Eisenberg, 1978; Kerr, 1983; Marmor & Zabeck, 1976; also see Jonides, Kahn & Rozin, 1975; Paivio & Okovita, 1971; Zimler & Keenan, 1983). In tests involving mental rotation, or image scanning, these subjects yield data quite similar to those obtained with *sighted* subjects—with response times proportionate to the "distance" traveled, and so on.

It seems unlikely that blind subjects are using *visual* imagery to perform these tasks. Therefore, these subjects must have some *other means* of thinking about spatial layout and spatial relations. This "spatial imagery" might be represented in the mind in terms of a series of imagined movements, so that it is "body imagery" or "motion imagery" rather than visual imagery. (Reisberg & Logie, 1993, provide a discussion of motion-based imagery; also Engelkamp, 1986, 1991; Saltz & Donnenwerth-Nolan, 1981.) Alternatively, perhaps spatial imagery is not tied to any sensory modality, but is part of our broader cognition about spatial arrangements and lay-out.

One way or another, though, it seems we do need to distinguish between visual imagery and spatial imagery and, moreover, it seems likely that sighted subjects have access to *both* of these types of imagery. As further evidence for this distinction, consider the interference observed between imagery and vision. We have already noted that many studies have documented this interference: It is difficult to image one stimulus while looking at another. (In addition to the studies already mentioned, pertinent data are reported by Johnson, 1982; Logie, 1986; Matthews, 1983.) Other studies, though, have not shown this pattern. For example, Baddeley and Lieberman (1980) asked their subjects to imagine a 4 × 4 matrix; within this matrix, the second square in the second row was designated as the starting square. Subjects then heard a series of sentences telling them how to "fill" this imagined matrix: "In the starting square, place a '1'; in the next square to the right, put a '2'; in the next square up, put a '3'," and so on. Then, after a short delay, subjects had to report back the "contents" of the matrix.

It seems likely that this task requires imagery, but what sort of imagery is relevant? In one condition, subjects tried to remember these matrices while simultaneously doing a visual interference task: As they were hearing the sentences, subjects were shown a series of lights, some of which were bright and others dim; their task was to press a key whenever they saw a bright stimulus. In a second condition, subjects had to remember the matrices while simultaneously doing a spatial interference task: They were required to move their hands in a particular spatial pattern, but they were blindfolded, so that they could not rely on vision in guiding their motions.

In this study, no interference was observed when subjects were asked to memorize the matrices while simultaneously doing the visual task. It would appear, therefore, that memorizing the matrices does *not* depend on "visual skills," and so it doesn't matter if these skills are otherwise occupied. Interference was observed, though, when the matrix task was combined with spatial interference—these two tasks, it seems, do overlap in their processing demands, and so cannot be done simultaneously. Apparently, then, memorizing this matrix depends on some sort of spatial skills and, correspondingly, it seems that the imagery relevant to this task is spatial, not visual, in nature. (For related evidence, see Logie & Marchetti, 1991; Morris, 1987; Quinn, 1988; Quinn & Ralston, 1986; Smyth & Pendleton, 1989.)

In short, some imagery tasks are disrupted by simultaneous visual activity; we used this as an argument that these tasks draw on visual imagery. Other imagery tasks, however, are not disrupted by simultaneous visual activity, but are disrupted by simultaneous spatial activity, with the implication that these tasks draw on spatial imagery, not visual. Apparently, we do need to distinguish different types of imagery, and it appears that both forms of imagery are available to most subjects.

The same claims are reflected in neuropsychological data. Consider the case of L.H., a brain-damaged subject studied by Farah, Hammond, Levine and Calvanio (1988). L.H.'s brain damage was the result of an automobile accident, but he has recovered remarkably well. Even after his recovery, however, he continued to have trouble with a variety of visual tasks: In one test, the experimenter named a number of common objects (e.g., "football"), and

L.H. had to report the color of each (for the football, "brown"). Control subjects got 19 of 20 items correct; L.H. got only 10 correct. In another test, the experimenter named an animal (e.g., "kangaroo"), and L.H. had to indicate whether the animal had a long tail or short, relative to its body size. Again, control subjects got 19 of 20 items correct on this test; L.H. got only 13 correct.

In contrast, L.H. does well in spatial tasks, including several of the tasks we have already described—image scanning, mental rotation, and the like. Indeed, on the Baddeley and Lieberman matrix task (described a few paragraphs back), L.H. was correct on 18 of 20 items, virtually identical to the performance of control subjects.

Thus, L.H. does poorly on tasks requiring judgments about visual appearance, or memory for visual appearance. He does quite well on tasks requiring spatial manipulations, or memory for spatial positions. To make sense of L.H.'s profile, therefore, it seems once again crucial to distinguish between visual tasks and spatial ones and, correspondingly, between visual imagery and spatial imagery.

Individual Differences

As we have already noted, both forms of imagery are available to most of us—visual imagery, relying on mechanisms usually involved in seeing, and spatial imagery, perhaps represented in the mind via imagery for movements, or perhaps represented in some abstract, "non-sensory" format.

Some tasks will surely require visual imagery rather than spatial. (Consider, for example, the tasks that L.H. could *not* do.) Other tasks may require spatial imagery rather than visual. In addition, still other tasks can go either way—that is, they can be supported by imagery of either type. In this last sort of task, which form of imagery we use will depend on our preferences, aspects of the instructions, and (probably) a variety of other factors. The choice between these forms of imagery may also be influenced by each individual's ability levels. In essence, some people may be poor visualizers, but good "spatializers"; these people would surely rely on spatial imagery, not visual, in most tasks.

We need to be careful, though, in describing these individual differences. The evidence suggests that it is too crude to speak of "good imagers" or "bad imagers" in general. Instead, some individuals seem quite adept at scanning their images, and so they do well on imagery tasks that involve a lot of scanning. These same individuals might be less talented, say, in elaborating their images, and so they will do less well on tasks that require elaboration. Other subjects have a different profile: They might be good at elaboration, but poor at *finding* things in their images, and so they will do well if an imagery task requires a lot of elaboration, and they will do poorly if the task requires a lot of finding. (For discussion, see Kosslyn, Brunn, Cave & Wallach, 1985.)

It would appear, therefore, that our analysis of imagery skill must be fairly fine-grained: Imagery tasks turn out to depend on a number of "subskills," and each of us seems to have our own profile of strengths and weaknesses, across these various subskills. Thus, rather than speaking of "good" and "bad" imagers, we need to be more specific, in describing which *aspects* of imagery a person can or cannot do well.

This still leaves us with a question about one rather striking way in which individuals seem to differ in their imagery, namely, *image vividness*. Recall Galton's data, mentioned early on in this chapter. Some of Galton's subjects described their imagery as rich and vivid and detailed, in short, very much like "seeing." Other subjects described their imagery as being relatively sparse, and not at all like vision. What should we make of these reports?

One research strategy would be this: Based on these self-reports about imagery vividness, we could categorize subjects as "vivid imagers," "sparse imagers," and so on. We could then test these subjects on tasks like image scanning or mental rotation. The obvious prediction would be that subjects with vivid imagery will do well in these tasks, while subjects with sparse imagery will do poorly. If this prediction worked out, we would have confirmation of the self-report data and, indeed, we would have indication that individuals do truly differ in how they consciously experience images.

A number of studies have tested these predictions, and the results are surprising: In a great many studies, there has been no relation between the vividness of subjects' imagery—assessed via self-report—and performance on these imagery tasks. (For reviews, see Ernest, 1977; Katz, 1983; Marks, 1983; Reisberg, Culver, Heuer & Fischman, 1986; Richardson, 1980.) There is no difference, for example, between vivid imagers and sparse imagers in how they do mental rotation, how quickly or accurately they scan across their images, or how effective their images are in supporting memory. Indeed, individuals who insist they have *no* imagery do as well as everyone else on these tasks; individuals who insist they have clear and detailed imagery show no corresponding performance advantage.

Given this pattern, we might choose to disbelieve the self-reports of imagery vividness. As we mentioned earlier in the chapter, perhaps individuals all have the same imagery experience, but simply choose to describe their experience in different ways. In this case, the vividness reports reflect different styles of talking about imagery, not differences in imagery. (These are precisely the concerns that made us wary of introspective data from the start.)

However, we would urge a different view of the evidence, guided by the distinction between visual and spatial imagery: When subjects describe their images as "vivid," they are, in general, describing the *visual* richness of their imagery. Indeed, many questionnaires, seeking to measure the imagery experience, explicitly ask subjects how much their image experience is "like seeing." In contrast, many imagery tasks require spatial judgments (e.g., judgments about relative distance or position) or spatial manipulations (scanning, rotation, folding). The obvious proposal, therefore, is that the self-reports assess visual imagery, while these laboratory tests require spatial imagery. No wonder, then, that there is little relation between the self-reports and the laboratory data—they are measuring different things.

If this view is correct, then subjects' vividness reports—a measure of visual imagery—should be related to performance on tasks that require visual imagery. For example, consider the two-point acuity experiment already described. This experiment seems to require little in the way of spatial judgments; instead, this test requires subjects to imagine exactly what something would *look like*. Therefore, this test seems likely to draw on visual, not spatial, imagery. And, consistent with our prediction, it turns out that performance in this test *is* related to imagery self-report: Subjects who describe their imagery as vivid yield data in this experiment in close correspondence to the perceptual data; subjects with less-vivid imagery do not show this correspondence (Finke & Kosslyn, 1980). This experiment (and many others—e.g., Heuer, Fischman & Reisberg, 1986; Reisberg & Leak, 1987) lends credibility to our claim: Subjects' reports on their conscious imagery experience reflect the *visual* richness of that experience. These reports are not related to how well subjects do on *spatial* tasks. However, these reports do seem related to how well subjects do on visual tasks. (For a broad review, see McKelvie, 1995.)

Images Are Not Pictures

Let's pause to take stock. We began this section by offering an informal comparison between imagery and "mental pictures." That comparison is hardly new—it is embedded in the way all of us talk about our imagery. Yet we have seen a number of cases in which this comparison may be misleading. First, the data tell us that images functionally preserve the lay-out of the imaged scene, but this does not mean that images physically preserve this lay-out. Thus, the image might *function* like a picture, but this is different from saying the image *is* (or *is like*) a picture. Second, we have seen that mental images can be three-dimensional; this too places limits on the image-picture comparison. Third, we have now seen grounds for distinguishing between visual images, which might be more picture-like, and spatial images, which may be movement-based or perhaps more abstract. Visual images are likely to draw on processes overlapping with those used in ordinary vision, but this is probably not the case for spatial images. Again, this implies that the idea of the "mind's eye" inspecting a "mental picture" often will be inappropriate.

Another line of research indicates a further way in which images and pictures differ. Pictures obviously have an existence independent of us, and independent of our understanding or perception. Thus, the raw material of the picture itself is separable from the interpretation we place on this raw material. As a consequence, illusions are possible, in which the picture has one set of characteristics, but our perception of it has some other characteristics. Similarly, pictures can be ambiguous, with more than one interpretation possible. For example, the cube at the top of Figure 10.7, the so-called Necker cube, can be perceived as a transparent version of either cube A or cube B. The Necker cube itself (that is, the *drawing* of the cube) is neutral with regard to interpretation; it is fully compatible with either interpretation A or interpretation B. Our perception, though, isn't neutral—it specifies one configuration or another, again emphasizing the distinction between the picture *per se* and our interpretation or understanding of it.

Is all of this true for images as well? Is there some raw material, akin to the picture, onto which we place an interpretation? Many psychologists would

Figure 10.7

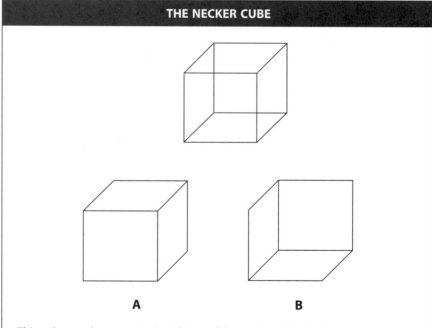

THE NECKER CUBE

A   **B**

This cube can be perceived as if viewed from above (in which case it is a transparent version of Cube A) or as if viewed from below (i.e., a transparent version of Cube B).

say "yes" to these questions (Finke, 1980; Kosslyn, 1980, 1983). Others, though, offer a different view. Images, they argue, are not physical things, with an existence independent of us. Instead, an image exists only because some person is imagining something. If the imager ceased visualizing, or decided to visualize something else, then the image would cease to exist. As a result, the image exists only in the context of the imager's understanding of it, and so the image and its comprehension are inseparable. There is no raw material, neutral with regard to interpretation. (For broad discussion of this perspective, see Casey, 1976; Fodor, 1981; Kolers & Smythe, 1984; Reisberg, 1994.)

This view of imagery has a number of consequences, and we can use these consequences to devise tests of this theoretical perspective. (For data that appear to challenge this claim, see Berbaum & Chung, 1981; Wallace, 1984a, 1984b; for a reply to these data, see Predebon & Wenderoth, 1985; Reisberg & Morris, 1985.) One line of evidence comes from the study of ambiguous figures: We know that pictures are reinterpretable; that was the point of our comments about the Necker cube. With pictures, you can set aside your initial interpretation, "return" to the raw material (the drawing itself), and then find a new interpretation—discovering, for example, that cube A and cube B are both possible interpretations of the drawing. Is the same true for images? Given the claims we have just made, it should not be true. On this view, one can't return to the "raw material" of the image, in order to reinterpret it, since there is no raw material—no free-standing icon existing independent of the imager's intentions.

A study by Chambers and Reisberg (1985) sought to test this claim. Their subjects were briefly shown a drawing of an ambiguous figure (such as the Necker cube, or the duck/rabbit—Figure 10.8). The subjects were then asked to form a mental image based on that drawing. All of the subjects had previously been trained so that they understood what was meant by an ambiguous figure and had successfully reinterpreted a series of practice figures. Subjects were then asked if they could reinterpret their image, just as they had reinterpreted the practice figures.

The results are easily summarized: Across several experiments, no subjects succeeded in reinterpreting their images: Subjects reliably failed to find the duck in a "rabbit image" or the rabbit in a "duck image." One might be concerned, though, that subjects did not understand their task, or perhaps did not remember the figure. To rule out these possibilities, subjects were given a blank piece of paper, immediately after their failure at reinterpreting their images, and asked to draw the figure, based on their image. Now, looking at their own drawings, all of the subjects were able to reinterpret the configuration in the appropriate way. Thus, we have 100% failure in reinterpreting these forms with images, and 100% success, a moment later, with the draw-

Figure 10.8

THE DUCK/RABBIT

This figure can be perceived either as a duck or as a rabbit. With the picture in view, subjects readily find both interpretations of the figure. However, if subjects are *imaging* the figure, they have great difficulty finding a different interpretation. That is, subjects imaging the "duck" have great difficulty in discovering the "rabbit"; subjects imaging the "rabbit" have great difficulty in discovering the "duck."

ings. This result is obviously problematic for the claim that images are neutral stimuli, subject to reinterpretation. Instead, this result seems strong confirmation of the claim that images are inherently meaningful, and so entirely unambiguous.

Learning from Images

In some ways, the results just cited are puzzling. It seems clear from common experience that mental images often surprise us, or remind us of something. We routinely consult our images in solving problems or in making decisions. Indeed, the history of science is filled with examples of discoveries apparently inspired by an image (see, for example, Miller, 1986). Many laboratory studies have also shown that subjects can invent new forms, or new devices, by inspecting and manipulating their images (Anderson & Helstrup, 1993; Finke, 1990; Finke & Slayton, 1988; Pinker & Finke, 1980; also see Chapter 13). Yet, in the Chambers and Reisberg study, subjects universally failed to make a discovery from imagery—even though they easily made the comparable discovery from a picture. How should we reconcile all these findings? Why are discoveries from imagery sometimes possible and sometimes not?

Perhaps some *types* of discovery can easily be made from imagery, while other types cannot. In this way, there might be no conflict between subjects' success in learning from imagery in a wide range of circumstances, and their *failure* to learn from imagery in the Chambers and Reisberg procedure. For example, Peterson, Kihlstrom, Rose and Glisky (1992) distinguish between "reconstruals" of an image and "reference-frame changes" of the image. Reconstruals require no change in one's perceptual understanding of the image. For example, you might first perceive Figure 10.8 as a rabbit, and then perceive it as child with her hair tied in pig-tails. In this case, there has been no change in your understanding of the figure's basic shape, including where its top is, where its front is, and so on. The reconstrual of images, defined in this way, happens easily and frequently, with no need for special hints or instructions.

In contrast, reference-frame changes do involve a shift in one's basic understanding of a form. For example, if you first perceive Figure 10.8 as a rabbit, and then as a duck, you have changed your understanding of the form's front, and also of the relations among the form's parts. Unlike reconstruals, discoveries of this sort seem to happen rarely with images, and are heavily dependent on hints and instructions. (For related data with verbal materials, see Keil, 1980.)

A study by Reisberg and Chambers (1991) provides evidence for these claims. Their subjects were asked to memorize a series of shapes; the tenth shape in the series, presented with no special notice, was the one depicted in Figure 10.9. Subjects had five seconds in which to memorize this shape, and then the picture was removed. Subjects were next asked to form an image of the shape, and then to imagine the shape rotated by 90° clockwise. At this point, subjects were told that the shape "resembles a familiar geographic form" and were asked to identify that form.

It seems likely that subjects understood the side topmost in the original drawing as being the shape's top. This understanding probably did not change when subjects imagined the rotation. In other words, when subjects imagined the rotation, they rotated both the form *and* its reference frame. As a consequence, subjects were, in this experiment, imaging the "right geometry" for Texas, but with the "wrong understanding," that is, specifying the wrong top. Therefore, in Peterson et al.'s terminology, discovering Texas in this image requires a reference-frame change—a shift in how the form is understood. As a result, we should predict that subjects will *not* make this discovery. This is correct: Exactly zero subjects were able to discover Texas in their image.

In a subsequent experiment, subjects were led through the same procedure, but this time they were explicitly instructed in how to *change* their understanding of the imaged form. That is, they were told directly to think of the form's left edge as being the "top." With this instruction, many subjects

When doing mental image rotations you often don't change your reference point (unless told to)

Figure 10.9

LIMITATIONS ON LEARNING FROM IMAGERY

Subjects imaged this form, thinking of it merely as an abstract shape. When asked to imagine the form rotated by ninety degrees, subjects failed to discover the familiar shape of Texas. Subjects' understanding of the imaged form (and, in particular, their understanding of the form's "top") prevented them from recognizing the Lone Star State. When subjects were explicitly instructed to change this understanding, many were able to discover Texas.

were able to discover Texas in the image. Apparently, then, the obstacle to discovery is indeed how subjects understand the image. When this understanding changes, there is a corresponding change in performance.

These results obviously fit with the claim that images are inherently understood in a certain way—a way that specifies, for example, which side of the form is the *top*, which side is the *front*, and so forth. This understanding then sets "boundaries" on what can be discovered about the image: Discoveries *compatible* with the imager's understanding of the form flow easily from the image; discoveries *incompatible* with the understanding are rare. Of course, imagers do have the option of changing how they understand the form. For example, we have just discussed a case in which subjects, with explicit instruction, change their assignment of the image's "top." And, once these changes occur, they can have powerful effects: When the imager's understanding of the form changes, a range of new discoveries, compatible with the new understanding, becomes available. Evidence suggests, however, that these changes in reference frame are surprisingly difficult, and often dependent on specific instructions, or specific training examples. Therefore, one's *initial* understanding of the form has a strong effect on what can be discovered from an image. (For further discussion, see Chapter 13; also Reisberg, 1996.)

Images and Pictures—An Interim Summary

Images, both visual and spatial, provide a distinctive means of representing the world, so that imagining a robot is quite different from thinking about the word, "robot" or describing a robot to yourself, or merely contemplating the idea "robot." As one distinctive attribute, images seem functionally to preserve the spatial lay-out of the imaged scene: Aspects of the scene that are, in fact, close together, are functionally close together in the image. Aspects of the scene that are large will, functionally, occupy a large portion of the image. Likewise, images depict a scene from a particular vantage point—as if the scene were viewed from a specific distance and a specific perspective.

In these regards, then, images (both visual and spatial) are indeed picture-like. At the same time, though, we have also highlighted ways in which images are *not* picture-like and, correspondingly, regards in which the processes of imagery are distinct from those of perception. A picture of the Necker cube (Figure 10.8) is neutral with regard to depth; an image of the Necker cube, in contrast, seems to specify an arrangement in depth, seems to specify whether it is cube A or cube B that is being thought about. In this sense, then, the image contains *more information* than the corresponding picture.

As one last example, consider these two pictures: One picture shows three rows of dots, with four dots in each row. The second picture shows four columns of dots, with three dots in each column. Needless to say, these two pictures would be identical. The corresponding images, though, turn out not to be identical. Subjects take longer, for example, to generate the second image, presumably because it contains a larger number of "units"—four columns, rather than three rows (cf. Kosslyn, 1983). Here, too, we have an example of an image more specific than a picture. Figure 10.10 contains no indication of whether we are looking at three rows of dots, or four columns. A mental image of Figure 10.11, though, does somehow specify this information.

We can thus catalog many instances in which images contain *more* than pictures. We should also mention that, in others ways, images can contain *less* than pictures. If a picture shows a cat sitting on a mat, then the picture will necessarily show whether the mat is one color or striped, smooth or textured. (Of course, the picture might be out of focus, or the mat might be obscured from view. But, in this case, there is still information about the mat—namely, that it is out of focus or hidden from view.) An *image* of a cat sitting on a mat, in contrast, might contain no indication of the mat's color or texture, and likewise might contain no information about whether the mat was in view or not. We will not pursue this point here, but let us note in passing that once again we find an important limit on the image-picture

Figure 10.10

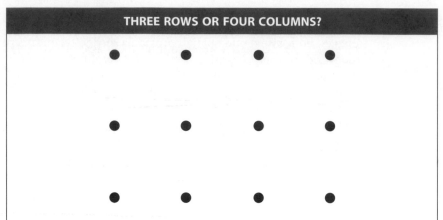

THREE ROWS OR FOUR COLUMNS?

This picture shows "three rows of dots." The same picture also shows "four columns of dots." There is, in short, no difference between a picture of "rows" and a picture of "columns." There is a difference, however, between a mental *image* of "three rows of dots" and a mental image of "four columns." The latter image, for example, takes longer to generate and is more difficult to maintain, presumably because it contains a larger number of "units"—four columns, rather than three rows.

comparison. (For discussion of these "image omissions," see Arnheim, 1969; Chambers & Reisberg, 1992; Dennett, 1981; James, 1890; Titchener, 1926.)

Where does all this leave us? Images are plainly different from pictures in important ways. However, this cannot distract us from how much images *do* have in common with pictures and, likewise, of the considerable overlap between imagery and perception. In short, images share *some* properties with pictures, and so images are, in many ways, picture-like. Nonetheless, images are not pictures.

Long-Term Visual Memory

So far, our discussion has focused on "active" images, images currently being contemplated, images presumably held in working memory. What about visual information in long-term memory? The images we have been considering are, of course, often based on this long-term storage. If you are asked to form an image of an elephant, you draw on information in long-term memory, information that records what you know about elephant appearances. But this long-term storage surely has other uses as well. For example, we obviously can remember scenes, pictures, and faces, and we use these memories to recognize these things if we encounter them again. How is this visual information recorded in memory?

Image Information in Long-Term Memory

We have already seen one way in which perceptual information might be encoded in memory. In our discussion of network models (Chapter 7), we considered the possibility that some nodes within the network are connected directly to the perceptual apparatus. These nodes played an important role in our account of how memory search begins, of how one "enters" the network (see, for example, pp. 257–259). Thus, the node for "apple" might be connected to nodes for "red," "round," and so on. These nodes would then be triggered by perceptual processes able to discern redness, roundness, and the like. In perceiving, these nodes would receive data-driven (or "bottom-up") activation, originating in the perceptual apparatus. In remembering appearances, or in forming an image, these same nodes might receive their activation from other nodes within the network; this would be concept-driven (or "top-down") activation. In both cases, though, these nodes would function as all nodes do—accumulating activation until they reach threshold, then letting their own activation spread out to their neighbors. In this way, there is no difficulty including nodes in the network for particular colors, or musical timbres, or smells.

One might extend this proposal to include intact visual images. In essence, one might have nodes containing entire pictures or templates, and these nodes could be triggered either by data-driven or concept-driven processes. However, evidence speaks against this idea. Research by Kosslyn (1980, 1983) and his associates indicates that images are not created by activating intact templates. Instead, one first creates an "image frame," depicting the form's global shape. Then elaborations can be added to this frame, as the imager wishes, to create a full and detailed image. Importantly, the image is created piece-by-piece, and the imager has some degree of control over how complete, and how detailed, the ultimate image will be.

This process of image construction depends on information in long-term memory, information specifying what a cat looks like, or what a circle looks like, and so on. This information is organized, Kosslyn argues, in **image files**, with each file specifying the appearance of a particular object, or a particular stimulus. Crucially, though, what is contained in these image files is *descriptive* information. In effect, the image file can be thought of as a set of instructions, or even a "recipe," for creating an image. By analogy, someone could instruct you in how to create a picture by uttering the appropriate sentences: "In the

info in LTM stored in non image format

top left, place a circle. Underneath it, draw a line, angling down . . . " and so on. Such instructions would allow you to create a picture, but there is nothing pictorial about the instructions themselves—the instructions are sentences, not pictures. In the same way, the instructions within an image file allow you to create a representation that, as we have seen, is picture-like in important ways. However, this information in long-term memory is not at all picture-like. These "imagery recipes" are probably encoded as propositions and, as such, they are easily analyzed in network terms.

This distinction between an active image and an image file is important for several reasons. For one, we have argued that the active image does have special status—it represents information in a distinctive way, compared to other forms of representation, and is operated on with special processes (such as "scan," "rotate," or "zoom"), processes that are irrelevant to other forms of thought. At the same time, though, image *files* may have no special status within long-term memory. These files can be encoded as propositions, and thus stored in the same fashion as other materials. Thus, we do want to distinguish imagery from other forms of thought, but this may have no consequences at all for our theorizing about long-term memory.

The distinction between active images and image files also matters for imagery function. Bear in mind that the image file will often contain more information than is represented in the currently active image. This "extra" information is not available to subjects scanning or inspecting the image— they are inspecting the active image, not the image file. As a result, we can find seemingly paradoxical cases in which subjects know quite well what something looks like, but fail to "see" this information in their image. But there is no paradox here; instead, this simply describes a case in which some information, perhaps information crucial for a task, is recorded in the image file but not represented in the currently active image. (For relevant data, see Chambers & Reisberg, 1992; for other evidence illuminating the contrast between active images and image files, see Hitch, Brandimonte & Walker, 1995.)

Verbal Coding of Visual Materials

In long-term memory, we have suggested, images are represented in some non-image format. That is, long-term memory contains a "recipe" for the image. In other cases, though, long-term memory will contain something even simpler—a verbal label.

For example, consider memory for color. It is appreciably easier to remember a color if one has a label for it, so that individuals with large "color vocabularies" have better color memories. This leads to striking contrasts if we gather data in different cultures, capitalizing on the fact that some languages have many words for describing and categorizing colors, while other languages have only a few. It turns out that this linguistic variation has no impact on how subjects *perceive* color, but does play an important role in memory—color memory is superior in those cultures with a greater number of color terms (Brown & Lenneberg, 1954; Rosch, 1977b). This implies that, in many cases, subjects are remembering a verbal description for the stimulus colors, rather than the colors themselves.

A related point was made by Carmichael, Hogan and Walter (1932). Their subjects were shown pictures like those in Figure 10.11. Half of the subjects were shown the top form and told, "This is a picture of eyeglasses." The other half were told, "This is a picture of a barbell." Subjects were later required to reproduce, as carefully as they could, the pictures they had seen. Subjects who had understood the picture as spectacles produced drawings that resembled spectacles; subjects who understood the picture as weights distorted their drawings appropriately. This is again what one would expect if subjects had memorized the description, rather than the picture itself, and were recreating the picture based on this description.

It seems that, in some cases, visual information may be stored in memory, not via imagery, but as a description of the previously-viewed object. Moreover, this is a *helpful* strategy: Memory is improved when an appropriate label, or appropriate description, is available. (This is certainly true in the color-memory studies.) However, this strategy can backfire: Subjects may end up recalling a picture in a fashion that is distorted by their understanding of it, or perhaps selective in ways that their description was selective. This obviously resembles the schema effects described in Chapter 6.

Imagery Helps Memory

We have so far been concerned with *how* visual information is represented in long-term memory. However, no matter how images are stored in memory, it is also clear that images *influence* long-term memory in important ways. More precisely, there are numerous ways in which imagery can improve memory. For example, materials that evoke imagery are considerably easier to remember than materials that do not evoke imagery. This can be demonstrated in many ways, including this two-step procedure: First, subjects are presented with a list of nouns, and asked to rate each noun, on a 1-to-7 scale, for how readily it evokes an image (Paivio, 1969; Paivio, Yuille & Madigan, 1968). Examples of words receiving high ratings are "church," with an average rating of 6.63, or "elephant," rated at 6.83. Words receiving lower ratings included "context" (2.13) and "virtue" (3.33).

As a second step, we ask whether these imagery ratings, generated by one group of subjects, can be used to predict memory performance with a new group of subjects. New subjects are asked to memorize lists of words, using

[handwritten margin note: their drawing was distorted b/c of their misunderstanding of it]

Figure 10.11

THE INFLUENCE OF VERBAL LABELS ON VISUAL MEMORY

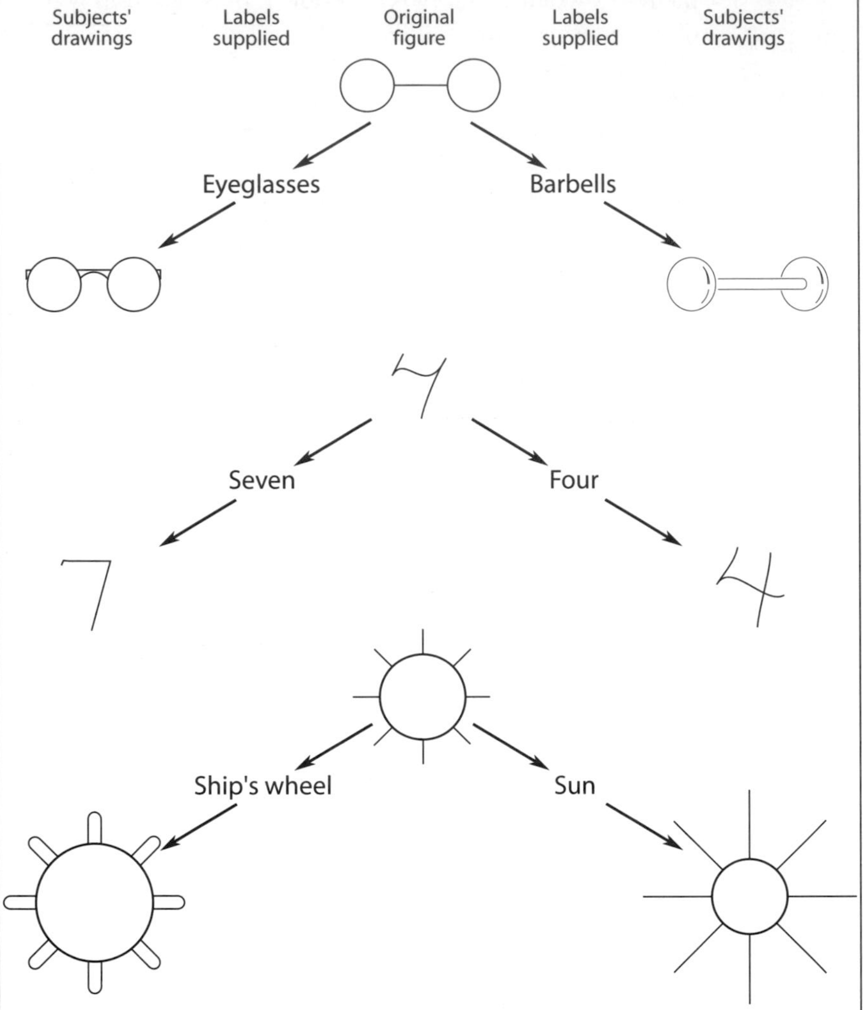

Subjects' drawings	Labels supplied	Original figure	Labels supplied	Subjects' drawings

Eyeglasses   Barbells

Seven   Four

Ship's wheel   Sun

Subjects were shown the figures in the middle column. If the top figure was presented with the label "eyeglasses," subjects were later likely to reproduce the figure as shown on the left. If the figure was presented with the label "barbells," subjects were likely to reproduce it as shown on the right. (And so on for the other figures.) One interpretation of these data is that subjects were remembering the verbal label and not the drawing itself and then, at the time of test, reconstructed what the drawing must have been based on the remembered label.

the words for which we have imagery ratings. The data indicate that subjects more readily learn high-imagery words than low-imagery words (Paivio, 1969). If asked to learn word-pairs, subjects perform best if both words in the pair are high-imagery words, perform worst if both are low-imagery words, and perform at intermediate levels if one word in the pair is a high-imagery word and the other is not (Paivio, Smythe & Yuille, 1968; but also see Marschark & Hunt, 1989).

In the same fashion, memory can be enormously aided by the use of imagery mnemonics. In one study, some subjects were asked to learn pairs of words by rehearsing each pair silently. Other subjects were instructed to make up a sentence for each pair of words, linking the words in some sensible way. Finally, other subjects were told to form a mental image for each pair of words, with the image combining the words in some interaction. The results showed poorest recall performance by the rehearsal group, and intermediate performance by the group that generated the sentences. Both of these groups, though, did appreciably less well than the imagery group (Bower & Winzenz, 1970; for discussion of other mnemonic techniques, see Chapter 4).

We might mention that imagery instructions have comparable effects with subjects who have been blind from birth. These subjects benefit from instructions to remember words by forming images, just as sighted subjects do (Jonides et al., 1975). Likewise, the memory advantage for easily imaged words can also be observed with blind subjects (Paivio & Okovita, 1971; Zimler & Keenan, 1983). Apparently, then, spatial images can improve memory just as much as visual images. (For further discussion of whether mnemonic images need be "visual," see Keenan, 1983; Keenan & Moore, 1979; Kerr & Neisser, 1983; Luria, 1968; Neisser & Kerr, 1973.)

We should also mention one side issue: In using imagery mnemonics, subjects are generally encouraged to make their images as elaborate or as bizarre as they like and, in fact, the suggestion is often made that bizarre images are more readily remembered. However, the evidence for this claim is mixed. For example, subjects in one study learned words pairs, with each pair illustrated by a line drawing. Four kinds of drawings were used, as shown in Figure 10.12. The drawings depicted the objects either interacting in some way or separate, and in either a bizarre, or non-bizarre fashion. The results show no memory impact of bizarreness. Memory was considerably improved, however, when the objects were shown in some interaction than when the objects were shown separately (Wollen, Weber & Lowry, 1972).

It is surely no surprise that memory is aided by interacting images. As we saw in Chapter 4, memory is improved in general if one can find ways to organize the material; interacting images provide one means of achieving this organization. But what about bizarreness? The Wollen et al. study shows no

Figure 10.12

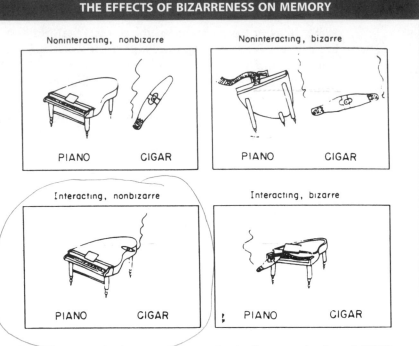

THE EFFECTS OF BIZARRENESS ON MEMORY

Noninteracting, nonbizarre

PIANO   CIGAR

Noninteracting, bizarre

PIANO   CIGAR

Interacting, nonbizarre

PIANO   CIGAR

Interacting, bizarre

PIANO   CIGAR

best one

Subjects were required to memorize word pairs (for example, the pair PIANO—CIGAR). The pairs were accompanied by drawings that were either nonbizarre (left column) or bizarre (right column), and that involved the two items either not interacting in any way or interacting. Memory was improved if the two items were shown as interacting; bizarreness had no effect. [After Wollen, Weber, & Lowry, 1972.]

memory advantage for bizarre images, but other studies do show an advantage, with subjects more likely to remember bizarre images than common ones. Einstein and McDaniel have argued that this effect will be observed only if the bizarre images are mixed together with more common images. If subjects only see a succession of bizarre images, then they cease thinking of the images as bizarre. In the context of more ordinary images, though, the bizarreness is noticed and contemplated, leading to a memory improvement. (For reviews, see Einstein, McDaniel & Lackey, 1989; McDaniel & Einstein, 1986, 1990; for related data, see Hunt & Elliott, 1980.) The benefits of bizarreness also depend on the form of test: Bizarre images are better remembered if subjects must *recall* the items later on; bizarreness has no impact on recognition testing. Given our earlier claims about recognition and recall (see

Chapter 5), this implies that bizarreness somehow facilitates memory search, so that bizarre images are more easily located within the memory network. (For a different perspective on these points, see Hirshman, Whelley & Palij, 1989; Kroll, Schepeler & Angin, 1986; Riefer & Rouder, 1993.)

Dual Coding

Setting aside the issue of "bizarreness," the message of the previous section is clear: Imagery improves memory. Materials that can be imaged are more easily remembered. Instructions to use imagery during memorization improve memory performance. Why is this? What memory aid does imagery provide?

One proposal is that imageable materials, such as high-imagery words, will be doubly represented in memory: The word itself will be remembered, and so will the corresponding picture. This pattern is referred to as **dual coding**, and the advantage of this should be obvious: When the time comes to retrieve these memories, either record, the verbal or the image, will provide the information you seek. You have a "double chance" of locating this information, thereby easing the process of memory search. Imagery mnemonics work the same way, by encouraging subjects to lay down two different memory records—a propositional record of the material, plus an image—rather than one.

In addition, Paivio (1971) has argued that these two memories—one verbal in character, one an image—will differ from each other in important ways. For example, *access* to the verbal memory will be easiest if one starts with a word, as in: "Do you know the word *squirrel*?" Access to the remembered image, in contrast, will be easiest if one begins with a picture, "Do you recognize this pictured creature?" Moreover, Paivio argues, some types of information—for example, semantic associations—are more easily stored via verbal memories. Other types of information, such as information about size or shape, are more readily accessed from the remembered images. (Also see Paivio & Csapo, 1969; Yuille, 1983.)

Putting these suggestions together, we are led to a series of predictions, many of which have been tested by Paivio and his collaborators. In one study, subjects were shown pairs of items and had to indicate whether there was a close association between the items in each pair (te Linde, 1983). If shown the pair "mouse-cheese," subjects should press the "yes" button; if shown the pair "car-tomato," they should press the "no" button. This task is hypothesized to draw heavily on the system of verbal memories, because it is here that abstract, semantic information is stored.

In another condition, subjects had to make a different judgment—they had to indicate whether the two items in the pair were of similar size. Subjects would respond "yes" to "thimble-acorn," and "no" to "key-dress." This judgment should draw on the system of remembered *images*, because this is where spatial information (including information about size) is represented.

For both of these tasks, some of the stimuli were presented in verbal form. Subjects might see the word "mouse" and the word "cheese," and then have to render the requested judgment. Other stimuli were presented pictorially—e.g., a picture of a mouse and a picture of cheese. The pictures were scaled so that all were of uniform size. That way, subjects making the size judgments could not respond based on the pictures themselves; instead, they had to draw on memory to recall the actual size of the depicted object.

We therefore have another 2 × 2 design, with two different judgments and two different types of stimulus information (see Figure 10.13). What should we expect here? The size task draws on remembered images, and these are more quickly accessed with picture stimuli than with words. Therefore, for this task, we expect to see a picture advantage—faster responses to pic-

Figure 10.13

THE TASKS AND STIMULI FOR TE LINDE'S DUAL-CODING EXPERIMENT

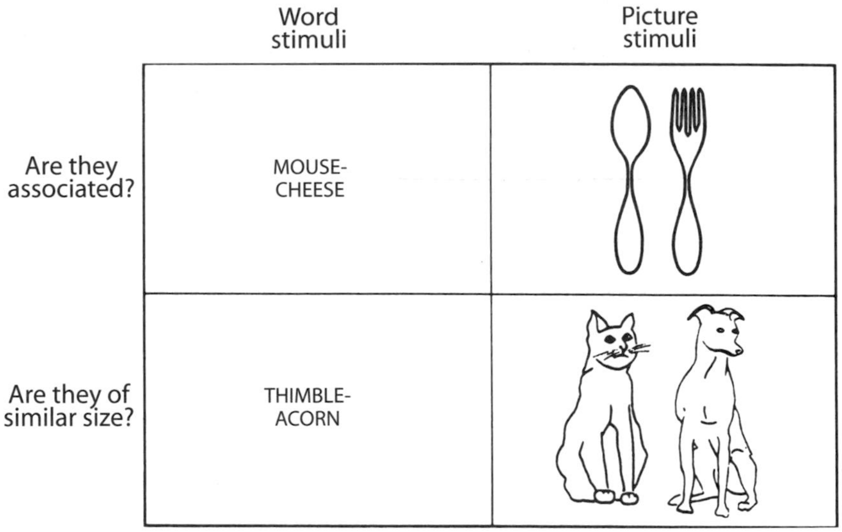

	Word stimuli	Picture stimuli
Are they associated?	MOUSE-CHEESE	
Are they of similar size?	THIMBLE-ACORN	

Subjects were asked either a question about association or a question about size. Half of the questions were presented in word form and half in pictorial form.

torial stimuli than to verbal stimuli. Things should reverse with the other task: Judgments about association depend on verbal memories, and these are more quickly accessed with word stimuli. For this task, we expect to see a disadvantage for pictures, with faster responses to the verbal stimuli.

Before we turn to the data, though, we need to add a complication. There is reason to believe that simple pictures are, overall, recognized more quickly than words, perhaps because pictures are more distinctive from each other than words are (Friedman & Bourne, 1976). This effect will, therefore, be superimposed on the effect we are after.

Let's think through what this means for our predictions: With questions about size, subjects should be quicker with pictures for two reasons: Pictures are quicker overall, and pictures are also just the right input with which to access size information. In answering questions about semantic associations, pictures have the advantage of being quickly recognized in general, but they also have the disadvantage of being an inappropriate input for accessing the desired information. These two effects should cancel each other, yielding no difference between pictures and words with the association questions.

As can be seen in Figure 10.14, the results fit with these predictions. For the size questions, response times were shortest when test items were presented as pictures. Responses were much slower if test items were presented as words. The association questions, however, yield a rather different pattern. These questions should be answered with information based on verbal memories, and these memories are best accessed with words. This effect is masked, however, by the overall quickness of pictures. With this task, therefore, we observe no difference between picture and word stimuli.

Memory for Pictures

Clearly, we do need to distinguish between visual memories and other, more symbolic memories, with these categories differing from each other both in their content and in their functioning. But how should we think about this? Paivio (1971) has proposed that there are two separate and distinct memory systems, one containing the verbal memories, the other containing images. However, many psychologists would argue instead that there is just a single, vast, long-term memory, capable of holding diverse contents. Within this single memory, each type of content would have its own traits, its own pattern of functioning—consistent with the data just reviewed. Nonetheless, there would still be one unified memory system, with images and verbal memories fully and intimately interwoven. (For discussion of this point, see Heil, Rösler & Hennighausen, 1994.)

To put this differently, images and verbal memories are distinct from each other in important ways—including how they are accessed, and also the types

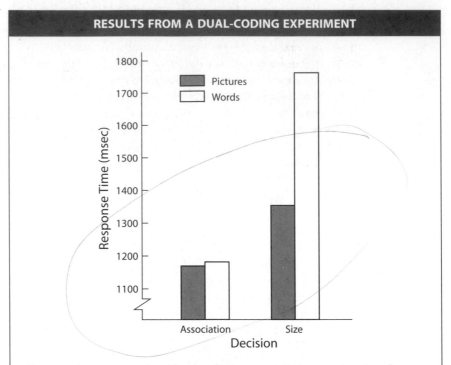

Figure 10.14

RESULTS FROM A DUAL-CODING EXPERIMENT

Size questions are answered by drawing on nonverbal memories; therefore, responses should be faster with picture stimuli (that is, short response times with picture stimuli, long response times with word stimuli). This prediction is confirmed. With questions about association, the information is coming from verbal memories, and so we expect faster responses with word stimuli. However, this effect is offset by the general advantage of picture stimuli over word stimuli. These two effects "cancel" each other, leaving us with no difference between picture and word stimuli for the association decision. [After te Linde, 1983.]

of information they contain. At the same time, these two types of memory also have a great deal in common, reflecting the fact that both types of memory reside within a single memory system. Thus, many of the claims we made in Chapters 4, 5, and 6 apply with equal force to visual memories and verbal memories: For example, recall of both memory types is dependent on memory connections; schema effects can be observed with both types of memory; encoding specificity is observed in both domains, and so on.

As a further illustration of this broad point, consider memory for *pictures*.

In many ways, the principles governing "picture memory" are the same as the principles governing memory for other materials. For example, recall our discussion of "schema effects," in Chapter 6. There we argued that subjects' memories are clearly influenced by generic knowledge, knowledge about how events unfold in general. In support of this claim, Chapter 6 relied largely on evidence for verbal memories, such as memory for sentences and stories. Similar effects, though, can easily be demonstrated with pictures.

In one study, Friedman (1979) showed subjects pictures of scenes such as a typical kitchen or a typical barnyard. In addition, the pictures also contained some unexpected objects. The kitchen picture included a stove and a toaster, but also included items less often found in a kitchen, such as a fireplace. Subjects were later given a recognition test, in which they had to discriminate between pictures they had actually seen, and altered versions of these pictures, in which something had been changed.

In some of the test pictures, one of the *familiar* objects in the scene had been changed. For example, subjects might be shown a test picture in which a different kind of stove appeared in the place of the original stove, or one in which the toaster on the counter was replaced by a radio. Subjects rarely noticed these changes, and so they tended (incorrectly) to respond "old" in these cases. This is sensible on schema-grounds: Both the original and altered pictures were fully consistent with the kitchen schema, and so both would be compatible with a schema-based memory.

On the other hand, subjects almost always noticed changes to the *unexpected* objects in the scene. If the originally viewed kitchen had a fireplace and the test picture did not, subjects consistently detected this alteration. Again, this is predictable on schema-grounds: The fireplace did not fit with the kitchen schema and so was likely to be specifically noted in memory. In fact, Friedman recorded subjects' eye movements during the original presentations of the pictures. Her data showed that subjects tended to look twice as long at the unexpected objects as they did at the expected ones—clearly these objects did catch subjects' attention.

In essence, then, what Friedman's subjects seemed to remember was that they had seen something we might label "kitchen plus a fireplace," a description that both identifies the relevant schema, and also notes what was special about this particular instance of the schema. If recognition memory is tested with a kitchen without a fireplace, subjects spot this discrepancy easily, since this picture does not fit with the remembered description. If tested with a kitchen plus or minus a toaster, this still fits with the "kitchen plus a fireplace" description, and so the alteration is likely not to be noticed. (See also Pezdek, Whetstone, Reynolds, Askari & Dougherty, 1989.)

A different line of evidence also shows schema effects in picture memory:

can have add-ons
on your schema
∴ something that doesn't
fit into your schema
can still be
recognized

Figure 10.15   BOUNDARY EXTENSION IN PICTURE MEMORY

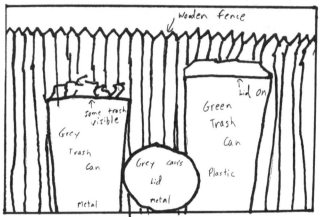

Subjects were initially shown the photograph at the top of this figure. The two panels below show drawings of the scene, drawn from memory by two different subjects. The subjects clearly recalled the scene as a "wide-angle" shot, revealing more of the background than it actually did. [After Intraub & Richardson, 1989.]

Recall our claim that, in understanding a story, subjects place the story within a schematic frame. As we have seen, this can often lead to intrusion errors, as subjects import their own expectations and understanding into the story, and so end up remembering the story as including more than it actually did.

A similar phenomenon can be demonstrated with picture memory: Intraub and her collaborators have documented a consistent pattern of *boundary extension* in picture memory (Intraub & Richardson, 1989; Intraub, Bender & Mangels, 1992; Intraub & Bodamer, 1993). That is, subjects remember a picture as including more than it actually did, in effect, "pushing out" the boundaries of the remembered depiction. For example, subjects shown the top panel in Figure 10.15 were later asked to sketch what they had seen. Two of subjects' drawings are shown in the bottom of Figure 10.15, and the boundary extension is clear—subjects remember the scene as less of a close-up view than it actually was and, correspondingly, they remember the scene as containing more of the backdrop than it actually did. This effect is observed whether subjects initially see a few pictures or many, whether they are tested immediately or after a delay, and even when subjects are explicitly warned about boundary extension and are urged to avoid this effect.

Intraub has argued that this boundary extension arises from the way in which subjects perceived these pictures in the first place. In essence, subjects understand a picture by means of a perceptual schema (e.g., Hochberg, 1978, 1986). This schema places the picture in a larger context, informing the perceiver about the real-world scene only partially revealed by the picture. This leads to a series of expectations about what subjects would see if they could somehow look beyond the photograph's edges. All of this influences memory, as the memory interweaves what subjects *saw* with what they *expected*, or what they knew they might see if they explored further. In important ways, this resembles the intrusion errors, produced by knowledge schemata, observed with verbal memory.

Theories of Picture Memory

Errors in picture memory, when they occur, follow a familiar pattern—with the errors predictable on schematic grounds. However, let us not make too much of these errors because, as it turns out, memory for pictures is, in many circumstances, astonishingly accurate. In an early study by Shepard (1967), subjects viewed a series of 612 pictures. Subjects were then given a recognition test, in which they were shown pairs of pictures, and had to decide, for each pair, which picture was from the previous set and which one was new. When this testing was immediate, subjects were 98% accurate. If the test was delayed by a week, subjects were still correct on 90% of the trials. Other experiments have reported comparable results (e.g., Nickerson, 1968; Standing, Conezio

& Haber, 1970; Standing, 1973), even when the initial series contained several thousand pictures.

How can we integrate these findings, showing high levels of performance, with the findings of the previous section, showing conspicuous errors? One option is to propose a two-part theory, allowing separate claims about what subjects remember, and what they don't. We have already seen one example of this, in the claim that subjects remember "kitchen *plus* a fireplace"—with an implicit distinction between the schematic knowledge relevant to the picture, and then more specific information pertinent to a particular picture. Likewise, Loftus and Bell (1975) have distinguished memory for *general visual information* about a picture and memory for *specific detail* with the suggestion that we are much more likely to remember the former than the latter. (Also see Mandler and Ritchey, 1977.)

Several pieces of evidence support these proposed distinctions. For example, Bahrick and Boucher (1968) showed subjects pictures of common objects, then tested for both recall of the objects' names, and also recognition. Bahrick and Boucher hypothesized that memory for schematic or descriptive information would be enough to support performance in the recall test. In the recognition test, however, subjects had to pick out the previously viewed picture from among choices all in the same category. For example, subjects had to choose which of several pictured coffee cups was the one they had previously been shown. For this test, memory for schematic information will not be enough, since all of the test items fit within the same schema. Instead, the recognition choice could only be made on the basis of memory for specific visual details.

The expectation, therefore, is that these two tests require different kinds of memory from the subject—schematic memory on the one hand, and detail memory on the other. Consistent with this, Bahrick and Boucher found that recognition and recall performance were independent of each other—one could not predict a subjects' recall score by knowing her recognition performance, and vice versa.

Similarly, Mandler and Ritchey (1977) report that these types of information differ in their longevity: Subjects seem to remember schematic information about a picture long after they have forgotten specific information about the picture's appearance. Likewise, Loftus and Bell (1975) found that memory for pictorial details is predictable from subjects' eye movements when they first inspected the picture, while subjects' memories for "general visual information" is *not* predictable from eye movements. This pattern isn't hard to understand: To remember the details, you have to have seen the details; hence, eye movements are crucial. For general visual information, though, if you see one aspect of the picture, then you can infer other aspects.

This obviously would weaken any connection between eye movements and memory for this information, since you don't have to look at something to infer its presence.

These two-part theories of picture memory echo, in miniature, our broader claim: In some regards, picture memory seems different from other forms of memory, particularly when we consider memory for pictorial detail. In other regards, picture memory follows the "standard" rules and is influenced by the same factors as memory for verbal materials. Schema effects, for example, can be found in both domains, with subjects showing better memory for the schema itself than for details of the particular stimulus. Intrusion errors can be documented in both domains. Similarly, subjects show *primacy* and *recency* effects when they learn a series of pictures (Tabachnick & Brotsky, 1976), just as they do when they learn a series of words (Chapter 4). Phenomena such as spread of activation and priming can be demonstrated with nonverbal materials (Kroll & Potter, 1984), just as they can be demonstrated with verbal materials (Chapter 7). In short, picture memory is distinct from other sorts of memory, but there is also enough communality to sustain our suggestion of a single memory system, containing diverse contents, but with a uniform set of operating principles.

Memory for Faces

What about memory for *faces*? What is the relation between face memory and the other categories of memories we have considered? As we saw in Chapter 2, face recognition does seem to involve specialized brain areas. This is indicated, for example, by the existence of prosopagnosia, a syndrome in which the ability to recognize familiar faces is disrupted, even though other aspects of recognition seem undisturbed. Moreover, it seems sensible that we might have specialized memories for faces. After all, our ancestors' survival, millions of years ago, may well have depended on the successful recognition of friends, foes, and family. This may have created evolutionary pressure for especially accurate face memory, which may, in turn, have demanded neural mechanisms specialized for this purpose.

Consistent with these comments about evolution, evidence indicates that memory for faces is quite good, with accuracy at high levels even after long retention intervals (Bahrick, Bahrick & Wittlinger, 1975; Bruck, Cavanagh & Ceci, 1991). Nonetheless, memory for faces is far from perfect, and large-scale errors have been documented (e.g., Baddeley, 1982). A number of factors can erode the accuracy of face memory, including such unsurprising factors as brief exposure during the initial encounter. It is also well documented that individuals are better in remembering faces from their own race than in remembering faces of other races (Brigham, 1986; Deffenbacher & Loftus, 1982; Shapiro & Penrod, 1986).

As we described in Chapter 2, it seems certain that faces are remembered as complex configurations, and not feature by feature (Bruce, Doyle, Dench & Burton, 1991; Farah, Tanaka & Drain, 1995; Rhodes, Brake & Atkinson, 1993). Beyond this, however, it appears that face memory follows many of the same principles as other categories of memory. For example, a number of studies have alleged that "deep processing" of faces (e.g., thinking about the personality of the person, rather than about the size or shape of specific features) leads to better face memory. However, there is reason to believe this effect is best explained in terms of the number and variety of features attended to while doing deep processing (Bloom & Mudd, 1991; Reinitz, Morrissey & Demb, 1994; Shapiro & Penrod, 1986; Sporer, 1991). Just like other categories of memory, face memory is best if, when the face is being observed, one pays attention to many and diverse aspects of the stimulus. Likewise, rehearsal of a face (via visualization) seems to improve memory, just as with other forms of memory (Sporer, 1988).

Similarly, subjects often seem able to recognize a face as *familiar* without being able to identify *why* the face is familiar. As a result, subjects will sometimes *misattribute* a face's familiarity—that is, identify a person as having been encountered in one circumstance when the person was encountered in a rather different setting (Brigham & Cairns, 1988; Brown, Deffenbacher & Sturgill, 1977; for some contrary data, see Read, Tollestrup, Hammersley & McFadzen, 1990). This is the same separation between familiarity and source-memory that we discussed with other categories of memory in Chapter 5.

Once again, therefore, we find a familiar pattern: There are some attributes unique to face memory (e.g., the sensitivity to facial *configurations*) but, at the same time, there are numerous parallels between memory for faces and memory for verbal materials. These parallels allow us to leave intact our claim that we don't need to subdivide long-term memory. Instead, there is but a single long-term memory. The contents are diverse, so that the attributes of one sort of content (e.g., memory for faces) will be somewhat different from the attributes of other contents. Nonetheless, all of long-term memory's contents will be subject to the same broad rules.

Finally, we should mention one other line of research concerning face memory—a line of research with important consequences. Eyewitnesses to crimes are often called on to identify or to describe the crimes' perpetrators, and this has made face memory an important topic for eyewitness research. Eyewitness memory for faces is often assessed via a "line-up," in which the witness must select, from a group of people, the person observed during the original crime, and numerous studies have examined the factors that influence line-up identifications. As examples, it appears that identification is equally accurate from a live or from a videotaped line-up (e.g., Cutler, Fisher & Chicvara, 1989); the likelihood of correctly identifying a culprit is also surprisingly unaffected by clothing or disguise (Lindsay, Wallbridge & Drennan, 1987). However, an *innocent* suspect is more likely to be misidentified as the culprit if he or she is wearing clothes similar to those remembered for the suspect.

Crucial for line-up accuracy, though, is the appearance of the other individuals in the line-up. Likelihood of accurate identification is maximized when the others resemble the suspect in relevant ways—including age, race, height, and weight. In addition, if the eyewitness has verbalized other features of the culprit (e.g., that he was attractive, or looked fierce), the others must be matched on these features as well. Indeed, it seems more important that the others resemble the witnesses' *description* of the culprit, rather than resembling the suspect (Brigham, Ready & Spier, 1990; Deffenbacher, 1988; Loftus & Kallman, 1979; Luus & Wells, 1991; Nosworthy & Lindsay, 1990).

Line-up identifications are also heavily influenced by instructions to subjects (Malpass & Devine, 1981; Warnick & Sanders, 1980; but see also Kohnken & Maass, 1988), and by whether the members of the line-up are viewed one at a time, rather than simultaneously—in general, it seems that sequential presentation leads to better accuracy than simultaneous (Cutler & Penrod, 1988; Lindsay & Wells, 1985; Lindsay, Lea & Fulford, 1991; Lindsay, Lea, Nosworthy, Fulford, Hector, LeVan et al., 1991). Accuracy can also be improved by allowing witnesses to hear the suspects' voices, and to view the suspects in their customary posture and gait and in three-quarter profile (Bruce, Valentine & Baddeley, 1987; Cutler & Penrod, 1988; Logie, Baddeley & Woodhead, 1987; Wogalter & Laughery, 1987).

The Diversity of Knowledge

Several themes have appeared again and again in this chapter. It is plain that we have diverse types of memories and knowledge in diverse domains. It is equally clear that our theories must acknowledge and accommodate this diversity. To describe face memory, for example, we need to consider configural properties that may well be specific to faces. Similarly, to describe images, we need to consider processes of "scanning" and "image rotation," processes that seem irrelevant to other kinds of representation. Likewise, images seem able to support a number of discoveries and creations, not accessible from other routes, and this too needs to be accommodated by our theories.

At the same time, however, we have also seen important commonalties across these domains, particularly with regard to long-term remembering. Across domains, rehearsal promotes memory. Across domains, schema effects are observed, in which memories for specific cases become entangled with more generic knowledge. Across domains, familiarity seems separable from source memory, and priming effects are observed, and so on. Consistent with these observations, we have seen no reason to set aside the claim that there is a single long-term memory, with a set of rules consistently applicable to all its diverse contents.

Other Categories of Memories

We offer these claims with some reservation, though—especially our claims about the singularity of long-term memory. In this chapter, we have focused entirely on visual memories, and one might well ask whether similar conclusions would emerge with other categories of knowledge. For example, can memories for tastes or smells be encoded propositionally? Do these memories benefit from rehearsal, show schema effects, and the like? Little research speaks to these questions. We do know, however, that subjects have memories in these other modalities, often memories of impressive accuracy (e.g., Levitin, 1993).

In the same spirit, we might consider other divisions of memory, not tied to particular sensory modalities. For example, some researchers have argued for separate memory systems for generic knowledge and for knowledge of specific episodes and events (McKoon, Ratcliff & Dell, 1986; Tulving, 1983, 1989; Tulving, Hayman & Macdonald, 1991; for further discussion, also Chapter 5). Others have suggested that we need different storehouses to accommodate our procedural knowledge and our declarative knowledge (see, for example, Cohen, 1984; Squire & Cohen, 1984; again, we first met this argument in Chapter 5). To mention one last and very different possibility, Zajonc (1980) caused some controversy when he proposed that emotions and emotionality operate in a separate mental system, following separate principles, from so-called "cold cognitions," i.e., dispassionate and calm memories or thoughts. This proposal has evoked interesting discussion (Lazarus, 1982, 1984; Zajonc, 1984), but it is too soon to tell what implications this has for claims about memory.

Little that we have said in this chapter bears directly on these proposals, but we hope it is clear how the logic and methods pursued in this chapter could be applied to these other domains. In fact, as we mentioned at the start, our agenda has been as much methodological as it has been substantive. We have tried to show by example both what it would mean to propose a separate memory system, and also how one might go about investigating that proposal. The number of subdivisions one might still propose remains large, and we look forward to seeing the evidence examining these.

11

Judgment: Drawing Conclusions from Evidence

So far, we have said a great deal about the *acquisition* and *retention* of knowledge, but little about what people *do* with their knowledge, once they've acquired it. It is to this broad concern that we now turn. We begin with a discussion of *judgment*—processes through which we think about evidence, draw conclusions, and make inferences. More broadly, these are processes that allow us to build new knowledge, based on the individual experiences that fill our lives.

In beginning our discussion of judgment, it is important to realize that the knowledge we need in our day-to-day lives is typically not supplied by the world in neat, ready-to-use packages. When we act on the basis of what we know, it is generally not because we have memorized a single relevant fact, nor is it because we have received some specific instruction about what to do in that situation. Instead, our actions are typically based on knowledge that we have, in effect, created ourselves—by drawing inferences from things we have seen, or by extrapolating from what we have experienced.

Imagine that you wish to cheer up your friend Fred. Chances are that Fred has never said to you, "Flowers are a good way to cheer me up." Therefore, you will need to figure out what will do the trick, based on things you have seen Fred do or heard him say. Or, as a more consequential case: Should you vote for candidate X or candidate Y in the upcoming election? In this case, you *have* received instructions—you have seen X on television, over and over, saying "Vote for me!" and likewise for Y. You will probably ignore these instructions, though, in making your decision. Instead, you will try to recall what you have read about X and Y, you will make inferences about how each is likely to behave in the future, and you will need to decide which is more trustworthy.

Obviously, these cases involve an element of judgment: You will draw some conclusions from your knowledge, and then use these conclusions as a basis for action. In other situations, we use our judgment because we want to figure things out, because we want to understand the pattern of our experiences. "Why was I in such a bad mood today?" "Does she really like me?" "What will the consequences of the election be?" In these cases, too, we build on what we already know, as we seek to draw some conclusion from the information available to us.

In this chapter, we will examine how these judgments are made. What strategies do we rely on in evaluating evidence? What factors influence us? Our focus will be on cases involving inductive judgment. In induction, the evidence available to us consists of specific facts or observations, and we seek some general conclusion. Given specific recollections of Candidate X, can we draw a conclusion about how she will behave in the future? Given specific observations we have made about Fred, can we draw a conclusion about what things, in general, might cheer him up? In Chapter 12, we will consider the related topic of deductive judgment. In deduction, we usually begin with a general statement, and try to figure out what specific claims follow from it. You might know, in general, that people with allergies often suffer during the spring. What conclusions can you (deductively) draw from this concerning Alicia, who has allergies?

Induction and **deduction** are key elements of our intellectual life, and they are ubiquitous in human reasoning. But induction and deduction also play a role in a more specialized arena: The rules of deduction have been specified in detail by logicians; these rules tell us rather precisely which deductive conclusions are valid—that is, warranted by the available information—and which are invalid. Likewise, scientists and statisticians have formalized many rules of induction. In scientific discourse, for example, one cannot offer any conclusion one chooses. Instead, certain statistical and methodological principles govern how evidence is to be summarized and interpreted. Thus, one's inductive inferences are only valid if they are made in accordance with these principles.

We can think of logic as specifying the "correct" way to reason deductively—the pattern of deduction endorsed by the relevant scholars. Logic thus provides a **normative** account of deduction, as opposed to a **descriptive** account. Normative accounts tell us how things ought to go; descriptive accounts tell us merely how things are. In the same way, statistics and scientific methodology provide normative rules for inductive reasoning, telling us how this form of reasoning ought to proceed.

This invites a series of questions: In our informal, day-to-day reasoning, do we reason "correctly," in accord with the normative models? Most people have never studied logic or statistics; is their reasoning sound? Or are most people illogical and likely to draw unwarranted conclusions?

Availability

Judgments usually don't depend on single facts or single observations. Instead, judgments depend on *patterns* of observations. Hence, as a first step in making a judgment, we typically seek some means of summarizing the evidence, in order to discern the pattern. This summary often takes the form of a **frequency estimate**—how often has this event occurred?

Frequency estimates are crucial in many domains, including any case in which you are trying to figure out some cause-and-effect relation. You are in a particularly good mood, for example, and you wonder why. Could it be the sunny weather? You could check this by drawing on memory; in a straight-forward way, this judgment will rely on frequency estimates: How often have you been in a good mood on sunny days? How often have you been in a bad mood on these days? How often have you been in a good mood despite the weather?

Frequency judgments are also needed when you are looking for *predictors* or *diagnostic tools*. Your friend just recommended a new movie; should you take his recommendation? Again, a frequency judgment is pertinent. (How often has he recommended movies that turned out to be terrific, and how often has he recommended films that were real losers?) Country X has just threatened to attack a neighboring country; should we take the threat seriously? Here, one might consult historical patterns, asking how often such threats have been indicators of violence-to-come, and how often not.

It seems that frequency estimates are at the root of a wide range of inductive judgments. How do we make this first step in inductive reasoning?

The Availability Heuristic

Are there more words in the dictionary beginning with the letter "r" (rose, rock, rabbit) or more words with an "r" in the third position (tarp, bare, throw)? Most people assert that there are more words beginning with "r" (Tversky & Kahneman, 1973, 1974), but the reverse is true, by a margin of two to one. Why do people get this wrong, and by so much?

In judging these word frequencies, subjects have several strategies open to them. As one option, they could take the time to search through a dictionary and count the words in the respective categories. If subjects used this strategy, they would come up with the correct answer. Likewise, subjects could find some systematic means of searching through their own memories, examining all the words in their vocabulary. This, too, would lead to the correct answer. A different strategy would be to scan through memory quickly, to see how many words they can come up with in each of the two categories. As it turns out, a first-letter cue allows a much more effective memory search than a third-letter cue. This presumably tells us something important about memory's organization but, for present purposes, it simply means that words in the first group will come to mind more easily than words in the second. That is, words in the first group are more available, producing a bias in what is retrieved from memory.

If one uses this last strategy, therefore, and relies on the sample that comes easily to mind, this will lead to error. Words beginning with "r" will *appear* more frequent, because they are more readily available from memory, even though they are *less* frequent in the language. Of course, we already know that subjects answer this question about "r-words" incorrectly, implying that they do indeed use this efficient but misleading strategy and not one of the more accurate strategies.

Notice the trade-off that is in place here: On the one side, subjects could select a cumbersome strategy, guaranteed to yield the correct answer. Alternatively, they could select a more efficient strategy, at the cost of risking error. This trade-off between accuracy and efficiency has appeared in our discussion several times already. In Chapter 8, this trade-off led us to introduce the notion of a **heuristic**—a strategy that risks some error in order to gain efficiency. Tversky and Kahneman (1973, 1974) speak, in fact, of the **availability heuristic** as a means of judging frequency: The idea, basically, is that we judge frequency by doing a quick count of examples. If instances of a category come easily to mind, then we conclude that the category has many members. If instances come to mind more slowly, or only with great effort, then we judge the category to be rare. This strategy is surely efficient, and will often serve us well. In many cases, though, this strategy will lead to error.

Use of this heuristic seems quite sensible in the "r-word" task. After all, this task isn't very interesting, and subjects probably don't want to spend much effort in choosing their response. The evidence suggests, though, that our use of this strategy is enormously widespread. Thus, we use this heuristic in making both trivial and consequential judgments.

Availability Effects from Biases in What We Notice

In many cases, "availability in memory" does correspond to "frequency in the world" and, therefore, one can use the first of these to gauge the second. After all, each encounter with an event provides an opportunity to learn about the event. More frequent encounters will probably lead to more learning, which will lead to greater prominence in memory. This creates an obvious link between frequency-of-encounter and memory, just as the availability heuristic requires.

However, other factors, beyond frequency-of-encounter, also influence memory availability, and this is why availability is, at best, an imprecise index of frequency. We have seen one example of this in the "r-word" task, but other examples are easy to find. For instance, consider the fact that subjects often overestimate the frequency of events that are, in actuality, quite rare (Attneave, 1953; Lichtenstein, Slovic, Fischhoff, Layman & Combs, 1978). This probably plays a part in people's willingness to buy lottery tickets—they overestimate the likelihood of winning! Sadly, it also can play a role in more important domains. For example, there is evidence that physicians may, in many circumstances, overestimate the likelihood of a rare disease and, in the process, fail to pursue other, perhaps more appropriate, courses of treatment.

(For a clear example of this, see Elstein, Holzman, Ravitch, Metheny, Holmes, Hoppe, Rothert, & Rovner, 1986.)

What causes this pattern? Events that are unusual or peculiar are, by their nature, likely to catch your attention. You will notice these events and think about them, ensuring that these events are well-recorded in memory. This will, in turn, make these events easily available to you. As a consequence, if you rely on the availability heuristic, you will overestimate the frequency of these unusual events and, correspondingly, you will overestimate the likelihood of similar events happening in the future.

Related effects are easily demonstrated in the laboratory. For example, Tversky and Kahneman presented subjects with a list of names; subjects were later asked to judge whether the list contained more names of men, or more names of women. For some subjects, the men on the list were quite famous (e.g., Richard Nixon) while the women on the list were less famous (e.g., Lana Turner). These subjects recalled the list as containing more men's names than women's. For other subjects, it was the women on the list who were quite famous (e.g., Elizabeth Taylor). These subjects recalled the list as containing more women's names than men's.

In this procedure, the famous names are more likely to catch subjects' attention, and so are more likely to be remembered. Thus, when subjects think back over the list, the famous names are more available, and this biases subjects' assessments of the list's membership. Once again, availability governs frequency estimates. (For other examples of availability effects, including effects in the social sphere, see Ross & Sicoly, 1979; Taylor, 1982; Taylor, Fiske, Etcoff & Ruderman, 1978.)

Other Sources of Availability Bias

It seems that our conclusions, inferences, and extrapolations often depend on frequency judgments, which in turn depend on availability. The pattern of what's available then depends, in large measure, on memory. Therefore, virtually any factor that influences memory will, sooner or later, influence the pattern of our conclusions and the quality of our judgments. For example, availability is influenced by memory's organization, since this organization makes some memories more retrievable than others. (This was crucial for the "r-word" task.) Availability is likewise influenced by what we notice and what we pay attention to. (This was central for some of the examples in the previous section.) Availability is also influenced by recency, and thus we are likely to overestimate the frequency of events recently encountered. (For relevant data, see Johnson & Tversky, 1983.)

In fact, we can put this more broadly: In making inferences, or in drawing conclusions, the information we need is often supplied to us by memory.

When you decide how to vote, you draw on memories of the candidates' positions and past deeds. If you are wondering why your friend is in a foul mood, you will try to recall events or conversations that might have led to the mood. In this context, failures of memory take on new importance. If memory is selective, or inaccurate, this will play a crucial role in shaping the progress of thought.

Factors external to memory can also bias availability. For example, imagine that you have been asked to advise the government on next year's budget. In particular, you are trying to decide how much money to spend on various research projects, all aimed at saving lives. It would be plausible to spend your resources on the more frequent causes of death, rather than investigating rare problems, and that leads to our questions: Should we spend more on preventing death from motor vehicle accidents or death from stomach cancer? Which is more common? Should we spend more on preventing homicides, or diabetes? People reliably assert that motor vehicle accidents and homicide are the more frequent in each pair, although the opposite is true both times,

Table 11.1

AVAILABILITY BIAS IN ESTIMATES OF FREQUENCY OF DEATH FROM VARIOUS CAUSES	
Most Overestimated	**Most Underestimated**
All accidents	Smallpox vaccination
Motor vehicle accidents	Diabetes
Pregnancy, childbirth, and abortion	Stomach cancer
Tornadoes	Lightning
Flood	Stroke
Botulism	Tuberculosis
All cancer	Asthma
Fire and flames	Emphysema
Venomous bite or sting	
Homicide	

Note: Subjects estimated how many deaths are caused by each of these factors. Subjects were clearly influenced by how often each factor is reported in the media: Stomach cancer is usually not reported; homicide and death from fires are often reported.

[From Slovic, Fischhoff, & Lichtenstein, 1982.]

as shown in Table 11.1 (Combs & Slovic, 1979; Slovic, Fischhoff & Lichtenstein, 1982). Why is this?

In estimating the likelihood of these events, people are heavily influenced by the pattern of media coverage. Homicide makes the front page, while diabetes does not, and this is reflected in subjects' estimates of frequency. Indeed, these estimates, for each of the causes of death, correspond rather closely to frequency-of-report in the media, rather than to actual frequency-of-occurrence. Thus, once again, we find an influence of availability. Just as some information is less available to us via the selectivity of memory, some information is less available via the selectivity of the media. And it is the available data that people use, making the media bias as important as the memory bias.

In the same vein, it is noteworthy that media critics have expressed considerable concern over how often African Americans are portrayed as criminals on television. Given the data we have just described, it is plausible that this pattern of media misrepresentation may well influence national estimates of who is committing crimes, a prospect with obvious political and social ramifications.

Anchoring

In some ways, these availability effects should not be surprising. After all, it is no shock that we are more influenced by the facts we remember, rather than the facts we fail to remember. Likewise, it is hardly news that some facts catch our attention, while other facts do not. And, of course, we are influenced by the pattern of how things are reported in the media.

What seems more surprising, though, is our apparent inability to overcome these effects, even when we are alerted to them. For example, you surely knew that homicide is generally considered newsworthy, while death from diabetes is not. You might, therefore, adjust for this media-bias in making your estimates—increasing your estimate of diabetes deaths, since you know these are underreported. However, it seems that subjects do *not* make these adjustments, do *not* compensate for availability bias, even when the bias is out in plain view.

A tendency known as **anchoring** is relevant here: This term refers to the fact that, once an answer to a question is on the scene, subjects seem to use this answer as a reference point, and select their own judgments only by making adjustments to this "anchor." Strikingly, subjects show this tendency even when the initial answer—that is, the anchor—is obviously not worth trusting.

Subjects in one study were asked to estimate the proportion of African nations in the United Nations. (The correct answer was 35%.) Subjects first watched while the experimenter spun a wheel marked with numbers from 1 to 100. As far as the subjects knew, this wheel was just a "random-number generator" but, in truth, the wheel was rigged, so that for half of the subjects it stopped at "10," and for half it stopped at "65." Subjects were asked whether the actual percentage is above or below this first "estimate" obtained from the wheel, and then they were asked to give their own estimate. Subjects who saw the wheel stop at 10 offered, on average, an estimate of 25%. Subjects who saw the wheel stop at 65 offered, on average, an estimate of 45%. Even in this case, subjects are apparently taking the wheel's "selection" as a reference point, and making their own estimate with reference to this anchor (Tversky & Kahneman, 1974).

Likewise, it is no accident that fundraisers often ask you how much you wish to contribute: "$100? $50? $30? $10?" Note that they don't phrase the question this way: "$10? $30? $50? $100?" It seems likely that the fund raisers are capitalizing on your tendency to treat the first-viewed numbers as anchors and to set your contribution relative to this anchor. (See Loftus & Zanni, 1975, for many related cases.)

Anchoring effects are important for several reasons but, for our purposes, they indicate that, once an error is made, it may be difficult for subjects to set the error aside and start again. Thus, if subjects' initial estimates are biased by media reporting, or by the selectivity of memory, we can't remove these effects by reminding subjects about media bias or memory selection. In both cases, the initial response, even though clearly in error, will serve as an anchor for subsequent judgments. Once an initial estimate is made, its effect seems long-lived. (For related claims, see Wilson & Brekke, 1994.)

Judgments of Quantity

We have catalogued many factors influencing information availability and, as we have seen, these factors have a direct impact on our judgments. All of this serves to confirm the claim that these judgments rely on the availability heuristic, so that our estimates of frequency are heavily influenced by how easily the relevant examples come to mind.

Similar heuristics allow us to make a number of related judgments, for example, judgments of *quantity*. Imagine that you are working on a paper for your English course; have you offered enough arguments to make your claims persuasive? Or imagine an attorney trying to persuade a jury; at what point has enough evidence been presented to "make the case"? These judgments, like frequency judgments, are often made via heuristics.

As an illustration, Josephs, Giesler and Silvera (1994) asked their subjects to write an essay on "Why it is better to buy American cars than Japanese

[handwritten margin note: eg. how many pages to make an essay (regardless of double or single spaced still say, 3 pages)]

cars." Subjects were given no instructions about how *long* the essay should be, but were told to continue working until they felt they had written an essay "that, if submitted for a grade, would earn an A." Half the subjects wrote their essays in a single-spaced format, with a small type-font; the other subjects wrote their essays in a double-spaced format, with a much larger font. Subjects in the former group ended up writing essays, on average, 25% longer than subjects in the latter group. Apparently, subjects judged the adequacy and the completeness of their essay in a fairly crude fashion, and so thought the essay "finished" when it had the appropriate number of pages.

We don't want to suggest that all judgments are made in such a crude way, and surely we can find circumstances in which subjects use more precise, more systematic strategies for estimating quantity. (For research examining *when* subjects rely on the heuristics and when they use other grounds for judging frequency, see Brown & Siegler, 1993; Bruce, Hockley & Craik, 1991; Watkins & LeCompte, 1991.) Nonetheless, the fact remains that we often do rely on these short-cuts in judging quantity or frequency. Let's emphasize that this is, in many cases, a sensible strategy—efficient and generally leading to a reasonable estimate. As we have seen, however, it is easy to find cases in which these heuristics lead us astray to estimates far from the truth. Given the impact of anchoring, these errors, once they occur, may have an enduring influence on our judgments.

Representativeness

It seems that we often use short-cuts when trying to summarize and assess the information to which we've been exposed. Note, though, that we usually want to do more than this. We want to extrapolate from this information, and so we draw inferences, offer conclusions, and make predictions, all based on the experiences we have already encountered. How do we go about making these steps?

Once again, evidence points to the prominent use of a heuristic strategy, a strategy closely related to one we first met in Chapter 8. In that context, we saw that people often categorize by use of prototypes. This strategy exploits the fact that, while "typicality" is different from "membership in a category," these qualities do overlap: Something that resembles a "typical bird" is likely to be a bird when closely inspected. This allows us to use typicality as an efficient, and usually successful, categorization strategy.

It turns out that this categorization strategy is just a special case of a broader heuristic, namely the **representativeness heuristic**. This heuristic involves making the assumption that, in general, the instances of a category will resemble the prototype for that category and, likewise, that the prototype resembles each instance. Or, as a different way of putting it, this heuristic amounts to an assumption of homogeneity in the categories you are reasoning about. "We expect instances to look like the categories of which they are members; thus, we expect someone who is a librarian to resemble the prototypical librarian. We expect effects to look like their causes, . . . and so we are more inclined to see jagged handwriting as a sign of a tense rather than a relaxed personality" (Gilovich, 1991, p. 18).

It should be clear that this reliance on similarity, and this assumption of homogeneous categories, will often be helpful: Many categories *are* homogeneous, and so reasoning in this fashion will bring us to warranted conclusions. However, like most heuristics, this strategy can also lead to error.

Reasoning from the Population to an Instance

If we operate on the assumption that each instance resembles the prototype, then we should expect each instance to show the properties that we perceive in the category overall. This expectation is clearly visible in something called the "gambler's fallacy."

Imagine tossing a coin over and over; let's say that the coin has landed heads up six times in a row. Many people (and many gamblers) believe that, in this situation, the coin is more likely to come up tails on the next toss than heads. The "logic" in this case seems to be that, if the coin is fair, then a series of tosses should contain equal numbers of heads and tails. If no tails have appeared for a while, then some are "overdue" to bring about this balance.

But how could this be? The coin has no "memory," so it has no way of knowing how long it has been since the last tails. More generally, there simply is no mechanism through which the history of the previous tosses could influence the current one. Therefore, the likelihood of a tail on toss #7 is 50-50 (i.e., .50), just as it was on the first toss, and as it is on every toss. Where, then, does our belief come from, and where does it go wrong?

The explanation lies in our assumption of category homogeneity. We know that, over the long haul, a fair coin will produce equal numbers of heads and tails. Thus, the category of "all tosses" has this property. Our assumption of homogeneity, though, leads us to expect that any "representative" of the category will also have this property—that is, any sequence of tosses will also show the 50-50 split. But this isn't true: Some sequences of tosses are 75% heads, some are 5% heads, some are 100% heads. It is only when we combine all these sequences that the 50-50 split emerges.

A different way to say this appeals to the notion of sample size. If we examine a large number of cases, we will find patterns close to those in the population at large. This is what statisticians refer to as the "law of large numbers." There is, however, no "law of small numbers": There is no tendency for small samples to approximate the pattern of the population. Indeed, small samples can often stray rather far from the population values. But people seem not to appreciate this, and act as though they expect small samples to show the pattern of the whole.

Here is a related example, from a study by Kahneman and Tversky (1972). Subjects are given the following problem:

> In a small town nearby, there are two hospitals. Hospital A has an average of 45 births per day; Hospital B is smaller, and has an average of 15 births per day. As we all know, overall the number of males born is 50%. Each hospital recorded the number of days in which, on that day, at least 60% of the babies born were male. Which hospital recorded more such days, (a) Hospital A, (b) Hospital B, (c) both equal?

The majority of the subjects chose response "both equal," but this answer is statistically unwarranted. All of the births in the country add up to a 50-50 split between male and female babies. The larger the sample one examines, the more likely one is to approximate this ideal. Conversely, the *smaller* the sample one examines, the more likely one is to stray from this ideal. Days with 60% male births, straying from the ideal, are therefore more likely in the smaller hospital, Hospital B.

If you don't see this, consider a more extreme case. Hospital C has 1,000 births per day; Hospital D has exactly one birth per day. Which hospital records more days with "at least 90% male births"? This value will be observed in Hospital D rather often since, on many days, all the babies born (one out of one) will be male. This value is surely less likely, though, in Hospital C: 900 male births, with just 100 female, would be a remarkable event indeed. In this case, it seems clear that the smaller hospital can more easily stray far from the 50-50 split.

In the hospital problem, just like in the gambler's fallacy, subjects seem not to take sample size into account. They seem to think a particular pattern is just as likely with a small sample as with a large sample, although this is plainly not true. This belief, however, is just what one would expect if subjects were making the assumption that each instance of a category or, in this case, each subset of a larger set, should show the properties associated with the entire set.

Reasoning from a Single Case to the Entire Population

In the cases just described, subjects seem to expect that each individual in a category will have the properties of the category overall. The reverse error can also be demonstrated: Subjects expect the overall category to have the properties of the individuals, and they are quite willing to extrapolate from a few instances to the entire set. In fact, evidence suggests that they generalize in this fashion even when they are explicitly told that the instance is *not* representative of the larger group.

Hamill, Wilson and Nisbett (1980) showed subjects a videotaped interview in which a person identified as a prison guard discussed his job. In one condition, the guard was compassionate and kind, and expressed great concern for rehabilitation. In the other condition, the guard expressed contempt for the prison inmates, and he scoffed at the idea of rehabilitation. Before seeing either of these videotapes, some subjects were told that this guard was quite typical of those at the prison; other subjects were told that he was quite atypical, chosen for the interview precisely because of his extreme views. Still other subjects were given no information about whether the interviewed guard was typical or not.

Subjects were later questioned about their views of the criminal justice system, and the data show that they were clearly influenced by the interview they had seen: Subjects who had seen the humane guard indicated that they believed prison guards to be decent people in general; subjects who had seen the inhumane guard reported more negative views of guards. What is remarkable, though, is that subjects seemed largely to ignore the information about whether the interviewed guard was typical or not. Subjects who were explicitly told the guard was *atypical* were influenced by the interview just as much, and in the same way, as subjects who were told that the guard was typical.

These data, and other laboratory findings (e.g., Hamill et al., 1980), make it clear that subjects are quite willing to draw conclusions from a single case, even when they have been explicitly warned that the case is not representative. This is exactly what we would expect if subjects are using the representativeness heuristic. If one makes the assumption that categories are homogeneous, then it is reasonable to extrapolate from one observation to the entire category, and that seems sadly close to what subjects are doing.

Similar data are easily observed outside of the laboratory. Consider what Nisbett and Ross (1980) have referred to as "man who" arguments. You are shopping for a new car. You have read various consumer magazines and decided, based on their reports of test data and repair records, that you will buy a Smacko brand car. You report this to your father, who is aghast. "Smacko?! You must be crazy. Why, I know a man who bought a Smacko, and the transmission fell out two weeks after he got it. Then the alternator went. Then the brakes. How could you possibly buy a Smacko?"

What should you make of this argument? The consumer magazines tested many cars, and reported that 20% of all Smackos break down. In your father's "data," 100% of the Smackos (one out of one) break down. Should this "sample of one" outweigh the much larger sample tested by the magazine? Your father presumably believes he is offering a persuasive argument, but what is the basis for this? The only basis we can see is the presumption that the category will resemble the instance; only if that were true would reasoning from the instance be appropriate.

If you listen to conversations around you, you will regularly hear "man who" (or "woman who") arguments. "What do you mean cigarette-smoking causes cancer?! I have an aunt who smoked for 50 years, and she runs in marathons!" Often, these arguments seem persuasive. But these arguments have force only by virtue of the representativeness heuristic—our assumption that categories are homogeneous, and therefore our peculiar willingness to take a small sample of data as seriously as a larger sample.

Detecting Covariation

We seem to be moving toward an unsettling indictment of human reasoning. Subjects place too much faith in the easily available evidence, even when they know the evidence to be biased. Subjects "anchor" their judgments, even when they know the anchor to be arbitrary. Subjects take small samples of evidence too seriously and treat evidence as though it were representative even if told explicitly that it is not. Is this grim picture correct? Is human reasoning as poor as the evidence so far suggests? We will have more to say about this before we are through. First, though, we need to add some further "charges" to the indictment.

Many of the judgments we informally make hinge on questions about covariation. This term has a technical meaning but, for our purposes, we can define it this way: X and Y "covary" if X tends to be on the scene whenever Y is, and if X tends to be absent whenever Y is absent. X might also covary with the *absence* of Y—X is present when Y is absent and absent when Y is present.

For example, exercise and stamina covary—people who do the first tend to have a lot of the second. Owning audio CDs and going to concerts also covary, although less strongly than exercise and stamina. (Some people own many CDs but rarely go to concerts.) Note then that covariation is a matter of degree—covariation can be strong or weak. Having a disease symptom and having the disease covary, not surprisingly, since one is an index of the other's presence. High temperatures and increased thirst also covary, again not surprisingly, since one is the cause of the other.

These examples should make clear why we so often care about covariation.

Covariation is what we look at in assessing the quality of a diagnostic technique. Can we diagnose schizophrenia on the basis of some blood test? We can find out by asking whether schizophrenic symptoms covary with some blood value. Covariation is also what we look at to test a hypothesis about cause and effect. Does education lead to a higher paying job? If so, then degree of education and salary should covary. Likewise, does taking aspirin prevent heart attacks? If so, then aspirin use and heart attacks should covary negatively, with the presence of one being associated with the absence of the other.

Assessing covariation is of crucial importance for scientific data analysis, and it is no less important in day-to-day reasoning. Do my colleagues at work act in a friendlier fashion when I am formal, or when I'm casual? Can you study more effectively if you have a period of physical exercise early in the day? These are, once again, questions about covariation, and they are the sort of questions we frequently ask. So how well do we do, when we think about covariation?

"Illusions" of Covariation

Psychologists have developed a wide variety of tests designed to measure personality characteristics or behavioral inclinations. One well-known example is the Rorschach test, in which subjects are shown ink-blots, and asked to describe them. These descriptions are then examined, looking for certain patterns. A mention of humans in motion is said to indicate imagination and a rich inner life; responses that describe the white spaces around the ink-blot are taken as indications of rebelliousness.

Is this valid? Do specific responses, or signs, as they are called, really covary with certain personality traits? And how astutely do psychologists detect this covariation? To attack these questions, Chapman and Chapman (1971) created a number of Rorschach protocols, that is, written transcripts of a subject's responses. The protocols were actually fictional, made up for this study, but were designed to resemble real subjects' responses. The Chapmans also made up fictional descriptions of the people who had supposedly offered these responses: One protocol was attributed to someone who "believes other people are plotting against him." Another protocol was attributed to someone who "has sexual feelings toward other men."

The Chapmans *randomly* paired the protocols and the personality descriptions—one protocol and one description, the next protocol and a different description. These randomly assembled protocol-profile pairs were then shown to a group of undergraduates, students who had no prior experience with the Rorschach test, and who did not know the theory behind the test. These students were asked to examine the pairs, and asked to determine what signs covaried with what traits. In particular, the students were asked which signs covaried with homosexuality.

Before pressing on, we should mention the fact that the Chapmans' research was done more than two decades ago, in a period of time when many psychologists viewed homosexuality as a "disorder" to be diagnosed. Let's note, though, that psychologists have long since abandoned this view. We discuss the Chapmans' research because it is a classic study of covariation, and not because it tells us anything about homosexuality.

Returning to the study itself, we know that, thanks to the random pairing, there was no covariation in this set of "data" between protocols and descriptions, between signs and personality traits. Nonetheless, the students reported seeing a pattern of covariation. Certain signs, they reported, seemed consistently good indicators that the respondant was a homosexual. For example, they reported that homosexual respondants were particularly likely to perceive buttocks in the inkblots. Therefore, mention of buttocks was a reasonable indicator, they claimed, of homosexuality.

We emphasize that there was no pattern in these made-up data, and therefore the covariation subjects are perceiving is illusory—"observed" in the data even though it is plainly not there. And, oddly enough, the covariation "perceived" by these subjects was identical to that alleged by professional clinicians. Clinicians, based on extensive experience with patients, are convinced that certain signs *are* valid indicators of homosexuality, and the signs they mention are, remarkably, exactly the ones nominated by the Chapman and Chapman subjects. The clinicians, like the Chapmans' subjects, report that use of the "buttocks" response does covary with sexual orientation, with homosexuals much more likely to use this response.

Is this just a coincidence—that the pattern "observed" by the undergraduates, in bogus data, matches the pattern reported by professionals, based on "real" data? Further evidence suggests it is not at all a coincidence: A number of researchers have examined the actual Rorschach responses from homosexuals and heterosexuals, and asked statistically whether "buttocks" responses are more likely from one group than the other. As it turns out, the two groups do not differ in the likelihood of this response; that is, there is no covariation between sexual orientation and use of the "buttocks" response. Therefore, this is not a valid indicator. Nonetheless, a wide range of clinicians, the Chapmans found, continue to insist that this response is indicative of homosexuality.

Notice where this leaves us: In the Chapmans' laboratory studies, we know there was no pattern of covariation in the Rorschach data; nonetheless, subjects perceived a pattern, perceived, specifically, covariation between sexual orientation and a particular response. Likewise, in *authentic* Rorschach data, professional clinicians see the same pattern, the same covariation. When the data are carefully tabulated, though, there is no such covariation. The clinicians, just like the undergraduates, are seeing something that isn't there; the professionals, with years of experience and training, are vulnerable to the same <u>illusory covariations</u> as the laboratory subjects. (For related evidence, see Arkes & Harkness, 1983; Schustack & Sternberg, 1981; Shaklee, & Mims, 1982; Smedslund, 1963.)

Theory-Driven and Data-Driven Detection of Covariation

Each of us seeks to learn from our experiences—both the experiences of daily life, and also experiences in our professional domains. Indeed, in our professional worlds we can accumulate great quantities of experience—a physician has seen many cases of the flu; a salesperson has seen many customers; a teacher, many students. Therefore, each of us has had enormous opportunity to accumulate "professional wisdom" within our area of special expertise.

The clear message of the Chapmans' data, though, is that we might be wary of this "professional wisdom." Their data remind us that professional training does not make you immune to illusions, that professionals, just like everyone else, are fully capable of "projecting" their beliefs onto the evidence and perceiving patterns that aren't there. Thus, if one starts with the intuition that there is some association between homosexuality and rear-ends, then one will "detect" a pattern, "confirming" this intuition, in the data.

Given all this, perhaps we should be cautious when a police officer assures us that crimes are more frequent under a full moon, or when a hair cutter tells us that a certain shampoo cures split ends. In each of these cases, a professional is making a claim about covariation, and we all tend to trust such claims, as they are based on so much first-hand experience. Nonetheless, we might want to ask how these conclusions were drawn. Was the evidence systematically recorded and rigorously reviewed? Or are these claims simply derived in an informal way, based on the professional's "global impression" of the facts? If the latter, one might argue that these claims can't be taken seriously, since they could turn out merely to be further examples of illusory covariation. (For other evidence, echoing this concern about "professional wisdom," see the studies reviewed by Shanteau, 1992.)

For that matter, if experts show these effects, what about the rest of us? Does each of us project our own biases onto the data, seeing only the pattern of covariation we expect to see? We are not surprised if such errors happen to someone very dogmatic, e.g., to the sexist who believes all women are moody (that is, expects to see, and "sees," covariation between gender and moodiness), or to the racist who believes all blacks are lazy (again, a covariation claim). Someone dogmatic would surely distort the evidence, in order to "support" these ugly beliefs. But we discover the same patterns of prejudice in ourselves.

In a study by Jennings, Amabile and Ross (1982), college students were asked to make covariation judgments in two types of situations: situations in which they had no prior expectations or biases, and situations in which they did. For example, in the "prior belief" (or "theory-based") case, subjects were asked to estimate how strong the covariation is between (a) children's dishonesty as measured by false report of athletic performance, and (b) children's dishonesty as measured by amount of cheating in solving a puzzle. If a child is dishonest according to one of these indices, is he or she also dishonest according to the other? Or, as a different example, subjects estimated the covariation between (a) how highly a student rated U.S. Presidents' performance in the last decade, and (b) how highly the student rated business leaders' performance in the last decade. If you think highly of our Presidents, do you also think highly of the business community?

Subjects presumably made these judgments by reflecting on their prior experience and their intuitions; no new data were presented in the experimental procedure. Subjects expressed these judgments by selecting a number between 0 and 100, where 0 indicated that the two traits were unrelated, did not covary, and 100 indicated that the traits covaried perfectly. Subjects could also use negative values (to -100) to indicate the belief that the two traits covary, but with the presence of one indicating the absence of the other.

Subjects were also asked to make a comparable judgment in a "no prior belief" (or "data-based") case, that is, with variables they had never met or considered before. For example, subjects were presented with ten pictures, each showing a man holding a walking stick. The heights of the men varied in the pictures, as did the length of the walking stick, and subjects had to judge whether these two variables covaried, again choosing a value between -100 and $+100$.

Figure 11.1 shows the results from the data-based cases, i.e., the cases in which subjects had no prior beliefs. Here, subjects' estimates were reasonably regular: the stronger the covariation, the stronger the estimate. Subjects also tended to be rather conservative; their estimates exceeded $+30$ only when the objective correlation was very strong. Figure 11.2 shows a very different picture for the theory-based cases. Subjects tended to be far more extravagant in these estimates, with estimates of $+60$ and $+80$. Subjects were also far less regular in the theory-based cases, with only a weak relation between the magnitude of the estimated covariation and the magnitude of the actual covariation. For example, the "children's dishonesty" pair, mentioned earlier, is shown as the black square in the figure. In this case, the objective correlation, statistically measured, is fairly small. That is, children who are dishonest in one context are often honest in other contexts. Subjects estimated this cov-

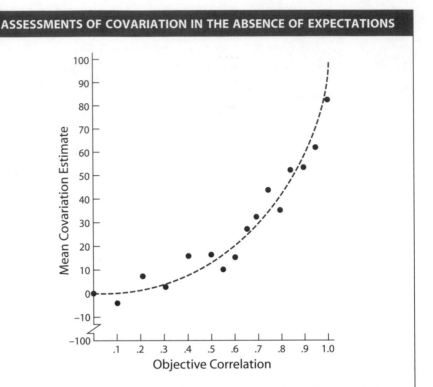

Figure 11.1

ASSESSMENTS OF COVARIATION IN THE ABSENCE OF EXPECTATIONS

When subjects enter a situation with no expectations about the data, their estimates of covariation are quite orderly: The estimates grow stronger and stronger as the actual (objective) correlation grows stronger and stronger. In addition, subjects give low estimates unless the actual correlation is very strong. [After Jennings, Amabile, & Ross, 1982.]

ariation to be quite large, though, with an average estimate of +60. For the "Presidents and business leaders" case (the black star in the figure), the objective correlation is much stronger than in the "dishonesty" pair, but subjects estimated it to be much weaker.

At the very least, subjects are performing differently in the theory-based and data-based judgments. The former judgments are often extravagant; the latter tend to be conservative. The data-based judgments track the objective facts fairly well; the theory-based judgments do not. It is difficult to avoid the conclusion that theory biased what subjects "saw" in the data, and led them to see much stronger (or weaker) covariation than was there. (Other relevant data are reviewed by Allan, 1993; Alloy & Tabachnik, 1984; Baron, 1988.)

Figure 11.2

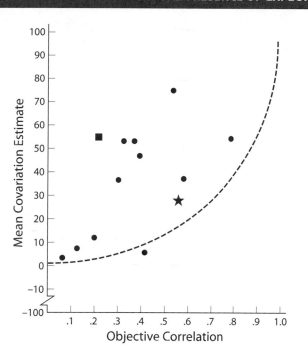

When subjects enter a situation with expectations about the data, their estimates of covariation are often inaccurate. In this instance, subjects were asked to assess the covariation in 16 cases. The square and the star indicate the two cases discussed in the text. Subjects often estimated the covariation as strong even when it was quite weak, or as being weak even when it was strong. The systematic pattern observed in Figure 11.1 is clearly absent here. (For purposes of comparison, this figure includes the curve describing the data from Figure 11.1). [After Jennings, Amabile, & Ross, 1982.]

Illusory Covariation: Another Availability Effect?

Why do beliefs and expectations mislead subjects in judgments of covariation? One possibility is that subjects are being dogmatic, and so it is a case of "I've already made up my mind; don't distract me with the facts." This is surely true in some occasions, but unpromising as a general explanation: In the experiments we have considered, subjects seem to be taking their task seriously—carefully examining the Rorschach responses, for example, and giving every indication that they are weighing the evidence as well as they can. Hence, we do not believe subjects simply ignore the facts in these experiments.

A different possibility is that perhaps subjects don't know how to compute covariation, so they end up using an estimation strategy that bears little resemblance to the correct formulae. However, if this were the problem, then subjects' performance in judging covariation should be uniformly poor. But that is not the case: Subjects do well in judging covariation in data-driven cases, when they don't have a prior theory. Plainly, subjects do have the means of computing covariation, at least in some circumstances.

Why do subjects go astray in the theory-based cases? At least part of the explanation can be cast in familiar terms, namely, availability. (Our proposal follows that offered by Jennings, Amabile & Ross, in accounting for their own data; see also Baron, 1988; Evans, 1989. For a related, but somewhat broader treatment, see Gilovich, 1991.) In short, the idea is that having a theory guides which cases we pay attention to, and this leads to a biased set of data. It is this bias in the data—or, more precisely, in the psychologically available data—that undercuts subjects' judgment.

Think back to Kahneman and Tversky's "r-word" experiment. In assessing how many words have an "r" in the third position, one *could* do a complete search of one's vocabulary. Or one could just use the words that come easily to mind, and so reach an answer much more quickly. As we have seen, evidence indicates that subjects use the latter approach, that is, they rely on information that is readily available. By the same token, in judging covariation, we could spend the time and effort needed to search out all the relevant data, or we could rely on the cases that come easily to mind. Given what we know about the "r" case, it seems a safe assumption that subjects will use the more efficient route, and consider only the available data.

This forces us to ask, therefore, which observations subjects are likely to consider, which observations are available, in assessing covariation. Will it be a random set? A representative sample? Or perhaps a biased sample? To answer this, we need some further theory, telling us what factors cause an observation to catch one's attention. In fact, much evidence indicates that one's attention is likely to be caught by "confirming" instances, instances that fit with one's beliefs. This tendency has been dubbed a **confirmation bias**, and can be demonstrated in various ways (Nisbett & Ross, 1980; Tweney, Doherty & Mynatt, 1981). We will have more to say about this topic in Chapter 12 but, for present purposes, we note only that the bias exists, and is clearly relevant to the cases we are discussing.

Let us imagine that you have the belief that big dogs tend to be vicious. When thinking about dogs, or looking at dogs, confirmation bias will lead you to notice big dogs that are, in fact, vicious, and little dogs that are friendly. Your memory schemata will also help you to remember episodes that fit with this belief and will work against remembering counter-examples. (Recall that one effect of these schemata is to "regularize" our past experiences, bringing our recollections into line with the schematic pattern—see Chapter 6.) Thanks to these various mechanisms, a biased sample of dogs is available to you. If asked to estimate covariation between dog size and temperament, you will therefore overestimate the covariation, thanks to this biased sample. There is nothing wrong with your skills in judging covariation. The problem instead is that, if your data are biased, so will be your judgment.

How often does this kind of error happen? How many of our covariation estimates are in error? We do not know, but it seems worth some concern. We have mentioned sexist hypotheses that depend on "observed covariation" for their support, and racist hypotheses in the same boat. Many medical hypotheses also hinge on covariation. Thus, the stakes are often quite high in judgments involving covariation. If misjudging covariation merely meant missing out on a fine meal at Chez Jose, then we might not worry about these errors. But, the cost of these errors is potentially far greater than this.

Base Rates

A further line of evidence also concerns our reasoning about covariation. More precisely, this evidence highlights information we often overlook in our assessment of covariation. As a way of entering these issues, consider the following problem (after Kahneman & Tversky, 1973; Nisbett & Ross, 1980):

> I have a friend who is a professor. He likes to write poetry, is rather shy, and is small in stature. Which of the following is his field: (a) Chinese studies or (b) psychology?

This is once again a question about covariation; in this case, we are asking whether certain traits (writing poetry, being shy) covary with profession. In response to this question, most subjects conclude that the friend is in Chinese studies. Presumably, this judgment is based on something like the representativeness heuristic: The example describes someone close to many people's stereotype of a Chinese scholar, and so subjects draw the appropriate conclusion.

However, this judgment overlooks an important bit of information. As you can probably guess, the number of psychologists in this country is much greater than the number of scholars in Chinese studies. To see how this matters, let us assume, just for sake of argument, that virtually all Chinese scholars—let's say, 90%—fit the stereotype. Let us assume further that only

5% of the psychologists fit the stereotype. In this case, "fitting the stereotype" would be high quality **diagnostic information**—information that does indeed indicate that you are in one category rather than another.

But now we need to factor in how many psychologists there are and how many Chinese scholars. Remember that there are relatively few Chinese scholars in this country; even if 90% of these fit the description, this is still 90% of a small number. In contrast, merely 5% of the psychologists fit the description, but this will be 5% of a much larger number. To make this concrete, let's say there are 10,000 Chinese scholars in this country, and 200,000 psychologists. In this case, 9,000 Chinese scholars fit the description (90% of 10,000), but 10,000 psychologists do as well (5% of 200,000). Therefore, even though the *proportion* of Chinese scholars fitting the description is larger than the *proportion* of psychologists (90% vs. 5%), the *number* of psychologists who fit the description is greater than the number of Chinese scholars fitting the description. As a result, chances are that the friend is a psychologist, since the description is compatible with more psychologists than Chinese scholars.

To put this more generally, in order to make judgments like this, one needs two types of information: the diagnostic information and the **base rates** or, as they are sometimes called, the prior probabilities. Prior to any other information, prior to hearing the sketch of my friend, you knew something about the relative numbers of scholars in psychology and in Chinese studies. This base rate information can offset the diagnostic information: In our example, a "small percentage of a big number" turned out to be larger than a "large percentage of a small number." Thus, the diagnostic information by itself favored the conclusion of "Chinese studies." However, the diagnostic information in conjunction with base rates can point toward a different conclusion.

Base rates are essential to a wide range of judgments. For example, we are testing a new drug, and discover that 70% of the patients who take this drug recover. Does that mean the drug is effective? The answer depends on the base rate: In general, how many patients recover? If the answer is 70%, then the drug is having no effect whatsoever. Likewise, do good-luck charms help? Let's say that you wear your lucky socks whenever your favorite team plays, and the team has won 85% of their games. We again need to ask about base rates: How many games has your team won over the last few years? Perhaps they have won 90% overall, but only 85% when you are wearing your lucky socks; in that case, your socks are actually a jinx.

Base Rates and Diagnostic Information

A number of studies have examined how subjects employ base rates. For example, Kahneman and Tversky (1973) asked subjects this question: If someone is chosen, at random, from a group of 70 lawyers and 30 engineers, what is his profession likely to be? Quite obviously, chances are that he is a lawyer. To be precise, there is a 70% chance that the individual selected will be a lawyer. Subjects seemed to understand this perfectly well: When asked the *probability* that this randomly chosen individual would be a lawyer, they respond .70. Thus, in this setting, subjects made full and accurate use of the base-rate information.

Other subjects were asked a different question. They were told that a "panel of psychologists" had interviewed and administered personality tests to a group of engineers and lawyers. No base rates were provided. Instead, subjects were given "thumbnail descriptions" of these individuals, allegedly based on the "personality tests." Subjects were asked to use this information to judge whether that individual was more likely to be an engineer or a lawyer.

The "thumbnail descriptions" provided to subjects were carefully designed, so that some evoked the subjects' engineer stereotype, while others evoked a lawyer stereotype. For example, a description favoring the engineer stereotype described a man whose hobbies include home carpentry, sailing, and mathematical puzzles, and who has no interest in political or social issues. Thus, from the subjects' point of view, the "thumbnail descriptions" provided reasonably clear indications of the individuals' professions.

In this set-up, subjects are being given diagnostic information but, as we noted, no information about base rates. Subjects were easily able to use this information, and thus their judgments sensibly reflected the content of the thumbnail sketches.

In short, therefore, subjects are responsive to base rates if this is the only information they have, indicating that they do know that base rates are relevant to this judgment. Likewise, subjects make appropriate use of the diagnostic information, if this is all they have. But now let's ask: What happens if we provide subjects with both sorts of information—the base rates *and* the diagnostic information?

Subjects in a third group were again provided with the thumbnail descriptions, but these subjects were told, in addition, that the individuals being described had been selected, at random, from a group of 30 engineers and 70 lawyers. We have just seen evidence that subjects understand the value of *both* pieces of information—the thumbnail sketch and the overall composition of the group. Therefore, we should expect subjects, when given both, to consider both, and to *combine* these two sources of information, as best they can. Thus, if the base rate and the diagnostic information both favor the lawyer response, subjects should offer this response with some confidence. If the base rate indicates one response, and the diagnostic information the other response, then subjects should temper their estimates accordingly.

However, this is not what subjects do. When subjects are provided with base rates and diagnostic information, they neglect the first, and base their responses entirely on the second. Thus, in the lawyer/engineer problem, subjects' responses were completely determined by the degree of resemblance between the individual described and their stereotype of a lawyer or an engineer. Indeed, subjects responded the same way if the base rates were as already described (70 lawyers, 30 engineers) or if the base rates were *reversed* (30 lawyers, 70 engineers). This reversal had no impact on subjects' judgments, confirming that subjects were ignoring the base rates.

Dilution Effects

We have already seen that if subjects' only information is the base rates, they use base rates. If subjects are given base rates *and* diagnostic information, they ignore the base rates. What happens if we go a step further and give subjects even more information? In a study by Nisbett, Zukier and Lemley (1981), subjects were asked to make predictions about their fellow students, including predictions about movie attendance. Some subjects were given diagnostic information, such as whether the target student was majoring in the sciences or the humanities. (According to the subjects, science majors go to half as many movies as humanities majors.) Other subjects were given this diagnostic information, plus some *irrelevant* information, for example the target individual's home town. This irrelevant information clearly influenced subjects: It caused them to pay less attention to the diagnostic information. In Nisbett et al.'s terms, the irrelevant information *diluted* the diagnostic information, diminishing its impact. Just as diagnostic information causes subjects to set aside base rates, the irrelevant information causes subjects to discount diagnostic information. (Also see Zukier, 1982.)

Irrelevant information can also dilute base-rate information. In one variation of the lawyer/engineer problem, subjects were told that a particular individual was "a 30-year-old man, married with no children, well liked by his colleagues." This obviously provides no information at all about the person's profession. Subjects were also told the base rates—they knew this individual was chosen from a group containing 30 engineers and 70 lawyers. Thus, subjects have one irrelevant piece of information and one useful bit. Their predictions should be determined entirely by the useful information—the base rates.

We emphasize again that subjects understand the usefulness of base rates—they use this information accurately if it is all the information they have. In the procedure just described, base rates are all the *useful* information subjects have. Subjects should in this case claim that there is a 30% chance of the person described being an engineer. What subjects did, however, was rather different: They paid attention to the worthless information and ignored the base rates. As a result, subjects estimated that there was a 50-50 chance of this individual being an engineer (Kahneman & Tversky, 1973; but see also Ginosar & Trope, 1980; Manis, Dovalina, Avis & Cardoze, 1980; Wells & Harvey, 1977).

How should we think about this pattern, summarized in Figure 11.3? Holland, Holyoak, Nisbett and Thagard (1986) have argued that subjects have a preference for "specific-level evidence." Given this preference, subjects seek to think about people and situations in the most specific way they can. If subjects are merely told an individual was "chosen at random" from a group, they have minimal information, and so they must think about this individual as a faceless, anonymous figure. The only thing the subjects do know is that the individual is from the group, and so information about the group is applied. That is, subjects consider base rates.

If, however, subjects are given some information about this individual, they can begin to think about him or her as an actual person. In the experiments described, the diagnostic information is designed to suggest that the individual is a member of a particular category—lawyer or engineer, humanities major or science major. In these cases, subjects are likely to rely on the representativeness heuristic and, as a result, they think about this individual with reference to their prototype for the appropriate category. The individual is thus categorized according to his or her resemblance to the prototype;

Figure 11.3

THE BIAS TOWARD "SPECIFIC-LEVEL EVIDENCE"

If subjects have information about:

Base rates .... ➡ they use base rates.

Base rates + Diagnostic information .... ➡ they use the diagnostic information.

Base rates ....+ Irrelevant information ➡ they use irrelevant information.

.... Diagnostic information + Irrelevant information ➡ they use both ("the dilution effect")

In each situation, we have double-underlined the information subjects seem to rely on: If base rate information is all subjects have, then they use this information. If they have the base rate information and some diagnostic information, they don't combine these two. Instead, they ignore base rates, and use the diagnostic. If subjects are given the base rate information and some *useless* information, they again ignore the base rates and focus on the useless information. Finally, if subjects are given some diagnostic information and some useless information, they once again give too much weight to the useless information, and end up "diluting" the diagnostic information.

likewise, the individual is assumed to have the properties associated with the prototype.

What is striking is that thinking about the individual in this fashion seems to interfere with thinking about the individual in other ways. Specifically, thinking about the individual with reference to the prototype seems to exclude thinking about the individual with reference to the more abstract group information. As a consequence, once subjects are thinking in terms of the category, they use the diagnostic information, but ignore the base rates.

Finally, if subjects are given still more information about the individual, they start to think about him or her as a specific character, with specific traits, and not merely as an exemplar of a larger category. In this case, neither the category information (the prototype) nor the group information (the base rate) is applied. Instead, the individual is thought of as just that: an individual. This individual is still a member of a group, but this is no longer considered. This individual is still a member of certain categories, but this also is ignored. These other considerations about this person are disregarded or, in the terms we have been using, diluted.

With all of this said, let's make certain that the key point is clear: It is easy to demonstrate, in laboratory studies, that subjects underutilize base-rate information. Subjects do use this information, if it is all they have. But, if more specific information is also available, subjects jettison the base rates, and attend only to the specific information. In the laboratory, this can easily lead to judgments not warranted by statistics or logic. Unfortunately, the same can be demonstrated outside of the laboratory.

Base Rates in the Real World

Imagine reading about Julia, age 42, who is worried about breast cancer. We might start by asking: How common is breast cancer for women of Julia's age, with her family history, her dietary pattern, and so on? Let us assume that, for this group, the statistics show an overall 1% likelihood of cancer. This is the base rate, the probability we estimate prior to any diagnostic testing. And it should be reassuring to Julia: There is a 99% chance that she is cancer-free.

It seems clear that this base rate is relevant to Julia's case. If the base rate were higher (30%), then we would expect Julia to be that much more anxious. If the base rate were lower (.000001%), then the odds are heavily in Julia's favor, and her anxiety should diminish. Without question, it seems reasonable to consider the base rates, in considering Julia's case.

Of course, we can also gather more information, since reasonably accurate procedures are available for detecting breast cancer. Let's say that mammograms are approximately 85% accurate. This is the likelihood of a positive test if cancer is on the scene. If there is no cancer, let's say that there is a 90% chance the test will correctly come back negative; that is, the possibility of a false positive is just 10%. (After Eddy, 1982.)

What should Julia conclude, therefore, if her mammogram comes back indicating that cancer is present? She might well schedule surgery as quickly as possible: We have just said that the diagnostic tests are quite reliable. However, we have also agreed that the base rate is relevant to Julia's case. Therefore, the base rate needs somehow to be integrated with the diagnostic information.

How should this information be combined? As a way of thinking this through, let's start with the information in Figure 11.4. We have laid out the diagnostic "credentials" of the mammogram, with 85% of all cancer cases correctly diagnosed, and 15% misdiagnosed. Of all the non-cancer cases, 90% will be correctly diagnosed; 10% will be misdiagnosed.

But now let us place *number* of occurrences in the table, rather than percentages. The correct numbers are shown in Figure 11.5. To understand this table, bear in mind that the base rate shows a 1% likelihood of cancer for the patient group we are considering. This means there are 99 patients in the bottom row of the table (cancer absent) for every one in the top row (cancer present). To keep our arithmetic straightforward, let us imagine that there are 99,000 patients in the bottom row (without cancer) and 1,000 in the top row (with cancer).

Of the 1,000 patients with cancer, we know that 85% (850 cases) will be correctly diagnosed by the mammogram. Of the 99,000 patients not having cancer, the mammogram will be correct for 90% of them, or a total of 89,100

Figure 11.4

MAMMOGRAM ACCURACY EXPRESSED AS PERCENT			
	MAMMOGRAM INDICATES		
	Cancer	**No Cancer**	**Total**
Cancer present	85%	15%	100%
Cancer absent	10%	90%	100%

Diagnostic mammography is reasonably accurate. The correct detection rate is close to 85%, the "false alarm" rate is only 10%. (These numbers are approximate, and intended only for purposes of illustration.) [After Eddy, 1982.]

Figure 11.5

MAMMOGRAM ACCURACY EXPRESSED AS NUMBER OF CASES			
	MAMMOGRAM INDICATES		
	Cancer	**No Cancer**	**Total**
Cancer present	850	150	1,000
Cancer absent	9,900	89,100	99,000

This table combines the percentage information (from Figure 11.5) with the *base rates* for cancer. The base rates are reflected in the right-most column: With an (estimated) base rate of 1%, there are 99,000 cases with *no* cancer for every 1,000 cases with cancer. Of these 99,000 cases, 10% will be misdiagnosed (see Figure 11.5). Hence, 9,900 of the women without cancer will be misdiagnosed; for the remaining 89,100, the mammogram will correctly indicate no cancer. Of the 1,000 cases with cancer, 15% will be misdiagnosed (again, see Figure 11.5). Hence, 150 women with cancer will be misdiagnosed; for the remaining 850, the mammogram will correctly indicate the presence of cancer. What then should we conclude if a mammogram indicates cancer? This places us in the left-hand column of the table; in this column, 850 women have cancer, out of a total of 10,750 (850 + 9,900). Therefore, with a base rate of 1%, a positive mammogram indicates an 8% chance of cancer (850/10,750). [After Eddy, 1982.]

patients. The mammogram will be incorrect, though, for 10%, a total of 9,900 patients.

We are now in a position to ask what it means if Julia's mammogram indicates cancer. In Figure 11.6, a positive mammogram result places us in the left-hand column ("Mammogram indicates cancer"). But note that, within this column, the "cancer absent" cases far outnumber the "cancer present" cases, by a margin of 9,900 to 850, or more than 10 to 1. In short, with this patient group, a mammogram indicating cancer is *wrong* more than ten times as often as it is right. This is not because the mammogram is a poor test. Just the opposite: We have already commented that mammograms are, overall, very accurate as diagnostic tools. A mammogram's being correct is, proportionally, much more likely than a mammogram's being incorrect. But, given the base rate, there are more opportunities for the less-likely event to occur, with the result evident in the table.

Thus, the likelihood of Julia having cancer, given a positive test, and given the numbers quoted, is about 8%. For most women, this risk is serious enough to warrant further action—for example, other tests. Nonetheless, this probability is much lower than one might have guessed, based simply on the mammogram's accuracy. One's response and, indeed, one's anxiety level, might be rather different, based on the diagnostic information *plus* the base rate, than it would have been on the basis of the diagnostic information alone.

Our discussion of this case has so far been statistical, not psychological: All we have done is to show how important it is, in understanding this diagnostic information, to take base rates into account. If one looks only at the mammogram's reliability as a test, one might conclude that a positive test on a mammogram is a sure sign of cancer. If one looks at both the mammogram and the base rate, one draws a different conclusion. What we need to ask now, though, is whether medical professionals are sensitive to these issues. We have already seen that laboratory subjects do poorly on base-rate problems, but one might hope that doctors, trained in the use of diagnostic information, might do better. In fact, this is not the case. Evidence suggests that doctors, just like the rest of us, do not take base rate information into account when evaluating evidence (Dawes, 1988; Eddy, 1982; Klayman & Brown, 1993; although also see Weber, Böckenholt, Hilton & Wallace, 1993). Doctors (and other professionals) show the same patterns of reasoning that we have already observed in laboratory subjects—with errors, in this case, that can lead to serious misassessments of a patient's status.

Assessing the Damage

We have painted an unflattering portrait of human reasoning. We have discussed several sources of error, and we have suggested that these errors are rather widespread. These studies have been run on many different campuses, including some of the world's most prestigious colleges and universities. Thus, the subjects are, presumably, talented and intelligent. The errors occur nonetheless. (For reviews, see Arkes, 1991; Einhorn & Hogarth, 1981; Gilovich, 1991; Kahneman, Slovic & Tversky, 1982; Nisbett & Ross, 1980.)

Even experts make these errors. We have discussed poor diagnostic reasoning in physicians and illusory correlations in experienced therapists. Likewise, if we add just a little subtlety to our problems, these errors are observed even among those with considerable training in statistics and methodology (Kahneman & Tversky, 1982a; Tversky & Kahneman, 1971, 1983; also see Mahoney & DeMonbreun, 1978; Shanteau, 1992). In some cases, the experts do avoid error, but only if the problems fit precisely into their areas of expertise. If we ask these same experts to make relatively unpracticed judgments, the errors appear in full force (e.g., Smith & Kida, 1991).

Finally, we make these errors even when the stakes are high. In a number of studies, subjects have been offered cash bonuses if they perform accurately; these incentives have little impact on performance (Arkes, 1991; Gilovich, 1991). More strongly, we have discussed errors in the context of cancer diagnosis; surely the stakes here are high indeed, yet the errors occur nonetheless. There is, in fact, even some suggestion that errors are *more* likely to occur (or, perhaps, more likely to be tolerated) when the stakes are high. For example, in one study, scientists were asked to evaluate brief descriptions of (fictitious) research. Some of the research involved important topics (e.g., heart disease), and some, less important topics (e.g., heartburn). In each case, though, the research contained an important flaw. The scientists were more likely to overlook the flaws and were more likely to recommend publication of the study, when the topic was an important one (Wilson, DePaulo, Mook & Klaaren, 1993).

Are the Normative Models Appropriate?

One might draw rather cynical conclusions from these findings: Human reasoning is fundamentally flawed; errors are appallingly common. No wonder that racism and warfare are so common. However, this view of things leaves many questions unanswered. If our reasoning is so poor, then how is it possible that we have survived at all? Indeed, the history of humanity is filled with a huge number of egregious deeds, but our history is also filled with great intellectual accomplishments and enormous technological progress. How was all of this achieved, given our flawed reasoning skills?

Perhaps there is nothing wrong with human reasoning. Perhaps instead there is something wrong with the research we have presented. As we have already mentioned, however, the subjects in these studies were well-motivated and, one would think, adequately skilled; the problems themselves are generally straightforward. Some scholars have expressed concern about the instructions in these studies (perhaps the instructions are obscure or misleading), but it seems unlikely that this could explain the full pattern of evidence. (For discussion, see Kahneman & Tversky, 1982a; Schwartz, Strack, Hilton & Naderer, 1991; Wolford, Taylor & Beck, 1990.)

Perhaps the problem lies in how we have assessed subjects' responses. In all of these studies, the researchers themselves have designated one answer or another as "preferable" or "correct." What if this designation were wrong? In this case, we would have counted subjects' responses as incorrect when, in actuality, their answers were fully justified. If this were so, then obviously we would have made things appear far worse than they are.

A suggestion along these lines is already contained in our appeal to heuristics. Heuristics, by definition, do allow errors to occur, but there is a reason for this: Heuristics provide efficiency. A heuristic is therefore valuable if this gain in efficiency is worth more to us than the cost. If this tradeoff is worthwhile, then we should cease lamenting the errors—they are simply the price we pay in order to live our lives at a sane and reasonable pace. Indeed, one might argue that our lives are filled with countless occasions requiring a judgment of one sort or another. If we took too much time in each of these judgments, we would spend our days frozen in thought, unable to move forward in any way. On this view, it might be madness *not* to use the heuristics, even if they do, on occasion, lead us astray. Some alternate strategy might avoid the errors, but perhaps at an intolerable cost.

The classic statement of this view comes from Simon (1957). In many cases, Simon argues, it is foolish to seek an *optimal* decision, or an *optimal* choice, since this may require more time, and more effort, than the decision is actually worth. If you are shopping for a car, you could test-drive every model on the market, and this would guarantee that you would find the *best* car on the market. But this would require an enormous amount of your time. Therefore, Simon argues, we compromise in a sensible way: Rather than searching for the optimal choice, we instead search only for a choice that is *good enough* to satisfy us, and then we cut short our search. In Simon's terms, it's more sensible to **satisfice** than to optimize—seeking a satisfactory outcome rather than seeking the best possible outcome.

It is easy to see how this applies to human reasoning. We could seek judgment strategies that would yield error-free performance. However, "optimizing" in this fashion would require more resources than we have. We therefore elect to "satisfice"—relying on judgment strategies that are *good enough*: accurate more often than not and, above all, efficient. On this view, therefore, there may be nothing wrong with human reasoning. Yes, we do make errors, but these are the exception and not the rule. Moreover, the errors need to be balanced against the enormous savings—in time, in effort—afforded by our use of heuristics. (For discussion, see Einhorn & Hogarth, 1981; Nisbett & Ross, 1980; von Winterfeldt & Edwards, 1986.)

Successful Statistical Reasoning

Even if Simon's argument is correct, we might still hope to improve human reasoning in a variety of ways—perhaps seeking strategies that are *both* efficient and accurate. (For surveys of some attempts to improve human reasoning, see Baron, 1988; Baron & Sternberg, 1987.) Indeed, one group of psychologists has argued that we already *have* these strategies—strategies that are quick and easy to use and also immune to many of the errors we have discussed. The problem, they assert, is that we *under-use* these important reasoning tools.

For example, many of the errors reviewed in this chapter seem to imply a profound misunderstanding of statistical principles. Subjects seem not to understand, for example, that small samples are less reliable than large samples. However, Nisbett and his colleagues (e.g., Nisbett, Krantz, Jepson & Kunda, 1983) have argued that subjects *do* understand these principles; the subjects' problem is that they don't *apply* what they know. Indeed, it is easy to show that subjects' untutored, informal intuitions are fully in line with statistics. For example, all subjects would endorse these claims: "We know that accidents happen. But accidents don't keep on happening. If something happens over and over, it is probably not an accident." Endorsing these claims is tantamount to endorsing the "law of large numbers": Small samples are vulnerable to accidents, but accidents don't keep happening—that is, large samples are less vulnerable to accidents.

Likewise, Nisbett et al. (1983) ask us to imagine hearing this comment: "I can't understand it. I have nine grandchildren, and all of them are boys." This sounds like a sensible statement; something does seem odd in this case if 100% of the cases (nine out of nine) are of the same gender. But now imagine this comment: "I can't understand it. I have three grandchildren, and all of them are boys." This statement sounds peculiar; it seems unlikely that anyone would ever utter these words. With this small sample (three babies), we easily believe that 100% of the cases (three out of three) could be of the same gender, just by accident. Again, it looks like we understand the law of large numbers.

In the same vein, we earlier lamented subjects' blanket assumption that categories are homogeneous. This led to subjects' overgeneralizing from a single case (as in "man who" arguments), or to subjects' expectation that small samples would preserve the pattern of the larger set (as in the gambler's fallacy). But, in some studies, subjects don't make this blanket assumption. Instead, subjects are sensitive to the degree of homogeneity within a category and temper their judgments accordingly.

In one study, Nisbett et al. (1983) asked subjects to imagine that they had encountered a new bird, the shreeble. The one shreeble observed so far was blue; how likely, therefore, is it that all shreebles are blue? In other trials, subjects were told about a new element, floridium. This sample of floridium, when heated, burned with a blue flame; how likely is it that all floridium, when heated, burns with a blue flame? Finally, in still other trials, subjects were told about a previously unknown tribe, living on a Pacific island. One member of the tribe has been observed, and was obese. How likely is it that all members of this tribe are obese?

For floridium, subjects were quite willing to believe that a single instance allows generalization to the whole set, and so they asserted that all floridium would burn blue when heated. Subjects were less willing to extrapolate, however, in thinking about shreebles, and even less willing to extrapolate when thinking about obese islanders. In these cases, subjects were clearly influenced by the number of cases observed: They were more willing to extrapolate on the basis of three shreebles than on the basis of one, and even more willing on the basis of 20 observations.

In this study, then, subjects are sensibly using information about sample size and are more willing to draw conclusions based on larger samples. Moreover, subjects are also being appropriately sensitive to category homogeneity, on the assumption that instances of an element are quite likely to resemble each other, while the weight of one native might easily be rather different from the weight of another. The first category is homogeneous, encouraging generalization; the second category is not.

Applying Statistical Knowledge

Nisbett and his colleagues therefore conclude that subjects do understand the importance of sample size and also the role of category homogeneity. Moreover, when subjects employ this knowledge, they seem to do so easily and efficiently. The demands of efficiency, therefore, need not lead to error. Indeed, Nisbett et al. assert that subjects' knowledge in these cases can be thought of as providing a set of statistical heuristics, efficient strategies allowing them to think about a variety of facts, observations, and experiences in statistical terms.

How should we reconcile these claims with evidence, throughout this chapter, showing poor reasoning, even among trained experts? Nisbett et al. argue that the problem lies in "triggering" the use of these heuristics. In many cases, we don't realize that our statistical knowledge is relevant, or we don't understand how to apply our statistical knowledge. As a result, we end up reasoning poorly—in a fashion we have seen reflected in study after study.

Specifically, Nisbett et al. propose that three factors are critical in triggering the use of these statistical heuristics. First, these strategies are likely to be applied if the role of *chance*, or of *accident*, is prominent in the problem under scrutiny. Consistent with this claim, manipulations that highlight the role of chance do increase the likelihood of subjects reasoning in a statistically appropriate manner.

As an example, consider the neglect of base rates, a phenomenon we explored with the lawyer/engineer problem. In a variation of this procedure, Gigerenzer, Hell and Blank (1988) presented subjects with an urn containing 100 pieces of paper. Thirty of the pieces of paper, subjects were told, contained descriptions of engineers; 70 contained descriptions of lawyers. The subjects themselves were then required to draw the "thumbnail descriptions" out of the urn, and to render a judgment about the likelihood that the individual selected was a lawyer. This manipulation emphasized for subjects the role of chance in the selection of these descriptions and, accordingly, much improved the quality of subjects' reasoning—that is, it diminished subjects' neglect of base rates. (For related data, see Gigerenzer, 1991; Tversky & Kahneman, 1982.)

As a second "trigger" for statistical heuristics, subjects seem more likely to use these heuristics if the problem highlights the role of *sampling*, so that subjects can, in particular, understand an experience as a sample of data drawn from a larger set of potential observations. This is particularly useful if the "data" arrive in a format that supports ready comparisons from one sample to the next.

Consider a study by Kunda and Nisbett (1986). Subjects were asked to judge covariation with two different types of cases: Some of the judgments were made about events that were easily coded in terms of single, repeatable observations—athletic performance or academic achievement. As such, these events are easily quantified, in terms of points per game or test scores. Other judgments were made about less easily coded events. For example, subjects made judgments about things like friendliness and honesty. "Such events are manifestly difficult to code reliably . . . Should friendliness be measured in smiles per minute, 'good vibrations' per encounter, or what?" (Holland et al., 1986, p. 212).

Kunda and Nisbett predicted that subjects would be more accurate in assessing covariation with the codable data, like athletic performance—these are data that should trigger the use of statistical heuristics. Subjects should be less accurate with cases that are difficult to code, like social behaviors. The data clearly support this prediction.

Finally, the use of statistical heuristics is also influenced by certain background beliefs, perhaps beliefs built into our cultural knowledge. For example, each of us has certain beliefs about the role of luck in certain achievements, and this will shape whether we think about these achievements with reference to luck, and therefore with reference to chance, and therefore with reference to statistical principles. Likewise, each of us has beliefs about the homogeneity or heterogeneity of certain sets, and this too will influence our thinking about these sets. (For related discussion, see Bar-Hillel, 1982; Tversky & Kahneman, 1982, 1983; Kahneman & Tversky, 1982c; Wilson & Brekke, 1994.)

Training Subjects to Use Statistics

We should emphasize that the triggering of statistical knowledge is far from trivial. Subjects' use of mental short-cuts seems a well-entrenched habit, and so will often continue even in situations emphasizing the role of chance, or situations with "codable" data. These situations do make it more likely that subjects will consider sample size, sample bias, and base rates but, even in these settings, subjects' sensitivity to these statistical factors is far from guaranteed. That's why it has been so easy, throughout this chapter, to catalog cases of poor-quality, unwarranted reasoning.

Is there anything we can do to change this situation, to make it more likely that subjects will reason in a statistically sensible fashion? One might expect that *training* of the appropriate sort might be helpful, and several studies confirm this optimistic prediction. For example, Fong, Krantz and Nisbett (1986) provided subjects with just a half-hour of training, focusing on the law of large numbers (LLN). Subjects were taught (or, perhaps we should say, "reminded") that accidents do indeed happen, but that accidents don't keep on happening, over and over. Therefore, a small sample of data might be the result of some accident, but a large sample probably isn't. Consequently, large samples are more reliable, more trustworthy, than small samples.

Some of the subjects in this study were taught about the LLN in a fairly abstract way—the law was illustrated by drawing samples of red or blue gumballs out of a jar. Other subjects were given examples during the training, showing them how the LLN applied to real-world cases (e.g., a public opinion poll). The results showed that even this brief training was remarkably effective: After training, the subjects (adults and high-school students) were more likely to apply the LLN to test cases, and their application of the law tended to be reasonable and appropriate. Interestingly enough, roughly the same benefit was observed following the formal training as was observed with the examples training. (See also Fong & Nisbett, 1991.)

If a half-hour's training in statistics improves subjects' reasoning, what about an entire course in statistics? Fong et al. conducted a telephone survey of "opinions about sports," calling subjects who were taking an undergraduate course in statistics. Half of the subjects were contacted during the first week of the semester; half were contacted during the last week. Note, though, that there was no indication to the subjects that the telephone interview was connected to their course; as far as the subjects knew, they had been selected entirely at random.

Subjects in this study were asked several questions, to increase the likelihood that they would indeed think they were simply being interviewed about sports, and to ensure that subjects didn't perceive the relation between the

Figure 11.6

The Problem

"In general, the major league baseball player who wins Rookie of the Year does not perform as well in his second year. This is clear in major league baseball in the past 10 years. In the American League, eight Rookies of the Year have done worse in their second year; only two have done better. In the National League, the Rookie of the Year has done worse the second year 9 times out of 10. Why do you suppose the Rookie of the Year tends not to do as well his second year?"

Non-statistical answer:

When a player does well in his first year, he receives an enormous amount of media attention. This puts great pressure on the player, and most players have a difficult time continuing to do well amidst all that pressure.

Statistical answer:

All of the players in the Major Leagues are talented—otherwise they wouldn't have made it into the Major Leagues! To stand out from the pack, then, you need more than talent—you need talent *and* some degree of luck—good health during the season, no distraction from personal problems, a lucky selection of pitchers, and so on. The Rookie of the Year, therefore, is probably someone who's talented *and* lucky, during his first year. Therefore, the first year performance probably *overestimates* the player's true talent. And, of course, the problem with luck is that it's unreliable and may not continue into a second year.

The "non-statistical answer" offered here is plausible, and may be true. The statistical answer, however, is better than "merely plausible," it is virtually certain to be true! It is surely the case that any performance, athletic or otherwise, depends both on talent and on some number of chance factors. It is also extremely likely that the Rookie of the Year has benefited from some degree of luck: Chance factors will favor some players, and will work against others. If chance works against you, you are unlikely to emerge as Rookie of the Year. Therefore, the Rookie of the Year is someone who is benefiting from some degree of luck. And, of course, lucky breaks—like any other sort of accident—don't keep happening, over and over. Therefore, as the "sample size" grows (two years of observation versus just the rookie year), factors like luck will play a smaller role. Hence, the Rookie of the Year won't continue to benefit from good luck, and so his performance will decline.

interview and their statistics course. Then subjects were asked the question quoted in Figure 11.6. The results clearly showed that subjects' reasoning about this question was influenced by their training: For those contacted early in the term, only 16% gave statistical answers. For those contacted later, the number of statistical answers more than doubled (to 37%). The quality of the answers also increased, with subjects more likely to articulate the relevant principles correctly at the end of the semester than at the beginning.

Let's note, though, that the effects of statistical training were modest in size. It is true that the training doubled the likelihood of statistically warranted answers, but it is also true that, even after a statistics course, only 37% of the subjects gave such an answer; almost two-thirds of the subjects, in other words, did not. This echoes our earlier remarks about the "triggers" for statistical reasoning: The triggers make this reasoning *more likely*, but the triggers leave many of the errors untouched. Likewise, training in statistics improves the quality of one's reasoning but, again, many of the errors remain in place.

Even with this caution, however, these are rather cheerful data: Subjects' reasoning about evidence, it seems, can be improved, and the improvement applies to problems in new domains and in new contexts. Training in statistics, it seems, can have widespread benefits.

Other Forms of Training

What about other forms of training? For example, think about students who major in psychology, or who go to psychology graduate school. These students are likely to take many courses that include discussion of methodological issues. Does this training carry over into other domains? If so, then one might expect that majoring in psychology will broadly improve one's reasoning.

Consistent with this suggestion, Lehman, Lempert and Nisbett (1988) showed that graduate training in psychology does improve one's ability to reason about evidence, including evidence having little to do with psychology. Similar results have been observed as a function of undergraduate training (Lehman & Nisbett, 1990). Subjects were tested during their first term at the university, and then retested in the middle of their senior year. The question of interest lies in the *change* scores for these subjects: How much have they learned from their four years of undergraduate study? What problems can they solve at the end of their college career that they couldn't solve when they were fresh out of high school?

Test problems in this study included problems in scientific domains (see Figure 11.7), and also problems in everyday life (Figure 11.6). As Figure 11.8 shows, a college education did indeed help subjects in solving these problems—in all of the groups, the seniors significantly out-performed the first-year students (i.e., all improvement scores were positive). This improvement

Figure 11.7

EXAMPLE OF A PROBLEM USED BY LEHMAN AND NISBETT
A recent study sought to determine whether *noise* harms plants. In the study, two identical coleus plants were transplanted from the same greenhouse and grown under identical conditions, except that the first plant was exposed to loud noise—approximately the same as a person would hear while standing on a busy subway platform—while the other plant grew in quiet conditions. After 1½ weeks of continuous exposure, only the sound-treated plant wilted.
Response indicating sensitivity to statistical factors:
With only two plants in the study, there is a possibility that the sound-treated plant was just weaker to begin with. This sort of chance difference between the two conditions would be less likely if a larger number of plants were included in the study. That way, it would be quite improbable that *all* of the sound-treated plants, just by luck, were weaker to begin with than the plants growing in quiet.
College seniors were more likely to give statistical responses to this problem, in comparison with first-year students.

was considerably larger, though, for students who had majored in social science or psychology. These are students who had majored in disciplines that emphasize problems of sampling and statistical variation. Apparently, this training pays off, not only helping these students to do work in their specific major, but also helping them to solve problems with content some distance away from their academic studies.

In looking at Figure 11.8, though, one might ask why social science training seemed superior to training in natural science. Let's emphasize that the natural science students did improve (a gain of about 25%), but they clearly gained less than the psychologists and social scientists, and the natural science students showed no advantage relative to the humanities students. Why is this? Students in natural science obviously do a great deal of quantitative work, but they also have the good fortune to work with homogeneous populations: One carbon atom behaves rather similarly to every other carbon atom; the properties of one electron are similar to the properties of all other electrons. Hence, issues of variability and sampling loom less large in these

Figure 11.8

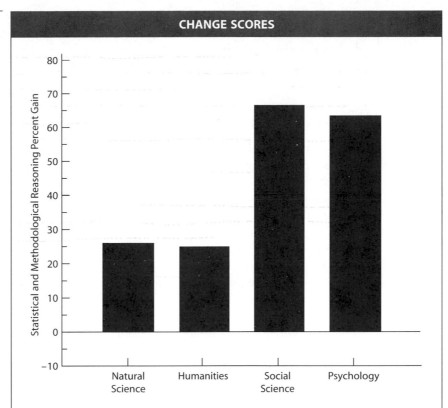

CHANGE SCORES

Shown here are change scores (average scores for college seniors *minus* average scores for first-year students) in statistical and methodological reasoning. All change scores are positive (seniors out-performed first-year students), but the change is particularly large for psychology and social science majors. Somewhat surprisingly, training in the natural sciences has only a modest impact on these tests—no larger than the impact from training in the humanities.

[handwritten margin note: b/c of psych & soc. more training in variability + sampling]

domains. As a consequence, students in the natural sciences receive less training in issues of sampling and the like. The implications of this are clear in Figure 11.8.

Let's also acknowledge that the pattern of Figure 11.8 would be rather different if we looked at improvement in other domains—for example, improvement in generating literary criticism, or improvement in thinking through the steps of a chemical reaction. In these domains, we obviously wouldn't expect an advantage for psychology or social science students. But there is a reason for focusing on statistical problems such as those sketched in Figures 11.6 and 11.7. These are problems that do indeed correspond to the sorts of reasoning we all need to do every day of our lives. There is a great deal not covered in, and not improved by, undergraduate training in psychology. But what is covered turns out to yield benefits of extraordinary breadth.

Thinking about Evidence: Some Conclusions

How, then, should we think about the results described throughout this chapter? As we have seen, it is easy to document judgment errors in bright, motivated undergraduates or in highly-trained professionals. These errors are made even when the consequences are extreme—e.g., errors in diagnosing a serious medical problem. At the same time, the fact remains that the intellectual accomplishments of our species—in science, in technology, in social matters—are huge. Apparently, our reasoning errors can't be too damaging.

How should we reconcile these observations? For a start, it is important to realize that the accomplishments of our species often derive from collective enterprises. Therefore, even if 90% of the participants make an error, the remaining 10% may detect the error and bring it to the attention of the group. (For a less sanguine view of group problem-solving, see Janis, 1972.) In addition, many intellectual achievements are rooted in domains that employ formal, explicitly defined means of data collection and data analysis, domains that should therefore be immune to the effects of informal reasoning, described in this chapter.

In addition, we have now catalogued several factors that reliably improve the quality of our judgment—factors that seem to trigger our statistical knowledge, and certain forms of training that make these errors less likely. This training probably helps us by making the statistical principles more prominent in memory and, therefore, easier to trigger. The training also helps us to see how our statistical intuitions apply to a range of new cases. Thus, with training, one realizes that an interview can be thought of as a small sample of data, and perhaps should be trusted less than some other source of information based on a larger sample of evidence. Likewise, one can think of an athlete's rookie year in these terms, or a dancer's audition, or a patient's symptom. Once the situation is coded in this fashion, the application of statistical rules is much more straightforward, and much more likely.

Moreover, we have emphasized the fact that there is a *reason* for our making mistakes: The world around us offers a wealth of information; still more information is provided by our memories. In addition, there is a wide range of options available to us, in considering what to do with this corpus of information. It is this great wealth—of information, of options—that forces us to be selective in our information processing: We cannot consider every fact or pursue every path. Pressure towards efficiency is created and, correspondingly, a demand that we "satisfice" rather than optimize. If we make errors in reasoning, therefore, this is the price we pay for efficiency.

One might still lament that we use the efficient path even when we shouldn't. We do, after all, appear to use the short-cuts even when making crucially important decisions. It may turn out, however, that this, too, is a matter of efficiency. Imagine that you had to decide, before answering any question or addressing any problem, whether to use some *careful* strategy this time around, or some *efficient* strategy. This determination by itself would require time and attention and might, therefore, be inefficient. If you want to preserve efficiency, it may be necessary to *skip* this determination, and proceed instead on the blithe assumption that it is always okay to be efficient. To put this differently, it would be inefficient to make a regular practice of asking yourself about efficiency. To be efficient, you have to assume that the efficient short-cuts are adequate, and live with the occasional errors that result.

With all these points made, the fact remains that errors in judgment are ubiquitous and often troubling. We close the chapter, then, with an optimistic note: We have seen that training can help in reducing the frequency of error, and we have seen indications that it is sometimes possible to be *both* efficient and accurate. In some situations, we do realize how to apply our statistical knowledge, and how to adjust for sample size or sample bias. All of this implies that judgment, as one might expect, is a skill, a skill that we all have to some extent, and a skill that can be improved by suitable training and practice. Errors in drawing conclusions, and in making inferences, are remarkably widespread, but the path is open to reducing these errors, and improving the quality of human judgment.

12

Reasoning: Thinking through the Implications of What You Know

I n Chapter 11, we examined how humans make judgments about evidence. Sometimes the evidence is provided to us directly through the senses; other times, it is supplied by memory. In either case, the evidence is often concerned with a specific event, or a specific observation, and so we focused on how humans draw conclusions from this singular evidence.

This type of reasoning—from specific bits of evidence to more general conclusions—is called induction. In induction, we confront a sample of evidence, and seek to extrapolate from this sample. That is why considerations of sample size and sample bias played such a large role in our discussion.

Obviously, though, not all thinking is inductive in character. Perhaps we have already concluded that a certain rash is regularly accompanied by a fever. We might then want to ask: What follows from this? What implications does this claim have for our other beliefs or actions? These questions rely on deduction—a process through which we start with general claims, or general assertions, and ask what follows from these premises.

Among its other roles, deduction allows us to make predictions about upcoming events: If you are meeting a particular six-year-old for the first time, you can anticipate many of her characteristics, based on your knowledge of six-year-olds in general. These anticipations rely on *deductions* from your general knowledge. Likewise, if you are going for a job interview, you can predict many of the questions you'll be asked, and again these predictions are deduced from your general knowledge.

The power to make predictions is obviously quite useful, and this is one of the important functions of deduction. But predictions also provide a way of keeping our beliefs in touch with reality: If our predictions turn out to be *wrong*, this implies that something is awry in our beliefs. Conversely, if a set of premises leads to a *correct* prediction, this obviously lends support to those premises.

Does our reasoning respect these principles? If you encounter evidence confirming your beliefs, does this strengthen your convictions? If evidence challenging your beliefs should come your way, do you adjust? And what if you realize, from the start, that you are uncertain about a belief? Perhaps you have drawn a tentative conclusion, and want to check on the conclusion before taking action. What evidence do you seek out to verify or disprove your view?

Confirmation and Disconfirmation

How should one go about testing a belief? What evidence might strengthen the belief? What would undermine it? These normative questions—about how one *ought to* reason—have been discussed at length by philosophers of science. How should scientists proceed, in testing their theories? What evidence would be most useful to them?

One important point, emerging from this discussion, concerns the ambiguity of *confirming* evidence and, correspondingly, the great value of *disconfirming* evidence. To see this, consider a concrete case: You believe that Natasha likes you, because she always smiles at you. You seek to *confirm* this belief, by arranging to encounter Natasha over and over. In each encounter, she smiles. Does this justify your belief?

These repeated smiles appear to confirm your belief, but the confirmations are actually ambiguous. It may be true that Natasha smiles at you because she likes you. But perhaps Natasha is just friendly in general, and smiles at everybody. Or perhaps she is quite unfriendly, and smiles only to be polite. Collecting more confirmations won't remove this ambiguity. If you continue to encounter Natasha, over and over, and she continues to smile, this is consistent with your initial belief, but it is also consistent with these other possibilities.

Similar examples are easy to find. The rooster is said to believe that his crowing each morning brings the sun into the sky. Plenty of evidence confirms his belief: Day after day he has crowed, and each time the sun has risen. Despite these confirmations, though, we believe the rooster's hypothesis to be false. Apparently, confirmations—no matter how numerous—cannot show a belief to be true.

Disconfirmations, on the other hand, can be enormously informative. Thus it might be useful for the rooster to ask: "What if I'm wrong? How else might I think about the evidence?" This might lead the rooster to the obvious experiment—to let one morning pass *without* crowing. The sun's arrival on that morning would surely tell the rooster a great deal.

Confirmation Bias

It is for these reasons that disconfirmation, rather than confirmation, plays such an important role in science. Indeed, the philosopher Karl Popper (e.g., 1959) argued that the search for disconfirming evidence is the earmark of science: Unless one seeks out this evidence, potentially challenging one's views, one is not doing science at all. Other scholars have expressed reservations about Popper's claim (e.g., Friedrich, 1993; Klayman & Ha, 1987; Lakatos, 1970; Tweney, Doherty & Mynatt, 1981) but, on anyone's account, it is clear that evidence that might disconfirm a belief is generally useful and often worth seeking. Likewise, consideration of alternative hypotheses is usually helpful: In asking, "Is there another way to explain the facts?" one will often discover that the evidence is indeed ambiguous.

However, despite the usefulness of disconfirmation, and the utility of considering alternatives, subjects seem to do neither. Instead, subjects display a strong tendency to seek out confirming evidence, and to rely on that evidence in drawing their conclusions. We first met this pattern, usually called the **confirmation bias**, in Chapter 11. Confirmation bias emerges in numerous forms: First, when subjects are assessing a belief or a hypothesis, they are far more likely to seek evidence that confirms the hypothesis than evidence that might disconfirm it. Second, when disconfirming evidence is made available to them, subjects often fail to use it, in adjusting their beliefs. Third, subjects often seem to *forget* disconfirming cases, and show a memory bias toward cases consistent with their beliefs. Finally, subjects regularly fail to consider alternative hypotheses, which might explain the available data just as well as their current hypothesis. (For reviews, see Evans, 1982; Gilovich, 1991; Higgins & Bargh, 1987; Rothbart, Evans & Fulero, 1979; Stangor & McMillan, 1992; Tweney et al., 1981).

In a classic demonstration of confirmation bias, Wason (1966, 1968) presented subjects with a series of numbers, such as "2, 4, 6." The subjects were told that this trio of numbers conformed to a specific rule, and their task was to figure out what the rule was. Subjects were allowed to propose their own trios of numbers ("Does 8, 10, 12 follow the rule?") and, in each case, the experimenter responded appropriately ("Yes, it does follow the rule" or "No, it doesn't"). Then, once subjects were satisfied they had discovered the rule, they announced their "discovery."

The rule was, in fact, quite simple: The three numbers had to be in ascending order. Thus "1, 3, 5" follows the rule; so does "18, 19, 236." The trio, "6, 4, 2" does not follow the rule, nor does "10, 10, 10." Despite this simplicity, though, subjects had considerable difficulty in discovering the rule, often requiring many minutes. This was in part due to the kinds of information subjects requested, as they sought to evaluate candidate rules: To an overwhelming extent, subjects sought to confirm the rules they had proposed; requests for disconfirmation were relatively rare. Attempts to test alternate hypotheses were also rare. (For related data, see Mynatt, Doherty & Tweney, 1977, 1978; Shaklee & Fischoff, 1982; Snyder & Swann, 1978. For similar results with trained scientists, see Mitroff, 1981, or Mahoney & DeMonbreun, 1978. For a review of this domain, see Baron, 1988.)

In short, subjects fail to reason in the fashion "recommended" by philosophers of science—that is, they fail to seek out disconfirming evidence. As one consequence of this, the subjects are less effective in their reasoning: In the Wason task, the number rule was discovered more quickly by the occasional subjects who *did* seek disconfirmation, in comparison to the (more typical) subjects who displayed confirmation bias. Thus, confirmation bias is plainly on the scene and interferes with subjects' performance.

Belief Perseverance

A different manifestation of confirmation bias is more troubling: Even when disconfirming evidence is out in plain view, subjects seem not to use it. Tweney et al. (1981) review a variety of studies making this point, but the most striking studies are those concerned with belief perseverance.

Subjects in one study were asked to read a series of suicide notes; their task was to figure out which notes were authentic, collected by the police, and which were fake, written by other students as an exercise. As subjects offered their judgments, they were provided with feedback about how well they were doing—that is, how accurate they were in detecting the authentic notes. The trick, though, was that the feedback was pre-determined, and had nothing to do with subjects' actual judgments. Some subjects were told that they were well above average in this task (again, independent of their judgments); other subjects were told the opposite—that they were much below average (Ross, Lepper & Hubbard, 1975; also Ross & Anderson, 1982).

Later on, subjects were debriefed. They were told that the feedback they had received was utterly bogus and had nothing to do with their performance. Indeed, they were shown the experimenter's instruction sheet, which assigned them to the "success" or "failure" group. Subjects were then asked a variety of further questions, including questions for which subjects had to assess their own "social sensitivity." Specifically, subjects were asked to rate their actual ability, as they perceived it, in tasks like the suicide-note task.

Let's emphasize that subjects were making these judgments about themselves *after* they had been told the truth about the feedback. That is, they had been told clearly and explicitly that the feedback was randomly determined and had no credibility whatsoever. Nonetheless, subjects were clearly influenced by the feedback: Subjects who had received the "above average" feedback continued to think of their social sensitivity as being above average, and likewise their ability to judge suicide notes. Subjects who had received the "below average" feedback showed the opposite pattern. The subjects, in other words, persevered in their beliefs even when the basis for the belief had been completely discredited. (For reviews of similar results, see Baron, 1988, especially Chapter 5; Nisbett & Ross, 1980.)

This finding has many implications. Among them, we might need to re-think the procedure, often used within psychology, of deceiving subjects during an experiment, and then "debriefing" them later on. We tend to view the debriefing as "undoing the damage" created by the initial deception, making us feel ethically comfortable with the fact that we had misled subjects in the first place. The data just described obviously raise questions about this common research practice.

In addition, we need to ask *why* subjects continue to believe in, and be influenced by, information that has been thoroughly discredited. Part of the answer, we have already said, rests on confirmation bias: Let's say that we tell you that you are particularly bad at the suicide-note task. Initially, you take this feedback quite seriously, and this leads you to wonder whether, perhaps, you are in general a less discerning person than you previously thought. To check on this possibility, you might search through your own memory, looking for evidence that might help you evaluate this suggestion.

What sort of evidence will you seek in memory? Given the broader pattern of confirmation bias, chances are good that you will specifically seek other facts or other prior episodes that might *confirm* your lack of social perception. Therefore, you will soon have *two* sources of evidence for your social insensitivity: the (bogus) feedback provided by us, and the supporting information you came up with yourself, thanks to your selective memory search. Thus, even if we discredit the information we provided, you will still have the information *you* provided and, on this basis, then, you might maintain your belief. (For discussion, see Nisbett & Ross, 1980; also Johnson & Seifert, 1994. For a similar account, applied to the phenomenon of "hindsight bias," see Baron, 1988; Fischhoff, 1977; Slovic & Fischhoff, 1977.)

Notice that, in this experiment, subjects could be led either to an enhanced estimate of their own social sensitivity, or to a diminished estimate, depending on which false information they were given in the first place. Presumably, this is because the range of episodes in subjects' memories is rather wide—in some previous episodes, subjects have been sensitive, and in some, they haven't been. Therefore, if they search through their memories seeking to confirm the hypothesis that they have been sensitive in the past, they will find confirming evidence. If, on the other hand, they search through memory seeking to confirm the opposite hypothesis, this too will be possible. In short, they can confirm *either* hypothesis, via a suitably selective memory search. Indeed, we could probably lead them to a wide range of different conclusions, simply by leading them to launch one type of memory search or another. This highlights the dangers built into a selective search of the evidence and, more broadly, the danger associated with confirmation bias. (For discussion of some ways to *avoid* or *undo* confirmation bias, see Koriat, Lichtenstein & Fischhoff, 1980; Lord, Lepper & Preston, 1984; Slovic & Fischhoff, 1977.)

Logic

We seem to be moving toward a picture of human reasoning that is as unflattering as the portrait we considered in Chapter 11: If subjects encounter evidence that contradicts one of their views, they maintain the view anyhow. Likewise, subjects regularly fail to notice that some other belief, some other hypothesis, fits with the facts just as well as their own beliefs do. They fail to realize that the evidence is *consistent* with their belief, but doesn't *favor* their belief (since the evidence is also consistent with other views).

In short, subjects in these experiments seem to be reasoning in a fashion that is not logical. Indeed, that invites a question: How well do subjects do if we explicitly invite them to think things through logically? Is thought logical?

Reasoning about Syllogisms

The relationship between *thought* and *logic* has been discussed by philosophers for thousands of years. Indeed, in developing systems of logic, mathematicians and philosophers have often asserted that they were doing nothing more than formalizing the rules of everyday thought, the rules we all use in our thinking and reasoning (Boole, 1854; Mill, 1874). On this view, there is no question about whether humans are "logical" or not. By definition, we are, since logic (allegedly) does nothing more than describe us, and our rules of thought. If we make reasoning errors, therefore, it cannot be because we are illogical; instead the errors come from some other source—carelessness, or an initial misreading of the problem, or some such. (For one version of this argument, see Henle, 1962, 1978.)

It turns out, however, that errors in logical reasoning are ubiquitous. If we are careless, or misread problems, we do so with great frequency. Much of the research relevant to this claim comes from studies employing **categorical syllogisms**. These begin with two assertions—the problem's premises—each containing a statement about a category. These statements usually involve quantifiers, such as "some," "all," or "none." A premise might state: "All men are mortal," or "Some houses are not wooden."

The syllogism can then be completed by specifying what conclusion follows from these premises. Examples of categorical syllogisms are shown in Figure 12.1. These are all valid syllogisms—that is, the conclusion does follow from the premises in each case. Here is an example of an invalid syllogism:

All P are M.
All S are M.   *invalid syllogism*
Therefore, all S are P.

To see that this is invalid, try translating it into concrete terms, such as "All professional plumbers are mortal," and "All sadists are mortal." Both of these are surely true, but it doesn't follow from this that "All sadists are professional plumbers." This *might* be true (although it seems extraordinarily unlikely),

Figure 12.1

EXAMPLES OF CATEGORICAL SYLLOGISMS

All M's are B.
All D's are M's.
    Therefore all D's are B.

All X's are Y.
Some A's are X's.
    Therefore some A's are Y.

Some A's are not B's.
All A's are G's.
    Therefore some G's are not B's.

compare for diagonally for valid syllogisms

All of the syllogisms shown here are valid—that is, if the two premises are true, then the conclusion must be true.

but there is surely no way in which this conclusion is demanded by these premises.

As you can see, syllogisms can involve concrete statements (such as "All men are mortal") or abstract statements ("All A are B"). The logic of a syllogism, however, depends only on its form: No matter how we fill in, "All A are B," the logical status of this statement remains the same. (Indeed, this dependence only on the *form* of a statement is the basis for the term, *formal logic.*)

Subjects, asked to reason about syllogisms, do remarkably poorly. Chapman and Chapman (1959) gave their subjects a number of syllogisms, including the one just discussed, with premises of "All P are M," and "All S are M." The vast majority of subjects, 81%, endorsed the *invalid* conclusion, "All S are P." Another 10% of the subjects endorsed other invalid conclusions; only 9% of the subjects got this problem right. Other studies, with other problems, yield similar data—with error rates regularly as high as 70–90%. (Gilhooly, 1988, provides a review.) Subjects' performance is somewhat better when the syllogisms are spelled out in concrete terms, but here, too, performance remains relatively low (Wilkins, 1928).

Subjects also show a pattern dubbed **belief bias**: If a syllogism's conclusion happens to be something subjects believe true anyhow, they are more likely to judge the conclusion as following logically from the premises. Conversely, if the conclusion happens to be something subjects believe false, they are likely to reject the conclusion as invalid. (For reviews, see Evans, Over & Manktelow, 1993; Newstead, Pollard, Evans & Allen, 1992; Oakhill & Garnham, 1993; Revlin, Leirer, Yopp & Yopp, 1980.)

In displaying belief bias, subjects are endorsing claims they believe to be true, based on the totality of their knowledge, and rejecting claims they believe to be false. Note, though, that this is *not* what these logic problems require: Logic is instead concerned with more "local" issues of reasoning—specifically, whether a particular conclusion is warranted by a particular set of premises. Thus, when subjects show the belief-bias pattern, they are failing to differentiate between good arguments (those that are logical and persuasive) and bad: They are willing to endorse a bad argument, if it happens to lead to conclusions they already believe true, and they are willing to reject a good argument, if it leads to conclusions already believed false.

Atmosphere Errors and Conversion

A misunderstanding of logic is also suggested by the so-called **atmosphere pattern**, first described by Woodworth and Sells (1935). The claim, in essence, is that the premises of a logic problem create a certain "atmosphere" in which some conclusions seem more appropriate, and some less. For example, premises involving the word "all" create an "atmosphere" in which conclusions about "all" seem appropriate; premises containing the word "some" make conclusions containing "some" seem appropriate. Thus, if one sees a premise such as "All A are B," and another premise such as "All D are B," one is "primed" to accept a conclusion that contains the word "all." None of this is logically sensible, but many of subjects' errors fall into this pattern, suggesting that subjects' reasoning is somehow influenced by these atmosphere effects. You might, for example, look back at the syllogism concerned with sadists and professional plumbers; subjects' errors in this case plainly do conform with the atmosphere pattern.

There has been considerable argument over what processes or strategies lie behind the atmosphere pattern. Moreover, while many of the errors made by subjects do fall into this pattern, some do not. As a result, it may be best to think of the atmosphere pattern as providing a reasonable—albeit crude— summary of the data and, as such, it implies that subjects approach these logic problems in a superficial manner and with minimal understanding. (For discussion, see Begg & Denny, 1969; Gilhooly, 1988; Johnson-Laird, 1983. For discussion of "matching" errors similar to the atmosphere errors, see Gilhooly, Logie, Wetherick, & Wynn, 1993; Wetherick, 1989.)

Another pattern is also prominent in subjects' errors: Subjects often interpret "All A are B" as though it were identical to "All B are A." (Of course this isn't warranted: "All trees are plants" isn't the same as "All plants are trees.") Likewise, subjects treat these as equivalent: "Some F are not G" and "Some G are not F." These errors are referred to as **conversion errors**, since subjects are "converting" these statements from one form into another.

Chapman and Chapman (1959) suggest that these conversions are unsurprising, given the content of ordinary conversation. In day-to-day discourse, they point out, we often do hear statements that are reversible in this fashion ("All three-sided figures are triangles"). Hence, our conversion of statements within logic exercises may simply be the consequence of a well-practiced habit, a habit useful in many contexts (e.g., normal conversation), even if it is inappropriate here. Whatever one makes of this account, the fact remains that many of subjects' errors do fit within the "conversion" pattern, and this contributes to their poor performance in tests of logical reasoning.

Where does all this leave us? Errors in logical reasoning seem ubiquitous. Moreover, these errors don't look like the product of carelessness; instead, there is a systematic pattern to the errors, a pattern that implies a profound misunderstanding of logic. In reasoning through logic problems, subjects are regularly influenced by their prior beliefs, clearly contrary to the rules of logic. Subjects seem generally unable to focus on the form or structure of statements, as logic requires; instead, subjects are influenced by the semantics or content of the problem. In addition, subjects regularly misinterpret logic problems, "converting" them in ways that might be sensible within casual conversation, but that are illegitimate here. All of this obviously undermines the claim that our thought follows the rules of logic or, conversely, that logic describes the rules of thought.

Reasoning about Conditional Statements

Similar conclusions derive from research on a different aspect of logic, namely, reasoning about **conditional statements**. These are statements of the familiar "If X, then Y" format, with the first statement providing a "condition" under which the second statement is guaranteed to be true.

Just as with syllogisms, subjects make enormous numbers of errors when asked to reason about conditional statements. Once again, errors are more common if subjects are asked to reason about abstract problems ("If P, then Q"), in comparison to performance with concrete problems ("If John plays baseball, then he is tense"). Errors are also more common if the logic problems involve negatives ("If John does not play baseball, then he won't be late"). Moreover, and again just like syllogisms, belief bias can be demonstrated: Subjects will endorse a conclusion if they happen to believe it true, even if the conclusion doesn't follow from the stated premises. Conversely, subjects will reject a conclusion if they happen to believe it false, even if the conclusion is logically demanded by the premises. (For broad reviews in this domain, see Evans, 1982; Evans, Newstead, & Byrne, 1993; Rips, 1990; Wason & Johnson-Laird, 1972.)

In reasoning about conditionals, subjects also make many conversion errors. With syllogisms, we suggested that these conversions are encouraged by our ordinary conversational habits, and the same is true here, since many terms have a different meaning in day-to-day conversation than they do within logic. For example, in logic the statement "A *or* B" means that either A is true, or B is true, or perhaps both are true. In ordinary conversation, though, we use "or" somewhat differently, usually ruling out this third possibility (namely, that *both* A and B are true). To see this, imagine that a child rings your doorbell and announces, "Trick or treat!" You are likely to understand this as an "exclusive" use of the word "or"—that is, you don't expect that both clauses will turn out to be true. (That is, the truth of either clause *excludes* the truth of the other.) You would feel betrayed if you provided the treat, but got the trick nonetheless.

Similarly, logicians interpret "If P then Q" this way: If P is true, then Q is guaranteed to be true. If P is *false*, then Q may turn out to be true anyhow. Once again, this is different from common usage: I might tell you, "If you touch my computer, I'll punish you." You therefore prudently leave my computer alone. If I punish you anyhow, surely you would feel this unjust. To put this in technical terms, we routinely interpret conditionals as if they were **biconditionals**, which are statements of the form, "If X, *and only if* X, then Y." In that case, if X isn't true, then Y won't be, either. To continue our example, a biconditional would imply that, if you didn't touch my computer, then you won't be punished—"Punish if touch, and *only if* touch." (For further discussion of these conversions, see Evans, 1982; Staudenmayer, 1975; Staudenmayer & Bourne, 1978; Wason & Johnson-Laird, 1972.)

Given these comments, one might argue that subjects' "errors" in logic may not be errors at all. Subjects understand these logic problems in their own terms and, in particular, they understand them in a fashion consonant with the ordinary usage of words like "or" and "if." Perhaps subjects then reason sensibly about the premises *interpreted in this fashion*. In this case, subjects might not offer the same responses as a logician, but that is not because their reasoning is bad. Instead, they are simply understanding the terms differently than a logician would. Thus, we don't have illogical subjects; instead, we simply have two different "dialects" in play—one the dialect of ordinary English, and one the dialect of logic. Each dialect is legitimate, each leads to its own interpretation of the problems, and each, therefore, leads to its own set of responses.

A number of psychologists have endorsed claims along these lines, arguing that subjects do reason well, but with a vocabulary somewhat different from that of standard logic. Once subjects' performance is understood, therefore, from the subjects' own perspective, the performance does not look so dismal. Indeed, we might even push this one step further: Perhaps subjects also have their own set of logical *rules*—rules that are sensible and coherent, but rules that are different from those used by the logicians. In effect, the subjects have their own "natural logic," a system somewhat different from logic as the logicians define it, but defensible nonetheless. (For discussion of this view, see Braine, 1978; Braine, Reiser & Rumain, 1984; Braine & O'Brien, 1991; Rips, 1983; Henle, 1962.)

This view has much to recommend it, but let's hold it to the side for now. There is another line of results we need to consider, before we can start assembling the pieces into an overall account.

The Four-Card Task

In the **four-card task** (sometimes called the selection task), subjects are shown four playing cards, as in Figure 12.2 (after Wason, 1966, 1968). Subjects are told that each card has a number on one side, and a letter on the other. Their task is to evaluate this rule: "If a card has a vowel on one side, it must have an even number on the other side." Which cards must be turned over to put this rule to the test?

Many subjects assert that the "A" card must be turned over, checking for an even number. Other subjects assert that the "6" card must also be turned over, checking for a vowel. Other subjects assert that both of these must be turned over. In Wason's research, 46% of the subjects turned over the "A" and the "6". Thirty-three percent turned over just the "A". The correct an-

Figure 12.2

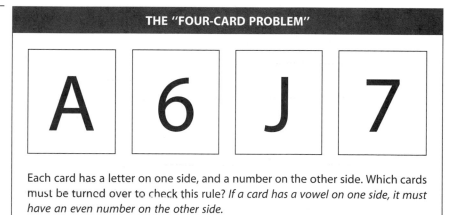

THE "FOUR-CARD PROBLEM"

Each card has a letter on one side, and a number on the other side. Which cards must be turned over to check this rule? *If a card has a vowel on one side, it must have an even number on the other side.*

swer was obtained by only 4% of the subjects—turning over the "A" and the "7." In brief, then, performance is atrocious in this problem, with 96% of the subjects giving wrong answers.

Why is "A and 7" the right answer? If we turn over the "A" card and find an odd number on the reverse, that would be inconsistent with the rule. Hence, there is a chance that we will find something informative by checking this card. What about the "J"? The rule makes no claims about what is on the flip-side of a consonant card, so, whatever is on the card's other side will be consistent with the rule. Hence, there is nothing to be learned by turning over this card. How about the "6"? If we find a vowel on the reverse side of this card, this would fit with the rule. If we find a consonant on the reverse, this also fits since, again, the rule makes no claims about what is on the reverse of a consonant card. We will learn nothing by turning over the "6"—no matter what we find, it is consistent with the rule. Finally, if we turn over the "7" and a vowel is on the other side, this would disprove the rule. Therefore, we do want to turn over this card—there is a chance we might find something informative.

Several hypotheses have been offered to explain the errors in this task. As one possibility, subjects might be converting the proposed rule, and then reasoning about this rule. They might, in particular, be interpreting this rule as a biconditional, rather than a conditional. Thus, they would be trying to test the rule, "If a vowel on one side, *and only if* a vowel on one side, then an even number on the other side." If this were subjects' understanding, though, then they should turn over *all* the cards to test the rule. However, this pattern—turning over all the cards—is shown by relatively few subjects (generally less than 20%). This seems a poor account of subjects' performance.

A different possibility is that subjects understand some logical rules, but not other rules, including a rule needed for this task. For example subjects do seem to understand the logical rule called ***modus ponens***, which justifies the conclusion in this case:

> If P then Q.
> P is true.
> Therefore, Q must be true.

Subjects generally reason well with problems resting on *modus ponens*, such as: "If Herbert waves at me, I'll be happy. Herbert did wave at me. What follows from this?"

Subjects have difficulty, though, with the rule of ***modus tollens***, which justifies the conclusion in this case:

hard for people

*modus tollens -
conclusion is
false.*

If P then Q.
Q is false.
Therefore, P must also be false.

In simple cases, subjects do understand this rule: "If Herbert waves at me, I'll be happy. I'm not happy. Therefore, it must be the case that Herbert didn't wave at me—if he had, I'd be happy." If we add any complexity at all, though, subjects are easily confused by problems resting on *modus tollens*, often rejecting conclusions if they are based on this rule (Braine & O'Brien, 1991; Evans, 1982; Rips, 1983, 1990; Taplin & Staudenmayer, 1973).

Could this be the problem in the four-card task? Because of their understanding of *modus ponens*, subjects would realize that they need to turn over the card with a vowel on it (that is, the "A"). That is because *modus ponens* tells them that a conclusion can be drawn from the combination of the rule ("if a vowel, then an even number") and the presence of a vowel. If subjects also fail to understand *modus tollens*, then they will fail to realize they should turn over cards with odd numbers (the "7"). This is because they won't see that a conclusion can be drawn from the combination of the rule ("if a vowel, then an even number") and the presence of a "not-even" number.

Therefore, a subject who understands *modus ponens* but not *modus tollens* will turn over the "A" card, but not the "7". This describes 33% of the subjects, so perhaps we are on the right track in understanding subjects' performance. But we have not explained why even more subjects (46%) chose the "A" and also the "6". Thus, a failure to understand *modus tollens* seems relevant here, but cannot provide our full account.

Case-Based Reasoning

We know that subjects do convert logic problems, but the most plausible conversion (turning a conditional into a biconditional) leaves unexplained most of the errors in the four-card task. We also know that subjects have trouble with *modus tollens*, but this too fails to explain the data from the four-card task. What, therefore, is going on?

Poor performance in the four-card task has been widely replicated. However, some studies, using variations on this problem, have found much better performance. For example, Johnson-Laird, Legrenzi and Legrenzi (1972) showed Italian subjects the figure illustrated in Figure 12.3, and asked them to test this rule: "If a letter is sealed, then it has a 50-lire stamp on it." Subjects did reasonably well in this version of the test, although, in its form, this test is identical to the original four-card problem.

Other studies, also using concrete materials, have likewise observed rea-

Figure 12.3

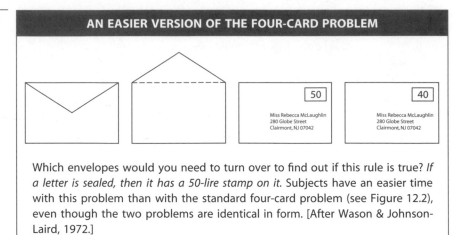

AN EASIER VERSION OF THE FOUR-CARD PROBLEM

Which envelopes would you need to turn over to find out if this rule is true? *If a letter is sealed, then it has a 50-lire stamp on it.* Subjects have an easier time with this problem than with the standard four-card problem (see Figure 12.2), even though the two problems are identical in form. [After Wason & Johnson-Laird, 1972.]

sonable levels of performance. For example, Griggs and Cox (1982) asked subjects to test this rule: "If a person is drinking beer, then the person must be over 19 years of age." As in the other studies, subjects were shown four cards, and asked which cards they would need to turn over, to test the rule. In this version, subjects did quite well: 73% of the subjects (correctly) selected the card labeled "drinking a beer," and also the card labeled "16 years of age." They did not select "drinking a Coke" or "22 years of age." Griggs and Cox also tested subjects with the "standard" version of the test (if vowel, then even number), and none of their subjects got this problem right. (For discussion, see Cheng & Holyoak, 1985; Evans, 1982; Evans, Newstead et al., 1993; Griggs, 1983; Legrenzi, Girotto & Johnson-Laird, 1993; Wason, 1983.)

Could it simply be the *concreteness* of these examples that improves performance? Other results argue against this suggestion: As just noted, the "envelope" problem produced good performance with Italian subjects. However, when the same problem was given to British subjects or to American subjects, poor performance was observed (Griggs & Cox, 1982; Johnson-Laird et al., 1972).

Perhaps the problem has to be concrete and also *familiar.* The Italian subjects actually had experience with the envelope rule, since it is pertinent to Italian postal regulations. (The Italian postal system requires slightly higher postage for sealed letters than for unsealed letters.) Neither the British nor the American subjects have had experience with this rule, and their performance with this problem was poor. In addition, it turns out that a postal regulation, similar to the one in the problem, used to be in effect in England,

and hence older British subjects are familiar with this rule, even though younger subjects are not. It is striking, therefore, that the older subjects do well with the envelope problem, suggesting indeed that familiarity with the rule is the key. (This result, reported by Golding, is summarized by Cheng & Holyoak, 1985.)

A number of authors have drawn a strong claim from these results. For the last several sections, we have been pursuing the hypothesis that *logic* describes the rules of thought—either logic as the logicians define it, or some "natural logic," building on the vocabulary of everyday conversation. On either of these views, thinking proceeds on a rather abstract level since, after all, logic depends only on the form or syntax of the assertions being considered, and not at all on their content. *Modus ponens*, for example, applies to any assertions of the form "If P, then Q," and also "P". It does not matter for *modus ponens* what P is or what Q is.

Other psychologists, however, have offered a rather different view (Griggs & Cox, 1982; Kolodner, 1992; Reich & Ruth, 1982). They suggest that we do not employ abstract rules in our reasoning; instead, our reasoning is much more concrete, based on specific knowledge we have about specific situations. In other words, we reason by thinking of experiences relevant to the problem now before us, and then we draw analogies based on these experiences. In short, reasoning is typically **case-based**, or instance-based. (There is an obvious tie between this suggestion and the claim of "exemplar-based categorization," which we discussed in Chapter 8.)

The evidence we have reviewed certainly seems consistent with this claim. If a test problem is familiar to subjects—that is, if the problem triggers case-based knowledge—then subjects do well with the problem. If the test problem contains unfamiliar materials, then subjects do poorly because, in this case, there is nothing to "trigger" prior experiences, and this leaves subjects with no basis from which to draw conclusions. (For discussion, see Braine et al., 1984; Henle, 1962; Holland, Holyoak, Nisbett & Thagard, 1986; Nisbett, 1993; Rips, 1983.)

Pragmatic Reasoning Schemata

We are on the brink of a complete reversal in our perspective: The proposal that we think according to the rules of logic is a proposal that thinking is enormously abstract and determined by form, not content. The case-based approach, in contrast, implies that thinking is rather concrete and determined by content, not form.

As it turns out, though, other conceptions of reasoning are also available, effectively "splitting the difference" between these two perspectives. One of these approaches emphasizes the role of **mental models** in reasoning; we will turn to this approach shortly. A different approach emphasizes the role of **pragmatic reasoning schemata**.

Like all schemata, reasoning schemata are derived from experience and so summarize that which is redundant and repetitive in our world. Reasoning schemata are defined in terms of goals, or event relationships, and so we have a *cause-and-effect* schema, which summarizes our experiences with cause-and-effect relations, and which we use in reasoning about causal relations. We also have an *obligation* schema, which we use in reasoning about social relations of the appropriate sort; we also have a *permission* schema, and so on.

These schemata embody rules that are quite similar to the rules of logic and so these schemata can be used to guide reasoning. For example, the permission schema includes rules like "If one wishes to take a certain action, then one must have permission," and "If one has permission to take a certain action, then one may take the action." We use these rules whenever we are trying to think about a situation requiring permission. Let's emphasize, though, that these rules support reasoning *about permission*; they are not general, abstract if-then rules. In this way, reasoning schemata are more concrete than logical rules.

At the same time, reasoning via these schemata is less concrete than case-based reasoning. This is because the schemata apply to broad *classes* of situations—e.g., any situation involving permission. Even if you are unfamiliar with the particular case under scrutiny, you might still recognize it as involving permission, or obligation, allowing you to apply the relevant schema. (For discussion, see Cheng & Holyoak, 1985; Cheng, Holyoak, Nisbett & Oliver, 1986; Nisbett, 1993.)

Reasoning Schemata and the Four-Card Task

How does all of this apply to the four-card problem? The standard version of this problem contains no practical or meaningful relations; the rule of "if a vowel, then an even number" is completely arbitrary. The problem is therefore unlikely to evoke a reasoning schema, and this leaves subjects at a complete loss: With their primary reasoning strategy not called into play, it is no wonder that subjects do poorly on this task.

On this view, we should be able to improve performance on the four-card task by altering the problem so that it *will* trigger a pragmatic reasoning schema. Then subjects will be able to employ their usual means of reasoning and should perform quite well. To this end, subjects in one experiment were given several variations of the basic problem (one example is illustrated in Figure 12.4). Their task was to decide which cards to turn over to test the

Figure 12.4

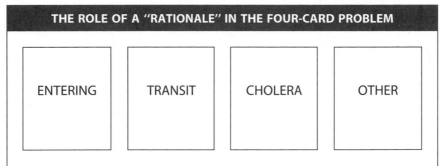

THE ROLE OF A "RATIONALE" IN THE FOUR-CARD PROBLEM

| ENTERING | TRANSIT | CHOLERA | OTHER |

Subjects were asked which cards they would need to turn over to find out if this rule is true: *If the form says ENTERING on one side, then the other side includes cholera among the list of diseases.* Subjects perform well on this problem if they are provided with a rationale; otherwise they perform poorly.

rule "If the form says ENTERING on one side, then the other side includes cholera among the list of diseases."

For half of the subjects, this problem was given with no further rationale. The prediction here is that no schema will be evoked and performance should be poor. The other subjects, however, were given a rationale, designed to trigger the permission schema. These subjects were told that the cards listed diseases against which airline passengers had been inoculated. In addition, they were told that cholera inoculation was required of all passengers seeking to enter the country. These subjects were then given the same rule as stated above, but now the rule can be understood in permission terms, something like "If a passenger wishes to enter the country, he or she must first receive a cholera inoculation." Thus, with the rationale in view, the problem should trigger a schema, and subjects should perform well.

Subjects were also given the "envelope" version of the problem, with the rule of "If an envelope is sealed, then it must have the higher value stamp." Half of the subjects were given no rationale; half were told that first-class mail was always sealed, and that the post office charged a higher rate for first-class mail.

As can be seen in Figure 12.5, subjects did rather well with the rationale versions of these problems, averaging about 90% correct. Without rationale, subjects did quite poorly (about 60%). The figure shows one exception to this pattern: Subjects run in Hong Kong did well with the envelope problem, even when no rationale was provided by the experimenters. This result is not difficult to understand: Residents of Hong Kong were familiar with an actual

Figure 12.5

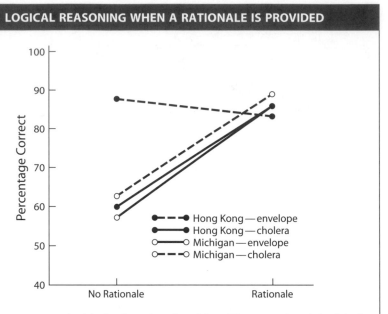

LOGICAL REASONING WHEN A RATIONALE IS PROVIDED

Subjects were tested with the "envelope" problem (Figure 12.3) and the "cholera" problem (Figure 12.4). When a rationale was provided, subjects performed well with both problems. When no rationale was provided, only the Hong Kong subjects working on the envelope problem did well. These subjects, familiar with the envelope rule, could provide a rationale for themselves. [After Cheng & Holyoak, 1985.]

postal rule similar to the one described within the experiment. These subjects had no trouble coming up with the rationale on their own, since the problem involved a familiar case.

In terms of their form, all of the problems used in this study are identical, all involving simple inferences about an "if-then" rule. Therefore, if subjects were reasoning about these problems by use of logic, then we should have observed equivalent performance in all conditions. This clearly is not the pattern we observe in the figure.

If familiarity is the key, then we should have observed low levels of performance with all versions of the problem except the Hong Kong-envelope condition. This condition presented a familiar problem to subjects; all other conditions presented novel problems. But, once again, this is not the pattern we observe. Performance is good in the Hong Kong-envelope condition, but it is equally good in several other conditions. This speaks against a case-based reasoning interpretation of these data.

REASONING IN THE ABSTRACT WITH A RATIONALE

| Has taken Action *A* | Has *not* taken Action *A* | Has fulfilled Precondition *P* | Has *not* fulfilled Precondition *P* |

Which cards would you turn over to test this rule? *If one is to take Action A, then one must satisfy precondition P.* This rule is relatively abstract, but does trigger the reasoning schema for *permission*. With the schema triggered, subjects perform well with this problem.

Finally, if subjects were reasoning by using pragmatic schemata, then we expect good performance when the schemata are called into play and poor performance otherwise. In this case, we predict high performance either with a familiar case, *or* with a case accompanied by a rationale triggering a specific schema. This is, of course, exactly what the data show.

Moreover, even with *abstract* problems, performance is improved the moment a reasoning schema is triggered. Subjects in one study were told, "Suppose you are an authority checking whether or not people are obeying certain regulations. The regulations all have the general form, "If one is to take Action A, then one must first satisfy Precondition P" (Cheng & Holyoak, 1985). Subjects were then given four cards, labeled as shown in Figure 12.6. In this task, 61% of the subjects solved the problem correctly, compared to 19% correct in a control group, given the standard problem. This makes it clear that concreteness is not crucial for correct reasoning—here subjects are doing reasonably well with an abstract problem.

Training Studies Using Reasoning Schemata

A number of scholars have expressed concerns about the reasoning-schemata proposal (Gigerenzer & Hug, 1992; Jackson & Griggs, 1990; Kirby, 1994; Klaczynski & Laipple, 1993; Manketelow & Over, 1991; Platt & Griggs, 1993). Nonetheless, a considerable quantity of evidence does fit with this proposal. Subjects reason well if a problem—familiar or not, concrete or abstract— triggers a reasoning schema; otherwise, reasoning seems to be extraordinarily poor, with errors far outnumbering the correct responses. Most of the research in this domain has focused on the permission schema, but related effects have been observed when subjects reason about cause-and-effect relations (Cheng & Nisbett, 1993; Lehman, Lempert & Nisbett, 1988; Morris & Nisbett, 1993; Thompson, 1994).

The idea of reasoning schemata has also been used as a basis for training subjects to reason more effectively. It should be said, first, that subjects' reasoning is *not* improved by courses in formal logic. For example, Morris and Nisbett (1993) tested subjects using a number of variants of the four-card task. Their subjects were graduate students in philosophy—some in their first year in the program, and some in their third year. The graduate training included several courses in logic and so, if these courses helped subjects, we would expect the third-year students to out-perform the first-year students. This was not the case: Both groups performed poorly. When the content of the problems was unfamiliar, for example, first-year students got 33% correct; third-year students got 32% correct. (As an interesting contrast, Morris & Nisbett also examined these students' performance with categorical syllogisms, like the ones we described earlier in this chapter. Graduate training in philosophy did help with these, with first-year students getting 63% correct, and third-year students, 83%. See also Galotti, Baron & Sabini, 1986.)

Similar results have been obtained when subjects are trained in logic within the context of the experimental procedure: This training has little impact on subjects' performance in the four-card task (Cheng et al., 1986). Likewise, an undergraduate course in logic seems not to improve performance on this task: Cheng et al. (1986) tested subjects both in the first week of a logic course, and again in the final week of the semester. While these subjects obviously learned a great deal during the term, this knowledge did not carry over into the four-card task, and performance was basically the same at the end of the course as it was initially.

However, a rather different result is obtained if subjects are trained to use reasoning schemata, rather than formal rules. Cheng et al. (1986) gave their subjects a two-page booklet detailing the nature of obligations and the procedures necessary for checking to see if a violation of the obligation had occurred. Subjects were also given an example of an obligation statement, framed in if-then terms. This training, brief as it was, had a dramatic impact on performance. These subjects were 92% correct with test problems designed to trigger the obligation schema (e.g., a problem involving the rule "If a steel support is intended for the roof, then it must be rustproof"). Subjects who received *no* training were only 64% correct. For more abstract problems (such as the "If vowel, then even number" problem), subjects trained in the nature of obligation got 55% right, compared to 27% for the control group.

In short, performance is little influenced by training in logic: There is little impact from a brief logic course within the experiment, or a full undergraduate course in logic, or even years of graduate training. In marked contrast, just a few minutes training in the use of reasoning schemata *does* improve performance, even with arbitrary problems.

Deductive Logic—An Interim Summary

Before pressing on, let's summarize where we are. As a start, common sense tells us that some people, in some circumstances, can use the rules of logic. Logic teachers, for example, can obviously use these rules. Even those untutored in logic can use "natural logic." Natural logic comes into play, for example, if I tell you "If G is true, then H is true. G happens to be true." With no difficulty, subjects draw the conclusion that H, too, is true. This problem, abstract and unfamiliar, relies on our intuitive understanding of *modus ponens*, and we use this understanding to draw the correct conclusion.

In other circumstances, though, we seem to rely on other reasoning strategies. If case-based knowledge is available to us, we are likely to use it. If not, the problem might nonetheless trigger a reasoning schema. This is more likely for people who have been trained to use these schemata and also more likely if the problem contains features triggering these rules. These pragmatic rules are more concrete than the rules of logic, and the specific inferences licensed by the schemata differ somewhat from those warranted by logic (Cheng & Holyoak, 1985). Nonetheless, in a range of problems, these schemata lead to the same responses as logical rules.

If no schema is triggered, and if no case-based knowledge is available, we might try to solve the problem through other means. The atmosphere hypothesis, for example, can be thought of as describing inferences you will try if you don't know how else to proceed. Likewise, if we can't figure out a problem, we might try to help ourselves by "smuggling in" other knowledge, external to the problem. In this case, we will show the pattern that we earlier called belief bias. This inclusion of other knowledge isn't warranted according to logic, but it may be your best bet, if you don't have some other plan available.

This suggests that there is no one strategy through which we tackle all reasoning problems. Instead, the rules of logic, reasoning schemata, and various heuristics may all co-exist in our mental repertoire, and each will surface in appropriate circumstances. Some of these reasoning strategies are more likely to yield the correct conclusion than others, and it is striking how often we rely on strategies that can lead to error. But this simply reflects the fact that the more "sophisticated" strategies come into play only when appropriately triggered—by cues in the problem setting or by virtue of relevant training.

Note the parallels between all of this and the pattern we saw in Chapter 11: When you are trying to make a judgment about evidence, there are several paths you might follow. If you have been trained in statistics and methodology, you may elect to translate the problem into these terms, and thus reason it through. This is likely to require some time and effort, but it is also likely to yield the right answer. As a second option, you may elect to think about the problem using statistical heuristics—heuristics, we suggested, that capture the gist of important statistical principles, such as the law of large numbers. Use of these heuristics, it seems, is more likely if you have been trained to use them, and more likely if the problem contains features that trigger these heuristics—for example, if the problem highlights the role of *chance* in determining an outcome. If all else fails, though, you will rely on a different set of heuristics, such as availability and representativeness. These may produce error, but they probably work more often than not, and at least they are efficient.

Clearly, this resembles the pattern described in the present chapter. We should emphasize, however, an interesting contrast between the data in this chapter and those in Chapter 11: In Chapter 11, we saw that a single undergraduate course in statistics has a large benefit for everyday reasoning; in this chapter, we have seen that a course in logic does not have this benefit. In Chapter 11, we saw that even brief instruction in statistics can improve reasoning; in this chapter, we've failed to find a parallel benefit from brief instruction in logic. What produces this contrast?

One possibility is that statistics courses are able to build on intuitions we already have and to remind us of beliefs we already hold. There is, for example, a reasonable correspondence between our intuitive understanding of chance events and the statistician's law of large numbers, and statistics courses can exploit this correspondence in conveying the law. One might argue that the same is not true for logic courses—apparently, there are important divergences between formal logic, as it is generally taught, and the natural logic that each of us already holds. For example, *modus tollens* is routinely included in logic courses, but seems foreign to our intuitions.

A related possibility is that statistics courses are, by their nature, often concerned with pragmatic examples; statistics textbooks are filled with problems asking you to apply statistical concepts to real-world cases. The study of formal logic, on the other hand, is more self-contained; logic texts rarely require you to translate commonsense problems into logical terms. This probably contributes to the fact that statistics courses do have an impact on everyday reasoning, while logic courses do not. (For broader discussion of this contrast between statistics and logic training, see Nisbett, 1993.)

Mental Models

An important message in the previous section was that different reasoning strategies may exist side-by-side in the mind and are called into play in different situations. If we sometimes reason poorly, this is largely because we are using inappropriate strategies. If we can change the reasoner's strategies (by means of instruction) or change the situation (so that different strategies are triggered), reasoning can be much improved.

It is against this backdrop that we consider one further reasoning strategy that people use, a strategy that, like reasoning schemata, is more concrete than reasoning via formal rules, yet more abstract than reasoning about specific cases. It is a strategy of creating, and then reasoning about, mental models. (Let's note from the start that there is some risk of confusion here, since we used the term "mental model" differently in Chapter 8. Unfortunately, though, it just is the case that researchers interested in concepts use this term in one fashion, while researchers interested in logic use the term differently. It will be best, therefore, if you hold the following sections separate from the themes we discussed in Chapter 8.)

Models and Categorical Syllogisms

Let us return for the moment to categorical syllogisms, like this one:

All of the artists are beekeepers.
Some of the beekeepers are chemists.

What follows from these premises? One way to think about this problem is by imagining a room full of people. Some of the people in the room are artists (perhaps you imagine them as wearing sweatshirts with a big "A" on the front). Others in the room are not artists (they have no sweatshirts). Perhaps you then imagine all of the artists as having a bee perched on their heads, and perhaps you also imagine some non-artists as having bees on their heads, as well. (After all, the premise said that all artists are beekeepers, but it *didn't* say that all beekeepers are artists.) Continuing in this fashion, you will end up imagining a little world, or a mental model, in which all of the premises are fulfilled. You can then inspect this model in order to ask what else is true about it: Once the premises are fulfilled, what other claims are entailed? Does it follow, for example, that some artists are chemists? (As it turns out, this *doesn't* follow from these premises, and so would be an invalid conclusion. You might confirm this by constructing a suitable mental model—"staffing" the imagined room as needed.) Other premises can also be represented in

Figure 12.7

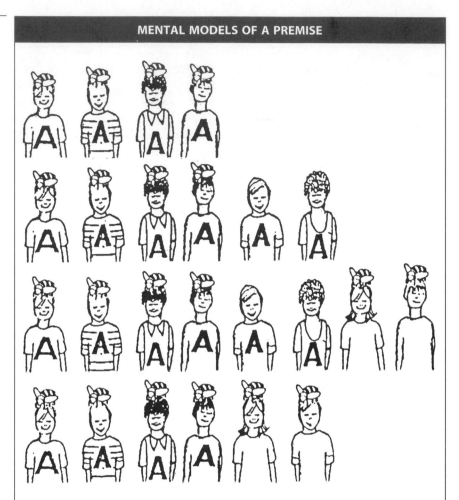

MENTAL MODELS OF A PREMISE

Many premises can be modeled in more than one way. For example, the figure shows several possible models for the premise: "Some of the artists are beekeepers." In other words, each row within the figure depicts a situation in which this premise is true. Artists are shown with A's on their shirts; non-artists don't have A's. Beekeepers are shown with bees on their heads; non–beekeepers are bare-headed.

this fashion. For example, if the premise were "No artists are beekeepers," you could imagine a room divided by a barrier, with the artists on one side, and the beekeepers on the other.

Johnson-Laird and his colleagues have argued that <u>mental models are widely used in reasoning</u>. Broadly put, the idea is that one first constructs a mental model of a problem (or perhaps multiple models). Next, one scrutinizes the model, seeking to discover what conclusions follow from the modeled premises. Finally, one can check on these conclusions by trying to discover counterexamples—models that are compatible with the premises, but not with the proposed conclusion. If no counterexamples are found, then one concludes that the conclusion is valid (Johnson-Laird, 1983, 1990; Johnson-Laird & Byrne, 1989, 1991; Johnson-Laird & Steedman, 1978; for related views, see Gentner & Stevens, 1983; Guyote & Sternberg, 1981; Kahneman & Tversky, 1982b).

Subjects in reasoning studies sometimes, on their own, mention the use of such models. One widely quoted subject commented, "I thought of all the little artists in the room and imagined that they all had beekeeper's hats on." As more formal evidence, though, the mental-model approach leads to a number of predictions about reasoning performance, and many of these predictions have been confirmed. For example, some premises can be modeled in more than one way (see Figure 12.7). In these cases, subjects trying to reason about these premises will have to examine multiple models, or else keep track of mental models with "optional" parts. One would expect this to make a problem more difficult, and this is indeed the case: The greater the number of models needed in reasoning through the problem, the more likely errors are to occur (Johnson-Laird, Byrne & Tabossi, 1989; Johnson-Laird & Steedman, 1978).

Mental Models and Deduction

Researchers have also suggested a role for mental models when subjects are reasoning about conditional problems (Evans, 1993; Johnson-Laird, Byrne & Schaeken, 1992; Legrenzi et al., 1993). Imagine that we tell you: "If it is sunny, the boys play baseball." You might then construct a mental model of this conditional—perhaps by contemplating a sunny day, with the boys out on the field. Imagine that we now add: "Today, it is sunny." This is obviously consistent with the model you've constructed, implying that it is okay to draw conclusions from this model. Therefore, you correctly conclude: "Today, the boys play baseball." In this way, the mental model will support an inference consistent with *modus ponens*.

Alternatively, imagine that we tell you, "If it is sunny, the boys play baseball," and, again, you think about a sunny day, with the teams out on the field. But now we add: "The boys didn't play baseball today." This sentence *isn't* compatible with your mental model and so, since the model isn't consistent with all the premises, you realize that you shouldn't draw conclusions from this model. In this case, you would *fail* to draw the correct conclusion: "Therefore, it is not sunny today." This is, of course, in accord with the fact that subjects often fail to draw conclusions which rest, as this one does, on *modus tollens*.

Of course, you could have modeled the initial premise in other ways. The conditional, "If sunny, then baseball" is *also* consistent with a model showing a rainy day, and no one on the field. If you had considered this model as well as the model already described, then you would draw the correct conclusion when told "The boys didn't play baseball today." However, you are unlikely to do this, because it requires some effort to maintain multiple models simultaneously. That is why performance suffers if a problem requires consideration of more than one model.

Consider what will happen, though, if we change the problem slightly, by presenting the *modus tollens* argument in inverted order: "The boys didn't play baseball today. If it is sunny, the boys play baseball. What follows from this?" In this case, subjects know, from the start, that the boys didn't play baseball. Therefore, when they get to the second premise, they won't construct a model showing boys playing happily on a sun-drenched field. Their model, therefore, must depict one of the other scenarios consistent with this conditional—for example, the model of "game canceled on account of rain." Inspection of this model would lead to the proper conclusion.

In terms of logic, or case-based reasoning, or reasoning schemata, this change in the premises' sequence should have no impact. But, as we just illustrated, the switch in sequence may have an influence on modeling. And, in fact, this change in sequence has a large impact: For subjects given the problem in "standard" sequence, only 40% drew the correct conclusion. For subjects given the "inverted" sequence, 69% got it right.

This result provides interesting confirmation for the mental-models conception, and so provides evidence that our thinking can, in many cases, be aided by mental models. Presumably, these models help us by making a problem concrete, perhaps via a visual image, or perhaps via some other form of mental representation. Hence, mental models take their place as part of the repertoire of human reasoning strategies, inviting future researchers to explore more fully the pattern of triggers that lead us on one occasion to use one strategy, and on another occasion some other strategy. (For further discussion of mental models, see Evans, 1993; Ford, 1995; Johnson-Laird et al., 1992; Rips, 1986, 1989b.)

Decision Making

We turn now to one last category of reasoning—reasoning about *choices*. How do we choose what courses to take next semester or what movie to see on Saturday? How do we choose which candidate to support in an election? How do we choose an apartment or a job? Choices like these fill our lives. Often, little is at stake in these decisions, but in other cases a decision can have enormous consequences—e.g., when a cancer patient must decide between surgery and radiation (or no treatment at all), or when a government must decide how to treat a hostile neighbor.

Sometimes, choices are based on aesthetic or emotional grounds, and we will have little to say about choices of this sort. In other cases, though, one tries to make a decision that is "reasonable"; one tries to select the option that is "more sensible." It is these choices, these decisions, which are of interest to us here.

Utility Theory

There is an obvious and seemingly simple way one might make decisions: Each of us has our own values—things we like, things we prize and, for that matter, things we hope to avoid. Likewise, each of us has a series of goals—things we hope to accomplish or things we hope to see—including both near-term goals (what we hope to accomplish soon) and longer term goals. The obvious suggestion, then, is that we use these values and goals in making decisions: In choosing courses for next semester, you will choose courses that are interesting and also courses that help fill the requirements for your major. In choosing a medical treatment, you will hope to avoid pain, and you will also hope to retain all of your physical capacities as long as possible.

To put this a bit more formally, each decision will have certain costs attached to it (that is, consequences that will carry us further from our goals) and also certain benefits (consequences moving us toward our goals, and providing us with things we value). In deciding, we weigh the costs against the benefits and seek a path that will minimize the former and maximize the latter. When we have several options open to us, we will presumably choose the one that provides the most favorable balance of benefits and costs.

This weighing of benefits against costs allows us to accommodate the fact that many decisions pose trade-offs of one sort or another. Should you go to Miami for your vacation this year, or to Tucson? The weather is better in Tucson, but the flight to Miami is less expensive. Hence, you have got to trade off the more desirable weather against the more attractive plane fare.

Likewise, should you drive a less comfortable car, if it happens to pollute less? Here, the trade-off is between your comfort and protection of the environment.

Notice, though, that these trade-offs involve factors that are, to say the least, highly disparate—comfort versus pollution, the pleasure made possible by good weather versus the $50 you might save in airfare. Can you really translate your pleasure into dollar amounts? Is your pleasure worth more than, or less than, $50? Likewise, how do you compare a 10% reduction in comfort with a .0001% reduction in pollution levels? In these examples (and, indeed, in most decisions), comparing these factors seems like the proverbial comparison of apples and oranges—the values at stake seem incommensurable.

Somehow, though, we do make these comparisons. We have to, if we are going to make these choices. Presumably, we compare them in a rather subjective way, by asking how important each factor is *to us*. This is often expressed as the subjective utility of each factor, meaning, quite simply, the value of that factor for us. These utilities can then be summed (e.g., the utility of a pleasant vacation minus the "disutility" of spending more on airfare) to evaluate the overall utility for each outcome. These summed-utilities for the various options can then be compared to each other, with the goal of selecting the option with the greatest overall utility.

In most decisions, though, there is also a degree of uncertainty or risk. Is Professor X an interesting instructor? Four of your friends have said she is, but two have said she is not. How should you factor these "mixed reviews" into your decision? Should you go to Miami for your vacation? At this time of year, let's say there is a 20% chance of rain. Do you want to take that chance?

One way to think about these risks follows a model formalized by von Neumann and Morgenstern (1947). Within their model, one calculates the **expected utility** or expected value of each option, using the simple equation:

$$\text{Expected Utility} = (\text{probability of a particular outcome}) \times (\text{utility of the outcome})$$

Thus, imagine that I offer you a lottery ticket. The ticket costs $5 but gives you a one-in-a-hundred chance of winning $200. In this case, the expected value of the ticket is (.01 × $200), or $2. At a cost of $5, then, I'm selling the ticket for far more than it is worth.

With more complicated decisions, you will calculate the expected value of each factor, and then add these up to compute the *overall* expected value associated with a particular choice. Let's say that you are choosing courses for next year. Course 1 looks interesting, but also has a heavy workload. To evaluate this course, you will first need to estimate the subjective utility of taking an interesting course and also the *disutility* of being burdened by a heavy workload. Next, you will have to factor in the uncertainties. Perhaps there is a 70% chance that the course will be interesting, but a 90% chance that it will have a heavy workload. In this case, the overall utility for this course will be (.70 × the utility of an interesting course) *minus* (.90 × the disutility of a heavy workload). You could then make similar calculations for the other courses available to you and choose the one with the greatest expected value.

All of this points the way toward a theory of choice: The claim is that, in making choices, we seek to maximize utility—that is, to gain as much as we can of those things we value, and to avoid those things we don't like. We do this by consistently selecting the option with the greatest *expected utility*, calculated as described. (For discussion, see von Neumann & Morgenstern, 1947; also Baron, 1988; Savage, 1954.)

Before continuing, though, let's be clear that the term "utilities" is used here in a very broad sense, referring to whatever it is that is important to you. Hence, there is no connection between, say, seeking to maximize utilities and being *greedy* or *materialistic*. If you happen to value money, then the attempt to maximize utilities will turn out to be an attempt to gather wealth. But if you happen to value leisure, or happiness in those around you, or a reduction of world hunger, then these will be the utilities you seek to maximize. Thus, there is no stigma attached to the notion of utility maximization, and it surely seems sensible to make decisions that move you, as efficiently as possible, toward your goals.

Framing of Outcomes

There is no doubt that many of our choices and decisions do follow the principle of utility maximization. Which would you rather have—$90 or $100? Which gamble would you prefer, a 1% chance of winning a prize, or a 5% chance of winning the same prize? In each case, we are (rather obviously) sensitive to both the value of the "pay-off" associated with a decision (i.e., its utility) and also to the probability of a pay-off.

However, an enormous number of studies show that, in many circumstances, we are *not* utility maximizers and, more broadly, that we are profoundly influenced by factors having little to do with utilities. In the process, we regularly make choices that are flatly inconsistent with other choices we have made. We will first review a number of these cases, and then turn to how a theory of choice might accommodate them.

Consider the question posed in Figure 12.8. Subjects show a clear preference between these options, and 72% choose program A (Tversky & Kahneman, 1987). Now consider the question posed in Figure 12.9. Note that

Figure 12.8

THE ASIAN DISEASE PROBLEM

Imagine that the U.S. is preparing for the outbreak of an unusual Asian disease, which is expected to kill 600 people. Two alternative programs to combat the disease have been proposed. Assume that the exact scientific estimates of the consequences of the programs are as follows:

• If Program A is adopted, 200 people will be saved.

• If Program B is adopted, there is a ⅓ probability that 600 people will be saved, and a ⅔ probability that no people will be saved.

There is clearly no "right answer" to this question—one could defend selecting the "risky" choice (Program B) or the less-rewarding, but less-risky choice (Program A). The clear majority of subjects, however, lean toward Program A, with 72% choosing it over Program B. Note that this problem is "positively" framed in terms of "lives *saved*."

Figure 12.9

THE ASIAN DISEASE PROBLEM, NEGATIVELY FRAMED

Imagine that the U.S. is preparing for the outbreak of an unusual Asian disease, which is expected to kill 600 people. Two alternative programs to combat the disease have been proposed. Assume that the exact scientific estimates of the consequences of the programs are as follows:

• If Program A is adopted, 400 people will die.

• If Program B is adopted, there is a ⅓ probability that nobody will die, and ⅔ probability that 600 people will die.

This problem is identical in content to the one shown in Figure 12.8: 400 dead, out of 600 people, is the same as 200 saved, out of 600. Nonetheless, subjects react to the problem shown here rather differently than they do to the one in Figure 12.8: In the "lives saved" version, 72% choose Program A. In the "dies" version, 78% choose Program B. Thus, by changing the phrasing, we reverse the pattern of subjects' preferences.

this problem is the same as the one in Figure 12.8—200 people saved out of 600 is identical to 400 people dead out of 600. Therefore, the utilities involved in this problem have not changed one whit. Nonetheless, this change in how the problem is phrased—that is, the **frame** of the decision—has a strong impact on subjects' choices. In the "lives saved" frame, subjects favor program A by almost a 3-to-1 margin. In the "dies" frame, this pattern of preferences *reverses*, and 78% of the subjects opt for Program B.

It should be emphasized that there is nothing wrong with subjects' individual choices. In either Figure 12.8 or Figure 12.9, there is no "right answer," and one can persuasively defend either the decision to avoid risk, by selecting Program A, or the decision to take the chance, by selecting Program B. The problem, though, lies in the *contradiction* created by choosing Program A in one context and Program B in the other context. Indeed, if a single subject is given both frames, on slightly different occasions, the subject is quite likely to contradict himself. For that matter, if a propagandist wanted to manipulate voters' evaluations of these programs, framing provides an effective way to do this.

Framing effects of this sort are easy to demonstrate. Figure 12.10 shows another example, in which subjects are urged to choose between two different medical treatments. When subjects were given the "survival frame," only 18% chose radiation over surgery. When subjects were given the "mortality frame," this number more than doubled—with 44% now favoring radiation (Tversky & Kahneman, 1987).

As one final example, consider the two problems shown in Figure 12.11. When subjects are given the first problem, almost three-quarters of them (72%) choose the first option—the sure gain of $100. Subjects contemplating the second problem, though, generally choose the second option, with only 36% selecting the sure loss of $100 (Tversky & Kahneman, 1987). Note, though, that the problems are once again identical. Both pose the question of whether you would rather end up with a certain $400, or with an even chance between $300 and $500. Despite this equivalence, subjects treat these problems very differently, preferring the sure thing in one case, and the gamble in the other.

Framing effects are common and powerful. Quite consistently, subjects who are contemplating a loss seem eager to gamble, with the obvious suggestion that they are hoping to avoid or reduce the loss. In short, subjects contemplating losses tend to be **risk seeking**. In contrast, subjects contemplating a gain tend to be **risk averse**. They try to avoid risk, choosing instead to hold tight to what they already have. We reiterate that neither of these, by itself, is problematic—there is nothing wrong with being risk averse, nor with being risk seeking. The problem arises when subjects flip-flop between these strategies, depending on how the problem is framed. This leaves subjects wide open to manipulation, to inconsistency, and to self-contradiction.

Figure 12.10

FRAMING EFFECTS IN MEDICAL DECISION MAKING

SURVIVAL FRAME

Surgery: Of 100 people having surgery, 90 live through the post-operative period, 68 are alive at the end of the first year, and 34 are alive at the end of five years.

Radiation: Of 100 people having radiation therapy, all live through the treatment, 77 are alive at the end of one year, and 22 are alive at the end of five years.

MORTALITY FRAME

Surgery: Of 100 people having surgery, 10 die during surgery, 32 die by the end of the first year, and 66 die by the end of five years.

Radiation: Of 100 people having radiation therapy, none die during the treatment, 23 die by the end of one year, and 78 die by the end of five years.

The options shown in the "survival" frame are identical to the options shown in the mortality frame. The only difference between the frames is in how the options are described. With the survival frame, only 18% of the subjects choose radiation over surgery. With the mortality frame, this number more than doubles, with 44% now choosing radiation.

Framing of Questions and Evidence

So far we have shown that subjects are influenced by how a problem's outcomes are framed. Related effects can be demonstrated by changing how the question itself is framed. For example, imagine that you serve on a jury in a relatively messy divorce case; the parents are battling over who will get custody of their only child. The two parents have the attributes listed in Figure 12.12. To which parent will you award sole custody of the child?

Subjects asked this question tend to favor Parent B, by a 64% to 36% margin. After all, this parent does have a close relationship with the child, and has a good income. Note, though, that we have asked to which parent you will *award* custody. Things are different if we ask subjects to which parent they would *deny* custody. This is, in obvious ways, the same question—if you

Figure 12.11

FRAMING EFFECTS IN MONETARY CHOICES

CHOICE 1

Assume yourself richer by $300 than you are today. You have to choose between
- a sure gain of $100
- 50% chance to gain $200 and 50% chance to gain nothing

CHOICE 2

Assume yourself richer by $500 than you are today. You have to choose between
- a sure loss of $100
- 50% chance to lose nothing and 50% chance to lose $200

These two choices are identical. In both cases, the first option leaves you with $400, while the second option leaves you with an even chance between $300 and $500. Despite this identity, subjects prefer the first option in Choice 1 (72% select this option), and the second option in Choice 2 (64% select this option). Once again, by changing the frames, we reverse the pattern of subjects' preferences.

are awarding custody to one parent, you are simultaneously denying it to the other parent. But, in this case, 55% of the subjects choose to *deny* custody to Parent B (and so, by default, end up awarding custody to A). Thus, the decision is simply reversed: With the "award" question, the majority of subjects awards custody to B. With the "deny" question, the majority of subjects denies custody to B, and so gives custody to A.

This effect has been observed in a number of contexts, including problems involving monetary gambles, problems involving which courses a student will take and, most troubling, problems involving decisions about political candidates (Shafir, 1993). As a related effect, subjects rate a basketball player more highly if the player has made 75% of his free-throws, compared to their ratings of a player who has missed 25% of his free-throws. They are more likely to endorse a medical treatment with a "50% success rate" than they are to endorse one with a "50% failure rate." And so on (Levin & Gaeth, 1988; Levin, Schnittjer & Thee, 1988; also see Dunning & Parpal, 1989).

None of this makes any sense from the perspective of utility theory, since these differences in framing have no impact on the expected utilities of the options. Yet these differences in framing can dramatically change subjects'

Figure 12.12

THE INFLUENCE OF HOW A QUESTION IS FRAMED

Imagine that you serve on the jury of an only-child sole-custody case following a relatively messy divorce. The facts of the case are complicated by ambiguous economic, social, and emotional considerations, and you decide to base your decision entirely on the following few observations. To which parent would you award sole custody of the child?

Parent A   average income
average health
average working hours
reasonable rapport with the child
relatively stable social life

Parent B   above-average income
very close relationship with the child
extremely active social life
lots of work-related travel
minor health problems

When asked the question shown here, 64% of the subjects decided to award custody to Parent B. Other subjects, however, were asked a different question: "To which parent would you *deny* sole custody?" Asked this question, 55% of the subjects chose to deny custody to B (and so, by default, to award custody to A). Thus, with the "award" question, a majority votes for granting custody to B; with the "deny" question, a majority votes for granting custody to A.

---

choices and, in many cases, can actually reverse their pattern of preferences. (For further, related evidence, see Mellers, Chang, Birnbaum & Ordez, 1992; Schneider, 1992; Wedell & Bockenholt, 1990.)

Influence of Other Alternatives

Consider the pair of problems shown in Figure 12.13 (Shafir et al., 1993). In the first problem, students show a strong preference for buying the Sony player: 66% choose this option, and only 34% choose to continue shopping. The second problem is identical except for the addition of a further option—an Aiwa player, costing $70 more than the Sony. Thus, subjects still have, within this problem, the same option of choosing the Sony over continuing

Figure 12.13

THE INFLUENCE OF OTHER ALTERNATIVES ON DECISION MAKING

VERSION 1

Suppose you are considering buying a compact disk player and have not yet decided which model to buy. You pass a store that is having a one-day clearance sale. They offer a popular Sony player for just $99, well below the list price. Do you
  a. buy the Sony player
  b. wait until you learn more about the various models

VERSION 2

Suppose you are considering buying a compact disk player and have not yet decided which model to buy. You pass a store that is having a one-day clearance sale. They offer a popular Sony player for just $99, and a top-of-the-line Aiwa player for just $169, both well below the list price. Do you
  a. buy the Sony player
  b. buy the Aiwa player
  c. wait until you learn more about the various models

When subjects were given the choice shown in Version 1, 66% chose to buy the Sony player, and only 34% chose to continue shopping. In Version 2, however, 46% of the subjects chose to continue shopping, and only 27% chose the Sony. Thus, in the first context, subjects think that the Sony is a better choice than shopping but, in the second choice, they think that shopping is a better choice than the Sony.

to shop around. However, that is not what subjects do—now they prefer shopping around over *both* the Aiwa and the Sony. To be precise, 46% choose to continue shopping, compared to only 27% choosing the Sony (and then the other 27% choosing the Aiwa). To put this bluntly, in the first context, subjects think that the Sony is a better choice than shopping and, in the second context, they think that shopping is a better choice than the Sony.

Related cases have been reported by Wedell (1991, 1993). Imagine that you are shopping for a car, and you have narrowed things down to three choices. The choices are generally similar to each other, but do differ on two dimensions, as shown in Figure 12.14. (Before reading on, you might examine the figure, and make your choice.)

Subjects in this setting clearly prefer the Asteroid—with 69% choosing it

Figure 12.14

CHOOSING WHICH CAR TO PURCHASE		
Model	**Ride Quality**	**Gas Mileage**
Asteroid	100	27
Bravo	80	33
Comet	100	21

Subjects are asked to imagine that they are shopping for a new car, and they have narrowed their choices down to the three models shown here. The numbers shown for "ride quality" and "gas mileage" are based on reports in a consumer magazine. In this setting, subjects strongly prefer the Asteroid, with 69% choosing it, 29% choosing the Bravo, and only 2% choosing the Comet.

Figure 12.15

CHOOSING WHICH CAR TO PURCHASE, IN A DIFFERENT CONTEXT		
Model	**Ride Quality**	**Gas Mileage**
Asteroid	100	27
Bravo	80	33
Clarion	60	33

The options shown here are similar to the ones shown in Figure 12.14. All we have done is remove the Comet (which was chosen by only 2% of the subjects), and replaced it with the Clarion. In this setting, though, subjects strongly prefer the Bravo, with 79% choosing it, compared to 19% for the Asteroid. Thus subjects rarely choose the Comet or the Clarion, but these less-preferred cars have a strong influence on subjects' choices.

over a mere 29% choosing the Bravo. But now consider a different scenario, shown in Figure 12.15: Your choices are the Asteroid, described as before, and also the Bravo, described as before. Now, however, there is no mention of the Comet. Instead, your third choice is the Clarion, with a ride quality of 60 (lower than either the Asteroid or the Bravo) and getting 33 mpg. Which would you choose?

In this set-up, subjects overwhelmingly prefer the Bravo over the Asteroid, by a margin of 79% to 19%. You will notice, then, that subjects virtually never choose either the Comet or the Clarion. Nonetheless, these less-preferred cars do play an important role, in setting the "agenda" for the choice. When the Comet is on the scene, subjects prefer the Asteroid over the Bravo, by more than 2-to-1. When the Clarion is on the scene, subjects prefer the Bravo over the Asteroid, by more than 4-to-1.

Dealing with Complex Decisions

Uutility theory does a poor job of explaining human decision making. If the expected utility of owning an Asteroid is greater than the utility of the Bravo, then we should always prefer the Asteroid over the Bravo. Adding or subtracting other options might change our ultimate decision (we might discover a car that we prefer over *both* the Asteroid *and* the Bravo), but shouldn't change our evaluation of the Asteroid and Bravo relative to each other. Likewise, utilities shouldn't be influenced by how a question is posed or how the outcomes are framed. But, as we have seen, all of these claims from utility theory fail to match the data. We are reliably influenced by factors having nothing to do with utility, and these factors can lead us to reverse our preferences and even to contradict ourselves. (For broad discussion of these data, from the perspective of utility theory, see Allais, 1953; Arkes & Blumer, 1985; Hoskin, 1983; Kahneman & Tversky, 1979; Lichtenstein & Slovic, 1971; Tversky & Kahneman, 1987.)

How, then, should we think about these data? One possibility is that humans try to be utility-maximizers, but just aren't able to carry through on this strategy. To put it simply, many decisions are too hard for us and, as a result, we are forced to rely on short-cuts in our decision making, or to rely on strategies that simplify the situation in some helpful way. This is obviously more likely with complex decisions, but we can even be overtaxed by simple decisions—for example, if these involve considerations of *risk*. This is because many subjects seem inept in reasoning about probabilities, particularly extreme probabilities (Tversky & Kahneman, 1987). We first saw this in Chapter 11, when we discussed the fact that subjects treat highly improbable events as though they are reasonably likely. Similarly, subjects seem too much impressed by "certainty"—i.e., a probability of 100%. Subjects are keenly sensitive to the contrast between an event that is 25% likely and one that is certain to occur; they are much less sensitive to the contrast between 20% and 80%. Yet the actual increment in probability is the same in both cases—in each pair, one event is four times as likely as the other event. Finally, subjects also seem inept in thinking about *conjunctions* of events—e.g., the probability that *both* A *and* B will be true, and subjects regularly overestimate the likelihood of these conjunctions (Shafir, Smith & Osherson, 1990; Tversky & Kahneman, 1983).

If utility maximization is often beyond our reach, what decision strategies *do* we rely on? We mentioned one candidate in Chapter 11, when we discussed the strategy of "satisficing," as opposed to "optimizing." The idea is that, in many decisions, we don't seek the *optimal* choice, that is, the choice that would maximize utilities. Instead, we make things easier for ourselves by searching only for a *satisfactory* choice, one that leaves us better off in the end than we were before. This strategy doesn't require us to pay attention to all of the available information or to consider all of the available options. Instead, this strategy allows a much more efficient process of decision making, with attention only to some subset of the information, and some subset of the options (Simon, 1957).

A related possibility is that, in many cases, we don't try to calculate the *overall* utility of this or that option. Instead, we simplify things for ourselves by evaluating the options in a *step-by-step* fashion, one attribute at a time. For example, imagine that you are shopping for a new tent. You might first focus on the tent's design. Perhaps you have decided you want a dome, and so you could eliminate all but the dome tents. You could then focus on each tent's weight. Perhaps you have decided you want a tent that weighs less than 8 pounds, and so you might eliminate all tents heavier than this. This strategy, called **elimination by aspects**, would allow you to sort through the alternatives in a systematic fashion, but might also lead you to a less-than-optimal choice (Tversky, 1972). Perhaps there is a truly terrific tent that is light-weight, inexpensive, easy to set up, and stable in stormy weather, but that happens not to be a dome. Given the positive features of this tent, it might be your best choice—its positive features outweigh the fact that it is not the design you prefer. But the decision process we just described, which starts by rejecting the non-domes, would never lead you to this tent. (For a review of evidence showing how and when this strategy is employed, see Baron, 1988.)

The Instability of Values

What about less complicated decisions? Many of the examples we have reviewed involve simple problems, with relatively few dimensions. For these problems, considerations of "satisficing" or decision-complexity never come into play. Therefore, we need some more theory to explain these cases.

In order to maximize utilities, you need, first, to calculate the expected utility of each option available to you. Sometimes, though, this can be rather difficult: For example, imagine that your employer asks you to give up your vacation, and to spend those days working, for a $500 bonus. To evaluate this proposal, you need to figure out the value of your vacation and, in particular, whether the vacation is worth more or less than $500. For most of us, this is far from straightforward.

Moreover, the assessment of values often requires that we predict the future, and this, obviously, is an uncertain enterprise. For example, imagine that you are looking for a new apartment. You find one, but you don't like the fact that it faces a noisy street. Will you just grow used to the noise so that it ceases to bother you? If so, then you should take the apartment. Or will the noise grow more and more obnoxious to you as the weeks go by? Evidence suggests that we are rather *inept* in making this sort of prediction, and this will clearly erode our ability to assess utilities—in this case, the utility of a quiet apartment (Kahneman & Snell, 1992.)

Finally, there is reason to believe that our values may *fluctuate* from one occasion to another, and this certainly will undermine utility calculations. For example, how valuable would it be for you to lose weight? It is possible that the value you place on losing weight may be relatively small right now but might be larger after the weight loss is actually done: Only then would you realize how much better you felt, and how much more you were able to do. Likewise, how much inconvenience would you tolerate in order to reduce air pollution? This, too, might vary, according to the context: When you have just come back from a camping trip, for example, you might be particularly sensitive to the value of clean air.

In fact, think about how we might try to *assess* your values: To figure out how much you value clean air, we could ask you a series of questions: Which do you think is more valuable, clean air or $100? (Concretely, would it be fair if we asked each citizen in the nation to contribute $100 to the improvement of air quality?) Which is more valuable, clean air or the reduction of crime? (Again: Imagine that the government is reallocating the budget. Should they give an extra million dollars for pollution control or to crime prevention?)

Questions like these would, presumably, provide information about your (relative) values for $100, clean air, and crime prevention. Notice, though, that these questions bear a strong resemblance to the questions posed in Figures 12.8, 12.9, 12.10, and so on. As we have seen, your responses to these questions flip-flop back and forth, depending on how the outcomes are framed, or how the question is phrased. If we use these questions as a way of assessing your values, it would seem that your values themselves flip-flop from one occasion to the next, one question to the next.

In short, these imagined choices seem to provide a direct and straightforward way of assessing your values. But, interpreted in this fashion, these questions reveal enormous instability in your values, with your preferences changing from question to question, occasion to occasion. Note where this leaves us: According to utility theory, we evaluate an action by asking: Does the action bring you the things you value? This requires us, in turn, to ask: What is it that you value? This question may not be answerable, though, if your values fluctuate from one moment to the next, depending on exactly what question you have just been asked. No wonder, then, that the predictions of utility theory are often at odds with the actual decisions that we make. (For reviews of research on values, see Fischhoff, 1991; Guagnano, Dietz & Stern, 1994; Kahneman, Ritov, Jacowitz & Grant, 1993; Kahneman, Fredrickson, Schreiber & Redelmeier, 1993; Payne, Bettman & Johnson, 1992; Slovic, 1990, 1995; Stevenson, 1993.)

Loss Aversion

Similar comments apply to a phenomenon known as **loss aversion**—a tendency to be far more sensitive to losses than to gains. We have already referred to the research indicating an asymmetry between how we perceive gains and losses, and loss aversion certainly fits into this larger pattern. As it turns out, though, loss aversion is often in conflict with the maximization of utility.

Consider the case illustrated in Figure 12.16 (after Thaler, 1980): The consumer is put off by the (potential) loss of a 5¢ per gallon "credit card surcharge," and so will elect to pay cash. The same consumer is less impressed by the (potential) gain of a 5¢ per gallon "cash discount," and may choose to forego this discount—that is, he will choose the convenience of using a credit card. (This is, of course, what the oil companies prefer.) Economically, the scenarios are identical but, within these scenarios, the loss of a nickel is enough to influence a decision, but the gain of a nickel isn't.

Similarly, imagine that we toss a coin. If it comes up heads, you win $10; if it comes up tails, you have to pay $10. Most subjects refuse this gamble. The risk of *losing* $10 is apparently more compelling than the attraction of *gaining* $10—again, we are more sensitive to losses than we are to (comparable) gains. Even though this is, economically, a fair bet, it is not fair from the subjects' point of view. Indeed, subjects still refuse to bet on a coin toss if we make the game more attractive: If the coin comes up heads, you gain $20; tails, you pay $10. Subjects generally refuse this bet as well (Kahneman & Tversky, 1984). Even with a "double pay-off," subjects are more repelled by the (potential) loss than they are attracted by the (potential) gain.

Loss aversion is also evident when we are invited to give up something we already own. For example, subjects in one experiment were each given a coffee mug and asked at what price they would be willing to sell this new possession. Other subjects were given the opportunity to buy the same mug, and asked at what price they would make the purchase. On average, the "sellers" set a price for the mug of $7.12; the "buyers," a price of $2.87

Figure 12.16

FRAMING EFFECTS IN THE MARKETPLACE

In both of these gas stations, one pays $1.25 per gallon for a *cash* purchase, and $1.30 per gallon for a *credit card* purchase. However, consumers react quite differently to these two situations. The 5¢ discount (a gain, from the consumer's point of view) seems meager, and so the consumer is willing to forego the discount, in order to obtain the convenience of paying via credit card. (This is, of course, what the gasoline stations prefer.) The 5¢ surcharge, however, a loss from the consumer's point of view, seems unacceptable, and so the consumer is likely to pay cash in this setting. Which pricing scheme do the gas stations actually use?

(Kahneman, Knetsch & Thaler, 1991). Owning something, it seems, endows it with special worth.

Now let's combine this pattern with our earlier discussion of framing effects: By manipulating the frame, we can describe problems relative to the best-possible outcome, so that all other options would be perceived as losses, relative to this ideal. In this setting, loss aversion comes into play, so subjects are willing to take substantial risks in hopes of *avoiding* the loss. This is consistent with the data: Subjects are risk seeking when outcomes are framed negatively.

Conversely, we can describe problems relative to the worst-possible outcome, so that all other options would be perceived as gains, relative to this worst-case scenario. In this case, we would expect subjects to seize whatever gain they can, and then take no chances with it—that is, they will avoid any risk of losing what they have gained. Again, this is consistent with the data: When outcomes are framed positively, subjects are markedly risk averse.

Likewise, we can influence what counts as a loss, and what counts as a gain, by manipulating your *basis for comparison*. It is in this way that your choice between two options can often be influenced by some other option, or by your current status. Imagine that you are looking for a new job (Kahneman et al., 1991). Let's say that you are unhappy about the fact that your current job is located so far from your apartment, requiring an 80-minute commute each way. But you do like the fact that your job involves much pleasant social interaction with your coworkers. Now, consider the two jobs described in Figure 12.17. Job A would provide a large reduction in your commuting time, but also a large loss in the social contact you will enjoy. Job B provides a much smaller reduction in your commuting time, but also a smaller loss in social contact. If you focus on the advantages of each, therefore, Job A wins (with a much-reduced commute). If you focus on the disadvantages, Job A *loses* (with much reduced social interaction). In this situation, a clear majority of subjects (67%) choose Job B: Thanks to loss aversion, subjects are much more impressed by A's disadvantages than by its advantages.

For contrast, imagine that your present job involves only a ten-minute commute, but leaves you isolated from your coworkers for long periods of time. In this case, a move to Job A would provide a small improvement in social contact, but at the cost of a slightly lengthened commute. Job B provides a large improvement in social contact, but at the cost of a much longer commute. Thus, if you focus on gains, Job B is the winner. If you focus on losses, you should go with Job A. In this setting, subjects are again guided by loss aversion: The disadvantage of B outweighs its advantage, and most subjects (70%) choose Job A.

Obviously, then, what counts as an advantage or a disadvantage in these decisions depends on your current state and your current focus. By changing

Figure 12.17

WHAT COUNTS AS A GAIN DEPENDS ON YOUR "REFERENCE POINT"

VERSION 1

You have decided to leave your current job, because it is located so far from your apartment, requiring an *80-minute* commute each way. But you do like the fact that your job involves much pleasant social interaction with your coworkers.

Your search for a *new* job has given you two options, and now you must choose between them. Which job would you prefer?

Job A   Limited contact with others   Commuting time = 20 minutes

Job B   Moderately sociable   Commuting time = 60 minutes

VERSION 2

You have decided to leave your current job. The job involves only a ten-minute commute, which you rather like. But your job leaves you isolated from your coworkers for long periods of time.

Your search for a *new* job has given you two options, and now you must choose between them. Which job would you prefer?

Job A   Limited contact with others   Commuting time = 20 minutes

Job B   Moderately sociable   Commuting time = 60 minutes

In the first problem shown here, Job A provides a large reduction in your commuting time, but at the price of a large loss in social contact. Job B provides a much smaller reduction in your commute, but also a smaller loss in social contact. Therefore, if you focus on the gains (the shorter commute), Job A is preferable. If you focus on the losses (diminished social contact), Job B is preferable. In this setting, subjects are more alert to the losses, and so most (67%) choose Job B. In the second setting, the job possibilities are the same; all that is changed is the description of your *current* job. Compared to this "reference point," Job A provides a small improvement in your social contact, but a slightly longer commute. Job B provides a large improvement in social contact, but a much longer commute. Now, in terms of gains (in social contact), Job B is preferable; if you focus on the losses (the longer commute), Job A is better. Once again, subjects are more alert to the losses, and so, in this setting, most (70%) choose Job A.

your focus, or by changing your starting point, we can reverse the decision. In the study just quoted, a change in starting point turns a 67–33 advantage for B into a 70–30 advantage for A—quite literally flipping things around.

We should also mention one further phenomenon, closely related to loss aversion: Imagine that you have invested some time or effort in a project, or imagine that you have taken a gamble and *lost*. In these circumstances, people seem extraordinarily sensitive to the fact that they have given up something they used to own and, as a result, they will often take extravagant steps to ensure that their investment, or their loss, "was not in vain." People do this even when their best strategy would be to *abandon* the now-lost resources and move on. This pattern is referred to as the <u>sunk-cost effect</u>, and is illustrated by the example shown in Figure 12.18. In this case, the $100 deposit is the "sunk cost"—a cost that has already occurred and is now irreversible. In the example, your best bet would be to abandon this sunk cost and not

shows our sensitivity to losses

Figure 12.18

THE SUNK-COST EFFECT

Some weeks ago, you saw an ad in the newspaper for a reduced-rate weekend at a nearby resort. Attracted by the ad, you sent a $100 non-refundable deposit to the resort.

The weekend has now arrived, and you and a companion have driven half-way to the resort. Unfortunately, though, both you and your companion are feeling slightly ill, and your assessment of the situation is that you would probably have a more pleasurable weekend at home, rather than at the resort.

You decide to press on, however. After all, you have already sent in the deposit, and you can't get it back. You have also already driven half-way to the resort. If you turn around at this point, your deposit will be lost—wasted!—and your driving will have been for nothing.

Is this sensible? Should you drive on, or should you turn back?

In the problem shown here, many people believe you *should* drive on, in order to avoid wasting the $100 deposit. However, this makes little sense. You have already spent the $100, whether you go to the resort or whether you go home. No matter what you do, you won't get the $100 back. Therefore, continuing to drive toward the resort won't "redeem" the $100. Thus, in deciding to drive on, you are being influenced by a "sunk cost," a cost that, in this case, leads you to spend the weekend at a place you would rather not be! [After Dawes, 1988.]

continue on the journey. However, that is not what people do; instead, they end up "throwing good money after bad"—that is, they end up investing even more resources, as though this would somehow "redeem" the sunk cost. This pattern is consistent with other evidence showing our keen sensitivity to losses, but this pattern is, once again, not consistent with utility theory. (For discussion of the sunk cost effect, see Arkes & Blumer, 1985; Dawes, 1988; Thaler, 1980.)

Maximizing Utility versus Seeing Reasons

Over and over, we have seen evidence of decisions not in accord with utility theory. And perhaps this evidence isn't so surprising: Utility theory requires that we be able to judge risks and that we be able to assess our own values. Evidence suggests, though, that subjects are quite incompetent in judging risks and that our values and utilities change, from context to context.

In response to all this, a number of alternative theories have been proposed. (For examples, see Bell, 1982; Fishburn, 1982; Kahneman & Tversky, 1979; Loomes, 1987.) Many of these theories preserve the spirit of utility theory, arguing that, with some repairs or adjustments, utility theory, in modified form, *can* handle the data. Other theories, though, have taken a rather different approach.

For example, a number of authors have argued that, in making decisions, the maximization of utility is not our goal. Instead, our goal is to make decisions that we believe to be reasonable or justified. Thus, we select one option over another, not because of some calculation of risks and payoffs, but because we have discovered a compelling argument for that selection. Therefore, we will need a theory of decision making that is less "economic" in its emphasis and more "psychological," a theory resting, in effect, on a consideration of what it is that makes an argument seem compelling, and what it is that makes an explanation seem persuasive. (For discussion, see Shafir et al., 1993; Slovic, 1975.)

As an illustration, we have already seen that *confirmation bias* plays a large role when we are evaluating an argument and so, on the account just sketched, confirmation bias may be pertinent to decision making. (Of course, confirmation bias is irrelevant for utility calculations.) To see this in action, let's reconsider a problem already discussed: the divorce/custody problem shown in Figure 12.12. You will recall that half the subjects presented with this problem were asked to which parent they would *award* custody. These subjects, influenced by confirmation bias, therefore ask themselves: "What would *justify* giving custody to one parent or another?" This draws their attention to one subset of the parental attributes—e.g., Parent B's close relationship with the child, and this in turn leads them to favor awarding custody to B.

Figure 12.19

THE ROLE OF "JUSTIFICATION" IN DECISION MAKING

VERSION 1: Passed

Imagine that you have just taken a tough qualifying examination. It is the end of the fall quarter, you feel tired and run-down, and you find out that you passed the exam. You now have an opportunity to buy a very attractive 5-day Christmas vacation package in Hawaii at an exceptionally low price. The special offer expires tomorrow. Would you

   a. buy the vacation package

   b. not buy the vacation package

   c. pay a $5 non-refundable fee in order to retain the rights to buy the package at the same exceptional price the day after tomorrow

VERSION 2: Failed

Imagine that you have just taken a tough qualifying examination. It is the end of the fall quarter, you feel tired and run-down, and you find out that you failed the exam. You will have to take it again in a couple of months—after the Christmas holiday. You now have an opportunity to buy a very attractive 5-day Christmas vacation package in Hawaii at an exceptionally low price. The special offer expires tomorrow. Would you

   a. buy the vacation package

   b. not buy the vacation package

   c. pay a $5 non-refundable fee in order to retain the rights to buy the package at the same exceptional price the day after tomorrow

VERSION 3: Don't know yet if passed of failed

Imagine that you have just taken a tough qualifying examination. It is the end of the fall quarter, you feel tired and run-down, and you are not sure whether you passed the exam. In case you failed, you have to take the exam again in a couple of months—after the Christmas holiday. You now have an opportunity to buy a very attractive 5-day Christmas vacation package in Hawaii at an exceptionally low price. The special offer expires tomorrow. Would you

   a. buy the vacation package

   b. not buy the vacation package

   c. pay a $5 non-refundable fee in order to retain the rights to buy the package at the same exceptional price the day after tomorrow, after you find out whether or not you passed the exam

In Version 1 of this problem, 54% of the subjects decide to buy the vacation package—presumably as a celebration for their having passed the exam. In Version 2, 57% choose to buy—presumably as consolation for having failed. Apparently, then, subjects will buy the package whether they pass or whether they fail. Therefore, information about passing or failing isn't relevant to the decision! Nonetheless, when subjects don't have this (irrelevant) information, as in Version 3, they behave rather differently: Here, only 32% buy the package.

The other half of the subjects were asked to which parent they would *deny* custody and, with confirmation bias in place, this leads them to ask: "What would justify denying custody to one parent or another?" This question draws attention to a different subset of attributes—e.g., B's travel schedule or health problems. Thus, these subjects easily find a basis for denying custody to B. (For related discussion, see Legrenzi et al., 1993.)

Here is another illustration of how decision making is governed by "perceived justification." Tversky and Shafir (1992b) presented their subjects with the problem posed in Figure 12.19. In the first version of the problem, subjects are asked to imagine that they have just *passed* an important exam; in this situation, subjects generally elect to buy the vacation package (54% buy), presumably as a celebration for their good exam performance. In the second version, subjects imagine that they have *failed* the exam. These subjects, too, elect to buy the package (57% buy), this time, one assumes, as a "consolation" for their failure. In the third version of the problem, however, subjects imagine that they don't yet know if they have passed the exam or not. In this condition of uncertainty, most subjects choose *not* to buy the package (only 32% buy).

What is going on here? If you pass the exam, you buy. If you fail, you buy. Hence, it doesn't matter if you pass or fail. Nonetheless, if you *don't know yet* whether you have passed or failed, you don't buy. Subjects are deterred by their ignorance about the exam's outcome, even though the outcome is irrelevant to their decision. None of this makes sense if our decisions depend on utilities. But it does make sense if our decisions depend on *reasons* and *justifications*. It is the exam's outcome that gives you a compelling reason for buying the package. Possible outcomes, or hypothetical outcomes, aren't compelling enough. Therefore, until you know the exam's outcome, you don't have a firm reason to buy the package, and so you don't buy.

In the same way, Tversky and Shafir (1992a) note that physicians often request medical tests that are, in fact, irrelevant to their choice of treatment—no matter how the test turns out, the treatment will be the same. Thus, in ordering the tests, the physicians are acting just like the subjects described. (Cf. Baron, 1988.)

Selecting a Normative Theory

Perhaps we shouldn't think of decision making as a matter of quantification and calculation, selecting the option that maximizes utility. Instead, decision making may be more a matter of argument and justification: We make the choices that we can best explain and defend to ourselves and to others. We make the choices that will leave us, in the end, content that we have made a rational choice.

Ironically, though, this process will sometimes lead us to choices that seem highly *irrational*. As we have seen, subjects can routinely be led to contradict themselves, depending on how a problem has been framed. Does this mean, therefore, that we are all making decisions in the "wrong way"?

In thinking this through, let's note that some decisions *are* made in accord with utility maximization. This is particularly likely if the problems are quite simple and if the utilities relevant to the problem are stated in a "transparent" fashion (Tversky & Kahneman, 1987). Moreover, this turns out to be another domain in which *training* matters: For example, economics professors are more likely to reason in accord with cost-benefit rules than are, say, biology or humanities professors (Larrick, Morgan & Nisbett, 1990). Similarly, students who have taken economics courses are more likely to reason in economic terms, even in decisions rather distant from those discussed within their training.

It also turns out that those who make decisions in accord with economic principles do indeed thrive in the end—for example, they end up making higher salaries (Larrick, Nisbett & Morgan, 1993). Likewise, the evidence suggests that *smart* people are more likely to make decisions in accord with cost-benefit reasoning: Such reasoning is more likely, for example, among students with higher grade-point averages; such reasoning is also associated with higher SAT scores, particularly in the verbal test (Larrick et al., 1993). This seems to imply that utility theory *is* a sensible normative theory and, therefore, that most of us *do* make decisions in a less-than-optimal fashion.

However, other normative theories can be developed. For example, it is obvious that each of us wishes to reach our goals and wishes to gain the things we value. But we also have other needs—for example, people generally don't want to feel foolish or capricious; instead, we all want to feel like our lives make some sense, and have some integrity. Therefore, it is important to feel that the choices we have made have been reasonable choices and that, if these choices were ever challenged, we could explain and defend our selections.

From this perspective, if a decision brings us utility, but leaves us feeling insecure or uncomfortable, then it is a bad decision, and one ought to avoid making such a decision. Notice the "ought." This is an assertion about how decisions *should* be made; it is, in other words, a normative assertion, and so we are moving toward a normative theory in which considerations of utility are not our only concern.

Moreover, some would argue that there are decisions that *shouldn't* be reduced to questions of utility. For example, consider choices involving morality—choices about theft or homicide or choices about respecting other people's rights. Should one calculate the utility of "doing the moral thing"? If so, then perhaps there is some other utility (for example: a large enough bribe) that would outweigh the demands of morality. For many people, this seems an inappropriate way to talk about moral values, but it is the *right* way to talk about moral decisions if utility theory is our normative theory.

Moral values can be treated differently, however, within a theory of decision making resting on *justification.* From this perspective, one shouldn't ask the "economic" question, "What *gain* would justify an immoral act?" Instead, one should ask the question: "What argument, or principle, would justify such an act?" Thus, on this view, there may be no pay-off, no matter how large, to justify immorality. Instead, the only justification for an immoral action would be something like an even stronger, more compelling, moral claim.

This seems an attractive position, but let's emphasize that utility theory also has much to recommend it. We are certainly not going to settle here the choice between these two normative views—one based on utilities, one based on justification. We do hope, though, that these comments have made it clear that the choice between these views is not straightforward; intriguing arguments can be presented on either side of the debate.

There is, to be sure, ample evidence that we don't make decisions in accord with utility theory. Instead, it does seem that our decisions are guided by principles of justification—we make decisions that seem sensible and defensible to us. Over the last few paragraphs, though, we have tried to indicate that how these decisions should be evaluated, from the standpoint of a normative theory, is still a matter open to discussion.

13

Solving Problems

I n Chapter 11, we considered the processes through which people form new beliefs, based on information they have encountered. In Chapter 12, we then examined how people reason about these beliefs—what implications they draw, and how they adjust their beliefs (or fail to), as new evidence comes in. That chapter also carried us one further step: People often use their beliefs as a basis for choosing among options or for selecting a course of action. Chapter 12 was concerned with how we take these steps and, thus, with how we make decisions.

Once we have formed a belief, though, drawn out its implications, and chosen a course of action, what happens next? In some cases, this is a straightforward matter: If you decide to buy one jacket, rather than another, your next steps will be easy: You go to the store and get the jacket. In many other cases, though, what you select is a *goal*, and that still leaves the question of how you will reach that goal. This is the domain of problem solving, the process through which you figure out how to reach your goals, starting from your current state.

We solve problems all the time. "I want to reach the store, but Sol borrowed my car. How should I get there?" "I really want Amy to notice me; how should I arrange it?" "I'm trying to prove this theorem; how can I do it, based on these premises?" Some of the problems we face are trivial, but some have enormous consequences. Some problems are well-defined, so that it is clear from the start what you need to accomplish, and what your options are. Other problems, though, are more diffuse. For example, what is the best way to educate the children of our country? In this case, there is obviously room for debate about how we should define our goal or what the options are in reaching the goal.

In this chapter, we will examine how people solve problems, both the trivial and the consequential, the well-defined and the diffuse. We will begin by considering strategies relevant to problems of all sorts. We will then turn to more specialized strategies, applicable only to some sorts of problems.

General Problem-Solving Methods

It is obvious that some problems do require special expertise: If you are trying to achieve some bit of genetic engineering, you need the relevant training in biology and biochemistry. If you are trying to repair a computer, you need knowledge of electronics. Some problems, though, draw on more general skills and strategies, which are available to all of us. What are these strategies?

Problem Solving as Search

Many authors have found it useful to compare problem solving to a process of search, as though one were navigating though space, seeking a path towards one's goal. Some paths will lead to the goal; others will lead to dead ends or to the wrong goal. Some paths will be blocked, perhaps because they involve insurmountable obstacles, or perhaps because the path is ruled out by something in the problem's definition.

This idea of "problem solving as search" was central to the thinking of Newell and Simon (1972). They describe problem solving as starting with an **initial state**, which includes the knowledge and resources you have at the outset, and working toward a **goal state**. The problem solver has a set of **operators**, that is, tools or actions that can change her current state, and it is with these operators that the problem solver seeks to move from the initial state to the goal state. In addition, there is likely to be a set of **path constraints**, ruling out some options or some solutions. These constraints might take the form of resource limitations (limited time or money) or other limits (ethical limits on what you can do).

Given one's initial state, the operators, and the path constraints, there is a limited number of intermediate states that one can reach, on route to the goal. For example, consider the "Hobbits and Orcs" problem, described in Figure 13.1. Figure 13.2 then shows the states one can reach, early on, in solving this problem. Notice that these states can be depicted as a "tree," with each step leading to more and more branches. All of these branches together form the **problem space**, that is, the set of all states that can be reached in solving this problem. In these terms, what one is seeking, in solving a problem, is quite literally a path through this space, leading, step-by-step, from the initial state to the goal.

One option in solving a problem would be to trace through the entire problem space, exploring each branch in turn. This would guarantee that you would eventually find the solution (if the problem is solvable at all). However, for most of the problems we face, this sort of "brute force" approach would be hopeless. Consider, for example, the game of chess: Your goal is to win the game, so how should you proceed? Let's say that you move first. In opening the game, you have exactly 20 moves available to you. For each of these, your opponent has 20 possible responses. Therefore, for the first "cycle" of play, there are 400 possibilities (20 × 20) for how things might go. If you are going to choose the best move, you need to inspect all 400 of these possibilities.

Your best move, however, probably depends on what you are planning to do next—it depends on what defense you are looking to establish or what attack you are planning to launch. Therefore, in evaluating your options, you

Figure 13.1

THE HOBBITS AND ORCS PROBLEM

Five Orcs and five Hobbits are on the east bank of the Muddy River. They need to cross to the west bank, and have located a boat. In each crossing, at least one creature must be in the boat, but no more than three creatures will fit in the boat.

And, of course, if the Orcs ever out-number the Hobbits, on either side of the river, they will eat the Hobbits! Therefore, in designing the crossing, we must make certain that the Hobbits are never out-numbered, either on the east bank of the river, or on the west.

How can the creatures get across, without any Hobbits being eaten?

This problem has been used in many studies of problem-solving strategies. Can you solve it?

will probably want to ask, "Will this lead me where I want to go?" and that requires some looking ahead. Before you select your move, you might want to think through three or four cycles of play, and not just one.

There are 400 possibilities for how the first cycle can unfold, but there are more options for subsequent cycles, as the pieces get spread out, leaving more room to move. Let's estimate, therefore, that there are 40 different moves you might make next and, for each of these, 40 possible responses from your opponent. Thus, for two cycles of play, there are 640,000 (400 × 40 × 40) possible outcomes. If, at that point, there are again 40 options open to you, and 40 possible responses for each, three cycles of play leave us with 1,024,000,000 different options; four cycles of play, 16,384,000,000,000 options. If you are truly seeking the best possible move, maybe you will want to consider all sixteen trillion of these, to find the best one. (For further discussion, see Gilhooly, 1988, Newell & Simon, 1972.)

This proliferation of moves obviously rules out the strategy of "check every possibility." If you needed one second to evaluate each sequence, you would still need 455 million hours to evaluate the full set of possibilities for four cycles of play. And, of course, there is nothing special about chess. Let's say that you are having dinner with Percy, and you want him to think you are witty. Your problem is to find things to say that will achieve this goal. How many possibilities are there for sentences you might utter? How many possible rejoinders are available to Percy? How many responses could you

Figure 13.2

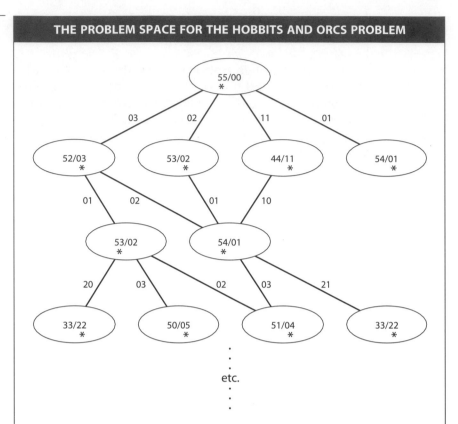

THE PROBLEM SPACE FOR THE HOBBITS AND ORCS PROBLEM

Each circle shows a possible problem state. The state 54/01, for example, indicates that five Hobbits and 4 Orcs are on the east bank; there are no Hobbits, but one Orc, on the west bank. The star shows the position of the boat. The numbers alongside of each line indicate the number of creatures in the boat during each river crossing. The move 02, for example, transports no Hobbits, but two Orcs. The problem states shown here are all the *legal* states. (Other states, and other moves, would result in some of the Hobbits getting eaten.) Thus, there are four "legal" moves one can make, starting from the initial state. From these, there are four possible moves one can make, but these lead to just two problem states (53/02, and 54/01). From these two states, there are four new states that can be reached, and so on. We have here illustrated the first three moves that can be made, in solving this problem; the shortest path to the problem's solution involves eleven moves.

then make? Again, the number is vast. If you consider them all, searching for the best choice, you will impress Percy with your long pauses, but not with your wit.

It would be helpful if you could somehow "narrow" your search, so that you only consider a *subset* of your options, rather than searching the entire problem space. Of course, this would involve an element of risk: If you only consider *some* options, you take the risk of overlooking the *best* option. However, you may have no choice about this, since the alternative—the strategy of considering *every* option—would be absurd for most problems.

In essence, then, what you need is a problem-solving *heuristic*. Heuristics, you will recall, are strategies that are reasonably efficient, but at the cost of tolerating occasional errors. In the domain of problem solving, a heuristic is a strategy that guides you through the problem space—narrowing your search appreciably, but (one hopes) in a fashion that still leads you to the problem's solution. What problem-solving heuristics do we employ?

General Problem-Solving Heuristics

Several problem-solving heuristics are revealed if we ask subjects to think out loud, while working on a problem. By inspecting these running commentaries, or "problem-solving protocols," we can locate strategies that are deliberately and wittingly in use. Other heuristics have been discovered in a different fashion: A number of researchers have tried to program computers to solve problems, including the Hobbits and Orcs problem in Figure 13.1, or the so-called Tower of Hanoi (Figure 13.3). We will have more to say about these computer models later on. For now, notice that these models provide a means of discovering and then evaluating problem-solving strategies: By programming a computer to use this or that strategy, we can literally ask how well problem solving would proceed with that strategy in place.

One often used heuristic is the so-called hill-climbing strategy. To understand the term, imagine that you are hiking through the woods and trying to figure out which trail leads to the mountain-top. You obviously need to climb *up-hill* to reach the top so, whenever you come to a fork in the trail, you select the path that is going up-hill. The hill-climbing strategy works the same way: At each point, you simply choose the option that moves you in the direction of your goal.

This strategy is helpful for some problems: Imagine that there is a bad smell in your house, and you are trying to figure out where it's coming from. You might stand at the doorway between the kitchen and the dining room, and then figure out in which direction the smell is stronger. If it is stronger in the kitchen, then that is the direction to explore. If the smell gets stronger as you approach the sink, then explore that area. By always moving in the direction of the stronger smell, you will eventually discover the smell's source.

Figure 13.3

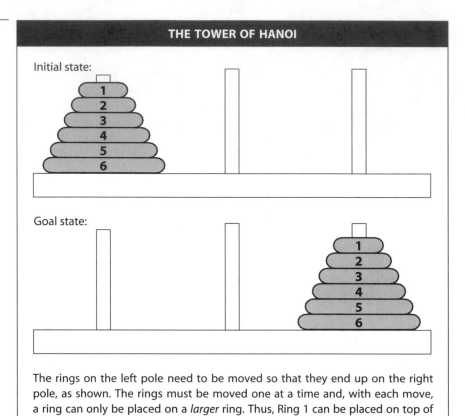

THE TOWER OF HANOI

Initial state:

Goal state:

The rings on the left pole need to be moved so that they end up on the right pole, as shown. The rings must be moved one at a time and, with each move, a ring can only be placed on a *larger* ring. Thus, Ring 1 can be placed on top of Ring 2, but Ring 2 can never be placed on Ring 1. Can you solve this?

This strategy, however, is of limited use, largely because many problems require that you start by moving *away* from your goal; only then, from this new position, can the problem be solved. We have illustrated this in Figure 13.4, and other examples are easy to find. For instance, if you want Mingus to notice you more, it might help if you went away for a while; that way, he will be more likely to notice you when you come back. This ploy would never be discovered, though, if you relied on the hill-climbing strategy.

Despite these limitations, subjects do often rely on a hill-climbing strategy. As a result, they have difficulties whenever a problem requires them to move "backward in order to go forward"—that is, whenever the problem requires subjects to move (briefly) away from their goal in order (ultimately) to reach the goal. For example, solving the Hobbits and Orcs problem (Figure 13.1) requires, at various points, that one carry creatures from the east bank back to the west—i.e., from the goal state back to the initial state. These points of

Figure 13.4

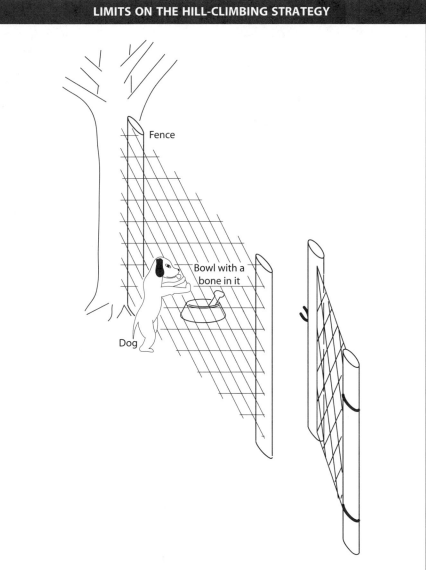

LIMITS ON THE HILL-CLIMBING STRATEGY

According to the hill-climbing strategy, the dog should, at each step, choose a path that moves it closer and closer to the goal. However, this strategy will *fail* here, since the dog needs first to move *away* from the bone in order to reach the bone.

"backward movement" turn out to be very difficult for subjects. Often, at these points, subjects will become convinced they are on the wrong track, and seek some other solution to the problem: "This must be the wrong strategy; I'm going the wrong way." (See, for example, Jeffries, Polson, Razran & Atwood, 1977; Thomas, 1974.)

Fortunately, though, subjects also have other, more sophisticated, heuristics available to them. For example, subjects often rely on a strategy called means-end analysis. To use this strategy, one starts by comparing the current state and the goal state. One then asks: "What means do I have available to get from here to there?" To see how this plays out, consider this commonsense example, offered by Newell and Simon (1972):

> I want to take my son to nursery school. What's the difference between what I have and what I want? One of distance. What changes distance? My automobile. My automobile won't work. What is needed to make it work? A new battery. What has new batteries? An auto repair shop. I want the repair shop to put in a new battery; but the shop doesn't know I need one. What is the difficulty? One of communication. What allows communication? A telephone . . .

A means-end analysis will generally lead you to break up a problem into smaller "sub-problems." By solving these, one at a time, the larger problem gets dealt with. In fact, some have suggested that this identification of sub-problems is itself a powerful problem-solving heuristic: By breaking a problem into smaller pieces, we make the initial problem easier to solve.

A related idea is that one can often solve a problem by focusing on the goal, rather than on one's current state, and then working backward from the goal. This strategy is quite useful for the "water-lilies" problem, described in Figure 13.5, or the "pennies" problem shown in Figure 13.6. Here, too, one

---

Figure 13.5

THE WATER LILIES PROBLEM

Water lilies are growing on Blue Lake. The water lilies grow rapidly, so that the amount of water surface covered by lilies *doubles* every *24* hours.

On the first day of summer, there was just one water lily. On the 90th day of the summer, the lake was entirely covered. On what day was the lake *half covered*?

Working backward from the goal is useful in solving this problem. Can you solve it?

Figure 13.6

THE PENNIES PROBLEM

Ten pennies are placed on a table. Two players take turns picking up pennies and, on each turn, each player has a choice of picking up one, two, or three pennies. The goal is to make the other player pick up the last penny. Is there a strategy that will guarantee that you will win if you go first?

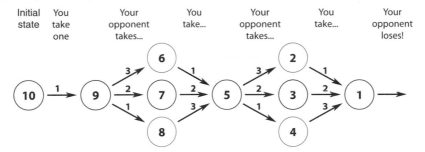

| Initial state | You take one | Your opponent takes... | You take... | Your opponent takes... | You take... | Your opponent loses! |

One could try to solve this problem by reasoning forward from the initial state. Thus, you could try to reason this way: "Let's see, if I take one penny initially, my opponent might then take. . . ." You could then, in principle, count through the (many) possibilities, seeking the solution. However, the solution is more easily found by *working backward from the goal*, in this fashion: On your opponent's last turn, you want there to be just one penny on the table. That way, your opponent will be forced to pick up that last penny. How can you bring about this state of affairs? On *your* last turn, you need to have either 2, 3, or 4 pennies left on the table. If there are 2, you pick up one, leaving your opponent with one. If there are 3, you pick up two; if there are four, you pick up three. In each case, you have left your opponent just where you want her! How can you guarantee that you will end up in the desired situation, with either 2, 3, or 4 pennies? You do this by leaving your opponent, on the prior turn, with *five* pennies. No matter how many of the five she picks up (1, 2, or 3), you are left in the situation you desire. How can you guarantee that your opponent ends up in this situation, with five pennies? In the immediately prior move, you need either 6, 7, or 8 pennies on the table. You will then pick up 1, 2, or 3 (respectively), leaving your opponent with five. How can you guarantee that you will find yourself with 6, 7, or 8? By leaving your opponent, on the prior move, with 9. How can you leave your opponent with 9? By picking up just one penny, on the very first move! (If you have trouble following this, look at the diagram.) [After Baron, 1988.]

is using means-end analysis, but now in reverse—asking how the goal state can be made more similar to the current state.

Means-end analysis and working backwards turn out to be effective strategies, applicable to a large number of problems. (Baron, 1988, provides a clear analysis of why working backwards is useful in solving the Tower of Hanoi problem.) It is fortunate, then, that these strategies seem often to be in use. For example, both these strategies are often reflected in subjects' problem-solving protocols.

Concretizing a Problem—Mental Models and Mental Images

In many cases, it also helps to translate a problem into concrete terms, perhaps relying on a mental image or a mental model. This will often make the elements of the problem easier to remember (see Chapter 10), and easier to think about (see Chapter 12). Moreover, an image or mental model is particularly likely to be useful if the problem hinges on spatial arrangements:

Figure 13.7

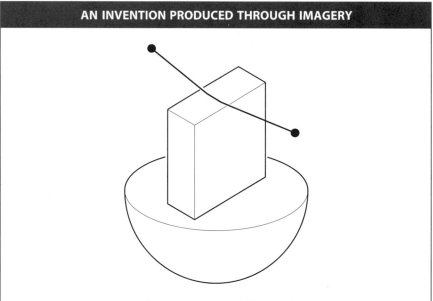

AN INVENTION PRODUCED THROUGH IMAGERY

A subject was told to make something useful by combining, in imagination, a *half sphere*, some *wire*, and a *rectangular block*. The subject invented this "hip exerciser." To use the exerciser, one stands on the flat side of the half sphere, and holds onto the wires. By shifting weight from side to side, one can exercise one's hips.

Using our "mind's eye," we can envision how the elements will look, once in their appropriate positions, and likewise we can visualize how the elements might look, if rearranged.

A number of studies have examined the role of imagery in problem solving (e.g., Cooper, 1990; Palmer, 1977; Shepard & Feng, 1972). Perhaps the most interesting studies, though, are those concerned with the role of imagery in *invention*. For example, subjects in one procedure were asked to imagine how a half sphere, a wire, and a rectangular block might be combined to

Figure 13.8

IMAGERY HELPS IN SOLVING VERBAL PROBLEMS

PROBLEM 1

A man is standing on a bridge, 300 feet from the near side and 500 feet from the far side. A train is approaching the near side. If the man runs at a speed of 10 mph toward the train, he will reach the near end of the bridge just as the train does. If he runs at a speed of 10 mph away from the train, he will reach the far end of the bridge just as the train overtakes him. What is the speed of the train?

PROBLEM 2

A monk has decided to climb a mountain near his monastery. He starts his climb promptly at sunrise, but hikes at varying speeds, and stops at several points in his journey to rest and to meditate. He reaches the mountain top just as the sun is setting.

The next day, he begins his descent, again starting just at sunrise. Once again, though, he hikes at varying speeds, stopping several times to rest and meditate. His descent is somewhat faster, however, than his climb, and he reaches the monastery again at 3:30 P.M.

Is there any point, anywhere on the monk's path, that he reached at precisely the same time of day on his ascent and on his descent?

In solving these problems, it may help to visualize the states of affairs described in them. It may help, in solving the first problem, to try visualizing where the man will be if he runs away from the train when the train reaches the near end of the bridge. For the second problem, try imagining two monks, one climbing uphill, one down, both starting their journey at the same moment.

create something that "might have practical value" (Finke, 1990, 1993; Finke & Slayton, 1988). The task allowed the subject to imagine these constituents at different sizes, and in different positions or orientations. One subject's invention is shown in Figure 13.7. To use this "hip exerciser," you stand on the flat side of the hemisphere, and shift your weight from side to side while holding onto the post. (For related discussion, see Kaufmann, 1990; Koestler, 1964; McKim, 1980. For discussion of imagery's role in scientific discoveries, see Miller, 1986; Reed, 1993; Shepard, 1988.)

Imagery can also help us in solving some *verbal* problems, such as those shown in Figure 13.8 (after Reed, 1993). If you can't solve the first of these, try answering this question first: If the man runs away from the train, where will he be when the train reaches the near end of the bridge? As an aid in solving the second problem in the figure, try imagining two monks, one climbing up the mountain, and one down, both starting their journey at the same moment.

Pictures and Diagrams

Consider the "bookworm" problem, described in Figure 13.9. Most subjects try an algebraic solution to this problem (width of each volume, multiplied by the number of volumes, divided by the worm's eating rate), and end up with the wrong answer. Subjects generally get this problem right, though, if they start by *drawing a diagram* (like the one in Figure 13.10).

Figure 13.9

THE BOOKWORM PROBLEM

Solomon is proud of his 26-volume encyclopedia, placed neatly, with the volumes in alphabetical order, on his bookshelf. Solomon doesn't realize, though, that there's a bookworm sitting on the front cover of the "A" volume. The bookworm begins chewing his way through the pages, on the shortest possible path toward the back cover of the "Z" volume.

Each volume is 3 inches thick (including pages and covers), so that the entire set of volumes requires 78 inches of bookshelf. The bookworm chews through the pages + covers at a steady rate of 3/4 of an inch per month. How long will it take before the bookworm emerges from the "Z" volume?

Subjects who try an algebraic solution to this problem often end up with the wrong answer.

Figure 13.10

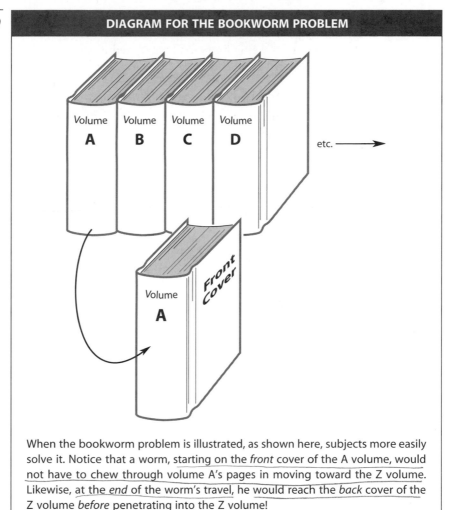

DIAGRAM FOR THE BOOKWORM PROBLEM

When the bookworm problem is illustrated, as shown here, subjects more easily solve it. Notice that a worm, starting on the *front* cover of the A volume, would not have to chew through volume A's pages in moving toward the Z volume. Likewise, at the *end* of the worm's travel, he would reach the *back* cover of the Z volume *before* penetrating into the Z volume!

In this problem and in many others, diagrams help us by bringing spatial positions and relationships into clear view—once you discern the actual position of the worm's "starting point," the problem is easily solved. Note, though, that subjects might derive the same benefit from inspecting a *mental image* of the problem's lay-out and, indeed, for many purposes, pictures and images may be interchangeable. Consistent with this idea, several studies have found no difference between problem solving via picture and problem solving via imagery (Anderson, 1993; Anderson & Helstrup, 1993; Reed, 1993).

For other purposes, though, there are important differences between mental images and pictures, with some problems more readily solved via imagery, and other problems showing the reverse. For example, mental images have the advantage of being more easily modified than diagrams: If one wishes to make a form larger, or a different shape, this is easy in imagination—one can, after all, imagine anything one wishes. Likewise, one can easily imagine *moving* patterns; it is much harder to depict motion with a diagram. Therefore, if a problem solution depends on motion (e.g., Figure 13.8), then the problem may be more easily solved with imagery than with a picture.

At the same time, however, it takes some effort to create and maintain a mental image (see Chapter 10); this can divert attention away from the problem under scrutiny, and so this provides an advantage for problem solving via *pictures*. Likewise, elaborate or detailed forms are difficult to image clearly. If a problem depends on such forms, then, problem solving via image will be difficult.

In addition, Chapter 10 presented evidence indicating that, in important

Figure 13.11

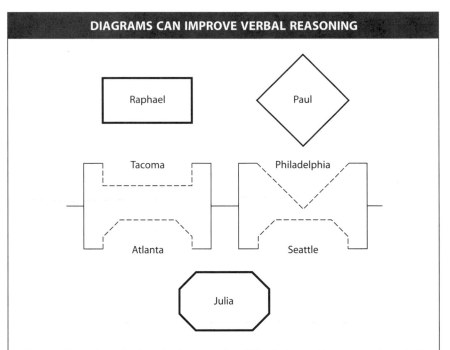

DIAGRAMS CAN IMPROVE VERBAL REASONING

The problem described in the text is quite difficult, but subjects solve it easily if provided with the right diagram. Think through the problem in the text while moving the "assistants"—Raphael, Paul, and Julia—into the appropriate positions. [After Bauer & Johnson-Laird, 1993.]

ways, mental images are different from pictures. Images, we argued, are created with a particular understanding in mind, and this understanding seems to set "boundaries" on what can be discovered within the image: Discoveries flow readily from an image if the discoveries are compatible with how the imager understands the depicted form. Image-based discoveries seem far less likely when they are not compatible with this understanding (or, equivalently, if they require a change in this understanding). None of this, however, applies to discoveries about pictures. For these, one can easily *set aside* one's initial understanding, inspect the picture again, and reach new discoveries. In many cases, it really does pay to draw a picture, since discoveries unreachable from an image may be effortlessly gained from the corresponding drawing. (For elaboration of this point, see Hayes, 1989; Reisberg, 1987, 1996.)

Finally, we should note one point relevant to *both* images and pictures: It is surely not the case that an image or picture *always* helps problem solving. In some cases, these concrete representations can introduce superfluous and misleading detail, and can be confusing. (Think back to your high-school algebra class, where it was often easier to think through equations than it was to think through a more concrete, more detailed, word problem.) Likewise, an image or picture will help us only if it is the "right" image or the "right" picture. For example, consider this problem (after Bauer & Johnson-Laird, 1993):

> In order for Maria to close the deal, she needs to have her assistants in the right locations. In particular, she needs either to have Raphael in Tacoma, or Julia in Atlanta, or both. She also needs either to have Julia in Seattle or Paul in Philadelphia, or both. Now, it turns out that Maria did close the deal. What can we infer from this?

Can you solve this? For example, is the following inference valid? "Since we know that she closed the deal, we know that, if Julia was in Atlanta, then Paul must have been in Philadelphia." (This is, in fact, a valid inference from the problem.)

Subjects' find these problems quite difficult, and they endorse invalid inferences about 75% of the time. Subjects do far better, though, if we give them a diagram like the one shown in Figure 13.11; now they endorse invalid inferences only 40% of the time—in other words, the number of correct inferences more than doubles (from 25% to 60%). However, subjects offered diagrams like the one in Figure 13.12 were helped not at all. Thus, it is not enough merely to make a problem concrete and easy to remember; instead, the diagram needs somehow to convey important relations within the problem. (Also see Boden, 1991, 1994; Larkin & Simon, 1987; Lovett & Anderson, 1994.)

Figure 13.12

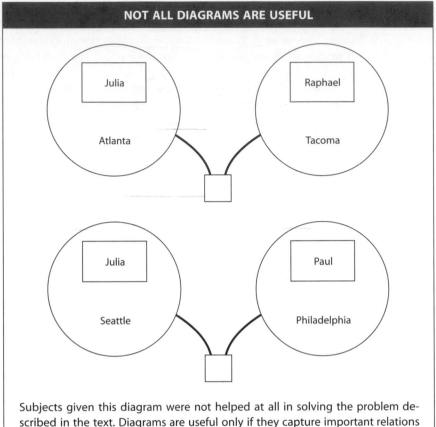

NOT ALL DIAGRAMS ARE USEFUL

Subjects given this diagram were not helped at all in solving the problem described in the text. Diagrams are useful only if they capture important relations within the problem. [After Bauer & Johnson-Laird, 1993.]

Computer Models of Problem Solving

We have now catalogued several of the problem-solving strategies that people have available to them. However, this catalog still leaves a great deal unspecified. For example, imagine that you are using a means-end analysis, and discover that your current state differs from the goal state in three different ways. Does it matter which of these differences you attack first? If so, what should the sequence be?

To answer questions like these, researchers are working on the development of more specific, more precise theories of problem solving, theories that pull together all of the pieces we have considered so far. Often, these theories are realized in the form of computer programs. The basic idea is that, if the program fails to solve a problem that people can solve, we know that the theory embodied in the program is inadequate. Likewise, if the computer program quickly solves problems that are difficult for human subjects, then again we know we are on the wrong track. In these ways, both the successes and the failures of the program provide a powerful means for assessing our theories.

Just as important, the mere step of translating a theory into a program is often quite useful. Computers do precisely what they are told. If they are not told what to do, they make no progress. Likewise, one can't give the computer vague instructions such as, "Oh, you know what I mean, so just do it." Instead, instructions to the computer must be clear, unambiguous, and complete. Therefore, if your theory is to be embodied in these instructions, then your theory, too, must be fully spelled out, with all the gaps filled. Getting the theory to this state is certain to be valuable and so, even if the program is never run, this exercise will improve the quality of our theorizing.

Many computer models of problem solving are being developed, each seeking to realize a particular researcher's conception. The "classic" model, though, is that created by Newell and Simon (1972). Their model is designed to solve a wide range of problems, and thus its name: General Problem Solver, or "GPS" for short. GPS is intended not merely to solve problems, but to solve them in the same way humans do. Development of this model was heavily influenced by consideration of problem-solving protocols, and by consideration of the specific profile of human problem solving—i.e., which problems we solve easily and which we don't.

GPS relies heavily on heuristics and, in particular, means-end analysis. Thus, the program compares the current state to the goal state, to detect the differences. GPS then considers the set of operators it has available, to determine which would reduce (or eliminate) these differences. The operators are applied, and then the cycle is repeated: Given the progress just made, what differences remain between current state and goal state? Which operators will reduce this difference?

GPS's operators generally involved actions, so that an operator might move some object to a new position, or might change an object from one specific form into another. More recent models, however, have considered other means of describing the operators. For example, many models rely on **production systems**, where each production involves (a) a goal, (b) some conditions that must be met before the action can be taken, and (c) a specific action (Anderson, 1993; Brown & Van Lehn, 1980; Holland, Holyoak, Nisbett & Thagard, 1986; Newell, 1973). A production might say: "IF the goal is to light the fire, and IF the fuel is ready, THEN strike the match." Or, as a more general production, "IF the goal is to transform the current state into the goal state, and IF D is the largest difference between these two states, THEN set as subgoals (1) to eliminate the difference D, and (2) to convert the resulting state into the goal state" (after Anderson, 1990).

With operators like these, computer models are able to solve an impressive range of problems. GPS, for example, is able to solve the Tower of Hanoi problem (Figure 13.3) and "transport" problems (like the Hobbits and Orcs); it is also able to prove logic theorems and to solve a variety of trigonometry problems. Moreover, GPS's performance in these problems seems well matched to that of humans: GPS takes longer with more difficult problems and makes errors roughly in the same ways that humans do. We can also compare GPS's step-by-step progress with subjects' problem-solving protocols. The correspondence between these is reasonably good, suggesting that GPS follows the same path in solving the problem that humans do. (For reviews, see Gardner, 1985; Kotovsky, Hayes & Simon, 1985; Simon, 1975.)

We can also assess these computer models in one other way: As subjects work on a problem, sometimes they work quickly, and sometimes they pause to consider their next move. Why is this? One possibility is that subjects move most slowly when they are contemplating a "stack" of subgoals: "What I next want to do is X. I can't do X, though, since I first need to do Y. And I can't do Y, because I first need to do Z. . . ." Consistent with this suggestion, Anderson (1993) reports a strong correlation between the number of subgoals active at any particular moment (determined via the computer model), and the actual speed with which subjects proceed (determined by assessing actual performance).

Finally, we should also note that computer models of problem solving can be useful in important ways: Imagine that the computer has trouble with a particular problem and always gets bogged down at a certain point in trying to solve the problem. We obviously can look "inside" the computer in ways that we can't look inside a human subject, and so we can figure out exactly what is causing the hang-up. If it then turns out that humans have trouble with the same problem, we can use the computer model to figure out the source of the humans' difficulty.

In this fashion, computer models can be used to design educational programs: The computer model can tell us a great deal about the sources of a student's errors, and then we can use this information to fine-tune the instruction given to that student. The computer can also be used to model an expert's performance, allowing us to define exactly what skills should be taught, en route to expertise. Anderson (1993) describes one such endeavor, designed to improve instruction in mathematics; other similar projects are underway (e.g., Polson & Richardson, 1988; Reed & Bolstad, 1991).

[handwritten margin note: can look inside a computer + figure out what causes problems figuring out certain problems ∴ helpful for educational purposes]

Relying on Past Knowledge

Our discussion so far has focused on strategies that apply to problem solving in general, problem solving of all sorts. This emphasis has highlighted a number of principles that do indeed seem to be general principles—for example, the role of heuristics or the widespread use of means-end analysis. Likewise, this emphasis has led researchers to computer models that are in many ways impressive. As a matter of technology, these models can solve an interesting range of problems. As a boon to education, these models can be used to design curricula, and then to guide instruction step-by-step as a student progresses. Finally, these models also point us toward explanations for a number of phenomena, providing insights, for example, into why some problems are harder than others and why problem solving sometimes proceeds slowly, sometimes quickly.

It turns out that problem solving also draws on particular and specialized knowledge, in addition to the flexible, widely applicable heuristics we have considered so far. To the extent that this is true, we need to turn away from models of problem solving in general, and ask instead how problem solving unfolds in more specialized domains.

Problem Solving via Analogy

Often, in solving a problem, we are reminded of some other problem we have already solved, and this will tell us, by analogy, how to solve the problem now before us. Of course, this is possible only if we have the relevant prior experience, providing a base from which we can draw analogies. In an obvious way, analogy use depends on specialized knowledge—that is, knowledge relevant to the problem now at hand.

Many authors have argued that the ability to draw analogies is a central intellectual tool. Certainly, within the history of science, analogies have often played an important role—with scientists furthering their understanding of the heart by comparing it to a pump, extending their knowledge of gases by comparing the molecules to billiard balls, and so on (cf. Gentner & Jeziorski, 1989). It is no wonder that analogies appear prominently in the SAT's and on many versions of the IQ test (for discussion, see Holyoak, 1984; Spearman, 1923).

Likewise, many writers have recommended the use of analogies as a *teaching* tool. Thus, the atom is described to students as (very roughly) resembling the solar system, memory is compared to a library, and the like. In fact, evidence suggests that analogies do make for effective instruction. For ex-

Figure 13.13 **ANALOGIES ARE A USEFUL WAY TO CONVEY NEW INFORMATION**

LITERAL VERSION:

Collapsing stars. Collapsing stars spin faster and faster as they fold in on themselves and their size decreases. This phenomenon of spinning faster as the star's size shrinks occurs because of a principle called "conservation of angular momentum."

Earth's rotation. The spinning Earth rotates in the solar system at a constant tilt. This tilted spinning, which is called "precession," is due to a balance between the spin of the Earth, which acts to straighten the Earth up, and gravity, which acts to pull the Earth down.

ANALOGY VERSION:

Collapsing stars. Collapsing stars spin faster as their size shrinks. Stars are thus like ice skaters, who pirouette faster as they pull in their arms. Both stars and skaters operate by a principle called "conservation of angular momentum."

Earth's rotation. The spinning Earth behaves like a slowing toy top that wobbles at a tilt (but never topples). This tilted spinning, called "precession," is due to a balance between the spin, which straightens the Earth (or the top), and gravity, which pulls the Earth (or the top) down.

QUESTIONS:

What would happen if a star "expanded" instead of collapsing?

a. Its rate of rotation would increase.
b. Its rate of rotation would decrease.
c. Its orbital speed would increase.
d. Its orbital speed would decrease.

What would happen if there were no gravity affecting the Earth's orbit?

a. The Earth would continue to rotate, which would cause it to fall on its side.
b. The Earth would continue to rotate, which would cause it to straighten up.
c. The Earth would stop rotating and so it would fall on its side.
d. The Earth would stop rotating and so it would freeze at its original tilt.

Subjects were presented with new materials either in a "literal version" or in an "analogy version." Later, subjects were asked questions about these materials. Subjects instructed via analogy reliably did better. [After Donnelly & McDaniel, 1993.]

Figure 13.14

THE TUMOR PROBLEM

Suppose you are a doctor faced with a patient who has a malignant tumor in his stomach. To operate on the patient is impossible, but unless the tumor is destroyed, the patient will die. A kind of ray, at a sufficiently high intensity, can destroy the tumor. Unfortunately, at this intensity the healthy tissue that the rays pass through on the way to the tumor will also be destroyed. At lower intensities the rays are harmless to healthy tissue, but will not affect the tumor. How can the rays be used to destroy the tumor without injuring the healthy tissue?

The tumor problem, designed by Duncker (1945), has been studied extensively. Can you solve it? One solution is to aim *multiple* low-intensity rays at the tumor, each from a different angle. The rays will "meet" at the site of the tumor and so, at just that location, will "sum" to full strength.

ample, Donnelly and McDaniel (1993) presented some of their subjects with literal accounts of new scientific materials; other subjects were given analogies of these same materials (Figure 13.13). When subjects were later asked to make inferences about these new ideas, those instructed via analogy did better.

In addition, analogies plainly do help subjects in solving problems. For example, the "tumor" problem (Figure 13.14) is quite difficult, but subjects generally solve it if they are able to use an analogy: Gick and Holyoak (1980) first had their subjects read about a related situation (Figure 13.15), and then presented them with the tumor problem. When subjects were encouraged to use this hint, 75% were able to solve the tumor problem. For subjects not given the hint, only 10% solved the tumor problem.

Difficulties in Finding an Appropriate Analogy

However, despite the clear benefit of using analogies, subjects routinely fail to use them. For example, Gick and Holyoak had another group of subjects read the "General and Fortress" story, but no further hints were given. In particular, these subjects were not told that this story was relevant to the tumor problem. Only 30% of these subjects solved the tumor problem—far fewer than the 75% explicitly told that the "fortress" story was relevant to their task.

Similarly, Reed (1977; Reed, Ernst & Banerji, 1974) first had subjects solve the "jealous-husbands" problem, shown in Figure 13.16; subjects were then

Figure 13.15

THE GENERAL AND FORTRESS PROBLEM

A small country was ruled from a strong fortress by a dictator. The fortress was situated in the middle of the country, surrounded by farms and villages. Many roads led to the fortress through the countryside. A rebel general vowed to capture the fortress. The general knew that an attack by his entire army would capture the fortress. He gathered his army at the head of one of the roads, ready to launch a full-scale direct attack. However, the general then learned that the dictator had planted mines on each of the roads. The mines were set so that small bodies of men could pass over them safely, since the dictator needed to move his own troops and workers to and from the fortress. However, any large force would detonate the mines. Not only would this blow up the road, but it would also destroy many neighboring villages. It seemed impossible to capture the fortress. However, the general devised a simple plan. He divided his army into small groups and dispatched each group to the head of a different road. When all was ready, he gave the signal and each group marched down a different road. Each group continued down its road to the fortress, so that the entire army arrived together at the fortress at the same time. In this way, the general captured the fortress and overthrew the dictator.

This problem is analogous in its structure to the tumor problem (Figure 13.14). If subjects read this problem, and then try the tumor problem, they are far more likely to solve the latter. [After Gick & Holyoak, 1980.]

asked to solve the Hobbits and Orcs problem (Figure 13.1). When the close relationship between these two problems was pointed out to subjects, they were considerably faster in solving the second problem. However, if this relationship was not pointed out to subjects, they showed no benefit at all from this "training." (See also Hayes & Simon, 1977; Ross, 1984, 1987, 1989; Weisberg, DiCamillo & Phillips, 1978.)

Apparently, then, subjects do use analogies if suitably instructed, but *spontaneous, uninstructed* use of analogies seems to be quite rare. Why is this? Part of the answer lies in how subjects search through their memories when seek-

Figure 13.16

THE JEALOUS HUSBANDS PROBLEM

Three jealous husbands and their wives, who have to cross a river, find a boat. However, the boat is so small that it can hold no more than two persons. Find the simplest schedule of crossings that will permit all six persons to cross the river so that no woman is left in the company of any other woman's husband unless her own husband is present. It is assumed that all passengers on the boat debark before the next trip and that at least one person has to be in the boat for each crossing.

If the experimenter points out the relationship between the jealous husbands problem and the Hobbits and Orcs problem (Figure 13.1), then subjects benefit from first solving the jealous husbands problem. If this relationship is not pointed out to subjects, however, they show no benefit from this "training." [After Reed, Ernst, & Banerji, 1974.]

ing an analogy. In solving a problem about tumors, subjects seem to ask themselves, "What else do I know about tumors?" They will remember other situations in which they thought about, or learned about, tumors but, of course, this memory search *won't* lead them to the "General and Fortress" problem. This (potential) analogue will therefore lie dormant in memory and provide no help. Likewise, hobbit problems remind subjects of other hobbit problems, even though problems on other topics might point the way to a solution.

Consistent with this perspective, spontaneous use of analogies is observed in some circumstances—namely, circumstances in which the current problem reminds subjects of a previously solved relevant problem. Thus, subjects solving hobbit problems will spontaneously use analogies if the previously studied problems also involved hobbits. In this case, the (rather obvious) relation between the current problem and the prior problems guarantees that the former will call the latter to mind. Subjects are less likely to draw analogies if they have previously solved problems involving actors of a different sort. (For relevant evidence, see Bassok, Wu & Olseth, 1995; Cummins, 1992; Holyoak & Koh, 1987, Novick, 1988; Ross, 1984, 1987; Spencer & Weisberg, 1986; Wharton, Holyoak, Downing & Lange, 1994.)

These similarities, between the current problem and the previously studied case, also help subjects in another way: In order to create, or even to understand, an analogy, subjects need to get beyond the superficial features of the problem and have to think instead about the principles governing the problem. Put differently, subjects can use analogies only if they figure out how to **map** the prior case onto the problem now being solved, only if they realize, for example, that converging groups of soldiers correspond to converging beams, and that a fortress-to-be-captured corresponds to a tumor-to-be-destroyed. This mapping process is often complicated and, in any case, requires insight into both the current problem and also the analogous case being drawn from memory. (For discussion of how this process of mapping unfolds, see Gentner, 1983, 1989; Holyoak, 1984; Holyoak & Thagard, 1989.) Failures to figure out this mapping are common, and these failures are another reason why subjects regularly fail to find, and fail to use, analogies.

Mapping one problem onto another is easier if the two problems are similar in their particulars: If you have recently solved one Hobbits and Orcs problem, it is easy to apply this experience to a new Hobbits and Orcs problem—what you earlier learned about hobbits can be mapped onto the new hobbits, what you earlier discovered about boats is immediately applicable to the boat in the current problem. If, instead, you have recently solved the jealous-husbands problem, then the principles learned in this experience might be applicable to the new problem, but only via a step of translation (hobbits become husbands; "cannot outnumber" is replaced with "cannot be left alone with"). This, by itself, makes use of the analogy more difficult, and provides a further reason for why analogy use is facilitated by similarity between the target problem and the analogous problem drawn from memory. (For discussion of other factors impeding or facilitating the use of analogies, see Bassok, Wu & Olseth, 1995; Gick & Holyoak, 1980; Novick & Holyoak, 1991; Needham & Begg, 1991.)

There are, to be sure, many differences between the tumor problem and the "General and Fortress" problem. But these differences are irrelevant to the analogy between these two problems; the analogy rests on the fact that these problems are governed by the same principles. In other words, the analogy depends entirely on what we might call the problem's "deep structure." The "surface structure"—that is, the way the deep structure is manifested—is *irrelevant* to the analogy. Subjects, though, are very much influenced by the "surface structure": If two problems don't share these superficial features, subjects are unlikely to spot the analogy, even though these superficial features don't matter at all for the analogy.

Strategies to Make Analogy Use More Likely

When considering the tumor problem, subjects are likely to ask themselves, "What else do I know about tumors?" Of course, there is nothing rigid about this: Subjects could, if suitably instructed, ask themselves a different question, along the lines of, "This problems involves converging forces; what else do I know about converging forces?" In this case, they might well be reminded of a suitable analogue, even if the analogue differed from the current problem in a dozen superficial ways.

Similarly, we have noted that what is shared between two analogous problems is usually the underlying dynamic (the pattern of causal relations within the problem, or how the problem's parts are interrelated), rather than the problem's superficial details. Thus, if subjects pay attention to this dynamic in the first place, rather than attending to the problem's superficial content, they will have focused on the information that is crucial for seeing the analogy. This suggests that the right orientation, when working with a problem, may ease the chore of *mapping*, later on.

This leads to an optimistic prediction: If we could motivate subjects, from the start, to think about these deeper aspects of a problem, then the subjects will be more likely to notice analogies, to use those analogies, and to benefit from those analogies. Several results confirm this suggestion. For example, we have already seen that subjects are unlikely, on their own, to notice the analogy between the "General and Fortress" problem (for which they know the solution), and the "tumor" problem (which they are currently trying to solve). In a related procedure, though, subjects were initially given *two* analogous stories, prior to the test problem, rather than just one (Gick & Holyoak, 1983). These subjects were much more likely to draw analogies from these stories in solving the tumor problem, than subjects who had only read one (potential) analogue.

Why are two analogues better than one? The two analogues both involved the same principles (one was the "General and Fortress" problem, the other problem involved the use of many small hoses to put out a large fire). This may have been enough to call subjects' attention to these principles (e.g., the use of converging forces). This would, in turn, highlight the underlying structure of the stories, paving the way for the analogy.

A similar point emerges from an experiment by Cummins (1992). She presented her subjects with a series of algebra word problems. One group of subjects was asked to analyze these training problems, one by one; these subjects tended to categorize the problems in terms of superficial features, and were unlikely, later on, to apply these analogies to new problems. Subjects in a second group were explicitly asked to *compare* the training problems to each other. These subjects tended to describe and categorize the problems in terms of their structures—in other words, they paid attention to the problems' underlying dynamic. These subjects were much more likely to use these problems as a basis for analogies, when later solving new problems. (For related evidence, see Catrambone & Holyoak, 1989.)

Likewise, Needham and Begg (1991) presented their subjects with a series of training problems. Some subjects were told that they would need to recall these problems later on and were encouraged to work hard at remembering them. Other subjects were encouraged to take a "problem-oriented" attitude during this training: They were encouraged to work at *understanding* each solution, so that they would be able to explain it later on.

When the time came for the test problems, subjects in the second group were much more likely to transfer what they had earlier learned. As a result, subjects who had taken the "problem-oriented" approach were able to solve 90% of the test problems; subjects who had taken the "memory-oriented" approach solved only 69%. Interestingly, it didn't matter whether the training examples were presented as unsolved problems (so that the subjects had worked on solving them) or as stories that included the solution. It also didn't matter whether subjects had successfully solved the training problems or tried and failed to solve these problems. That is, what mattered *wasn't* a history of solving the problems. Instead, what mattered was a history of *thinking* about the problems in a certain way.

For purposes of problem solving, therefore, there is a "preferred" way to learn. In essence, you want to attend to the *structure* of a problem rather than to its surface; this increases the likelihood of finding analogies later on, and thus the likelihood of benefiting from analogies later on. Comparing problems to each other, seeking parallels and points of similarity, seems to bring this about. As we have seen, a similar effect is observed if subjects simply spend time thinking about a problem's solution and, in particular, thinking about *why* the solution gets the job done. Subjects are also helped by getting the *right* training problems, problems that call attention to the problems' underlying structure (Catrambone, 1994; Gick & Holyoak, 1983). There seem many ways to promote analogy use, ways that provide subjects both with the relevant analogues and with the "sagacity to apply the knowledge to a new problem" (Needham & Begg, 1991; after James, 1890).

Expert Problem Solvers

Our discussion so far has obvious implications for education. Let's say that we want students to be better problem solvers; how should we proceed? First, we could teach our students some of the heuristics that appear useful for problem solving in general. Second, analogies are plainly helpful in problem solving, and so we could provide students with experience in the relevant domains, so that they would have a basis from which to draw analogies. Third, we now see that this training may have little effect unless we take steps to ensure students will use this knowledge when it is needed. To this end, we need to encourage students to approach the training problems in an appropriate way, to make certain the training problems will be retrievable from memory later on, and also to provide a basis for seeing the mapping between the training and test problems.

These training steps are designed to produce better problem solving; in the extreme, these steps might even produce expert problem solving. But can we characterize *expertise* in the terms used so far? We have claimed an advantage, for example, in thinking about problems in terms of their structure; is this the way experts think about problems? We have likewise claimed that analogies often help problem solving; is analogy use common among experts?

Even with moderate levels of expertise, subjects do categorize problems in terms of their structure and type of solution, rather than in terms of superficial features (Hinsley, Hayes & Simon, 1977). For example, college students, moderately well-versed in algebra, categorized word problems as "river-current problems" whenever the problem involved one object moving with or against some countervailing force—be it a boat sailing upstream, a fish swimming against the tide, or an airplane flying into the wind. Apparently, then, it is only the novices who attend exclusively to a problem's superficial features.

Likewise, Chi, Feltovish and Glaser (1981) asked subjects to categorize simple physics problems. Novices tended to place together all the problems involving inclined planes, all the problems involving springs, and so on, in each case focusing on the surface form of the problem, independent of what physical principles were needed to solve the problem. In contrast, expert subjects (Ph.D. students in physics) ignored the details of the problems and, instead, sorted according to the physical principles relevant to the problem's solution. (Also see Adelson, 1981; Chase & Simon, 1973; Chi, Glaser & Farr, 1988; Cummins, 1992; Hardiman, Dufresne & Mestre, 1989; Schoenfeld & Herrmann, 1982.)

Of course, we have already said that attention to a problem's structure promotes analogy use. Therefore, if experts are more attentive to this structure, then experts should be more likely to use analogies. Several studies indicate that this is correct. For example, Novick and Holyoak (1991) examined subjects' skill in using mathematical analogies (an example is shown in Figure 13.17). They first provided their subjects with a training problem; subjects then tried to solve several analogous problems.

Novick and Holyoak assessed "math expertise" by looking at subjects' SAT scores, and they found a consistent relation between these scores and subjects' ability to form mathematical analogies. There was no relation between analogy use and verbal SAT's, or between analogy use and what they called "general analogy skill." (This was measured via a series of verbal analogies, such as "_____ is to horses as worms are to _____.") What

Figure 13.17

USING ANALOGIES TO SOLVE MATHEMATICAL PROBLEMS

Problem

Mr. and Mrs. Renshaw were planning how to arrange vegetable plants in their new garden. They agreed on the total number of plants to buy, but not on how many of each kind to get. Mr. Renshaw wanted to have a few kinds of vegetables and ten of each kind. Mrs. Renshaw wanted more different kinds of vegetables, so she suggested having only four of each kind. Mr. Renshaw didn't like that because if some of the plants died, there wouldn't be very many left of each kind. So they agreed to have five of each vegetable. But then their daughter pointed out that there was room in the garden for two more plants, although then there wouldn't be the same number of each kind of vegetable. To remedy this, she suggested buying six of each vegetable. Everyone was satisfied with this plan. Given this information, what is the fewest number of vegetable plants the Renshaws could have in their garden?

Solution for Garden Problem

Since at the beginning Mr. and Mrs. Renshaw agree on the total number of plants to buy, 10, 4, and 5 must all go evenly into that number, whatever it is. Thus the first thing to do is to find the smallest number that is evenly divisible by those 3 numbers, which is 20. So the original number of vegetable plants the Renshaws were thinking of buying could be any multiple of 20 (that is, 20 or 40 or 60 or 80 etc.). But then they decide to buy 2 additional plants, that they hadn't been planning to buy originally, so the total number of plants they actually end up buying must be 2 more than the multiples of 20 listed above (that is, 22 or 42 or 62 or 82 etc.). This means that 10, 4, and 5 will now no longer go evenly into the total number of plants. Finally, the problem states that they agree to buy 6 of each vegetable, so the total number of plants must be evenly divisible by 6. The smallest total number of plants that is evenly divisible by 6 is 42, so that's the answer.

The Marching Band Problem

Members of the West High School Band were hard at work practicing for the annual Homecoming Parade. First they tried marching in rows of twelve, but Andrew was left by himself to bring up the rear. The band director was annoyed because it didn't look good to have one row with only a single person in it, and of course Andrew wasn't very pleased either. To get rid of this problem, the director told the band members to march in columns of eight. But Andrew was still left to march alone. Even when the band marched in rows of three, Andrew was left out. Finally, in exasperation, Andrew told the band director that they should march in rows of five in order to have all the rows filled. He was right. This time all the rows were filled and Andrew wasn't alone any more. Given that there were at least 45 musicians on the field but fewer than 200 musicians, how many students were there in the West High School Band?

The Seashell Problem

Samantha's mother asked her how many sea shells she has in her collection. Samantha said she wasn't sure, but it was a lot—somewhere between 80 and 550. And she could count them by sevens without having any left over. However, if she counted them by threes, there was one shell left over. Things were even worse if she counted the shells by fives, by sixes, by nines, or by tens—there were always four shells left over. Samantha's mother promptly told her how many sea shells she had in her collection. What number did Samantha's mother come up with?

Subjects first solved the "garden" problem, and then were tested with the "band" and "seashell" problems. Subjects with greater math expertise (measured via SAT scores) were more likely to rely on analogies in solving these problems, and so were more likely to apply what they had learned in the training problems to the subsequent test problems. [After Novick & Holyoak, 1991.]

seems to matter in drawing analogies, therefore, is not some sort of generalized skill. Instead, analogy use depends specifically on expertise within the relevant domain. (For related results, see Clement, 1982; Novick, 1988.)

Chunking and Subgoals

Experts' sensitivity to a problem's structure is also evident in a series of classic studies of chess experts (DeGroot, 1965, 1966; also Chase & Simon, 1973). These studies indicate that these experts are particularly skilled in organizing a chess game—in seeing the structure of the game, understanding its parts, and perceiving how these parts are related to each other. This is revealed in how chess masters remember board positions: In one procedure, chess masters were able to remember the positions of twenty pieces, after viewing the board for just five seconds. Moreover, there was a clear pattern to the experts' recollection: In recalling the lay-out of the board, the experts would place four or five pieces in their proper positions, then pause, then another group, then pause, and so on. In each case, the group of pieces was one that made "tactical sense," e.g., the pieces involved in a "forked" attack, a chain of mutually defending pieces, and the like.

This memory pattern suggests that the masters had memorized the board in terms of *groups* of pieces, rather than individual pieces, with these groups characterized according to their function within the game. Consistent with this suggestion, the masters showed no memory advantage if asked to memorize random configurations of chess pieces. In this case, there were no sensible groupings, and so the masters were unable to organize (and thus memorize) the board.

All of this should sound familiar to you. In Chapter 4, we discussed the fact that memory is generally improved if one can organize the to-be-remembered materials. More specifically, it often helps to repackage the materials into a small number of memory "chunks," allowing more effective use of working memory's limited capacity. Given this backdrop, it should be no surprise that chess experts, with their ability to organize a board and to perceive the large-level units, have superior memories for chess positions. Indeed, similar memory advantages have been reported in other domains—e.g., masters in the game of Gō memorizing board positions (Reitman, 1976) or experts in electronics memorizing circuit diagrams (Egan & Schwartz, 1979).

This memory advantage will, by itself, aid problem solving. If you are trying to remember the locations of 20 pieces, this will demand virtually all of your mental resources, with little left over for other chores—e.g., choosing your next move. If these 20 locations can be chunked as four tactical units, the burden on working memory is reduced, freeing capacity for the task at hand.

Hand in hand with this, the perception of a problem's higher order units will draw attention to these units and to how they are related to each other. This allows the expert problem solver to focus on the overall structure of the problem, rather than getting bogged down in the details. Thus, problem solution can proceed at the level of "I'm being attacked, and I need to move away," without worrying about whether the attack comes from a bishop or a rook, from an opponent close by or one far away.

In addition, the perception of a problem's parts often leads directly to the identification of sub-problems and, with it, to the creation of "subgoals."

[handwritten margin note: chunking will aid problem solving (frees memory capacity for the task at hand)]

Having perceived an opponent's "knight fork," one realizes the need to defend against this attack. Having realized how few pieces defend a rook, one sets the subgoal of shoring up those defenses. In this fashion, breaking a problem into "chunks" can sometimes allow the expert to deal with the problem "one piece at a time," rather than all at once.

Consistent with all these suggestions, DeGroot's data show that the chess experts often didn't consider that many options in selecting their next move. That is because their perception of the game's organization allowed them to focus on just those options that were particularly promising in that situation. Indeed, the evidence suggests that the experts often considered fewer options in selecting their next move than less talented players.   *chess*

The Nature of Expertise

We have now suggested that experts may have several advantages in comparison to novices. But what exactly is "expertise" in a problem area? And what does it take to become an "expert"? It seems clear that experts know more about their domains of expertise than novices. Hayes (1985) estimates that it takes at least ten years to become an expert in a domain, presumably because it takes that long to accumulate the relevant experience. (Also see Holding, 1985.) This is consistent with a claim we made in Chapter 8: There we argued that expert dermatologists routinely draw on remembered exemplars in reaching their diagnoses; part of their expertise, therefore, lies in having a large set of exemplars on which they can draw. (For further discussion of medical expertise, see Lesgold, Rubinson, Feltovich, Glaser, Klopfer & Wang, 1988.)

Experts also have different types of knowledge than novices do. We have just suggested, for example, that chess masters are particularly conversant with higher order patterns on the chess board, patterns often involving six or seven different pieces. Indeed, the expert may know a huge number of these patterns; it has been estimated that a chess master has roughly 50,000 different chess patterns in memory, compared to the 1,000 patterns known to someone who is merely a "good" player (Chase & Simon, 1973; also Bédard & Chi, 1992). Similar claims have been made for experts in a variety of other domains, including experts in the games of Gō, bridge, and poker (Gilhooly, 1988).

There are also indications that experts organize their knowledge more effectively than novices. In particular, studies indicate that experts' knowledge is heavily "cross-referenced," so that each bit of information has associations to many other bits (e.g., Bédard & Chi, 1992; Eylon & Reif, 1984; Heller & Reif, 1984). As a result, not only do experts know more, but they have faster, more effective access to what they know.

As an example of how this all plays out, consider the strategies chosen by experts when they are solving a problem. Both experts and novices make heavy use of means-end analysis, a strategy we discussed earlier in this chapter. However, in trying to reach their ends, novices often find it useful to work backward from the goal—to seek operators that will gradually make the goal state more and more similar to their current state. In contrast, experts are less likely to use this working-backwards strategy (Bédard & Chi, 1992; Gick, 1986; Larkin, McDermott, Simon & Simon, 1980; Sweller, Mawer & Ward, 1983); instead, they work forwards, from the initial state toward the goal.

One might think that the experts are using a risky strategy: If you start at the initial state and work forward, it is possible that the path you have selected might not lead where you want to go. However, this risk is relatively small for experts: Since they quickly recognize what type of problem they are working on, they realize what type of solution will be appropriate. Therefore, they are essentially guaranteed, as they work forward from their initial state, that they are moving in the right general direction.

Notice that we are suggesting that experts work forward on a problem only because they recognize the type of problem and know how to tackle it. If this is right, then even experts will resort to the working-backwards strategy with *unfamiliar* problems, problems that they cannot categorize. This is correct: When experts don't recognize a problem, they work backward from the goal to their current state, exactly as a novice would (Bhaskar & Simon, 1977; Gick, 1986). Thus, the experts' strategy choice is, in the end, dependent on the experts' knowledge base.

Finally, one other advantage for the experts should also be mentioned: In addition to their advantages in knowledge, experts are also, rather obviously, well-practiced in working in their domain, well-practiced in solving problems. As we discussed in Chapter 3, this allows the expert to "automatize" many tasks. Similarly, the expert has established certain routines for dealing with commonplace tasks or, as some would say, has "proceduralized" these tasks. In many cases, an expert will realize that a problem is functionally identical to problems met earlier, and so give the problem no further thought, relying instead on the well-rehearsed routine. (For discussion, see Anderson, 1982, 1983, 1987.)

Limits of Expertise

There are important limits, however, on the function of (and advantages of) expertise. We have already suggested that a large part of an expert's advantage derives from his or her knowledge base: The expert knows more, and knows more higher order patterns, than the novice does. However, if this knowledge can't be applied to a problem, then much of the expert's advantage will disappear. We've already seen some evidence for this claim: Experts generally work forwards toward their goal, rather than working backwards toward their current state. This contrast between experts and novices disappears, however, if experts fail to recognize a problem, and so fail to apply their base of knowledge.

Similarly, experts show no advantage in solving problems outside their domain. Thus, expert surgeons and psychiatrists show no special skill in solving cardiology problems (Patel, Evans & Groen, 1989). Likewise, in solving political problems, expert chemists do no better than novice political scientists. Both groups, however, are (by far) out-performed by expert political scientists (Voss, Blais, Means, Greene, and Ahwesh, 1989; Voss & Post, 1988).

Finally, we should also note that, in some circumstances, expertise may actually convey disadvantages. Imagine that you want to solve a problem, but also want to remember the problem, later on. If you were an expert in that domain, you would pay little attention to the problem's details, and instead focus on the problem's gist or structure. This would help you in solving the problem, and also in remembering the gist. However, this emphasis on gist will probably undermine your memory for the problem's detail. Consistent with this suggestion, several studies indicate that experts are less able to remember problems' details, and also commit many intrusion errors, as they import their own knowledge into the problem-as-remembered (Arkes & Freedman, 1984; also Adelson, 1984; Bédard & Chi, 1992). *b/c they don't pay attention to details often*

Defining the Problem

One of the features of expertise lies in how experts define a problem: Novices are likely to understand a problem in terms of its superficial features, while experts are likely to understand a problem in terms of its structure or dynamic. As a result, the experts are more likely to realize what other problems are analogous to the current problem and are more likely to benefit from analogies. Apparently, there are better and worse ways to think about a problem—ways that will lead to a solution and ways that will obstruct it. This turns out to be a crucial point, and we need to explore this effect of "problem representation"—an effect, in essence, of how exactly the problem solver defines the problem.

Ill-Defined and Well-Defined Problems

For many problems, the initial state, goal state, and operators are clearly defined from the start. In the Hobbit and Orcs problem, you know exactly where all the creatures stand at the beginning of the problem. You know exactly where you want the creatures to be at the problem's end. And you know exactly what operators you have available.

Many problems—including problems we encounter in our day-to-day lives—are rather different. We all hope for peace in the world, but what exactly will this goal look like? There will be no fighting, of course, but what other traits will the goal have? Will the nations currently on the map still be in place? How will disputes be settled? How will resources be allocated? It is also unclear what the operators should be for reaching this goal. Should we try making diplomatic adjustments? Or would economic measures be more effective—perhaps some pattern of commerce through which nations become more dependent on each other?

Problems like this one are said to be ill-defined, with no clear statement at the outset of how the goal should be characterized or what steps one might try in reaching that goal. Many problems are ill-defined—"having a good time while on vacation," "saving money for college," "choosing a good paper topic" (Halpern, 1984; Kahney, 1986; Reitman, 1964; Simon, 1973).

Problem solvers have several options available, when they confront ill-defined problems. An obvious option is one we have already met: Establish subgoals. For many ill-defined problems, there may be well-defined sub-problems and, by solving each of these, one can move toward solving the overall problem. A different strategy is to add some structure to the problem—by adding extra constraints or extra assumptions. In this way, you might gradually render the problem well-defined, instead of ill-defined—with a narrower set of options perhaps, but with a clearly specified goal state and, eventually, with a manageable set of operators to try.

This adding of structure to an ill-defined problem turns out to be one more way in which expert and novice problem solvers differ: Before they even start working on a problem, experts spend time defining the problem and elaborating its problem states, far more time than novices do (Voss et al., 1983; Voss & Post, 1988; see also Getzels & Csikszentmihalyi, 1976).

Functional Fixedness

Even for well-defined problems, there is often more than one way to understand the problem and more than one way to structure the problem. We have already met an example of this, in the contrast between superficial and deeper level descriptions of a problem. But other examples are easy to find.

Consider the "mutilated checkerboard" problem, described in Figure 13.18. The most obvious treatment of this problem represents it in terms of spatial positions. It doesn't matter how large the board is (as long as the dominoes are sized accordingly), nor does it matter what colors the board is decorated in, nor how much the board weighs. The operators to consider also

Figure 13.18

THE MUTILATED CHECKERBOARD PROBLEM

A checkerboard contains 8 rows and 8 columns, or 64 squares in all. You are given 32 dominoes, and asked to place the dominoes on the checkerboard so that each domino covers two squares. With 64 squares and 32 dominoes, there are actually many arrangements of dominoes that will cover the board.

We now take out a knife, and cut away the top-left and bottom-right squares on the checkerboard. We also remove one of the dominoes. Therefore, you now have 31 dominoes with which to cover the remaining 62 squares on the checkerboard.

Is there an arrangement of the 31 dominoes that will cover the 62 squares? Each domino, as before, must cover two adjacent squares on the checkerboard.

Solving this problem usually requires a change in problem representation. Can you solve it?

involve spatial positions—locating each domino here or there, on route to a solution.

But a rather different representation is possible, one that largely ignores spatial position, and instead focuses on the color of the squares. In this representation, different operators are relevant, different aspects of the problem are highlighted, and different aspects ignored. And it is this representation that leads speedily to the problem's solution. (See Figure 13.19.) Indeed, this particular problem is rarely solved if represented in spatial terms; the same problem is readily solved if represented with an emphasis on which colors

Figure 13.19

SOLUTION TO THE MUTILATED CHECKERBOARD PROBLEM

The squares on a checkerboard obviously have an alternating color scheme, and so the squares might be white–black–white–black (or any other alternating scheme). Therefore, if a domino covers two adjacent squares, it will necessarily cover one white square and one black. Said differently, we need one white square and one black square for each domino and so, more broadly, we need equal numbers of white squares and black squares—one of each, for each domino.

On a "normal" checkerboard, that is easy—there are 32 white squares and 32 black, and so there are enough of each for the 32 dominoes.

Notice, though, that the top-left and bottom-right squares on a checkerboard *are the same color*. Therefore, if we cut away these squares, we no longer have equal numbers of white squares and black—we are left with 32 white squares, and 30 black. Therefore, we can't provide one square of each color for each domino. For the first 30 dominoes, we are fine—for each of these, we have one white square and one black. But, for the thirty-first domino, we are left with two more white squares, in need of cover.

Therefore, the mutilated checkerboard *cannot be covered* by the 31 dominoes!

The initial representation of this problem typically emphasizes spatial positions and various arrangements of the dominoes. The solution shown here, however, largely ignores these factors. Instead, the solution emphasizes the *color* of the checkerboard's squares.

get covered. Obviously, then, how a problem gets represented is of considerable importance—with one representation making the problem difficult, while another representation speeds you toward the problem's solution.

As a different example of this, consider the "candle" problem presented in Figure 13.20. To solve this problem, subjects need to cease thinking of the box as a "container." They need instead to think of it as a potential platform. Solving the problem depends heavily on how the box is represented.

As a way of emphasizing this point, we can compare two groups of subjects: One group is given the "equipment" shown in Figure 13.20—some

Figure 13.20

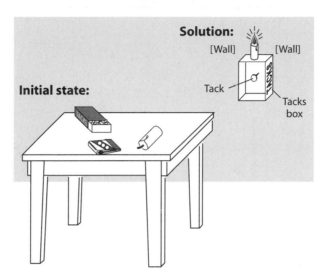

THE CANDLE PROBLEM

You are given the objects shown below—a candle, a book of matches, and a box of tacks. No other objects are available to you. Your task is to find a way to attach the candle to the wall of the room, at eye-level, so that it will burn properly and illuminate the room.

Solution:

[Wall]   [Wall]

Tack

Tacks box

Initial state:

What makes this problem difficult is the tendency to think of the box of tacks *as a box*—i.e., as a container. The problem is readily solved, though, once subjects think of the box as a potential platform.

matches, a box of tacks, and a candle. This configuration (implicitly) underscores the box's conventional function—namely, as a container. As a result, this configuration increases **functional fixedness**—that is, the tendency to be rigid in how one thinks about an object's function. With this fixedness in place, the problem is rarely solved.

If empty box less functional fixedness to use the box as a container

Other subjects are given the same tools, but configured differently. They are given some matches, a pile of tacks, the box (now empty), and a candle. In this setting, subjects are less likely to think of the box as a container for the tacks, and so they are less likely to think of the box *as a container*. And, in this setting, subjects are more likely to solve the problem (Duncker, 1945; also Adamson, 1952; Glucksberg & Danks, 1968; Weisberg & Suls, 1973).

Functional fixedness is also evident in studies of the "two string" problem (Figure 13.21). Few subjects solve this problem, presumably because they are thinking of the pliers as a tool for grabbing and holding. In this situation,

Figure 13.21

THE TWO STRING PROBLEM

You enter a room in which two strings are hanging from the ceiling. Your task is to tie the two strings together. Unfortunately, though, the strings are positioned far enough apart so that you can't grab one string and hold onto it while reaching for the other. How can you tie them together?

To solve the problem, you should tie the pliers to one string, then push them gently *away* from the other string. Then grab the *second* string, and wait until the pliers, as a pendulum, swing back to you. [After Maier, 1931.]

though, the pliers play a much simpler role, serving only as a *weight*, and subjects will realize this only if they ignore the pliers' customary function. And, once again, we can make this problem even more difficult if we take steps to emphasize the pliers' standard function—if, for example, we use the pliers to pull a tack out of the table-top, while instructing the subject in the overall task. Under these circumstances, fixedness is maximal, and virtually no subjects solve the problem.

"Einstellung" -have to have a switch in training / problem type

In the cases just described, subjects represent a problem in a fashion that emphasizes a particular function for some crucial object—a representation that emphasizes the "pulling" function of pliers, or the "containing" function of a box. If we can change that representation, subjects immediately benefit—

that is, they are able to solve the problem. Changing this representation, though, turns out not to be easy, and subjects instead display a counterproductive rigidity, a rigidity we referred to as functional fixedness.

Subjects also display other forms of rigidity in problem solving, and this rigidity in general is referred to as *Einstellung*, the German word for "attitude." The idea is that, in solving a problem, subjects develop a certain attitude or perspective and then approach all subsequent problems with the same rigid attitude. Functional fixedness provides one example of an *Einstellung* effect, but the classic demonstration of this effect employs the so-called water-jar problem. You are initially given three jars, A, which holds 18 ounces; B, which holds 43 ounces; and C, which holds 10 ounces. You have access to an unlimited supply of water. You also have a large, uncalibrated bucket. Your task is to pour exactly 5 ounces of water into the bucket. How would you do it?

The solution is to fill jar B (43 ounces), then to pour water from jar B into jar A (which holds 18). Twenty-five ounces now remain in B. Now, from this, fill jar C (which holds 10 ounces); 15 ounces now remain in B. Dump jar C, then fill it again from B. Now, 5 ounces remain in jar B, so you are done.

Once subjects have solved this problem, we give them a new problem. Jar A now holds 9 ounces, B holds 42, and C holds 6. The goal is to end up with 21 ounces. We then give subjects a third problem: Jar A holds 21; B holds 127; C holds 3; you are seeking 100 ounces.

The series of problems is carefully designed, such that all can be solved in the same way: One starts by filling the largest jar (B), pouring from it once into the middle-sized jar (A), then pouring from it twice into the smallest jar (C), leaving the desired amount.

After solving four problems of this form, subjects are given one more problem: Jar A holds 18 ounces; Jar B holds 48 ounces; Jar C holds 4 ounces; the goal is 22 ounces. Subjects solve this problem the same way they have solved the previous problems. Subjects fail to see that a different, more direct route to the goal is possible—by filling A, filling C, and then combining these (18 + 4). Their prior success in using the same procedure over and over renders them blind to this alternative.

More troubling, consider what happens if subjects are given the "training" problems, all solved via the same path, and then are given this problem: Jar A holds 28 ounces; B holds 76; C holds 3. The goal is 25 ounces. Subjects attack this problem by using their tried-and-true method: B minus A minus C twice. But this time the method fails (yielding 42 ounces, instead of the desired 25). When subjects realize this, they are often stymied—their well-practiced routine won't work here, and they fail to see the much simpler path that would work (28 minus 3 equals 25). Remarkably, 64% of the subjects fail to solve this problem, thanks to their history of using a now inapplicable strategy (Luchins, 1942; Luchins & Luchins, 1950, 1959).

In a sense, subjects are doing something sensible here: Once you discover a strategy that "gets the job done," you might as well use the strategy. Correspondingly, once you discover a strategy that works, there is little reason to continue hunting for other, alternative strategies. It is a little unsettling, though, that this mechanization of problem solving prevents subjects from discovering other, simpler strategies. Worse, this mechanization actually interferes with subjects' problem solving: Once they have learned one strategy for solving water-jar problems, they seem less able to discover new strategies. When a new problem arrives that is *not* solvable with the prior formula, performance suffers. (For a related phenomenon, see Schwartz, 1982.)

Problem-Solving Set — happens before you start · what you go in w̄

In the water-jar experiments, subjects develop a strategy within the experiment itself, and then continue applying that strategy in a rigid, mechanical fashion. In other cases, though, subjects seem to approach a problem *from the start* with certain assumptions—about how the problem should be handled and what sorts of strategy are likely to be productive. These starting assumptions are referred to as a problem-solving set. Often, this "set" is quite helpful and gets subjects started on the right path toward solving the problem. If the set turns out to be inappropriate, though, problem solving suffers.

An often-quoted example of problem-solving set involves the nine-dot problem, illustrated in Figure 13.22. In tackling this problem, subjects seem to assume that the lines they draw must remain within the "square" formed by the nine dots. This assumption isn't stated anywhere in the problem; instead, it is supplied by the subjects. As it turns out, though, this assumption is *wrong*: To solve this problem, your lines must go *outside* this square (Figure 13.23). It is not surprising, then, that subjects find this problem quite hard.

Problem-solving sets are often characterized as bad things, blocking the solution of a problem. Indeed, in the nine-dot problem, subjects do seem misled by their initial set. Likewise, functional fixedness can also be counted as a species of problem-solving set and, as we have seen, fixedness often impedes problem solution. These points must be balanced, though, with an equal emphasis on the *benefits* of a problem-solving set. In confronting an ill-defined problem, you often need to add some structure. If you add an appropriate structure, this will help problem solving enormously. "Adding structure" is, of course, equivalent to approaching the problem with a particular set.

Even with well-defined problems, the number of options you might consider as you work your way toward a solution is often quite large. In the terms

Figure 13.22

THE NINE DOT PROBLEM

Draw four straight lines, passing through all nine of these dots, without lifting your pencil from the page.

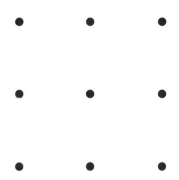

Most subjects have difficulty with this problem, probably because of an inappropriate problem-solving set.

Figure 13.23

SOLUTION TO THE NINE DOT PROBLEM

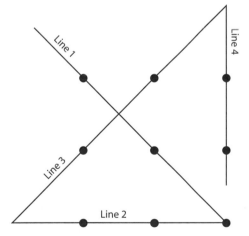

In solving the nine-dot problem, subjects seem to assume that their dots must remain inside the "square" formed by the dots. However, the solution requires lines outside of this square.

used earlier, a problem-solving space can be enormous, involving many thousands of options. A problem-solving set, therefore, serves to narrow your options, which, in turn, eases your search for a solution. For example, in solving the "candle problem" (Figure 13.20), you didn't waste any time wondering whether Martians might be summoned to hold the candle in place. You also didn't waste time trying to think of ways to melt the thumbtacks, in order to transform them into a candelabra. These are obviously silly options, so you brushed past them. But what identifies them as silly? It is your problem-solving set, which tells you, among other things, what options are plausible, which are physically possible, and the like.

In sum, there are benefits and costs to a problem-solving set. A set can blind you to important options, and thus can, in some cases, be an enormous obstacle to problem solution. But a set also blinds you to a wide range of futile or impractical options, and this is a good thing: It allows you to focus, much more productively, on options likely to work out. Therefore, the key is not to approach a problem without a set. Instead, all depends on finding the right set.

Creativity

Our argument so far can be easily summarized: For ill-defined problems, one often needs to make assumptions and to add constraints; otherwise, there are too many options to think through. Even for well-defined problems, there are often many ways to represent the problem, with some representations leading swiftly to a solution, while others render the problem quite difficult. Moreover, if one selects the wrong representation, it is often hard to "shift gears," thanks to phenomena like fixedness or *Einstellung*.

Briefly put, it seems that approaching a problem with the *right* set—the right assumptions, the right representation—helps us in important ways. How, then, does one find an appropriate problem-solving set? How does one figure out how to approach a problem?

Brainstorming

We have already noted that a problem's *solution* can, in many cases, be suggested by an analogy to a previously solved problem. In the same fashion, a *set* can also be suggested by analogy: If the current problem reminds you of a previously solved case, you are likely to adopt the same set that worked previously: You will make the same assumptions, you will try the same operations, as you did on the prior occasion.

What if no analogy comes to mind? In this case, you will be forced to use some less insightful, more laborious strategy—perhaps trial and error, or hill-climbing, or working backwards from the problem's solution.

What if you are already working on the problem and making no headway? Given our discussion so far, it seems plausible that you are being stymied by an inappropriate set. To help yourself along, therefore, you could try "relaxing" this set—you could try to be as open-minded as possible about how the problem might be approached. This will often help, for reasons that are quite straightforward: If you try being more open-minded, you might, by luck, stumble across a more productive approach to the problem. Likewise, if you continue rummaging through memory, seeking some alternative approach, you might well come across a useful analogue that you hadn't spotted before.

Our suggestion, then, is that "relaxing" your set, and "letting the ideas flow," simply leads to more ideas, more options to be considered. This will, in turn, often suggest a new approach. Some authors, however, have suggested a more ambitious conception of what happens when you "let the ideas flow." In particular, some have argued that the ideas produced under these free-flowing circumstances will be *better* ideas, more creative ideas, than those produced with more deliberate, careful cogitation.

Relevant evidence comes from studies of **brainstorming**. This is a technique, pioneered by Osborn (1957), in which one really does try to "let the ideas flow." In brainstorming sessions, one tries to generate as many ideas, and as many new approaches, as possible. Criticism of these ideas is deliberately put on hold, to make sure the ideas are generated in a free, uninhibited fashion. Later, one can separate the wheat from the chaff.

A number of researchers have examined the output of "brainstorming sessions" and, while some of the evidence is encouraging, most is not. The uninhibited atmosphere of brainstorming does indeed increase the number of ideas generated, and often that is just what one needs. For these purposes, then, brainstorming is a good strategy. However, there is no evidence that brainstorming increases the *quality* of ideas being produced. (For reviews, see Baron, 1988; Gilhooly, 1988; Weisberg, 1986; for a more positive assessment of brainstorming, though, see Flower, 1980; Stein, 1975.)

A similar point emerges from a study by Weisberg and Alba (1981). They asked their subjects to solve several problems, including the nine-dot problem (Figure 13.22). To help subjects along, Weisberg and Alba provided a hint: They told subjects directly that the solution required lines outside of the square.

One might think that this hint will "free up" subjects' thinking, so that new ideas (including the solution) can flow forth. However, even with the hint, 80% of the subjects still failed to solve the problem in the time allowed. It should be said that the hint did help, since, without it, *no* subjects solved the problem. <u>Nonetheless</u>, the benefit of the hint was clearly modest, suggesting, once again, that <u>"letting the ideas flow" provides no special path to problem solution.</u> (Also see Dominowski, 1981; Weisberg & Alba, 1982.)

Measures of Creativity

Brainstorming seems not to unleash a flood of creative ideas. Instead, brainstorming seems to involve memory search, the use of analogies, and perhaps the use of a greater range of heuristics. This helps, but there is nothing mysterious about it.

Surely, though, there is more to problem solving than this. What about cases of *insight*, or cases in which one suddenly finds a new and creative way

Figure 13.24

CREATIVITY AS "DIVERGENT THINKING"

Tests of divergent thinking require you to think of new uses for simple objects, or new ways to think about familiar ideas.

How many different uses can you think of for a *brick*?
As a paperweight.
As the shadow-caster in a sun dial (if positioned appropriately).
As a means of writing messages on a sidewalk.
As a step-ladder (if you want to grab something just slightly out of reach).
As a nut-cracker.
As a pendulum useful for solving the two string problem.

Choose five names, at random, from the telephone directory. In how many different ways could these names be classified?
According to the number of syllables.
According to whether there is an even or odd number of vowels.
According to whether their third letter is in the last third of the alphabet.
According to whether they rhyme with things that are edible.

Guilford argued that creativity lies in the ability to take an idea in a new, unprecedented direction. Among its other items, his *test* of creativity asks subjects to think of new uses for a familiar object. Some possible responses are listed here.

to approach a problem? These don't seem like cases of searching-through-memory for an analogy or cases based on heuristic use. What, then, can we say about these cases?

To tackle these questions, we first need to be more specific about what insight and creativity are. Psychologists generally define a creative discovery as one that is novel, and also valuable or useful. Let's be clear, though, that this definition is still in need of explication: How do we decide, for example, if a discovery or a work of art is "valuable"? In the world of music, for instance, many new pieces have been reviled when they first premiered; years later, though, these pieces have been reevaluated and judged to be master-pieces. In these cases, we would first judge the piece of music not to be valuable and, therefore, the composition of this music not to be creative. Later on, both of these decisions would be reversed. (For discussion, see Baron, 1988; Gilhooly, 1988; Hennessey & Amabile, 1988; Murray, 1959; Perkins, 1981; Stein, 1956.)

Even with these concerns, this rough definition of creativity has allowed research to proceed. Indeed, psychologists have sought not only to define creativity, but to *measure* it. For example, Guilford (1967, 1979) argued that the heart of creativity lies in discovering new, unanticipated approaches to a problem. Therefore, he sought directly to measure someone's effectiveness in this sort of "divergent thinking"—i.e., her ability to take an idea in a new, unprecedented direction. In his test of creativity, therefore, one is asked to think of new uses for a familiar object. How many different uses can you think of for a brick? (See Figure 13.24 for some suggestions.)

A different approach was suggested by Mednick (1962; Mednick & Mednick, 1967), who proposed that creativity often depends on finding new *connections* among ideas. His measure of creativity is designed to evaluate how readily a person finds these connections. The Remote Associates Test (or RAT) provides trios of words; your task is to find some fourth word that "belongs" with each of the three. A test item might be "snow, down, out." A good solution would be "fall" (as in "snowfall, downfall, and fallout"). Other test items are shown in Figure 13.25.

Both of these measures have received some validation. For example, individuals judged to be creative by their coworkers score somewhat higher on tests of divergent thinking (Guilford, 1967). Likewise, graduate students who score highly on the RAT are more likely to be judged creative by their advisors (Mednick & Mednick, 1967). These correlations are weak, however, so neither of these tests seems that effective at predicting creativity. Nonetheless, the correlations do suggest that these tests tap into at least some aspect of creativity. (For discussion, see Andrews, 1975; Nickerson, Perkins & Smith, 1985; Wallach, 1976. Sternberg & Lubart, 1992, offer a somewhat different approach to the study of individual differences in creativity.)

Figure 13.25

CREATIVITY AS THE ABILITY TO FIND NEW CONNECTIONS

For each trio of words, think of a fourth word that is related to each of the first three. For example, for the trio "snow, down, out," the answer would be "fall." (Snowfall; downfall; fallout.)

1. off   top   tail
2. ache   sweet   burn
3. dark   shot   sun
4. arm   coal   peach
5. tug   gravy   show

Mednick argued that creativity lies in the ability to find new connections among ideas. This ability is measured in the Remote Associates Test, for which some sample items are shown here. The solutions are: (1) spin (spin-off, top-spin, tail-spin); (2) heart; (3) glasses; (4) pit; (5) boat.

Case Studies of Creativity

A great deal of what we know about creativity comes from case studies of enormously creative individuals, with the evidence often coming from the individuals themselves. The poet Samuel Taylor Coleridge, for example, described in some detail how his poems came to be; the mathematician Poincaré wrote about how he discovered the proofs to certain theorems; Tchaikovsky wrote about his experiences in composing music; Crick and Watson have written a great deal about how they discovered the structure of DNA. (Many of these accounts are in Baron, 1988; Gilhooly, 1988; Weisberg, 1986.)

We need to be cautious, though, in interpreting these case studies. For one concern, these reports were often recorded years after the creative event, raising questions about whether the event was remembered correctly. (See, for example, Schunn & Dunbar, in press.) In addition, one might worry about some degree of self-service, as individuals seek to portray themselves (and their discoveries) in the most favorable light. Finally, it seems likely that creative discoveries often rely on nonverbal thoughts, and this raises questions about whether the discoveries can be adequately represented via verbal reports—even if the reporter is sincere and remembering accurately. (For further discussion of the limits of self-report, see Chapters 1 and 14.)

Even with these cautions in view, several researchers have argued that there is a systematic pattern to these self-reports. The classic formulation of this pattern comes from Wallas (1926), who argued that creative thought proceeds through four stages. In the first stage, **preparation**, the problem solver gathers information about the problem. This stage is typically characterized by periods of effortful, often frustrating, work on the problem, generally with little progress. In the second stage, **incubation**, the problem solver sets the problem to the side and seems not to be working on it. Wallas argued, though, that the problem solver was continuing to work on the problem during this stage, albeit unconsciously. Thus, the problem solution is continuing to develop, unseen, just as the baby bird develops, unseen, inside the egg. This period of incubation leads to the third stage, **illumination**, in which some key insight or new idea emerges, paving the way for the fourth stage, verification, in which one confirms that the new idea really does lead to a problem solution, and works out the details.

This view of creativity has been endorsed by some authors but has been roundly criticized by others. For example, Patrick (1935, 1937) asked subjects to think aloud as they worked on a piece of poetry; her data largely conform with the four-stage view. (Also see Ghiselin, 1952; Harding, 1940.) In contrast, Weisberg (1986) argues that the data, including the historical accounts, do *not* fit with Wallas's formulation. Many of these accounts, he argues, do not include all four stages. In other cases, the four stages do occur, but in a complex, back-and-forth sequence. In still other cases, Weisberg suggests, the self-reports fit with Wallas's view, but there is reason to believe the self-reports are false. It is therefore of no interest that these *fictions* happen to conform to Wallas's scheme. (For further skepticism about Wallas's claims, see Baron, 1988; Weber & Dixon, 1989.)

The "Moment of Illumination"

It seems clear, then, that the case studies of creativity are at best ambiguous, and this has led researchers to seek more persuasive evidence concerning creativity. Can we, for example, study creativity in a well-documented, well-controlled laboratory setting?

Consider Wallas's third stage, illumination. Illumination typically signals a new *approach* to a problem, rather than a *solution* and so, at the moment of illumination, the problem is not yet solved, and there is still work to be done. Nonetheless, illumination generally arrives with the conviction that—at last—you are on the right track. Is this correct? Even before solving a problem, can you detect when you are nearing the solution?

Metcalfe (1986; Metcalfe & Weibe, 1987) gave her subjects a series of "insight problems," like those shown in Figure 13.26. As subjects worked on each problem, they rated their progress, using a judgment of "warmth." ("I'm getting warmer . . . I'm getting warmer. . . .") These ratings did capture the

Figure 13.26

STUDIES OF "INSIGHT PROBLEMS"

PROBLEM 1

A stranger approached a museum curator and offered him an ancient bronze coin. The coin had an authentic appearance and was marked with the date 544 B.C. The curator had happily made acquisitions from suspicious sources before, but this time he promptly called the police and had the stranger arrested. Why?

PROBLEM 2

A landscape gardener is given instructions to plant four special trees so that each one is exactly the same distance from each of the others. How could the trees be arranged?

As subjects worked on these problems, they were asked to judge their progress, using an assessment of "warmth" ("I'm getting warmer ... I'm getting warmer ... I'm getting hot!"). For the first problem, realize that no one in the year 544 B.C. realized that it was 544 B.C.—that is, no one could have known that Christ would be born exactly 544 years later. For the second problem, the gardener needs to plant one of the trees at the top of a hill, and then plant the other three at the base of the hill, with the three together forming an equilateral triangle, and with the four forming a triangle-based pyramid (i.e., a tetrahedron).

"moment of insight": Initially, subjects didn't have a clue how to proceed and gave "warmth ratings" of "1" or "2". Then, rather abruptly, subjects saw how to solve the problem and, at that instant, their "warmth ratings" shot up to the top of the scale.

To understand this pattern, though, we need to look separately at those subjects who subsequently announced the *correct* solution to the problem, and those who announced an *incorrect* solution. As you can see in Figure 13.27, the pattern is the same for these two groups. Thus, some subjects announce that they are getting "hot," and moments later solve the problem. Other subjects make the same announcement, and moments later slam into a dead end. Indeed, if there is any difference at all between these two groups, it appears that the subjects who are on the *wrong* track are more confident in their progress than subjects who are on the right track.

There seems to be nothing magical about the "moment of illumination," nothing special about the "Aha!" experience. Sometimes we say "Aha!" when we finally perceive the right path. Just as often, though, and just as fervently, we say "Aha!" when we discover an apparently promising dead end.

Figure 13.27

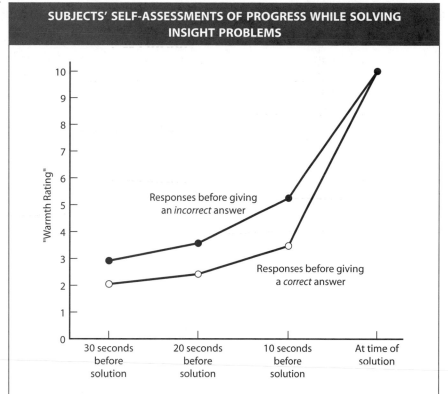

SUBJECTS' SELF-ASSESSMENTS OF PROGRESS WHILE SOLVING INSIGHT PROBLEMS

Initially, subjects had little idea about how to proceed with these problems, and gave very low "warmth" ratings. Then, abruptly, they saw how to solve the problem and, at that moment, their "warmth ratings" shot up to the top of the scale. Importantly, though, the same pattern was observed for subjects who then announced a *correct* solution to the problem *and* for subjects who then announced an *incorrect* solution. Thus, it seems that subjects really *can't tell* when they are on the verge of correctly solving a problem. Sometimes, they shout "Aha!" only to slam into a dead end a moment later.

Incubation

What about Wallas's second stage, the stage of "incubation?" In this stage, you will recall, subjects seem to set the problem aside, but (allegedly) they continue to work on it unconsciously and, as a result, make considerable progress.

Many people find this an appealing idea, since most of us have had an experience along these lines: You are working on a problem, but getting no-where. After a while, you give up and turn your thoughts to other matters.

Some time later, though, you try the problem again and are able to solve it. Or perhaps, later on, you are thinking about something altogether different, when the solution suddenly "pops" into your thoughts.

Many examples of this pattern have been recorded, with a number of authors pointing out that great scientific discoveries have often been made in this manner (e.g., Kohler, 1969). As a more modest example, consider the tip-of-the-tongue (TOT) phenomenon, which we described in Chapter 7. In this phenomenon, you are struggling to think of a specific word, but can't. Often, your best strategy is to give up and try again later. When you do, there is a reasonable likelihood that the word will come to you.

Let's be careful, though, in how we interpret these observations. After you "give up" on finding the word, are you unconsciously continuing to search for it? If so, then your subsequent discovery is presumably the fruit of this unconscious work. But here is a different way to think about the facts: Notice that, when you return to a problem, you are, quite simply, devoting more time to it: First you worked on the problem for 5 minutes, then you set the problem aside for an hour, and then you worked on the problem for another five minutes, and solved it. Did your hour's break help you? Perhaps the problem simply required ten minutes of work. In that case, you would have solved it in the second try, with or without the break.

This hypothesis is easy to test: We can allow one group of subjects to work on a problem for ten minutes. A second group is allowed to work on the same problem for five minutes, then they are interrupted and forced to work on something else for a while. Then, this second group is allowed to return to the initial problem, for another five minutes. Thus, in the end, both groups have worked on the problem for ten minutes. If, in addition, time away from the problem allows incubation, then subjects in the second group should benefit from the interruption, and should be more likely to solve the problem than subjects given no time away (and hence no opportunity for incubation).

Many studies, designed in this way, have been carried out, and the results are, at best, mixed. A few studies have shown improved problem solving after an interruption, consistent with the incubation claim. A larger number of studies, however, have shown no such advantage. (See, among others, Dominowski & Jenrick, 1972; Fulgosi & Guilford, 1968; Goldman, Wolters & Winograd, 1992; Murray & Denny, 1969; Olton, 1979; Olton & Johnson, 1976; Peterson, 1974.) As a consequence, many researchers are skeptical about the claim that incubation fosters problem solution.

Let's focus, though, on just those studies that do show a benefit of time away from the problem, that *do* show that an interruption promotes problem solving. How should we interpret these findings? Wallas's explanation, of course, is that the interruption allows unconscious problem-solving activity.

Others, however, offer more prosaic hypotheses. In some studies, the interruption may simply provide an opportunity for subjects to gather new information. Perhaps, during the time away from the problem, they stumble across some clue in the environment, or in their own memories, that will help them when they return to the problem. In this case, time away will aid problem solution, but not because of any unconscious work on the problem.

Figure 13.28

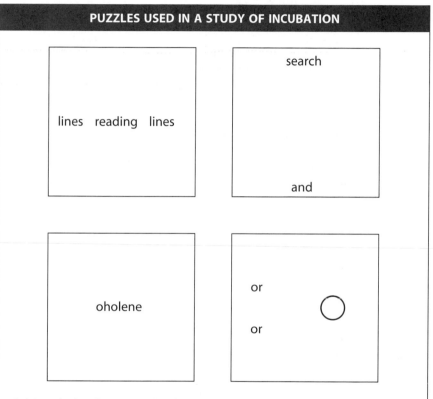

PUZZLES USED IN A STUDY OF INCUBATION

Subjects had to figure out what familiar phrase was represented by each picture. For example, the first picture represents the phrase "reading between the lines"; the second represents the phrase "search high and low"; the third represents "a hole in one"; the fourth represents "double or nothing." For some stimuli, these pictures were accompanied by helpful clues (for example, the last picture might be accompanied by the word "nothing"). For other stimuli, the clues were *misleading* (e.g., the third picture might be accompanied by the clue "chemical"). Time away from these puzzles, however, allowed subjects to *forget* the misleading cues and, as a result, they were no longer misled by the clues, and were more likely to solve the puzzles. [After Smith & Blakenship, 1989, 1991.]

In other cases, the interruption may simply allow problem solvers a "fresh start" on a problem. Subjects' early efforts with a problem may be tiring, or frustrating, and the interruption may provide an opportunity for this frustration or fatigue to dissipate. Likewise, your early efforts with a problem may be dominated by a particular approach, a particular set. If you put the problem aside for a while, it is possible for you to forget these earlier tactics, and this will then free you to explore other, more productive, avenues.

There is some evidence for this "forgetting" account of incubation. Smith and Blankenship (1989, 1991) gave their subjects puzzles to solve like those shown in Figure 13.28. To make these problems even more difficult, clues were given but, for many of the problems, the clues were designed to be misleading. Control subjects had a minute to work on each puzzle; other subjects worked on each puzzle for 30 seconds, then were interrupted, and later returned to the puzzle for an additional 30 seconds.

This interruption did improve performance, so that problem solution was more likely for the "incubation" group. Crucially, though, Smith and Blakenship also tested subjects' memory for the misleading clues, and found that the incubation subjects were less likely to remember the clues. Smith and Blakenship argue that this forgetting is what created the "incubation" advantage: After the interruption, subjects were no longer misled by the bad clues, and their performance improved accordingly.

Let's emphasize, though, that it is *not* the problem itself that subjects forget; instead, they forget their own *strategies*, and their unproductive lines of attack on the problem. Indeed, evidence suggests we are quite likely to remember problems we have not yet solved—more likely, in fact, than we are to remember problems we *have* solved. (For classic data, see Zeigarnik, 1927; for more recent findings, see Patalano & Seifert, 1994.) This memory pattern may actually contribute to the romance that surrounds incubation: We are particularly likely to recall unsolved problems, and therefore we are likely to return regularly to these problems, trying them again and again. As a consequence, we are likely, sooner or later, to discover the solution. But this doesn't speak to the utility of incubation. Instead, it testifies to the value of repeated efforts, and repeated tries, in tackling any difficult task.

The Nature of Creativity

One stands in awe of creative geniuses like DaVinci, Einstein, or Mozart. So remarkable are their accomplishments, so different from what you and I produce, that it is natural to assume their thought processes are no less distinctive. You and I, equipped with heuristics and analogies, have troubles enough with Hobbits and Orcs. It seems unlikely, therefore, that these same intellectual tools could have led to the creativity obvious in great works of art, great innovations of science, or great inventions. The presumption, then, is that this creativity must arise from some other source—some different form of thinking, some other approach to problem solving.

Of course, we have not studied DaVinci or Mozart in the laboratory, nor have we asked subjects to create great art or great inventions. Nonetheless, one might hope that the laboratory data would provide some hint of this "special" form of thinking, this "other" approach to problem solving. What the data show, though, is much more mundane. On the positive side, we have seen that brainstorming—a technique alleged to promote creative thinking—does lead to new ideas. There is little evidence, though, that brainstorming leads to *better* or more *creative* ideas, compared to other, more careful, forms of thought.

Likewise, it is clear that subjects do sometimes experience a sense of "illumination" when working on a problem, as though they have suddenly achieved some deep insight into the problem. When closely examined, though, we find that there is nothing magical about this "moment of illumination." This experience seems to occur when subjects discover a new line of attack on the problem. In essence, subjects realize that they now have new things to try, new approaches to explore. However, with this experience comes no guarantee of subsequent success. In many cases, subjects stumble onto a new approach, and shout "Aha!" only to discover that the new approach leads them no closer to their goal.

Similarly, the topic of incubation has fascinated many authors, and much has been written about the role of incubation within the creative process. However, the evidence for incubation is uneven: It is unclear whether time off from a problem provides any consistent benefit, in contrast to continued effort on the same problem. Even when an "incubation" effect is observed, the mechanisms behind the effect are unclear. There is no persuasive evidence for an unconscious process of problem solving. Instead, incubation seems best explained in terms of dissipation of fatigue, opportunity for discovering new clues, forgetting of previous false starts, and the like.

Finally, we have seen that subjects in the laboratory do, sometimes, produce ideas that seem genuinely creative—consider the hip exerciser, in Figure 13.7. However, there is every reason to believe that these creative ideas are the product of processes similar to the ones already discussed—heuristics, analogies, and the like. (For discussion, see Finke, 1990; Finke, Ward & Smith, 1992.) For the matter, there is some indication that creativity *outside* of the lab can also be understood in these terms. (Cf. Gruber, 1989; McGuire, 1989; Simonton, 1989; Weber, 1993.)

Given all these results, is it possible that there is nothing "special" about the mental processes underlying creativity? To be sure, the creative *product* is extraordinary, but could it be that this product is the result of the same processes, the same forms of thinking, as more "ordinary" thought? Several authors have endorsed this idea, arguing that we need no special mental mechanisms to explain creativity. (See, for example, Langley & Jones, 1988; Perkins, 1981; Sternberg, 1988; Weisberg, 1986, 1988.) The "ingredients" of creativity are available to all of us—or, perhaps, *would* be available, if we acquired expertise in the relevant domain.

What, then, is so special about Newton, or Picasso, or Bach? We are suggesting that it is *not* the case that these individuals had some special intellectual tools, or some unusual thought process, that led them to their towering greatness. Instead, these individuals simply had *all* the relevant ingredients—the heuristics, the expertise, the strategies, plenty of motivation and, it would seem, a personality of just the right sort (cf. Sternberg & Lubart, 1992). It is this extraordinary convergence of ordinary elements that may, perhaps, be the recipe for their astonishing creative prowess.

Is this the final word on creativity? Probably not. It does look like there is less to incubation, illumination, and brainstorming than first meets the eye. Nonetheless, a number of concerns remain. For one, it is certainly possible that we have not yet figured out how to study creativity in the laboratory. Perhaps something in the studies we have reviewed discourages creativity. In that case, creativity, no matter what its nature, might not appear in the data. Likewise, perhaps we haven't been studying the right subjects. Yes, creative inventions have been produced in the lab but, as we acknowledged, Darwin has not participated in our laboratory studies, nor has Beethoven. If we have uncovered no extraordinary "creative process," perhaps that is because we have not yet studied "true creativity" in the laboratory.

Yet another concern lies in what still remains *unsaid* about creativity. We have suggested that creative problem solutions (just like problem solutions in general) rely on memory search, as we seek out related problems or relevant principles. But how exactly does this memory search proceed? Is it possible that this memory search involves a different dynamic for creative discoveries? These are important questions; until they are adequately addressed, we must remain open-minded about what creativity involves and what creativity is. For the moment, creativity appears to involve no special or magical processes. Quite plainly, though, the final word on creativity has not yet been written. (For further discussion of these themes, see Baer, 1993; Baron, 1988; Boden, 1991, 1994; Holyoak & Thagard, 1989; Koestler, 1964; Langley & Jones, 1988; Langley, Simon, Bradshaw & Zytkow, 1987; Mednick, 1962.)

14

Conscious Thought, Unconscious Thought

I t was only a century ago that the field of psychology emerged as a separate discipline, distinct from philosophy or biology. And in those early years of our field, the topic of *consciousness* was a central concern: In Wilhelm Wundt's laboratory, in Germany, researchers sought to understand the "elements" of consciousness. William James, in America, sought to understand the "stream of consciousness."

However, in its eagerness to be objective and scientific, the young field of psychology soon rejected this focus on consciousness, arguing that this research was both subjective and unscientific. By the early twentieth century, the topic of consciousness was largely gone from psychological research, and little was written on the topic for the next half-century. As we have seen in the previous chapters, though, psychologists have now realized that we *can* do scientific research on this topic, and so the field is, once again, ready to explore the issue of consciousness.

There is certainly much about consciousness that we still do not understand. What exactly is consciousness? How is it possible for a biological mechanism, namely the human brain, to be conscious at all? How is it possible for this mass of living tissue to be aware of itself, to be able to reflect on its own state and its own situation, to be able to feel such things as pain and love and gladness and remorse? Are other organisms conscious? Could machines (perhaps complex computers) be conscious? These questions remain the subject of debate and, generally speaking, philosophers have more to say about them than psychologists do. (For a survey of these philosophical discussions, see Churchland, 1988; Dennett, 1992; Flanagan, 1991. For other perspectives, see Crick, 1994; Greenwald, 1992; Jackendoff, 1987; Kihlstrom, 1987; Marcel & Bisiach, 1988; Reber, 1993.)

Psychological research has, however, illuminated several important issues about consciousness, and these will be our focus in this final chapter. Ironically, much of our progress has come, not from examining consciousness directly, but by studying what happens in the *absence* of conscious awareness. By detailing what can be done *without* consciousness, we can refine our understanding of when consciousness is needed and, correspondingly, our understanding of just what it is that consciousness contributes to our functioning. This understanding of what consciousness is *for* can in turn illuminate questions about what consciousness *is*.

As it turns out, much of the information we need for this discussion is already out in view—presented and discussed in previous chapters. Therefore, in this final chapter, we will draw repeatedly on topics covered earlier in this book. By weaving these strands together, we will see that we already have a great deal to say about the topic of consciousness.

Introspection

In the last three chapters, we have been discussing the nature of thought—how we think when we make a judgment; how we think when we reason; how we think when we solve problems. One might expect that research in this domain would be rather easy: Surely each of us is aware of our own thoughts, and this might be an arena in which we could plausibly rely on introspection as a research tool. We could ask subjects to look within themselves, and in this fashion we could effortlessly discover what the subjects were thinking, how the thought was expressed and, ultimately, how thinking proceeds.

Of course, we argued, in the very first chapter of this book, that introspection is limited in important ways, either as a means of conducting scientific inquiry or as a means of knowing ourselves. Let's spend a moment, though, in reexamining those limitations: It is probably no surprise that we can't introspect about the processes of pattern recognition or the microprocesses of memory search. But is it truly the case that we can't introspect about our own thoughts?

The Limits of Introspection

Let's start by quickly cataloguing the limits on introspection. As one broad concern, we often need to worry about the *sincerity* of introspective self-report. This point came up in our discussion of creativity (Chapter 13), but the point is actually a broad one. In many cases, the nature of our thought is personal, or somehow embarrassing, and so we might be tempted to "clean up" our introspection before giving it a voice. This obviously compromises introspection as a source of data.

In addition, self-report data are generally based on memory, and this invites questions about the accuracy of this memory. If the introspection is concerned with a distant event, then we might worry about schema effects or intrusion errors (see Chapter 6; for discussion of schema-based errors in remembering the self, see Ross, 1989). Even if the introspection concerns a recent event, accurate memory is not guaranteed. This kind of recollection draws on working memory and, as we saw in Chapter 4, working memory is quite fragile. The contents of this memory can be displaced by any newly arriving thought, and this will undermine your ability to introspect about these displaced and therefore forgotten ideas.

In addition, much of our thought may turn out, in important ways, not to be "introspectable." As one problem, thinking often proceeds very quickly, and so is over before we know it. Consider the scanning of a mental image

(Chapter 10). This scanning plays an important role in the inspection of, and use of, mental images, but this scanning is simply too quick for introspection: When looking within, you can not discern whether you scan your image at a constant rate, or at an accelerating pace, or what. As a result, introspection tells us little about this event.

What about longer, slower paced mental events? Even for these, introspection is often of limited worth. A great deal of our thought is *nonverbal* in its content (again, see Chapter 10). Therefore, if asked to report on our thoughts, we must first "translate" these thoughts into words. This introduces a risk: Our verbal description might not capture the essence of our experience, and so the "translation" may give a distorted impression of our thoughts. Imagine someone who has never tasted chocolate; could you describe the taste of chocolate for them? Imagine what goes through your mind when you design a picture you are about to draw. Could these processes be fully captured in words?

Even if words are available, there is still no guarantee that different people will use the words in the same way in describing their thoughts. We first met this problem in Chapter 1, and then again in Chapter 10: You might have an experience you call a "vivid image," and so might I. But how could we find out whether your "vivid image" is comparable to mine? Perhaps your image is quite impoverished, relative to mine; it only *seems* vivid to you because you have never had a truly vivid image. Hence, my "vivid image" might, in fact, be vastly more detailed than your "vivid image" but, with no way for you to experience my image, or I yours, there is no way we could discover this contrast. Concerns like these have been a major obstacle to the study of imagery vividness, but the concern also applies to self-report in many other domains.

How deep are these problems about self-report? Many researchers have argued that, despite these concerns, self-report can provide a valuable source of data—although, to be sure, data to be handled with caution, data to be checked against other measures. (For advocates of this position, see Davison, Navarre & Vogel, 1995; Ericsson & Simon, 1980; Hayes, 1989.) You will notice that we did rely on introspective data in Chapter 13, since some of the evidence for heuristic use in problem solving comes from "problem-solving protocols"—moment-by-moment narrations, by the subjects themselves, of what they are thinking as they work on a problem.

Others, however, have taken a more negative view of self-report, suggesting that self-report provides, at best, an incomplete portrait of mental events and, at worst, a distorted portrait. More strongly, some have suggested that self-report may even be *disruptive* of mental events—not just mischaracterizing thought, but also changing and undermining thought's progress. Why should this be? One possibility is that the attempt at introspection may lead you to focus on just those aspects of your thought that are easily verbalized. This may lead you to give these aspects more attention than they deserve—both in your report and, crucially, in your subsequent thinking. As a result, the requirement of self-report may redirect the sequence of thought, sometimes in ways that are counterproductive.

As an example, Schooler, Ohlsson and Brooks (1993) asked their subjects to solve a series of problems, such as this one: "A dealer in antique coins got an offer to buy a beautiful bronze coin. The coin had an emperor's head on one side, and the date 544 B.C. stamped on the other. The dealer examined the coin, but instead of buying it, he called the police. Why?" After working on each problem for two minutes, subjects were interrupted. Half of the subjects were then asked to describe their thoughts about the problem, and the strategies they were using. The remaining subjects spent the interruption time working on an unrelated activity (a crossword puzzle).

The results showed significant *disruption* from the self-report: Subjects who had verbalized their thoughts were able to solve 36% of the problems; subjects who had not been asked to introspect solved 46%. Apparently, introspection can in some circumstances disrupt thought. (For related data, see Schooler & Engstler-Schooler, 1990; Wilson & Schooler, 1991. Also see Crutcher, 1994; Payne, 1994; Wilson, 1994. For evidence, though, that it sometimes helps to "think out loud," see Berardi-Coletta, Buyer, Dominowski & Rellinger, 1995.)

Introspections that Are False

In many cases, though, we feel that we can offer a self-report on mental processes. We are convinced that we remember the processes well and have no trouble expressing them in words. We feel no embarrassment about the events, so there is no concern about our "polishing" the report to put ourselves into the best light. Even with all of these factors in place, however, our "introspections" can still fail to reflect our thoughts.

Nisbett and Wilson (1977) review a number of studies relevant to this claim. In general, the pattern of the studies is this: In each study, some factor is manipulated and is shown to influence subjects' behavior. However, when asked, subjects steadfastly deny that this factor influenced them. Instead, subjects offer their own account about why they acted as they did—an account that omits the factor we know to be relevant. In short, it seems that subjects are simply *mistaken* about why they acted as they did. (For broad surveys of this evidence, see Greenwald & Banaji, 1995, Uleman & Bargh, 1989.)

As an example, subjects in one study were presented with four pairs of nylon stockings, laid side-by-side on a table (Nisbett & Wilson, 1977). Subjects were asked to evaluate the stockings and were asked, in particular, which was of the best quality. (In fact, the stockings were identical to each other, but subjects didn't know this.) Then, after subjects had announced their choice, they were asked *why* they had chosen as they did.

The data revealed a pronounced effect of *position*: Subjects showed a clear preference for the right-most pair of stockings; indeed, this pair was preferred over the left-most pair by almost four-to-one. When asked about the reasons for their choice, however, zero subjects (out of 52) mentioned that they had been influenced by position. Subjects were then asked directly whether the stockings' positions had influenced their choice; virtually all subjects denied such an influence.

Similarly, subjects in another study read a brief excerpt from the novel *Rabbit Run*. Subjects were then asked to describe what emotional impact the excerpt had had on them. Subjects were also asked *why* the excerpt had the impact it did: Which sentences or which images, within the excerpt, led to the emotional "kick"? Subjects were impressively unanimous in their judgments, with 86% pointing to a particular passage (describing the messiness of a baby's crib) as playing an important role in creating the emotional tone of the overall passage. However, it appears that subjects' judgments were simply wrong: Another group of subjects read the same excerpt, but minus the passage about the crib. These subjects reacted to the overall excerpt in exactly the same way as did the earlier subjects. Apparently, the passage about the crib was not crucial at all (Nisbett & Wilson, 1977).

Surely it is no surprise that we are often influenced by unnoticed factors. Likewise, it seems unsurprising that we often have little idea of *why* we acted as we did. ("Gee, I don't know . . . it just seemed like the right thing to do.") What is striking about these cases, though, is that subjects *think* they know why they acted as they did, but they are wrong. The subjects' self-reports are offered with full confidence—subjects report that they carefully and deliberately thought about their actions, and so the various causes and influences were, it seems, out in plain view. Indeed, subjects' self-reports in these studies are generally quite plausible, so that, as "interviewers," we would surely accept these introspective reports at face value. However, from our perspective as researchers, we can see that these introspective reports are mistaken—omitting factors we know to be crucial, highlighting factors we know to be largely irrelevant.

Indeed, one might argue that these "introspective reports" are not, in fact, introspections at all. If they were, then it is puzzling that these reports are often at odds with the facts. If subjects were able to "look within," if they had genuine insight into why they acted as they did, then these errors in the self-reports seem inexplicable. Consequently, Nisbett and Wilson offer a different account of these "introspections." These self-reports, they claim, do not derive from some direct process of self-perception. Instead, when asked to "introspect," what subjects do is ask themselves: "Why did I act that way? Well, let me think about why, *in general*, people would act in a certain way in this situation. Then let me build, from that general knowledge, a plausible, after-the-fact *inference* about why I acted as I did." In terms we used in an earlier chapter, subjects are engaging in a "schema-based reconstruction"— building on generic knowledge to reconstruct what must have occurred in a particular episode. Let's emphasize, though, that subjects don't realize that this is what they are doing. Instead, the subjects are convinced that they are simply *remembering* their mental processes—and remembering easily, since the target events took place just moments earlier. Hence, these reconstructions *feel like* introspections.

Is this truly what "introspection" is all about? This claim has been widely debated. (See, for example, Sabini & Silver, 1981; Smith & Miller, 1978; White, 1988.) There is no disagreement, though, that this is a sensible account of *some* introspections. There is likewise no disagreement about the fact that self-reports are sometimes in error. The issue still debated lies in how often these errors occur, and also in whether some types of self-report might be immune to error. For our purposes, though, the message is clear: Self-report is, at best, a worrisome tool.

Unconscious Mental Events

The data reviewed so far make it clear that the causes of subjects' behavior, and various influences on that behavior, are often hidden from the subjects' view. In other words, the relevant causes and influences appear to be unconscious. This places profound limits on what we can learn via introspection, since introspection assumes self-awareness. If a great deal of our thinking happens without our being aware of it, then much of our cognition is inaccessible to introspection.

In addition, we can also draw an important theoretical claim from the same evidence: Apparently, a broad range of activities, including rather complex activities, can go forward without the actor being conscious of the activity. We can remember, we can see, we can understand language, and we can reason, all with no awareness of the mental processes involved, and with no conscious supervision of these processes. All of this has important implications for our thinking about consciousness and, in particular, for our thinking about the function of consciousness.

Unconscious Processes; Conscious Products

Evidence pertinent to these claims has entered our discussion at several points. In general, we have seen that our intellectual life requires an elaborate support structure, with a great deal of mental activity taking place "behind the scenes." The suggestion, therefore, is that we are often unaware of the *process* of our thoughts; we are instead aware only of the *products* that result from that process. (For discussion of the process/product distinction, see Nisbett & Wilson, 1977; Smith & Miller, 1978; White, 1988.)

Consider these mundane bits of memory retrieval: What is your mother's first name? What is your father's first name? Odds are that the answers just "popped into" your mind. You presumably had no awareness of searching through memory, of "traveling" from node to node within a network. You presumably had no awareness of activation spreading out from the node for MOTHER'S NAME, activation that then facilitated the retrieval of your father's name. Yet, as we saw in Chapter 7, there is reason to believe that all of these processes were relevant to this bit of memory retrieval. The processes were hidden from your view; all that you were aware of was the product—in this case, the two sought-after names.

Consider also *implicit* memory, which, by definition, is a memory of which we are unaware. As we saw in Chapter 5, we are often influenced by this kind of memory and, thus, are often unaware how our thoughts and actions are shaped by prior episodes. Moreover, the prior episode frequently has its influence only via some attribution steps: "That name surely 'rings a bell,' but I'm not sure why. But the experimenter is asking me about other famous names, and there are other clearly famous names on this list. I guess, therefore, that this one must also be the name of some famous person." This kind of inference surely sounds like something that we want to count as "thinking," but it is thinking, the evidence suggests, of which we are not conscious.

Unconscious processes are also crucial in other domains. For example, in Chapter 2, we mentioned that our recognition of words is often guided by *inferences*, and that we are, in general, unaware of these inferences. This was pivotal in our discussion of proofreading; there we argued that we are systematically unable to distinguish letters we have *read* from letters we have *inferred*. That is why misspelled words often look correct, even when you are staring right at them. Thus, we are aware of the product (our perceptual apparatus reports that the word was "CAKE"), but not the process (we can't tell if the word was actually perceived or merely inferred).

Similar themes emerged in Chapter 6, when we discussed the seamless manner in which our experiences are fused together with our prior knowledge. Many of the scenes we observe, or the sentences we hear, are ambiguous or leave out important materials. However, we easily draw on our knowledge to fill the gaps and resolve the ambiguities. The same is true when we are trying to remember some previous event or scene: We rely on unnoticed schema-based inferences to fill gaps in our recollection. Thus, by using our general understanding of how events unfold, we are able to *reconstruct* that which we cannot recall.

As we have discussed, this use of schemata provides important advantages, because it allows us to grasp a huge range of inputs with extraordinary efficiency. This same process, however, can also lead to problems—e.g., these "seamless" combinations can lead to memory errors. One way or the other, though, this combination of "old" knowledge and "new experience" is done entirely without our awareness. We are, for example, often unable to distinguish facts we have remembered (i.e., drawn from memory) from facts we have reconstructed. This provides another case in which we are conscious of the product (the event as experienced, the event as remembered) but not the process (perception versus inference; recall versus reconstruction).

The Influence of Unconscious Attributions

Our unconscious thinking is often impressively sophisticated, involving multiple steps of logical reasoning. Many studies illustrate this point but, as one example, consider an early experiment by Nisbett and Schachter (1966). Their subjects were asked to endure a series of electric shocks, with each shock slightly more severe than the one before. The question of interest was how far into the series the subjects would go. What was the maximum shock they would voluntarily accept?

Before beginning the series of shocks, some of the subjects were given a pill, which, they were told, would diminish the pain, but which would also have several side-effects: The pill would cause their hands to shake, would cause butterflies in the stomach, irregular breathing, and the like. The pill was in fact a placebo and had no analgesic properties, nor did it produce any of these side-effects. Yet this inert pill was remarkably effective: Subjects given the pill and told about its side-effects, were willing to accept four times as much amperage as control subjects.

Why was the placebo so effective? Nisbett and Schachter proposed that their *control* subjects noticed that their hands were shaking, that their stomachs were upset, and so on. (These are standard reactions to electric shock.) Subjects then used these self-observations as evidence in judging that they were quite uncomfortable in the experiment. It is as if subjects said to themselves: "Oh look, I'm trembling! I guess I must be scared. Therefore, these shocks must really be bothering me." This led them to terminate the shock series relatively early. Placebo subjects, in contrast, attributed these same physical symptoms *to the pill*. "Oh look, I'm trembling! That's just what the experimenter said the pill would do. I guess I can stop worrying, therefore, about the trembling. Let me look for some other indication of whether the shock is bothering me." As a consequence, these subjects were less influenced by their own physical symptoms—they discounted the symptoms, attributing them to the pill, not to the shock. In effect, these subjects overruled the evidence of their own anxiety and so misread their own internal state. (For related studies, see Nisbett & Wilson, 1977.)

Of course, subjects' reasoning about the pill was entirely unconscious. It seems plain that they were thinking about the pill, since subjects who received the pill (plus the instructions about the side-effects) behaved in a fashion dramatically different from other subjects. Nonetheless, when subjects were specifically asked *why* they had accepted so much shock, they rarely mentioned the pill. When asked directly, "While you were taking the shock, did you think about the pill at all?" subjects responded with answers like, "No, I was too worried about the shock to think of anything else." Thus, once again we have a factor demonstrably influencing subjects but entirely absent from their introspections.

More important, this study serves to illustrate the complexity of the processes underlying our conscious thoughts. Subjects in this experiment seem to be reasoning about themselves in an intellectually sophisticated manner: They are observing "symptoms," generating hypotheses about those symptoms, drawing conclusions from this, and so on. Of course, in this case, the subjects reached erroneous conclusions, because they have been misled about the pill by the experimenter. But that takes nothing away from what the subjects are doing intellectually—and unconsciously.

Unconscious Guides to Our Conscious Thinking

So far, then, we have argued for a distinction between the *processes* involved in thought and the *products* that result from these processes. We need to acknowledge that there is room for debate about how exactly this distinction should be drawn. Nonetheless, the distinction does support a useful rule-of-thumb: In general, it seems that we are aware of the products that result from our thought processes, but unaware of the processes themselves. Thus, we arrive at a conclusion, but the steps leading to the conclusion are likely to be hidden from view. We reach a decision but, again, we are unable to introspect about the processes leading to that decision. We may be able to reconstruct what those processes or steps must have been, but this is different from saying that we were aware of those processes in the first place.

Sometimes, though, the processes of thought do seem to be conscious. Sometimes, you reason carefully and deliberately, weighing each step, scrutinizing each bit of logic. This surely sounds like a case in which your thoughts are conscious. Even here, though, an elaborate unconscious support structure is needed—a support structure which exists at the "fringe" or the "horizon" of your conscious thoughts (cf. Husserl, 1931; James, 1890).

Let's look a bit more closely at how this "careful, deliberate" thought proceeds. Often, when thinking in this manner, we try to put our thoughts into words. Perhaps we hold a silent debate with ourselves, formulating clear, verbal arguments for or against some position. Perhaps we even "think out loud" as we navigate our way through a difficult problem. What should we make of this inner narration, this internal monologue?

Consider how you would think about these two arguments:

1. The toy was in the carton.
   The carton was in the closet
   Therefore, the toy was in the closet.

2. The pain was in his foot.
   His foot was in his shoe.
   Therefore, the pain was in his shoe.

The first of these arguments seems acceptable, but not the second. Yet, in their wording, the arguments are obviously similar. If you were guided only by the wording, you would treat both arguments in the same way. But of course, you don't. Apparently, your thinking goes "beyond" the wording in important ways.

In this example, the arguments are out on the page for you to peruse. The issue would be the same, though, if you were articulating these words as a verbalization of your own thoughts. In either case, there seems to be more to the argument, and more to the thought, than is directly expressed in the words themselves.

Related examples are easy to find. Thus, when you think, "I saw the sage," you are not puzzled about whether you saw an herb or a wise fellow. Likewise, if you were to think, "I saw the man with the binoculars," you might not even detect the ambiguity. In either case, your thought is embedded in a context of understanding that resolves the ambiguity, a context that tells you, in effect, how the thought is to be understood. The context isn't expressed in the words themselves, but is needed to avoid confusion, ambiguity, or slips. Notice that, even with explicit, clearly articulated, verbally expressed thoughts, thinking requires an unspoken, unnoticed support structure—a support structure that, in this case, specifies how the thought is to be interpreted. (For other discussion of the intertwining of thought and language, see Bloom,

1981; Clark & Clark, 1977; Hardin & Banaji, 1993; Hunt & Agnoli, 1991; Rosch, 1977b; Whorf, 1956.)

Roughly the same claims can be made about nonverbal thought, for example, cases in which you think carefully and deliberately about a mental image. Here, too, an unnoticed, unspoken support structure is on the scene, guiding how the image is to be understood. In Chapter 10, we referred to this support structure as a "perceptual reference frame," and there we argued that this frame renders a mental image unambiguous: A *picture* of a black disk on a white field is ambiguous—the same picture could also represent a white field with a circular hole in it, through which you see the darkness beyond. But your image of this scene is unambiguous—specifying what is figure, what is ground, what is close and what is far. This context of understanding isn't depicted in the image itself but seems, nonetheless. to be a crucial part of your thinking about the image. (For discussion, see Casey, 1976; Fodor, 1975.)

In fact, this point can be extended to many other domains: In our discussion of decision making, we emphasized the role played by how a decision is framed (Chapter 12; also see Bassok, Wu & Olseth, 1995). In our discussion of problem solving, we emphasized the role of set (Chapter 13). These again provide instances in which our thinking is done within a context, within a framework, which colors our thoughts and which plays a large role in determining the outcome of our thoughts—e.g., how a decision will be made or whether a problem will be solved.

Let's be clear, though, that one is usually not aware of this context of understanding—in decision making, in imagery, or in verbally expressed thoughts. Our awareness, instead, is filled with the specific content of the thought—our ideas about the sage, our hypotheses about how the problem should be solved. The context of understanding certainly shapes this awareness, but is not itself part of the awareness—much as we see *through* our glasses, while we (typically) don't see our glasses. Here, too, unnoticed mental processes are guiding our thinking and shaping the sequence of our thoughts.

Automatic Actions

Let's pause to take stock. We have argued that introspection is of limited value as a research tool for many different reasons. Among the other concerns, though, failures of introspection often seem best attributed to the fact that our thought processes are unconscious and therefore not introspectable. This led us to a distinction between the processes of thought and the resulting products, and we argued that it is the latter, not the former, that are consciously available. This remains true even when the processes are quite complex: It seems that we can engage in multiple steps of logical reasoning, with all the steps entirely hidden from view.

In some cases, the processes of thought do seem introspectable, do seem conscious. Even here, though, we argued that an unconscious support structure was needed—a support structure that guides our interpretation of the thoughts, that fills in many assumptions, and that, in general, directs our thinking in one direction rather than another. Thus, an unnoticed frame can lead us to be risk seeking rather than risk averse; an unnoticed set can block our path to a problem's solution; an unnoticed reference frame can lead us to interpret a mental image one way rather than another.

In short, we have so far described two broad categories of unconscious mental events—the processes that produce our conscious thoughts, and the unconscious framework (and assumptions) that guide our interpretations of our conscious thoughts. Yet another category of unconscious thought grows out of our discussion of automaticity (in Chapter 3) and also our discussion of routinizing problem solutions (Chapter 13). We will return to automaticity later in this chapter, when we offer some conjectures about what consciousness is *for*. For immediate purposes, though, note that automatization substantially broadens the range of activities performed without conscious supervision.

To put this in concrete terms, we noted in Chapter 3 that practice in a task has many consequences. Among them, practice allows us to perform the task without close monitoring and, in the end, without being aware of the task at all. We mentioned an extreme case in Chapter 3—the study by Spelke, Hirst and Neisser (1976) in which subjects learned to read a book while simultaneously taking dictation. This is, needless to say, a stunning achievement, equivalent to your being able to take notes in a chemistry lecture while simultaneously doing the reading for your literature class.

Subjects were able to achieve this remarkable feat after many weeks of practice. Let's emphasize, though, that the subjects themselves did not realize what they had accomplished: When asked whether they could remember the material dictated to them, subjects claimed they could not. When actually tested for their memory for this material, subjects insisted they were guessing. But, in fact, the test indicated that subjects had reasonably complete memory for the dictated material. Indeed, the evidence indicates that subjects had understood the dictated material's meaning, and had integrated different sentences to form a coherent tale. Thus, subjects seem to have comprehended the dictated material without being aware of it, without consciousness.

Blind-Sight and Amnesia

We are accumulating an impressive catalogue of what can be done *without* consciousness. Further evidence comes from patients who have suffered one or another form of brain damage. Consider, for example, the cases of memory pathology that we described in Chapter 5. Patients suffering from Korsakoff's amnesia often have no conscious awareness of events they have witnessed or things they have done. If asked directly about these events, the patients will insist that they have no recollection. If asked to perform tasks that require recollection, the patients will fail. Yet the patients do remember these events in some sense—they are influenced, in their present beliefs and behaviors, by the specific content of the prior episodes. Apparently, amnesics can remember, and can be influenced by their memories, with no conscious awareness that they are recalling the past. This is a pattern that Jacoby and Witherspoon (1982) dubbed "memory without awareness."

A similar pattern is evident in the phenomenon of "blind sight." This is a pattern observed in patients who have experienced damage to the striate cortex. As a result of this brain damage, these patients are, for all practical purposes, blind: If asked to move around a room, they will bump into objects. They do not react to flashes of bright light, and so on. However, in one experiment, visual stimuli were presented to these patients, and they were forced to *guess* whether the stimuli were (for example) X's or O's, or circles or squares. Quite reliably, these patients "guessed" correctly (Marcel, 1988; Weiskrantz, 1986). Similarly, if the patients were forced to guess where various objects were placed and to reach toward those objects, they tended to reach in the right direction with the appropriate hand position (given the shape and size of the target object). Subjects did this, all the while asserting that the task was silly, that they could not see the targets, and insisting that they were reaching out at random. There is no indication that these patients are lying about their blindness. Instead, it seems that these patients can, in a sense, "see," but they are not aware of seeing.

The Cognitive Unconscious and the Freudian Unconscious

It is clear, therefore, that our ordinary intellectual commerce with the world relies on a great many unconscious, undetected mental steps, steps including memory retrieval and inference. Before pressing ahead, though, we should say a few words more about what these "unconscious" steps are all about.

Many people's understanding of the unconscious has been shaped by the ideas of Sigmund Freud. For Freud, some thoughts and memories will be confined to the unconscious mind because they are threatening or because they provoke anxiety. Moreover, Freud viewed the unconscious mind as being in a continual struggle with the conscious mind, with the conscious mind constantly working to keep unconscious thoughts out of awareness and to keep unconscious wishes from being acted upon. Finally, Freud viewed the unconscious mind as being similar to the conscious mind in important ways. To be sure, each was ruled by its own principles (the conscious mind, according to Freud, was governed largely by considerations of pragmatic reality, while the unconscious, he argued, was governed by basic instincts and a constant quest for pleasure). Nonetheless, each had its own wishes and its own goals. In effect, the unconscious mind was a separate but largely autonomous player in the drama of mental life.

The unconscious mechanisms relevant to this book are rather different. To be sure, unconscious processes are highly active and have a considerable degree of autonomy, since they are able to function without the guidance of our conscious thoughts. In addition, these unconscious processes do have access to knowledge not available to the conscious mind (e.g., implicit memories). But here the resemblance to the Freudian unconscious ends. The unconscious processes we have discussed are not an adversary to the conscious mind. Instead, the cognitive unconscious functions as a sophisticated support service, working in harmony with our conscious thoughts and, indeed, making possible our conscious thoughts.

[handwritten margin note: unlike Freud]

In addition, there is no indication that ideas are "confined" to the cognitive unconscious because of anxiety or pain. Quite simply, psychic distress is irrelevant to the procedures we have discussed. The cognitive unconscious is not, therefore, the place we hide our forbidden wishes. Indeed, there is remarkably little evidence that such a place exists. That is, there is little evidence for the unconscious mind as Freud described it. Instead, the cognitive unconscious simply provides the machinery, the inner workings, of our ordinary intellectual functioning. The cognitive unconscious is rich and complex, and influences us in often surprising ways. But it is enormously different from the unconscious that Freud described.

It should also be said that, throughout his career, Freud generated both a body of theory, and also a large number of observations about human nature and human behavior. We have expressed skepticism about the theory, but we should nevertheless try to preserve Freud's observations and seek some other explanation for them. The mechanisms described in this book may provide that explanation. For example, in Chapter 6, we discussed Freud's explanation of childhood amnesia, but we also discussed a more promising explanation, framed in cognitive terms. Likewise, Freud described a pattern that he called the repetition compulsion—a tendency to treat situations as if they were echoes of some previous situation, to act now as one did then. Freud explained this in terms of repressed memories and wishes, but we would explain it instead as an instance of schema use (Chapter 6), in which you comprehend the current situation (or, perhaps, distort the current situation) by relying on some schematic knowledge. Similarly, Freud pointed out a number of contradictions and bits of seeming irrationality in human thought. As we have seen, however, these can be explained in cognitive terms (Chapters 11 and 12), rather than in terms of unconscious motives. Other examples, translating Freudian phenomena into cognitive terms, are easily found. (For discussion, see Erdelyi, 1974, 1985; Erdelyi & Goldberg, 1979.)

The Function of Consciousness

Clearly, a broad range of activities, including rather complex activities, can be accomplished unconsciously. This provides certain advantages—chief among them, efficiency—but it creates certain problems. By understanding both the advantages and the problems, we get an important clue about consciousness.

The Advantages and Disadvantages of Routine

Let's consider a simple case: When you first learned how to tie your shoes, you had to pay close attention to what you were doing, and you were surely aware of your individual actions (cross the laces, put the end of the right-hand lace through the loop). With practice, though, you became less and less aware of the details of your performance. Thus, if you were asked, as an adult, to list the steps of shoe-tying (as if instructing a child), you would probably fail to provide an adequate account. In a real sense, you have learned how to perform this task on "auto-pilot," outside of awareness.

Why does practice allow this "withdrawal" of attention? We offered one proposal in Chapter 3: With practice, fewer *decisions* are needed as you step through a complex task. As a practiced shoe-tyer, you do not have to choose what to do after the initial loop is formed. Instead, you simply draw on the memory of what you did last time. In fact, you have probably stored in memory a complete routine for shoe-tying, encapsulating all of the steps of the procedure. Once the routine is launched, no further decisions are needed—you simply repeat the familiar steps.

In short, the idea is that it is the *decisions* that require attention. With fewer decisions to be made, less attention is required, and this is why routine allows you to perform tasks without awareness.

This reliance on routine has many advantages. For one, it allows mental tasks to run much more quickly, and we have seen many indications that speed is a desirable feature in our intellectual functioning. (This is, of course, one of the reasons why we so often draw on "mental shortcuts" of one sort or anther—e.g., Chapters 8, 11, 12 or 13.) In addition, this "withdrawal" of attention, made possible by the routine, allows you to devote more attention to other aspects of the task, with important consequences for performance. Think back to our discussion of expertise, in Chapter 13. Experts, well-practiced in their domain, no longer need to attend to the low-level details of task performance. This allows them to attend to higher order factors, including the overall organization of the task. As a result, they are more sensitive to these organizational factors, better able to plan, and so on.

However, we also noted in Chapter 3 that these advantages of routinization are purchased at a price: Reliance on routine sacrifices flexibility. As long as one is attending to the individual steps, one has the option of substituting one step, or one sequence, for another. If the steps are run off as a routinized sequence, this control is gone. One can elect to run off the entire sequence or not, but cannot fine-tune the steps.

There are, in fact, a number of ways to demonstrate the inflexibility of unconscious processing. For example, the inferences used to fill gaps in memory generally serve us well—these inferences are likely to be correct more often than not and so genuinely supplement what we remember. However, as we have seen, these memory inferences can on occasion lead us astray. Knowing this, though, is no protection at all: Just as one cannot choose to avoid a perceptual illusion, one cannot choose to avoid memory error. The process of inference is automatic and effortless, but it is also irresistible. In the same fashion, the automatization of word recognition allows much quicker reading (Chapter 2), but also leaves us vulnerable to the Stroop effect (Chapter 3). Again, knowing about this effect is no protection—the processes are not open to control.

A Suggestion about Consciousness

All of this leads to an obvious suggestion: In a wide range of situations, we are willing to sacrifice flexibility in order to gain efficiency. But, for many tasks, we can't afford this sacrifice. For these tasks, we need to be flexible, and so we cannot rely on routine; we must, instead, continue to select each individual step, and then launch it, then select the next, and so forth. This slows down the sequence appreciably, but preserves control. For these tasks, therefore, we continue paying attention to what we are doing—monitoring the task and deliberately guiding performance. For these tasks, we remain *conscious* of what we are doing.

The suggestion is that consciousness may be needed for just those tasks in which we must preserve flexibility, and for which we cannot rely on routine. What tasks fall into this category? For novel tasks, obviously, we don't yet have a routine and, for these, conscious control will be needed. Other tasks, by their nature, require frequent choices and adjustments. These tasks will be difficult to automatize and so will continue to require conscious monitoring. For still other tasks, a routine may be available, but we might choose not to use the routine. In these cases, we need to remain "mindful" of the task in order to *inhibit* a habitual action. In other words, "mindfulness" (i.e., conscious self-awareness) may be needed to avoid becoming the victim of habit, to avoid falling into the rut of always relying on routine activities (cf. Langer, 1989).

Related proposals have been offered by other authors. For example, Jacoby, Kelley, Brown and Jasechko (1989) invite us to consider cases like this: You offer a suggestion to a friend, perhaps about how to write a paper, or how to deal with a troubling situation. Your friend rejects the idea, but then, sometime later, your friend reintroduces this same idea as if it were an insight that she just had. In this case, the unconscious retrieval of the earlier conversation serves as the source for your friend's "insight." However, in the absence of any conscious recollection of the prior conversation, your friend claims the idea as her own, confusing a memory with an insight.

This sort of inadvertent plagiarism might happen often if we simply relied on primed pathways and established channels in evaluating ideas or in choosing courses of action. This reliance on familiarity, moreover, is what we might expect if we relied on habitual or customary actions. Jacoby et al. suggest, however, that such plagiarism (and a variety of related problems) is generally blocked by conscious recollection: In evaluating ideas, we *don't* simply rely on what's habitual, customary, or familiar. Instead, we *reflect* on our thoughts, and also on the *sources* of these thoughts. This allows us to avoid the sort of plagiarism just described and saves us (most of the time) from telling and retelling the same jokes to the same audience or endorsing sentiments merely because we have heard them uttered by others. (Related examples are discussed by Baddeley and Wilson, 1994.)

These cases rest on the fact that unconscious processes can accomplish a great deal. However, consciousness allows us to control and regulate these processes, and, in particular, to make sure that our actions are appropriate to the situation. (We should mention that early versions of these ideas were offered by Angell, 1907, 1908; Dewey, 1903; James, 1890; and others. For a discussion of this early literature, see Pani, in press.)

Consciousness as "Justification" for Action

A further, different role for consciousness is also suggested by the data. Consider the blind-sight patients. We have so far emphasized the fact that these patients are sensitive to some visual information, and this tells us something important: Apparently, some aspects of vision can go forward with no conscious awareness, with no conscious monitoring. But it's also striking that these patients do insist that they are blind—they are fearful of walking across a room (lest they bump into something); they fail to react to many stimuli; and so on. How is this possible? Why don't these patients realize what they see? Why can't these patients take action (e.g., navigate across a room) based on what they see?

Roughly the same words can be said about amnesics. We have emphasized how much amnesics do remember, when properly tested. We drew from this the claim that memory encoding and memory retrieval seem not to depend on consciousness—this is the pattern of "memory without awareness." But note that we still need to explain the fact of amnesia itself: It is of course striking that the amnesic insists that he or she doesn't remember the prior event. How is it possible to retrieve a memory without becoming aware of the memory? Why don't (objectively) familiar events *seem* familiar?

Similar points can be made about neurologically intact subjects. For example, subjects in one study were shown a list of words and then, later on, were tested in either of two ways (Graf, Mandler & Haden, 1982). Some subjects were explicitly asked to recall the earlier list, and were given word stems as cues: "What word on the prior list began 'CLE'?" Other subjects were tested indirectly: "Tell me the first word which comes to mind beginning 'CLE'."

The results show rather poor memory in the explicit test, but much better performance in the implicit test. This echoes many findings we have reviewed: We often have *implicit* memories for episodes we have *explicitly* forgotten. But note that there is something peculiar in this result: Subjects could, in principle, proceed this way: "I don't recall any words from the list beginning 'CLE.' Perhaps I'll just *guess*. Let's see: What words come to mind which begin 'CLE'?" In this way, subjects could use their implicit memory to *supplement* what they remember explicitly. If they did this, then the performance difference between the two conditions would be erased—performance on the explicit test would be just as good as performance on the implicit test. Given the results, though, subjects are obviously not using this strategy. For some reason, subjects in this situation seem unable to use their implicit memories to guide explicit responding.

What is going on in these cases? Why are we sometimes willing to rely on implicit memories, in offering a response, and sometimes not? Why are blind-sight patients unable to *use* what they apparently can see? The answer, broadly, seems to be this: In many situations, we need to take action, based on remembered or perceived information. In some cases, the action is overt (walking across the room, or making a verbal response); other times, the action is mental (reaching a decision, or drawing a conclusion). In either case, though, it seems *not enough* merely to have access to the relevant information. In addition, we also seem to need some justification, some reason, to take the relevant information seriously.

By analogy, imagine that you are trying to remember some prior event, and some misty thoughts about that event come to mind. You vaguely recall that friends were present on the target occasion; you have a dim idea that food was served. You might refuse to give these thoughts a voice, though, because you are not convinced that these thoughts are memories. (Perhaps they are chance associations or dreams you once had.) You will only report your memory if you're satisfied that you are, in fact, *remembering*. In other words, you need more than the remembered information; you also need some reason to believe that the remembered information is credible.

Against this backdrop, the suggestion is that the justification for action is generally provided by the conscious presentation of information. In other words, it is the nature and quality of our conscious experience that persuades us to take information seriously (or not to). When this experience is rich and detailed, this convinces us that the presented information is more than a passing fantasy, more than a chance association. When the conscious presentation is impoverished, though, as it seems to be in blind sight, or in amnesia, we fail to take seriously the information provided to us by our own eyes, or our own memory, and so we are paralyzed into inactivity.

This claim must be offered tentatively, since we are here reaching well beyond the evidence. Moreover, we have said little about what exactly it is, within the conscious experience, that makes information persuasive or compelling. Nonetheless, the unwillingness of blind-sight patients to acknowledge what they see, and the inability of amnesics to act on the basis of what they (implicitly) remember, does need explanation. Likewise, while it is clear that many judgments are routinely influenced by implicit memory, other judgments seem not to be, and this too needs to be explained. Our comments in this section provide at least one way to approach these issues. (For further discussion, see Johnson, Hashtroudi & Lindsay, 1993; Marcel, 1988; Reisberg & Heuer, 1989.)

Consciousness: What Is Left Unsaid

Many of our remarks in this chapter have been speculative, and future research may force us to refine our conception of what consciousness is, and what consciousness is for. Likewise, it seems certain that consciousness has other functions in addition to the ones just discussed. For example, several authors have argued that consciousness plays a crucial role for each of us in forming our sense of who we are; this sense of self then plays an important part in guiding our thoughts and actions (e.g., Greenwald & Pratkanis, 1984). Here, too, further research is sure to illuminate these claims.

Perhaps most important, we should emphasize how much is still left unsaid. We have suggested that we must distinguish two broad categories of thought—one that is highly efficient, but inflexible; and one that is maximally flexible, but much slower. We have not explained, however, why this second category of thought needs to be conscious. Could there be a category of thought that is slow, deliberate, flexible, but unconscious?

In describing consciousness, philosophers speak of **qualia**—the "raw feels" of sensory experience. When you see a red apple, for example, you gain the information that a red apple is before you, but the red also *looks* a certain way to you, has a certain appearance that you are aware of. Likewise, when you feel pain, you *know* you are feeling pain, but you also have a specific sensory experience—the pain feels a certain way. These sensory experiences provide the basic "stuff" of which our awareness, our subjective states, is built. In these terms, we can refine our question: Could there be a category of thought that is slow, deliberate, flexible, but *without qualia*? With such a category of thought, you would be sensitive to the relevant information—you would know that a red apple was present, you would know that there was pain—but you would not have the subjective experience. It would be like knowing that *someone else* was seeing red or feeling pain. In this case, you might know what this other person knows, but you wouldn't be experiencing what he or she is experiencing.

Does deliberate thought, reflective thought, require *qualia*? We have no ready answer for this; the data we have described do not bear directly on this question. (For further discussion of this issue, see Flanagan, 1991.) We close this chapter, therefore, as we began it—by emphasizing that psychologists can only provide a small piece of the puzzle of consciousness. There is no question, though, that the discussion will be informed by the data we have reviewed in this chapter—e.g., data about unconscious attributions, or blind sight, or implicit memory. This by itself—the mere fact that research can address these issues—is a source of considerable satisfaction for psychologists.

Glossary

activated node A *node* for which the current *activation level* has reached or passed that node's *response threshold*. An activated node will often trigger a response or summon attention, and can, in addition, serve as a source of activation for other nodes.

activation level A measure of the current activation state for a *node* or *detector*. Activation level is increased if the node or detector receives the appropriate input from its associated nodes or detectors; activation level will be high if input has been received frequently or recently.

agnosia An inability to recognize familiar objects, typically caused by specific forms of brain damage.

amnesia A broad inability to remember events within a certain category, due in many cases to brain damage.

anarthria A disorder involving an inability to control the muscles needed for ordinary speech; hence, anarthric individuals cannot speak, although other aspects of language functioning are unimpaired.

anchoring A tendency to use an initial answer to a question as an "anchor," so that subsequent answers to the question are selected by making (often inadequate) adjustments from this "reference point."

anomia A disruption of language abilities, usually resulting from specific brain damage, in which the individual loses the ability to name objects, including highly familiar objects.

anterior attention system A set of brain locations, identified largely through *brain-imaging techniques*, hypothesized as the brain's "traffic director" coordinating various ongoing activities, and keeping track of different inputs.

anterograde amnesia An inability to remember experiences that occurred *after* the event that triggered the memory disruption. Often contrasted with *retrograde amnesia*.

aphasia A disruption of language function caused by brain damage.

articulatory rehearsal loop One of the *slave systems* hypothesized as part of the *working memory system*. This slave system draws on subvocalized speech, which serves to create a record in the *phonological buffer*. Materials in this buffer then fade, but can be refreshed by another cycle of covert speech, with this cycle initiated by working memory's *central executive*.

associations Functional connections hypothesized as linking *nodes* within a mental network, or *detectors* within a detector network; these associations are often hypothesized as the "carriers" of activation, from one node or detector to the next.

atmosphere pattern A tendency to endorse a conclusion in a logic problem if that conclusion is consistent with the "atmosphere" of the premises. Thus, two premises containing the word "not" make it more likely that subjects will endorse a conclusion containing the word "not"; premises containing "all" make it more likely that subjects will endorse a conclusion containing "all."

attended channel In *selective-attention* experiments, subjects are exposed to simultaneous inputs, and instructed to ignore all of these except one. The attended channel is the input subjects are instructed to attend.

automaticity A state achieved by some tasks and some forms of processing, in which the task can be performed with little or no attention. Automatized actions can, in many cases, be combined with other activities without interference. Automatized actions are also often difficult to control, leading many to refer to them as "mental reflexes."

availability heuristic A strategy used to judge the frequency of a certain type of object, or the likelihood of a certain type of event. This strategy begins by assessing the ease with which examples of the object or event come to mind; this "availability" of examples is then used as an index of frequency or likelihood.

base rate Information about the broad likelihood of a particular type of event (also referred to as "prior probability"). Base-rate information is distinguished from *diagnostic information.*

baseline activation (or resting) level A *detector* or *node*'s activation level prior to the arrival of any inputs.

basic-level category A level of categorization hypothesized as the "natural" and most informative level, neither too specific nor too general. It is proposed that we tend to use basic-level terms (such as "chair," rather than the more general "furniture" or the more specific

"armchair") in our ordinary conversation and in our reasoning.

behaviorist theory Broad principles concerned with how behavior changes in response to different configurations of stimuli (including stimuli often called "rewards" and "punishments"). In its early days, behaviorist theory sought to avoid *mentalistic* terms.

belief bias A tendency, within logical reasoning, to endorse a conclusion if the conclusion happens to be something one believes is true anyhow. In displaying this tendency, subjects seem to ignore both the premises of the logical argument, and logic itself, and rely instead on their broader pattern of beliefs about what is true and what is not.

biconditionals Logical statements of the form, "If X, and only if X, then Y." Such a statement is equivalent to asserting that *both* "X implies Y" *and* "Y implies X."

bigram A pair of letters. For example, the word "FLAT" contains the bigrams "FL," "LA" and "AT."

brain-imaging techniques Techniques developed for medical diagnosis, which allow us to examine the moment-by-moment activity levels of different brain areas.

brainstorming A technique sometimes used for problem solving in which one tries to relax all constraints and to "let the ideas flow." In brainstorming sessions, one tries to generate as many ideas, and as many new approaches, as possible.

Broca's aphasia A form of *aphasia* caused by damage to specific sites within the left frontal lobe of the brain. Patients suffering from this aphasia show relatively good language comprehension but disrupted production. Moreover, the speech they produce is "agrammatic."

case-based reasoning A form of reasoning in which one tries to think of experiences relevant to the problem under scrutiny, and then draws analogies based on these experiences.

categorical perception The tendency to hear speech sounds "merely" as members of a category—the category of "z" sounds, or the category of "p" sounds, and so on. As a consequence, one tends to hear sounds *within* the category as being rather similar to each other; sounds from different categories, however, are perceived as quite different.

categorical syllogism   A logical argument containing two premises and a conclusion, and concerned with the properties of, and relations between, categories. An example is "All trees are plants. All plants require nourishment. Therefore all trees require nourishment." This is a valid syllogism, since the truth of the premises guarantees the truth of the conclusion.

center-surround cells   Neurons in the visual system with a "donut-shaped" *receptive field*; stimulation in the *center* of the receptive field has one effect on the cell, whereas stimulation in the surrounding ring has the opposite effect.

central executive   The hypothesized director of the *working-memory system*. This is the component of the system needed for any interpretation or analysis; in contrast, mere storage of materials can be provided by working memory's *slave system*, which work under the control of the central executive.

channel segregation   In performing simultaneous tasks, one needs to keep track of which task elements belong with which task. The task of keeping these elements separate, so that elements from one task do not intrude into the other task, is called channel segregation.

childhood amnesia   The difficulty, experienced by most adults, in remembering events that took place before one's third or fourth birthday.

chronometric studies   Literally "time-measurement" studies; generally, studies that measure the amount of time a task takes, often used as a means of examining the task's components, or used as a means of examining which *brain* events are simultaneous with specific *mental* events.

chunk   The hypothetical storage unit in working memory; it is estimated that working memory can hold 7 ± 2 chunks. An unspecified quantity of information can be contained within each chunk, since the context of each chunk depends on how the memorizer has organized the to-be-remembered materials.

clustering   A pattern often observed in free recall tasks in which subjects will recall the earlier-learned materials category by category, independent of the sequence in which these materials were initially presented.

coarticulation   A trait of speech production in which the way a sound is produced is altered slightly by the immediately previous and the next sounds. Because of this "overlap" in speech production, the acoustic properties of each speech sound vary, according to the context in which that sound appears.

cognitive economy   The need to manage one's mental resources, including time, effort, and specific processing tools. Performance will suffer if one seeks to perform tasks (or combinations of tasks) that demand more resources than are available, and this leads people to use a variety of cognitive "short-cuts."

competence   The pattern of skills and knowledge that might be revealed under optimal circumstances. Competence is generally distinguished from "performance," which refers to the pattern of skills and knowledge revealed under ordinary circumstances.

complex cell   A neuron within the visual system that fires maximally in response to lines or angles of a specific orientation; however, position of the line within the field of view is not critical.

concept-driven processing   A type of processing in which the sequence of mental events is influenced by a broad pattern of knowledge and expectations (sometimes referred to as "top-down" processing).

concurrent-articulation task   A task, used in many studies of working memory, in which subjects are required to repeat a phrase or word over and over out loud. Concurrent articulation can be used to block use of *subvocalization*, and therefore can be used to study the function of subvocalization.

conditional statements   These are statements of the format "If X then Y," with the first statement (the "if" clause) providing a "condition" under which the second statement (the "then" clause) is guaranteed to be true.

confirmation bias   A family of effects in which

subjects seem more sensitive to evidence *confirming* their beliefs than they are to evidence *challenging* their beliefs. Thus, if subjects are given a choice about what sort of information they would like in order to evaluate their beliefs, they request information that is likely to confirm their beliefs. Likewise, if subjects are presented with both confirming and disconfirming evidence, they are more likely to pay attention to, to be influenced by, and to remember the confirming evidence, rather than the disconfirming.

connection weight   The strength of a connection between two *nodes* in a network. The greater the connection weight, the more efficiently activation will flow from one node to the other.

consistent mapping   An experimental procedure in which the response required to each stimulus is held constant across a block of trials. Thus, if a button-press is the appropriate response for, say, a "T" viewed on the first trial, then this button-press will be the appropriate response whenever a "T" appears. Often contrasted with *varied mapping.*

content morphemes   *Morphemes* that carry meaning; generally contrasted with *function morphemes* (like the plural morpheme "s" or past-tense morpheme "ed"), which signal the relations among words.

converging evidence   A pattern of evidence in which various procedures, or various results, all point toward the same conclusion.

conversion errors   An error in which subjects convert statements from one form into another, for example, treating, "All A are B" as though it is identical to "All B are A," or treating "If A then B" as though it were "If B then A."

crosstalk   A pattern of errors in which elements of one task intrude into a second simultaneous task.

data-driven processing   A type of processing in which the sequence of mental events is largely determined by the pattern of incoming information (sometimes referred to as "bottom-up" processing).

decay theory of forgetting   The hypothesis that

with the passage of time, memories may fade or erode.

declarative memories   Memories, including both *episodic* and *generic knowledge*, that can be described as "remembering *that*" such and such is true. Often contrasted with *procedural memories*, which are remembering *how* to do something.

deduction   A process through which we start with claims, or general assertions, and ask what follows from these premises.

default values   Values we fill in unless we have some reason or information to the contrary.

descriptive accounts   An account of how things actually are; often contrasted with *normative* or *prescriptive* accounts, which describe how things *ought* to be.

detectors   A *node* within a processing network that fires primarily in response to a specific target contained within the incoming perceptual information.

diagnostic information   Information about an individual case, which indicates whether the case belongs in one category or another; often contrasted with base-rate information, which is information about the overall category (primarily: how common that category is), rather than information about the individual case.

dichotic listening   A task in which subjects hear two simultaneous verbal messages, one presented via headphones to the left ear, while a second is presented to the right ear. In typical experiments, subjects are asked to pay attention to one of these inputs (the *attended channel*) and urged to ignore the other.

digit-span task   A task often used for measuring working-memory's storage capacity. Subjects are read a series of digits (e.g., "8 3 4") and must immediately repeat them back. If subjects do this successfully, they are given a slightly longer list (e.g., "9 2 4 0"), and so forth. The length of the longest list a subject can remember in this fashion is that subject's digit span.

direct memory testing   A form of memory testing in which subjects are asked explicitly to remember some previous event. *Recall* and standard *recognition* testing are both forms of direct testing.

distributed representation A mode of representing ideas or contents in which there is no one *node* representing the content, and no one place at which the content is stored. Instead, the content is represented via a pattern of simultaneous activity across many nodes. Those same nodes will also participate in other patterns, and so those same nodes will also be part of other distributed representations. Often contrasted with *local representation.*

divided attention The skill of performing multiple tasks simultaneously.

dual-coding theory A theory that imaginable materials, such as high-imagery words, will be doubly represented in memory: the word itself will be remembered, and so will the corresponding mental image.

echolalia A disorder in which patients turn into virtual echo-boxes, repeating back anything they hear. However, these patients show no sign of understanding the speech they are echoing, nor do they produce speech on their own.

Einstellung The phenomenon in problem-solving in which subjects develop a certain attitude or perspective on a problem, and then approach all subsequent problems with the same rigid attitude.

elaborative rehearsal A way of engaging to-be-remembered materials, such that one pays attention to what the materials mean, and how they are related to each other or to other things in the surroundings, or to other things one already knows. Often contrasted with *maintenance rehearsal.*

elimination by aspects A decision-making strategy often used when making complicated decisions. Within this strategy, one evaluates the options one dimension, or one attribute, at a time, discarding unwanted alternatives if they are inadequate with regard to the specific attribute now being considered (independent of what other attributes that alternative might have).

encoding specificity The tendency, when memorizing, to place in memory *both* the to-be-learned materials *and also* some amount of the context of those materials. As a result, these materials will be recognized as familiar, later on, only if the materials appear again in a similar context.

episodic knowledge Knowledge about specific episodes in one's life; often contrasted with *generic knowledge.*

error signal A flow of activation proportional to the magnitude of error (i.e., proportional to the difference between output-produced and output-desired).

error trapping Procedures that detect and correct errors before the errors cause further confusion.

excitatory connection Links from one *node*, or one *detector*, to another, such that activation of one node activates the other. Often contrasted with *inhibitory connections.*

exemplar-based reasoning Reasoning that draws on knowledge about specific category members, rather than drawing on more general information about the overall category.

expected utility An estimate of the value of a particular course of action, calculated as the *utility* of the likely outcome of that action, multiplied by the probability of reaching that outcome. (Also referred to as "expected value.")

explicit memories Memories revealed by *direct memory testing*, and typically accompanied by the conviction that one is remembering a specific prior episode. Often contrasted with *implicit memories.*

false alarm A detection even though the specified target is actually absent.

family resemblance The notion that members of a category (all dogs, or all games) resemble each other. In general, family resemblance relies on some number of *features* shared by any group of category members, even though these features may not be shared by *all* members of the category. Therefore, the basis for family resemblance may shift from one subset of the category to another.

feature One of the small set of elements out of which more complicated patterns are composed. Features can be identified in many ways and are, for example, reflected in the *search asymmetries* evident in many *visual search* tasks.

flashbulb memories   Memories of extraordinary clarity, typically for highly emotional events, retained despite the passage of many years.

four-card task   A task used in many studies of deductive reasoning. In this task, subjects are shown four playing cards and are told that each card has a number on one side, and a letter on the other. Their task is to evaluate this rule: If a card has a vowel on one side, it must have an even number on the other side. (Also known as the "selection task.")

frame   Aspects of how a decision is phrased, which are, in fact, irrelevant to the decision, but which influence subjects' choices nonetheless.

frequency estimate   Subjects' assessment of how often they have encountered examples of a particular category and how likely they believe they are to encounter new examples of that category.

function morphemes   *Morphemes* that signal the relations among words within a sentence, such as the morpheme "s" indicating a plural, or the morpheme "ed" indicating past tense. Often contrasted with *content morphemes*.

functional fixedness   A tendency to be rigid in how one thinks about an object's function. This generally involves a strong tendency to think of an object only in terms of its *typical* function.

fuzzy boundary   A distinction between categories that identifies each instance only as "more" or "less likely" to be in a category, rather than specifying whether each instance is or is not included in the category.

garden-path sentences   Sentences that initially lead the reader to one understanding of how the sentence's words are related, but that then require a change in this understanding in order to comprehend the sentence. Examples are "The old man ships," or "The horse raced past the barn fell."

generic knowledge   Knowledge of a general sort, as opposed to knowledge about specific episodes. Often contrasted with *episodic knowledge*.

general resources   Mental resources that are relevant to virtually all cognitive tasks, so that virtually all tasks, no matter what their nature, will compete for this limited pool. Often contrasted with *task-specific resources*.

generativity   The idea that one can combine and recombine basic units to create (or "generate") new and more complex entities. Linguistic rules, for example, are generative, and so govern how a limited number of words can be combined and recombined to produce a vast number of sentences.

goal state   The state one is working towards in trying to solve a problem. Often contrasted with *initial state*.

geons   One of the basic shapes proposed as the "building blocks" of all complex three-dimensional forms. Geons take the form of cylinders, cones, blocks, and the like, and are combined to form "geon assemblies." These are then combined to produce entire objects.

graded membership   The idea that some members of a category are "better" members, and therefore are "more firmly" in the category than other members.

grammatical   Conforming to the rules that govern the sequence of words acceptable within the language.

"hasa" links   Associative links representing possessive relations, such as "Sam *hasa* dog." Often contrasted with *"isa" links*.

heuristics   Strategies that are reasonably efficient, and work most of the time. In using a heuristic, one is in effect choosing to accept some risk of error in order to gain efficiency.

homunculus   The classic "little man in the head" used (wrongfully) in explaining the intelligence of behavior. Appeals to the homunculus amount to claiming that intelligent processes are produced by some mental processes that are themselves intelligent—providing, in essence, no real explanation.

hypermnesia   A process through which earlier-forgotten memories are now remembered.

Sometimes referred to as "unforgetting," hypermnesia often results merely from continued efforts at remembering, with these efforts spread out over a period of time and a variety of circumstances.

illumination   The third in a series of stages often hypothesized as crucial for creativity. Illumination refers to the stage in which some new key insight or new idea suddenly comes to mind.

illusory covariation   A pattern that subjects "perceive" in data, leading them to believe that the presence of one factor allows them to predict the presence of another factor. However, this perception occurs even in the absence of any genuine relationship between these two factors. As an example, subjects perceive that a child's willingness to cheat in an academic setting is an indicator that the child will also be willing to cheat in athletic contests. However, this perception is incorrect, and so the covariation that subjects perceive is "illusory."

image   A mental representation *depicting* an object or event, rather than *describing* the object or event. Generally, images have a strong subjective resemblance to perceptual experiences, and so visual images are described as being similar to actual pictures.

image files   Visual information stored in long-term memory, specifying what a particular object or shape looks like. Information within the image file can then be used as a "recipe" or set of instructions for how to construct an active image of this object or shape.

implicit memories   Memories revealed by *indirect memory testing* usually manifest as *priming effects* in which current performance is guided or facilitated by previous experiences. Implicit memories are often accompanied by no conscious realization that one is, in fact, being influenced by specific past experiences. Often contrasted with *explicit memories.*

incubation   The second in a series of stages often hypothesized as crucial for creativity. Incubation refers to (hypothesized) events that occur when one puts a problem being worked on *out of* one's conscious thoughts, but continues nonetheless to work on the problem unconsciously. Many current psychologists are skeptical about this process, and propose alternative accounts for data ostensibly documenting incubation.

indirect memory testing   A form of memory testing in which subjects are not told that their memories are being tested. Instead, subjects are tested in a fashion in which previous experiences can influence current behavior. Examples of indirect tests include *word-stem completion, lexical decision,* and tachistoscopic recognition.

induction   A pattern of reasoning in which one seeks to draw general claims from specific bits of evidence. Often contrasted with *deduction.*

information processing   A particular approach to theorizing in which complex mental events, such as learning, remembering, and deciding, are understoood as being built up out of a large number of discrete steps. These steps occur one-by-one, with each providing as its "output" the input to the next step in the sequence.

inhibitory connections   Links from one *node*, or one *detector*, to another, such that activation of one node decreases the *activation level* of the other. Often contrasted with *excitatory connections.*

initial state   The state one begins in, in working towards the solution of a problem. In other words, problem solution can be understood as the attempt to move, with various operations, from the initial state to the goal state.

insight problems   Problems in which one's initial approach to the problem is likely to be unproductive, and for which a more appropriate approach often arrives quite abruptly.

interactive models   Models of cognitive processing that rely on an ongoing interplay between *data-driven* and *concept-driven processing.*

interference theory of forgetting   The hypothesis that materials are lost from memory because of *interference* from other materials also in memory. If the interference is caused by materials learned prior to the learning episode, this is called *proactive interference;* if the interference is caused by materials learned after the learning episode, this is *retroactive interference*.

introspection The process through which one "looks within," to observe and record the contents of one's own mental life.

intrusion errors Memory errors in which one recalls elements not part of the original episode one is trying to remember.

"isa" links Associative links representing equivalence (or partial equivalence) relations, such as "Sam *isa* dog." Often contrasted with "*hasa*" *links*.

Korsakoff's syndrome A clinical syndrome characterized primarily by dense *anterograde amnesia*. Korsakoff's syndrome is caused by damage to specific brain regions, and is often precipitated by a form of malnutrition common among long-term alcoholics.

letter span A traditional measure of working-memory's capacity, obtained by determining how many letters subjects can repeat back, without error, moments after hearing them. (Similar to a *digit-span task*.)

lexical-decision task A test in which subjects are shown strings of letters and must indicate, as quickly as possible, whether the string of letters is a word in English or not. It is supposed that subjects perform this task by "looking up" these strings in their "mental dictionary."

linguistic universals Rules that appear to apply to every human language.

linguistics The academic study of language.

local representation Representations of information that are encoded in some small number of identifiable *nodes*. Representations of this sort are sometimes spoken of as "one-idea-per-node," or "one-content-per-location." Often contrasted with *distributed representations*.

long-term recency A *recency effect* observed in circumstances in which *all* the materials being recalled are drawn from long-term memory. Traditional accounts attribute the recency effect to the ease of retrieval from *working memory*, and so these accounts cannot explain long-term recency.

loss aversion A tendency to be far more sensitive to losses than to gains, often accompanied by a willingness to take chances in hopes of avoiding losses.

maintenance rehearsal A rote, mechanical process, in which items are continually cycled through working memory, merely by repeating them over and over. Also called "item-specific rehearsal," and often contrasted with *elaborative rehearsal*.

manner of production In producing speech-sounds, the speaker momentarily obstructs the flow of air out of the lungs. This obstruction can take several forms. For example, the air-flow can be fully stopped for a moment, as it is in the /t/ or /b/ sound, or the air can continue to flow, as it does in the pronunciation of /f/ or /v/. These differences in how the air-flow is restricted are referred to as the manner of production for that speech sound.

mapping The assignment of individual responses to individual stimuli. Some mappings are easy to learn, whereas others are more difficult (e.g., press a high button in response to a stimulus at the bottom of the computer screen; press a low button in response to a stimulus at the top of the screen).

memory rehearsal Any mental activity that has the effect of maintaining information in working memory. Two types of rehearsal are often distinguished: *maintenance* (or item-specific) *rehearsal*, and *elaborative rehearsal*.

mental model An internal representation in which an abstract description is translated into a relatively concrete representation, with that representation serving to illustrate how that abstract state of affairs might be realized.

mentalism The view that human actions must be understood with theories that refer to unseen mental entities, such as beliefs, expectations, plans, and strategies.

metacognitive judgments Judgments in which one must stand back from a particular mental activity, and comment on the activity, rather than participating in it.

metalinguistic judgments A particular type of *metacognitive judgment*, in which one must stand back from one's ordinary language use, and instead comment on language or linguistic processes.

method of loci   A *mnemonic strategy* in which the to-be-remembered materials are each associated with a particular location. When the time comes to remember, one imagines that one is "returning" to these remembered locations, and "finds" at each spot the target materials.

minimal attachment   A *heuristic* used in sentence perception. In using this heuristic, the listener or reader proceeds through the sentence seeking the simplest possible phrase structure that will accommodate the words heard so far.

misinformation effect   An effect in which subjects' reports about an earlier event are influenced by misinformation they received after experiencing the event. In the extreme, misinformation can be used to create false memories concerning an entire event that, in truth, never occurred.

mnemonic strategies   Techniques designed to improve memory. These techniques seek to improve memory accuracy, and to make learning easier; in general, these strategies seek in one fashion or another to help memory by imposing an organization on the to-be-learned materials.

modal model   This nickname refers to a specific conception of the "architecture" of memory. In this model, working memory serves both as the storage site for material now being contemplated, and also the "loading platform" for long-term memory. Information can reach working memory through the processes of perception, or it can be drawn from long-term memory. Once in working memory, material can be further processed, or can simply be "recycled" for subsequent use.

modularity   The claim that different aspects of processing work independently of each other, so that information available to one processing module may have no influence on the function of some other module.

modus ponens   A logical rule that stipulates that, from these two premises: "If p then q," and "p is true," one can draw the conclusion: "Therefore, q is true."

modus tollens   A logical rule that stipulates that, from these two premises: "If p then q," and "q is false," one can draw the conclusion: "Therefore, p is false."

morphemes   The smallest language units that carry meaning. Psycholinguists distinguish *content morphemes* (the primary carriers of meaning) from *function morphemes* (which specify the relations among words).

necessary conditions   Conditions that *must* be fulfilled in order for a certain consequence to occur. However, these conditions may not guarantee that the consequence will occur, since it may be true that other conditions must also be met. Often contrasted with *sufficient conditions*.

neuropsychology   The branch of psychology concerned with the relation between various forms of brain dysfunction and various forms of mental functioning. Neuropsychologists study, for example, *amnesia*, *agnosia*, and *aphasia*.

nodes   Individual units within an associative network. In a scheme employing *local representations*, *nodes* represent single ideas or concepts. In a scheme employing *distributed representations*, ideas or contents are represented by a pattern of activation across a wide number of nodes; the same nodes may also participate in other patterns and therefore in other representations.

normative accounts   Accounts of how an event or a process *should* or *ought to* unfold. Also referred to as *prescriptive* accounts.

operators   The tools or actions that one can use, in problem solving, to move from the problem's *initial state* to the *goal state*.

over-regularization errors   Errors in which one perceives or remembers a word or event as being closer to the "norm" than it really is. For example, misspelled words are read as though they were spelled correctly; atypical events are misremembered in a fashion that brings them closer to more typical events; words with an irregular past tense (such as "ran") are replaced with a regular past tense ("runned").

parsing The process through which one divides an input into its appropriate elements—for example, divides the stream of incoming speech into its constituent words.

path constraints Limits that rule out some operations in problem solving. These might take the form of resource limitations (limited time to spend on the problem, or limited money), or limits of other sorts (perhaps ethical limits on what one can do).

pattern recognition The process of identifying or categorizing the objects in one's environment.

peg-word systems A type of *mnemonic strategy* using words or locations as "pegs" on which one "hangs" the to-be-remembered materials.

phonemes The basic categories of sound used to convey language. For example, the words "peg" and "beg" differ in their initial phoneme—/p/ in one case, /b/ in the other.

phonological buffer A passive storage device that serves as part of the *articulatory rehearsal loop*. The phonological buffer serves as part of the mechanisms ordinarily needed for hearing. In rehearsal, however, the buffer is loaded by means of *subvocalization*. Materials within the buffer then fade, but can be refreshed by new covert speech, under the control of the *central executive*.

phonology The study of the sounds that are used to convey language.

phrase-structure ambiguity Ambiguity in how a sentence should be interpreted, resulting from the fact that more than one phrase structure is compatible with the sentence. An example of such ambiguity is "I saw the bird with my binoculars."

phrase-structure rules Constraints governing the pattern of branching in a phrase-structure tree. Equivalently, these are rules governing what the constituents must be for any syntactic element of a sentence.

place of articulation In producing speech sounds, the speaker momentarily obstructs the flow of air out of the lungs. This obstruction can occur at several different positions, depending on the position of the tongue, teeth, and lips. The position at which this obstruc-tion occurs is called the place of articulation. For example, the "place" for the /b/ sound is the lips; the "place" for the /d/ sounds is created by the tongue briefly touching the roof of the mouth.

post-stimulus mask A pattern displayed after a visual stimulus has been shown, designed to block sensory memory for that just-presented stimulus.

pragmatic reasoning schema A collection of rules, derived from ordinary practical experience, that defines what inferences are appropriate in a specific situation. These reasoning schemata are usually defined in terms of a goal or theme, and so one schema defines the rules appropriate for reasoning about situations involving "permission," whereas a different schema defines the rules appropriate for thinking about situations involving cause-and-effect relations.

pragmatic rules Rules governing how language is ordinarily used, and also governing how this language will be interpreted. As an example, "Do you know the time?" is literally a question about one's knowledge, but this question is interpreted as a request that one *tell* what time it is.

preparation The first in a series of stages often hypothesized as crucial for creativity. Preparation refers to the stage in which one commences effortful work on the problem, often with little progress.

prescriptive rules Rules describing how things are *supposed* to be. Often called *normative rules*, and often contrasted with *descriptive rules*.

primacy effect An often-observed advantage in remembering the early-presented materials within a sequence of materials. This advantage is generally attributed to the fact that one can focus attention on these items, because, at the beginning of a sequence, one is obviously not trying to divide attention between these items and other items in the series.

priming effect An improvement in processing created by an earlier experience of working on the same task with the same stimulus materials. Many tasks show priming effects, including *lexical decision, word-fragment completion,* and tachistoscopic recognition.

proactive interference Interference observed when earlier-learned materials disrupt memory for later-learned materials. Often contrasted with *retroactive interference.*

problem space The set of all states that can be reached in solving a problem, as one moves, by means of the problem's *operators,* from the problem's *initial state* toward the problem's *goal state.*

procedural memories Memories for how to do something, not easily described in propositions. Often contrasted with *declarative memories.*

proceduralism The claim that what is stored in memory is a record of the *procedures* one followed on an earlier occasion.

processing fluency An improvement in the speed or ease of processing, which results from prior practice in using those same processing steps.

production systems A system for representing actions. Each "production" within this system involves (a) a goal, (b) some conditions that must be met before the action can be taken, and (c) a specific action to be taken, when the conditions have been met.

prosody The pattern of pauses and pitch changes that characterize speech production. Prosody can be used to emphasize elements of a spoken sentence, to highlight the sentence's intended structure, or to signal the difference between a question and an assertion.

prosopagnosia A syndrome in which patients lose their ability to recognize faces and to make other fine-grained discriminations within a highly-familiar category, even though their other visual abilities seem relatively intact.

prototype theory The claim that mental categories are represented by means of a single "best example," or prototype, identifying the "center" of the category. In this view, decisions about category membership, and inferences about the category, are made with reference to this best example, often an "average" of the examples of that category that one has actually encountered.

pseudowords Letter strings designed to resemble actual words, even though they are not. Examples include "blar," "plome," or "tuke."

psycholinguistics The study of how linguistic knowledge is acquired, represented, and used, by the human mind.

qualia The subjective qualities that provide the "raw feel" of sensory experience.

recall The task of memory retrieval in which the rememberer must come up with the desired materials, sometimes in response to a cue that names the context in which these materials were earlier encountered ("Name the pictures you saw earlier."), sometimes in response to a question that requires the sought-after information ("Name a fruit," or "What is the state-capital of California?"). Often contrasted with *recognition.*

receptive field The portion of the visual field to which a cell within the visual system responds. Thus, if the appropriately shaped stimulus appears in the appropriate position, the cell's firing rate will change. The cell's firing rate will not change if the stimulus is of the wrong form or is in the wrong position.

recency effect The tendency to remember materials that occur late in a series. In "standard" recency, the late-occurring items are probably being retrieved from working memory; in *long-term recency,* the late-occurring items are drawn from long-term memory, and probably gain their memory advantage from distinctiveness.

recognition The task of memory retrieval in which the to-be-remembered items are presented to the subject, and the subject must decide whether or not the item was encountered in some earlier circumstance. Thus, for example, one might be asked, "Have you ever seen this person before?" or "Is this the poster you saw in the office yesterday?" Often contrasted with *recall.*

recognition by components model A model (often referred to by its initials: RBC) of object recognition. In this model, a crucial role is played by *geons,* the (hypothesized) basic building blocks out of which all the objects we recognize are constructed.

recognition threshold The briefest exposure duration for a stimulus that still allows accurate *recognition* of that stimulus. For words, the recognition threshold typically lies between 10 and 40 msec. Words shown for longer durations are usually easily perceived; words shown for briefer durations are typically difficult to perceive.

reconstruction A process in which one draws on broad patterns of knowledge in order to figure out how a prior event actually unfolded. In some circumstances, we rely on reconstruction to fill gaps in what we recall; in other circumstances, we rely on reconstruction because it requires less effort than actual recall.

recursion A property of rule systems that allows a symbol to appear both on the left-side of a definition (the part being defined) and on the right-side (the part providing the definition). Recursive rules within syntax, for example, allow sentences to include another sentence, as one of its constituents, as in the example: "Solomon says that Jacob is talented."

referent That object or event in the world that a word or phrase refers to. For example, the word "apple" refers to a particular type of fruit that grows on trees; "Daniel Reisberg" refers to the man who wrote this text.

representativeness heuristic A strategy often used in making judgments about categories. This strategy is broadly equivalent to making the assumption that, in general, the instances of a category will resemble the prototype for that category, and, likewise, that the prototype resembles each instance.

repression A (hypothesized) process through which anxiety-provoking thoughts are denied access to the conscious mind. Most researchers are skeptical about the existence of repression, although many clinical psychologists insist that the process is well-documented.

response selector A (hypothesized) mental resource needed for the selection and initiation of a wide range of responses, including overt responses (e.g., moving in a particular way) and covert responses (e.g., initiating a memory search).

response threshold The quantity of information, or quantity of activation, needed in order to trigger a response.

restoration effect A perceptual illusion in hearing, in which one "hears" sounds that are actually missing from the stimulus presented.

retention interval The amount of time that passes between the initial learning of some material and the subsequent memory retrieval of that material.

retrieval failure A mechanism that probably contributes to a great deal of forgetting. Retrieval failure occurs when a memory is, in fact, in long-term storage, but one is unable to locate that memory when trying to retrieve it.

retrieval path A connection (or series of connections) that can lead to a sought-after memory in long-term storage.

retroactive interference Interference observed when memory for earlier-observed materials is disrupted by later-learned materials. Often contrasted with *proactive interference*.

retrograde amnesia An inability to remember experiences that occurred *before* the event that triggered the memory disruption. Often contrasted with *anterograde amnesia*.

rewrite rule One of the rules governing the possible forms that a sentence's phrase structure can take. Rewrite rules specify how each constituent within a phrase structure can be expanded (or "rewritten"). Thus, the rule "S → NP VP" indicates that a sentence can be expanded into a noun phrase followed by a verb phrase; the rule "NP → det N" indicates that a noun phrase can be expanded into a determiner followed by a noun.

risk aversion A tendency toward avoiding risk. Subjects tend to be risk averse when contemplating gains, choosing instead to hold tight to what they already have. Often contrasted with *risk seeking*.

risk seeking A tendency toward seeking out risk. Subjects tend to be risk seeking when contemplating losses, as they are willing to gamble in hopes of avoiding (or diminishing) their losses.

satisficing A decision-making procedure in which one seeks a satisfactory outcome, rather than searching more ambitiously for the *optimal* outcome. In satisficing, one seeks a choice that is "good enough," even if other (not yet detected) choices might be even better.

schema (plural: schemata)   A pattern of knowledge describing what is typical or frequent in a particular situation. Thus a "kitchen schema" would stipulate that a stove and refrigerator are likely to be present, whereas a coffeemaker may be or may not be present, and a piano is likely not to be present.

search asymmetry   A data pattern sometimes observed in *visual-search* tasks, and often used as a basis for identifying the basic features used by the visual system. As an example, it is relatively easy to locate a tilted line against a background of verticals, but difficult to find a vertical line against a background of tilted lines. This implies that "tilt" may be a basic feature for the visual system, whereas "vertical" is not.

selective attention   The skill through which one pays attention to one input or one task, while ignoring other stimuli that are also on the scene.

semantics   The study of how a word's meaning is represented in the mind.

sense   The meaning of a word is determined both by the word's *referent* and also by how the word identifies that referent. Thus the "Morning Star" and the "Evening Star" both refer to the same object (the planet Venus) but they identify that object in different ways. This means of identifying the referent is called the word's (or phrase's) sense.

serial position curve   A data pattern summarizing the relationship between some performance measure (often, likelihood of *recall*) and the order in which the test materials were presented. In memory studies, the serial position curve tends to be U-shaped, with subjects best able to recall the first-presented items (the *primacy effect*) and also the last-presented items (the *recency effect*).

set   The assumptions one brings to a task concerning how the task should be approached, and also what sorts of strategies are likely to be productive in performing the task.

shadowing   A task in which subjects are required to repeat back a verbal input, word for word, as they hear it.

simple cell   A neuron within the visual system that fires maximally to lines or angles of a specific orientation and at a specific position within the visual field.

single-cell recording   A technique for recording the moment-by-moment *activation level* of an individual neuron, within a healthy, normally functioning brain.

slave systems   A part of the *working-memory system* useful for temporary storage, much as a scratch-pad stores information not in use at that moment, but likely to be needed soon. Just like a scratch-pad, the slave systems serve only to store the target information; any analyses or interpretations of this information require the *central executive*. Examples of slave systems include the *visuospatial buffer* and the *articulatory rehearsal loop*.

source confusion   A memory error in which one misremembers where a bit of information was learned, or where a particular stimulus was last encountered.

source memory   A form of memory that allows one to recollect the spisode in which learning took place, or the time and place in which a particular stimulus was encountered.

speech segmentation   The process through which a stream of speech is "sliced" into its constituent words and, within words, into the constituent *phonemes*.

spreading activation   A process through which acitivation travels from one *node* to another, via associative links. As each node becomes activated, it serves as a source for further activation, spreading onward through the network.

Stroop effect   A classic demonstration of *automaticity*, in which subjects are asked to name the color of ink used to print a word, and the word itself is a color name. For example, subjects might see the word "yellow" printed in blue ink, and are required to say "blue." Considerable interference is observed in this task, with subjects apparently unable to ignore the word's content, even though it is irrelevant to their task.

subthreshold activation Activation levels below *response threshold*. Subthreshold activation, by definition, will not trigger a response; nonetheless, this activation is important because it can accumulate, leading eventually to an activation level that exceeds the response threshold.

subvocalization Covert speech, in which one goes through the motions of speaking, or perhaps forms a detailed motor plan for speech movements, but without making any sound.

sufficient conditions Conditions that, if satisfied, guarantee that a certain consequence will occur. However, these conditions may not be necessary for that consequence (since the same consequence might occur for some other reasons). Often contrasted with *necessary conditions*.

summation The addition of two or more separate inputs so that the effect of these combined inputs is greater than the effect caused by any one of the inputs.

sunk-cost effect A tendency toward taking extravagant steps to ensure that a previous expense was not "in vain." The previous expense is the "sunk cost," that is, a commitment already made. Often, it is more sensible to abandon this commitment, rather than expending further resources to justify the commitment. However, this abandonment is precisely what subjects tend not to do.

surface structure The representation of a sentence that is actually expressed in speech. In some treatments, this structure is referred to as the "s-structure" and is often contrasted with the *underlying structure* (or d-structure, with the "d" an abbreviation for deep).

syntax Rules governing the sequences and combinations of words in the formation of phrases and sentences.

tachistoscope A device that allows presentation of stimuli for precisely controlled amounts of time, including very brief presentations.

task-specific resources Mental resources needed for some tasks but not others; thus the nature of each task determines which resources will be needed. Often contrasted with *general resources*.

time-sharing A process through which one rapidly switches attention from one task to another, creating the appearance of doing two things at the same time.

token A specific example or instance of a category, and therefore used in propositions concerned with specific events and individuals. Often contrasted with *type*.

T.O.T. phenomenon An often-observed effect in which subjects are unable to remember a particular word, even though they are certain the word (typically identified via its definition) is in their vocabulary. Subjects in this state often can remember the starting letter for the word and its number of syllables, and insist the word is "on the tip of their tongue" (hence the T.O.T label).

trace The hypothesized remnant left when a word has been shifted from one position to another in a sentence's *underlying structure*. Although unexpressed, the trace can be detected in various ways.

transcendental inference A step in reasoning in which one uses observed circumstances to figure out what causes brought about these circumstances, or what preconditions made these circumstances possible.

transfer-appropriate processing Processing of a stimulus that prepares the subject for an upcoming test. To judge processing as "transfer-appropriate," one must consider both the initial processing, which promotes a set of skills, and the subsequent processing, to which those skills may be applied (or "transferred").

type A broad category; often contrasted with *token*, a term devoting an individual within the category.

typicality effects Any of a number of experimental effects in which "typical" category members have an advantage, relative to atypical category members. Thus subjects are quicker to verify "A robin is a bird," than they are to verify "A heron is a bird." Likewise, subjects are more likely to name "robin" if asked to name a bird than they are to name "heron."

underlying structure An abstract representation of the sentence to-be-expressed, sometimes called "deep structure" (or d-structure) and often contrasted with *surface structure.*

unilateral neglect syndrome   A pattern of symptoms in which patients ignore all inputs coming from one side of space. Thus, patients with this syndrome put only one of their arms into their jackets, eat food from only one half of their plates, read only one half of words (and so read "output" as "put"), and so on.

utility theory   A view proposing that humans make decisions in a fashion that maximizes "utility." Utility is defined as the subjective value asssociated with a particular circumstance.

varied mapping   An experimental procedure in which the response required for each stimulus varies from one trial to another. Thus, if an "X" is a target on one trial (and so demands a "yes" response), "X" might be a distractor on the next trial (and so demand a "no" response). Often contrasted with *consistent mapping.*

visual acuity   A measure of one's ability to see fine detail.

visual cortex   The portion of the brain primarily responsible for vision.

visual search   An experimental task in which subjects must scan through a set of visual stimuli, searching for a particular target.

visuospatial buffer   One of the *slave systems* used as part of the *working-memory system.* This buffer plays an important role in storing visual or spatial representations, including visual images.

voicing   One of the properties that distinguishes different categories of speech sounds. A sound is considered "voiced" if the vocal folds are vibrating while the sound is produced. If the vocal folds start vibrating sometime after the sound begins (that is, with a long *voice-onset time*), the sound is considered "unvoiced."

voice-onset time (VOT)   The time period that elapses between the start of a speech sound and the onset of *voicing.* VOT is the main feature distinguishing "voiced" consonants (such as /b/, with a near-zero VOT) and "unvoiced"

consonants (such as /p/, with a VOT of approximately 60 msec).

weapon-focus effect   A pattern, often alleged for witnesses to violent crimes, in which one pays close attention to some crucial detail (such as the weapon, within a crime scene) to the exclusion of much else.

Wernicke's aphasia   A language disorder in which patients seem largely unable to comprehend speech, even though the speech that they produce sounds effortless and fluent, with the function words and the appropriate suffixes correctly in place. Typically, though, the speech produced by these patients makes no sense.

word-fragment completion   A task in which subjects are given fragments of a word (e.g., "A-S-S-I-") and must figure out what the full word is ("assassin"). This task is often used to study *implicit memory.*

word-length effect   A phenomenon observed in tests of working memory, such that memory is poorer for words that take a longer time to pronounce. This effect is attributed to the fact that these words take longer to subvocalize, and are therefore more difficult to rehearse efficiently.

word-stem completion   A task in which subjects are given the beginning of a word (e.g., "TOM . . .") and must provide a word that starts with the letters provided. In some versions of the task, only one solution is possible, and so performance is measured by counting the number of words completed. In other versions of the task, several solutions are possible for each stem, and performance is assessed by determining which of the subjects' responses fulfill some other criterion.

working-memory system   A system of mental resources used for holding information in an easily-accessible form. The *central executive* is at the heart of this system, and the executive then relies on a number of *slave systems,* including the *visuospatial buffer* and the *articulatory rehearsal loop.*

References

Aaronson, D., & Scarborough, H. (1977). Performance theories for sentence coding: Some quantitative models. *Journal of Verbal Learning and Verbal Behavior, 16,* 277–304.

Abelson, R. P. (1981). Psychological status of the script concept. *American Psychologist, 36,* 715–729.

Abney, S., & Johnson, M. (1991). Memory requirements and local ambiguities of parsing strategies. *Journal of Psycholinguistic Research, 20,* 233–250.

Ackley, D. H., Hinton, G. E., & Sejnowski, T. J. (1985). A learning algorithm for Boltzmann machines. *Cognitive Science, 9,* 147–169.

Adamson, R. (1952). Functional fixedness as related to problem solving: A repetition of three experiments. *Journal of Experimental Psychology, 44,* 288–291.

Adelson, B. (1981). Problem solving and the development of abstract categories in programming languages. *Memory & Cognition, 9,* 422–433.

Adelson, B. (1984). When novices surpass experts: The difficulty of the task may increase with expertise. *Journal of Experimental Psychology: Learning, Memory and Cognition, 10,* 483–495.

Alba, J. W., Alexander, S. G., Hasher, L., & Caniglia, K. (1981). The role of context in the encoding of information. *Journal of Experimental Psychology: Human Learning and Memory, 7,* 283–292.

Alba, J. W., & Hasher, L. (1983). Is memory schematic? *Psychological Bulletin, 93,* 203–231.

Alexander, M. P., & Albert, M. L. (1983). The anatomical basis of visual agnosia. In A. Kertesz (Ed.), *Localization in neuropsychology.* New York: Academic Press.

Algom, D., & Cain, W. (1991). Remembered odors and mental mixtures: Tapping reservoirs of olfactory knowledge. *Journal of Experimental Psychology: Human Perception and Performance, 17,* 1104–1119.

Algom, D., & Lubel, S. (1994). Psychophysics in the field: Perception and memory for labor pain. *Memory & Cognition, 55,* 133–141.

Allais, M. (1953). Le comportement de l'homme rationnel devant le risque: Critique des postulats et axiomes de l'Ecole americaine. *Econometrica, 21,* 503–546.

Allan, L. (1993). Human contingency judgments: Rule based or associative. *Psychological Bulletin, 114,* 435–448.

Alloy, L. B., & Tabachnik, N. (1984). Assessment of covariation by humans and animals: The joint influence of prior expectations and current situational information. *Psychological Review, 91,* 112–149.

Allport, A. (1989). Visual attention. In M. Posner (Ed.), *Foundations of cognitive science* (pp. 631–682). Cambridge, MA: MIT Press.

Allport, A., Styles, E., & Hsieh, S. (1994). Shifting intentional set: Exploring the dynamic control of tasks. In C. Umiltà & M. Moscovitch (Eds.), *Attention and performance XV.* Cambridge, MA: MIT Press.

Allport, D., Antonis, B., & Reynolds, P. (1972). On the division of attention: A disproof of the single channel hypothesis. *Quarterly Journal of Experimental Psychology, 24,* 225–235.

Anderson, J. (1974). Verbatim and propositional representation of sentences in immediate and long-term memory. *Journal of Verbal Learning and Verbal Behavior, 13*, 149–162.

Anderson, J. (1976). *Language, memory, and thought.* Hillsdale, NJ: Lawrence Erlbaum.

Anderson, J. (1980). *Cognitive psychology and its implications.* San Francisco: Freeman.

Anderson, J. (1982). Acquisition of cognitive skill. *Psychological Review, 89*, 369–406.

Anderson, J. (1983). *The architecture of cognition.* Cambridge, MA: Harvard University Press.

Anderson, J. (1985). *Cognitive psychology.* New York: W. H. Freeman & Co.

Anderson, J. (1987). Skill acquisition: Compilation of weak-method problem solutions. *Psychological Review, 94*, 192–210.

Anderson, J. (1990). *The adaptive character of thought.* Hillsdale, NJ: Lawrence Erlbaum.

Anderson, J. (1993). Problem solving and learning. *American Psychologist, 48*, 35–44.

Anderson, J., & Bower, G. H. (1972). Recognition and retrieval processes in free recall. *Psychological Review, 79*, 97–123.

Anderson, J., & Bower, G. H. (1973). *Human associative memory.* Washington, DC: Winston & Sons.

Anderson, R., & Helstrup, T. (1993). Visual discovery in mind and on paper. *Memory & Cognition, 21*, 283–293.

Anderson, R. C., & Pichert, J. (1978). Recall of previously unrecallable information following a shift in perspective. *Journal of Verbal Learning and Verbal Behavior, 17*, 1–12.

Andrews, F. (1975). Social and psychological factors which influence the creative process. In I. A. Taylor & J. W. Getzels (Eds.), *Perspectives in creativity.* Chicago: Aldine.

Angell, J. R. (1907). The province of functional psychology. *Psychological Review, 14*, 61–91.

Angell, J. R. (1908). *Psychology* (4th ed.). New York: Holt.

Arkes, H. (1991). Costs and benefits of judgment errors: Implications for debiasing. *Psychological Bulletin, 110*, 486–498.

Arkes, H., & Blumer, C. (1985). The psychology of sunk cost. *Organizational Behavior and Human Decision Processes, 35*, 124–140.

Arkes, H., & Freedman, M. (1984). A demonstration of the costs and benefits of expertise in recognition memory. *Memory & Cognition, 12*, 84–89.

Arkes, H., & Harkness, A. (1983). Estimates of contingency between two dichotomous variables. *Journal of Experimental Psychology: General, 112*, 117–135.

Armstrong, S. L., Gleitman, L. R., & Gleitman, H. (1983). What some concepts might not be. *Cognition, 13*, 263–308.

Arnheim, R. (1969). *Visual thinking.* Berkeley: University of California Press.

Atkinson, R. C., & Juola, J. F. (1974). Search and decision processes in recognition memory. In D. H. Krantz, R. C. Atkinson & P. Suppes (Eds.), *Contemporary developments in mathematical psychology.* San Francisco: Freeman.

Atkinson, R. C., & Shiffrin, R. M. (1968). Human memory: A proposed system and its control processes. In K. W. S., & J. T. Spence (Eds.), *The psychology of learning and motivation* (pp. 89–105). New York: Academic Press.

Attneave, F. (1953). Psychological probability as a function of experienced frequency. *Journal of Experimental Psychology, 46*, 81–86.

Austin, J. (1962). *How to do things with words.* Cambridge, MA: Harvard University Press.

Baddeley, A. D. (1963). A Zeigarnik-like effect in the recall of anagram solutions. *Quarterly Journal of Experimental Psychology, 15*, 63–64.

Baddeley, A. D. (1966). Short-term memory for word sequences as a function of acoustic, semantic and formal similarity. *Quarterly Journal of Experimental Psychology, 18*, 362–365.

Baddeley, A. D. (1976). *The psychology of memory.* New York: Basic Books.

Baddeley, A. D. (1978). The trouble with "levels": A reexamination of Craik and Lockhart's framework for memory research. *Psychological Review, 85*, 139–152.

Baddeley, A. D. (1982). *Your memory: A user's guide.* New York: Macmillan.

Baddeley, A. D. (1986). *Working memory.* Oxford: Clarendon Press.

Baddeley, A. D. (1988). But what the hell is it for? In M. Gruneberg, P. Morris, & R. Sykes (Eds.), *Practical aspects of memory: Current research and issues.* Chichester: Wiley.

Baddeley, A. D. (1990). *Human memory: Theory and practice.* Needham Heights, MA: Allyn & Bacon.

Baddeley, A. D. (1992). Is working memory working? The fifteenth Bartlett lecture. *Quarterly Journal of Experimental Psychology, 44A,* 1–31.

Baddeley, A. D. (1993). Working memory or working attention? In A. Baddeley & L. Weiskrantz (Eds.), *Attention: Selection, awareness and control: A tribute to Donald Broadbent* (pp. 152–170). Oxford: Oxford University Press.

Baddeley, A. D., & Dale, H. C. A. (1966). The effect of semantic similarity on retroactive interference in long- and short-term memory. *Journal of Verbal Learning and Verbal Behavior, 5,* 417–420.

Baddeley, A. D., & Hitch, G. (1974). Working memory. In G. Bower (Ed.), *Recent advances in learning and motivation.* New York: Academic Press.

Baddeley, A. D., & Hitch, G. (1977). Recency reexamined. In S. Dornic (Ed.), *Attention and performance VI* (pp. 646–667). Hillsdale, NJ: Lawrence Erlbaum.

Baddeley, A. D., & Hitch, G. (1993). The recency effect: Implicit learning with explicit retrieval? *Memory & Cognition, 21,* 146–155.

Baddeley, A. D., & Lieberman, K. (1980). Spatial working memory. In R. Nickerson (Ed.), *Attention and performance VIII* (pp. 521–539). Hillsdale, NJ: Lawrence Erlbaum.

Baddeley, A. D., Logie, R., Nimmo-Smith, I., & Brereton, J. (1985). Components of fluent reading. *Journal of Memory and Language, 24,* 119–131.

Baddeley, A. D., Papagno, C., & Vallar, G. (1988). When long-term learning depends on short-term storage. *Journal of Memory and Language, 27,* 586–595.

Baddeley, A. D., Thomson, N., & Buchanan, M. (1975). Word length and the structure of short-term memory. *Journal of Verbal Learning and Verbal Behavior, 14,* 575–589.

Baddeley, A. D., & Wilson, B. (1994). When implicit learning fails: Amnesia and the problem of error elimination. *Neuropsychologia, 32,* 53–68.

Baer, J. (1993). *Creativity and divergent thinking: A task-specific approach.* Hillsdale, NJ: Lawrence Erlbaum.

Bahrick, H. (1984). Semantic memory content in permastore: 50 years of memory for Spanish learned in school. *Journal of Experimental Psychology: General, 113,* 1–29.

Bahrick, H., Bahrick, L., Bahrick, A., & Bahrick, P. (1993). Maintenance of foreign language vocabulary and the spacing effect. *Psychological Science, 4,* 316–321.

Bahrick, H., Bahrick, P. O., & Wittlinger, R. P. (1975). Fifty years of memory for names and faces: A cross-sectional approach. *Journal of Experimental Psychology: General, 104,* 54–75.

Bahrick, H., & Boucher, B. (1968). Retention of visual and verbal codes of the same stimuli. *Journal of Experimental Psychology, 78,* 417–422.

Bahrick, H., & Hall, L. (1991). Lifetime maintenance of high school mathematics content. *Journal of Experimental Psychology: General, 120,* 20–33.

Bahrick, H., & Hall, L. (1993). Long intervals between tests can yield hypermnesia: Comments on Wheeler and Roediger. *Psychological Science, 4,* 206–208.

Bainbridge, J. V., Lewandowsky, S., & Kirsner, K. (1993). Context effects in repetition priming are sense effects. *Memory & Cognition, 21,* 619–626.

Balch, W., Bowman , K., & Mohler, L. (1992). Music-dependent memory in immediate and delayed word recall. *Memory & Cognition, 20,* 21–28.

Banks, W. P., Thompson, S., Henry, G., & Weissmann, T. (1986). Mental models of physiological function in health and illness. Presentation at the 27th annual meeting of the Psychonomic Society, November 1986, New Orleans.

Bar-Hillel, M. (1982). Studies of representativeness. In D. Kahneman, P. Slovic, & A. Tversky (Eds.), *Judgment under uncertainty: Heuristics and biases.* New York: Cambridge University Press.

Bargh, J. (1989). Conditional automaticity: Varieties of automatic influence in social perception and cognition. In J. Uleman & J. Bargh (Eds.), *Unintended thought.* New York: Guilford Press.

Baron, J. (1977). Mechanisms for pronouncing printed words: Use and acquisition. In S. J. Samuels (Ed.), *Basic processes in reading: Perception and comprehension.* Hillsdale, NJ: Lawrence Erlbaum.

Baron, J. (1988). *Thinking and reasoning.* Cambridge: Cambridge University Press.

Baron, J. B., & Sternberg, R. J. (1987). *Teaching thinking skills: Theory and practice.* New York: W. H. Freeman & Co.

Barsalou, L. (1982). Context-independent and context-dependent information in concepts. *Memory & Cognition, 10,* 82–93.

Barsalou, L. (1983). Ad hoc categories. *Memory & Cognition, 11,* 211–227.

Barsalou, L. (1985). Ideals, central tendency, and frequency of instantiation. *Journal of Experimental Psychology: Learning, Memory and Cognition, 11,* 629–654.

Barsalou, L. (1987). The instability of graded structure: Implications for the nature of concepts. In U. Neisser (Ed.), *Concepts and conceptual development.* Cambridge: Cambridge University Press.

Barsalou, L. (1988). The content and organization of autobiographical memories. In U. Neisser & E. Winograd (Eds.), *Remembering reconsidered.* Cambridge: Cambridge University Press.

Barsalou, L., & Sewell, D. R. (1985). Contrasting the representation of scripts and categories. *Journal of Memory and Language, 24,* 646–665.

Bartlett, F. C. (1932). *Remembering: A study in experimental and social psychology.* Cambridge: Cambridge University Press.

Bartlett, J. C., Till, R. E., & Levy, J. C. (1980). Retrieval characteristics of complex pictures: Effects of verbal encoding. *Journal of Verbal Learning and Verbal Behavior, 19,* 430–449.

Bartz, W. H. (1976). Rehearsal and retrieval processes in recall and recognition. *Bulletin of the Psychonomic Society, 8,* 258.

Bassock, M., Wu, L.-L., & Olseth, K. (1995). Judging a book by its cover: Interpretive effects of content on problem-solving transfer. *Memory & Cognition, 23,* 354–367.

Bates, E., Masling, M., & Kintsch, W. (1978). Recognition memory for aspects of dialogue. *Journal of Experimental Psychology: Human Learning and Memory, 4,* 187–197.

Bateson, G. (1958). *Naven.* Stanford, CA: Stanford University Press.

Bauer, M., & Johnson-Laird, P. (1993). How diagrams can improve reasoning. *Psychological Science, 4,* 372–378.

Beach, C. M. (1991). The interpretation of prosodic patterns at points of syntactic structural ambiguity: Evidence for cue trading relations. *Journal of Memory and Language, 30,* 644–663.

Beaman, A., Barnes, J., Klentz, B., & McQuirk, B. (1978). Increasing helping rates through information dissemination: Teaching pays. *Personality and Social Psychology Bulletin, 4,* 406–411.

Bédard, J., & Chi, M. (1992). Expertise. *Current Directions in Psychological Science, 1,* 135–139.

Begg, I., Anas, A., & Farinacci, S. (1992). Dissociation of processes in belief: Source recollection, statement familiarity, and the illusion of truth. *Journal of Experimental Psychology: General, 121,* 446–458.

Begg, I., Armour, V., & Kerr, T. (1985). On believing what we remember. *Canadian Journal of Behavioral Science, 17,* 199–214.

Begg, I., & Denny, J. (1969). Empirical reconciliation of atmosphere and conversion interpretations of syllogistic reasoning errors. *Journal of Experimental Psychology, 81,* 351–354.

Begg, I., & Wickelgren, W. A. (1974). Retention

functions for syntactic and lexical vs. semantic information in sentence recognition memory. *Memory & Cognition, 2,* 353–359.

Behrman, M., Moscovitch, M., & Winocur, G. (1994). Intact visual imagery and impaired visual perception in a patient with visual agnosia. *Journal of Experimental Psychology: Human Perception and Performance, 20,* 1068–1087.

Bell, D. (1982). Regret in decision making under uncertainty. *Operations Research, 30,* 961–981.

Belli, R. (1989). Influences of misleading postevent information: Misinformation interference and acceptance. *Journal of Experimental Psychology: General, 118,* 72–85.

Belli, R., Lindsay, S., Gales, M., & McCarthy, T. (1994). Memory impairment and source misattribution in postevent misinformation experiments with short retention intervals. *Memory & Cognition, 22,* 40–54.

Belli, R., Windschitl, P., McCarthy, T., & Winfrey, S. (1992). Detecting memory impairment with a modified test procedure: Manipulating retention interval with centrally presented event items. *Journal of Experimental Psychology: Learning, Memory and Cognition, 18,* 356–367.

Bellugi, U., Klima, E. S., & Siple, P. (1975). Remembering in signs. *Cognition, 3,* 93–125.

Berardi-Coletta, B., Buyer, L., Dominowski, R., & Rellinger, E. (1995). Metacognition and problem-solving: A process-oriented approach. *Journal of Experimental Psychology: Learning, Memory and Cognition, 21,* 205–223.

Berbaum, K., & Chung, C. (1981). Muller-Lyer illusion induced by imagination. *Journal of Mental Imagery, 5,* 125–128.

Berko, J. (1958). The child's learning of English morphology. *Word, 14,* 150–177.

Bermant, G., & Starr, M. (1972). Telling people what they are likely to do: Three experiments. In *Proceedings of the 80th Annual Convention of the American Psychological Association,* (pp. 171–172).

Bever, T. (1970). The cognitive basis for linguistic structures. In J. R. Hayes (Ed.), *Cognition and the development of language* (pp. 279–362). New York: Wiley.

Bhaskar, R., & Simon, H. (1977). Problem solving in semantically rich domains: An example from engineering thermodynamics. *Cognitive Science, 1,* 193–215.

Bickerton, D. (1984). The language bioprogram hypothesis. *Behavioral and Brain Sciences, 7,* 173–221.

Bickman, L. (1975). Bystander intervention in a crime: The effect of a mass-media campaign. *Journal of Applied Social Psychology, 5,* 296–302.

Biederman, I. (1985). Human vision understanding: Recent research and a theory. *Computer Vision, Graphics, and Image Processing, 32,* 29–73.

Biederman, I. (1987). Recognition by components: A theory of human image understanding. *Psychological Review, 94,* 115–147.

Biederman, I., & Cooper, E. (1991). Priming contour-deleted images: Evidence for intermediate representations in visual object recognition. *Cognitive Psychology, 23,* 393–419.

Biederman, I., & Cooper, E. (1992). Size invariance in visual object priming. *Journal of Experimental Psychology: Human Perception and Performance, 18,* 121–133.

Biederman, I., & Gerhardstein, P. (1993). Recognizing depth-rotated objects: Evidence and conditions for three-dimensional viewpoint invariance. *Journal of Experimental Psychology: Human Perception and Performance, 19,* 1162–1182.

Biederman, I., Glass, A. L., & Stacy, E. W. (1973). Searching for objects in real world scenes. *Journal of Experimental Psychology, 97,* 22–27.

Bisiach, E., & Luzzatti, C. (1978). Unilateral neglect of representational space. *Cortex, 14,* 129–133.

Bisiach, E., Luzzatti, C., & Perani, D. (1979). Unilateral neglect, representational schema, and consciousness. *Brain, 102,* 609–618.

Bjork, R. A., & Whitten, W. B. (1974). Recency-sensitive retrieval processes. *Cognitive Psychology, 6,* 173–189.

Blaney, P. H. (1986). Affect and memory: A review. *Psychological Bulletin, 99,* 229–246.

Blaxton, T. A. (1989). Investigating dissociations among memory measures: Support for a transfer-appropriate processing framework. *Journal of Experimental Psychology: Learning, Memory and Cognition, 15,* 657–688.

Bliss, D., Sledjeski, M., & Leiman, A. (1971). State dependent choice behavior in the rhesus monkey. *Neuorpsychologia, 9,* 51–59.

Bloom, A. (1981). *The linguistic shaping of thought: A study of the impact of language on thinking in China and the West.* Hillsdale, NJ: Lawrence Erlbaum.

Bloom, L., & Mudd, S. (1991). Depth of processing approach to face recognition: A test of two theories. *Journal of Experimental Psychology: Learning, Memory and Cognition, 17,* 556–565.

Bloom, P. (Ed.), (1994). *Language acquisition.* Cambridge, MA: MIT Press.

Bobrow, S., & Bower, G. H. (1969). Comprehension and recall of sentences. *Journal of Experimental Psychology, 80,* 455–461.

Boden, M. (1991). *The creative mind: Myths and mechanisms.* New York: Basic.

Boden, M. (Ed.). (1994). *Dimensions of creativity.* Cambridge, MA: Bradford Books.

Bohannon, J. N. (1988). Flashbulb memories of the space shuttle disaster: A tale of two theories. *Cognition, 29,* 179–196.

Bohannon, J. N. (1993). Affect and accuracy in recall: Studies of "flashbulb" memories. In E. Winograd & U. Neisser (Eds.), *Affect and accuracy in recall: Studies of "flashbulb" memories.* New York: Cambridge University Press.

Boole, G. (1854). *An investigation of the laws of thought, on which are founded the mathematical theories of logic and probabilities.* London: Walton G. Maberly.

Borges, J. L. (1964). *Labyrinths.* New York: New Directions Publishing Co.

Bornstein, B. (1963). Prosopagnosia. In L. Halpern (Ed.), *Problems of dynamic neurology.* Jerusalem: Hadassah Medical Organization.

Bornstein, B., Sroka, H., & Munitz, H. (1969). Prosopagnosia with animal face agnosia. *Cortex, 5,* 164–169.

Bothwell, R. K., Deffenbacher, K. A., & Brigham, J. C. (1987). Correlation of eyewitness accuracy and confidence: Optimality hypothesis revisited. *Journal of Applied Psychology, 72,* 691–695.

Bousfield, W. A. (1953). The occurrence of clustering in the recall of randomly arranged associates. *Journal of General Psychology, 49,* 229–240.

Bower, G. H. (1970). Analysis of a mnemonic device. *American Scientist, 58,* 496–510.

Bower, G. H. (1972). Mental imagery and associative learning. In L. W. Gregg (Ed.), *Cognition in learning and memory.* New York: Wiley.

Bower, G. H. (1981). Mood and memory. *American Psychologist, 36,* 129–148.

Bower, G. H., Black, J. B., & Turner, T. J. (1979). Scripts in memory for text. *Cognitive Psychology, 11,* 177–220.

Bower, G. H., Clark, M. C., Lesgold, A. M., & Winzenz, D. (1969). Hierarchical retrieval schemes in recall of categorized word lists. *Journal of Verbal Learning and Verbal Behavior, 8,* 323–343.

Bower, G. H., & Karlin, M. B. (1974). Depth of processing pictures of faces and recognition memory. *Journal of Experimental Psychology, 103,* 751–757.

Bower, G. H., Karlin, M. B., & Dueck, A. (1975). Comprehension and memory for pictures. *Memory & Cognition, 3,* 216–220.

Bower, G. H., & Reitman, J. S. (1972). Mnemonic elaboration in multilist learning. *Journal of Verbal Learning and Verbal Behavior, 11,* 478–485.

Bower, G. H., Thomson-Schill, S., & Tulving, E. (1994). Reducing retroactive interference: An interference analysis. *Journal of Experimental Psychology: Learning, Memory and Cognition, 20,* 51–66.

Bower, G. H., & Winzenz, D. (1970). Comparison of associative learning strategies. *Psychonomic Science, 20,* 119–120.

Bowers, R., Mollenhauer, M., & Luxford, J. (1990). Short-term memory for tactile and temporal stimuli in a shared-attention recall task. *Perceptual and Motor Skills, 70,* 903–913.

Boyce, S., & Pollatsek, A. (1992). Identification of objects in scenes: The role of scene background in object naming. *Journal of Experimental Psychology: Learning, Memory and Cognition, 18,* 531–543.

Braine, M. (1978). On the relation between the natural logic of reasoning and standard logic. *Psychological Review, 85,* 1–21.

Braine, M., & O'Brien, D. (1991). A theory of *if*: A lexical entry, reasoning program, and pragmatic principles. *Psychological Review, 98,* 182–203.

Braine, M., Reiser, B. J., & Rumain, B. (1984). Some empirical justification for a theory of natural propositional logic. In G. H. Bower (Ed.), *The psychology of learning and motivation.* New York: Academic Press.

Bransford, J. (1979). *Human cognition: Learning, understanding and remembering.* Belmont, CA: Wadsworth.

Bransford, J., Barclay, J. R., & Franks, J. J. (1972). Sentence memory: A constructive versus interpretive approach. *Cognitive Psychology, 3,* 193–209.

Bransford, J., & Franks, J. J. (1971). The abstraction of linguistic ideas. *Cognitive Psychology, 2,* 331–350.

Bransford, J., Franks, J. J., Morris, C. D., & Stein, B. S. (1979). Some general constraints on learning and memory research. In L. S. Cermak & F. I. M. Craik (Eds.), *Levels of processing in human memory.* Hillsdale, NJ: Lawrence Erlbaum.

Bransford, J., & Johnson, M. K. (1972). Contextual prerequisites for understanding: some investigations of comprehension and recall. *Journal of Verbal Learning and Verbal Behavior, 11,* 717–726.

Bransford, J., & Johnson, M. K. (1973). Considerations of some problems of comprehension. In W. G. Chase (Ed.), *Visual information processing.* New York: Academic Press.

Brennen, T., Baguley, T., Bright, J., & Bruce, V. (1990). Resolving semantically induced tip-of-the-tongue states for proper nouns. *Memory & Cognition, 18,* 339–347.

Brewer, W. (1977). Memory for the pragmatic implications of sentences. *Memory & Cognition, 5,* 673–678.

Brewer, W. (1987). Schemas vs. mental models in human memory. In P. Morris (Ed.), *Modeling cognition* (pp. 187–197). New York: Wiley.

Brewer, W. (1988). Memory for randomly sampled autobiographical events. In U. Neisser & E. W. Winograd (Eds.), *Remembering reconsidered.* Cambridge: Cambridge University Press.

Brewer, W., & Treyens, J. C. (1981). Role of schemata in memory for places. *Cognitive Psychology, 13,* 207–230.

Brewin, C., Andrews, B., & Gotlib, I. (1993). Psychopathology and early experience: A reappraisal of retrospective reports. *Psychological Bulletin, 113,* 82–98.

Briand, K., & Klein, R. (1987). Is Posner's "beam" the same as Treisman's "glue"? *Journal of Experimental Psychology: Human Perception and Performance, 13,* 228–241.

Brigham, J. (1986). The influence of race on face recognition. In H. D. Ellis, M. A. Jeeves, F. Newcombe, & A. Young (Eds.), *Aspects of face processing* (pp. 170–177). Dordrecht, Netherlands: Martinus Nijhoff.

Brigham, J. (1990). Target person distinctiveness and attractiveness as moderator variables in the confidence-accuracy relationship in eyewitness identifications. *Basic and Applied Social Psychology, 11,* 101–115.

Brigham, J., & Cairns, D. L. (1988). The effect of mugshot inspections on eyewitness identification accuracy. *Journal of Applied Social Psychology, 18,* 1394–1410.

Brigham, J., Ready, D., & Spier, S. (1990). Standards for evaluating the fairness of photograph lineups. *Basic and Applied Social Psychology, 11,* 149–163.

Brigham, J., & Wolfskiel, M. P. (1983). Opinions

of attorneys and law enforcement personnel on the accuracy of eyewitness identification. *Law and Human Behavior, 7*, 337–349.

Broadbent, D. E. (1958). *Perception and communication.* London: Pergamon.

Brooks, L. (1967). The suppression of visualization by reading. *Quarterly Journal of Experimental Psychology, 19*, 289–299.

Brooks, L. (1968). Spatial and verbal components of the act of recall. *Canadian Journal of Psychology, 22*, 349–368.

Brooks, L. (1978). Non-analytic concept formation and memory for instances. In E. Rosch & B. Lloyd (Eds.), *Cognition and Categorization.* Hillsdale, NJ: Lawrence Erlbaum.

Brooks, L. (1987). Decentralized control of categorization: the role of prior processing episodes. In U. Neisser (Ed.), *Concepts and conceptual development.* Cambridge: Cambridge University Press.

Brooks, L. (1990). Concept formation and particularizing learning. In P. Hanson (Ed.), *Information, language and cognition.* Vancouver, BC: University of British Columbia Press.

Brooks, L., Norman, G., & Allen, S. (1991). Role of specific similarity in a medical diagnostic task. *Journal of Experimental Psychology: General, 120*, 278–287.

Brown, A. (1991). A review of the tip-of-the-tongue experience. *Psychological Bulletin, 109*, 204–223.

Brown, A., Neblett, D., Jones, T., & Mitchell, D. (1991). Transfer of processing in repetition priming: Some inappropriate findings. *Journal of Experimental Psychology: Learning, Memory and Cognition, 17*, 514–525.

Brown, A. L. (1979). Theories of memory and the problems of development: Activity, growth, and knowledge. In L. S. Cermak & F. I. M. Craik (Eds.), *Levels of processing in human memory.* Hillsdale, NJ: Lawrence Erlbaum.

Brown, A. S., & Halliday, H. E. (1990). Multiple-choice tests: Pondering incorrect alternatives can be hazardous to your knowledge. Paper presented at the meeting of the Psychonomics Society, November 1990, New Orleans.

Brown, E., Deffenbacher, K., & Sturgill, W. (1977). Memory for faces and the circumstances of encounter. *Journal of Applied Psychology, 62*, 311–318: .

Brown, J. (1958). Some tests of the decay theory of immediate memory. *Quarterly Journal of Experimental Psychology, 10*, 12–21.

Brown, J. S., & Van Lehn, K. (1980). Repair theory: A generative theory of bugs in procedural skills. *Cognitive Science, 4*, 379–426.

Brown, N., & Siegler, R. (1993). Metrics and mappings: A framework for understanding real-world quantitative estimation. *Psychological Review, 100*, 511–534.

Brown, R., & Kulik, J. (1977). Flashbulb memories. *Cognition, 5*, 73–99.

Brown, R., & Lenneberg, E. H. (1954). A study in language and cognition. *Journal of Abnormal and Social Psychology, 49*, 454–462.

Brown, R., & McNeill, D. (1966). The "tip of the tongue" phenomenon. *Journal of Verbal Learning and Verbal Behavior, 5*, 325–337.

Bruce, D. (1989). The how and why of ecological memory. *Journal of Experimental Psychology: General, 114*, 78–90.

Bruce, D., Hockley, W., & Craik, F. (1991). Availability and category-frequency estimation. *Memory & Cognition, 19*, 301–312.

Bruce, V. (1988). *Recognizing faces.* Hillsdale, NJ: Lawrence Erlbaum.

Bruce, V., Doyle, T., Dench, N., & Burton, M. (1991). Remembering facial configurations. *Cognition, 38*, 109–144.

Bruce, V., Valentine, T., & Baddeley, A. (1987). The basis of the 3/4 view advantage in face recognition. *Applied Cognitive Psychology, 1*, 109–120.

Bruck, M., Cavanagh, P., & Ceci, S. (1991). Fortysomething: Recognizing faces at one's 25th reunion. *Memory & Cognition, 19*, 221–228.

Bruner, J., Goodnow, J., & Austin, G. (1956). *A study of thinking.* New York: Wiley.

Burke, A., Heuer, F., & Reisberg, D. (1992). Remembering emotional events. *Memory & Cognition, 20*, 277–290.

Burton, A. M., Young, A., Bruce, V., Johnston,

R., & Ellis, A. (1991). Understanding covert recognition. *Cognition, 39,* 129–166.

Burtt, E. A. (1954). *The metaphysical foundations of modern science.* Garden City, NY: Double-day Anchor Books.

Buschke, H. (1977). Two-dimensional recall: Immediate identification of clusters in episodic and semantic memory. *Journal of Verbal Learning and Verbal Behavior, 16,* 201–215.

Cahill, L., Prins, B., Weber, M., & McGaugh, J. (1994). β-Adrenergic activation and memory for emotional events. *Nature, 371,* 702–704.

Cann, A., & Ross, D. (1989). Olfactory stimuli as context cues in human memory. *American Journal of Psychology, 2,* 91–102.

Cantor, J., & Engle, R. (1993). Working-memory capacity as long-term memory activation: An individual-differences approach. *Journal of Experimental Psychology: Learning, Memory and Cognition, 19,* 1101–1114.

Caplan, D. (1987). *Neurolinguistics and linguistic aphasiology.* New York: Cambridge University Press.

Caplan, D. (1992). *Language: Structure, processing and disorders.* Cambridge, MA: MIT Press.

Carey, S. (1985). *Conceptual change in childhood.* Cambridge, MA: Bradford/MIT Press.

Carmichael, L. C., Hogan, H. P., & Walters, A. A. (1932). An experimental study of the effect of language on the reproduction of visually perceived form. *Journal of Experimental Psychology, 15,* 73–86.

Carpenter, P., & Eisenberg, P. (1978). Mental rotation and the frame of reference in blind and sighted individuals. *Perception & Psychophysics, 23,* 117–124.

Carpenter, P., Just, M., & Shell, P. (1990). What one intelligence test measures: A theoretical account of the processing in the Raven Progressive Matrices Test. *Psychological Review, 97,* 404–431.

Casey, E. (1976). *Imagining: A phenomenological study.* Bloomington: Indiana University Press.

Castiello, U., & Umiltà, C. (1990). Size of the attentional focus and efficiency of processing. *Acta Psychologica, 73,* 195–209.

Castiello, U., & Umiltà, C. (1992). Splitting focal attention. *Journal of Experimental Psychology: Human Perception and Performance, 18,* 837–848.

Catrambone, R. (1994). Improving examples to improve transfer to novel problems. *Memory & Cognition, 22,* 606–615.

Catrambrone, R., & Holyoak, K. (1989). Overcoming contextual limitations on problem-solving transfer. *Journal of Experimental Psychology: Learning, Memory and Cognition, 15,* 1147–1156.

Cattell, J. M. (1885). Uberdi Aeit der Erkennung and Benennung von Schriftzeichen, Bildern and Farben. *Philos, 2,* 635–650.

Ceci, S., & Bruck, M. (1993). Suggestibility of the child witness: A historical review and synthesis. *Psychological Bulletin, 113,* 403–439.

Ceci, S., Huffman, M., & Smith, E. (1994). Repeatedly thinking about a non-event: Source misattributions among preschoolers. *Consciousness and Cognition, 3,* 388–407.

Challis, B., & Brodbeck, D. (1992). Level of processing affects priming in word fragment completion. *Journal of Experimental Psychology: Learning, Memory and Cognition, 18,* 595–607.

Challis, B., Chiu, C.-Y., Kerr, S., Law, J., Schneider, L., Yonelinas, A., & Tulving, E. (1993). Perceptual and conceptual cueing in implicit and explicit retrieval. *Memory, 1,* 127–151.

Chambers, D., & Reisberg, D. (1985). Can mental images be ambiguous? *Journal of Experimental Psychology: Human Perception and Performance, 11,* 317–328.

Chambers, D., & Reisberg, D. (1992). What an image depicts depends on what an image means. *Cognitive Psychology, 24,* 145–174.

Chandler, C. (1994). Studying related pictures can reduce accuracy, but increase confidence, in a modified recognition test. *Memory & Cognition, 22,* 273–280.

Chapman, J., & Chapman, J. (1959). Atmosphere effect re-examined. *Journal of Experimental Psychology, 58,* 220–226.

Chapman, L. J., & Chapman, J. (1971). Test results are what you think they are. *Psychology Today*, November, 18–22, 106–110.

Charniak, E. (1972). *Toward a model of children's story comprehension.* Unpublished doctoral dissertation, M.I.T.

Charniak, E., & McDermott, D. (1987). *Introduction to artificial intelligence.* Reading, MA: Addison-Wesley.

Chase, W., & Ericsson, K. A. (1978). Acquisition of a mnemonic system for digit span. Paper presented at the annual meeting of the Psychonomic Society, San Antonio, Texas.

Chase, W., & Ericsson, K. A. (1979). A mnemonic system for digit span: One year later. Paper presented at the annual meeting of the Psychonomic Society, Phoenix, Arizona.

Chase, W., & Ericsson, K. A. (1982). Skill and working memory. In G. H. Bower (Ed.), *The psychology of learning and motivation.* New York: Academic Press.

Chase, W., & Simon, H. (1973). Perception in chess. *Cognitive Psychology, 4*, 55–81.

Cheng, P. (1985). Restructuring versus automaticity: Alternative accounts of skill acquisition. *Psychological Review, 92*, 414–423.

Cheng, P., & Holyoak, K. J. (1985). Pragmatic reasoning schemas. *Cognitive Psychology, 17*, 391–416.

Cheng, P., Holyoak, K. J., Nisbett, R. E., & Oliver, L. M. (1986). Pragmatic versus syntactic approaches to training deductive reasoning. *Cognitive Psychology, 18*, 293–328.

Cheng, P., & Nisbett, R. (1993). Pragmatic constraints on causal deduction. In R. Nisbett (Ed.), *Rules for reasoning.* Hillsdale, NJ: Lawrence Erlbaum.

Cherry, E. C. (1953). Some experiments on the recognition of speech with one and with two ears. *Journal of the Acoustical Society of America, 25*, 975–979.

Chi, M. T. H. (1976). Short-term memory limitations in children: Capacity or processing deficits? *Memory & Cognition, 4*, 559–572.

Chi, M., Feltovish, P., & Glaser, R. (1981). Categorization and representation of physics problems by experts and novices. *Cognitive Science, 5*, 121–152.

Chi, M., Glaser, R., & Farr, M. (Eds.). (1988). *The nature of expertise.* Hillsdale, NJ: Lawrence Erlbaum.

Chomsky, N. (1957). *Syntactic structures.* The Hague: Mouton.

Chomsky, N. (1965). *Aspects of a theory of syntax.* Cambridge, MA: MIT Press.

Chomsky, N. (1975). *Reflections on language.* London: Temple-Smith.

Chomsky, N. (1981). *Lectures on government and binding.* Dordrech, Netherlands: Foris.

Chomsky, N. (1986). *Knowledge of language: Its nature, origin and use.* New York: Praeger.

Chomsky, N., & Halle, M. (1968). *The sound pattern of English.* New York: Harper Row.

Christen, F., & Bjork, R. A. (1976). On updating the loci in the method of loci. Paper presented at the meeting of the Psychonomic Society, November 1976, St. Louis.

Christensen-Szalanski, J., Beck, D., Christensen-Szalanski, C., & Koepsell, T. (1983). The effect of journal coverage on physicians' perception of risk. *Journal of Applied Psychology, 68*, 278–284.

Christiaansen, R., Sweeney, J., & Ochalek, K. (1983). Influencing eyewitness descriptions. *Law and Human Behavior, 7*, 59–65.

Christianson, S.-Å. (1989). Flashbulb memories: Special, but not so special. *Memory & Cognition, 17*, 435–443.

Christianson, S.-Å. (1992). Emotional stress and eyewitness memory: A critical review. *Psychological Bulletin, 112*, 284–309.

Christianson, S.-Å., & Loftus, E. (1990). Some characteristics of people's traumatic memories. *Bulletin of the Psychonomic Society, 28*, 195–198.

Christianson, S.-Å., & Loftus, E. (1991). Remembering emotional events: The fate of detailed information. *Cognition & Emotion, 5*, 693–701.

Churchland, P. (1988). *Matter and consciousness.* Cambridge, MA: MIT Press.

Churchland, P. (1989). *A neurocomputational*

perspective: The nature of mind and the structure of science. Cambridge, MA: MIT Press.

Clapar de, E. (1911/1951). Reconnaissance et moiité. In D. Rapaport (Ed.), *Organization and pathology of thought.* New York: Columbia University Press.

Clark, H., & Clark, E. (1977). *Psychology and language.* New York: Harcourt, Brace, Jovanovich.

Clement, J. (1982). Analogical reasoning patterns in expert problem solving. Paper presented at the 4th Annual Conference of the Cognitive Science Society, August 1982, Ann Arbor.

Clifton, C., Speer, S., & Abney, S. (1991). Parsing arguments: Phrase structure and argument structure as determinants of initial parsing decisions. *Journal of Memory and Language, 30,* 251–271.

Cofer, C. N., Bruce, D. R., & Reicher, G. M. (1966). Clustering in free recall as a function of certain methodological variations. *Journal of Experimental Psychology, 71,* 858–866.

Cohen, N. J. (1984). Preserved learning capacity in amnesia: Evidence for multiple memory systems. In L. R. Squire & N. Butters (Eds.), *Neuropsychology of memory.* New York: Guilford.

Cohen, N. J., & Squire, L. R. (1980). Preserved learning and retention of pattern analyzing skill in amnesics: Dissociation of knowing how and knowing that. *Science, 210,* 207–210.

Cole, R. A., & Jakimik, J. (1980). A model of speech perception. In R. A. Cole (Ed.), *Perception and the production of fluent speech* (pp. 133–163). Hillsdale, NJ: Lawrence Erlbaum.

Collins, A. M., & Loftus, E. F. (1975). A spreading activation theory of semantic processing. *Psychological Review, 82,* 407–428.

Collins, A. M., & Quillian, M. R. (1969). Retrieval time from semantic memory. *Journal of Verbal Learning and Verbal Behavior, 8,* 240–247.

Coltheart, V. (1993). Effects of phonological similarity and concurrent irrelevant articulation on short-term-memory recall of repeated and novel word lists. *Memory & Cognition, 21,* 539–545.

Combs, B., & Slovic, P. (1979). Causes of death: Biased newspaper coverage and biased judgments. *Journalism Quarterly, 56,* 837–843, 849.

Comrie, B. (1981). *Language universals and linguistic typology.* Chicago: University of Chicago Press.

Conrad, C. (1972). Cognitive economy in semantic memory. *Journal of Experimental Psychology, 92,* 149–154.

Conrad, R. (1964). Acoustic confusion in immediate memory. *British Journal of Psychology, 55,* 75–84.

Conrad, R., & Hull, A. J. (1964). Information, acoustic confusion and memory span. *British Journal of Psychology, 55,* 429–432.

Conway, M., Anderson, S., Larsen, S., Donnelly, C., McDaniel, M., McClelland, A. G. R., Rawles, R., & Logie, R. (1994). The formation of flashbulb memories. *Memory & Cognition, 22,* 326–343.

Conway, M., Cohen, G., & Stanhope, N. (1991). On the very long-term retention of knowledge acquired through formal education: Twelve years of cognitive psychology. *Journal of Experimental Psychology: General, 120,* 395–409.

Conway, M., Cohen, G., & Stanhope, N. (1992). Why is it that university grades do not predict very long term retention? *Journal of Experimental Psychology: General, 121,* 382–384.

Cook, V. J. (1988). *Chomsky's universal grammar: An introduction.* Cambridge, MA: Basil Blackwell.

Cooper, L. (1990). Mental representation of three-dimensional objects in visual problem solving and recognition. *Journal of Experimental Psychology: Learning, Memory and Cognition, 16,* 1097–1106.

Cooper, L., & Schacter, D. (1992). Dissociations between structural and episodic representations of visual objects. *Current Directions in Psychological Science, 1,* 141–145.

Cooper, L., Schacter, D., Ballesteros, S., & Moore, C. (1992). Priming and recognition of transformed three-dimensional objects: Effects of size and reflection. *Journal of Experimental*

Psychology: Learning, Memory and Cognition, 18, 43–57.

Cooper, L., & Shepard, R. N. (1973). Chronometric studies of the rotation of mental images. In W. G. Chase (Ed.), *Visual information processing.* New York: Academic Press.

Corbetta, M., Miezin, F., Dobmeyer, S., Shulman, G., & Petersen, S. (in press). Selective and divided attention during visual discriminations of shape, color, and speed: Functional anatomy by positron emission tomography. *Behavioral Neuroscience.*

Corteen, R. S., & Dunn, D. (1974). Shock-associated words in a nonattended message: A test for momentary awareness. *Journal of Experimental Psychology, 102*, 1143–1144.

Corteen, R. S., & Wood, B. (1972). Autonomic responses to shock-associated words in an unattended channel. *Journal of Experimental Psychology, 94*, 308–313.

Corter, J., & Gluck, M. (1992). Explaining basic categories: Feature predictability and information. *Psychological Bulletin, 111*, 291–303.

Costermans, J., Lories, G., & Ansay, C. (1992). Confidence level and feeling of knowing in question answering: The weight of inferential processes. *Journal of Experimental Psychology: Learning, Memory and Cognition, 18*, 142–150.

Cowan, N., Wood, N., & Borne, D. (1994). Reconfirmation of the short-term storage concept. *Psychological Science, 5*, 103–107.

Craik, F. I. M., & Lockhart, R. S. (1972). Levels of processing: A framework for memory research. *Journal of Verbal Learning and Verbal Behavior, 11*, 671–684.

Craik, F. I. M., Moscovitch, M., & McDown, J. (1994). Contributions of surface and conceptual information to performance on implicit and explicit memory tasks. *Journal of Experimental Psychology: Learning, Memory and Cognition, 20*, 864–875.

Craik, F. I. M., & Tulving, E. (1975). Depth of processing and the retention of words in episodic memory. *Journal of Experimental Psychology: General, 104*, 269–294.

Craik, F. I. M., & Watkins, M. J. (1973). The role of rehearsal in short-term memory. *Journal of Verbal Learning and Verbal Behavior, 12*, 599–607.

Crick, F. (1989). The recent excitement about neural networks. *Nature, 337*, 129–132.

Crick, F. (1994). *The astonishing hypothesis: The scientific search for the soul.* New York: Charles Scribners' Sons.

Crowder, R. (1982). *Principles of learning and memory.* Hillsdale, NJ: Lawrence Erlbaum.

Crowder, R. (1993). Short-term memory: Where do we stand? *Memory & Cognition, 21*, 142–145.

Crowder, R., & Wagner, R. (1992). *The psychology of reading* (2nd ed.). New York: Oxford University Press.

Crutcher, R. (1994). Telling what we know: The use of verbal report methodologies in psychological research. *Psychological Science, 5*, 241–244.

Crystal, D. (1987). *The Cambridge encyclopedia of language.* Cambridge, MA: Cambridge University Press.

Cummins, D. (1992). Role of analogical reasoning in induction of problem categories. *Journal of Experimental Psychology: Learning, Memory and Cognition, 18*, 1103–1124.

Cutler, B. L., Fisher, R. P., & Chicvara, C. L. (1989). Eyewitness identification from live versus videotaped lineups. *Forensic Reports, 2*, 93–106.

Cutler, B. L., & Penrod, S. D. (1988). Improving the reliability of eyewitness identification: Lineup construction and presentation. *Journal of Applied Psychology, 73*, 281–290.

Cutler, B. L., & Penrod, S. D. (1989). Forensically relevant moderators of the relation between eyewitness identification accuracy and confidence. *Journal of Applied Psychology, 74*, 650–652.

Cutler, B. L., Penrod, S. D., & Stuve, T. E. (1988). Juror decision making in eyewitness identification cases. *Law and Human Behavior, 12*, 41–55.

da Costa Pinto, A., & Baddeley, A. (1991). Where did you park your car? Analysis of naturalistic long-term recency effect. *European Journal of Cognitive Psychology, 3*, 297–313.

Dale, H. C. A., & Baddeley, A. D. (1969). Acoustic similarity in long-term paired-associate learning. *Psychonomic Science, 16*, 209–211.

Damasio, A. , Damasio, H., & Van Hoesen, G. W. (1982). Prosopagnosia: Anatomic basis and behavioral mechanisms. *Neurology, 32*, 331–341.

Damasio, A., Tranel, D., & Damasio, H. (1990). Face agnosia and the neural substrates of memory. *Annual Review of Neuroscience, 13*, 89–109.

Daneman, M., & Carpenter, P. (1980). Individual differences in working memory and reading. *Journal of Verbal Learning and Verbal Behavior, 19*, 450–466.

Daneman, M., & Stainton, M. (1991). Phonological coding in silent reading. *Journal of Experimental Psychology: Learning, Memory and Cognition, 17*, 618–632.

Daniloff, R., & Hammarberg, R. (1973). On defining coarticulation. *Journal of Phonetics, 1*, 185–194.

Darley, J., & Batson, D. (1973). "From Jerusalem to Jericho": A study of situational and dispositional variables in helping behavior. *The Journal of Personality and Social Psychology, 27*, 100–108.

Darley, J., & Latane, B. (1968). Bystander intervention in emergencies: Diffusion of responsibility. *Journal of Personality and Social Psychology, 10*, 202–214.

Davison, G., Navarre, S., & Vogel, R. (1995). The articulated thoughts in simulated situations paradigm: A think-aloud approach to cognitive assessment. *Current Directions in Psychological Science, 4*, 29–33.

Dawes, R. M. (1988). *Rational choice in an uncertain world*. San Diego: Harcourt Brace Jovanovich.

De Groot, A. (1965). *Thought and choice in chess*. The Hague: Mouton.

De Groot, A. (1966). Perception and memory versus thought: Some old ideas and recent findings. In B. Kleinmuntz (Ed.), *Problem solving*. New York: Wiley.

De Jong, R. (1993). Multiple bottlenecks in overlapping task performance. *Journal of Experimental Psychology: Human Perception and Performance, 19*, 965–980.

De Jong, R., & Sweet, J. (1994). Preparatory strategies in overlapping-task performance. *Memory & Cognition, 55*, 142–151.

Deese, J., & Kaufman, R. A. (1957). Serial effects in recall of unorganized and sequentially organized verbal material. *Journal of Experimental Psychology, 54*, 180–187.

Deffenbacher, K. (1980). Eyewitness accuracy and confidence: Can we infer anything about their relationship. *Law and Human Behavior, 4*, 243–260.

Deffenbacher, K. (1988). Eyewitness research: The next ten years. In M. Gruneberg, P. Morris, & R. Sykes (Eds.), *Practical aspects of memory: Current research and issues* (pp. 20–26). New York: Wiley.

Deffenbacher, K., & Loftus, E. F. (1982). Do jurors share a common understanding concerning eyewitness behavior? *Law and Human Behavior, 6*, 15–30.

Demers, R. (1989). Linguistics and animal communication. In F. Newmeyer (Ed.), *Linguistics: The Cambridge Survey. III. Language: Psychological and biological aspects*. Cambridge, MA: Cambridge University Press.

Dempster, F. N. (1981). Memory span: Sources of individual and developmental differences. *Psychological Bulletin, 89*, 63–100.

Dennett, D. (1981). The nature of images and the introspective trap. In N. Block (Ed.), *Imagery* (pp. 51–61). Cambridge, MA: MIT Press.

Dennett, D. (1992). *Consciousness explained*. Boston: Little, Brown.

De Renzi, E., Faglioni, P., Grossi, D., & Nichelli, P. (1991). Apperceptive and associative forms of prosopagnosia. *Cortex, 27*, 213–221.

Dewey, J. (1903). *Studies in logical theory—The decennial publications, 2nd ser.: vol. 11*. Chicago: University of Chicago Press.

DeWitt, L., & Samuel, A. (1990) The role of

knowledge-based expectations in music perception: Evidence from musical restoration. *Journal of Experimental Psychology: General, 119*, 123–144.

Diamond, R., & Carey, S. (1986). Why faces are and are not special: An effect of expertise. *Journal of Experimental Psychology: General, 115*, 107–117.

Dinges, D., Whitehouse, W., Orne, E., Powell, J., Orne, M., & Erdelyi, M. (1992). Evaluation of hypnotic memory enhancement (hypermnesia and reminiscence) using multitrial forced recall. *Journal of Experimental Psychology: Learning, Memory and Cognition, 18*, 1139–1147.

Dingwall, W. O. (1993). The biological bases of human communicative behavior. In J. Berko Gleason & N. Bernstein Ratner (Eds.), *Psycholinguistics*. New York: Harcourt Brace Jovanovich.

Dominowski, R. (1981). Comment on "An examination of the alleged role of 'fixation' in the solution of several insight problems" by Weisberg and Alba. *Journal of Experimental Psychology: General, 110*, 193–198.

Dominowski, R., & Jenrick, R. (1972). Effects of hints and interpolated activity on solution of an insight problem. *Psychonomic Science, 26*, 335–338.

Donnelly, C., & McDaniel, M. (1993). Use of analogy in learning scientific concepts. *Journal of Experimental Psychology: Learning, Memory and Cognition, 19*, 975–986.

Dooling, D. J., & Christiaansen, R. E. (1977). Episodic and semantic aspects of memory for prose. *Journal of Experimental Psychology: Human Learning and Memory, 3*, 428–436.

Dooling, D. J., & Lachman, R. (1971). Effects of comprehension on retention of prose. *Journal of Experimental Psychology, 88*, 216–222.

Dreyfus, H. (1979). *What computers can't do* (rev. ed.). New York: Harper Colophon Books.

Dudycha, G. J., & Dudycha, M. M. (1941). Childhood memories: A review of the literature. *Psychological Bulletin, 38*, 668–682.

Duncan, J. (1984). Selective attention and the organization of visual information. *Journal of Experimental Psychology: General, 113*, 501–517.

Duncan, J. (1994). Attention, intelligence, and the frontal lobes. In M. Gazzaniga (Ed.), *The cognitive neurosciences*. Cambridge, MA: MIT Press.

Duncker, K. (1945). On problem-solving. *Psychological monographs, 58*, No. 270 (entire).

Dunning, D., & Parpal, M. (1989). Mental addition versus subtraction in counterfactual reasoning. *Journal of Personality and Social Psychology, 57*, 5–15.

Durso, F., Rea, C., & Dayton, T. (1994). Graph-theoretic confirmation of restructuring during insight. *Psychological Science, 5*, 94–98.

Dywan, J., & Bowers, K. (1983). The use of hypnosis to enhance recall. *Science, 222*, 184–185.

Easterbrook, J. A. (1959). The effect of emotion on cue utilization and the organization of behavior. *Psychological Review, 66*, 183–201.

Eddy, D. M. (1982). Probabilistic reasoning in clinical medicine: Problems and opportunities. In D. Kahneman, P. Slovic, & A. Tversky (Eds.), *Judgment under uncertainty: Heuristics and biases*. Cambridge: Cambridge University Press.

Egan, D., & Greeno, J. (1974). Theories of rule induction: Knowledge acquired in concept learning, serial pattern learning, and problem solving. In L. Gregg (Ed.), *Knowledge and cognition* (pp. 43–104). New York: Wiley.

Egan, D., & Schwartz, B. (1979). Chunking in the recall of symbolic drawings. *Memory & Cognition, 7*, 149–158.

Egeth, H. (1993). What do we *not* know about eyewitness identification? *American Psychologist, 48*, 577–580.

Eich, E. (1995). Mood as a mediator of place dependent memory. *Journal of Experimental Psychology: General, 124*, 293–308.

Eich, E., & Metcalfe, J. (1989). Mood dependent memory for internal versus external events. *Journal of Experimental Psychology: Learning, Memory, and Cognition, 15*, 443–455.

Eich, E., Reeves, J., Jaeger, B., & Graff-Radford,

S. (1985). Memory for pain: Relation between past and present pain intensity. *Pain, 23,* 375–380.

Eich, J. E. (1980). The cue-dependent nature of state dependent retrieval. *Memory & Cognition, 8,* 157–173.

Eich, J., Weingartner, H., Stillman, R. C., & Gillin, J. C. (1975). State-dependent accessibility of retrieval cues in the retention of a categorized list. *Journal of Verbal Learning and Verbal Behavior, 14,* 408–417.

Eimas, P., & Corbit, J. (1973). Selective adaptation of linguistic feature detectors. *Cognitive Psychology, 4,* 99–109.

Einhorn, H., & Hogarth, R. (1981). Behavioral decision theory: Processes of judgment and choice. *Annual Review of Psychology, 32,* 53–88.

Einstein, G. O., McDaniel, M. A., & Lackey, S. (1989). Bizarre imagery, interference, and distinctiveness. *Journal of Experimental Psychology: Learning, Memory, and Cognition, 15,* 137–146.

Ekstrand, B. R. (1967). Effect of sleep on memory. *Journal of Experimental Psychology, 75,* 64–72.

Ekstrand, B. R. (1972). To sleep, perchance to dream (about why we forget). In C. P. Duncan, L. Sechrest & A. W. Melton (Eds.), *Human memory: Festschrift for Benton J. Underwood* (pp. 59–82). New York: Appleton-Century-Crofts.

Elias, C. S., & Perfetti, C. A. (1973). Encoding task and recognition memory: The importance of semantic encoding. *Journal of Experimental Psychology, 99,* 151–156.

Ellis, H. (1989). Past and recent studies of prosopagnosia. In J. Crawford & D. Parker (Eds.), *Developments in clinical and experimental neuropsychology* (pp. 151–166). New York: Plenum.

Ellis, H. C., & Ashbrook, P. W. (1989). The "state" of mood and memory research: A selective review. *Journal of Social Behavior and Personality, 4,* 1–21.

Ellis, N., Detterman, D., Runcie, D., McCarver,

R., & Craig, E. (1971). Amnesic effects in short-term memory. *Journal of Experimental Psychology, 89,* 357–361.

Ellis, N., & Henneley, R. A. (1980). A bilingual word-length effect: Implications for intelligence testing and the relative ease of mental calculation in Welsh and English. *British Journal of Psychology, 71,* 43–52.

Elstein, A., Holzman, G., Ravitch, M., Metheny, W., Holmes, M., Hoppe, R., Rothbert, M., & Rovner, D. (1986). Comparison of physicians' decisions regarding estrogen replacement therapy for menopausal women and decisions derived from a decision analytic model. *American Journal of Medicine, 80,* 246–258.

Engelkamp, J. (1986). Motor programs as part of the meaning of verbal items. In I. Kurcz, E. Shugar, & J. H. Danks (Eds.), *Knowledge and language.* Amsterdam: North-Holland.

Engelkamp, J. (1991). Imagery and enactment in paired-associate learning. In R. H. Logie & M. Denis (Eds.), *Mental images in human cognition* (pp. 119–128). Amsterdam: Elsevier.

Engelkamp, J., Zimmer, H., Mohr, G., & Sellen, O. (1994). Memory of self-performed tasks: Self-performing during recognition. *Memory & Cognition, 22,* 34–39.

Engle, R., Cantor, J., & Carullo, J. (1992). Individual differences in working memory and comprehension: A test of four hypotheses. *Journal of Experimental Psychology: Learning, Memory and Cognition, 18,* 972–992.

Epstein, W. (1961). The influence of syntactical structure on learning. *American Journal of Psychology, 74,* 80–85.

Erdelyi, M. (1974). A new look at the New Look: Perceptual defense and vigilance. *Psychological Review, 81,* 1–25.

Erdelyi, M. (1985). *Psychoanalysis.* New York: W. H. Freeman & Co.

Erdelyi, M., & Becker, J. (1974). Hypermnesia for pictures: Incremental memory for pictures but not words in multiple recall trials. *Cognitive Psychology, 6,* 159–171.

Erdelyi, M., Buschke, H., & Finkelstein, S. (1977). Hypermnesia for Socratic stimuli: The growth of recall for an internally generated memory list abstracted from a series of riddles. *Memory & Cognition, 5,* 283–286.

Erdelyi, M., Finkelstein, S., Herrell, N., Miller, B., & Thomas, J. (1976). Coding modality vs. input modality in hypermnesia: Is a rose a rose a rose? *Cognition, 4,* 311–319.

Erdelyi, M., & Goldberg, B. (1979). Let's not sweep repression under the rug: Toward a cognitive psychology of repression. In J. F. Kihlstrom & F. J. Evans (Eds.), *Functional disorders of memory.* Hillsdale, NJ: Lawrence Erlbaum.

Erdelyi, M., & Kleinbard, J. (1978). Has Ebbinghaus decayed with time?: The growth of recall (hypermnesia) over days. *Journal of Experimental Psychology: Human Learning and Memory, 4,* 275–289.

Ericsson, K., Chase, W. G., & Faloon, S. (1980). Acquisition of a memory skill. *Science, 208,* 1181–1182.

Ericsson, K., & Simon, H. (1980). Verbal reports as data. *Psychological Review, 87,* 215–251.

Eriksen, C., & St. James, J. (1986). Visual attention within and around the field of focal attention. A zoom lens model. *Perception & Psychophysics, 40,* 225–240.

Eriksen, C., & Yeh, Y. (1985). Allocation of attention in the visual field. *Journal of Experimental Psychology: Human Perception and Performance, 11,* 583–597.

Ernest, C. (1977). Imagery ability and cognition: A critical review. *Journal of Mental Imagery, 2,* 181–216.

Ervin-Tripp, S. (1993). Conversational discourse. In J. B. Gleason & N. B. Ratner (Eds.), *Psycholinguistics.* New York: Harcourt Brace Jovanovich.

Estes, W. (1972). An associative basis for coding and organization in memory. In A. W. Melton & E. Martin (Eds.), *Coding processes in human memory.* Washington, DC: Winston.

Estes, W. (1973). Memory and conditioning. In F. J. McGuigan & D. B. Lumsden (Eds.), *Contemporary approaches to conditioning and learning.* Washington, DC: Winston.

Estes, W. (1976). Structural aspects of associative models for memory. In C. N. Cofer (Ed.), *The structure of human memory.* San Francisco: Freeman.

Estes, W. (1993). Concepts, categories and psychological science. *Psychological Science, 4,* 143–153.

Etcoff, N., & Magee, J. (1992). Categorical perception of facial expressions. *Cognition, 44,* 227–240.

Evans, J. (1993). The mental model theory of conditional reasoning: Critical appraisal and revision. *Cognition, 48,* 1–20.

Evans, J., Over, D., & Manktelow, K. (1993). Reasoning, decision making and rationality. *Cognition, 49,* 165–187.

Evans, J. S. B. T. (1982). *The psychology of deductive reasoning.* London: Routledge & Kegan Paul.

Evans, J. S. B. T. (1989). *Bias in human reasoning.* Hillsdale, NJ: Lawrence Erlbaum.

Evans, J. S. B. T., Barston, J., & Pollard, P. (1983). On the conflict between logic and belief in syllogistic reasoning. *Memory & Cognition, 11,* 295–306.

Evans, J. S. B. T., Newstead, S. E., & Byrne, R. M. J. (1993). *Human reasoning: The psychology of deduction.* London: Lawrence Erlbaum.

Eylon, B., & Reif, F. (1984). Effects of knowledge organization on task performance. *Cognition and Instruction, 1,* 5–44.

Eysenck, M. W. (1982). *Attention and arousal: Cognition and performance.* Berlin: Springer Verlag.

Farah, M. (1985). Psychophysical evidence for a shared representational medium for mental images and percepts. *Journal of Experimental Psychology: General, 114,* 91–103.

Farah, M. (1988). Is visual imagery really visual? Overlooked evidence from neuropsychology. *Psychological Review, 95,* 307–317.

Farah, M. (1989). Mechanisms of imagery-perception interaction. *Journal of Experimental Psychology: Human Perception and Performance, 15,* 203–211.

Farah, M. (1990). *Visual agnosia: Disorders of ob-*

ject recognition and what they tell us about normal vision. Cambridge, MA: MIT Press.

Farah, M. (1992). Is an object an object an object? Cognitive and neuropsychological investigations of domain specificity in visual object recognition. *Current Directions in Psychological Science, 1,* 164–169.

Farah, M. J., Hammond, K. M., Levine, D. N., & Calvanio, R. (1988). Visual and spatial mental imagery: Dissociable systems of representation. *Cognitive Psychology, 20,* 439–462.

Farah, M., & Smith, A. (1983). Perceptual interference and facilitation with auditory imagery. *Perception & Psychophysics, 33,* 475–478.

Farah, M., Soso, M., & Dasheiff, R. (1992). Visual angle of the mind's eye before and after unilateral occipital lobectomy. *Journal of Experimental Psychology: Human Perception and Performance, 18,* 241–246.

Farah, M., Tanaka, J., & Drain, H. M. (1995). What causes the face inversion effect? *Journal of Experimental Psychology: Human Perception and Performance, 21,* 628–634.

Ferreira, F., & Clifton, C. (1986). The independence of syntactic processing. *Journal of Memory and Language, 25,* 348–368.

Ferreira, F., & Henderson, J. (1990). The use of verb information in syntactic parsing: A comparison of evidence from eye movements and word-by-word self-paced reading. *Journal of Experimental Psychology: Learning, Memory and Cognition, 16,* 555–568.

Fillenbaum, S. (1971). On coping with ordered and unordered conjunctive sentences. *Journal of Experimental Psychology, 87,* 93–98.

Fillenbaum, S. (1974). Pragmatic normalization: Further results for some conjunctive and disjunctive sentences. *Journal of Experimental Psychology, 103,* 913–921.

Fillmore, C. (1982). Towards a descriptive framework for spatial deixis. In R. J. Jarvella & W. Klein (Eds.), *Speech, place and action: Studies in deixis and related topics.* Chichester, England: Wiley.

Finke, R. (1980). Levels of equivalence in imagery and perception. *Psychological Review, 87,* 113–132.

Finke, R. (1989). *Principles of mental imagery.* Cambridge, MA: MIT Press.

Finke, R. (1990). *Creative imagery: Discoveries and inventions in visualization.* Hillsdale, NJ: Lawrence Erlbaum.

Finke, R. (1993). Mental imagery and creative discovery. In B. Roskos-Ewoldsen, M. J. Intons-Peterson, & R. Anderson (Eds.), *Imagery, creativity, and discovery* (pp. 255–285). New York: North-Holland.

Finke, R., & Kosslyn, S. (1980). Mental imagery acuity in the peripheral visual field. *Journal of Experimental Psychology: Human Perception and Performance, 6,* 126–139.

Finke, R., & Slayton, K. (1988). Explorations of creative visual synthesis in mental imagery. *Memory & Cognition, 16,* 252–257.

Finke, R., Ward, T., & Smith, S. (1992). *Creative cognition: Theory, research and applications.* Cambridge, MA: MIT Press.

Fischhoff, B. (1975). Hindsight ≠ foresight: The effect of outcome knowledge on judgment about uncertainty. *Journal of Experimental Psychology: Human Perception and Performance, 1,* 288–299.

Fischhoff, B. (1977). Perceived informativeness of facts. *Journal of Experimental Psychology: Human Perception and Performance, 3,* 349–358.

Fischhoff, B. (1991). Value elicitation: Is there anything in there? *American Psychologist, 46,* 835–847.

Fishburn, P. (1982). Nontransitive measurable utility. *Journal of Mathematical Psychology, 26,* 31–67.

Fisher, D. L. (1984). Central capacity limits in consistent mapping, visual search tasks: Four channels or more? *Cognitive Psychology, 16,* 449–484.

Fisher, R., & Craik, F. I. M. (1977). The interaction between encoding and retrieval operations in cued recall. *Journal of Experimental Psychology: Human Learning and Memory, 3,* 701–711.

Fisher, R., & Geiselman, R. (1992). *Memory-enhancing techniques for investigative interviewing: The cognitive interview.* Springfield, IL: Charles C. Thomas.

Fisher, R., Geiselman, R., & Amador, M. (1989). Field tests of the cognitive interview: Enhancing the recollection of actual victims and witnesses of crime. *Journal of Applied Psychology, 74,* 722–727.

Fisher, R., Geiselman, R. E., Raymond, D. S., & Jurkevich, L. M. (1987). Enhancing enhanced eyewitness memory: Refining the cognitive interview. *Journal of Police Science and Administration, 15,* 291–297.

Fisher, R., & McCauley, M. (1994). Improving eyewitness memory with the cognitive interview. In D. Ross, J. Read, & M. Toglia (Eds.), *Eyewitness memory: Current trends and development.* New York: Springer-Verlag.

Fivush, R. (1988). The functions of event memory: Some comments on Nelson and Barsalou. In U. Neisser & E. Winograd (Eds.), *Remembering reconsidered.* Cambridge: Cambridge University Press.

Flanagan, O. (1991). *The science of the mind* (2nd ed.). Cambridge, MA: MIT Press.

Fleet, M. L., Brigham, J. C., & Bothwell, R. K. (1987). The confidence-accuracy relationship: The effects of confidence assessment and choosing. *Journal of Applied Social Psychology, 17,* 171–187.

Flexser, A. J., & Tulving, E. (1978). Retrieval independence in recognition and recall. *Psychological Review, 85,* 153–172.

Flower, L. (1980). *Problem solving strategies for writing.* New York: Harcourt, Brace, Jovanovich.

Fodor, J. (1975). *The Language of Thought.* New York: Thomas Y. Crowell.

Fodor, J. (1981). Imagistic representation. In N. Block (Ed.), *Imagery* (pp. 63–86). Cambridge, MA: MIT Press.

Fodor, J. (1983). *The modularity of mind.* Cambridge, MA: MIT Press.

Fodor, J. (1985). Précis and multiple book review of "The modularity of mind." *Behavioral and Brain Sciences, 8,* 1–42.

Fodor, J., & Pylyshyn, Z. W. (1988). Connectionism and cognitive architecture: A critical analysis. *Cognition, 28,* 3–71.

Fong, G., Krantz, D., & Nisbett, R. (1986). The effects of statistical training on thinking about everyday problems. *Cognitive Psychology, 18,* 253–292.

Fong, G., & Nisbett, R. (1991). Immediate and delayed transfer of training effects in statistical reasoning. *Journal of Experimental Psychology: General, 120,* 34–45.

Ford, M. (1995). Two modes of mental representation and problem solution in syllogistic reasoning. *Cognition, 54,* 1–71.

Ford, M., Bresnan, J., & Kaplan, R. (1982). A competence-based theory of syntactic closure. In J. Bresnan (Ed.), *The mental representation of grammatical relations.* Cambridge, MA: MIT Press.

Fox, E. (1994). Interference and negative priming from ignored distractors: The role of selection difficulty. *Perception & Psychophysics, 56,* 565–574.

Fox, E. (1995). Negative priming from ignored distractors in visual selection: A review. *Psychonomic Bulletin & Review, 2,* 145–173.

Frazier, L. (1989). Against lexical generation of syntax. In W. Marslen-Wilson (Ed.), *Lexical representation and process.* Cambridge, MA: MIT Press.

Frege, G. (1892/1952). On sense and reference. In P. Geach & M. Black (Eds.), *Philosophical writings of Gottlob Frege.* Oxford: Oxford University Press.

Fried, L. S., & Holyoak, K. J. (1984). Induction of category distributions: A framework for classification learning. *Journal of Experimental Psychology: Learning, Memory and Cognition, 10,* 234–257.

Friedman, A. (1979). Framing pictures: The role of knowledge in automatized encoding and memory for gist. *Journal of Experimental Psychology: General, 108,* 316–355.

Friedman, A., & Bourne, L. E., Jr. (1976). Encoding the levels of information in pictures and words. *Journal of Experimental Psychology: General, 105,* 169–190.

Friedrich, J. (1993). Primary error detection and minimizatin (PEDMIN) strategies in social cognition: A reinterpretation of confirmation bias phenomena. *Psychological Review, 100,* 298–319.

Fromkin, V. (1993). Speech production. In J. B. Gleason & N. B. Ratner (Eds.), *Psycholinguistics.* New York: Harcourt Brace Jovanovich.

Fulgosi, A., & Guilford, J. (1968). Short term incubation in divergent production. *American Journal of Psychology, 81,* 241–246.

Galotti, K., Baron, J., & Sabini, J. (1986). Individual differences in syllogistic reasoning: Deduction rules or mental models? *Journal of Experimental Psychology: General, 115,* 16–25.

Galton, F. (1883). *Inquiries into human faculty.* London: Dent.

Gardiner, J., & Java, R. (1991). Forgetting in recognition memory with and without recollective experience. *Memory & Cognition, 19,* 617–623.

Gardner, H. (1974). *The shattered mind.* New York: Vintage.

Gardner, H. (1985). *The mind's new science: A history of the cognitive revolution.* New York: Basic Books.

Garfield, J. (Ed.). (1987). *Modularity in knowledge representation and natural-language understanding.* Cambridge, MA: MIT Press.

Garnes, S., & Bond, Z. (1976). The relationship between semantic expectation and acoustic information. In W. Dressler & O. Pfeiffer (Eds.), *Proceedings of the Third International Phonology Meeting.* Innsbruck: Phonologische Tagung.

Gathercole, S., & Baddeley, A. D. (1989). Evaluation of the role of phonological STM in the development of vocabulary in children: A longitudinal study. *Journal of Memory and Language, 28,* 200–213.

Gathercole, S., & Baddeley, A. D. (1990). The role of phonological memory in vocabulary acquisition: A study of young children learning arbitrary names of toys. *British Journal of Psychology, 81,* 439–454.

Geiselman, R. E. (1984). Enhancement of eyewitness memory: An empirical evaluation of the cognitive interview. *Journal of Police Science and Administration, 12,* 74–80.

Geiselman, R. E., & Padilla, J. (1988). Cognitive interviewing with child witnesses. *Journal of Police Science & Administration, 16,* 236–242.

Gelman, S., & Wellman, H. (1991). Insides and essences: Early understandings of the nonobvious. *Cognition, 38,* 213–244.

Gentner, D., & Jeziorski, M. (1989). Historical shifts in the use of analogy in science. In B. Gholson, W. Shadish, R. Neimeyer, & A. Houts (Eds.), *Psychology of science: Contributions to metascience.* Cambridge: Cambridge University Press.

Gentner, D., & Stevens, A. L. (1983). *Mental models.* Hillsdale, NJ: Lawrence Erlbaum.

Gentner, D. (1983). Structure mapping: A theoretical framework for analogy. *Cognitive Science, 7,* 155–170.

Gentner, D. (1989). The mechanisms of analogical learning. In S. Vosniadou & A. Ortony (Eds.), *Similarity, analogy, and thought* (pp. 199–241). Cambridge: Cambridge University Press.

Getzels, J., & Csikszentmihalyi, M. (1976). *The creative vision: A longitudinal study of problem finding in art.* New York: Wiley.

Ghiselin, B. (1952). *The creative process.* New York: New American Library.

Gibson, E., Bishop, C., Schiff, W., & Smith, J. (1964). Comparison of meaningfulness and pronounceability as grouping principles in the perception and retention of verbal material. *Journal of Experimental Psychology, 67,* 173–182.

Gick, M. (1986). Problem-solving strategies. *Educational Psychologist, 21,* 99–120.

Gick, M., & Holyoak, K. (1980). Analogical problem solving. *Cognitive Psychology, 12,* 306–355.

Gick, M., & Holyoak, K. (1983). Schema induction and analogical transfer. *Cognitive Psychology, 15*, 1–38.

Gigerenzer, G. (1991). From tools to theories: A heuristic of discovery in cognitive psychology. *Psychological Review, 98*, 254–267.

Gigerenzer, G., Hell, W., & Blank, H. (1988). Presentation and content: The use of base rates as a continuous variable. *Journal of Experimental Psychology: Human Perception and Performance, 14*, 513–525.

Gigerenzer, G., & Hug, K. (1992). Domain-specific reasoning: Social contracts, cheating and perspective change. *Cognition, 43*, 127–172.

Gilhooly, K. (1988). *Thinking: Direct, undirected and creative* (2nd ed.). New York: Academic Press.

Gilhooly, K., Logie, R., Wetherick, N., & Wynn, V. (1993). Working memory and strategies in syllogistic-reasoning tasks. *Memory & Cognition, 21*, 115–124.

Gilligan, S. G., & Bower, G. H. (1984). Cognitive consequences of emotional arousal. In C. E. Izard, J. Kagan & R. B. Zajonc (Eds.), *Emotions, cognitions, and behavior*. Cambridge: Cambridge University Press.

Gilovich, T. (1991). *How we know what isn't so.* New York: Free Press.

Ginosar, Z., & Trope, Y. (1980). The effects of base rates and individuating information on judgments about another person. *Journal of Experimental Social Psychology, 16*, 228–242.

Glanzer, M., & Adams, J. (1985). The mirror effect in recognition memory. *Memory & Cognition, 13*, 8–20.

Glanzer, M., & Cunitz, A. R. (1966). Two storage mechanisms in free recall. *Journal of Verbal Learning and Verbal Behavior, 5*, 351–360.

Glass, A. L., Holyoak, K. J., & Kiger, J. I. (1979). Role of antonymy relations in semantic judgments. *Journal of Experimental Psychology: Human Learning and Memory, 5*, 598–606.

Glass, A. L., Holyoak, K. J., & O'Dell, C. (1974). Production frequency and the verification of quantified statements. *Journal of Verbal Learning and Verbal Behavior, 13*, 237–254.

Gleitman, H. (1995). *Psychology* (4th ed.). New York: W. W. Norton.

Glenberg, A., & Adams, F. (1978). Type I rehearsal and recognition. *Journal of Verbal Learning and Verbal Behavior, 17*, 455–463.

Glenberg, A., Smith, S. M., & Green, C. (1977). Type I rehearsal: Maintenance and more. *Journal of Verbal Learning and Verbal Behavior, 16*, 339–352.

Glisky, E., Schacter, D., & Tulving, E. (1986). Computer learning by memory impaired patients: Acquisition and retention of complex knowledge. *Neuropsychologia, 24*, 313–328.

Gluck, M., & Rumelhart, D. (1990). *Neuroscience and connectionist theory.* Hillsdale, NJ: Lawrence Erlbaum.

Glucksberg, S., & Danks, J. (1968). Effects of discriminative labels and of nonsense labels upon availability of novel function. *Journal of Verbal Learning and Verbal Behavior, 7*, 72–76.

Glucksberg, S., & McCloskey, M. (1981). Decisions about ignorance: Knowing that you don't know. *Journal of Experimental Psychology: Learning, Memory and Cognition, 7*, 311–325.

Godden, D. R., & Baddeley, A. D. (1975). Context-dependent memory in two natural environments: On land and underwater. *British Journal of Psychology, 66*, 325–332.

Gold, P. (1987). Sweet memories. *American Scientist, 75*, 151–155.

Gold, P. (1995). Modulation of emotional and non-emotional memories: Same pharmacological systems, different neuroanatomical systems. In J. McGaugh & N. Weinberger (Eds.), *Brain and memory.* New York: Oxford University Press.

Goldman, P., Wolters, N., & Winograd, E. (1992). A demonstration of incubation in anagram problem solving. *Bulletin of the Psychonomic Society, 30*, 36–38.

Goldstone, R. (1994). Similarity, interactive activation, and mapping. *Journal of Experimental Psychology: Learning, Memory and Cognition, 20*, 3–28.

Goldstone, R., & Medin, D. (1994). Time course

of comparison. *Journal of Experimental Psychology: Learning, Memory and Cognition, 20,* 29–50.

Goodman, N. (1972). Seven strictures on similarity. In N. Goodman (Ed.), *Problems and projects* (pp. 437–446). New York: Bobbs-Merrill.

Gordon, P. (1986). Level-ordering in lexical development. *Cognition, 21,* 73–93.

Gordon, P., & Scearce, K. (1995). Pronominalization and discourse coherence: Discourse structure and pronoun interpretation. *Memory & Cognition, 23,* 313–323.

Gorenstein, G., & Ellsworth, P. (1980). Effect of choosing an incorrect photograph on later identification by an eyewitness. *Journal of Applied Psychology, 65,* 616–622.

Graesser, A., Woll, S., Kowalski, D., & Smith, D. (1980). Memory for typical and atypical actions in scripted activities. *Journal of Experimental Psychology: Human Learning and Memory, 6,* 503–515.

Graf, P., & Komatsu, S. (1994). Process dissociation procedure: Handle with caution! *European Journal of Cognitive Psychology, 6,* 113–129.

Graf, P., & Mandler, G. (1984). Activation makes words more accessible, but not necessarily more retrievable. *Journal of Verbal Learning and Verbal Behavior, 23,* 553–568.

Graf, P., Mandler, G., & Haden, P. E. (1982). Simulating amnesic symptoms in normals. *Science, 218,* 1243–1244.

Graf, P., & Masson, M. (Eds.). (1993). *Implicit memory: New directions in cognition, development and neuropsychology.* Hillsdale, NJ: Lawrence Erlbaum.

Graf, P., & Ryan, L. (1990). Transfer-appropriate processing for implicit and explicit memory. *Journal of Experimental Psychology: Learning, Memory and Cognition, 16,* 978–992.

Graf, P., & Schacter, D. L. (1985). Implicit and explicit memory for new associations in normal and amnesic subjects. *Journal of Experimental Psychology: Learning, Memory and Cognition, 11,* 501–18.

Green, E., & Barber, P. (1981). An auditory Stroop effect with judgments of speaker gender. *Perception & Psychophysics, 30,* 459–466.

Greenberg, J., Ferguson, C., & Moravcsik, E. (Eds.). (1978). *Universals of human language.* Stanford, CA: Stanford University Press.

Greene, E., Flynn, M., & Loftus, E. (1982). Inducing resistance of misleading information. *Journal of Verbal Learning and Verbal Behavior, 21,* 207–219.

Greenwald, A. (1972). Evidence of both perceptual filtering and response suppression for rejected messages in selective attention. *Journal of Experimental Psychology, 94,* 58–67.

Greenwald, A. (1992). New Look 3—Unconscious cognition reclaimed. *American Psychologist, 47,* 766–790.

Greenwald, A., & Banaji, M. (1995). Implicit social cognition: Attitudes, self-esteem and stereotypes. *Psychological Review, 102,* 4–27.

Greenwald, A., & Pratkanis, A. (1984). The self. In R. S. Wyer & T. K. Srull (Eds.), *Handbook of social cognition* (pp. 129–178). Hillsdale, NJ: Lawrence Erlbaum.

Grice, H. P. (1975). Logic and conversation. In P. Cole & J. L. Morgan (Eds.), *Syntax and semantics 3: Speech acts.* New York: Academic Press.

Griggs, R. (1983). The role of problem content in the selection task and in the THOG problem. In J. S. B. Evans (Ed.), *Thinking and reasoning: Psychological approaches.* London: Routledge & Kegan Paul.

Griggs, R., & Cox, J. R. (1982). The elusive thematic-materials effect in Wason's selection task. *British Journal of Psychology, 73,* 407–420.

Grimshaw, J. (1990). *Argument structure.* Cambridge, MA: MIT Press.

Gruber, H. (1989). Networks of enterprise in creative scientific work. In B. Gholson, W. Shadish, R. Neimeyer, & A. Houts (Eds.), *Psychology of science: Contributions to metascience.* Cambridge: Cambridge University Press.

Guagnano, G., Dietz, T., & Stern, P. (1994). Willingness to pay for public goods: A test of the contribution model. *Psychological Science, 5,* 411–415.

Guilford, J. (1967). *The nature of human intelligence.* New York: Scribner.

Guilford, J. (1979). Some incubated thoughts on incubation. *Journal of Creative Behavior, 13,* 1–8.

Guyote, M., & Sternberg, R. (1981). A transitive-chain theory of syllogistic reasoning. *Cognitive Psychology, 13,* 461–525.

Halle, M. (1990). Phonology. In D. Osherson & H. Lasnik (Eds.), *Language: An invitation to cognitive science.* Cambridge, MA: MIT Press.

Halligan, P., & Marshall, J. (1994). Toward a principled explanation of unilateral neglect. *Cognitive Neuropsychology, 2,* 167–206.

Halpern, D. (1984). *Thought and knowledge: An introduction to critical thinking.* Hillsdale, NJ: Lawrence Erlbaum.

Hamann, S. (1990). Level-of-processing effects in conceptually driven implicit tasks. *Journal of Experimental Psychology: Learning, Memory and Cognition, 16,* 970–977.

Hamill, R., Wilson, T. D., & Nisbett, R. E. (1980). Insensitivity to sample bias: Generalizing from atypical cases. *Journal of Personality and Social Psychology, 39,* 578–589.

Handel, S. (1989). *Listening: An introduction to the perception of auditory events.* Cambridge, MA: MIT Press.

Hardiman, P., Dufresne, R., & Mestre, J. (1989). The relation between problem categorization and problem solving among experts and novices. *Memory & Cognition, 17,* 627–638.

Hardin, C., & Banaji, M. (1993). The influence of language on thought. *Social Cognition, 11,* 277–308.

Harding, R. (1940). *An anatomy of inspiration.* London: Cass.

Harris, J. (1982). The VVIQ and imagery-produced McCollough effects: An alternative analysis. *Perception & Psychophysics, 32,* 290–292.

Hart, J. T. (1965). Memory and the feelings of knowing experience. *Journal of Educational Psychology, 56,* 208–216.

Hart, J. T. (1967). Memory and the memory-monitoring process. *Journal of Verbal Learning and Verbal Behavior, 6,* 685–691.

Hasher, L., Goldstein, D., & Toppino, T. (1977). Frequency and the conference of referential validity. *Journal of Verbal Learning and Verbal Behavior, 16,* 107–112.

Hasher, L., & Griffin, M. (1978). Reconstructive and reproductive processes in memory. *Journal of Experimental Psychology: Human Learning and Memory, 4,* 318–330.

Haugeland, J. (Ed.). (1981). *Mind design.* Cambridge, MA: MIT Press.

Haugeland, J. (1986). *Artificial intelligence: The very idea.* Cambridge, MA: MIT Press.

Hawkins, J. (Ed.). (1988). *Explaining language universals.* London: Basil Blackwell.

Hawley, K., & Johnson, W. (1991). Long-term perceptual memory for briefly exposed words as a function of awareness and attention. *Journal of Experimental Psychology: Human Perception and Performance, 17,* 807–815.

Hay, D., Young, A., & Ellis, A. (1991). Routes through the face recognition system. *Quarterly Journal of Experimental Psychology: Human Experimental Psychology, 43A,* 761–791.

Hayes, J. (1985). Three problems in teaching general skills. In S. Chipman, J. Segal & R. Glaser (Eds.), *Thinking and learning skills* (pp. 391–406). Hillsdale, NJ: Lawrence Erlbaum.

Hayes, J. (1989). *The complete problem solver* (2nd ed.). Hillsdale, NJ: Lawrence Erlbaum.

Hayes, J., & Simon, H. (1977). Psychological differences among problem solving isomorphs. In N. Castellan, D. Pisoni, & G. Potts (Eds.), *Cognitive theory* (pp. 21–42). Hillsdale, NJ: Lawrence Erlbaum.

Hayman, C., & Tulving, E. (1989). Contingent dissociation between recognition and fragment completion: The method of triangulation. *Journal of Experimental Psychology: Learning, Memory and Cognition, 15,* 228–240.

Healy, A. F. (1981). The effects of visual similarity on proofreading for misspellings. *Memory & Cognition, 9,* 453–460.

Healy, A. F., Volbrecht, V. J., & Nye, T. R. (1983).

The effects of perceptual condition on proofreading for misspellings. *Memory & Cognition, 11*, 528–538.

Hecaen, H. (1981). The neuropsychology of face recognition. In G. Davies, H. Ellis, & J. Shephard (Eds.), *Perceiving and remembering faces*. New York: Academic Press.

Heeger, D. (1994). The representation of visual stimuli in primary visual cortex. *Current Directions in Psychological Science, 3*, 159–163.

Heil, M., Rösler, F., & Hennighausen, E. (1993). Imagery-perception interaction depends on the shape of the image: A reply to Farah. *Journal of Experimental Psychology: Human Perception and Performance, 19*, 1313–1319.

Heil, M., Rösler, F., & Hennighausen, E. (1994). Dynamics of activation in long-term memory: The retrieval of verbal, pictorial, spatial and color information. *Journal of Experimental Psychology: Learning, Memory and Cognition, 20*, 169–184.

Heilman, K., Watson, R., & Valenstein, E. (1985). Neglect and related disorders. In K. Heilman & E. Valenstein (Eds.), *Clinical neuropsychology* (pp. 243–293). New York: Oxford University Press.

Heit, E., & Rubinstein, J. (1994). Similarity and property effects in inductive reasoning. *Journal of Experimental Psychology: Learning, Memory and Cognition, 20*, 411–422.

Heller, J., & Reif, F. (1984). Prescribing effective human problem-solving processes: Problem description in physics. *Cognition and Instruction, 1*, 177–216.

Henik, A., Friedrich, F., Tzelgov, J., & Tramer, S. (1994). Capacity demands of automatic processes in semantic priming. *Memory & Cognition, 22*, 157–168.

Henle, M. (1962). On the relation between logic and thinking. *Psychological Review, 69*, 366–378.

Henle, M. (1978). Foreword. In R. Revlin & R. Mayer (Eds.), *Human reasoning* (pp. xiii-xviii). New York: Wiley.

Hennessey, B., & Amabile, T. (1988). The conditions of creativity. In R. J. Sternberg (Ed.), *The nature of creativity* (pp. 11–35). Cambridge: Cambridge University Press.

Heuer, F., Fischman, D., & Reisberg, D. (1986). Why does vivid imagery hurt colour memory? *Canadian Journal of Psychology, 40*, 161–175.

Heuer, F., & Reisberg, D. (1990). Vivid memories of emotional events: The accuracy of remembered minutiae. *Memory & Cognition, 18*, 496–506.

Heuer, F., & Reisberg, D. (1992). Emotion, arousal and memory for detail. In S.-Å. Christianson (Ed.), *Handbook of emotion and memory* (pp. 151–180). Hillsdale, NJ: Lawrence Erlbaum.

Higbee, K. L. (1977). *Your memory: How it works and how to improve it*. Englewood Cliffs, NJ: Prentice-Hall.

Higgins, E. T., & Bargh, J. A. (1987). Social cognition and social perception. *Annual Review of Psychology, 38*, 1–95.

Hilgard, E. R. (1968). *The experience of hypnosis*. New York: Harcourt Brace Jovanovich.

Hillis, A., & Caramazza, A. (1991). Category-specific naming and comprehension impairment: A double dissociation. *Brain, 114*, 2081–2094.

Hilton, D. (1995). The social context of reasoning: Conversational inference and rational judgment. *Psychological Bulletin, 118*, 248–271.

Hinsley, D., Hayes, J., & Simon, H. (1977). From words to equations: Meaning and representation in algebra word problems. In P. Carpenter & M. Just (Eds.), *Cognitive processes in comprehension*. Hillsdale, NJ: Lawrence Erlbaum.

Hinton, G., & Anderson, J. (1981). *Parallel models of associative memory*. Hillsdale, NJ: Lawrence Erlbaum.

Hintzman, D. L. (1986). "Schema abstraction" in a multiple-trace memory model. *Psychological Review, 93*, 411–428.

Hirsh-Pasek, K., Reeves, L., & Golinkoff, R. (1993). Words and meaning: From primitives to complex organization. In J. Berko Gleason & N. Bernstein (Eds.), *Psycholinguistics*. New York: Harcourt Brace Jovanovich.

Hirshman, E., Whelley, M., & Palij, M. (1989). An investigation of paradoxical memory effects. *Journal of Memory and Language, 28,* 594–609.

Hirst, W. (1986). The psychology of attention. In J. E. LeDoux & W. Hirst (Eds.), *Mind and brain* (pp. 105–141). Cambridge: Cambridge University Press.

Hirst, W., & Kalmar, D. (1987). Characterizing attentional resources. *Journal of Experimental Psychology: General, 116,* 68–81.

Hirst, W., Spelke, E., Reaves, C., Caharack, G., & Neisser, U. (1980). Dividing attention without alternation or automaticity. *Journal of Experimental Psychology: General, 109,* 98–117.

Hitch, G., Brandimonte, M., & Walker, P. (1995). Two types of representation in visual memory: Evidence from the effects of stimulus contrast on image combination. *Memory & Cognition, 23,* 147–154.

Hochberg, J. (1978). *Perception* (2nd ed.). Englewood Cliffs, NJ: Prentice-Hall.

Hochberg, J. (1986). Representation of motion and space in video and cinematic displays. In K. J. Boff, L. Kaufman, & J. P. Thomas (Eds.), *Handbook of perception and human performance* (pp. 22:1–22:64). New York: Wiley.

Hockey, G. (1978). Arousal and stress in human memory: Some methodological and theoretical considerations. In M. Gruneberg, P. Morris, & R. Sykes (Eds.), *Practical aspects of memory* (pp. 295–302). New York: Academic Press.

Hockey, G. R., Davies, S., & Gray, M. M. (1972). Forgetting as a function of sleep at different times of day. *Quarterly Journal of Experimental Psychology, 24,* 386–393.

Holding, D. (1985). *The psychology of chess.* Hillsdale, NJ: Lawrence Erlbaum.

Holland, J. H., Holyoak, K. F., Nisbett, R. E., & Thagard, P. R. (1986). *Induction.* Cambridge, MA: MIT Press.

Hollingworth, H. (1910). The obliviscence of the disagreeable. *Journal of Philosophical and Psychological Sciences Methods, 7,* 709–714.

Holm, J. (1988). *Pidgins and creoles.* New York: Cambridge University Press.

Holmes, D. (1991). The evidence for repression: An examination of sixty years of research. In J. L. Singer (Ed.), *Repression and dissociation: Implications for personality theory, psychopathology and health* (pp. 85–102). Chicago: University of Chicago Press.

Holyoak, K. (1984). Analogical thinking and human intelligence. In R. J. Sternberg (Ed.), *Advances in the psychology of human intelligence.* Hillsdale, NJ: Lawrence Erlbaum.

Holyoak, K. (1987). Review of parallel distributed processing. *Science, 236,* 992.

Holyoak, K., & Koh, H. (1987). Surface and structural similarity in analogical transfer. *Memory & Cognition, 15,* 332–340.

Holyoak, K., & Thagard, P. (1989). Analogical mapping by constraint satisfaction. *Cognitive Science, 13,* 295–355.

Homa, D., Dunbar, S., & Nohre, L. (1991). Instance frequency, categorization, and the modulating effect of experience. *Journal of Experimental Psychology: Learning, Memory and Cognition, 17,* 444–458.

Homa, D., Sterling, S., & Trepel, L. (1981). Limitation of exemplar-based generalization and the abstraction of categorical information. *Journal of Experimental Psychology: Human Learning and Memory, 7,* 418–439.

Hornby, P. (1974). Surface structure and presupposition. *Journal of Verbal Learning and Verbal Behavior, 13,* 530–538.

Hoskin, R. (1983). Opportunity cost and behavior. *Journal of Accounting Research, 21,* 78–95.

Howes, D., & Solomon, R. (1951). Visual duration thresholds as a function of word probability. *Journal of Experimental Psychology, 41,* 401–410.

Howes, M., Siegel, M., & Brown, F. (1993). Early childhood memories: Accuracy and affect. *Cognition, 47,* 95–119.

Hubel, D., & Wiesel, T. (1959). Receptive fields of single neurones in the cat's visual cortex. *Journal of Physiology, 148,* 574–591.

Hubel, D., & Wiesel, T. (1968). Receptive fields and functional architecture of monkey striate cortex. *Journal of Physiology, 195,* 215–243.

Hulse, S. H., Egeth, H., & Deese, J. (1980). *The psychology of learning.* New York: McGraw-Hill.

Hummel, J., & Biederman, I. (1992). Dynamic binding in a neural network for shape recognition. *Psychological Review, 99*, 480–517.

Hunt, E., & Agnoli, F. (1991). The Whorfian hypothesis: A cognitive psychology perspective. *Psychological Review, 98*, 377–389.

Hunt, R., & Elliott, J. (1980). The role of nonsemantic information in memory: Orthographic distinctiveness effects on retention. *Journal of Experimental Psychology: General, 109*, 49–74.

Hunt, R., & Ellis, H. D. (1974). Recognition memory and degree of semantic contextual change. *Journal of Experimental Psychology, 103*, 1153–1159.

Husserl, E. (1931). *Ideas.* New York: Collier.

Hyams, N. (1986). *Language acquisition and the theory of parameters.* Dordrecht, Holland: Reidel.

Hyde, T. S., & Jenkins, J. J. (1969). Differential effects of incidental tasks on the organization of recall of a list of highly associated words. *Journal of Experimental Psychology, 82*, 472–481.

Hyde, T. S., & Jenkins, J. J. (1973). Recall for words as a function of semantic, graphic, and syntactic orienting tasks. *Journal of Verbal Learning and Verbal Behavior, 12*, 471–480.

Hyman, I., Husband, T., & Billings, F. (1995). False memories of childhood experiences. *Applied Cognitive Psychology, 9*, 181–198.

Intons-Peterson, M., & White, A. (1981). Experimenter naiveté and imaginal judgments. *Journal of Experimental Psychology: Human Perception and Performance, 7*, 833–843.

Intraub, H., Bender, R., & Mangels, J. (1992). Looking at pictures but remembering scenes. *Journal of Experimental Psychology: Learning, Memory and Cognition, 18*, 180–191.

Intraub, H., & Bodamer, J. (1993). Boundary extension: Fundamental aspect of pictorial representation or encoding artifact? *Journal of Experimental Psychology: Learning, Memory and Cognition, 19*, 1387–1397.

Intraub, H., & Richardson, M. (1989). Wide-angle memories of close-up scenes. *Journal of Experimental Psychology: Learning, Memory and Cognition, 15*, 179–187.

Isen, A. (1985). The asymmetry of happiness and sadness in effects on memory in normal college students. *Journal of Experimental Psychology: General, 114*, 388–391.

Isen, A. (1987). Positive affect, cognitive processes and social behavior. In L. Berkowitz (Ed.), *Advances in experimental social psychology* (pp. 203–253). New York: Academic Press.

Isen, A., Shalker, T. E., Clark, M., & Karp, L. (1978). Affect, accessibility of material in memory, and behavior: A cognitive loop? *Journal of Personality and Social Psychology, 36*, 1–12.

Isha, A., & Sagi, D. (1995). Common mechanisms of visual imagery and perception. *Science, 268*, 1772–1774.

Jackendoff, R. (1972). *Semantic interpretation in generative grammar.* Cambridge, MA: MIT Press.

Jackendoff, R. (1987). *Consciousness and the computational mind.* Cambridge, MA: MIT Press.

Jackson, S., & Griggs, R. (1990). The elusive pragmatic reasoning schemas effect. *Quarterly Journal of Experimental Psychology, 42A*, 353–373.

Jacobs, W. J., & Nadel, L. (1985). Stress-induced recovery of fears and phobias. *Psychological Review, 92*, 512–531.

Jacoby, L. L. (1978). On interpreting the effects of repetition: Solving a problem versus remembering a solution. *Journal of Verbal Learning and Verbal Behavior, 17*, 649–667.

Jacoby, L. L. (1983). Remembering the data: analyzing interactive processes in reading. *Journal of Verbal Learning and Verbal Behavior, 22*, 485–508.

Jacoby, L. L. (1988). Memory observed and memory unobserved. In U. Neisser & E. Winograd (Eds.), *Remembering reconsidered.* Cambridge: Cambridge University Press.

Jacoby, L. L. (1991). A process dissociation

framework: Separating automatic from intentional uses of memory. *Journal of Memory and Language, 30,* 513–541.

Jacoby, L. L., Allan, L., Collins, J., & Larwill, L. (1988). Memory influences subjective experience: Noise judgments. *Journal of Experimental Psychology: Learning, Memory and Cognition, 14,* 240–247.

Jacoby, L. L., & Brooks, L. R. (1984). Nonanalytic cognition: Memory, perception and concept learning. In G. H. Bower (Ed.), *The psychology of learning and motivation: Advances in research and theory.* New York: Academic Press.

Jacoby, L. L. & Craik, F. I. M. (1979). Effects of elaboration of processing at encoding and retrieval: Trace distinctiveness and recovery of initial context. In L. S. Cermak & F. I. M. Craik (Eds.), *Levels of processing in human memory.* Hillsdale, NJ: Lawrence Erlbaum.

Jacoby, L. L., & Dallas, M. (1981). On the relationship between autobiographical memory and perceptual learning. *Journal of Experimental Psychology: General, 3,* 306–340.

Jacoby, L. L., & Hayman, C. A. G. (1987). Specific visual transfer in word identification. *Journal of Experimental Psychology: Learning, Memory and Cognition, 13,* 456–463.

Jacoby, L. L., & Hollingshead, A. (1990). Reading student essays may be hazardous to your spelling: Effects of reading incorrectly and correctly spelled words. *Canadian Journal of Psychology, 44,* 345–258.

Jacoby, L. L., & Kelley, C. (1992). A process-dissociation framework for investigating unconscious influences: Freudian slips, projective tests, subliminal perception, and signal detection theory. *Current Directions in Psychological Science, 1,* 174–179.

Jacoby, L. L., Kelley, C. M., Brown, J., & Jasechko, J. (1989). Becoming famous overnight: Limits on the ability to avoid unconscious influences of the past. *Journal of Personality and Social Psychology, 56,* 326–338.

Jacoby, L. L., Levy, B. A., & Steinbach, K. (1992). Episodic transfer and automaticity: Integration of data-driven and conceptually-driven processing in rereading. *Journal of Experimental Psychology: Learning, Memory and Cognition, 18,* 15–24.

Jacoby, L. L., Toth, J., & Yonelinas, A. (1993). Separating conscious and unconscious influences of memory: Measuring recollection. *Journal of Experimental Psychology: General, 122,* 139–154.

Jacoby, L. L., & Whitehouse, K. (1989). An illusion of memory: False recognition influenced by unconscious perception. *Journal of Experimental Psychology: General, 118,* 126–135.

Jacoby, L. L., & Witherspoon, D. (1982). Remembering without awareness. *Canadian Journal of Psychology, 36,* 300–324.

James, W. (1890). *The principles of psychology, vol. II.* New York: Dover Publications.

Janis, I. (1972). *Victims of groupthink.* Boston: Houghton Mifflin.

Jarvella, R. (1970). Effects of syntax on running memory span for connected discourse. *Psychonomic Science, 19,* 235–236.

Jarvella, R. (1971). Syntactic processing of connected speech. *Journal of Verbal Learning and Verbal Behavior, 10,* 409–416.

Jeffries, R., Polson, P., Razran, L., & Atwood, M. (1977). A process model for missionaries-cannibals and other river-crossing problems. *Cognitive Psychology, 9,* 412–440.

Jenkins, J. G., & Dallenbach, K. M. (1924). Oblivescence during sleep and waking. *American Journal of Psychology, 35,* 605–612.

Jennings, D. L., Amabile, T. M., & Ross, L. (1982). Informal covariation assessment: Data-based versus theory-based judgments. In D. Kahneman, P. Slovic, & A. Tversky (Eds.), *Judgments under uncertainty: Heuristics and biases.* Cambridge: Cambridge University Press.

Jepson, D., Krantz, D., & Nisbett, R. (1983). Inductive reasoning: Competence or skill? *Behavioral and Brain Sciences, 6,* 494–501.

Jobe, J., Tourangeau, R., & Smith, A. (1993). Contributions of survey research to the understanding of memory. *Applied Cognitive Psychology, 7,* 567–584.

Johnson, E., & Tversky, A. (1983). Affect, generalization, and the perception of risk. *Journal of Personality and Social Psychology*, 20–31.

Johnson, H., & Seifert, C. (1994). Sources of the continued influence effect: When misinformation affects later inferences. *Journal of Experimental Psychology: Learning, Memory and Cognition, 20*, 1420–1436.

Johnson, M. K., Bransford, J. D., & Solomon, S. (1973). Memory for tacit implication of sentences. *Journal of Experimental Psychology, 98*, 203–205.

Johnson, M. K., Hashtroudi, S., & Lindsay, S. (1993). Source monitoring. *Psychological Bulletin, 114*, 3–28.

Johnson, M. K., Kim, J. K., & Risse, G. (1985). Do alcoholic Korsakoff's syndrome patients acquire affective reactions? *Journal of Experimental Psychology: Learning, Memory and Cognition, 11*, 27–36.

Johnson, P. (1982). The functional equivalence of imagery and movement. *Quarterly Journal of Experimental Psychology, 34A*, 349–365.

Johnson-Laird, P. (1983). *Mental models.* Cambridge, MA: Harvard University Press.

Johnson-Laird, P. (1987). The mental representation of the meaning of words. *Cognition, 25*, 189–211.

Johnson-Laird, P. (1988). A computational analysis of consciousness. In A. Marcel & E. Bisiach (Eds.), *Consciousness in contemporary science.* Oxford: Oxford University Press.

Johnson-Laird, P. (1990). Mental models. In M. Posner (Ed.), *Foundations of cognitive science* (pp. 469–500). Cambridge, MA: Bradford Press.

Johnson-Laird, P., & Byrne, R. (1989). Only reasoning. *Journal of Memory and Language, 28*, 313–330.

Johnson-Laird, P., & Byrne, R. (1991). *Deduction.* Hillsdale, NJ: Lawrence Erlbaum.

Johnson-Laird, P., Byrne, R. M. J., & Schaeken, W. (1992). Propositional reasoning by model. *Psychological Review, 99*, 418–439.

Johnson-Laird, P., Byrne, R., & Tabossi, P. (1989). Reasoning by model: The case of multiple quantification. *Psychological Review, 96*, 658–673.

Johnson-Laird, P., Herrmann, D. J., & Chaffin, R. (1984). Only connections: A critique of semantic networks. *Psychological Bulletin, 96*, 292–315.

Johnson-Laird, P., Legrenzi, P., & Legrenzi, M. S. (1972). Reasoning and a sense of reality. *British Journal of Psychology, 63*, 395–400.

Johnson-Laird, P., & Shafir, E. (1993). The interaction between reasoning and decision making: An introduction. *Cognition, 49*, 1–9.

Johnson-Laird, P., & Steedman, M. (1978). The psychology of syllogisms. *Cognitive Psychology, 10*, 64–99.

Johnston, W. A., & Dark, V. J. (1986). Selective attention. *Annual Review of Psychology, 37*, 43–75.

Johnston, W., Hawley, K., & Elliott, J. (1991). Contribution of perceptual fluency to recognition judgments. *Journal of Experimental Psychology: Learning, Memory and Cognition, 17*, 210–223.

Jonides, J. (1981). Voluntary versus automatic control over the mind's eye's movement. In J. Long & A. Baddeley (Eds.), *Attention and performance IX* (pp. 187–203). Hillsdale, NJ: Lawrence Erlbaum.

Jonides, J. (1983). Further toward a model of the mind's eye movement. *Bulletin of the Psychonomic Society, 21*, 247–250.

Jonides, J., Kahn, R., & Rozin, P. (1975). Imagery instructions improve memory in blind subjects. *Bulletin of the Psychonomic Society, 5*, 424–426.

Joordens, S., & Merikle, P. (1993). Independence or redundancy? Two models of conscious and unconscious influences. *Journal of Experimental Psychology: General, 122*, 462–467.

Josephs, R., Giesler, R. B., & Silvera, D. (1994). Judgment by quantity. *Journal of Experimental Psychology: General, 123*, 21–32.

Just, M., & Carpenter, P. (1987). *The psychology of reading and language comprehension.* Boston: Allyn & Bacon.

Just, M., & Carpenter, P. (1992). A capacity theory of comprehension: Individual differences in working memory. *Psychological Review, 99,* 122–149.

Kahneman, D. (1973). *Attention and effort.* Englewood Cliffs, NJ: Prentice-Hall.

Kahneman, D., & Chajczyk, D. (1983). Tests of the automaticity of reading: Dilution of Stroop effects by color-irrelevent stimuli. *Journal of Experimental Psychology: Human Perception and Performance, 9,* 497–509.

Kahneman, D., Fredrickson, B., Schreiber, C., & Redelmeier, D. (1993). When more pain is preferred to less: Adding a better end. *Psychological Science, 4,* 401–405.

Kahneman, D., Knetsch, J., & Thaler, R. (1991). The endowment effect, loss aversion, and status quo bias. *Journal of Economic Perspectives, 5,* 193–206.

Kahneman, D., Ritov, I., Jacowitz, K., & Grant, P. (1993b). Stated willingness to pay for public goods. *Psychological Science, 4,* 310–315.

Kahneman, D., Slovic, P., & Tversky, A. (Eds.). (1982). *Judgment under uncertainty: Heuristics and biases.* New York: Cambridge University Press.

Kahneman, D., & Snell, J. (1992). Predicting a changing taste: Do people know what they will like. *Journal of Behavioral Decision Making, 5,* 187–200.

Kahneman, D., & Treisman, A. (1984). Changing views of attention and automaticity. In R. Parasuraman & D. R. Davies (Eds.), *Varieties of attention* (pp. 29–62). New York: Academic Press.

Kahneman, D., Treisman, A. & Gibbs, B. (1992). The re-viewing of object files: Object-specific integration of information. *Cognitive Psychology, 24,* 175–219.

Kahneman, D., & Tversky, A. (1972). Subjective probability: A judgment of representativeness. *Cognitive Psychology, 3,* 430–454.

Kahneman, D., & Tversky, A. (1973). On the psychology of prediction. *Psychological Review, 80,* 237–251.

Kahneman, D., & Tversky, A. (1979). Prospect theory: An analysis of decision under risk. *Econometrica, 47,* 263–291.

Kahneman, D., & Tversky, A. (1982a). On the study of statistical intuitions. *Cognition, 11,* 237–251.

Kahneman, D., & Tversky, A. (1982b). The simulation heuristic. In D. Kahneman, P. Slovic, & A. Tversky (Eds.), *Judgment under uncertainty: Heuristics and biases* (pp. 201–208). New York: Cambridge University Press.

Kahneman, D., & Tversky, A. (1982c). Variants of uncertainty. *Cognition, 11,* 143–158.

Kahneman, D., & Tversky, A. (1984). Choices, values and frames. *American Psychologist, 39,* 341–350.

Kahney, H. (1986). *Problem solving: A cognitive approach.* Milton Keynes, England: Open University Press.

Kanizsa, G. (1979). *Organization in vision.* New York: Praeger.

Kassin, S. M. (1985). Eyewitness identification: Retrospective self-awareness and the accuracy-confidence correlation. *Journal of Personality and Social Psychology, 49,* 878–893.

Katona, G. (1940). *Organizing and memorizing.* New York: Columbia University Press.

Katz, A. (1983). What does it mean to be a high imager? In J. Yuille (Ed.), *Imagery, memory and cognition.* Hillsdale, NJ: Lawrence Erlbaum.

Katzev, R., & Averill, A. (1984). Knowledge of the bystander problem and its impact on subsequent helping behavior. *The Journal of Social Psychology, 123,* 223–230.

Kaufmann, G. (1990). Imagery effects on problem solving. In P. Hampson, D. Marks, & J. T. E. Richardson (Eds.), *Imagery: Current developments* (pp. 169–196). London: Routledge.

Keenan, J. M. (1983). Qualifications and clarifications of images of concealed objects: A reply to Kerr and Neisser. *Journal of Experimental Psychology: Learning, Memory and Cognition, 9,* 222–230.

Keenan, J. M., MacWhinney, B., & Mayhew, D. (1977). Pragmatics in memory: A study of natural conversation. *Journal of Verbal Learning and Verbal Behavior, 16,* 549–560.

Keenan, J. M., & Moore, R. E. (1979). Memory for images of concealed objects: A reexamination of Neisser and Kerr. *Journal of Experimental Psychology: Human Learning and Memory, 5,* 374–385.

Keil, F. C. (1979). *Semantic and conceptual development.* Cambridge, MA: Harvard University Press.

Keil, F. (1980). Development of the ability to perceive ambiguities: Evidence for the task specificity of a linguistic skill. *Journal of Psycholinguistic Research, 9,* 219–230.

Keil, F. C. (1986). The acquisition of natural-kind and artifact terms. In W. Demopoulos & A. Marras (Eds.), *Language, learning, and concept acquisition.* Norwood, NJ: Ablex.

Keil, F. C. (1989). *Concepts, kinds, and cognitive development.* Cambridge, MA: MIT Press.

Kent, G. (1985). Memory of dental pain. *Pain, 21,* 187–194.

Kerr, N. H. (1983). The role of vision in "visual imagery" experiments: Evidence from the congenitally blind. *Journal of Experimental Psychology: General, 112,* 265–277.

Kerr, N. H., & Neisser, U. (1983). Mental images of concealed objects: New evidence. *Journal of Experimental Psycholgy: Learning, Memory and Cognition, 9,* 212–221.

Kihlstrom, J. (1987). The cognitive unconscious. *Science, 237,* 1445–1452.

Kim, J., Pinker, S., Prince, A., & Prasada, S. (1991). Why no mere mortal has ever flown out to center field. *Cognitive Science, 15,* 173–218.

Kinsbourne, M. (1981). Single channel theory. In D. Holding (Ed.), *Human skills* (pp. 375–381). Chichester, England: Wiley.

Kintsch, W. (1994). Text comprehension, memory, and learning. *American Psychologist, 49,* 294–303.

Kirby, K. (1994). Probabilities and utilities of fictional outcomes in Wason's four-card selection task. *Cognition, 51,* 1–28.

Kirsner, K., Milech, D., & Standen, P. (1983).

Common and modality-specific processes in the mental lexicon. *Memory & Cognition, 11,* 621–630.

Klaczynski, P., & Laipple, J. (1993). Role of content domain, logic training, and IQ in rule acquisition and transfer. *Journal of Experimental Psychology: Learning, Memory and Cognition, 19,* 653–672.

Klayman, J., & Brown, K. (1993). Debias the environment instead of the judge: An alternative approach to reducing error in diagnostic (and other) judgment. *Cognition, 49,* 97–122.

Klayman, J., & Ha, Y. (1987). Confirmation, disconfirmation, and information in hypothesis-testing. *Psychological Review, 94,* 211–228.

Klein, S., Loftus, J., Trafton, R. G., & Fuhrman, R. W. (1992). The use of exemplars and abstractions in trait judgments: A model of trait knowledge about the self and others. *Journal of Personality and Social Psychology, 63,* 739–753.

Klentz, B., & Beaman, A. (1981). The effects of type of information and method of dissemination on the reporting of a shoplifter. *Journal of Applied Social Psychology, 11,* 64–82.

Kluender, R., & Kutas, R. (1993). Bridging the gap: Evidence from ERPs on the processing of unbounded dependencies. *Journal of Cognitive Neuroscience, 5,* 196–214.

Knowlton, B., & Squire, L. (1993). The learning of categories: Parallel brain systems for item memory and category knowledge. *Science, 262,* 1747–1749.

Koehler, D. (1991). Explanation, imagination, and confidence in judgment. *Psychological Bulletin, 110,* 499–519.

Koestler, A. (1964). *The act of creation.* London: Hutchinson.

Kohler, W. (1969). *The task of Gestalt psychology.* Princeton, NJ: Princeton University Press.

Kohnken, G., & Maass, A. (1988). Eyewitness testimony: False alarms on biased instructions? *Journal of Applied Psychology, 73,* 363–370.

Kolers, P. (1983). Perception and representation. *Annual Review of Psychology, 34,* 129–166.

Kolers, P., & Roediger, H. (1984). Procedures of

mind. *Journal of Verbal Learning and Verbal Behavior, 23,* 425–449.

Kolers, P., & Smythe, W. (1984). Symbol manipulation: Alternatives to the computational view of mind. *Journal of Verbal Learning and Verbal Behavior, 23,* 289–314.

Kolodner, J. (1992). An introduction to case-based reasoning. *Artificial Intelligence Review, 6,* 3–34.

Komatsu, L. (1992). Recent views of conceptual structure. *Psychological Bulletin, 112,* 500–526.

Koriat, A. (1993). How do we know that we know? The accessibility model of the Feeling of Knowing. *Psychological Review, 100,* 609–639.

Koriat, A., Lichtenstein, S., & Fischhoff, B. (1980). Reasons for confidence. *Journal of Experimental Psychology: Human Learning and Memory, 6,* 107–118.

Kosslyn, S. M. (1976). Can imagery be distinguished from other forms of internal representation? Evidence from studies of information retrieval times. *Memory & Cognition, 4,* 291–297.

Kosslyn, S. M. (1980). *Image and mind.* Cambridge, MA: Harvard University Press.

Kosslyn, S. M. (1983). *Ghosts in the mind's machine.* New York: W. W. Norton.

Kosslyn, S. M., Ball, T. M., & Reiser, B. J. (1978). Visual images preserve metric spatial information: Evidence from studies of image scanning. *Journal of Experimental Psychology: Human Perception and Performance, 4,* 1–20.

Kosslyn, S. M., Brunn, J., Cave, K., & Wallach, R. (1985). Individual differences in mental imagery ability: A computational analysis. *Cognition, 18,* 195–243.

Kotovsky, K., Hayes, J., & Simon, H. (1985). Why are some problems hard? Evidence from Tower of Hanoi. *Cognitive Psychology, 17,* 248–294.

Kripke, S. (1972). Naming and necessity. In D. Davidson & G. Harman (Eds.), *Semantics of natural language.* Dordrecht: D. Reidel.

Kroll, J. F., & Potter, M. C. (1984). Recognizing words, pictures, and concepts: A comparison of lexical, object, and reality decisions. *Journal of Verbal Learning and Verbal Behavior, 23,* 39–66.

Kroll, N. E., Schepeler, E. M., & Angin, K. T. (1986). Bizarre imagery: The misremembered mnemonic. *Journal of Experimental Psychology: Learning, Memory and Cognition, 12,* 42–54.

Kucera, H., & Francis, W. N. (1967). *Computational analysis of present-day American English.* Providence, RI: Brown University Press.

Kumon-Nakamura, S., Glucksberg, S., & Brown, M. (1995). How about another piece of pie: The allusional pretense theory of discourse irony. *Journal of Experimental Psychology: General, 124,* 3–21.

Kunda, Z. (1990). The case for motivated reasoning. *Psychological Bulletin, 108,* 480–498.

Kunda, Z., & Nisbett, R. E. (1986). The psychometrics of everyday life. *Cognitive Psychology, 18,* 195–224.

Kunen, S., & May, J. (1981). Imagery-induced McCollough effects: Real or imagined. *Perception & Psychophysics, 30,* 99–100.

Kwiatkowski, S., & Parkinson, S. (1994). Depression, elaboration, and mood congruence: Differences between natural and induced mood. *Memory & Cognition, 22,* 225–233.

Kyllonen, P. C., & Cristal, R. E. (1990). Reasoning ability is (little more than) working-memory capacity? *Intelligence, 14,* 389–433.

LaBerge, D. (1975). Acquisition of automatic processing in perceptual and association learning. In P. M. A. Rabbit & S. Dornic (Eds.), *Attention and performance V.* London: Academic Press.

Labov, W. (1973). The boundaries of words and their meanings. In C.-J. N. Bailey & R. W. Shuy (Eds.), *New ways of analyzing variations in english.* Washington, DC: Georgetown University Press.

Lachter, J., & Bever, T. G. (1988). The relation between linguistic structure and associative theories of language learning—a critique of some connectionist learning models. *Cognition, 28,* 195–247.

Lakatos, I. (1970). Falsification and the methodology of scientific research programmes. In I. Lakatos & A. Musgrave (Eds.), *Criticism and the growth of scientific knowledge* (pp. 91–196). New York: Cambridge University Press.

Lakoff, G. (1987). Cognitive models and prototype theory. In U. Neisser (Ed.), *Concepts and conceptual development*. Cambridge: Cambridge University Press.

Landau, B. (1982). Will the real grandmother please stand up? The psychological reality of dual meaning representations. *Journal of Psycholinguistic Research, 11*, 47–62.

Langer, E. (1989). *Mindfulness*. Reading, MA: Addison-Wesley Publishing Co.

Langley, P., & Jones, R. (1988). A computational model of scientific insight. In R. J. Sternberg (Ed.), *The nature of creativity* (pp. 177–201). Cambridge: Cambridge University Press.

Langley, P., Simon, H., Bradshaw, G., & Zytkow, J. (1987). *Scientific discovery: Computational explorations of the creative process*. Cambridge, MA: MIT Press.

Larkin, J., McDermott, J., Simon, D., & Simon, H. (1980). Expert and novice performance in solving physics problems. *Science, 208*, 1335–1342.

Larkin, J., & Simon, H. (1987). Why a diagram is (sometimes) worth 10,000 words. *Cognitive Science, 4*, 317–345.

Larrick, R., Morgan, J., & Nisbett, R. (1990). Teaching the use of cost-benefit reasoning in everyday life. *Psychological Science, 1*, 362–370.

Larrick, R., Nisbett, R., & Morgan, J. (1993). Who uses the normative rules of choice? In R. Nisbett (Ed.), *Rules for reasoning* (pp. 277–294). Hillsdale, NJ: Lawrence Erlbaum.

Lazarus, R. S. (1982). Thoughts on the relations between emotion and cognition. *American Psychologist, 37*, 1019–1024.

Lazarus, R. S. (1984). On the primacy of cognition. *American Psychologist, 39*, 124–129.

LeCompte, D. (1995). Recollective experience in the revelation effect: Separating the contributions of recollection and familiarity. *Memory & Cognition, 23*, 324–334.

Legrenzi, P., Girotto, V., & Johnson-Laird, P. (1993). Focussing in reasoning and decision making. *Cognition, 49*, 37–66.

Lehman, D. R., Lempert, R. O., & Nisbett, R. E. (1988). The effects of graduate training on reasoning: Formal discipline and thinking about everday-life events. *American Psychologist, 43*, 431–442.

Lehman, D. R., & Nisbett, R. (1990). A longitudinal study of the effects of undergraduate education on reasoning. *Developmental Psychology, 26*, 952–960.

Lesgold, A., Rubinson, H., Feltovich, P., Glaser, R., Klopfer, D., & Wang, Y. (1988). Expertise in a complex skill: Diagnosing x-ray pictures. In M. Chi, R. Glaser, & M. Farr (Eds.), *The nature of expertise*. Hillsdale, NJ: Lawrence Erlbaum.

Levelt, W. J. M. (1970). A scaling approach to the study of syntactic relations. In F. B. F. d'Arcais & W. J. M. Levelt (Eds.), *Advances in psycholinguistics*. New York: Elsevier.

Levin, I., & Gaeth, G. (1988). How consumers are affected by the framing of attribute information before and after consuming the product. *Journal of Consumer Research, 15*, 374–378.

Levin, I., Schnittjer, S., & Thee, S. (1988). Information framing effects in social and personal decisions. *Journal of Experimental Social Psychology, 24*, 520–529.

Levitin, D. (1993). Absolute representation in auditory memory: Evidence from the production of learned melodies. *Perception & Psychophysics, 56*, 414–423.

Lewis, C. H., & Anderson, J. R. (1976). Interference with real world knowledge. *Cognitive Psychology, 7*, 311–335.

Liberman, A. (1970). The grammars of speech and language. *Cognitive Psychology, 1*, 301–323.

Liberman, A., Harris, K., Hoffman, H., & Griffith, B. (1957). The discrimination of speech sounds within and across phoneme boundaries. *Journal of Experimental Psychology, 54*, 358–368.

Lichtenstein, S., & Slovic, P. (1971). Reversals of preference between bids and choices in gambling decisions. *Journal of Experimental Psychology, 89,* 46–55.

Lichtenstein, S., Slovic, P., Fischhoff, B., Layman, M., & Combs, B. (1978). Judged frequency of lethal events. *Journal of Experimental Psychology: Human Learning and Memory, 4,* 551–578.

Light, L. L., & Carter-Sobell, L. (1970). Effects of changed semantic context on recognition memory. *Journal of Verbal Learning and Verbal Behavior, 9,* 1–11.

Lindsay, D. S. (1993). Eyewitness suggestibility. *Current Directions in Psychological Science, 2,* 86–89.

Lindsay, R. C., Lea, J. A., & Fulford, J. A. (1991). Sequential lineup presentation: Technique matters. *Journal of Applied Psychology, 76,* 741–745.

Lindsay, R. C., Lea, J. A., Nosworthy, G., Fulford, J., Hector, J., LeVan, V., & Seabrook, C. (1991). Biased lineups: Sequential presentation reduces the problem. *Journal of Applied Psychology, 76,* 796–802.

Lindsay, R. C., Wallbridge, H., & Drennan, D. (1987). Do the clothes make the man? An exploration of the effect of lineup attire on eyewitness identification accuracy. *Canadian Journal of Behavioural Science, 19,* 463–478.

Lindsay, R. C., & Wells, G. L. (1985). Improving eyewitness identifications from lineups: Simultaneous versus sequential lineup presentation. *Journal of Applied Psychology, 70,* 556–564.

Linton, M. (1975). Memory for real-world events. In D. A. Norman & D. E. Rumelhart (Eds.), *Explorations in cognition* (pp. 376–404). San Francisco: Freeman.

Linton, M. (1978). Real world memory after six years: An in vivo study of very long term memory. In M. M. Gruneberg, P. E. Morris, & R. N. Sykes (Eds.), *Practical aspects of memory* (pp. 69–76). London: Academic Press.

Linton, M. (1982). Transformations of memory in everyday life. In U. Neisser (Ed.), *Memory observed: Remembering in natural contexts* (pp. 77–92). San Francisco: Freeman.

Linton, M. (1986). Ways of searching and the contents of memory. In D. C. Rubin (Ed.), *Autobiographical memory.* Cambridge: Cambridge University Press.

Linton, S. J., & Melin, L. (1982). The accuracy of remembering chronic pain. *Pain, 13,* 281–285.

Lockhart, R. (1989). The role of theory in understanding implicit memory. In S. Lewandowsky, J. C. Dunn, & K. Kirsner (Eds.), *Implicit memory: Theoretical issues.* Hillsdale, NJ: Lawrence Erlbaum.

Lockhart, R. S., Craik, F. I. M., & Jacoby, L. (1976). Depth of processing, recall, and recognition. In J. Brown (Ed.), *Recall and recognition.* New York: Wiley.

Loewenstein, R. (1993). Psychogenic amnesia and psychogenic fugue: A comprehensive review. In D. Spiegel (Ed.), *Dissociative disorder: A clinical review.* Lutherville, MD: Sidran Press

Loftus, E. (1975). Leading questions and the eyewitness report. *Cognitive Psychology, 7,* 560–572.

Loftus, E. (1979). *Eyewitness testimony.* Cambridge, MA: Harvard University Press.

Loftus, E. (1992). When a lie becomes memory's truth: Memory distortion after exposure to misinformation. *Current Directions in Psychological Science, 1,* 121–123.

Loftus, E. (1993). Desperately seeking memories of the first few years of childhood: The reality of early memories. *Journal of Experimental Psychology: General, 122,* 274–277.

Loftus, E., & Greene, E. (1980). Warning: Even memory for faces may be contagious. *Law and Human Behavior, 4,* 323–334.

Loftus, E., & Hoffman, H. G. (1989). Misinformation and memory: The creation of new memories. *Journal of Experimental Psychology: General, 118,* 100–104.

Loftus, E., Miller, D. G., & Burns, H. J. (1978). Semantic integration of verbal information into a visual memory. *Journal of Experimental Psychology: Human Learning and Memory, 4,* 19–31.

Loftus, E., & Palmer, J. C. (1974). Reconstruction of automobile destruction: An example of the interaction between language and memory. *Journal of Verbal Learning and Verbal Behavior, 13,* 585–589.

Loftus, E., & Zanni, G. (1975). Eyewitness testimony: The influence of the wording of a question. *Bulletin of the Psychonomic Society, 5,* 86–88.

Loftus, G., & Bell, S. M. (1975). Two types of information in picture memory. *Journal of Experimental Psychology: Human Learning and Perception, 104,* 103–113.

Loftus, G., & Kallman, H. (1979). Encoding and use of detail information in picture recognition. *Journal of Experimental Psychology: Human Learning and Memory, 5,* 197–211.

Logan, G. (1989). Automaticity and cognitive control. In J. Uleman & J. Bargh (Eds.), *Unintended thought.* New York: Guilford.

Logan, G., & Klapp, S. (1991). Automatizing alphabet arithmetic: I. Is extended practice necessary to produce automaticity? *Journal of Experimental Psychology: Learning, Memory and Cognition, 17,* 179–195.

Logan, G., & Stadler, M. (1991). Mechanisms of performance improvement in consistent mapping search: Automaticity or strategy shift? *Journal of Experimental Psychology: Learning, Memory and Cognition, 17,* 478–496.

Logie, R. (1986) Visuo-spatial processing in working memory. *Quarterly Journal of Experimental Psychology, 38A,* 229–247.

Logie, R., Baddeley, A., & Woodhead, M. (1987). Face recognition, pose and ecological validity. *Applied Cognitive Psychology, 1,* 53–69.

Logie, R. & Marchetti, C. (1991). Visuo-spatial working memory: Visual, spatial or central executive. In R. H. Logie & M. Denis (Eds.), *Mental images in human cognition* (pp 105–115). Amsterdam: Elsevier.

Loomes, G. (1987). Testing for regret and disappointment in choice under uncertainty. *Economic Journal, 97,* 118–129.

Lord, A. B. (1960). *The singer of tales.* Cambridge, MA: Harvard University Press.

Lord, C. G., Lepper, M. R., & Preston, E. (1984). Considering the opposite: A corrective strategy for social judgment. *Journal of Personality and Social Psychology, 47,* 1231–1243.

Lovett, M., & Anderson, J. (1994). Effects of solving related proofs on memory and transfer in geometry problem solving. *Journal of Experimental Psychology: Learning, Memory and Cognition, 20,* 366–378.

Luchins, A. (1942). Mechanization in problem solving: The effect of Einstellung. *Psychological Monographs, 54*(1), (entire).

Luchins, A., & Luchins, E. (1950). New experimental attempts at preventing mechanization in problem solving. *Journal of General Psychology, 42,* 279–297.

Luchins, A., & Luchins, E. (1959). *Rigidity of behavior: A variational approach to the effects of Einstellung.* Eugene: University of Oregon Books.

Luria, A. R. (1968). *The Mind of a Mnemonist.* Chicago: Henry Regnery Co.

Luus, C. E., & Wells, G. L. (1991). Eyewitness identification and the selection of distracters for lineups. *Law and Human Behavior, 15,* 43–57.

Lyman, B., & McDaniel, M. (1990). Memory for odors and odor names: Modalities of elaboration and imagery. *Journal of Experimental Psychology: Learning, Memory and Cognition, 16,* 656–664.

MacArdy, E., & Riccio, D. (1991). Increased generalization between drug-related interoceptive stimuli with delayed testing. *Behavior and Neural Biology, 36,* 213–219.

MacDonald, M. C. (1989). Priming effects from gaps to antecedents. *Language and Cognitive Processes, 4,* 1–72.

MacLeod, C. (1991). Half a century of research on the Stroop effect: An integrative review. *Psychological Bulletin, 109,* 163–203.

MacWhinney, B., & Leinbach, J. (1991). Implementations are not conceptualizations: Revising the verb learning model. *Cognition, 29,* 121–157.

Mahoney, M., & DeMonbreun, B. (1978). Problem-solving bias in scientists. *Cognitive Therapy and Research, 1*, 229–238.

Maier, N. R. F. (1931). Reasoning in humans: II. The solution of a problem and its appearance in consciousness. *Journal of Comparative Psychology, 12*, 181–194.

Malpass, R. S., & Devine, P. G. (1981). Eyewitness identification: Lineup instructions and the absence of the offender. *Journal of Applied Psychology, 66*, 483–489.

Malt, B. C., & Smith, E. E. (1984). Correlated properties in natural categories. *Journal of Verbal Learning and Verbal Behavior, 23*, 250–269.

Mandler, G. (1980). Recognizing: The judgment of previous occurrence. *Psychological Review, 87*, 252–271.

Mandler, G. (1981). The recognition of previous encounters. *American Scientist, 69*, 211–218.

Mandler, G., Graf, P., & Kraft, D. (1986). Activation and elaboration effects in recognition and word priming. *Quarterly Journal of Experimental Psychology, 38*, 645–662.

Mandler, G., Nakamura, Y., & Van Zandt, B. (1987). Nonspecific effects of exposure on stimuli that cannot be recognized. *Journal of Experimental Psychology: Learning, Memory and Cognition, 13*, 646–658.

Mandler, G., & Pearlstone, Z. (1966). Free and constrained concept learning and subsequent recall. *Journal of Verbal Learning and Verbal Behavior, 5*, 126–131.

Mandler, J. M. (1984). *Stories, scripts, and scenes: Aspects of schema theory.* Hillsdale, NJ: Lawrence Erlbaum.

Mandler, J. M., & Ritchey, G. H. (1977). Long-term memory for pictures. *Journal of Experimental Psychology: Human Learning and Memory, 3*, 386–396.

Manis, M., Dovalina, I., Avis, N. E., & Cardoze, S. (1980). Base rates can affect individual predictions. *Journal of Personality and Social Psychology, 38*, 231–248.

Manketelow, K. I., & Over, D. E. (1991). Social roles and utilities in reasoning with deontic conditions. *Cognition, 39*, 85–106.

Marcel, A. (1988). Phenomenal experience and functionalism. In A. Marcel & E. Bisiach (Eds.), *Consciousness in contemporary science.* Oxford: Oxford University Press.

Marcel, A., & Bisiach, E. (Eds.). (1988). *Consciousness in contemporary science.* New York: Oxford University Press.

Marcus, G., Pinker, S., Ullman, M., Hollander, M., Rosen, T., & Xu, F. (1992). Overregularization in language acquisition. *Monographs of the Society for Research in Child Development, 57*, entire issue.

Marek, G. R. (1975). *Toscanini.* London: Vision Press.

Margolis, E. (1994). A reassessment of the shift from the classical theory of concepts to prototype theory. *Cognition, 51*, 73–89.

Marks, D. (1983). Mental imagery and consciousness: A theoretical review. In A. Sheikh (Ed.), *Imagery: Current theory, research and application.* New York: Wiley.

Marmor, G. S., & Zabeck, L. A. (1976). Mental rotation by the blind: Does mental rotation depend on visual imagery? *Journal of Experimental Psychology: Human Perception and Performance, 2*, 515–521.

Marschark, M., & Hunt, R. R. (1989). A reexamination of the role of imagery in learning and memory. *Journal of Experimental Psychology: Learning, Memory and Cognition, 15*, 710–720.

Marslen-Wilson, W., & Tyler, L. (1987). Against modularity. In J. L. Garfield (Ed.), *Modularity in knowledge representation and natural-language understanding.* Cambridge, MA: MIT Press.

Marslen-Wilson, W. D., & Teuber, H. L. (1975). Memory for remote events in anterograde amnesia: Recognition of public figures from news photographs. *Neuropsychologia, 13*, 353–364.

Martin, E. (1970). Toward an analysis of subjective phrase structure. *Psychological Bulletin, 74*, 153–166.

Masson, M., & MacLeod, C. (1992). Reenacting the route to interpretation: Enhanced perceptual identification without prior perception. *Journal of Experimental Psychology: General, 121,* 145–176.

Matthews, W. A. (1983). The effects of concurrent secondary tasks on the use of imagery in a free recall task. *Acta Psychologica, 53,* 231–241.

May, C., Kane, M., & Hasher, L. (1995). Determinants of negative priming. *Psychological Bulletin, 118,* 35–54.

McCann, R., & Johnston, J. (1992). Locus of the single-channel bottleneck in dual-task interference. *Journal of Experimental Psychology: Human Perception and Performance, 18,* 471–484.

McClelland, J. L., & Rumelhart, D. E. (1981). An interactive model of context effects in letter perception. Part 1. An account of basic findings. *Psychological Review, 88,* 375–407.

McClelland, J. L., & Rumelhart, D. E. (Eds.). (1986). *Parallel distributed processing, vol. 2.* Cambridge, MA: MIT Press.

McCloskey, M., & Cohen, N. J. (1989). Catastrophic interference in connectionist networks: The sequential learning problem. In G. H. Bower (Ed.), *The psychology of learning and motivation: vol. 23.* New York: Academic Press.

McCloskey, M., & Glucksberg, S. (1978). Natural categories. Well-defined or fuzzy sets? *Memory & Cognition, 6,* 462–472.

McCloskey, M., & Glucksberg, S. (1979). Decision processes in verifying category membership statements: Implications for models of semantic memory. *Cognitive Psychology, 11,* 1–37.

McCloskey, M., Wible, C. G., & Cohen, N. J. (1988). Is there a special flashbulb-memory mechanism? *Journal of Experimental Psychology: General, 117,* 171–181.

McCloskey, M., & Zaragoza, Z. (1985). Misleading postevent information and memory for events: Arguments and evidence against memory impairment hypotheses. *Journal of Experimental Psychology: General, 114,* 3–18.

McDaniel, M. (1981). Syntactic complexity and elaborative processing. *Memory & Cognition, 9,* 487–495.

McDaniel, M., & Einstein, G. (1986). Bizarre imagery as an effective mnemonic aid: The importance of distinctiveness. *Journal of Experimental Psychology: Learning, Memory and Cognition, 12,* 54–65.

McDaniel, M., & Einstein, G. (1990). Bizarre imagery: Mnemonic benefits and theoretical implications. In R. Logie & M. Denis (Eds.), *Mental images in human cognition* (pp. 183–192). New York: North Holland.

McDermott, K., & Roediger, H. (1994). Effects of imagery on perceptual implicit memory tests. *Journal of Experimental Psychology: Learning, Memory and Cognition, 20,* 1379–1390.

McElree, B., & Griffith, T. (1995). Syntactic and thematic processing in sentence comprehension: Evidence for a temporal dissociation. *Journal of Experimental Psychology: Learning, Memory and Cognition, 21,* 134–157.

McGhee, P. (1983). The role of arousal and hemispheric lateralization in humor. In P. McGhee & J. Goldstein (Eds.), *Handbook of humor research: Basic issues.* New York: Springer-Verlag.

McGovern, J. B. (1964). Extinction of associations in four transfer paradigms. *Psychological Monographs, 78.*

McGuire, W. (1989). A perspectivist approach to the strategic planning of programmatic scientific research. In B. Gholson, W. Shadish, & R. Neimeyer (Eds.), *Psychology of science: Contributions to metascience.* Cambridge: Cambridge University Press.

McKelvie, S. (1995). The VVIQ as a psychometric test of individual differences in visual imagery vividness: A critical quantitative review and plea for direction. *Journal of Mental Imagery,* 1–106.

McKim, R. (1980). *Experiences in visual thinking.* Belmont, CA: Wadsworth.

McKoon, G., & Ratcliff, R. (1992). Spreading activation versus compound cue accounts of priming: Mediated priming revisited. *Journal of Experimental Psychology: Learning, Memory and Cognition, 18,* 1155–1172.

McKoon, G., Ratcliff, R., & Dell, G. (1986). A critical evaluation of the semantic/episodic distinction. *Journal of Experimental Psychology: Learning, Memory, and Cognition, 12,* 295–306.

McNamara, T. (1992a). Priming and constraints it places on theories of memory and retrieval. *Psychological Review, 99,* 650–662.

McNamara, T. (1992b). Theories of priming: I. Associative distance and lag. *Journal of Experimental Psychology: Learning, Memory and Cognition, 18,* 1173–1190.

McNamara, T. (1994). Theories of priming: II. Types of primes. *Journal of Experimental Psychology: Learning, Memory and Cognition, 20,* 507–520.

Mecklinger, A., Schriefers, K., Steinhauer, K., & Fridererici, A. (1995). Processing relative clauses varying on syntactic and semantic dimensions: An analysis of event-related potentials. *Memory & Cognition, 23,* 477–494.

Medin, D. (1975). A theory of context in discrimination learning. In G. H. Bower (Ed.), *The psychology of learning and motivation.* New York: Academic Press.

Medin, D. (1976). Theories of discrimination learning and learning set. In W. K. Estes (Ed.), *Handbook of learning and cognitive processes.* Hillsdale, NJ: Lawrence Erlbaum.

Medin, D., Altom, M. W., Edelson, S. M., & Freko, D. (1982). Correlated symptoms and simulated medical classification. *Journal of Experimental Psychology: Learning, Memory, and Cognition, 8,* 37–50.

Medin, D., Goldstone, R., & Gentner, D. (1993). Respects for similarity. *Psychological Review, 100,* 254–278.

Medin, D., & Ortony, A. (1989). Psychological essentialism. In S. Vosniadou & A. Ortony (Eds.), *Similarity and analogical reasoning* (pp. 179–195). New York: Cambridge University Press.

Medin, D., & Schaffer, M. (1978). Context theory of classification learning. *Psychological Review,* 207–238.

Mednick, S. (1962). The associative basis of the creative process. *Psychological Review, 69,* 220–232.

Mednick, S., & Mednick, M. (1967). *Examiner's manual, Remote Associates Test.* Boston: Houghton Mifflin.

Mellers, B., Chang, S.-j., Birnbaum, M., & Ordóñez, L. (1992). Preferences, prices, and ratings in risky decision making. *Journal of Experimental Psychology: Human Perception and Performance, 18,* 347–361.

Mervis, C. B., Catlin, J., & Rosch, E. (1976). Relationships among goodness-of-example, category norms and word frequency. *Bulletin of the Psychonomic Society, 7,* 268–284.

Metcalfe, J. (1986). Premonitions of insight predict impending error. *Journal of Experimental Psychology: Learning, Memory and Cognition, 12,* 623–634.

Metcalfe, J., Schwartz, B., & Joaquim, S. (1993). The cue-familiarity heuristic in metacognition. *Journal of Experimental Psychology: Learning, Memory and Cognition, 19,* 851–861.

Metcalfe, J., & Weibe, D. (1987). Intuition in insight and noninsight problem solving. *Memory & Cognition, 15,* 238–246.

Meudell, P. (1983). The development and dissolution of memory. In A. Mayes (Ed.), *Memory in animals and humans* (pp. 83–133). Workingham, UK: Van Nostrand Reinhold.

Meyer, D. E., & Schvaneveldt, R. W. (1971). Facilitation in recognizing pairs of words: Evidence of a dependence between retrieval operations. *Journal of Experimental Psychology, 90,* 227–234.

Meyer, D. E., Schvaneveldt, R. W., & Ruddy, M. G. (1974). Functions of graphemic and phonemic codes in visual word recognition. *Memory & Cognition, 2,* 309–321.

Mill, J. S. (1874). *A system of logic* (8th ed.). New York: Harper.

Miller, A. (1986). *Imagery in scientific thought.* Cambridge, MA: MIT Press.

Miller, G. (1951). *Language and communication.* New York: McGraw-Hill.

Miller, G. (1956). The magical number seven plus or minus two: Some limits on our capacity for processing information. *Psychological Review, 63,* 81–97.

Miller, G. (1991). *The science of words.* New York: Freeman.

Miller, G., Bruner, J., Postman, L. (1954). Familiarity of letter sequences and tachistoscopic identification. *Journal of General Psychology, 50,* 129–139.

Miller, G., Galanter, E., & Pribram, K. (1960). *Plans and the structure of behavior.* New York: Holt, Rinehart and Winston.

Miller, G., & Nicely, P. (1955). An analysis of perceptual confusions among some English consonants. *Journal of the Acoustical Society of America, 27,* 338–352.

Milner, B. (1966). Amnesia following operation on the temporal lobes. In C. W. M. Whitty & O. L. Zangwill (Eds.), *Amnesia.* London: Butterworths.

Milner, B. (1970). Memory and the medial temporal regions of the brain. In K. H. Pribram & D. E. Broadbent (Eds.), *Biology of memory.* New York: Academic Press.

Minami, H., & Dallenbach, K. M. (1946). The effect of activity upon learning and retention in the cockroach. *American Journal of Psychology, 59,* 1–58.

Mitroff, I. (1981). Scientists and confirmation bias. In R. Tweney, M. Doherty, & C. Mynatt (Eds.), *On scientific thinking* (pp. 170–175). New York: Coumbia University Press.

Miyashita, Y. (1995). How the brain creates imagery: Projection to primary visual cortex. *Science, 268,* 1719–1720.

Moore, C. (1994). Negative priming depends on probe-trial conflict: Where has all the inhibition gone? *Perception & Psychophysics, 56,* 133–147.

Moray, N. (1959). Attention in dichotic listening: Affective cues and the influence of instructions. *Quarterly Journal of Experimental Psychology, 11,* 56–60.

Moray, N. (1969). *Attention: Selective processes in vision and hearing.* London: Hutchingson Educational Ltd.

Moreland, R. L., & Zajonc, R. B. (1977). Is stimulus recognition a necessary condition for the occurrence of exposure effects? *Journal of Personality and Social Psychology, 35,* 191–199.

Morris, C. D., Bransford, J. D., & Franks, J. J. (1977). Levels of processing versus transfer appropriate processing. *Journal of Verbal Learning and Verbal Behavior, 16,* 519–533.

Morris, M., & Nisbett, R. (1993). Tools of the trade: Deductive schemas taught in psychology and philosophy. In R. Nisbett (Ed.), *Rules for reasoning.* Hillsdale, NJ: Lawrence Erlbaum.

Morris, N. (1987). Exploring the visuo-spatial scratch pad. *Quarterly Journal of Experimental Psychology, 39A,* 409–430.

Morton, J. (1969). Interaction of information in word recognition. *Psychological Review, 76,* 165–178.

Morton, J. (1970). A functional model of human memory. In D. Norman (Ed.), *Models of human memory.* New York: Academic Press.

Moscovitch, M. (1982). Multiple dissociations of function in amnesia. In L. S. Cermak (Ed.), *Human memory and amnesia.* Hillsdale, NJ: Lawrence Erlbaum.

Mullen, M. (1994). Earliest recollections of childhood: A demographic analysis. *Cognition, 52,* 55–79.

Murdock, B. B., Jr. (1962). The serial position effect of free recall. *Journal of Experimental Psychology, 64,* 482–488.

Murname, K., & Phelps, M. (1994). When does a different environmental context make a difference in recognition? A global activation model. *Memory & Cognition, 22,* 584–590.

Murname, K., & Shiffrin, R. (1991). Interference and the representation of events in memory. *Journal of Experimental Psychology: Learning, Memory and Cognition, 17,* 855–874.

Murphy, G., & Shapiro, A. (1994). Forgetting of verbatim information in discourse. *Memory & Cognition, 22,* 85–94.

Murray, D., Ward, R., & Hockley, W. (1975). Tactile short-term memory in relation to the two-point threshold. *Quarterly Journal of Experimental Psychology, 27,* 303–312.

Murray, H. (1959). Vicissitudes of creativity. In H. Anderson (Ed.), *Creativity and its cultivation.* New York: Harper & Row.

Murray, H., & Denny, J. (1969). Interaction of ability level and interpolated activity (opportunity for incubation) in human problem solving. *Psychological Reports, 24,* 271–276.

Mynatt, C., Doherty, M., & Tweney, R. (1977). Confirmation bias in a simulated research environment: An experimental study of scientific inference. *Quarterly Journal of Experimental Psychology, 29,* 85–95.

Mynatt, C., Doherty, M., & Tweney, R. (1978). Consequences of confirmation and disconfirmation in a simulated research environment. *Quarterly Journal of Experimental Psychology, 30,* 395–406.

Nadel, L., & Zola-Morgan, S. (1984). Infantile amnesia: A neurobiological perspective. In M. Moscovitch (Ed.), *Infant memory.* New York: Plenum.

Nairn, J., & Pusen, C. (1984). Serial recall of imagined voices. *Journal of Verbal Learning and Verbal Behavior, 23,* 331–342.

Nakamura, G. V., Graesser, A. C., Zimmerman, J. A., & Riha, J. (1985). Script processing in a natural situation. *Memory & Cognition, 13,* 140–144.

Navon, D. (1977). Forest before trees: The precedence of global features in visual perception. *Cognitive Psychology, 9,* 343–383.

Navon, D. (1984). Resources—A theoretical soup stone? *Psychological Review, 91,* 216–234.

Navon, D. (1985). Attention division or attention sharing? In M. I. Posner & O. S. Marin (Eds.), *Attention and performance XI.* Hillsdale, NJ: Lawrence Erlbaum.

Needham, D., & Begg, I. (1991). Problem-oriented training promotes spontaneous analogical transfer: Memory-oriented training promotes memory for training. *Memory & Cognition, 19,* 543–557.

Neely, J. H. (1977). Semantic priming and retrieval from lexical memory: Role of inhibitionless spreading activation and limited capacity attention. *Journal of Experimental Psychology: General, 106,* 226–254.

Neely, J. H. (1991). Semantic priming effects in visual word recognition: A selective review of current findings and theories. In D. Besner & G. Humphreys (Eds.), *Basic processes in reading: Visual word recognition* (pp. 264–336). Hillsdale, NJ: Lawrence Erlbaum.

Neill, W. T. (1977). Inhibitory and facilitatory processes in selective attention. *Journal of Experimental Psychology: Human Perception and Performance, 3,* 444–450.

Neill, W. T., & Terry, K. (1995). Negative priming without reaction time: Effects on identification of masked letters. *Psychological Bulletin and Review, 2,* 121–123.

Neisser, U. (1964). Visual search. *Scientific American, 210,* 94–102.

Neisser, U. (1967). *Cognitive psychology.* New York: Appleton-Century-Crofts.

Neisser, U. (1976). *Cognition and reality.* New York: W. H. Freeman.

Neisser, U. (1981). John Dean's memory: A case study. *Cognition, 9,* 1–22.

Neisser, U. (1982). *Memory observed.* San Francisco: W. H. Freeman & Co.

Neisser, U. (1987). From direct perception to conceptual structure. In U. Neisser (Ed.), *Concepts and conceptual development.* Cambridge: Cambridge University Press.

Neisser, U., & Becklen, R. (1975). Selective looking: Attending to visually significant events. *Cognitive Psychology, 7,* 480–494.

Neisser, U., & Harsch, N. (1992). Phantom flashbulbs: False recollections of hearing the news about *Challenger.* In E. Winograd & U. Neisser (Eds.), *Affect and accuracy in recall: Studies of "flashbulb" memories* (pp. 9–31). Cambridge: Cambridge University Press.

Neisser, U., & Kerr, N. H. (1973). Spatial and mnemonic properties of visual images. *Cognitive Psychology, 5,* 138–150.

Nelson, D., Schreiber, T., & Holley, P. (1993).

The retrieval of controlled and automatic aspects of meaning on direct and indirect tests. *Memory & Cognition, 20,* 671–684.

Neisser, U., Winograd, E., & Weldon, M. S. (1991). Remembering the earthquake: "What I experienced" vs. "How I heard the news." Paper presented at the meeting of the Psychonomic Society, San Francisco, November 24, 1991.

Nelson, K. (1988). The ontogeny of memory for real events. In U. Neisser & E. Winograd (Eds.), *Remembering reconsidered: Ecological and traditional approaches to the study of memory.* Cambridge: Cambridge University Press.

Nelson, K. (1993). The psychological and social origins of autobiographical memory. *Psychological Science, 4,* 7–14.

Nelson, R. L., Walling, J. R., & McEvoy, C. L. (1979). Doubts about depth. *Journal of Experimental Psychology: Human Learning and Memory, 5,* 24–44.

Nelson, T. O. (1976). Reinforcement and human memory. In W. K. Estes (Ed.), *Handbook of learning and cognitive processes, vol. 3.* Hillsdale, NJ: Lawrence Erlbaum.

Neuman, P. G. (1977). Visual prototype infomraton with discontinuous representation of dimensions of variability. *Memory & Cognition, 5,* 187–197.

Newell, A. (1973). Production systems: Model of control structures. In W. Chase (Ed.), *Visual information processing.* New York: Academic Press.

Newell, A., & Simon, H. (1972). *Human problem solving.* Englewood Cliffs, NJ: Prentice-Hall.

Newstead, S., Pollard, P., Evans, J., & Allen, J. (1992). The source of belief bias effects in syllogistic reasoning. *Cognition, 45,* 257–284.

Nickerson, R. A., & Adams, M. J. (1979). Long-term memory for a common object. *Cognitive Psychology, 11,* 287–307.

Nickerson, R. S. (1968). A note on long-term recognition memory for picture material. *Psychonomic Science, 11,* 58.

Nickerson, R., Perkins, D., & Smith, E. (1985).

The teaching of thinking. Hillsdale, NJ: Lawrence Erlbaum.

Nicol, J., & Swinney, D. (1989). The role of structure in coreference assignment during sentence comprehension. *Journal of Psycholinguistic Research, 18,* 5–19.

Nilsson, H. (1971). *The point* [film]. Directed by Fred Wolf. Produced by Murikami-Wolf-Swenson.

Nisbett, R. (Ed.). (1993). *Rules for reasoning.* Hillsdale, NJ: Lawrence Erlbaum.

Nisbett, R., Krantz, D. H., Jepson, C., & Kunda, Z. (1983). The use of statistical heuristics in everyday inductive reasoning. *Psychological Review, 90,* 339–363.

Nisbett, R., & Ross, L. (1980). *Human inference: Strategies and shortcomings of social judgment.* Englewood Cliffs, NJ: Prentice-Hall.

Nisbett, R., & Schachter, S. (1966). Cognitive manipulation of pain. *Journal of Experimental Social Psychology, 2,* 277–236.

Nisbett, R., & Wilson, T. (1977). Telling more than we can know: Verbal reports on mental processes. *Psychological Review, 84,* 231–259.

Nisbett, R., Zukier, H., & Lemley, R. E. (1981). The dilution effect: Nondiagnostic information weakens the implications of diagnostic information. *Cognitive Psychology, 13,* 248–277.

Norman, D., & Bobrow, D. (1975). On data-limited and resource-limited processes. *Cognitive Psychology, 7,* 44–64.

Norman, D., Rumelhart, D. E., & Group, T. L. R. (1975). *Explorations in cognition.* San Francisco: Freeman.

Norman, D., & Shallice, T. (1986). Attention to action: Willed and automatic control of behavior. In R. Davidson, G. Schwartz, & D. Shapiro (Eds.), *Consciousness and self-regulation.* New York: Plenum Press.

Nosofsky, R. (1986). Attention, similarity, and the identification-categorization relationship. *Journal of Experimental Psychology: General, 115,* 39–57.

Nosworthy, G. J., & Lindsay, R. C. (1990). Does

nominal lineup size matter? *Journal of Applied Psychology, 75,* 358–361.

Novick, L. (1988). Analogical transfer, problem similarity and expertise. *Journal of Experimental Psychology: Learning, Memory and Cognition, 14,* 510–520.

Novick, L., & Holyoak, K. (1991). Mathematical problem solving by analogy. *Journal of Experimental Psychology: Learning, Memory and Cognition, 17,* 398–415.

Oakhill, J., & Garnham, A. (1993). On theories of belief bias in syllogistic reasoning. *Cognition, 46,* 87–92.

Oakley, D. A. (1983). The varieties of memory: A phylogenetic approach. In A. R. Mayes (Ed.), *Memory in humans and animals.* Wokingham, UK: Van Nostrand Reinhold.

Ofshe, R. (1992). Inadvertent hypnosis during interrogation: False confession due to dissociative state; mis-identified multiple personality and the Satanic Cult Hypothesis. *International Journal of Clinical and Experimental Hypnosis, 40,* 125–136.

Oldfield, R. (1963). Individual vocabulary and semantic currency: A preliminary study. *British Journal of Social and Clinical Psychology, 2,* 122–130.

Oliphant, G. W. (1983). Repetition and recency effects in word recognition. *Australian Journal of Psychology, 35,* 393–403.

Olton, D. S. (1978). Characteristics of spatial memory. In S. H. Hulse, H. Fowler, & W. K. Honig (Eds.), *Cognitive processes in animal behavior* (pp. 341–373). Hillsdale, NJ: Lawrence Erlbaum.

Olton, R. (1979). Experimental studies of incubation: Searching for the elusive. *Journal of Creative Behavior, 13,* 9–22.

Olton, R., & Johnson, D. (1976). Mechanisms of incubation in creative problem solving. *American Journal of Psychology, 7,* entire.

Onifer, W., & Swinney, D. (1981). Accessing lexical ambiguities during sentence comprehension: Effects of frequency-of-meaning and contextual bias. *Memory & Cognition, 9,* 225–236.

Osborn, A. (1957). *Applied imagination.* New York: Charles Scribner's Sons.

Osherson, D. N., & Smith, E. E. (1981). On the adequacy of prototype theory as a theory of concepts. *Cognition, 9,* 35–58.

Overton, D. (1964). State-dependent or "dissociated" learning produced with pentobarbital. *Journal of Comparative and Physiological Psychology, 57,* 3–12.

Overton, D. (1985). Contextual stimulus effects of drugs and internal states. In P. D. Balsam & A. Tomie (Eds.), *Context and learning.* Hillsdale, NJ: Lawrence Erlbaum.

Owens, J., Bower, G. H., & Black, J. B. (1979). The "soap opera" effect in story recall. *Memory & Cognition, 7,* 185–191.

Paap, K., & Ogden, W. (1981). Letter encoding is an obligatory but capacity-demanding operation. *Journal of Experimental Psychology: Human Perception and Performance, 7,* 518–528.

Paivio, A. (1969). Mental imagery in associative learning and memory. *Psychological Review, 76,* 241–263.

Paivio, A. (1971). *Imagery and verbal processes.* New York: Holt, Rinehart & Winston.

Paivio, A., & Csapo, K. (1969). Concrete image and verbal memory codes. *Journal of Experimental Psychology, 80,* 279–285.

Paivio, A., & Okovita, H. W. (1971). Word imagery modalities and associative learning in blind and sighted subjects. *Journal of Verbal Learning and Verbal Behavior, 10,* 506–510.

Paivio, A., Smythe, P. C., & Yuille, J. C. (1968). Imagery versus meaningfulness of nouns in paired-associate learning. *Canadian Journal of Psychology, 22,* 427–441.

Paivio, A., Yuille, J. C., & Madigan, S. (1968). Concreteness, imagery, and meaningfulness values for 925 nouns. *Journal of Experimental Psychology Monograph, 78* (1, Pt. 2).

Palmer, S. (1977). Hierarchical structure in perceptual representation. *Cognitive Psychology, 9,* 441–474.

Palmer, S., Schreiber, C., & Fox, C. (1991). Remembering the earthquake: "Flashbulb" memory for experienced vs. reported events. Paper presented at the meeting of the Psychonomic Society, November 1991, San Francisco.

Pani, J. (in press). Mental imagery as the adaptationist views it. *Consciousness and Cognition*, 1995.

Papagno, C., Valentine, T., & Baddeley, A. D. (1991). Phonological short-term memory and foreign-language vocabulary learning. *Journal of Memory and Language, 30*, 331–347.

Paris, S. C., & Lindauer, B. K. (1976). The role of inference in children's comprehension and memory for sentences. *Cognitive Psychology, 8*, 217–227.

Parkin, A. J. (1984). Levels of processing, context, and facilitation of pronunciation. *Acta Psychologia, 55*, 19–29.

Parrott, W. G., & Sabini, J. (1990). Mood and memory under natural conditions: Evidence for mood incongruent recall. *Journal of Personality and Social Psychology, 59*, 321–336.

Parsons, L. M. (1996). How orientation matters for models of mental rotation. Manuscript submitted for publication.

Pashler, H. (1991). Dual-task interference and elementary mental mechanisms. In D. E. Meyer & S. Kornblum (Eds.), *Attention and performance XIV*. Hillsdale, NJ: Lawrence Erlbaum.

Pashler, H. (1992). Attentional limitations in doing two tasks at the same time. *Current Directions in Psychological Science, 1*, 44–47.

Pashler, H. (1994). Graded capacity-sharing in dual-task interference. *Journal of Experimental Psychology: Human Perception and Performance, 20*, 330–342.

Pashler, H., & Carrier, M. (in press). Structures, processes and the flow of information. In E. Bjork & R. Bjork (Eds.), *Handbook of perception and cognition*.

Pashler, H., & Johnston, J. (1989). Interference between temporally overlapping tasks: Chronometric evidence for central postponement with or without response grouping. *Quarterly Journal of Experimental Psychology, 41A*, 19–45.

Pashler, H., & O'Brien, S. (1993). Dual-task interference and the cerebral hemispheres. *Journal of Experimental Psychology: Human Perception and Performance, 19*: 315–330.

Patalano, A., & Seifert, C. (1994). Memory for impasses during problem solving. *Memory & Cognition, 22*, 234–242.

Patel, V., Evans, D., & Groen, G. (1989). Biomedical knowledge and clinical reasoning. In D. Evans & V. Patel (Eds.), *Cognitive science in medicine: Biomedical modeling*. Cambridge, MA: MIT Press.

Patrick, C. (1935). Creative thought in poets. *Archives of Psychology, 26*, 73.

Patrick, C. (1937). Creative thought in artists. *Journal of Psychology, 4*, 35–73.

Payne, J. (1994). Thinking aloud: Insights into information processing. *Psychological Science, 5*, 241–248.

Payne, J., Bettman, J., & Johnson, E. (1992). Behavioral decision research: A constructive process perspective. *Annual Review of Psychology, 43*, 87–131.

Penfield, W., & Roberts, L. (1959). *Speech and brain mechanisms*. Princeton, NJ: Princeton University Press.

Perfect, T., & Hanley, J. (1992). The tip-of-the-tongue phenomenon: Do experimenter-presented interlopers have any effect. *Cognition, 45*, 55–75.

Perkins, D. (1981). *The mind's best work*. Cambridge, MA: Harvard University Press.

Peterson, C. (1974). Incubation effects in anagram solution. *Bulletin of the Psychonomic Society, 3*, 29–30.

Peterson, L. R., & Peterson, M. J. (1959). Short-term retention of individual verbal items. *Journal of Experimental Psychology, 58*, 193–198.

Peterson, L. R., & Potts, G. R. (1982). Global and specific components of information integration. *Journal of Verbal Learning and Verbal Behavior, 21*, 403–420.

Peterson, M., Kihlstrom, J., Rose, P., & Glisky, M. (1992). Mental images can be ambiguous:

Reconstruals and reference-frame reversals. *Memory & Cognition, 20,* 107–123.

Peterson, S., Fox, P., Posner, M., Mintern, M., & Raichle, M. (1989). Positron emission tomographic studies of the processing of single words. *Journal of Cognitive Neuroscience, 1,* 153–170.

Peterson, S., Fox, P., Snyder, A., & Raichle, M. (1990). Activation of extrastriate and frontal cortical areas by visual words and word-like stimuli. *Science, 249,* 1041–1044.

Pezdek, K., Whetstone, T., Reynolds, K., Askari, N., & Dougherty, T. (1989). Memory for real-world scenes: The role of consistency with schema expectation. *Journal of Experimental Psychology: Learning, Memory, and Cognition, 15,* 587–595.

Pillemer, D. B. (1984). Flashbulb memories of the assassination attempt on President Reagan. *Cognition, 16,* 63–80.

Pillemer, D. (1992). Remembering personal circumstances: A functional analysis. In E. Winograd & U. Neisser (Eds.), *Affect and accuracy in recall: The problem of "flashbulb" memories.* New York: Cambridge University Press.

Pillsbury, W. B. (1987). A study in apperception. *American Journal of Psychology, 8,* 315–393.

Pinker, S. (1980). Mental imagery and the third dimension. *Journal of Experimental Psychology: General, 109,* 354–371.

Pinker, S. (1989). *Learnability and cognition: The acquisition of argument structure.* Cambridge, MA: MIT Press.

Pinker, S. (1991). Rules of language. *Science, 253,* 530–535.

Pinker, S. (1994). *The language instinct.* New York: Penguin Press.

Pinker, S., & Finke, R. (1980). Emergent two-dimensional patterns in images in depth. *Journal of Experimental Psychology: Human Perception and Performance, 6,* 244–264.

Pinker, S., & Prince, A. (1988). On language and connectionism: Analysis of a parallel distributed processing model of language acquisition. *Cognition, 28,* 73–193.

Pirolli, P., & Anderson, J. (1985). The role of learning from examples in the acquisition of recursive programming skills. *Canadian Journal of Psychology, 39,* 240–272.

Platt, R., & Griggs, R. (1993). Darwinian algorithms and the Wason selection task: A factorial analysis of social contract selection task problems. *Cognition, 48,* 163–192.

Podgorny, P., & Shephard, R. (1983). Distribution of visual attention over space. *Journal of Experimental Psychology: Human Perception and Performance, 9,* 380–393.

Pollack, I., & Pickett, J. (1964). Intelligibility of excerpts from fluent speech: Auditory versus structural context. *Journal of Verbal Learning and Verbal Behavior, 3,* 79–84.

Polson, M., & Richardson, J. (Eds.). (1988). *Handbook of intelligent training systems.* Hillsdale, NJ: Lawrence Erlbaum.

Popper, K. (1959). *The logic of scientific discovery.* New York: Basic Books.

Posner, M. (1978). *Chronometric explorations of mind.* Hillsdale, NJ: Lawrence Erlbaum.

Posner, M. (1992). Attention as a cognitive and neural system. *Current Directions in Psychological Science, 1,* 11–14.

Posner, M., & Petersen, S. (1990). The attention system of the human brain. *Annual Review of Neuroscience, 13,* 25–42.

Posner, M., Petersen, S., Fox, P., & Raichle, M. (1988). Localization of cognitive operations in the human brain. *Science, 240,* 1627–1631.

Posner, M., & Snyder, C. R. R. (1974). Attention and cognitive control. In R. L. Solso (Ed.), *Information processing and cognition: The Loyola symposium.* Hillsdale, NJ: Lawrence Erlbaum.

Posner, M., & Snyder, C. (1975). Facilitation and inhibition in the processing of signals. In P. Rabbitt & S. Dornic (Eds.), *Attention and performance V.* New York: Academic Press.

Posner, M., Snyder, C., & Davidson, B. (1980). Attention and the detection of signals. *Journal of Experimental Psychology: General, 109,* 160–174.

Postman, L. (1964). Short-term memory and incidental learning. In A. W. Melton (Ed.), *Cat-*

egories of human learning. New York: Academic Press.

Postman, L. (1975). Verbal learning and memory. *Annual Review of Psychology, 26,* 291–335.

Postman, L., & Phillips, L. W. (1965). Short-term temporal changes in free recall. *Quarterly Journal of Experimental Psychology, 17,* 132–138.

Postman, L., & Stark, K. (1969). Role of response availability in transfer and interference. *Journal of Experimental Psychology, 79,* 168–177.

Postman, L., Thompkins, B. A., & Gray, W. D. (1978). The interpretation of encoding effects in retention. *Journal of Verbal Learning and Verbal Behavior, 17,* 681–705.

Postman, L., & Underwood, B. J. (1973). Critical issues in interference theory. *Memory & Cognition, 1,* 19–40.

Potter, M., Moryadas, A., Abrams, I., & Noel, A. (1993). Word perception and misperception in context. *Journal of Experimental Psychology: Learning, Memory and Cognition, 19,* 3–22.

Potts, G. R. (1972). Information-processing strategies used in the encoding of linear orderings. *Journal of Verbal Learning and Verbal Behavior, 11,* 727–740.

Potts, G. R. (1974). Storing and retrieving information about ordered relationships. *Journal of Experimental Psychology, 103,* 431–439.

Predebon, J., & Wenderoth, P. (1985). Imagined stimuli: Imaginary effects? *Bulletin of the Psychonomic Society, 23,* 215–216.

Putnam, H. (1975). The meaning of "meaning". In K. Gunderson (Ed.), *Language, mind, and knowledge.* Minneapolis: University of Minnesota Press.

Pylyshyn, Z. (1984). *Computation and cognition.* Cambridge, MA: MIT Press.

Quinn, G. (1988). Interference effects in the visuo-spatial sketchpad. In M. Denis, J. Engelkamp & J. T. E. Richardson (Eds.), *Cognitive and neuropsychological approaches to mental imagery* (pp. 181–189). Dordrecht: Martinus Nijhoff.

Quinn, G. (1991). Encoding and maintenance of information in visual working memory. In R. H. Logie & M. Denis (Eds.), *Mental images in human cognition* (pp 105–115). Amsterdam: Elsevier.

Quinn, G., & Ralston, G. E. (1986). Movement and attention in visual working memory. *Quarterly Journal of Experimental Psychology, 38A,* 689–703.

Rachman, S., & Eyrl, K. (1989). Predicting and remembering recurrent pain. *Behavior Research and Therapy, 27,* 621–635.

Radvansky, G., & Zacks, R. T. (1991). Mental models and the fan effect. *Journal of Experimental Psychology: Learning, Memory and Cognition, 17,* 940–953.

Rajaram, S. (1993). Remembering and knowing: Two means of access to the personal past. *Memory & Cognition, 21,* 89–102.

Ramsey, W., Stich, S., & Rumelhart, D. (1991). *Philosophy and connectionist theory.* Hillsdale, NJ: Lawrence Erlbaum.

Rao, G. A., Larkin, E. C., & Derr, R. F. (1986). Biologic effects of chronic ethanol consumption related to a deficient intake of carbohydrates. *Alcohol and Alcoholism, 21,* 369–373.

Rayko, D. (1977). Does knowledge matter? Psychological information and bystander helping. *The Canadian Journal of Behavioral Sciences, 9,* 295–304.

Rayner, K. (1993). Eye movements in reading: Recent developments. *Current Directions in Psychological Science, 2,* 81–85.

Rayner, K., Carlson, M., & Frazier, L. (1983). The interaction of syntax and semantics during sentence processing: Eye movements in the analysis of semantically biased sentences. *Journal of Verbal Learning and Verbal Behavior, 22,* 358–374.

Read, J. D., & Bruce, D. (1982). Longitudinal tracking of difficult memory retrievals. *Cognitive Psychology, 14,* 280–300.

Read, J. D., Tollestrup, P., Hammersley, R., & McFadzen, E. (1990). The unconscious transference effect: Are innocent bystanders ever misidentified? *Applied Cognitive Psychology, 4,* 3–31.

Reason, J. T., & Lucas, D. (1984). Using cognitive

diaries to investigate naturally occurring memory blocks. In J. E. Harris & P. E. Morris (Eds.), *Everyday memory actions and absentmindedness.* London: Academic Press.

Reber, A. (1992). An evolutionary context for the cognitive unconscious. *Philosophical Psychology, 5,* 33–52.

Reber, A. (1993). *Implicit learning and tacit knowledge: An essay on the cognitive unconscious.* New York: Oxford University Press.

Reder, L. (1982). Plausibility judgment versus fact retrieval: Alternative strategies for sentence verification. *Psychological Review, 89,* 250–280.

Reder, L., & Ritter, F. (1992). What determines initial feeling of knowing? Familiarity with question terms, not with the answer. *Journal of Experimental Psychology: Learning, Memory and Cognition, 18,* 435–451.

Reder, L., & Ross, B. H. (1983). Integrated knowledge in different tasks: Positive and negative fan effects. *Journal of Experimental Psychology: Human Learning and Memory, 8,* 55–72.

Reed, S. (1972). Pattern recognition and categorization. *Cognitive Psychology, 3,* 383–407.

Reed, S. (1977). Facilitation of problem solving. In J. N Castellan, D. Pisoni, & G. R. Potts (Eds.), *Cognitive theory* (pp. 3–20). Hillsdale, NJ: Lawrence Erlbaum.

Reed, S. (1988). *Cognition: Theory and applications.* Pacific Grove, CA: Brooks/Cole.

Reed, S. (1993). Imagery and discovery. In B. Roskos-Ewoldsen, M. J. Intons-Peterson, & R. Anderson (Eds.), *Imagery, creativity, and discovery: A cognitive perspective* (pp. 287–312). New York: North-Holland.

Reed, S., & Bolstad, C. (1991). Use of examples and procedures in problem solving. *Journal of Experimental Psychology: Learning, Memory and Cognition, 17,* 753–766.

Reed, S., Dempster, A., & Ettinger, M. (1985). Usefulness of analogous solutions for solving algebra word problems. *Journal of Experimental Psychology: Learning, Memory and Cognition, 11,* 106–125.

Reed, S., Ernst, G., & Banerji, R. (1974). The role of analogy in transfer between similar problem states. *Cognitive Psychology, 6,* 436–450.

Reich, S. S., & Ruth, P. (1982). Wason's selection task: Verification, falsification and matching. *British Journal of Psychology, 73,* 395–405.

Reicher, G. M. (1969). Perceptual recognition as a function of meaningfulness of stimulus material. *Journal of Experimental Psychology, 81,* 275–280.

Reinitz, M., Lammers, W., & Cochran, B. (1992). Memory-conjunction errors: Miscombination of stored stimulus features can produce illusions of memory. *Memory & Cognition, 20,* 1–11.

Reinitz, M., Morrissey, J., & Demb, J. (1994). Role of attention in face encoding. *Journal of Experimental Psychology: Learning, Memory and Cognition, 20,* 161–168.

Reisberg, D. (1983). General mental resources and perceptual judgments. *Journal of Experimental Psychology: Human Perception and Performance, 9,* 966–979.

Reisberg, D. (1987). External representations and the advantages of externalizing one's thought. In E. Hunt (Ed.), *The ninth annual conference of the cognitive science society.* Hillsdale, NJ: Lawrence Erlbaum.

Reisberg, D. (Ed.). (1992). *Auditory imagery.* Hillsdale, NJ: Lawrence Erlbaum.

Reisberg, D. (1996). The non-ambiguity of mental images. In C. Cornold, R. Logie, M. Brandimonte, G. Kaufmann & D. Reisberg (Eds.), *Stretching the imagination: Representation and transformation in mental imagery.* New York: Oxford University Press.

Reisberg, D., Baron, J., & Kemler, D. (1980). Overcoming Stroop interference: The effects of practice on distractor potency. *Journal of Experimental Psychology: Human Perception and Performance, 6,* 140–150.

Reisberg, D., & Chambers, D. (1991). Neither pictures nor propositions: What can we learn from a mental image? *Canadian Journal of Psychology, 45,* 288–302.

Reisberg, D., Culver, C., Heuer, F., & Fischman,

D. (1986). Visual memory: When imagery vividness makes a difference. *Journal of Mental Imagery, 10*, 51–74.

Reisberg, D., & Heuer, F. (1989) The consequences of vivid imagery: An empirical handle on the function of phenomenal states? Paper presented at the meetings of the Society for Philosophy and Psychology, Tucson, Arizona, April 1989.

Reisberg, D., Heuer, F., McLean, J., & O'Shaughnessy, M. (1988). The quantity, not the quality, of affect predicts memory vividness. *Bulletin of the Psychonomic Society, 26*, 100–103.

Reisberg, D., & Leak, S. (1987). Visual imagery and memory for appearance: Does Clark Gable or George C. Scott have bushier eyebrows? *Canadian Journal of Psychology, 41*, 521–526.

Reisberg, D., & Logie, R. (1993). The in's and out's of working memory: Escaping the boundaries on imagery function. In B. Roskos-Ewoldsen, M. Intons-Peterson, & R. Anderson (Eds.), *Imagery, creativity and discovery: A cognitive approach* (pp. 39–76). Amsterdam: Elsevier.

Reisberg, D., & Morris, A. (1985). Images contain what the imager put there: A non-replication of illusions in imagery. *Bulletin of the Psychonomic Society, 23*, 493–496.

Reisberg, D., Rappaport, I., & O'Shaughnessy, M. (1984). The limits of working memory: The digit digit-span. *Journal of Experimental Psychology: Learning, Memory and Cognition, 10*, 203–221.

Reitman, J. (1976). Skilled perception in Go: Deducing memory structures from inter-response times. *Cognitive Psychology, 8*, 336–356.

Reitman, W. (1964). Heuristic decision procedures, open constraints, and the structure of ill-defined problems. In M. Shelley & G. Bryan (Eds.), *Human judgments and optimality.* New York: Wiley.

Remington, R. (1980). Attention and saccadic eye movements. *Journal of Experimental Psychology: Human Perception and Performance, 6*, 726–744.

Repp, B. (1992). Perceptual restoration of a "missing" speech sound: Auditory induction or illusion? *Perception & Psychophysics, 51*, 14–32.

Revlin, R., Leirer, V., Yopp, H., & Yopp, R. (1980). The belief bias effect in formal reasoning: The influence of knowledge on logic. *Memory & Cognition, 8*, 584–592.

Rhodes, G., Brake, S., & Atkinson, A. (1993). What's lost in inverted faces? *Cognition, 47*, 25–57.

Riccio, D., Rabinowitz, V., & Axelrod, S. (1994). Memory: When less is more. *American Psychologist, 49*, 917–926.

Richardson, J. (1980). *Mental imagery and human memory.* New York: St. Martin's.

Richardson, J. (1984). Developing the theory of working memory. *Memory & Cognition, 12*, 71–83.

Richardson-Klavehn, A., & Bjork, R. A. (1988). Measures of memory. *Annual Review of Psychology, 39*, 475–543.

Richardson-Klavehn, A., Lee, M., Joubran, R., & Bjork, R. (1994). Intention and awareness in perceptual identification priming. *Memory & Cognition, 22*, 293–312.

Riefer, D., & Rouder, J. (1993). A multinomial modeling analysis of the mnemonic benefits of bizarre imagery. *Memory & Cognition, 20*, 601–611.

Riemsdijk, H. V., & Williams, E. (1986). *Introduction to the theory of grammar.* Cambridge, MA: MIT Press.

Rips, L. (1975). Inductive judgements about natural categories. *Journal of Verbal Learning and Verbal Behavior, 14*, 665–681.

Rips, L. (1983). Cognitive processes in propositional reasoning. *Psychological Review, 90*, 38–71.

Rips, L. (1986). Mental muddles. In M. Brand & R. Harnish (Eds.), *The representation of knowledge and belief* (pp. 258–286). Tucson: University of Arizona Press.

Rips, L. (1989a). Similarity, typicality, and categorization. In S. Vosniadou & A. Ortony (Eds.), *Similarity and analogical reasoning* (pp.

21–59). Cambridge: Cambridge University Press.

Rips, L. (1989b). The psychology of knights and knaves. *Cognition, 31*, 85–116.

Rips, L. (1990). Reasoning. *Annual Review of Psychology, 41*, 321–353.

Rips, L., & Collins, A. (1993). Categories and resemblance. *Journal of Experimental Psychology: General, 122*, 468–489.

Rips, L., Shoben, E. J., & Smith, E. E. (1973). Semantic distance and the verification of semantic relations. *Journal of Verbal Learning and Verbal Behavior, 12*, 1–20.

Ritchie, J. M. (1985). The aliphatic alcohols. In A. G. Gilman, L. S. Goodman, T. W. Rall, & F. Murad (Eds.), *The pharmacological basis of therapeutics* (pp. 372–386). New York: Macmillan.

Roberts, W. A. (1981). Retroactive inhibition in rat spatial memory. *Animal Learning and Behavior, 9*, 566–574.

Rock, I. (1983). *The logic of perception.* Cambridge, MA: MIT Press.

Roediger, H. L. (1980). The effectiveness of four mnemonics in ordering recall. *Journal of Experimental Psychology: Human Learning and Memory, 6*, 558–567.

Roediger, H. L. (1990). Implicit memory: Retention without remembering. *American Psychologist, 45*, 1043–1956.

Roediger, H. L., & Blaxton, T. A. (1987a). Effects of varying modality, surface features, and retention interval on word fragment completion. *Memory & Cognition, 15*, 379–388.

Roediger, H. L., & Blaxton, T. A. (1987b). Retrieval modes produce dissociations in memory for surface information. In D. S. Gorfein (Ed.), *Memory and cognitive processes: The Ebbinghaus centennial conference* (pp. 349–379). Hillsdale, NJ: Lawrence Erlbaum.

Roediger, H. L., & Neely, J. H. (1982). Retrieval blocks in episodic and semantic memory. *Canadian Journal of Psychology, 36*, 213–242.

Roediger, H. L., & Payne, D. G. (1985). Recall criterion does not affect recall level or hypermnesia: A puzzle for generate/recognize theories. *Memory & Cognition, 13*, 1–7.

Roediger, H. L., & Payne, D. P. (1982). Hypermnesia: The role of repeated testing. *Journal of Experimental Psychology: Learning, Memory and Cognition, 8*, 66–72.

Roediger, H. L., Srinivas, K., & Weldon, M. (1989). Dissociations between implicit measures of retention. In S. Lewandowsky, J. Dunn & K. Kirsner (Eds.), *Implicit memory: Theoretical issues* (pp. 67–84). Hillsdale, NJ: Lawrence Erlbaum.

Roediger, H. L., & Thorpe, L. A. (1978). The role of recall of time in producing hypermnesia. *Memory & Cognition, 6*, 296–305.

Roediger, H. L., Weldon, M., & Challis, B. (1989). Explaining dissociations between implicit and explicit measures of retention: A processing account. In H. L. Roediger & F. I. M. Craik (Eds.), *Varieties of memory and consciousness: Essays in honor of Endel Tulving* (pp. 3–41). Hillsdale, NJ: Lawrence Erlbaum.

Roediger, H. L., & Wheeler, M. (1993). Hypermnesia in episodic and semantic memory: Response to Bahrick and Hall. *Psychological Science, 4*, 207–208.

Roitblat, H. (1987). *Introduction to comparative cognition.* New York: Freeman.

Rosch, E. (1973). On the internal structure of perceptual and semantic categories. In T. E. Moore (Ed.), *Cognitive development and the acquisition of language.* New York: Academic Press.

Rosch, E. (1975). Cognitive representations of semantic categories. *Journal of Experimental Psychology: General, 104*, 192–233.

Rosch, E. (1977a). Human categorization. In N. Warren (Ed.), *Advances in cross-cultural psychology.* London: Academic Press.

Rosch, E. (1977b). Linguistic relativity. In P. Johnson-Laird & P. Wason (Eds.), *Thinking: Readings in cognitive science* (pp. 501–519). New York: Cambridge University Press.

Rosch, E. (1978). Principles of categorization. In E. Rosch & B. B. Lloyd (Eds.), *Cognition and categorization* (pp. 27–48). Hillsdale, NJ: Lawrence Erlbaum.

Rosch, E., & Mervis, C. B. (1975). Family resemblances. Studies in the internal structure of categories. *Cognitive Psychology, 7*, 573–605.

Rosch, E., Mervis, C. B., Gray, W., Johnson, D., & Boyes-Braem, P. (1976). Basic objects in natural categories. *Cognitve Psychology, 3*, 382–439.

Rosch, E., Simpson, C., & Miller, R. S. (1976). Structural bases of typicality effects. *Journal of Experimental Psychology: Human Perception and Performance, 2*, 491–502.

Rosenbaum, D. (1991). *Human motor control.* San Diego, CA: Academic Press.

Ross, B. (1984). Remindings and their effects in learning a cognitive skill. *Cognitive Psychology, 16*, 371–416.

Ross, B. (1987). This is like that: The use of earlier problems and the separation and similarity effects. *Journal of Experimental Psychology: Learning, Memory and Cognition, 13*, 629–639.

Ross, B. (1989). Distinguishing types of superficial similarities: Different effects on the access and use of earlier problems. *Journal of Experimental Psychology: Learning, Memory and Cognition, 15*, 456–468.

Ross, J., & Lawrence, K. A. (1968). Some observations on memory artifice. *Psychonomic Science, 13*, 107–108.

Ross, L., & Anderson, C. (1982). Shortcomings in the attribution process: On the origins and maintenance of erroneous social assessments. In D. Kahneman, P. Slovic & A. Tversky (Eds.), *Judgment under uncertainty: Heuristics and biases.* New York: Cambridge University Press.

Ross, L., Lepper, M., & Hubbard, M. (1975). Perseverance in self perception and social perception: Biased attributional processes in the debriefing paradigm. *Journal of Personality and Social Psychology, 32*, 880–892.

Ross, M., & Buehler, E. (1994). Creative remembering. In U. Neisser & R. Fivush (Eds.), *The remembered self.* New York: Cambridge University Press.

Ross, M., & Sicoly, F. (1979). Egocentric biases in availability and attribution. *Journal of Personality and Social Psychology, 37*, 322–336.

Rothbart, M., Evans, M., & Fulero, S. (1979). Recall for confirming events: Memory processes and the maintenance of social stereotypes. *Journal of Experimental Social Psychology, 15*, 343–355.

Rozin, P. (1976). The evolution of intelligence and access to the cognitive unconscious. In E. Stellar & J. M. Sprague (Eds.), *Progress in psychobiology and physiological psychology* (vol. 6). New York: Academic Press.

Rubin, D. C., & Kontis, T. S. (1983). A schema for common cents. *Memory & Cognition, 11*, 335–341.

Rubin, D. C., & Kozin, M. (1984). Vivid memories. *Cognition, 16*, 81–95.

Rueckl, J. G., & Oden, G. C. (1986). The integration of contextual and featural information during word identification. *Journal of Memory and Language, 25*, 445–460.

Rumelhart, D., & McClelland, J. (1986a). On learning the past tenses of English verbs. In J. McClelland & D. Rumelhart (Eds.), *Parallel distributed processing: Explorations in the microstructure of cognition.* Cambridge, MA: MIT Press.

Rumelhart, D. E., & McClelland, J. L. (Eds.). (1986b). *Parallel distributed processing, vol. 1.* Cambridge, MA: MIT Press.

Rumelhart, D. E., & Norman, D. A. (1975). The active structural network. In D. A. Norman & D. E. Rumelhart (Eds.), *Explorations in cognition.* San Francisco: Freeman.

Rumelhart, D. E., & Ortony, A. (1977). The representation of knowledge in memory. In R. C. Anderson, R. J. Spiro, & W. E. Montague (Eds.), *Schooling and the acquisition of knowledge.* Hillsdale, NJ: Lawrence Erlbaum.

Rumelhart, D. E., & Siple, P. (1974). Process of recognizing tachistoscopically presented words. *Psychological Review, 81*, 99–118.

Rundus, D. (1971). Analysis of rehearsal processes in free recall. *Journal of Experimental Psychology, 89*, 63–77.

Ryan, C. (1983). Reassessing the automaticity—control distinction: Item recognition as a paradigm case. *Psychological Review, 90*, 171–178.

Sabini, J., & Silver, M. (1981). Introspection and causal accounts. *Journal of Personality and Social Psychology, 40*, 171–179.

Sachs, E., Weingarten, M., & Klein, N. (1966). Effects of chlordiazepoxide on the acquisition of avoiding learning and its transfer to the normal state and other drug conditions. *Psychopharmacologia, 9*, 17–30.

Sachs, J. D. S. (1967). Recognition memory for syntactic and semantic aspects of connected discourse. *Perception & Psychophysics, 2*, 437–442.

Sacks, O. (1985). *The man who mistook his wife for a hat and other clinical tales.* New York: Harper & Row.

Salame, P., & Baddeley, A. D. (1982). Disruption of short-term memory by unattended speech: Implications for the structure of working memory. *Journal of Verbal Learning and Verbal Behavior, 21*, 150–164.

Saltz, E., & Donnenwerth-Nolan, S. (1981). Does motoric imagery facilitate memory for sentences? A selective interference test. *Journal of Verbal Learning and Verbal Behavior, 20*, 322–332.

Samuel, A. G. (1986). The role of the lexicon in speech perception. In E. C. Schwab & H. C. Nusbaum (Eds.), *Pattern recognition by humans and machines* (pp. 89–111). Orlando, FL: Academic Press.

Samuel, A. (1987). Lexical uniqueness effects on phonemic restoration. *Journal of Memory and Language, 26*, 36–56.

Samuel, A. (1991). A further examination of attentional effects in the phonemic restoration illusion. *Quarterly Journal of Experimental Psychology: Human Experimental Psychology 43*, 679–699.

Sanitioso, R., Kunda, Z., & Fong, G. (1990). Motivated recruitment of autobiographical memories. *Journal of Personality and Social Psychology, 59*, 229–241.

Savage, J. (1954). *The foundation of statistics.* New York: Wiley.

Schab, F. (1990). Odors and the remembrance of things past. *Journal of Experimental Psychology: Learning, Memory and Cognition, 16*, 648–655.

Schab, F. (1991). Odor memory: Taking stock. *Psychological Bulletin, 109*, 242–251.

Schactel, E. G. (1947). On memory and childhood amnesia. *Psychiatry, 10*, 1–26.

Schacter, D. (1987). Implicit memory: History and current status. *Journal of Experimental Psychology: Learning, Memory and Cognition, 13*, 501–518.

Schacter, D. (1992). Understanding implicit memory: A cognitive neuroscience approach. *American Psychologist, 47*, 559–569.

Schacter, D., & Tulving, E. (1982). Amnesia and memory research. In L. S. Cermak (Ed.), *Human memory and amnesia.* Hillsdale, NJ: Lawrence Erlbaum.

Schacter, D., Tulving, E., & Wang, P. (1981). Source amnesia: New methods and illustrative data. Paper presented at the meeting of the International Neuropsychological Society, Atlanta.

Schank, R. C. (1982). *Dynamic memory: A theory of reminding and learning in computers and people.* New York: Cambridge University Press.

Schank, R. C., & Abelson, R. (1977). *Scripts, plans, goals, and understanding.* Hillsdale, NJ: Lawrence Erlbaum.

Schneider, S. (1992). Framing and conflict: Aspiration level contingency, the status quo, and current theories of risky choice. *Journal of Experimental Psychology: Learning, Memory and Cognition, 18*, 1040–1057.

Schneider, S., & Laurion, S. (1993). Do we know what we've learned from listening to the news? *Memory & Cognition, 21*, 198–209.

Schneider, W., & Shiffrin, R. (1977). Controlled and automatic human information processing: I. Detection, search, and attention. *Psychological Review, 84*, 1–66.

Schneider, W., & Shiffrin, R. M. (1985). Categorization (restructuring) and automatization: Two separable factors. *Psychological Review*, *92*, 424–428.

Schoenfeld, A., & Herrmann, D. (1982). Problem perception and knowledge structure in expert and novice mathematical problem solvers. *Journal of Experimental Psychology: Learning, Memory and Cognition*, *5*, 484–494.

Schooler, J., & Engstler-Schooler, T. (1990). Verbal overshadowing of visual memories: Some things are better left unsaid. *Cognitive Psychology*, *22*, 36–71.

Schooler, J., Ohlsson, S., & Brooks, K. (1993). Thoughts beyond words: When language overshadows insight. *Journal of Experimental Psychology: General*, *122*, 166–183.

Schunn, C., & Dunbar, K. (in press). Priming, analogy and awareness in complex reasoning. *Memory & Cognition*.

Schustack, M., & Sternberg, R. (1981). Evaluation of evidence in causal inference. *Journal of Experimental Psychology: General*, *110*, 101–120.

Schwartz, B. (1982). Reinforcement-induced behavioral stereotypy: How not to teach people to discover rules. *Journal of Experimental Psychology: General*, *111*, 23–59.

Schwartz, B., & Hashtroudi, S. (1991). Priming is independent of skill learning. *Journal of Experimental Psychology: Learning, Memory and Cognition*, *17*, 1177–1187.

Schwartz, B., & Reisberg, D. (1991). *Learning and memory*. New York: W. W. Norton.

Schwartz, B., & Robbins, S. (1995). *Psychology of learning and behavior*, 4th ed. New York: W. W. Norton.

Schwartz, N., Strack, F., Hilton, D., & Naderer, G. (1991). Base rates, representativeness and the logic of conversation: The contextual relevance of "irrelevant" information. *Social Cognition*, *9*, 67–84.

Segal, S., & Fusella, V. (1970). Influence of imaged pictures and sounds in detection of visual and auditory signals. *Journal of Experimental Psychology*, *83*, 458–474.

Segal, S., & Fusella, V. (1971). Effect of images in six sense modalities on detection of visual signal from noise. *Psychonomic Science*, *24*, 55–56.

Seidenberg, M., Tanenhaus, M., Leiman, M., & Bienkowski, M. (1982). Automatic access of the meanings of words in context: Some limitations of knowledge-based processing. *Cognition*, *7*, 177–215.

Selfridge, O. (1955). Pattern recognition and modern computers. Proceedings of the Western Joint Computer Conference, Los Angeles, CA.

Selfridge, O. (1959). Pandemonium: A paradigm for learning. In *The mechanisation of thought processes*. London: H. M. Stationery Office.

Seltzer, B., & Benson, D. F. (1974). The temporal pattern of retrograde amnesia in Korsakoff's Disease. *Neurology*, *24*, 527–530.

Sergent, J., & Poncet, M. (1990). From covert to overt recognition of faces in a prosopagnosic patient. *Brain*, *113*, 989–1004.

Shaffer, L. H. (1975a). Control processes in typing. *Quarterly Journal of Experimental Psychology*, *27*, 419–432.

Shaffer, L. H. (1975b). Multiple attention in continuous verbal tasks. In P. Rabbitt & S. Dornic (Eds.), *Attention and performance V*. New York: Academic Press.

Shafir, E. (1993). Choosing versus rejecting: Why some options are both better and worse than others. *Memory & Cognition*, *21*, 546–556.

Shafir, E., Simonson, I., & Tversky, A. (1993). Reason-based choice. *Cognition*, *49*, 11–36.

Shafir, E., Smith, E. E., & Osherson, D. N. (1990). Typicality and reasoning fallacies. *Memory & Cognition*, *18*(3), 229–239.

Shaklee, H., & Fischoff, B. (1982). Strategies of information search in causal analysis. *Memory & Cognition*, *10*, 520–530.

Shaklee, H., & Mims, M. (1982). Sources of error in judging event covariations. *Journal of Experimental Psychology: Learning, Memory and Cognition*, *8*, 208–224.

Shand, M. (1982). Sign-based short-term coding of American Sign Language signs and printed English words by congenitally deaf signers. *Cognitive Psychology*, *14*, 1–12.

Shanteau, J. (1992). The psychology of experts: An alternative view. In G. Wright & F. Bolger (Eds.), *Expertise and decision support* (pp. 11–23). New York: Plenum Press.

Shapiro, P. N., & Penrod, S. (1986). Meta-analysis of facial identification studies. *Psychological Bulletin, 100,* 139–156.

Shepard, R. N. (1967). Recognition memory for words, sentences, and pictures. *Journal of Verbal Learning and Verbal Behavior, 6,* 156–163.

Shepard, R. N. (1988). The imagination of the scientist. In K. Egan & D. Nadaner (Eds.), *Imagination and education* (pp. 153–185). New York: Teachers College Press.

Shepard, R. N., & Cooper, L. A. (1982). *Mental images and their transformations.* Cambridge, MA: MIT Press.

Shepard, R. N., & Feng, C. (1972). A chronometric study of mental paper folding. *Cognitive Psychology, 3,* 228–243.

Shepard, R. N., & Metzler, J. (1971). Mental rotation of three-dimensional objects. *Science, 171,* 701–703.

Shiffrin, R., & Schneider, W. (1977). Controlled and automatic human information processing: II. Perceptual learning, automatic attending and a general theory. *Psychological Review, 84,* 127–190.

Shiffrin, R., & Schneider, W. (1984). Automatic and controlled processes revisited. *Psychological Review, 91,* 269–276.

Shin, H., & Nosofsky, R. (1992). Similarity-scaling studies of dot-pattern classification and recognition. *Journal of Experimental Psychology: General, 121,* 278–304.

Shulman, G., & Wilson, J. (1987). Spatial frequency and selective attention to local and global structure. *Perception, 16,* 89–101.

Sieroff, E., Pollatsek, A., & Posner, M. (1988). Recognition of visual letter strings following damage to the posterior visual spatial attention system. *Cognitive Neuropsychology, 5,* 427–449.

Simon, H. (1957). *Models of man.* New York: Wiley.

Simon, H. (1973). The structure of ill-defined problems. *Artificial Intelligence, 4,* 181–201.

Simon, H. (1974). How big is a chunk? *Science, 183,* 482–488.

Simon, H. (1975). The functional equivalence of problem solving skills. *Cognitive Psychology, 7,* 268–288.

Simon, H., & Reed, S. (1976). Modeling strategy shifts in a problem-solving task. *Cognitive Psychology, 8,* 86–97.

Simonton, D. (1989). Chance-configuration theory of scientific creativity. In B. Gholson, W. Shadish, R. Neimeyer & A. Houts (Eds.), *Psychology of science: Contributions to metascience.* Cambridge: Cambridge University Press.

Simpson, G. (1984). Lexical ambiguity and its role in models of word recognition. *Psychological Bulletin, 96,* 316–340.

Simpson, G. B., Peterson, R. R., Castell, M. A., & Burgess, C. (1989). Lexical and sentence context effects in word recognition. *Journal of Experimental Psychology: Learning, Memory and Cognition, 15,* 88–97.

Singer, J., & Salovey, P. (1988). Mood and memory: Evaluating the network theory of affect. *Clinical Psychology Review, 8,* 211–251.

Slamecka, N. J., & Graf, P. (1978). The generation effect: Delineation of a phenomenon. *Journal of Experimental Psychology: Human Learning and Memory, 4,* 592–604.

Slobin, D. (1966). Grammatical transformations and sentence comprehension in childhood and adulthood. *Journal of Verbal Learning and Verbal Behavior, 5,* 219–227.

Slovic, P. (1975). Choice between equally valued alternatives. *Journal of Experimental Psychology: Human Perception and Performance, 1,* 280–287.

Slovic, P. (1990). Choice. In D. Osherson & E. Smith (Eds.), *An invitation to cognitive science: Thinking* (pp. 89–116). Cambridge, MA: MIT Press.

Slovic, P. (1995). The construction of preference. *American Psychologist, 50,* 364–371.

Slovic, P., & Fischhoff, B. (1977). On the psychology of experimental surprises. *Journal of*

Experimental Psychology: Human Perception and Performance, 3, 544–551.

Slovic, P., Fischhoff, B., & Lichtenstein, S. (1982). Facts versus fears: Understanding perceived risk. In D. Kahneman, P. Slovic, & A. Tversky (Eds.), *Judgment under uncertainty: Heuristics and biases.* Cambridge: Cambridge University Press.

Smedslund, J. (1963). The concept of correlation in adults. *Scandinavian Journal of Psychology, 4,* 165–173.

Smith, D., & Graesser, A. (191). Memory for actions in scripted activities as a function of typicality, retention interval, and retrieval task. *Memory & Cognition, 9,* 550–559.

Smith, E., & Miller, F. (1978). Limits on perception of cognitive processes: A reply to Nisbett & Wilson. *Psychological Review, 85,* 355–362.

Smith, E., & Zárate, M. (1992). Exemplar-based model of social judgment. *Psychological Review, 99,* 3–21.

Smith, E. E. (1978). Theories of semantic memory. In W. K. Estes (Ed.), *Handbook of learning and cognitive processes.* Potomac, MD: Lawrence Erlbaum.

Smith, E. E. (1988). Concepts and thought. In R. J. Sternberg & E. E. Smith (Eds.), *The psychology of human thought.* Cambridge: Cambridge University Press.

Smith, E. E., Adams, N., & Schorr, D. (1978). Fact retrieval and the paradox of interference. *Cognitive Psychology, 10,* 438–464.

Smith, E. E., Balzano, G. J., & Walker, J. H. (1978). Nominal, perceptual, and semantic codes in picture categorization. In J. W. Cotton & R. L. Klatzky (Eds.), *Semantic factors in cognition.* Hillsdale, NJ: Lawrence Erlbaum.

Smith, E. E., Langston, C., & Nisbett, R. (1992). The case for rules in reasoning. *Cognitive Science, 16,* 1–40.

Smith, E. E., & Medin, D. L. (1981). *Categories and concepts.* Cambridge, MA: Harvard University Press.

Smith, E. E., Rips, L. J., & Shoben, E. J. (1974). Structure and process in semantic memory: A featural model for semantic decisions. *Psychological Review, 81,* 214–241.

Smith, J., & Kida, T. (1991). Heuristics and biases: Expertise and task realism in auditing. *Psychological Bulletin, 109,* 472–489.

Smith, M. (1982). Hypnotic memory enhancement of witnesses: Does it work? Paper presented at the meeting of the Psychonomic Society, Minneapolis.

Smith, M., Besner, D., & Miyoshi, H. (1994). New limits to automaticity: Context modulates semantic priming. *Journal of Experimental Psychology: Learning, Memory and Cognition, 20,* 104–115.

Smith, S. (1979). Remembering in and out of context. *Journal of Experimental Psychology: Human Learning and Memory, 5,* 460–471.

Smith, S. (1985). Background music and context-dependent memory. *American Journal of Psychology, 6,* 591–603.

Smith, S. M., & Blankenship, S. (1991). Incubation and the persistence of fixation in problem solving. *American Journal of Psychology, 104,* 61–87.

Smith, S. M., & Blankenship, S. E. (1989). Incubation effects. *Bulletin of the Psychonomic Society, 27,* 311–314.

Smith, S. M., Glenberg, A., & Bjork, R. A. (1978). Environmental context and human memory. *Memory & Cognition, 6,* 342–353.

Smyth, M., & Scholey, K. (1994). Interference in immediate spatial memory. *Memory & Cognition, 22,* 1–13.

Smyth, M. M., & Pendleton, L. R. (1989). Working memory for movements. *Quarterly Journal of Experimental Psychology, 41A,* 235–250.

Snyder, M., & Swann, W. (1978). Behavioral confirmation in social interaction: From social perception to social reality. *Journal of Experimental Social Psychology, 14,* 148–162.

Spear, N. E. (1979). Experimental analysis of infantile amnesia. In J. F. Kihlstrom & F. S. Evans (Eds.), *Functional disorders of memory* (pp. 75–102). Hillsdale, NJ: Lawrence Erlbaum.

Spearman, C. (1923). *The nature of "intelligence"*

and the principles of cognition. London: Macmillan.

Spelke, E., Hirst, W., & Neisser, U. (1976). Skills of divided attention. *Cognition, 4,* 215–230.

Spencer, R., & Weisberg, R. (1986). Is analogy sufficient to facilitate transfer during problem solving? *Memory & Cognition, 14,* 442–449.

Sperling, G. (1960). The information available in brief visual presentations. *Psychological Monographs, 74,* entire issue.

Sperling, G., & Speelman, R. G. (1970). Acoustic similarity and auditory short-term memory: experiments and a model. In D. A. Norman (Ed.), *Models of human memory* (pp. 152–202). New York: Academic Press.

Spiro, R. J. (1977). Remembering information from text: The "state of schema" approach. In R. C. Anderson, R. J. Spiro, & W. E. Montague (Eds.), *Schooling and the acquisition of knowledge.* Hillsdale, NJ: Lawrence Erlbaum.

Sporer, S. (1988). Long-term improvement of facial recognition through visual rehearsal. In M. Gruneberg, P. Morris, & R. Sykes (Eds.), *Practical aspects of memory: Current research and issues* (pp. 182–188). New York: Wiley.

Sporer, S. (1991). Deep-deeper-deepest? Encoding strategies and the recognition of human faces. *Journal of Experimental Psychology: Learning, Memory and Cognition, 17,* 323–333.

Squire, L., & Cohen, N. J. (1984). Human memory and amnesia. In J. McGaugh, G. Lynch, & N. Weinberger (Eds.), *Proceedings of the conference on the neurobiology of learning and memory.* (pp. 3–64). New York: Guilford Press.

Squire, L., & McKee, R. (1993). Declarative and nondeclarative memory in opposition: When prior events influence amnesic patients more than normal subjects. *Memory & Cognition, 21,* 424–430.

Squire, L., & Zola-Morgan, S. (1991). The medial temporal lobe memory system. *Science, 253,* 1380–1386.

Srinivas, K. (1993). Perceptual specificity in nonverbal priming. *Journal of Experimental Psychology: Learning, Memory and Cognition, 19,* 582–602.

Srinivas, K., & Roediger, H. (1990). Classifying implicit memory tests: Category association and anagram solution. *Journal of Memory and Language, 29,* 389–412.

Standing, L. (1973). Learning 10,000 pictures. *Quarterly Journal of Experimental Psychology, 25,* 207–222.

Standing, L., Conezio, J., & Haber, R. (1970). Perception and memory for pictures: Single-trial learning of 2500 visual stimuli. *Psychonomic Science, 19,* 73–74.

Stangor, C., & McMillan, D. (1992). Memory for expectancy-congruent and expectancy-incongruent information: A review of the social and social developmental literatures. *Psychological Bulletin, 111,* 42–61.

Staudenmayer, H. (1975). Understanding conditional reasoning with meaningful propositions. In R. J. Falmagne (Ed.), *Reasoning: Representation and process in children and adults.* Hillsdale, NJ: Lawrence Erlbaum.

Staudenmayer, H., & Bourne, L. (1978). The nature of denied propositions in the conditional reasoning task: Interpretation and learning. In R. Revlin & R. Mayer (Eds.), *Human reasoning.* New York: Wiley.

Steblay, N. J. (1992). A meta-analytic review of the weapon focus effect. *Law and Human Behavior, 16,* 413–424.

Stein, M. (1956). A transactional approach to creativity. In C. W. Taylor (Ed.), *The 1955 University of Utah research conference on the identification of creative scientific talent.* Salt Lake City: University of Utah Press.

Stein, M. (1975). *Stimulating creativity.* New York: Academic Press.

Stern, L., Dahlgren, R., & Gaffney, L. (1991). Spacing judgments as an index of integration from context-induced relational processing: Implications for the free recall of ambiguous prose passages. *Memory & Cognition, 19,* 579–592.

Sternberg, R. (1988). A three-facet model of creativity. In R. J. Sternberg (Ed.), *The nature of creativity* (pp. 125–147). Cambridge: Cambridge University Press.

Sternberg, R., & Lubart, T. (1992). Buy low and sell high: An investment approach to creativity. *Current Directions in Psychological Science, 1*, 1–5.

Stevenson, M. (1993). Decision making with long-term consequences: Temporal discounting for single and multiple outcomes in the future. *Journal of Experimental Psychology: General, 122*, 3–22.

Stine, E. A. L. (1990). On-line processing of written text by younger and older adults. *Psychology and Aging, 5*, 68–78.

Strayer, D., & Kramer, A. (1994a). Strategies and automaticity: II. Dynamic aspects of strategy adjustment. *Journal of Experimental Psychology: Learning, Memory and Cognition, 20*, 342–365.

Strayer, D., & Kramer, A. (1994b). Strategies and automaticity: I. Basic findings and conceptual framework. *Journal of Experimental Psychology: Learning, Memory and Cognition, 20*, 318–341.

Stroop, J. (1935). Studies of interference in serial verbal reaction. *Journal of Experimental Psychology, 18*, 643–662.

Sulin, R. A., & Dooling, D. J. (1974). Intrusion of a thematic idea in retention of prose. *Journal of Experimental Psychology, 103*, 255–262.

Sumby, W. H. (1963). Word frequency and serial position effects. *Journal of Verbal Learning and Verbal Behavior, 1*, 443–450.

Svartik, J. (1966). *On voice in the English verb.* The Hague: Mouton.

Sweller, J., Mawer, R., & Ward, M. (1983). Development of expertise in mathematical problem solving. *Journal of Experimental Psychology: General, 112*, 639–661.

Swinney, D. (1979). Lexical access during sentence comprehension: (Re)consideration of context effects. *Journal of Verbal Learning and Verbal Behavior, 5*, 219–227.

Tabachnick, B., & Brotsky, S. (1976). Free recall and complexity of pictorial stimuli. *Memory & Cognition, 4*, 466–470.

Tanenhaus, M., Spivey-Knowlton, M., Eberhard, K., & Sedivy, J. (1995). Integration of visual and linguistic information in spoken language comprehension. *Science, 268*, 1632–1634.

Taplin, J., & Staudenmayer, H. (1973). Interpretation of abstract conditional sentences in deductive reasoning. *Journal of Verbal Learning and Verbal Behavior, 12*, 530–542.

Taraban, R., & McClelland, J. (1988). Constituent attachment and thematic role assignment in sentence processing: Influences of content-based expectations. *Journal of Memory and Language, 27*, 597–632.

Taylor, S. E. (1982). The availability bias in social perception and interaction. In D. Kahneman, P. Slovic, & A. Tversky (Eds.), *Judgments under uncertainty: Heuristics and biases.* Cambridge: Cambridge University Press.

Taylor, S. E., Fiske, S. T., Etcoff, N., & Ruderman, A. (1978). The categorical and contextual bases of person memory and stereotyping. *Journal of Personality and Social Psychology, 36*, 778–793.

Teasdale, J., Proctor, L., Lloyd, C., & Baddeley, A. (1993). Working-memory and stimulus-independent thought: Effects of memory load and presentation rate. *European Journal of Cognitive Psychology, 5*, 417–433.

te Linde, J. (1983). Pictures and words in semantic decisions. In J. C. Yuille (Ed.), *Imagery, memory, and cognition.* Hillsdale, NJ: Lawrence Erlbaum.

Tenpenny, P., & Shoben, E. (1992). Component processes and the utility of the conceptually-driven/data-driven distinction. *Journal of Experimental Psychology: Learning, Memory and Cognition, 18*, 25–42.

Thaler, R. (1980). Toward a positive theory of consumer choice. *Journal of Economic Behavior and Organization, 1*, 39–60.

Thapar, A., & Greene, R. (1993). Evidence against a short-term store account of long-term recency effects. *Memory & Cognition, 21*, 329–337.

Thapar, A., & Greene, R. (1994). Effects of level of processing on implicit and explicit tasks.

Journal of Experimental Psychology: Learning, Memory and Cognition, 20, 671–679.

Thomas, J. (1974). An analysis of behavior in the Hobbits-Orcs problem. *Cognitive Psychology, 6,* 257–269.

Thompson, P. (1980). Margaret Thatcher: A new illusion. *Perception, 9,* 483–484.

Thompson, V. (1994). Interpretational factors in conditional reasoning. *Memory & Cognition, 22,* 742–758.

Thorndike, E., & Lorge, I. (1963). *The Thorndike/Lorge teacher's word book of 30,000 words.* New York: Columbia University Press.

Thorndyke, P. W. (1976). The role of inferences in discourse comprehension. *Journal of Verbal Learning and Verbal Behavior, 15,* 437–446.

Thorndyke, P. W., & Bower, G. H. (1974). Storage and retrieval processes in sentence memory. *Cognitive Psychology, 5,* 515–543.

Till, R. E., & Jenkins, J. J. (1973). The effects of cued orienting tasks on the free recall of words. *Journal of Verbal Learning and Verbal Behavior, 12,* 489–498.

Tipper, S. (1985). The negative priming effect: Inhibitory effects of ignored primes. *Quarterly Journal of Experimental Psychology, 37A,* 571–590.

Tipper, S. (1992). Selection for action: The role of inhibitory mechanisms. *Current Directions in Psychological Science, 1,* 105–109.

Tipper, S., & Driver, J. (1988). Negative priming between picture and words in a selective attention task: Evidence for semantic processing of ignored stimuli. *Memory & Cognition, 16,* 64–70.

Tipper, S., Driver, J. & Weaver, B. (1991). Object-centered inhibition of return of visual attention. *Quarterly Journal of Experimental Psychology: Human Experimental Psychology, 43,* 289–298.

Titchener, E. B. (1926). *Lectures on the experimental psychology of the thought-process.* New York: Macmillan

Toth, J., Reingold, E., & Jacoby, L. (1994). Toward a redefinition of implicit memory: Process dissociations following elaborative processing and self-generation. *Journal of Experimental Psychology: Learning, Memory and Cognition, 20,* 290–303.

Tousignant, J., Hall, D., & Loftus, E. (1986). Discrepancy detection and vulnerability to misleading postevent information. *Memory & Cognition, 14,* 329–338.

Tranel, D., Damasio, A., & Damasio, H. (1988). Intact recognition of facial expression, gender, and age in patients with impaired recognition of face identity. *Neurology, 38,* 690–696.

Treisman, A. (1964). Verbal cues, language, and meaning in selective attention. *American Journal of Psychology, 77,* 206–219.

Treisman, A. (1986). Features and objects in visual processing. *Scientific American, 255,* 114B-125.

Treisman, A., & Gormican, S. (1988). Feature analysis in early vision: Evidence from search asymmetries. *Psychological Review, 95,* 15–48.

Treisman, A., & Souther, J. (1985). Search asymmetry: A diagnostic for preattentive processing of separable features. *Journal of Experimental Psychology: General, 114,* 285–310.

Trueswell, J., Tanenhaus, M., & Kello, C. (1995). Verb-specific constraints in sentence processing: Separating effects of lexical preference from garden paths. *Journal of Experimental Psychology: Learning, Memory and Cognition, 19,* 528–553.

Tulving, E. (1962). Subjective organization in free recall of "unrelated" words. *Psychological Review, 69,* 344–354.

Tulving, E. (1983). *Elements of episodic memory.* Oxford: Oxford University Press.

Tulving, E. (1986). What kind of a hypothesis is the distinction between episodic and semantic memory? *Journal of Experimental Psychology: Learning, Memory and Cognition, 12,* 307–311.

Tulving, E. (1989). Remembering and knowing the past. *American Scientist, 77,* 361–367.

Tulving, E., & Gold, C. (1963). Stimulus information and contextual information as determinants of tachistoscopic recognition of words. *Journal of Experimental Psychology, 92,* 319–327.

Tulving, E., Hayman, C., & Macdonald, C. (1991). Long-lasting perceptual priming and semantic learning in amnesia: A case experiment. *Journal of Experimental Psychology: Learning, Memory and Cognition, 17*, 595–617.

Tulving, E., Mandler, G., & Baumal, R. (1964). Interaction of two sources of information in tachistoscopic word recognition. *Canadian Journal of Psychology, 18*, 62–71.

Tulving, E., & Osler, S. (1968). Effectiveness of retrieval cues in memory for words. *Journal of Experimental Psychology, 77*, 593–601.

Tulving, E., & Psotka, J. (1971). Retroactive inhibition in free recall: Inaccessibility of information available in the memory store. *Journal of Experimental Psychology, 87*, 1–8.

Tulving, E., & Schacter, D. (1990). Priming and human memory systems. *Science, 247*, 301–306.

Tulving, E., Schacter, D., & Stark, H. (1982). Priming effects in word-fragment completion are independent of recognition memory. *Journal of Experimental Psychology: Learning, Memory and Cognition, 8*, 336–342.

Tulving, E., & Thomson, D. (1973). Encoding specificity and retrieval processes in episodic memory. *Psychological Review, 80*, 352–373.

Turtle, J., & Yuille, J. (1994). Lost but not forgotten details: Repeated eyewitness recall leads to reminiscence but not hypermnesia. *Journal of Applied Psychology, 79*, 260–271.

Tversky, A. (1972). Elimination by aspects: A theory of choice. *Psychological Review, 79*, 281–299.

Tversky, A., & Kahneman, A. (1987). Rational choice and the framing of decisions. In R. Hogarth & M. Reder (Eds.), *Rational choice: The contrast between economics and psychology.* Chicago: University of Chicago Press.

Tversky, A., & Kahneman, D. (1971). Belief in the law of small numbers. *Psychological Bulletin, 76*, 105–110.

Tversky, A., & Kahneman, D. (1973). Availability: A heuristic for judging frequency and probability. *Cognitive Psychology, 5*, 207–232.

Tversky, A., & Kahneman, D. (1974). Judgments under uncertainty: Heuristics and biases. *Science, 185*, 1124–1131.

Tversky, A., & Kahneman, D. (1982). Evidential impact of base rates. In D. Kahneman, P. Slovic, & A. Tversky (Eds.), *Judgment under uncertainty: Heuristics and biases.* New York: Cambridge University Press.

Tversky, A., & Kahneman, D. (1983). Extensional versus intuitive reasoning: The conjunction fallacy in probability judgment. *Psychological Review, 90*, 293–315.

Tversky, A., & Shafir, E. (1992a). Choice under conflict: The dynamics of deferred decision. *Psychological Science, 3*, 358–361.

Tversky, A., & Shafir, E. (1992b). The disjunction effect in choice under uncertainty. *Psychological Science, 3*, 305–309.

Tversky, A. (1977). Features of similarity. *Psychological Review, 84*, 327–352.

Tversky, B. (1973). Encoding processes in recognition and recall. *Cognitive Psychology, 5*, 275–287.

Tversky, B., & Tuchin, M. (1989). A reconciliation of the evidence on eyewitness testimony: Comments on McCloskey and Zaragoza (1985). *Journal of Experimental Psychology: General, 118*, 86–91.

Tweney, R. D., Doherty, M. E., & Mynatt, C. R. (1981). *On scientific thinking.* New York: Columbia University Press.

Tyler, L., & Marslen-Wilsen, W. (1977). The on-line effects of semantic context on syntactic processing. *Journal of Verbal Learning and Verbal Behavior, 16*, 683–692.

Uleman, J., & Bargh, J. (Eds.). (1989). *Unintended thought.* New York: Guilford.

Ullman, S. (1989). Aligning pictorial descriptions: An approach to object recognition. *Cognition, 32*, 193–254.

Usher, J. A., & Neisser, U. (1993). Childhood amnesia in the beginnings of memory for four early life events. *Journal of Experimental Psychology: General, 122*, 155–165.

Vallar, G., & Baddeley, A. D. (1982). Short-term forgetting and the articulatory loop. *Quarterly Journal of Experimental Psychology, 34*, 53–60.

Vallar, G., Papagno, C., & Baddeley, A. (1991). Long-term recency effects and phonological short-term memory: A neuropsychological case study. *Cortex, 27*, 323–326.

Vallar, G., & Shallice, T. (Eds.). (1990). *Neuropsychological impairments of short-term memory.* Cambridge: Cambridge University Press.

Van Lancker, D., Kreiman, J., & Emmorey, K. (1985). Familiar voice recognition: Patterns and parameters: I. Recognition of backward voices. *Journal of Phonetics, 13*, 19–38.

Van Lancker, D., Kreiman, J., & Wickens, T. (1985). Familiar voice recognition: Patterns and parameters: II. Recognition of rate altered voices. *Journal of Phonetics, 13*, 39–52.

Vicente, K., & Brewer, W. (1993). Reconstructive remembering of the scientific literature. *Cognition, 46*, 101–128.

von Neumann, J., & Morgenstern, O. (1947). *Theory of games and economic behavior.* Princeton, NJ: Princeton University Press.

von Winterfeldt, D., & Edwards, W. (1986). *Decision analysis and behavioral research.* New York: Cambridge University Press.

Voss, J., Blais, J., Means, M., Greene, T., & Ahwesh, E. (1989). Informal reasoning and subject matter knowledge in the solving of economics problems by naive and novice individuals. In L. Resnick (Ed.), *Knowing, learning and instruction: Essays in honor of Robert Glaser.* Hillsdale, NJ: Lawrence Erlbaum.

Voss, J., & Post, T. (1988). On the solving of ill-structured problems. In M. Chi, R. Glaser & M. Farr (Eds.), *The nature of expertise.* Hillsdale, NJ: Lawrence Erlbaum.

Wagenaar, W. A. (1986). My memory: A study of autobiographical memory over six years. *Cognitive Psychology, 18*, 225–252.

Wagenaar, W. A., & Groeneweg, J. (1990). The memory of concentration camp survivors. *Applied Cognitive Psychology, 4*, 77–88.

Wagner, A. (1979). Habituation and memory. In A. Dickinson & R. Boakes (Eds.), *Mechanisms of learning and motivation.* Hillsdale, NJ: Lawrence Erlbaum.

Wagner, A. (1981). SOP: A model of automatic memory processing in animal behavior. In N. E. Spear & R. R. Miller (Eds.), *Information processing in animals: Memory mechanisms.* Hillsdale, NJ: Lawrence Erlbaum.

Waldfogel, S. (1948). The frequency and affective character of childhood memories. *Psychological Monographs, 62*, entire issue.

Walker, S. (1993). Supernatural beliefs, natural kinds, and conceptual structure. *Memory & Cognition, 20*, 655–662.

Wallace, B. (1984a). Apparent equivalence between perception and imagery in the production of various visual illusions. *Memory & Cognition, 12*, 156–162.

Wallace, B. (1984b). Creating of the horizontal-vertical illusion through visual imagery. *Bulletin of the Psychonomic Society, 22*, 9–11.

Wallach, M. (1976). Tests tell us little about talent. *American Scientist, 64*, 57–63.

Wallas, G. (1926). *The art of thought.* New York: Harcourt, Brace.

Wang, M., & Bilger, R. (1973). Consonant confusion in noise: A study of perceptual features. *Journal of the Acoustical Society of America, 54*, 1248–1266.

Wardlaw, K. A., & Kroll, N. E. A. (1976). Autonomic responses to shock-associated words in a non-attended message: A failure to replicate. *Journal of Experimental Psychology: Human Perception and Performance, 2*, 357–360.

Warnick, D. H., & Sanders, G. S. (1980). Why do eyewitnesses make so many mistakes? *Journal of Applied Social Psychology, 10*, 362–366.

Wason, P. (1966). Reasoning. In B. Foss (Ed.), *New horizons in psychology.* Middlesex, England: Penguin.

Wason, P. (1968). Reasoning about a rule. *Quarterly Journal of Experimental Psychology, 20*, 273–281.

Wason, P. (1983). Realism and rationality in the selection task. In J. S. B. Evans (Ed.), *Thinking and reasoning: Psychological approaches.* London: Routledge & Kegan Paul.

Wason, P., & Johnson-Laird, P. (1972). *Psychol-*

ogy of reasoning: Structure and content. Cambridge, MA: Harvard University Press.

Watkins, M. J. (1977). The intricacy of memory span. *Memory & Cognition, 5*, 529–534.

Watkins, M., & Gibson, J. (1988). On the relation between perceptual priming and recognition memory. *Journal of Experimental Psychology: Learning, Memory and Cognition, 14*, 477–483.

Watkins, M., & LeCompte, D. (1991). Inadequacy of recall as a basis for frequency knowledge. *Journal of Experimental Psychology: Learning, Memory and Cognition, 17*, 1161–1176.

Watkins, M. J., & Tulving, E. (1975). Episodic memory: When recognition fails. *Journal of Experimental Psychology: General, 104*, 5–29.

Watkins, M. J., & Watkins, O. C. (1974). Processing of recency items for free recall. *Journal of Experimental Psychology, 102*, 488–493.

Wattenmaker, W. (1991). Learning modes, feature correlations, and memory-based categorization. *Journal of Experimental Psychology: Learning, Memory and Cognition, 17*, 908–923.

Waugh, N. C., & Norman, D. A. (1965). Primary Memory. *Psychological Review, 72*, 89–104.

Weaver, C. (1993). Do you need a "flash" to form a flashbulb memory? *Journal of Experimental Psychology: General, 122*, 39–46.

Weber, E., Böckenholt, U., Hilton, D., & Wallace, B. (1993). Determinants of diagnostic hypothesis generation: Effects of information, base rates and experience. *Journal of Experimental Psychology: Learning, Memory and Cognition, 19*, 1151–1164.

Weber, R. J. (1993). *Forks, phonographs, and hot air balloons: A field guide to inventive thinking.* New York: Oxford University Press.

Weber, R., & Dixon, S. (1989). Invention and gain analysis. *Cognitive Psychology, 21*, 283–302.

Wedell, D. (1991). Distinguishing among models of contextually induced preference reversals. *Journal of Experimental Psychology: Learning, Memory and Cognition, 17*, 767–778.

Wedell, D. (1993). Effects of different types of decoys on choice. Paper presented at the meeting of the Psychonomic Society, Washington, DC.

Wedell, D., & Bockenholt, U. (1990). Moderation of preference reversals in the long run. *Journal of Experimental Psychology: Human Perception and Performance, 16*, 429–438.

Wegner, D. (1994). Ironic processes of mental control. *Psychological Review, 101*, 34–52.

Wegner, D., Wenzlaff, R., Kerker, R., & Beattie, A. (1981). Incrimination through innuendo: Can media questions become public answers? *Journal of Personality and Social Psychology, 40*, 822–832.

Weingardt, K., Loftus, E., & Lindsay, D. S. (1995). Misinformation revisited: New evidence on the suggestibility of memory. *Memory & Cognition, 23*, 72–82.

Weingartner, H., Adefris, W., Eich, J. E., & Murphy, D. L. (1976). Encoding-imagery specificity in alcohol state-dependent learning. *Journal of Experimental Psychology: Human Learning and Memory, 2*, 83–87.

Weisberg, R. (1969). Sentence processing assessed through intrasentence word associations. *Journal of Experimental Psychology, 82*, 332–338.

Weisberg, R. (1986). *Creativity: Genius and other myths.* New York: W. H. Freeman.

Weisberg, R. (1988). Problem solving and creativity. In R. J. Sternberg (Ed.), *The nature of creativity* (pp. 148–176). Cambridge: Cambridge University Press.

Weisberg, R., & Alba, J. (1981). An examinagion of the alleged role of "fixation" in the solution of several "insight" problems. *Journal of Experimental Psychology: General, 110*, 169–192.

Weisberg, R., & Alba, J. (1982). Problem solving is not like perception: More on Gestalt theory. *Journal of Experimental Psychology: General, 111*, 326–330.

Weisberg, R., & Suls, J. (1973). An information processing model of Duncker's candle problem. *Cognitive Psychology, 4*, 255–276.

Weisberg, R., DiCamillo, M., & Phillips, D. (1978). Transferring old associations to new problems: A nonautomatic process. *Journal of*

Verbal Learning and Verbal Behavior, 17, 219–228.

Weiskrantz, L. (1986). *Blindsight: A case study and implications.* New York: Oxford University Press.

Weldon, M. (1993). The time course of perceptual and conceptual contributions to word fragment completion priming. *Journal of Experimental Psychology: Learning, Memory and Cognition, 19,* 1010–1023.

Weldon, M. S., & Jackson-Barrett, J. (1993). Why do pictures produce priming on the word-fragment completion test? A study of encoding and retrieval factors. *Memory & Cognition, 21,* 519–528.

Wells, G. L., & Harvey, J. H. (1977). Do people use consensus information in making causal attributions? *Journal of Personality and Social Psychology, 35,* 279–293.

Wells, G. L., Lindsay, R. C. L., & Ferguson, T. J. (1979). Accuracy, confidence, and juror perceptions in eyewitness identification. *Journal of Applied Psychology, 64,* 440–448.

Wells, G., Luus, C. A. E., & Windschitl, P. (1994). Maximizing the utility of eyewitness identification evidence. *Current Directions in Psychological Science, 3.* 194–197.

Werker, J., & Desjardins, R. (1995). Listening to speech in the first year of life: Experiential effects on phoneme perception. *Current Directions in Psychological Science, 4,* 76–80.

Wetherick, N. (1989). Psychology and syllogistic reasoning. *Philosophical Psychology, 2,* 111–124.

Wetzler, S. (1985). Mood state-dependent retrieval: A failure to replicate. *Psychological Reports, 56,* 759–765.

Wetzler, S., & Sweeney, J. A. (1986). Childhood amnesia: An empirical demonstration. In D. C. Rubin (Ed.), *Autobiographical memory.* Cambridge: Cambridge University Press.

Wexler, K. (1978). A review of John R. Anderson's language, memory, and thought. *Cognition, 6,* 327–351.

Wharton, C., Holyoak, K., Downing, P., & Lange, T. (1994). Below the surface: Analogical similarity and retrieval competition in reminding. *Cognitive Psychology, 26,* 64–101.

Wheeler, D. (1970). Processes in word recognition. *Cognitive Psychology, 1,* 59–85.

White, N. M. (1991). Peripheral and central memory-enhancing actions of glucose. In R. C. A. Frederickson, J. L. McGaugh, & D. L. Felten (Eds.), *Peripheral signaling of the brain: Neural, immune and cognitive function.* Toronto: Hogrefe and Huber.

White, P. (1988). Knowing more than we can tell: "Introspective access" and causal report accuracy 10 years later. *British Journal of Psychology, 79,* 13–45.

White, R. T. (1989). Recall of autobiographical events. *Applied Cognitive Psychology, 3,* 127–136.

White, S. H., & Pillemer, D. B. (1979). Childhood amnesia and the development of a socially accessibly memory system. In J. F. Kihlstrom & F. J. Evans (Eds.), *Functional disorders of memory.* Hillsdale, NJ: Lawrence Erlbaum.

Whittlesea, B., Brooks, L., & Westcott, C. (1994). After the learning is over: Factors controlling the selective application of general and particular knowledge. *Journal of Experimental Psychology: Learning, Memory and Cognition, 20,* 259–274.

Whittlesea, B., Jacoby, L., & Girard, K. (1990). Illusions of immediate memory: Evidence of an attributional basis for feelings of familiarity and perceptual quality. *Journal of Memory and Language, 29,* 716–732.

Whorf, B. L. (1956). *Language, thought, and reality.* Cambridge: Technology Press.

Wierzbicka, A. (1992). Defining emotion concepts. *Cognitive Science, 16,* 539–582.

Wilkins, M. (1928). The effect of changed material on ability to do formal syllogistic reasoning. *Archives of Psychology, 16,* 83.

Wilson, T. (1994). The proper protocol: Validity and completeness of verbal reports. *Psychological Science, 5,* 249–252.

Wilson, T., & Brekke, N. (1994). Mental contamination and mental correction: Unwanted influences on judgments and evaluations. *Psychological Bulletin, 116,* 117–142.

Wilson, T., DePaulo, B., Mook, D., & Klaaren, K. (1993). Scientists' evaluations of research: The biasing effects of the importance of the topic. *Psychological Science, 4,* 322–325.

Wilson, T., & Schooler, J. (1991). Thinking too much: Introspection can reduce the quality of preferences and decisions. *Journal of Personality and Social Psychology, 60,* 181–192.

Wingfield, A., & Butterworth, B. (1984). Running memory for sentences and parts of sentences: Syntactic parsing as a control function in working memory. In H. Bouma & D. G. Bouwhuis (Eds.), *Attention and performance X: Control of language processes.* Hillsdale, NJ: Lawrence Erlbaum.

Winnick, W., & Daniel, S. (1970). Two kinds of response priming in tachistoscopic recognition. *Journal of Experimental Psychology, 84,* 74–81.

Winograd, E. (1994). Factors influencing accuracy and distortion in remembering. Paper presented at the Practical Aspects of Memory Conference, College Park, MD.

Winograd, E., & Killinger, W. A., Jr. (1983). Relating age at encoding in early childhood to adult recall: Development of flashbulb memories. *Journal of Experimental Psychology: General, 112,* 413–422.

Winograd, E., & Neisser, U. (Eds.). (1993). *Affect and accuracy in recall: Studies of "flashbulb" memories.* New York: Cambridge University Press.

Winston, P. (1984). *Artificial intelligence* (2nd ed.). Reading, MA: Addison-Wesley.

Wiseman, S., & Neisser, U. (1974). Perceptual organization as a determinant of visual recognition memory. *American Journal of Psychology, 87,* 675–681.

Wittgenstein, L. (1953). *Philosophical investigations* (G. E. M. Anscombe, Trans.). Oxford: Blackwell.

Wixted, J. (1991). Conditions and consequences of maintenance rehearsal. *Journal of Experimental Psychology: Learning, Memory and Cognition, 17,* 963–973.

Wogalter, M., & Laughery, K. (1987). Face recognition: Effects of study to test maintenance and change of photographic mode and pose. *Applied Cognitive Psychology, 1,* 241–253.

Wolford, G., Taylor, H., & Beck, J. (1990). The conjunction fallacy? *Memory & Cognition, 18,* 47–53.

Wollen, K. A., Weber, A., & Lowry, D. (1972). Bizarreness versus interaction of mental images as determinants of learning. *Cognitive Psychology, 3,* 518–523.

Woodhead, M. M., Baddeley, A. D., & Simmonds, D. C. V. (1979). On training people to recognise faces. *Ergonomics, 22,* 333–343.

Woodward, A. E., Bjork, R. A., & Jongeward, R. H., Jr. (1973). Recall and recognition as a function of primary rehearsal. *Journal of Verbal Learning and Verbal Behavior, 12,* 608–617.

Woodworth, R., & Sells, S. (1935). An atmosphere effect in formal syllogistic reasoning. *Journal of Experimental Psychology, 18,* 451–460.

Wright, L. (1993). Remembering Satan—Part 2. *New Yorker,* May 24, pp. 54–76.

Yantis, S. (1993). Stimulus-driven attention capture. *Current Directions in Psychological Science, 2,* 156–161.

Yantis, S., & Johnston, J. (1990). On the locus of visual selection: Evidence from focused attention tasks. *Journal of Experimental Psychology: Human Perception and Performance, 16,* 135–149.

Yarmey, A. (1973). I recognize your face but I can't remember your name: Further evidence on the tip-of-the-tongue phenomenon. *Memory & Cognition, 1,* 287–290.

Yates, F. A. (1966). *The art of memory.* London: Routledge and Kegan Paul.

Yee, P., & Hunt, E. (1991). Individual differences in stroop dilution: Tests of the attention-capture hypothesis. *Journal of Experimental Psychology: Human Perception and Performance, 17,* 715–725.

Yeni-Komshian, G. (1993). Speech perception. In J. B. Gleason & N. B. Ratner (Eds.), *Psycholinguistics* (pp. 90–133). New York: Harcourt Brace Jovanovich.

Yin, R. (1969). Looking at upside-down faces. *Journal of Experimental Psychology, 81,* 141–145.

Young, A., & Bruce, V. (1991). Perceptual categories and the computation of "grandmother." *European Journal of Cognitive Psychology, 3,* 5–49.

Yuille, J. (Ed.), (1983). *Imagery, memory, and cognition.* Hillsdale, NJ: Lawrence Erlbaum.

Yuille, J. (1984). Research and teaching with police: A Canadian example. *International Review of Applied Psychology, 33,* 5–23.

Yuille, J., & Cutshall, J. L. (1986). A case study of eyewitness memory of a crime. *Journal of Applied Psychology, 71,* 291–301.

Yuille, J., & Kim, C. (1987). A field study of the forensic use of hypnosis. *Canadian Journal of Behavioral Sciences Review, 19,* 418–429.

Yuille, J., & Tollestrup, P. (1992). A model of the diverse effects of emotion on eyewitness memory. In S.-Å. Christianson (Ed.), *The handbook of emotion and memory: Research and theory* (pp. 201–215). Hillsdale, NJ: Lawrence Erlbaum.

Zajonc, R. B. (1980). Feeling and thinking. *American Psychologist, 35,* 151–175.

Zajonc, R. B. (1984). On the primacy of affect. *American Psychologist, 39,* 117–123.

Zangwill, O. L. (1972). Remembering revisited. *Quarterly Journal of Experimental Psychology, 24,* 123–138.

Zaragoza, M., & Lane, S. (1994). Source misattributions and the suggestibility of eyewitness memory. *Journal of Experimental Psychology: Learning, Memory and Cognition, 20,* 934–945.

Zbrodoff, N., & Logan, G. (1986). On the autonomy of mental processes: A case study of arithmetic. *Journal of Experimental Psychology: General, 115,* 118–130.

Zeigarnik, B. (1927). Das Behalten erledigter und unerledigter Handlungen. *Psychologische Forschungen, 9,* 1–85.

Zimler, J., & Keenan, J. M. (1983). Imagery in the congenitally blind: How visual are visual images? *Journal of Experimental Psychology: Learning, Memory and Cognition, 9,* 269–282.

Zukier, H. (1982). The dilution effect: The role of the correlation and the dispersion of predictor variables in the use of nondiagnostic information. *Journal of Personality and Social Psychology, 43,* 1163–1174.

Author Index

Subject Index

692